AREA HANDBOOK
for
SOUTH VIETNAM

Co-Authors

Harvey H. Smith

Donald W. Bernier
Frederica M. Bunge
Frances Chadwick Rintz
Rinn-Sup Shinn
Suzanne Teleki

Research and writing were completed on
April 15, 1966

Published
April 1967

DA Pam 550-55

Library of Congress Catalog Card Number: 67–62089

For sale by the Superintendent of Documents, U.S. Government Printing Office
Washington, D.C. 20402 - Price $6.75

FOREWORD

This volume is one of a series of handbooks prepared by Foreign Area Studies (FAS) of The American University, designed to be useful to military and other personnel who need a convenient compilation of basic facts about the social, economic, political and military institutions and practices of various countries. The emphasis is on objective description of the nation's present society and the kinds of possible or probable change that might be expected in the future. The handbook seeks to present as full and as balanced an integrated exposition as limitations on space and research time permit. It was compiled from information available in openly published material. Extensive bibliographies are provided to permit recourse to other published sources for more detailed information. There has been no attempt to express any specific point of view or to make policy recommendations. The contents of the handbook represent the work of the authors and FAS and do not represent the official view of the United States Government.

An effort has been made to make the handbook as comprehensive as possible. It can be expected, however, that the material, interpretations and conclusions are subject to modification in the light of new information and developments. Such corrections, additions and suggestions for factual, interpretive or other change as readers may have will be welcomed for use in future revisions. Comments may be addressed to:

THE DIRECTOR
Foreign Area Studies
The American University
5010 Wisconsin Avenue, N.W.
Washington, D.C. 20016

PREFACE

This volume is part of a second major revision of the *Area Hand-book for Vietnam*. The Handbook, originally prepared in 1957 by the Foreign Areas Studies Division (then known as the Washington Branch, Human Relations Area Files), was substantially revised in 1962, under the chairmanship of George L. Harris, for the Foreign Areas Studies Division, then associated with the Special Operations Research Office at The American University. Since publication of the 1962 revision, significant changes have occurred in the political, military and other aspects of the situation in South and North Vietnam, particularly South Vietnam.

Study of the society while it was undergoing crises of various types presented obvious difficulties. In many areas obtainable information was fragmentary and often contradictory. Moreover, the pace of events within the country and its neighboring states rapidly outdated the revision as it was being written. Because the changes occurring within the two Vietnams became so diverse and complex, revision of the 1962 Handbook was divided into two separate studies: this volume on South Vietnam, and another, to be completed later, on North Vietnam.

Many of the difficulties confronting the government in South Vietnam in 1966 could be traced to complications caused by the country's sudden change from the status of a colony to that of a sovereign state burdened with disadvantages incident to limited resources in leadership and to a society composed of widely varied, often disparate, ethnic, religious, political and social elements. From its beginning, or during the course of about 12 years, the state had to build its basic governmental structure, virtually under war conditions imposed by powerful and aggressive subversive forces, directed and liberally supported by Communist North Vietnam.

Despite administrative, social and economic reforms initiated by Prime Minister Ky's government, Buddhist opposition in early 1966 entered its most violent period since November 1963 and was continuing unabated at the time research on this study terminated. The announced objective of the Buddhists was the resignation of the military regime of Prime Minister Ky and its replacement by a government headed by civilians.

Apparently mollified somewhat by the Prime Minister's promise, on April 14, 1966, to hold national elections within 5 months, as a preliminary step to the transfer of power to a civilian government, the Buddhists announced that they would suspend their opposition campaign if the government met two conditions: first, to ensure fairly conducted elections; second, to guarantee amnesty to those demonstrators who had been incarcerated during the preceding month-long political crisis. Governmental silence on the proposal was met within 24 hours by intensified disturbances, particularly in Da Nang where dissidents, mostly youths, joined by military and police elements, seized control of the radio stations and some other government buildings.

Faced with increasing Buddhist pressure, Prime Minister Ky on April 24 announced that preparations were under way to appoint an Electoral Law Drafting Commission. The Buddhist leaders, unappeased, charged the government with using delaying tactics and extended their demonstrations to Saigon, where the placards and chants of some participants took on Communist, neutralist and anti-American tones.

To meet the increasing challenge, the Prime Minister, on May 16, sent, unannounced, about 1,000 South Vietnamese marines and 500 paratroopers to Da Nang by plane. They restored government authority and ended the disorders. Meanwhile, Buddhist agitation flared unopposed in Hue, where roaming bands of armed university students caused extensive property damage, including the sacking and burning of the United States Information Agency's library on May 26 and a similar assault on June 1 against the United States Consulate. These actions appeared, at the moment, to eliminate the possibility of a harmonious transition from military to civilian rule.

The government, nevertheless, proceeded with transition plans and announced on June 1 that elections for a constituent assembly were scheduled for September 11. On June 7 the Electoral Law Drafting Commission published a detailed schedule for election procedures. It fixed September 26 as the date for convening the elected constituent assembly, which was to draft a constitution within about 6 months. Under its plans the government envisaged retention of power for an additional 3 to 6 months, pending approval of the constitution and the election of a National Assembly. Buddhist leaders, however, seemed to expect that the constituent assembly would serve also as a legislative body authorized to appoint a new government. Charging the government with undue procrastination, the Buddhists, again manifesting impatience, called for the immediate resignation of the government's top leaders.

In protest against the alleged delaying tactics and the refusal of Chief of State Nguyen Van Thieu and Prime Minister Ky to resign, the militant Buddhist monk, Thich Tri Quang, on June 8, began a well-publicized hunger strike in Hue. In the continuing riotous disturbances within the city, some 500 army troops participated with the Buddhist demonstrators. Police with substantial reinforcements failed to maintain order. Dissenters were virtually unopposed in their activities, which included the obstruction of basic governmental processes by resorting to various measures, such as absenteeism and placing ancestral altars in the streets and highways to block traffic.

To placate civilian appeals for a voice in making national policy, the government, on June 6, added 10 civilians to The Directory (National Leadership Committee), the ruling body previously composed of 10 high-ranking military officers. Eight of the new members were laymen representing religious faiths: of the 8, 2 were Buddhists (unaffiliated with the Unified Buddhist Church of Vietnam), 2 were Catholics, and 2 each were from the Cao Dai and Hoa Hao sects. The remaining 2 were political personalities. Unified Buddhist Church leaders, still unsatisfied, refused to be represented.

Confronted with the continuing serious threat to governmental authority throughout the northern provinces and with virtual anarchy in Hue, the Prime Minister sent some 1,500 paratroopers and marines to the area between June 15 and 17 and declared martial law in the city. Government forces, in dealing with the dissidents, inflicted several casualities among the hard-core local Army insurgents attempting to march under Buddhist flags. With this evidence of loyalty within troop units stationed outside the trouble area, and of their effectiveness in dealing with unruly crowds, the influence of the agitators seemed to diminish. The disorders gradually subsided, and by June 20, Hue was again under government control. Thich Tri Quang was removed under police guard to a hospital in Saigon on June 22, and by the end of the month normal conditions were virtually restored in the major population centers.

Meanwhile, on June 19, Chief of State Thieu signed decrees establishing procedures for forming the constituent assembly, to be convened in September as previously announced. The decrees stipulated that the assembly would be dissolved upon promulgation of the new constitution. This ended speculation that the assembly might be given legislative powers and continue in service as a National Assembly.

Within the Unified Buddhist Church hierarchy the intensified antigovernment protests, such as those held at Hue, seemed to widen cleavages and develop new ones as various leaders competed for control of the organization. Street demonstrations by the militants aroused Catholic groups to organize counterdemonstrations. The Buddhist moderates denounced such manifestations and called for an attitude of tolerance toward the military government's leadership as long as it showed good faith in carrying out its promises for elections.

By mid-summer 1966 the moderates appeared to be gaining predominant influence.

In marked contrast to their previous antigovernment campaigns, the Buddhists this time lacked effective military support. Furthermore, factionalism and apparent disagreements among groups as to methods and objectives tended to detract from their influence on the public.

While preoccupied with the Buddhist problem, the government, on June 18, initiated a series of drastic reforms designed to alleviate the effects of inflation and ameliorate economic distress. The steadily depreciating piaster was devalued from an official rate of 35 to US$1 to 80 to US$1. The black-market rate was 180 to US$1. A special provision fixed the effective commercial exchange rate at 118 for US$1, replacing several varying rates used for different purposes. Civil servants, teachers and military personnel received graduated pay raises ranging from 20 to 30 percent. A new tax, amounting to about 49 percent of dollar value, was placed on imports. As an incentive to clear imports promptly through congested port areas, and to discourage price manipulations by withholding imports from markets, a special warehouse storage penalty tax was imposed.

It was not generally expected that these measures, although regarded by many as steps in the right direction, would cure the country's economic ills. Therefore, regardless of the outcome of elections and the transfer of power to civil authorities, economic distress appeared likely to persist as an unsettling influence on government.

Grateful acknowledgment must be given to various area specialists who helped in the preparation of this volume. Parts of the manuscript were checked by them for factual accuracy, but the complexity and changing nature of the subject matter made it impossible for errors to be avoided entirely.

Special credit is given to Dinh Van Ban for discovering and providing useful source material on Buddhist organizations in South Vietnam. Donald Luce contributed valuable firsthand information on living conditions in rural areas, especially in the mountain regions. Mrs. Klaus Loewald offered suggestions and criticisms for Chapter 7, Family, and Chapter 12, Social Values. Nguyen Ay Quang contributed translations and evaluations of Vietnamese material, particularly in the field of cultural history.

Nguyen Ngoc Bich, a graduate student at Columbia University, discovered and summarized important primary source material in Vietnamese, mainly on historical and sociological subjects. Nguyen Ngoc Ch'ac made suggestions and offered advice regarding religious and social matters. Miss Nguyen Dung, drawing on her extensive knowledge of Vietnamese laws and courts, contributed valuable information on the judiciary system and on various legal codes. Mrs.

Paula A. Sinanoglu provided helpful bibliographical data, wrote a preliminary draft for Chapter 15, Foreign Relations, and made available a historical study which she had recently completed.

In addition, special credit is given to W. Robert Warne for his advice and perceptive comments, relating particularly to Chapter 14, Political Dynamics. Appreciation is extended to the staff of the Military Assistance Institute, of the American Institutes for Research, for their cooperation in providing the use of facilities and important source materials, as well as giving advice and assistance in the revision of this study.

Grateful acknowledgment is also due many persons within and outside the United States Government, too numerous to mention individually, who gave of their time and special knowledge to provide data and objective criticism of preliminary chapter drafts.

A glossary is included as an appendix for the reader's convenience. The terms in the glossary are not in every case defined in the text. An attempt was made to avoid the use of non-Vietnamese foreign terms. In using Vietnamese words or titles, diacritical marks were omitted. The place names used are, wherever possible, those established by the United States Board on Geographic Names for South Vietnam as of 1962 and for North Vietnam as of 1964.

SOUTH VIETNAM

TABLE OF CONTENTS

LIST OF ILLUSTRATIONS

LIST OF TABLES

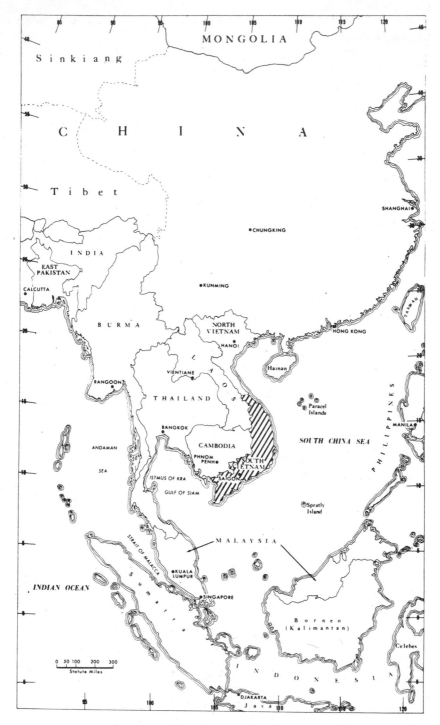

Figure 1. Position of South Vietnam in Southeast Asia.

SECTION I. SOCIAL

CHAPTER 1

GENERAL CHARACTER OF THE SOCIETY

The Republic of Vietnam, commonly referred to as South Vietnam, came into being as a result of circumstances following the Agreement on the Cessation of Hostilities in Vietnam concluded at Geneva on July 20, 1954. The Agreement ended 8 years of armed conflict with France, known as the Indochina War (1946–54), and fixed a "provisional Demarcation Line" across the State of Vietnam near the seventeenth parallel. This Line created two zones into which the opposing military forces were to withdraw pending a future political solution for the reunification of the country. The territory south of the Line became the anti-Communist Republic of Vietnam, aligned with France; the area to the north became the self-styled Democratic Republic of Vietnam, commonly called North Vietnam, in the orbit of the major Communist powers.

Before its partition, Vietnam's development and growth were repeatedly interrupted by foreign interventions. As "Nam Viet," the country was first recognized as an independent state in the tenth century by the Chinese, who had ruled over it for nearly 1,000 years. It retained its sovereignty until late in the nineteenth century, when the French made it a part of their colonial empire and administered the territory as three separate regions: Cochin China, in the south; Annam, in the center; and Tonkin, in the north. These regions, together with Laos and Cambodia, made up French Indochina.

The ideological differences in 1966 between South Vietnam and North Vietnam had begun during World War II when Vietnamese Communists, exploiting rising nationalist sentiments, organized armed resistance against the Japanese and French occupation authorities. It was this resistance, continuing against the French after the end of World War II, which developed into the Indochina War.

In order to enlist the support of anti-Communist Vietnamese nationalists and to weaken the armed resistance to its authority, France by mid-1949 had formally established the State of Vietnam, composed of Cochin China, Annam and Tonkin, under the leadership of Bao Dai, ex-emperor of Annam. The new State of Vietnam, the Kingdom of Laos and the Kingdom of Cambodia were recognized by France as independent states but were firmly bound to France within the French Union.

These efforts by the French to secure local support met with some success, as a sizable number of contingents composed of non-Communist nationalists from the State of Vietnam fought side by side with the French against the Communist-led resistance forces who called themselves the "National Liberation Army." This help from the Vietnamese nationalists, however, had little impact on the course of hostilities, which ended in the French defeat formalized by the Geneva Agreement.

South Vietnam, situated entirely within the tropics, has several geographic regions varying in type. The flat expanse of the Mekong Delta in the south joins a narrow coastal strip of lowlands extending northeastward more than 500 miles along the South China Sea to the Demarcation Line. Terrain inland from this coastal strip rises abruptly into the Chaîne Annamitique, a jungle-covered mountain range interspersed in its southern portion with some rather fertile plateaus. The mountains serve to impede passage to Laos and to Cambodia as far south as the Mekong Delta. Distances from the sea across South Vietnam to the frontiers with these two neighboring states are short, varying between 135 miles in the south to Cambodia and 35 miles in the north to Laos.

Because the boundaries are vaguely defined and in many places unmarked, border incidents and conflicts are frequent. Moreover, many minority groups live astride the boundary. Thick vegetation along the border areas, coupled with inaccessibility, makes effective surveillance of ground movement across or along frontiers almost impossible. Conditions are favorable for ambushes, for the concealment of troops and supplies and for the conduct of insurgency operations.

Lack of communications tends to isolate the peoples living in the mountainous areas from the central government in Saigon and from the rest of the world. Villagers of the coastal plains and the delta region have had more outside contacts, but, except for inhabitants of port cities and Saigon, the extent of their knowledge of and their interests in areas beyond their immediate environs has been extremely limited. For centuries the tightly knit clusters of families, the core of village life, have constituted self-contained units of social conservatism strongly resistant to external influences. This situation presents the central government with the difficult problem of developing a sense of civic responsibility extending beyond the local community and of creating the administrative bodies, particularly at the lower levels, required for a unified state.

The cultural impact of successive Chinese invasions and periods of domination is still evident in South Vietnam, but French colonial rule, coming in the late 1800's and lasting for nearly a century, also left an indelible imprint on the society. Initially Confucianism gave the people a sense of moral unity and a clearly defined pattern of authority which, far from resulting in their assimilation by the dominant Chinese, enabled them to rearticulate and preserve their own identity. Nevertheless, the French impact altered or weakened critical parts of the social system, precipitating the decline of traditional values and giving rise to new ideas, new attitudes toward authority and new social relationships.

Vietnamese resistance was never completely suppressed but was not strong enough at that time to prevail against French military might. The Vietnamese emperor and his mandarins could either oppose the French and face certain defeat or cooperate. For the most part, after the establishment in 1883 of the protectorate in Annam (a large part of which now constitutes the Central Lowlands and the Central Highlands), the tenure and prerogatives of the emperors depended upon the colonial administration. Similarly, those mandarins who retained their positions, instead of withdrawing or resisting, found that they had become no more than agents of the French. Demoralized, many of them developed a cynical disregard for the responsibilities of their positions and became increasingly self-seeking. Their value to France was that they represented a continuity with traditional patterns of authority, but their subordination to France undermined their attachment and that of the people to the traditional order which France wanted to preserve.

The economic changes wrought by France in the area that was to become South Vietnam had even more far-reaching effect. The appearance of large-scale agriculture, rubber plantations and large landholdings by absentee entrepreneurs required the services of landless peasants who were brought great distances to work in the burgeoning enterprises. Prosperous Vietnamese landowners moved to urban areas, leaving their ricefields to be tilled by the growing number of tenant farmers and hired laborers.

Exploitation of rice production in the Mekong Delta did not begin until late in the nineteenth century when the French colonial administration opened up large areas by digging complex systems of canals to provide drainage and transportation. Large landholdings and tenancy became characteristic of the area, and after 1900 the Mekong Delta began to produce a substantial surplus of rice for export. A relatively small group of Vietnamese closely associated with the French obtained large holdings in this area and acquired substantial wealth by exploiting the land. The worst abuses of landlordism and tenancy developed here.

The Vietnamese beneficiaries emerged as a new group in the society. Most were mandarins or of mandarin families, but, although they did not lose their traditional respect for learning, their status was no longer primarily based upon learning but upon wealth. Furthermore, the knowledge they and especially their children sought came not from the Confucian classics but from the science and literature of Europe. It was from the ranks of these Westernized incipient middle and upper classes that many of the leaders of South Vietnamese nationalism were to come.

Under the French colonial administration villages changed remarkably little in their external aspects. They continued to be the focal points of social, moral and religious life, for they had remained isolated from many of the transformations which became apparent in the cities and towns. The foundations of the traditional village order, however, had been undermined. The villager found himself at the bottom of a pyramid, the higher levels of which were crumbling under the weight of an alien authority. As it was impressed upon him that the traditional values and precepts were losing force with his superiors, he began to question them himself.

French intervention in local affairs depreciated the authority of village elders by reducing their powers of independent decision. Colonial economic demands, particularly those pertaining to increased production and higher taxes, imposed new burdens on the peasant without, however, providing corresponding rewards and incentives. The effect was not merely to arouse resentments, with which the Vietnamese had always reacted to foreign rule, but also to alter the character of the aspiration for independence.

Until the arrival of the French, Vietnamese nationalist sentiments, such as existed, were largely concerned with eliminating foreign rule and preserving the old order. The independence movement of the twentieth century looked not merely to the end of foreign rule but to the creation of a new social and political order. Differences quickly developed among the nationalists about the means and ends. In the mid-1960's these differences continued to be the basis for the military and political conflicts between South and North Vietnam.

Most of the population, estimated to be about 16.1 million in mid-1965, lives in the fertile delta of the Mekong River or in the lush coastal lowlands along the South China Sea. About 75 percent of the population is engaged in agriculture, rice being the principal crop. Inhabitants of the lowland areas are nearly all ethnically Vietnamese; major exceptions are some 1 million Chinese, located largely in the Saigon-Cho Lon area, and about 400,000 Khmers (Cambodians), most of whom live in the Mekong Delta.

The almost inaccessible Central Highland Region, comprising about two-thirds of the country's total area, is sparsely settled by about 700,000 persons from various indigenous ethnic groups. Collectively they are known among the Vietnamese as Nguoi Thuongs (highland people), frequently shortened to Thuongs. In French they are the *montagnards* (mountaineers), a term which is customarily employed by most foreigners and by many Vietnamese themselves. Despite government efforts to integrate these mountain groups into the national society, they customarily earn a livelihood from subsistence farming, separated from the bulk of the lowland population, who have a general aversion for life in the mountain areas.

Most people, with sizable exceptions among the Chinese, *montagnards* and Khmers, regard themselves as Vietnamese. Mixed marriages are not infrequent, however, and persons with ancestors from different ethnic groups are found at all levels of society. Many, especially among the older generation, speak French, but it is being gradually replaced by English as a second language, particularly among high school and college students.

South Vietnam is predominantly a Buddhist country, but less than half of those who regard themselves as Buddhists actually practice the faith. There are substantial minorities of Roman Catholics, Cao Dai and Hoa Hao. The *montagnards* subscribe to various animistic beliefs, although some have been converted to Christianity. The Chinese are mainly Confucianists or Taoists and, like the Vietnamese, are ancestor worshipers. Regardless of their adherence to a particular religious faith or belief, astrology, necromancy and superstitions in one form or another have a significant influence on many South Vietnamese and play an important role in governing their activities.

When South Vietnam became fully independent in 1954 with Ngo Dinh Diem as prime minister, the country, still known as the State of Vietnam, was on the brink of anarchy. The society was plagued by factionalism developed during decades of foreign rule. Cohesive efforts toward creating a sense of nationhood were thwarted by competing groups within military, political, religious and social organizations and even within the government itself. In general, leaders were inexperienced in dealing with national problems, and trained subordinates were lacking, particularly at provincial and district levels. Moreover, the Prime Minister faced the determined opposition of special interest groups which had acquired power under an alien administration.

The greatest threat, however, was the opposition of a well-organized Communist network which was created by agents remaining in the South after the Communist-led forces withdrew to the North in 1954. The agents soon developed armed bands of insurgents, commonly known in the South as Viet Cong (Vietnamese Communists), who were bent on undermining the authority of the newly established government. The Viet Cong insurgents, by exploiting the strong inherent desire for independence, reinforced by themes extolling nationalism and anticolonialism, gained widespread sympathetic reaction from the people.

By the end of 1960, Communist insurgency efforts were further strengthened by creation of the so-called "National Front for the Liberation of South Vietnam." The National Front, composed of figures taken from many segments of South Vietnamese society, attempted, with Hanoi backing, to establish itself as the sole representative of the South Vietnamese people.

In 1963 the situation rapidly deteriorated. Buddhist opposition to alleged discriminatory and dictatorial measures by the government of President Diem, a Catholic, sparked widespread riotous demonstrations. These antigovernment disturbances culminated in a military coup d'etat on November 1, 1963, that overthrew the Diem regime and resulted in the deaths of President Diem and his brother, a close political adviser. Rampant factionalism contributing to political instability was evidenced by a series of nine rapid changes in governing regimes. Some were accomplished peacefully; others were accompanied by violence. All except two were headed by military officers. Economic and social welfare programs suffered a setback, and even antiguerrilla operations were adversely affected.

Meanwhile, the counterinsurgency efforts entered a new phase. Under provisions of the pact establishing the Southeast Asia Treaty Organization (SEATO) in 1954, the United States military role in South Vietnam, hitherto limited to granting aid and advice, was expanded by June 1965 to include the employment of combat elements against the increasing Viet Cong threat. Australia and New Zealand, also SEATO members, likewise provided combat contingents at about the same time. Later in the year South Korea, at Saigon's request, dispatched an infantry division and some supporting troops to help in the conflict.

Conditions appeared to improve after June 1965, when Lieutenant General (then Major General) Nguyen Van Thieu became chief of state as chairman of the National Leadership Committee—the ruling military group—and Air Vice Marshal Nguyen Cao Ky, commander of the Air Force, was named prime minister by the Committee.

By early 1966 the people within a 3-year period had experienced many types of government, ranging from the one headed by civilians, with highly centralized authority closely controlled by President Diem and his brothers, to a collective leadership type with central authority shared by 10 military men of high rank comprising The Directory (National Leadership Committee). The Directory leaders, however, have declared that they were making arrangements for drafting a new constitution to provide for the transfer of power to duly elected authorities.

By mid-1966, Buddhist and student protest demonstrations had subsided, temporarily at least. Massive United States material aid, including increased numbers of combat forces, continued to arrive to help check the continuing Communist insurgency effort which was being strongly aided by troops and materiel from North Vietnam's military establishment. The government was plagued, however, by serious inflation, caused mainly by the increase in spending attributable to the large influx of United States military and civilian personnel and by the shortage of goods resulting from distribution bottlenecks.

Although the South Vietnamese Government considers that it has authority over all of the territory south of the Demarcation Line established by the Geneva Agreement, in practice the Viet Cong insurgents, in mid-1966, dominated many areas within that territory. The location and extent of the areas remaining outside the effective control of Saigon authorities varied in relation to the fortunes of the military combat. In general, the government was paramount more in the urban places and less so in many rural areas. Similarly, it had more control by day than by night, when Viet Cong groups had relative freedom of movement under the cover of darkness.

On the positive side, serious efforts were being made to gain the support of the rural population, and some success was indicated. A separate Department of Revolutionary Development, formerly the Department of Rural Reconstruction, under the Ministry of War and Reconstruction, was engaged in carrying out a program for bringing security, social justice, medical care, dispensaries, schools and other facilities to the villages.

The design is to give impetus to the efforts in the fields performed by the various ministries, with the overall objective of developing a desire for political and economic coherence within the state. In this respect, the national leadership was faced with many difficult problems. The most critical was the successful prosecution of a counterinsurgency war, but at the same time it was faced with the necessity of attempting to develop representative, competent and stable governmental processes capable of checking inflation, curbing venality and keeping opposition activities of political dissidents within the bounds of orderly procedures. It seemed clear that the ultimate favorable outcome of the prolonged conflict would depend primarily upon the government's capacity to win popular support from the countryside and to inspire the people with a sense of national consciousness.

CHAPTER 2

PHYSICAL ENVIRONMENT

South Vietnam is the southern part of prepartition Vietnam, one of the world's oldest nations. It occupies the lower eastern extremity of the Southeast Asian Peninsula which thrusts southward between India and China (see fig. 1). With an area of about 66,200 square miles, it is about equal in size to one of its western neighbors, Cambodia, with which it shares its longest land frontier. The population of approximately 16.1 million in mid-1965, however, was more than 2½ times greater than Cambodia's.

Saigon, the capital city, had a population of almost 1.5 million in mid-1965 and was also the country's chief port and major industrial center. It is approximately 900 air-miles from Hong Kong and about 1,000 miles from Manila.

In 1954, by the Geneva Agreement, the whole of Vietnam was divided provisionally into two approximately equal parts (see ch. 3, Historical Setting). The Demarcation Line separating South Vietnam from the Communist-controlled North runs along a small river, the Song Ben Hai, from its mouth to the village of Bo Ho Su, and from there due west to the Laotian border. Because the Song Ben Hai is very close to the 17th parallel, the Demarcation Line is usually referred to as the 17th parallel.

The natural land routes into prepartition Vietnam were from the north rather than from the west. The predominant Mongoloid component in the racial inheritance of the people is believed to have come into the country from southern China in the centuries before the Christian era (see ch. 5, Ethnic Groups and Languages). The existence of these routes, and also the ease with which the country could be reached by sea from coastal China, enabled China to exert a dominant role in Vietnamese history (see ch. 3, Historical Setting). The subsequent migration of the people along the coastal plain carried this Chinese influence into the delta of the Mekong River. There it came into contact with the Hindu culture and traditions of India which had slowly reached the delta area through the dense jungles of Thailand and along the difficult sea route around the Malay Peninsula. The passage of time has seen a gradual ascendancy of Chinese over Indian influences.

The land boundaries of the prepartition nation evolved over the course of centuries and, except in the Mekong Delta, generally ran through sparsely settled mountains and relatively inaccessible regions. By about 1800 the boundaries with Laos and Cambodia had been roughly defined by Vietnamese conquest and settlement at approximately their present-day limits. Between 1863 and 1893 the French gained control of Cambodia, Laos and Vietnam and formalized the boundaries between them by treaty and administrative decision. Vietnam was arbitrarily deprived of its name and divided into three parts: the colony of Cochin China in the south; the protectorate of Annam in the center; and the protectorate of Tonkin in the north (see ch. 3, Historical Setting). The partition of 1954 approximately bisected the original territory of Vietnam.

The boundaries with Laos and Cambodia, though based in part on the administrative convenience of the colonial power, France, also reflected, to a degree, ethnic and geographic divisions and were not a source of dispute for more than half a century. Since World War II, however, friction has developed with Cambodia over administration of Dao Phu Quoc, an island in the Gulf of Siam, which was assigned to Cochin China by the French authorities in 1939. More recently, the South Vietnamese Government has become increasingly concerned with broader problems arising from reported use of military approach routes and sanctuaries in both Cambodia and Laos by Communist-controlled North Vietnam in its aggression against Laos and South Vietnam.

Structurally, there are three major regions discernible in South Vietnam—the Mekong Delta, the southern portions of the Chaîne Annamitique and the Central Lowlands. The Mekong Delta occupies the southern two-fifths of the country, and its fertile alluvial plains, favored by heavy rainfall, make it one of the great ricegrowing areas of the world. The Chaîne Annamitique, with several high plateaus, dominates the area northward from the Mekong Delta to the Demarcation Line and continues on into North Vietnam. The Central Lowlands (still so designated even though they are central only to prepartition Vietnam and not to South Vietnam) consist of a fertile, narrow, coastal strip along the eastern slopes of the Chaîne Annamitique (see fig. 2).

Lying entirely below the Tropic of Cancer, the area has a hot and humid climate. The monthly mean temperature is about 80° F., and the annual rainfall is consistently heavy. The monsoons, blowing generally from the south in the summer and from the north in the winter, profoundly influence the temperature and rainfall. The strength and direction of the wind, as well as the amount and timing of the rainfall, however, vary considerably from place to place because of differences in latitude and the marked variety of physical relief.

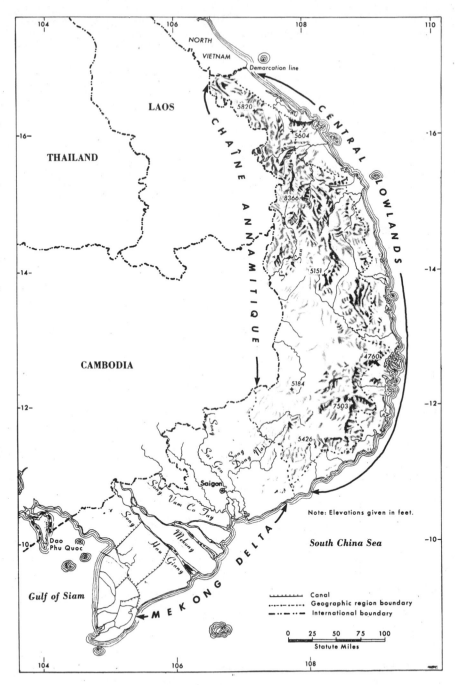

Figure 2.   Relief and Geographic Regions of South Vietnam.

11

The warm climate and heavy rainfall produce luxuriant vegetation and favor the existence of tropical forest conditions over broad portions of the country.

The population of approximately 16.1 million is heavily concentrated in the region of the Delta which includes about 40 percent of the country's total area. In contrast, the uplands and mountainous regions, comprising most of the remaining 60 percent of the country, are sparsely settled, certain portions being almost uninhabited. The overwhelming proportion of the population lives in rural communities.

About 85 percent of the population is of Vietnamese ethnic origin. Of the several minority groups, among the most important are the various highland tribes—usually known collectively as the *montagnards*—who number over half a million and live in the mountains and on the high plateaus. Originally they occupied the prosperous valleys of the coastal regions with easy access to the sea. With the rise of the Kingdom of Champa in the third century, the *montagnards* were eventually driven from the fertile lands along the coast into the highlands where they accommodated themselves to that environment. Later, in the fifteenth century, the Vietnamese virtually destroyed the Chams and extended their control to the southern slopes of the Chaîne Annamitique. The *montagnards* were effectively locked in the mountain hinterlands and accordingly have had little contact with the rest of Vietnamese society.

Another important minority is the Chinese, who total more than three-quarters of a million and live mainly in the cities as merchants, contractors, managers, rice brokers and moneylenders. Nearly half a million Khmers (akin to the principal population of Cambodia) form the third most important minority group, and exist as farmers in the provinces along the Cambodian border (see ch. 5, Ethnic Groups and Languages).

The people of South Vietnam are more than usually dependent upon their physical environment because of the primary agricultural base that supports their economy. Since they exist on a rice culture, the surface configuration, climate, vegetation, and soils all play a great part in determining the limits and potentialities of ricegrowing areas. The extent to which rice culture can be supplemented by other activities is also influenced to a measurable degree by these same factors.

GEOGRAPHICAL REGIONS

South Vietnam varies greatly in its topography. The three major geographic regions, the Mekong Delta, the Chaîne Annamitique, and the Central Lowlands, have served more as divisive rather than cohesive factors in the development of the country.

Mekong Delta

The 2,800-mile-long Mekong is one of the 12 great rivers of the world and, together with the Amur, the Hwang Ho (Yellow), and the Chang Chiang (Yangtze), provides the Pacific drainage of the Asian Continent. From its source in the high plateau of Tibet, not far from the headwaters of the Yangtze of China and the Salween of Burma, it flows through Tibet and China to the northern border of Laos. There it separates Burma from Laos and, farther downstream, Laos from Thailand. Flowing through Cambodia, it bifurcates at the capital, Phnom Penh, at the apex of the delta, the broad base of which is in Vietnam to the south and east on the South China Sea. The southern branch, the Song Hau Giang flows directly to the sea; the larger northern branch splits into four parts about 50 miles before reaching the sea (see fig. 3).

The heavily silted Mekong is navigable by seagoing craft of shallow draft only. These can proceed as far as the rapids at Kompong Cham, about 70 miles above Phnom Penh. Thereafter, frequent portages are required, and the river journey to Luang Prabang in central Laos takes about 37 days in the dry season and 27 days in the wet season.

A tributary, which enters the Mekong at Phnom Penh, drains the Tonle Sap. This large fresh-water lake, which was once an arm of the sea, covers approximately 1,000 square miles in central Cambodia and serves as a regulating reservoir to stabilize the flow of water through the lower Mekong. When the river is in flood, its silted delta outlets are unable to carry off the floodwaters, and they back up into the Tonle Sap, expanding the lake to cover as much as 4 times its low-water area. As the river flood subsides, the water reverses its course and flows from the lake to the sea. The effect is to reduce significantly the danger of serious floods in the Mekong Delta. The first major flood in 30 years occurred in October 1961, when the volume of water was too great for the Tonle Sap to hold. The disaster was worsened by being unexpected.

In South Vietnam the delta proper, approximately 26,000 square miles in area, was built up by the five branches of the Mekong, which total about 300 miles in length, and the system of three smaller rivers—the Song Vam Co, the Song Sai Gon and the Song Dong Nai. The low, level plain, nowhere more than 10 feet above sea level, is very fertile, and cultivated land extends to the immediate shoreline in the vicinity of the river mouths. So much sediment is brought to the sea that the coastline to the south is advancing as much as 250 feet per year. More than 9,000 square miles of delta land are under rice cultivation (see ch. 19, Agriculture). Drainage is effected chiefly by tidal action which differs greatly from place to place. The difference between high and low tides is about 3 feet on the Song Hau

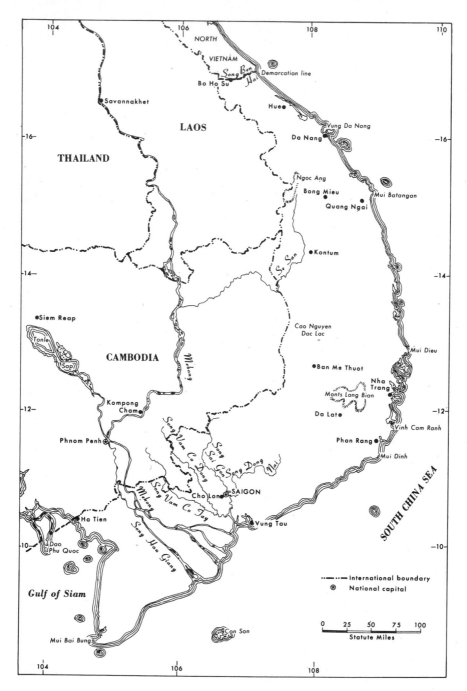

Figure 3.   South Vietnam.

Giang and double that along the northern outlets of the Mekong and the Song Sai Gon. The southernmost tip of the delta, known as the Mui Bai Bung (Ca Mau Peninsula), is covered with dense jungles and the shoreline by mangrove swamps.

The people of the delta region live in villages made up largely of bamboo houses with thatched roofs which are built directly on the ground. Village streets usually follow a regular pattern, and the entire community ordinarily is enclosed by a bamboo fence. Levees and dykes built for flood control are used extensively as village sites, and are often strung out along riverbanks and roads. During the flood period, the only dry land is that forming the banks of the canals and rivers. On such pieces of land, often isolated by the floodwaters from other communities and neighbors, stand the farmhouses with their small garden plots for growing vegetables and a few fruit trees.

Chaîne Annamitique

The Chaîne Annamitique is the southernmost spur, over 750 miles in length, of the rugged mountains which originate in Tibet and China. It extends southeastward, forming the border between South Vietnam and Laos and, later, between South Vietnam and Cambodia, until it reaches the Mekong Delta where it terminates about 50 miles north of Saigon. The Chaîne is irregular in height and form and gives off numerous spurs which divided the coastal strip into a series of compartments and render north-south communication difficult. The southern reaches of these mountains are quite extensive and form an effective natural barrier for the containment of the people who live in the Mekong basin.

The northern portion of the Chaîne, which extends into North Vietnam, is narrow and very rugged; within the southern portion is formed a plateau area, known as the Central Highlands, which is about 100 miles wide and 200 miles in length. The peaks of the Chaîne Annamitique range in height from about 5,000 feet to the 8,521-foot height of Ngoc Ang, which is about 75 miles inland from Mui Batangan (see fig. 3).

In the mountain and plateau areas the settlement patterns are varied. Most typical among the *montagnards* are the simple bamboo structures, built on pilings and having thatched roofs. Some tribes often construct extended family long houses, with a long communal house located centrally in the village. Along the hillsides, villages are usually made up of clusters of dwellings, fairly close together.

The Central Highlands, an area covering approximately 20,000 square miles, consists of two distinct parts. The northern part, called Cao Nguyen Dac Lac, extends some 175 miles north from the vicinity of Ban Me Thuot to the Ngoc Ang peak. Irregular in shape, it varies in elevation from about 600 feet to 1,600 feet, with a few peaks rising much higher. This area of approximately 5,400 square miles is covered mainly with bamboo and tropical broadleaf forests interspersed with farms and rubber plantations. The southern portion of the Central Highlands, much of it over 3,000 feet above sea level, includes about 4,000 square miles of usable land. Da Lat, a modern hill city in the center of the area, is overlooked by Monts Lang Bian, with an elevation of 7,380 feet. The forest growth is predominantly of broadleaf evergreens at higher elevations and bamboo on the lower slopes. Coffee, tea, tobacco and temperate-climate vegetables flourish in the fertile soil.

The sparsely settled plateaus of the Central Highlands, with their extensive forests and rich soil, are particularly important to South Vietnam for potential expansion room from the densely populated lowlands.

Central Lowlands

The Central Lowlands of South Vietnam extend along the sea from the Mekong Delta northward to the Demarcation Line. On the landward side, the Chaîne Annamitique rises precipitously above the Lowlands and, in some areas, is nearly 40 miles inland; elsewhere it veers shoreward and at several points crowds into the sea. In general, the land is fertile and is extensively cultivated. The chief crop is rice, and considerable sugarcane is also grown. Fishing is good along the entire coast and is important both as an industry and for local subsistence in the southern section near the Mekong Delta.

From the Mekong Delta an infertile coastal strip, generally narrow and covered with shifting sand dunes, extends northeastward some 100 miles to Mui Dinh. This region has less rainfall than any other part of Vietnam.

From Mui Dinh northward the coastal plain remains narrow for about 100 miles to Mui Dieu where a mountain spur presses against the shore. In this section there are occasional stretches of quite fertile land where rice is grown.

From Mui Dieu to Vung Da Nang, about 250 miles north, lie the most extensive and fertile plains of the Central Lowlands coast where two rice crops a year are grown. From Vung Da Nang to Hue, about 50 miles farther north, mountain spurs jut into the sea at several places. From Hue to the 17th parallel—50 miles beyond—much of the shore is fringed by a narrow line of sand dunes backed by an intensively cultivated flat fertile area.

In the Central Lowlands two distinct types of village predominate. The fishing village, strung out along the coastal plain, usually consists of a close-knit group of dwellings located in a sheltered cove or bay. In the second type of village, fishing is not the major economic activity and its formation follows a pattern similar to that of the delta with houses more dispersed over a broader area.

CLIMATE

The seasonal alternation of the monsoons determines both the rainfall and the temperature throughout the year, although geographical features alter patterns locally. During the winter monsoon, the high-pressure area in the interior of the continental landmass forces dry, cool air outward toward the sea, producing the country's dry season. During the summer monsoon, the heated air of the Gobi Desert rises, causing moist air to flow inland from the sea, depositing heavy rainfall in its passage. Even the northeast winter monsoon, blowing down along the China coast and across the South China Sea, picks up considerable moisture which makes this season in most parts of South Vietnam "dry" only by comparison with the wetter southwest summer monsoon. Typhoons off the South China Sea, bringing heavy rains, strike somewhere in the area on the average of 10 times a year, usually between June and November, and do great damage.

The annual rainfall is heavy in all regions and torrential in many (see figs. 4 and 5). It is heaviest at Hue, which has an annual average of 128 inches. The low of 28 inches at Mui Dinh results from the presence of a barrier of hills in the area. At Saigon, annual rainfall averages 80 inches.

The winter monsoon reaches the Central Lowlands by early October and the Mekong Delta area by November. Here, however, it skirts the receding coastline and brings little rain inland. The winter monsoon continues to blow until April, producing gradually decreasing rainfall in all areas and almost none in the Mekong Delta area. Precipitation increases during April and May, the transitional months between the winter and summer monsoons. By June the summer monsoon has arrived. Coming from the south and southwest, it brings, with important local variations, heavy rains to most parts of the country. The dry season in the Mekong Delta region lasts from December through March.

There is no extended foggy period over any portion of the country. In the northern section of the Central Lowlands area, however, poor visibility occurs during the first part of October, and occasionally from January to July. In the southern portion of the country there is almost no fog at any time of the year.

Except in a few mountainous areas, high temperatures prevail throughout the year. The humidity is generally high and debilitating. The average annual temperature range is not very pronounced, varying only a few degrees between the north (Hue, 77° F.) and the south (Saigon, 81.5° F.) On the mountains and plateaus of the Chaîne Annamitique the temperatures are much lower than in the plains to the west and south.

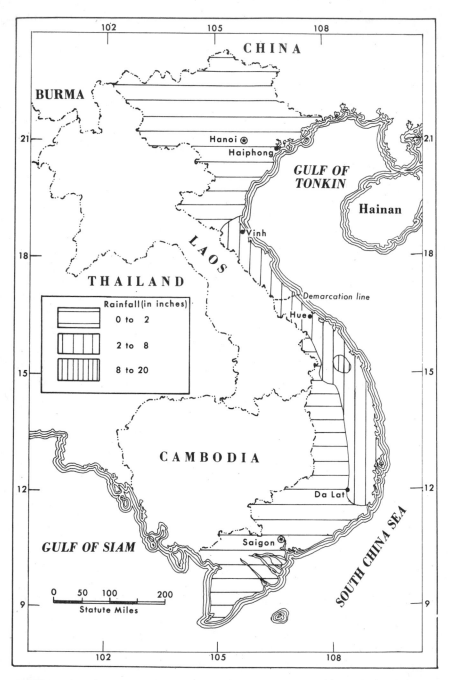

Figure 4. Mean Monthly Rainfall in South and North Vietnam, January.

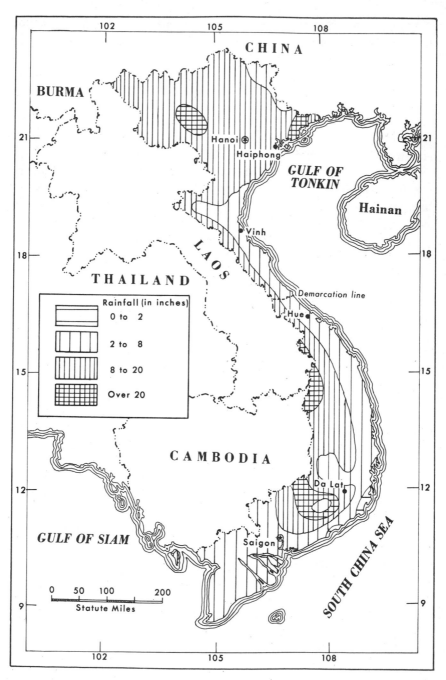

Figure 5. Mean Monthly Rainfall in South and North Vietnam, August.

SOILS AND VEGETATION

Soils range from the rich ricegrowing alluvium in the delta and river areas, through the red soils of the highland plateaus which will support dry crops, to uncultivable sand and rock formations. By far the most important are the delta soils.

In order to retain the great fertility necessary for a heavy rice yield, the alluvium must be renewed periodically. Only those soils nearest the mouths of rivers and streams contain enough phosphorus and potash to support rice cultivation. Soils in the upper delta region retain their productivity only by the use of chemical fertilizers, and some contain toxic quantities of alumina which must be leached out by the application of large quantities of water before they can be planted to rice. The area south of the Song Hau Giang has the best soil in the delta. By contrast, the older alluvial land near Saigon is extremely poor, consisting in many areas of nearly 90 percent pure silica in the form of fine sand (see ch. 19, Agriculture).

In the plateau areas a red laterite soil is found which varies greatly in fertility. Where heavy rains wash off the humus, the silica dissolves out more easily than do the alumina and iron oxides, and the residue produces a red color. Potassium is generally lacking, and the combination of the iron oxides in the laterite plus the effect of rain and sun results in the soil setting like cement. In some plateau areas, where the humus content of the soil has built up under heavy vegetation, plantation crops, particularly rubber, are favored. An estimated 4,000 square miles of such usable red soil exists in this region; very little of it is cultivated because of a lack of roads and other communications.

Approximately one-third of South Vietnam is covered by forests. Evergreen rain forest predominates in upland areas where rainfall is 80 inches or more annually. The less dense deciduous monsoon forests are also extensive in the hills where precipitation is under 80 inches a year. The coastal fringe of the deltas supports large stands of mangrove. Pine forests, bamboo thickets and sand dune growths make up the remainder of the wooded area (see fig. 6).

The nonforested parts of the country are under extensive rice and plantation cultivation except for the savanna areas. These grasslands were created for the most part from monsoon forests either as the result of cultivation or of fires. Other savannas have grown up where the soil was unfavorable to the growth of dense forests.

ANIMAL LIFE

The wild animals are generally of the same types found in Bengal and the Malay Peninsula. The plateaus north of Da Lat have long been considered one of the best hunting areas of the world. The large

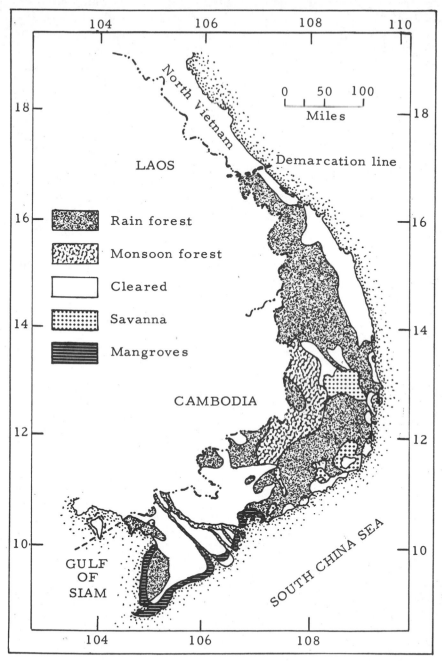

104   106   108   110

North Vietnam

18   0   50   100   18
                           Miles

Demarcation line

LAOS

16   Rain forest   16

        Monsoon forest

        Cleared

14   Savanna   14

        Mangroves

CAMBODIA

12   12

SOUTH CHINA SEA

10   10

GULF
OF
SIAM

104   106   108

Source: Adapted from Canada, Department of Mines and
Technical Surveys, Indo-China, A Geographical
Appreciation, p. 21.

Figure 6. Vegetation in South Vietnam.

species found there include elephants, bears, wild oxen and buffaloes, as well as tigers and leopards in particular abundance. Among smaller game are boar, goats, deer and hares. An interesting form of wild dog is found on the island of Dao Phu Quoc off the coast of Cambodia, with a broad strip of hair, turned the wrong way, running the whole length of its body from head to tail. Monkeys are found in all of the coastal areas. Wild fowl, both water and land birds, are plentiful in many parts of the country.

Crocodiles thrive in the Mekong Delta area, and some deaths from these are recorded each year. Although there are snakes of many varieties, including large pythons, they are seldom seen, and only the cobra and almost all varieties of salt-water snakes are highly dangerous. Deaths from snakebites are rare.

Both fresh- and salt-water fish are plentiful. In coastal areas sharks, dogfish, rays and shad are obtainable in various seasons of the year. Eels are numerous, and a great variety of fresh-water fish of the carp and catfish species are to be found in rivers, canals, lakes and flooded ricefields.

As in most tropical areas, appreciable numbers of insect pests are prevalent. Among them are ants, termites, mosquitoes, ticks and leeches. Leeches are particularly active after rains, possess an affinity for humans and cause acute discomfort.

MINERALS

The land is largely devoid of any great variety or volume of commercially exploitable minerals. Of those of commercial importance, only coal is found in appreciable quantity, in a single anthracite field at Tu Chanh Nong Son, about 30 miles southwest of Da Nang. Some gold is also mined at Bong Mieu in this same general area. White sands, reportedly containing more than 99 percent exploitable silica, stretch almost the full length of the coast. About 3 miles southwest of Hue considerable limestone deposits are known to exist, and other deposits are being exploited farther to the south along the Cambodian border in the coastal area of Ha Tien. Extensive reserves of phosphate rock also exist, and its mining is increasing under the stimulus of an increasing need for chemical fertilizer in rice cultivation, particularly in the Mekong Delta.

TRANSPORTATION

In 1966 the transport facilities showed the destructive effects of a long 6-year period of resurgency of military action. These modern facilities consisted of one railroad, a network of highways and a national airline (see fig. 7).

After the Geneva Agreement of 1954 and the withdrawal of the French forces the following year, the central government undertook, with appreciable United States assistance, an extensive program of rehabilitation, improvement and extension of all transportation facilities. Although much was accomplished, this has been largely offset by the increased destruction and sabotage which has occurred since 1959 as a result of Viet Cong activity.

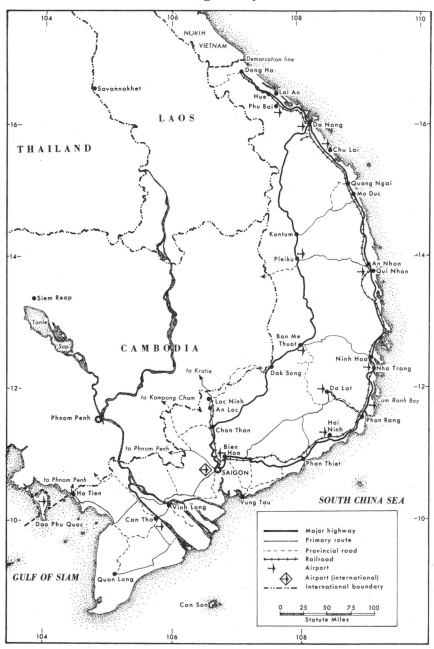

Figure 7. Ports, Railways, Roads and Airfields in South Vietnam.

Roads

In their improvement program, the government has given high priority to the development of modern roads. This program, however, has been nullified to a great degree by the efforts of the Viet Cong to disorganize the country by controlling or disrupting the general use of major roads. There were, in 1962, approximately 9,000 miles of roads, of which about 7,000 miles were considered in motorable condition. Of those so considered, over 2,000 miles were asphalted, about 3,000 were macadamized and about 2,000 were unsurfaced but fairly passable under average conditions. The condition of these roads has generally deteriorated since the Viet Cong have undertaken, at various times, to render strategic links of important routes unusable by sabotaging bridges, establishing roadblocks and ambushes, and by digging deep, wide trenches which require major repair efforts.

There are two principal highways which link Saigon, the capital city, with the north. The most heavily traveled is the old Mandarin route which formerly connected Saigon with Hanoi. It was cut at the Demarcation Line in 1954, and Dong Ha is now its northernmost terminus. The second route extends through the Central Highlands of the Chaîne Annamitique, linking the plateaus within them. It roughly parallels the first from Saigon via Chon Than, Dak Song, Ban Me Thuot, Pleiku, and Kontum to Da Nang. Three connecting highways link these two routes; one between Mo Duc and Kontum; a second between An Nhon (formerly Binh Dinh) and Pleiku and on into Cambodia; and a third between Ninh Hoa and Ban Me Thuot. Two other roads branch off from the old Mandarin route into the mountain regions. One extends westward from Dong Ha into Laos; and the other joins Da Lat with the coast at Phan Thiet. A good highway also runs from the health resort of Da Lat to Saigon.

Two major roads lead from Saigon to Cambodia—the Saigon-An Loc road and the Saigon-Phnom Penh road. One principal route extends generally southward from Saigon into the Mekong Delta. It divides at Vinh Long, one branch extending to Quan Long (formerly Ca Mau), and the other running to the Cambodia border at Ha Tien. Most of the remaining highway network radiates out from Saigon over the delta.

Railroads

The government-owned railroad system consists of approximately 780 miles of main and branch lines. The main line runs from Saigon to Dong Ha just south of the Demarcation Line and links the population centers along the coast. There is a branch line from Phan Rang to Da Lat, and a short line runs from Saigon to Loc Ninh. There are no lines south of Saigon into the Mekong Delta. The section between Da Nang and Nha Trang is the only portion that remains generally operable, requiring considerable assistance from United States troops.

Over 300 miles of the main line were destroyed during the war years up to 1954. Extensive damage had been done to stations, depots and workshops. Moreover, a large portion of the railroad bridges and two-thirds of the locomotives and rolling stock had been demolished.

In 1955 major reconstruction was undertaken with huge amounts of United States aid. Much had been accomplished by 1959, and by the end of 1962 restoration and rehabilitation had progressed appreciably. Since 1962, however, renewed destruction of facilities by the Viet Cong has taken place, reducing operating mileage at times to less than 100 miles, principally between Nha Trang and Da Nang.

Air Transport

The only national airline, Air Vietnam, provides both domestic and international flight services. The controlling interest in the company is held by the government; French interests—mainly Air France—own the remainder. Tan Son Nhut Airport at Saigon handles the bulk of the country's air traffic, and the most frequent flights are between Saigon and Hue. There are also commercial airports at Da Nang, Nha Trang, Qui Nhon, Bien Hoa, Da Lat, Ban Me Thuot, Pleiku, Hai Ninh, Can Tho and Dao Phu Quoc. United States forces are developing and improving additional airfields at Chu Lai and Cam Ranh Bay for the military support of United States and South Vietnamese forces. Also, the United States and South Vietnam military forces are providing aerial supply for many urban centers that have been isolated by the interdiction of ground supply routes by the Viet Cong.

Air Vietnam's regional service connects with Phnom Penh and Siem Reap in Cambodia, with Bangkok in Thailand and with Vientiane and Savannakhet in Laos. International service is also provided principally by Pan American Airways, British Overseas Airways Corporation, Royal Dutch Airways, Air France, Air Laos and Royal Air Cambodge.

Waterways

Water transport of any great magnitude is restricted to the Mekong Delta where roads are generally impracticable. Climatic and topographic factors limit the regional use of water transportation, and the lack of communication between river systems hampers the broad development of a countrywide network. Throughout the country area there are about 2,750 miles of inland waterways of which close to 1,350 are canals. The greater part of this river-canal system is located in the Mekong Delta and is oriented toward Saigon as a distribution center. Although it has carried well over 4 million tons of traffic annually in past years, its present capacity has been reduced appreciably by Viet Cong interference.

Navigation in the Mekong Delta is facilitated by the dredging of riverbeds and the constant improvement of the canals, particularly those which connect the principal rivers of the region. Sampans, junks and other shallow-draft vessels are mostly used, although small steamers are common on the lower reaches of the rivers. An exception is the Song Sai Gon which can accommodate ships of up to 19 feet of draft as far as Saigon, 45 miles inland. This is made possible by the relatively low silt-bearing nature of the Song Sai Gon and by the ocean tides which scour the approaches to the river's mouth twice a day.

Above the delta region, the rivers are short, swift and used very little for navigation. Shifting channels and variable depths also serve to limit their general use. Small motorized launches and steamers are capable of navigating the lower parts of most of the rivers during the period of high water. Sampans and other small indigenous craft can utilize the waterways at any time of the year, being little affected by climatic or tide conditions.

Ports

Before 1965 the nation had one chief port, Saigon, and three ports of much lesser commercial significance, Da Nang, Nha Trang, and Qui Nhon. Coincidental with the substantial increase of United States military support, in 1965, these smaller coastal ports have been improved and incorporated into a system of military supply bases extending from Hue to Vung Tau.

Saigon, situated 45 miles from the sea on the Song Sai Gon is one of the great ports of Southeast Asia and the largest city in the country. It has a population of almost 1,500,000, not including the more than 700,000 inhabitants of the adjacent city of Cho Lon. Saigon is a modern city and the business and commercial center of the port; Cho Lon is the industrial center, and contains the largest concentration of overseas Chinese in South Vietnam.

All overseas trade for the entire country focuses on Saigon. The important rubber plantations are easily accessible from the city, and its textile mills, sugar factories, papermills, cement plants and glassworks are taking on increasing importance (see ch. 20, Industry). All rice for export is collected in this port and constitutes 50 percent of the export tonnage in normal times. The international airport of Tan Son Nhut which serves Saigon has become one of the busiest in the world. In a peak period during 1965 it handled 1 million pounds of cargo, and its volume of traffic generally exceeds that of San Francisco.

Port facilities are ample for a trade which amounts to 1,300 overseas vessels a year and thousands of small river and coastal craft. The city is situated well inland, and seagoing ships must proceed through an adequate but circuitous channel to reach the docks in the city proper. The channel varies from 29 to 39 feet in depth; the riverfront docks are designed to take ships with a draft of no more than 19 feet, although larger ships can be accommodated on favorable tides.

Hue, situated 50 miles south of the 17th parallel, is the northernmost base in the military coastal supply system. It was the imperial capital of all Vietnam for two centuries, and, despite its population of more than 100,000, it has no industrial plants. The neighboring port of Lai An cannot accommodate oceangoing ships, but it serves as a naval and coast guard station. The nearby airfield of Phu Bai, with United States aid, has become its lifeline to the rest of the country because of Viet Cong control of the surrounding area.

Da Nang, also a city of over 100,000 is considered the best port in the entire Central Lowlands. It has adequate harbor facilities, but its deep anchorage is exposed to heavy winds from the northeast during the winter monsoon. It has a seaplane anchorage, and United States forces have built two 10,000-foot runways to modernize its airfield, now one of the most important in the northern area.

Lying between Da Nang and Quang Ngai is the expanding port area of Chu Lai. It is undergoing development under military impetus as an important supply port and will probably be an economic asset of considerable future commercial value. In addition, this strategic base contains two runways, 8,000 and 10,000 feet in length, respectively, and serves as a major airbase in the war against the Viet Cong.

Farther to the south are situated Quang Ngai and Qui Nhon, two small fishing ports which are serving as naval stations and military land bases in the predominant United States military effort against the Viet Cong to keep land routes open from the coast to the plateau areas of the Central Highlands. Both these ports have shallow beaches which permit lighterage of large cargo ships.

Halfway down the coast, at Nha Trang, the United States has developed its major logistic base for the entry and supply of military forces. This base extends 15 miles southward where it is linked with the harbor and newly developed port facilities of Cam Ranh Bay. Cam Ranh Bay, rated as one of the best natural harbors in Asia, contains sheltered deepwater facilities which have assisted in the rapid establishment of huge stockpiles and staging depots for military support purposes. The potential commercial value of this port complex to the economy of South Vietnam is further enhanced by the planned building of two parallel 10,000-foot jet runways.

Vung Tau is the southernmost port and coastal base, being located more than 400 miles south of Hue. Once known as Saint Jacques, this port is becoming the main support center for the entire southern region. It is situated at the entrance to the river system leading to the capital, and work is continuing to expand its harbor facilities to accommodate oceangoing vessels. When completed, fewer ships will have to wait during busy periods to go upriver to unload cargoes.

CHAPTER 3

HISTORICAL SETTING

Throughout 2,000 years of recorded history—to which legend adds 2,000 more—the Vietnamese have been sustained by a feeling of unity based on common origin, language and cultural heritage. They are intensely proud of having been an independent and unified nation for centuries, although they also experienced periods of disunity and foreign domination. They take equal pride in their cultural heritage, regarded by them as an eloquent testimony to their eclectic and creative talents for absorbing foreign cultures without themselves losing distinct political identity.

In the evolution of Vietnamese society and culture, much of the formative influence came from China, whose colonial officials and traders were largely responsible for the transmission of the Chinese way of life. The Chinese influences intermingled freely with the indigenous culture, known as Dong-Son (Indonesian), which dates from around the fourth century B.C. and was then centered in the Red River Delta.

A striking feature of Vietnam's history is the story of its relations with China, its vastly larger and more powerful neighbor to the north. Over the centuries the Vietnamese have admired China for its superior culture and feared it for its power. During the 1,000 years (second century B.C. to the tenth century A.D.) that the country was ruled directly by China, the people accepted discriminately much of the dominant culture, but politically they were inclined to be militantly anti-Chinese.

Freeing themselves from direct Chinese control in A.D. 938, they thereafter jealously guarded their independence by various means, at times holding off invading Chinese and Mongolian armies and at others, resorting to hard bargaining, the payment of tribute or the acceptance of nominal Chinese overlordship. Negotiating from weakness, they became adroit bargainers, expert in obtaining through suppleness and patience the best terms under a given circumstance.

In their long resistance to Chinese domination, they came to regard China as the traditional enemy. This old antagonism profoundly affects their thinking and attitude, and many Vietnamese continue to see danger in any relationship with China.

The Chinese rule was followed by varying degrees of independence under a succession of Vietnamese emperors presiding over a powerful bureaucracy of the Chinese type. Revolts were numerous and, with brief periods of reasserted Chinese control, one dynasty fell to be replaced by another but the outcome was always a transfer of authority without basic change in the sociopolitical structure.

The Vietnamese are prone to regard themselves as peaceful people, but they assign high importance to valor and fighting ability in their survival as a nation. The heroes and heroines of their history are those who rebelled against invading armies from the north. To the prowess of their ancestors they attribute not only successful resistance to Chinese encroachment but also the extension of their territory to the present boundaries of North and South Vietnam by victories over neighboring kingdoms to the south and west.

Because of powerful China to the north, and apart from defending themselves against occasional northern invaders, the main thrust of Vietnamese history usually has been directed southward, as epitomized in *nam-tien* (march southward). Aided by superior organizational skill and military techniques acquired from the Chinese, the people of the overcrowded Red River Delta moved down the coastline in search of more rice paddies. In the process they pushed the original settlers of the lowland coastal areas further back into the highlands to gain the fertile foothills for themselves. This process of southern expansion continued at the expense of the peoples of the Kingdom of Champa to the south of Hue and of Cambodia to the west until the Vietnamese acquired the fertile lands of the Mekong River Delta in the eighteenth century. Through the absorption of these peoples, who had been under the cultural influence of India, the Vietnamese came into contact with the Hindu civilization of India.

This pattern of expansion left an indelible imprint on the differing cultural orientation between the north-central section of the country on the one hand and the southern part of the country on the other. The people of the northern (Tonkin) and central (Annam) regions came to be regarded as keenly conscious of a traditional way of life. Those in the southern part (Cochin China)—perhaps because of their exposure to Indian influence—were thought to be more eclectic and less tradition-bound.

Moreover, during nearly a century of French rule, which had begun in the latter part of the nineteenth century, the varying pattern of French control gave further solidity to the country's cultural variation. Because the French rule was more direct and all-pervasive in the south than in the northern and central regions, the impact of French influence was correspondingly more pronounced in the south, resulting in a more culturally heterogenous society there.

The French, much more than the Chinese before them, remained alien to the people. The Vietnamese, as they always had, reacted to foreign control with reluctant acquiescence and, when they could, with open resistance. During World War II French rule was exercised by representatives of the Vichy regime at the sufferance of Japan until March 1945, when it was ended by a Japanese coup d'etat. After Japan's surrender, the French returned to a position which the events of the war years had made irretrievable.

In the Indochina War, which broke out at the end of 1946 and ended nearly 8 years later in the French defeat at Dien Bien Phu, the French found themselves confronted by the skillful and determined Communist leadership under Ho Chi Minh. The Communists, exploiting popular opposition to the continuation of any form of foreign control, soon came to the forefront in the increasingly bitter struggle. Under a nationalist disguise within the Viet Minh—a Communist-led coaliton group—they attracted the active or passive support of most of the population.

With the achievement of independence and the partitioning of the country in 1954, Vietnam entered a new phase of conflict. The struggle was between the non-Communist government in the South, supported by the United States and its allies, and the Communist regime in the North, backed by Communist China and the Soviet Union. Beginning in 1958 the northern regime stepped up its efforts to subjugate the South through a well-organized campaign of subversion and terror. Eventually the United States, at South Vietnam's request, intervened to help the Saigon government repel armed aggression from the North. In early 1966 the outcome of the North-South confrontation still remained bitterly contested.

HISTORIC ORIGINS

Legend establishes the first Vietnamese kingdom in what is now North Vietnam. According to one story, Lac Long Quan, the first Vietnamese king, was the descendant of a line of Chinese divine rulers. He married Au Co, an immortal, and, according to the legend, fathered 100 sons. The king and queen then parted, dividing sons between them. The king went south; the queen, north into the mountains near Hanoi. The eldest of the boys accompanying the king was then installed on the throne and founded the Hong Bang dynasty, the dates of which are given as 2879 to 258 B.C. This legendary account, which probably was not developed in literary form until after A.D. 1200, differs in substance from Chinese mythical history but shares some themes and figures with it. The resemblance suggests not only Chinese influence but an effort by the Vietnamese chroniclers to show that in origin and antiquity Vietnam (lit., the

Viet of the South or Southern Viet) was in no way inferior to dominant China.

The first historical records pertaining to the people in the Red River Delta were written by the Chinese after they had conquered the area in the third century B.C. Still earlier Chinese accounts mention a Viet (Yüeh in Chinese) kingdom which existed about 500 B.C. south of the Yangtze River. This kingdom fell in 333 B.C., and its inhabitants, one of the many tribal peoples in southern China at the time, moved further south.

Basically Mongoloid, like the Chinese, they seem to have shown, both physically and culturally, the results of mixture with Mon-Khmer- and Malayo-Polynesian-speaking peoples. Some of the Viets remained in China and over the centuries were integrated into the developing Chinese civilization, the dynamic center of which was then in northern China. Others, under pressure from the north, pushed south, reaching the Red River Delta in the mid-fourth century B.C., and encountered a mixed Indonesian population with which they both fought and mingled.

After the fall of the Ch'in dynasty of China (897–207 B.C.), there emerged a number of small, competing states, which, after 207 B.C., had been united as the Kingdom of Nam Viet under a Chinese general. This kingdom is referred to as Nan Yüeh (Southern Viet) in ancient Chinese chronicles. It controlled the areas west of the present site of Canton and extended through the Red River Delta down to Hai Van Pass, 40 miles south of Hue.

CHINESE DOMINATION

The overthrow of the Kingdom of Nam Viet in 111 B.C. by the armies of the Chinese Han dynasty (202 B.C. to A.D. 220) marked the end of the legendary period of Vietnamese history. The Red River valley and a coastal strip to the south as far as Hue became Giao Chi, the southernmost Chinese province, and for the next 1,000 years the events in the area were an integral part of imperial China.

The Chinese found the Viets organized on feudal lines. Villages and groups of villages led by hereditary local chiefs were in vassalage to provincial lords, who, in turn, owed allegiance to the king, to whom many of them were related. The primitive agriculture of the people included some knowledge of irrigation but not the plow and the water buffalo, which were introduced by the Chinese. Fish and game supplemented the cereals raised in the fire-cleared fields. Bronze had made its appearance in the form of ceremonial objects and arrowheads, but the principal agricultural tool was the stone hoe, and the people hunted and fought with spears and bows and arrows.

Chinese rule was not initially oppressive, and the Vietnamese feudal chiefs, although required to recognize the authority of a few Chinese high officials and pay taxes to the Chinese throne, were left largely undisturbed. Chinese agricultural technology, intellectual culture, and method of making weapons were readily accepted. Life in the delta was enriched but not overwhelmed. Later, when a growing Chinese officialdom began to expand its direct controls, the local aristocracy rallied against the alien encroachment on their hereditary prerogatives. Armed revolt in A.D. 39 briefly threw off the Chinese yoke. The struggle was led by two sisters, Trung Trac and Trung Nhi, who ruled jointly until A.D. 43, when, with the defeat of their forces by the Chinese, they drowned themselves. The memory of the warrior queens has been preserved in Vietnam as a symbol of resistance to foreign oppression.

The revolt was harshly suppressed, and those of its leaders who were not killed were exiled or degraded. With the old feudal order weakened, direct Chinese rule was imposed, and only subordinate places in the bureaucracy were left to the Vietnamese. The process of introducing Chinese culture, which now began in earnest, remade many aspects of Vietnamese life.

In attempts to strengthen central authority by destroying feudal vestiges at local levels, China introduced, around A.D. 50, a system of communal administration under which groups of 5 to 50 families formed communes. As the basic administrative and social unit, the commune had considerable freedom to manage local affairs through its council, which was chosen by influential villagers and family heads from among their own number. The council was responsible for public order, implementation of official decrees, the collection of taxes and the recruitment of conscripts for the army. In discharging these functions the village council was financially independent of the central government because its operating expenses were derived mostly from village communal land, which also served to support the landless and needy people of a village. By installing their own administrative institutions, the Chinese gave the Vietnamese a new political structure, the cohesion and strength of which later made it possible for Vietnam to resist and expel invaders from the north.

There were important areas of thought and action over which the process of acculturation simply spread a Chinese gloss without essentially altering the resistant material beneath. This was especially true of the peasantry from whom the Chinese rule meant mainly the payment of taxes and the giving of labor service. Conscious of their distinctive ethnic identity, the peasants continued to use their traditional language and clung to animism and other customs preserved from long before the arrival of the Chinese. When confronted with oppressive Chinese officials, the peasants resisted them, rallying around their communes which served as the focus of social and political activities. It was in acknowledgment of the debt the country owed to these village communes that all the Vietnamese dynasties after China took great care to preserve village autonomy. The autonomous village tradition is perhaps best epitomized by a popular saying, "the king's laws bow before village customs."

Vietnamese language, the origin of which remains controversial, was retained though it was enriched by Chinese words and expressions. Nevertheless, the Chinese language and learning were essential to any who aspired to office under the Chinese. Educated Vietnamese were largely oriented toward Chinese culture, but their native roots were also preserved through their continuing contacts with the ordinary people whom they helped the Chinese govern.

In a parallel process, Chinese officials, acquiring land and wealth and marrying Vietnamese, developed local loyalties and personal ambitions which rendered increasingly remote the claims of Peiping. Out of this mingling of cultures and convergence of interests there was to emerge a new breed of Chinese elite, owing allegiance to their homeland but displaying increasing Vietnamese orientation.

Chinese domination survived the collapse of the Han dynasty in A.D. 220 and the ensuing period of confusion, during which several anti-Chinese revolts were attempted. In A.D. 248, Trieu Au, a woman, incited an uprising which was put down the following year. Ly Bon led a revolt in 542 and proclaimed himself emperor in 544, but the Chinese ousted him by the following year. Ly Xuan in 589 and Ly Phat Tu in 602 also tried unsuccessfully to overthrow the Chinese authorities. The leaders of the revolts are honored as national heroes in Vietnam today.

In A.D. 679 the T'ang dynasty (618–907) made the province of Giao Chi a protectorate-general and renamed it Annam (Pacified South), a term resented by the Vietnamese. Under more liberal policies, Annam thrived, the population increased and reclamation and resettlement of the Red River Delta proceeded more vigorously. Culture was further enriched under Buddhist influence, first introduced by a Chinese monk around A.D. 188.

Prosperity and the continued penetration of Chinese influence did not, however, check the growth of incipient national feeling. The Vietnamese were frequently in revolt, and although these uprisings usually involved only upper-class elements and were invariably short lived, they produced an array of national heroes and heroines celebrated in Vietnamese history and still venerated at many village and city shrines.

INDEPENDENCE

The disorders following the fall of the T'ang dynasty provided the opportunity the Vietnamese had long sought. In A.D. 938 one of their generals, Ngo Quyen, in a struggle culminating in the battle of Bach Dang, drove out the occupying Chinese forces from the Red

River Delta and founded the short-lived Ngo dynasty. Chinese attempts to retake the Red River valley were repelled, and by 946, though by no means entirely secure and out of danger from the Chinese, the first independent Vietnam became a historical reality. With the exception of a 20-year interlude of Chinese reoccupation early in the fifteenth century, it remained independent for the next 900 years.

The Dinh Dynasty (968–980)

The formation of stable institutions of government which could function without the sustaining influence of a foreign occupying power proved difficult, and during the latter part of the tenth century there were no less than a dozen autonomous local leaders in the Red River valley. One of them, Dinh Bo Linh, defeated his rivals in 968 and called his new state Dai Co Viet (Great Viet State). The Chinese continued to refer to it as Annam.

Aware of the superior power that the newly established Chinese Sung dynasty (960–1126) could bring against him, Dinh Bo Linh embarked on a course which was to establish the basis for future relations with China for many centuries. He sent an embassy to the Sung court, requesting confirmation of his authority over Dai Co Viet. This embassy agreed to accept, on his behalf, the title of vassal king and to send a triennial tribute to China.

Acceptance of Chinese suzerainty was softened by the understanding that the Chinese would not attempt to restore their authority over the country. Moreover, Dinh Bo Linh was permitted to call himself emperor at home and in dealing with countries other than China. Peace with China was maintained during most of the Dinh dynasty. Relations with the Kingdom of Champa to the south, however, were unfriendly, and the two kingdoms were in frequent conflict. Champa was then within the Indian rather than the Chinese cultural sphere.

The Ly Dynasty (1009–1225)

The Dinh dynasty did not outlast the first emperor, whose throne was usurped. The Ly dynasty, established in 1009, was the first of the great Vietnamese dynasties and, after an interval of confusion, ushered in a period of population growth, territorial expansion, prosperity, cultural development and stability. An efficient central government with a strong administrative and military organization was formed. The Ly rulers, adapting the Confucian Chinese model, gave the government the form it retained until the French conquest.

The emperor had three roles. He was at once the father of the nation-family, the absolute temporal monarch in whom all powers of the state resided and, finally, the religious head of the realm and intermediary between it and heaven, the highest realm of the supernatural. The work of administering the country was carried on by a civil bureaucracy—the so-called mandarinate. Six administrative departments were created: personnel, finance, rites, justice, armed forces and public works. A board of censors kept watch over the civil servants and advised the emperor of any infractions.

The first literary examinations were held in the mid-eleventh century; a college for prospective civil servants and an imperial academy were founded—all geared to the mandarinate system. Ranked in nine grades, the mandarins were recruited through public examinations in which knowledge of the Chinese Confucian classics and skill in literary composition were the central requirements. This method of recruitment survived until the second decade of the twentieth century.

Public revenues were used to complete the drainage and resettlement of the Red River Delta and to build new dikes, canals and roads. More land was opened up for rice cultivation to feed the expanding population. An army was created which not only repelled a Chinese invasion in 1076 but also checked aggression from the Kingdom of Cambodia and seized territory from the Kingdom of Champa (A.D. 192–1471), which then controlled territories corresponding roughly to the present Central Lowlands and Central Highlands. It was after one of the victories over Champa in 1069 that Thanh-Tong, the third Ly emperor and one of the greatest Vietnamese sovereigns, renamed the country Dai-Viet (Greater Viet). The country kept this name until 1802, when Emperor Gia Long changed it to Viet Nam.

It was during the Ly dynasty that the expansionist policy of *nam-tien* began in earnest. This policy was continued down through Vietnamese history until 1780, when the southern tip of the Indochinese peninsula was acquired from Cambodia.

During this dynasty, Buddhism reached its height on the strength of royal patronage. It was made the state religion. Many of the better educated Buddhist monks filled high official posts. The Ly rulers also encouraged Confucianism and Taoism. Taoism, in particular, penetrated the countryside, adulterating popular Buddhism. Art depicting Buddhist themes also flourished. Another notable achievement was the perfection of ceramic art (see ch. 11, Religion).

The Tran Dynasty (1225–1400)

In 1225 the throne was seized by the Tran dynasty which held it for 175 years of repeated military crisis, including prolonged conflict with the Kingdom of Champa. Three invasions by the Mongol armies of Kublai Khan—in 1257, 1284 and 1287—were repelled. The Vietnamese victory under General Tran Hung Dao in the last of these encounters is one of the most celebrated in the annals of the country's history. After the Mongol withdrawal, the Tran monarch sent a mission to Kublai Khan and reestablished peace as a tributary of Mongol-ruled China.

During this dynasty, Confucianism, with its emphasis on learning, replaced Buddhism in importance. This scholarly atmosphere produced a number of literary accomplishments. The first extant historical records—a 30-volume official history of Dai-Viet (*Dai-Viet Su-ky*)—date from the Tran. Other historical writings and biographies also appeared—all written in Chinese (see ch. 10, Artistic and Intellectual Expression).

The Chinese Interregnum (1406–28)

Economic and social crises, following the devastation of war, were intensified by the aggrandizement of big landlords at the expense of the peasantry and by incompetence and corruption in the bureaucracy. An ambitious regent, Ho Qui Ly, took advantage of the situation to usurp the throne, thereby giving the Ming dynasty (1368–1662) of China the occasion to intervene on the pretext of restoring the Tran dynasty. Within a year of the Chinese invasion in 1406, Dai-Viet was again a province of China. Under the Ming the country was heavily exploited, and radical measures were instituted to Sinicize the Vietnamese. Within little more than a decade, oppression had brought into being a powerful movement of national resistance.

The Le Dynasty (1428–1788)

The leader of the movement to restore independence was Le Loi, an aristocratic landowner. Employing guerrilla tactics, he waged a 10-year fight against the Chinese, defeating them in 1427. Shortly after the Chinese left the country, he ascended the throne under the name of Le Thai To. His dynasty lasted for 360 years.

During the early years of the dynasty, the kindgom grew more powerful than it had ever been, particularly under Le Thanh-Tong, who is one of the most celebrated rulers in Vietnamese history. The triennial tribute to China was paid regularly, and relations with the Chinese were peaceful. At the same time, war was vigorously pushed against the Kingdom of Champa; when it was finally conquered in 1471, all Champa territory north of Mui Dieu (formerly Cap Varella or Varella Cape) was annexed. The remaining territory became a vassal state in tribute to Dai-Viet. The Vietnamese, however, continued to absorb Champa until it disappeared as a political entity. All that remains of this once-advanced culture in present-day Vietnam is a small rural ethnic minority called Cham and impressive ruins in the Central Lowlands.

The power and prestige of the Le dynasty declined after the death of Le Thanh-Tong in 1497. In 1527, General Mac Dang Dung usurped the throne and established a new dynasty for which he was able to purchase the unenthusiastic approval of the Chinese. Shortly thereafter, another powerful family, the Nguyen, set up a descendant of the deposed Le dynasty as head of the government-in-exile south of Hanoi—an event which marked the beginning of a century and a half of regional strife and of division between the north and the south which lasted until the latter part of the eighteenth century. In this struggle, the place of the Mac was taken by another family, the Trinh, which in 1592 defeated the Mac ruler and reinstalled a puppet Le emperor on the throne in the north. Meanwhile, the Nguyen were able to consolidate power in the region south of the seventeenth parallel.

It was in the name of the Le emperor, the symbol of national unity, that the Nguyen and the Trinh carried on their war against each other. Both the Trinh, who controlled the Le emperors at this time, and the Nguyen, who ruled as independent autocrats, claimed support of the Le as justification for the legitimacy of their respective regimes. In 1673, after half a century of bloody and inconclusive fighting, a truce was concluded which lasted for 100 years.

This 100 years of peace brought a great cultural resurgence, especially to the north, where the Vietnamese civilization was well established. Along with the Buddhist renaissance that occurred, there was much literary and artistic effort. The north produced great works of history and historical criticism.

Under the Nguyen, Vietnamese expansion, at the expense of Cambodia, was vigorously pursued. The remaining coastal territories of the Champa were gradually absorbed and, in the seventeenth and eighteenth centuries, a series of short but decisive wars were waged with the Cambodians, who then occupied the Mekong Delta and most of the south-central portion of the Indochinese peninsula. The acquisition of the vastly fertile Mekong Delta represented a gain of major proportion for the land-hungry Vietnamese. By the end of the eighteenth century, Vietnamese control extended to the limits of contemporary South Vietnam.

The Tay Son Uprising (1776–1802)

Late in the eighteenth century three brothers of a Nguyen family in the village of Tay Son in central Vietnam led an uprising against the ruling Nguyen (to whom they were not related). The rebellion had popular support, both of the peasants and of the merchants. The oldest of the brothers, Nhac, drove the Nguyen lords out of the south by 1778 and proclaimed himself emperor over southern Dai-Viet. The youngest brother, Hue, led the attack on the Trinh in the north, defeating them in 1786. In 1788, after abolishing the decrepit Le dynasty and extending his power to the south at the expense of his brother, he made himself emperor of a reunited Vietnam. A new

Chinese invasion attempt was repelled by him in 1788. He is known as the Quang-Trung Emperor. Hoping to cultivate a Vietnamese national consciousness free of Chinese influence, he substituted *chu nom* (the vulgate script using Chinese characters to express Vietnamese sounds) for Chinese in all public acts and military proclamations.

THE ARRIVAL OF EUROPEANS

The pioneering voyage of Vasco da Gama to India in 1498 showed the way from Europe to Asia by sea. The Portuguese ships which followed drove rapidly eastward, establishing, sometimes by peaceful means but often by force or the threat of force, a line of trading and missionary outposts which in two generations extended from Goa, through Malacca, the Indies and Macao, to Nagasaki. The Spanish, meanwhile, coming across the Pacific from their holdings in the New World, were installing themselves in the Philippines and seeking to challenge the Portuguese monopoly of the coveted spice trade. Other European powers—Holland, England and France—joined the maritime procession eastward, ultimately overshadowing the Portuguese in a sanguinary competition, at first for trade and later for colonial possessions.

The European wave reached Vietnam in 1535 with the arrival in Vung Da Nang (Da Nang Bay) of the Portuguese captain Antonio da Faria. For a century the Portuguese, trading through the port of Faifo (later named Hoi An), a few miles to the south, dominated European commerce with Vietnam. Confronting a strongly organized state power and a sophisticated, resourceful officialdom, they could not, as in the Indies, impose their will or deal purely on their own terms. In the Nguyen, locked in conflict with the Trinh, they found a market for Western weapons and advice. The Dutch, coming in 1636, similarly purveyed to the Trinh. The English and French finally got a commercial foothold in the latter part of the century, but, after the truce between the Nguyen and Trinh in 1673, Vietnamese interest in armaments, which had made up the bulk of the trade, subsided. The European merchants had been badly hurt by the ferocity of the Western political and economic rivalry of which they were the agents in Asia. Trade declined and after 1700 almost ceased.

The first Catholic missionaries entered Vietnam in the sixteenth century, and with the near halt in trade in the eighteenth century they remained almost the only Europeans in the country. Prominent among them were the French, who had been left a relatively clear field by the decline of Portuguese power and the preoccupation of the British and the Dutch with India and the Indies. In both northern and southern Vietnam the Confucian-oriented officials had their misgivings about the new religion. They suspected it as the possible forerunner of conquest, and they feared the effect upon the traditional order of a doctrine which founded its morality on the will of God rather than on a concept of duty to family and state. Missionary activity was forbidden, but only at intervals was the ban enforced. Christianity spread among the poor, and Jesuit scholars trained in the sciences were welcomed at the northern and southern courts where they were able to make their influence felt among the privileged and educated.

The rule of the Tay Son brothers was brief, and with their fall the West, through the agency of the French, assumed a new and larger role in the affairs of the country. Early in the Tay Son rebellion, Nguyen Anh, the last descendant of the southern Nguyen lords, escaped annihilation with the aid of a French missionary, Pigneau de Behaine, Bishop of Adran. In 1787 the Bishop, who had hopes of placing a Christian prince on the throne of Annam, arranged an alliance in which France promised military aid in return for extensive commercial concessions and the grant of the port of Da Nang and the islands of Con Son (Isles de Puolo Condore).

When disagreement in France blocked the promised assistance, Pigneau privately organized a small force of Frenchmen to help Nguyen Anh. The bloody struggle which followed ended with the defeat of the last Tay Son king in 1802 and the installation of Nguyen Anh as the Emperor Gia Long—Gia Long being the contraction of Gia Dinh (then Saigon) and Thanh Long (Hanoi). With the founding of the Nguyen dynasty at Hue, the reunified country was renamed Vietnam (the Viet of the South). In 1803 the emperor's authority was formally recognized by the Chinese Ch'ing dynasty, to which he agreed to pay tribute biannually. The Nguyen dynasty lasted until the abdication of Bao Dai at the end of World War II.

Gia Long, who regarded Christianity as potentially subversive, never accepted the faith as Bishop Pigneau had hoped, but, out of gratitude to him, he did not persecute Christians as his successors did. In general, he followed a policy of aloofness from the West, which succeeded primarily because, at the time, the Napoleonic wars were occupying all of France's attention.

Minh Mang, Thieu Tri and Tu Duc, Gia Long's immediate successors, were unfriendly to Europeans and suspicious of the motives of both the traders and the missionaries. Cruel and indiscriminate repressions and persecutions were launched against both the missionaries and the sizable convert communities.

Under this dynasty, more than two centuries of struggle between Vietnam and Siam (Thailand) for control of Cambodia reached a critical stage, and in the process the two competing powers earned the intense enmity of the Cambodians. Whenever opportunity presented itself, Vietnam proceeded to impose its own culture and institutions on the Cambodians, and after 1834 Cambodia was virtually subjected to direct Vietnamese rule. Shortly thereafter the Cambodians, encouraged by Siam, rebelled against the Vietnamese, and the ensuing inconclusive military conflict between Siam and Vietnam ended in 1845, when the two powers agreed to set up joint control over Cambodia. This dual vassalage was terminated in 1863 with the establishment of a French protectorate over the area.

The cultural outburst during this dynasty was one of the most brilliant in Vietnamese history. The *chu nom* was extended to many categories of literature. The national masterpiece, *Kim Van Kieu*, an epic poem, appeared in *chu nom*. After that the indigenous script became more and more widely used, to the exclusion of Chinese. Hue emerged as the center of literary and artistic activities. In addition to the architecture and sculpture, the bronzes and enamel work were also outstanding. Behind this rich facade, however, the economy was stagnant, and intellectual life received little fresh impetus from outside sources. At a time when the West was developing at an astounding pace, Vietnam was rehashing and reenacting philosophies and policies that had changed little over the centuries. The arrival of the new techniques and ideas from the West jolted Vietnam into a reevaluation of its traditions.

THE FRENCH CONQUEST (1858-83)

Toward the middle of the nineteenth century pressure was mounting in influential French quarters for positive action to establish a position for France in Vietnam of the kind other European powers enjoyed, or were acquiring, elsewhere in Asia. The missionaries had been roused to an angry militance by the imprisonment or execution of some of their number and by the periodic persecution of Vietnamese Christians. The imperial ban had not halted missionary activity in the country, but it was clear that the authorities would never cease to obstruct Christianity unless forced to do so. Considerations of French national prestige and military advantage were also present, as was the desire for a share of the economic benefits to be had from an aggressive policy in Asia.

In September 1857 all these factors led to France's decision to take Tourane (Da Nang). The city was captured in 1858, and the French thereafter turned their attention to the south. Inflicting heavy losses on the Vietnamese, they took Saigon by July 1861. In June 1862 the Vietnamese court at Hue ceded Saigon and the adjacent area to France and agreed to pay a war indemnity. They also promised not to cede territory to any other power without French permission. The western part of the southern delta, which was virtually cut off from the rest of Vietnam, was annexed by France in 1867, thus completing the territorial formation of what later became the French colony of Cochin China.

The French next turned their attention to the Red River, having found the Mekong unsuitable as a trade route to China because of its rapids. A treaty was signed in 1874 which opened the Red River to French traders, but Chinese pirates largely nullified the value of the concession. In 1883 an expeditionary force brought northern Vietnam under French control, and the signing of a Treaty of Protectorate on August 25, 1883, formally ended Vietnam's independence.

CONSOLIDATION OF COLONIAL RULE (1883–1900)

The treaty of 1883 and one of June 1884 established French protectorates over northern Vietnam (Tonkin) and central Vietnam (Annam). All of southern Vietnam (Cochin China) had been in French hands since the conquest in 1867 and now, with the abrogation of what was left of the country's independence, the name "Vietnam" itself was officially eliminated. In Annam, the emperor and his officials were left in charge of internal affairs, except for customs and public works, but they functioned under the eye of the French, who had the right to station troops in the area. The protectorate over Tonkin made few concessions to the appearance of autonomy, and French resident officers in the larger towns directly controlled the administration.

These developments did not go unchallenged. The Chinese denied the validity of treaties made with the Vietnamese without their approval. The French defeated a Chinese force sent in to win control of a part of Tonkin. China in 1885 formally recognized the French Protectorate over Tonkin and Annam. The Vietnamese were more difficult to cope with. Beginning in 1885, under the 12-year-old Emperor Ham Nghi, a general uprising broke out against the French. It failed and Ham Nghi was exiled in 1888. Active armed resistance, led by such men as De Tham and Phan Dinh Phung, continued into the early twentieth century but failed largely because the movements were localized and made no systematic attempts to arouse popular nationalist sentiments.

The final phase of French consolidation was marked by the formation of an Indochinese Union in 1887. Consisting of Tonkin, Annam, Cochin China and Cambodia (a French protectorate since 1863), the Union was administered under a French governor general who was responsible directly to the Ministry of Colonies in Paris. In 1893, Laos, following annexation by France, was also added to the Union (see fig. 8).

The basic political structure of French Indochina was completed by 1900. Each of Vietnam's three regions was treated differently, although basic policy decisions for all usually originated in Paris. Cochin China was administered directly by a French-staffed civil service under a governor and a colonial council. It also sent a representative to the Chamber of Deputies in Paris. The colonial council, a

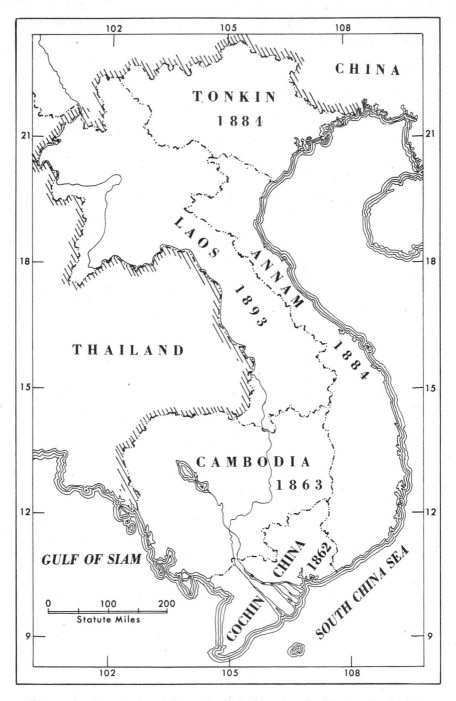

Figure 8. French Acquisitions in Indochina in the Nineteenth Century.

legislative body, consisted of both French and Vietnamese members. In the administrative apparatus, only subordinate positions were open for Vietnamese. In the protectorate of Tonkin, the mandarinate was retained for administrative purposes, but important executive powers were vested in a French senior resident at Hanoi. In Annam, where the emperor was still nominally in power and the mandarinate continued to function, French rule was only a little less direct.

On the whole, French rule was much more liberal in Cochin China than in Annam or Tonkin. Cochin China was administered under the French judicial system, whereas in Tonkin and Annam the traditional judicial system, marked by extreme severity, was retained and applied by using the mandarinate as a front.

THE IMPACT OF FRENCH RULE

French influence permeated nearly all walks of Vietnamese society. With the aid of modern science and technology, the French undertook to develop a society which would be patterned after their own but, at the same time, uncritically submissive to colonial rule. In the process, stabilizing forces of the traditional order were disrupted, and workable alternatives were lacking. The resulting social tensions and stresses paved the way for the political awakening of the people.

Meanwhile, French nationals took over all important governmental administrative and managerial positions. The traditional mandarinate declined sharply in social prestige and political influence. As a direct consequence, aspiring Vietnamese turned to Western-type rather than to Chinese-type schooling, traditionally the most important means for the attainment of power and wealth. This shift exposed educated Vietnamese to liberal and radical political ideals of the West, stimulating them to question the capability of their Confucian-oriented social order to withstand new challenges from the West. Direct contact with French culture, especially during World War I when about 100,000 Vietnamese served on the European front, further accelerated the introduction of new ideas. At the same time many educated people began to demand the right to self-determination.

French influence, especially pronounced in urban areas, also left a discernible imprint on the rural society. The traditional village institution was gradually affected by stimulating forces emanating from the highly centralized administrative system, the improved network of communications and transportation, and the penetration of cash economy. The village notables could no longer command the authority they once had, and, as a result, social cohesion weakened. The French policy of establishing large landed estates, especially in Cochin China, tended to strip villages of communal land, which had been the major source of social insurance to the needy peasants. Much of the communal land fell into the hands of speculators and absentee landowners. As a result, the rural society became increasingly subjected to disruptive forces beyond its control. A growing tax burden, combined with rapid increases in the number of landless peasants and in total population, brought about progressive impoverishment in rural areas. Surplus rural manpower was absorbed partially by industries in the north and by rubber plantations in the south, but in the absence of protective labor legislation the plight of urban workers proved to be equally distressing.

In the economic sphere the colonial policy was geared mainly to benefit metropolitan France. Indochina was transformed not only into a source of raw materials but also into an exclusive market for tariff-protected French goods. To facilitate French domination, canals, drainage systems, railroads, harbors and highways were extensively constructed. Large tracts of virgin land in the Mekong Delta were opened for rice cultivation, thereby making Indochina an important rice exporter. Most of the new land fell into French hands or into the hands of Vietnamese landlords who collaborated with the French. These landlords derived substantial portions of their wealth from high rents and from practices of usury.

Although much French profit went out of the country, some remained for investment in light industries and rubber plantations, from which the Vietnamese were virtually excluded. By 1938 nearly 95 percent of all foreign investments were in French hands. As a result, Vietnamese capital continued to be invested in land. On the whole, industry became the exclusive domain of the French investors, whereas the control of agriculture was shared by French and Vietnamese elements. The two sectors were linked by Chinese middlemen, dominating rice trade and retail business in both urban and rural areas.

The impact of French rule was most pronounced in Cochin China, which was directly ruled by French officials and dominated by French business. Western influences, however, also penetrated some industrial cities of Tonkin. Annam was least affected, as the area afforded little opportunity to French entrepreneurs, compared with the rubber plantations in the south and the industrial potential of the north. Furthermore, the presence of the Vietnamese court at Hue with its ceremonial rites kept alive the traditional structure.

THE RISE OF NATIONALISM

Early in the twentieth century nationalist movements began to develop, initially among urban intellectuals. Japan's victory over Russia in 1905 gave impetus to nationalist sentiment by demonstrating that an Asian nation with sufficient technical knowledge and equipment could prevail over a Western power. Despite the watchfulness of the French authorities, numerous anti-French secret societies sprang up, but most of them were loosely organized and had no well-defined political objectives. Nascent nationalism drew its inspiration mainly from outside sources—Europe, China and Japan.

A distinguished scholar, Phan Boi Chau, is popularly regarded as the founder of nationalist movements. Vietnamese independence, he thought, could best be achieved by enlisting the support of, or emulating Japan, and in 1906 he went to Japan to promote his cause. Through his writings and the leadership of a group of Vietnamese intellectuals who shared his exile, he gained a wide following. His activities were a source of embarrassment to the Japanese Government, and he was expelled in 1910, but he continued his work from exile in China, where he succeeded in uniting most of the nationalist groups outside of Vietnam in the Association for the Restoration of Vietnam (Viet Nam Quang Phuc Hoi). He organized a government-in-exile under Prince Cuong De, a direct descendant of Gia Long and claimant to the throne of Annam. Despite intensive clandestine propaganda efforts, his movement—whose objective was to oust the French and restore monarchical rule in traditional form and to promulgate a constitution on the Japanese model—failed to enlist mass support.

While Phan Boi Chau led a nationalist movement from outside the country, others worked in Vietnam for similar goals. Phan Chau Trinh, another scholar, led a group of nationalists who sought French rather than Japanese assistance. Believing that the French could be persuaded to prepare the Vietnamese for eventual independence, he presented a memorandum along these lines to the French governor general in 1906. His proposals were ignored, however, and when he continued to agitate for reforms and formed various study groups, he was imprisoned by the French authorities.

From the group of scholar-officials also came the leaders of an uprising in 1916 to which young Emperor Duy Tan lent his support. Several hundreds of the participants were executed or deported, and Duy Tan himself was sent into exile. After this disaster, resistance by the scholars subsided, but it did not disappear.

By the early 1920's a new socioeconomic group had emerged which had been made wealthy by the acquisition of newly developed lands through cooperation with the French. Many of these persons, especially in Cochin China, sought the privileges of French citizenship for themselves and frequently sent their children to France to be educated. Some of them, however, still cherished nationalist sentiments and advocated Franco-Vietnamese collaboration and gradual reform. In 1923 two such leaders, Bui Quang Chieu and Nguyen Phan Long, founded the Constitutionalist Party in Saigon. This was the first Vietnamese political organization to be sanctioned by the French authorities, but lukewarm French response and lack of mass support only brought disillusionment to its leaders.

A number of nationalist groups found inspiration in the Chinese nationalist movement. Of these, the best known and most important was the Vietnam Nationalist Party (Viet Nam Quoc Dan Dang—VNQDD). It was established first in 1925 in Canton, then the center of the revolutionary ferment in China, in opposition to the Association of Vietnamese Revolutionary Youth (Viet-Nam Thanh-Nieu Cach-Mang Dong-chi Hoi), precursor of the Indochinese Communist Party.

Two years later the VNQDD was also established secretly in Hanoi by Nguyen Thai Hoc, a schoolteacher. Impressed by the Chinese efforts to modernize their country and simultaneously to repel foreign encroachments, Nguyen Thai Hoc's supporters adopted the organization, methods and programs of the Chinese Nationalist Party (Kuomintang), but failed to create an effective organization within the country. Their greater shortcoming was the lack of an imaginative social program. An uprising staged in 1930 at Yen Bay, northwest of Hanoi, was severely repressed by the French. The VNQDD was nearly destroyed, and many of its surviving members fled to Yunnan in southwest China. They returned to Vietnam after World War II to confront both the French and the Communists.

After the Yen Bay insurrection, the leadership of the clandestine nationalist movement in Vietnam was taken over by the opportunist Indochinese Communist Party (Dong Duong Cong San Dang), which chose not to participate in that uprising. Formed in Hong Kong in 1930, it united several existing independent Communist groups under the leadership of Nguyen Ai Quoc (Nguyen the Patriot), later known as Ho Chi Minh.

UNFULFILLED REFORMS

The thoroughness with which the Yen Bay uprising was repressed for a time rendered the more militant nationalists inactive. Some Vietnamese did, however, attempt to advance the cause of national liberation through reforms from above. They looked to the young Emperor Bao Dai as their best hope. Bao Dai had ascended the throne in 1925 at the age of 12 on the death of his father, Emperor Khai Dinh, but did not return to Vietnam until 1932 after he had completed his education in France.

Bao Dai was greeted with enthusiasm by the Vietnamese, who expected that he would be able to persuade the French to install a more liberal regime. He attempted to reign as a constitutional monarch, according to the terms of the treaty of 1884 establishing the protectorate, and he strove to modernize the ancient imperial administration at Hue.

Among his young collaborators was Ngo Dinh Diem, governor of the Phan Thiet area in Binh Thuan Province, who was given the portfolio of minister of the interior and appointed head of the secretariat of a Vietnamese-French commission which was charged with the responsibility of implementing Bao Dai's reform proposals. When it became obvious that the French had no intention of granting real power to the Vietnamese administration and would make no concessions toward unification of the country, the youthful emperor appeared to lose interest, and Ngo Dinh Diem resigned his official position.

For a brief time in 1936, during the period of the Popular Front government in France, the Vietnamese had hopes that autonomy might be granted. The French Socialists, however, made no important concessions, and the colonial administration continued as before.

THE JAPANESE OCCUPATION (1940–45)

After the fall of France in June 1940, the Vichy government acceded to Japanese demands, which ultimately led to the establishment of Japanese controls over all of the French Indochina peninsula. In August 1940 the Vichy authorities agreed to accept Japan's "preeminent" position in the Far East and to grant the Japanese certain transit facilities in Tonkin in return for Japanese recognition of its sovereignty over Indochina. Under this accord the French colonial administrative structure was kept intact, and the French community maintained its privileged position with little change to indicate to the population the eclipse of French power in Indochina. This arrangement gave the Japanese the benefit of the services of the French officials and freed Japanese personnel for duties elsewhere. There were clashes between Japanese and French forces along the northern border of Tonkin, and Japanese aircraft bombed the port of Haiphong. But after the Vichy government had agreed, in September, to the stationing of Japanese troops in areas on the northern side of the Red River, the French troops did not offer further military opposition and continued their traditional garrison duties.

An economic agreement was signed in May 1941 which reserved all of the important exports of Indochina for Japan; these included rice, manganese, tungsten, antimony, tin and chrome. A shortage of Japanese shipping, however, contributed to a sharp decline in exports, which in turn drastically curtailed imports, and shortages developed in many items which the Vietnamese had been accustomed to import from Europe.

The Japanese position was further consolidated in July 1941 when the two governments signed a military agreement providing for the "common defense of French Indochina," under which Japan was permitted to station troops in southern Indochina. The agreement also enabled Japan to control virtually all airfields in the south and important port facilities and railroads elsewhere. Immediately after Japan's attack on Pearl Harbor, the French made another agreement reaffirming the existing Franco-Japanese cooperation, and this uneasy relationship continued until the Japanese coup d'etat in March 1945.

The Japanese occupation and French reaction to it had the effect of further stimulating nationalist sentiments. Fearing that Japan would capitalize on the strong anti-French feelings of the people, the French administration undertook to liberalize certain of its repressive policies. It improved technical and vocational education programs, opened new schools, and launched a youth movement, presumably in hopes of winning the support of youth groups. It also opened additional civil service posts for the Vietnamese. The French apparently intended, however, to reinforce the colonial order through these token concessions, while they continued to impose restrictions on nationalist activities.

COMMUNIST MOVEMENT

Nguyen Ai Quoc (Ho Chi Minh), a Communist since 1920 and founder of the united Indochinese Communist Party in 1930, was still in the forefront of the Vietnamese Communist movement 10 years later. Allied with and deftly exploiting the non-Communist nationalist groups, Nguyen Ai Quoc eventually emerged as the dominant political figure of the country.

To broaden the social and political bases of its activities, the Communist Party, in May 1941, adopted a policy of collaboration with all non-Communist nationalists. This decision led to the formation of a united front organization, the Vietnam Independence League (Viet Nam Doc Lap Dong Minh), better known as the Viet Minh.

One of the first actions of the Viet Minh was to form guerrilla bands, under the direction of Vo Nguyen Giap, to operate in Vietnamese territory against the Japanese and the French. He also began implanting agents and setting up intelligence networks in Tonkin. Meanwhile, comparable efforts by the non-Communist groups, beset by factional wranglings, were virtually nonexistent. Although Nguyen Ai Quoc was jailed for his Communist activity by the Chinese authorities in 1942, the Viet Minh continued its vigorous efforts to win popular support.

During the same period, the Chinese, who urgently needed intelligence on Japanese activities in Tonkin, attempted to make use of the non-Communist Vietnamese exiles for this purpose. At Chinese urging, a new organization, called the Revolutionary League of Vietnam (Vietnam Cach Minh Dong Minh Hoi), usually abbreviated to Dong Minh Hoi, was formed in October 1942 and given financial support by the Chinese Kuomintang. Although all the major nationalist groups—including the Vietnamese Nationalist Party and the Viet Minh—were represented in it, the new organization, without active Viet Minh cooperation, remained ineffective. It was against this background that in 1943 the Chinese released Nguyen Ai Quoc in exchange for his offer to help them. Thereupon he took the name of Ho Chi Minh (He Who Enlightens), presumably to conceal his Communist affiliation from the Vietnamese people (see ch. 14, Political Dynamics).

Ho Chi Minh was expected to work through the Dong Minh Hoi, but, in fact, he worked only through the Viet Minh and used the funds which the Dong Minh Hoi received from the Chinese Nationalist Government to strengthen his Communist organization. His organization produced some intelligence of use to the Allies, and Vo Nguyen Giap's guerrilla bands engaged in minor forays against the Japanese. In return, Ho Chi Minh received an undetermined amount of small arms, munitions and communication equipment from the United States for counteraction against the Japanese. This aid later formed the basis for his claim that the Viet Minh enjoyed Allied support.

Working in nationalist disguise, Ho Chi Minh effectively strengthened the organization of Communist cells throughout Vietnam. In the subsequent struggle for leadership in the nationalist movement as the war ended, the superior organization of the Communists enabled him to gain control of the Viet Minh and to claim all the credit for nationalist activities during the war. Capitalizing on the anticolonialist propaganda organized by Moscow, Vietnamese Communists claimed to be fighting only against economic misery and for national liberation. They were not recognized by Vietnamese as representing an alien force except by those with superior education and keen political insight (see ch. 14, Political Dynamics).

NATIONAL INDEPENDENCE REGAINED

In September 1944 the Tokyo government, alarmed over growing indications of anti-Japanese activities, decided to displace the French and grant independence to the Vietnamese. Initially, this plan was to be executed on April 25, 1945, but the reoccupation of the Philippine Islands by the United States forces in October and the growing awareness that Japan was losing the war advanced the date of the Japanese coup d'etat to March 9, 1945.

At the instigation of the Japanese, Emperor Bao Dai proclaimed the independence of Vietnam under Japanese "protection." He formed a new government at Hue, proclaimed a political amnesty, and attemped to create a Vietnamese administration to replace the French administration which had been ousted. An effective government could not be established, however, because of administrative difficulties arising from the sudden French ouster, the breakdown of communications owing to Allied bombing, crop failures and famine in Tonkin and Annam, and the imposition of direct Japanese military rule over Cochin China.

50

Meanwhile, at Hanoi, the Viet Minh went into action, refusing to support the Bao Dai regime. Ho Chi Minh began to refer to the Viet Minh guerrilla units as the "National Liberation Army" and announced the formation of a Committee for the Liberation of the Vietnamese People, with himself as president. By late August 1945 the Viet Minh partisans and agents gained administrative control over the Tonkin area by a show of force.

In Cochin China, where Communist activity had been negligible because of strict French control measures, nationalist groups of various political leanings formed a United National Front and took over administrative functions from the Japanese. It was, however, politically ineffective because of factional differences. The Viet Minh exploited this situation by launching a skillful propaganda campaign which portrayed the Viet Minh as a strong nationalist movement enjoying the support of the Allies. In ignorance of the organization's actual character, the United National Front agreed to accept Viet Minh leadership.

While these events were taking place, Bao Dai, apparently convinced that a united and independent nation offered the only possibility of preventing the return of French control, decided to abdicate. Recognizing only the nationalist character of the Viet Minh movement and assuming that it had Allied support, he abdicated in its favor on August 25, 1945, and handed over his imperial seal and other symbols of office to Ho Chi Minh. To the overwhelming majority of the people this clearly meant that Ho Chi Minh was endowed with legitimacy and that they would be expected to follow the Viet Minh leadership.

On September 2, Ho Chi Minh formally proclaimed the independence of Vietnam and the establishment of the Democratic Republic of Vietnam. To facilitate the negotiations directed toward gaining international recognition of its legitimacy, Communist domination of the new government was carefully concealed and emphasis placed on the "democratic," Vietnamese character of the regime. Bao Dai was made high counselor to the new government.

THE RETURN OF FRANCE

At the Potsdam Conference of July 1945, the Allies agreed that the British were to accept the surrender of the Japanese south of the sixteenth parallel, and the Chinese would perform a similar duty north of it. After World War II the Vietnamese expected the Allies to support their claims to independence. Nationalist China opposed the return of France to Indochina, apparently to reassert its traditional influence over Tonkin, and, in principle, the United States favored the formation of a provisional international trusteeship.

The first British troops arrived in Saigon on September 12, 1945, and although the Potsdam agreements made no explicit reference to French sovereignty over Indochina, by virtue of shrewd diplomacy in Allied councils, France was able to land its troops about 10 days later. Almost immediately Vietnamese of virtually all political persuasions rose up in defense of their newly won freedom. The British assisted the French and also ordered Japanese troops to help put down the resistance. By the end of November all strategic points within Cochin China had been taken. Even then resistance in the South did not cease; guerrilla forces were organized and continued to clash with French units.

In the meantime, the Chinese forces occupying the North during the fall of 1945 found that the Viet Minh regime was willing to cooperate with them and with non-Communist nationalist groups in the expectation of support for its nationalist aspirations. The Viet Minh ostensibly dissolved the Indochinese Communist Party in November 1945, held elections in January 1946 for a National Assembly (in which a number of seats were reserved for the Chinese-sponsored VNQDD and Dong Minh Hoi leaders) and formed a nationalist coalition government headed by Ho Chi Minh. But in February 1946, a Franco-Chinese agreement was concluded whereby China agreed to the return of the French to Indochina in exchange for various concessions, including France's surrender of its extraterritorial rights in China.

Faced with the loss of Chinese support, the Viet Minh was forced to reconsider its policy toward the French. Furthermore, with the French desire to return peacefully to the northern area without arousing intense feelings against themselves, an agreement between France and Ho Chi Minh was signed in March 1946, by which the Democratic Republic of Vietnam was recognized as a "free state" within the Indochinese Federation (yet to be created) and the French Union. The new state, which was not precisely defined in the agreement and interpreted by the Vietnamese as consisting of Tonkin, Annam and Cochin China, was to have its own national assembly, manage its own finances, and maintain its own army. (In Vietnamese these three areas are referred to as the three *ky* [region]: Bac-bo, Trung-bo and Nam-bo, northern, central and southern, respectively.) The French, however, did not appear to imply any recognition of a single government over the three regions. Details of the new state's relationship to France were to be decided by a future agreement.

As a result of this agreement, French forces were permitted to land in the North. Bao Dai, who had been acting as high counselor to Ho Chi Minh, was sent on a "goodwill" mission to China where he remained in exile, thus eliminating the possibility that he might provide a rallying point for groups not thoroughly aligned with the Viet Minh.

Differences between the French and the Democratic Republic of Vietnam immediately developed over the question of defining the "free state." A delegation of the Vietnamese representatives, headed by Ho Chi Minh, traveled to Paris to settle differences. The Paris conference was broken up in early June 1946 when a Republic of Cochin China was established in the South under the support of separatist French elements. In September 1946, however, Ho Chi Minh signed a modus vivendi on behalf of his government—an agreement which he reportedly described as "better than nothing." The agreement was designed to facilitate the resumption of French economic and cultural activities in return for French promises to introduce a more liberal regime.

The modus vivendi did not include recognition of Vietnamese unity or independence and was opposed by many within Ho Chi Minh's regime. French actions to enforce customs controls in October aroused further hostility. In November shooting broke out in Haiphong, and the subsequent French bombardment of the city reportedly killed more than 6,000 Vietnamese. The French demands which followed were so completely unacceptable to the Democratic Republic of Vietnam that it decided to risk a long war of liberation rather than to accept. On December 19, 1946, it launched the first attack on the French in what was to be known as the Indochina War. In this act of resistance against French troops, the Republic had the active or passive support of a majority of Vietnamese.

THE INDOCHINA WAR (1946–54)

The war touched off by the Viet Minh attack lasted for 8 years and caused unending misery to the Vietnamese. It was financially and militarily disastrous to the French and resulted in more than 35,000 of them killed and 48,000 wounded. The United States gave the state of Vietnam military and economic aid, reportedly totaling over $2 billion. Military aid was granted indirectly through France from December 1950 until late in 1954. Economic aid was sent directly to Vietnam, beginning in September 1951 (see ch. 23, Foreign Economic Relations; ch. 27, The Armed Forces). Large sums were also spent by Communist China and the Soviet-bloc countries on assistance to Ho Chi Minh's regime. The war, which started out as an anti-French struggle, became enmeshed with the worldwide conflict between East and West. During this period the Vietnamese people also witnessed the emergence of two governments, both competing for popular support.

In the early months of 1947, the French military forces reestablished their control over the principal towns in Tonkin and Annam and cleared the road between Haiphong and Hanoi. This forced the Viet Minh to resort to the guerrilla tactics which became the chief characteristic of the war. Ho Chi Minh's armed forces made use of the jungle to neutralize French mechanized mobility and power. By selecting their objectives and retiring when they met superior strength, they presented a problem with which the French could not cope. After 3 years of fighting, the Viet Minh controlled large areas throughout the country. The French had firm control only in the large cities.

Early in the struggle the French sought to encourage the Vietnamese anti-Communist nationalists to take a stand against the Viet Minh and to cooperate with France, but the effort failed as the nationalists claimed the French would not clarify their policy with respect to future Vietnamese unity and independence. In 1946 some of the anti-Communist nationalists in Nanking, China, formed a Front of National Union of Vietnam and appealed to Bao Dai to return from exile in Hong Kong and head a national government. The French, seeing another opportunity to make the nationalists an effective counterforce against Ho Chi Minh, offered Vietnam "liberty within the French Union." Bao Dai, apparently fearful of becoming a pawn of the French, cautiously agreed only to represent Vietnam in negotiations. Violent Viet Minh reaction to these maneuvers included the assassination of prominent nationalist leaders.

Negotiations with France continued for 2 years, but by June 1949 France finally approved of limited independence for "the State of Vietnam" within the French Union. Bao Dai assumed the role of chief of state, but the principal nationalists (including Ngo Dinh Diem) failed to unite behind him, since they claimed that the French did not offer real independence. Although the new government was permitted internal autonomy and an army of is own, strong safeguards to protect French nationals and economic interests were maintained, and the foreign policy of the new state was coordinated with that of France.

In the meantime, Ho Chi Minh rid his coalition government of the moderates and nationalists whom he had accepted earlier and showed himself to be completely Communist. In March 1951 the Indochinese Communist Party (dissolved in 1945) was revived as the Workers Party (Dang Lao Dong). Propaganda emanating from the government, however, continued to be solely nationalistic in tone.

After the defeat of the Chinese Nationalists by the Communists in China in late 1949, Communist China became the first state to recognize the North Vietnamese regime as the legitimate government of all Vietnam. Soviet-bloc countries quickly followed suit. In early 1950, after North Vietnam began to receive assistance from Communist China, offensive action was initiated against the French Union forces composed of French as well as Vietnamese soldiers. In 1951 the advance of the Communist forces was temporarily halted with the aid of American equipment, but in 1952 the Communists started a new offensive in several areas. Vigorous counterattacks brought no decisive results, and a military stalemate followed; where tanks could go, the French Union forces held, but in the mountains and in the mud of the rice paddies Ho Chi Minh consolidated his control.

In February 1950, Great Britain and the United States recognized the State of Vietnam headed by the ex-emperor Bao Dai as the legitimate government. When France concluded agreements with Laos and Cambodia similar to that with Vietnam, the three countries became the Associate States of Indochina and where accorded diplomatic recognition by more than 30 other nations. In May 1950 the United States announced a decision to give aid to Bao Dai through France, and a United States Economic Mission arrived in Saigon. In September 1951 a United States-Vietnamese agreement for direct economic assistance was also signed.

In its efforts to win popular support, the Bao Dai regime was unsuccessful. Confronted with a choice between French colonialism and the Communist-led nationalist movement, many Vietnamese, attracted by its appeal for independence and unity, tended to side with the Viet Minh organization.

THE GENEVA CONFERENCE

While the military battle was raging, steps were being taken to bring a negotiated end to the Indochina War. France was admittedly unable to continue the war, and Ho Chi Minh, under apparent Sino-Soviet pressure, had let it be known that he was ready to discuss peace. In February 1954 the Big Four (France, Great Britain, the Soviet Union and the United States) powers at Berlin agreed that a conference should be held to seek a solution for the Indochina War and Korea.

On April 28, 1954, 2 days after the opening of the conference at Geneva, a Franco-Vietnamese declaration, proclaiming Vietnam to be unequivocally sovereign and independent, was made public. It was only after May 8, however, that the conference began focusing its attention primarily on Indochina. The immediate cause was the decisive French defeat at Dien Bien Phu at the hands of the Viet Minh forces on May 7 and the resultant popular pressure in France for a rapid conclusion of the war. The Indochinese phase of the conference was attended, under the cochairmanship of Great Britain and the Soviet Union, by the representatives of the United States, France, the United Kingdom, the Soviet Union, Communist China, the State of Vietnam, the Democratic Republic of Vietnam, Cambodia and Laos.

Final negotiations for armistice were conducted directly between the French High Command and Ho Chi Minh's People's Army High Command. A truce agreement covering the territory of both North and South Vietnam was signed on July 20 between the two High Commands. Separate truce agreements were also concluded for Cambodia and Laos, respectively.

The agreement for Vietnam fixed a provisional military Demarcation Line roughly along the seventeenth parallel and provided for the total evacuation of Vietnam north of the Demarcation Line by the military forces of the French and the State of Vietnam, as well as for the evacuation of the South by the Viet Minh forces. It also provided for a period of 300 days during which freedom of movement was to be allowed for all persons wishing to move from one sector to the other. Under the agreement, the introduction into Vietnam of any troop reinforcements and additional military personnel was prohibited except for rotation purposes; imports of new weapons were similarly limited to replacement levels. It also imposed restrictions on the establishment of foreign military bases, and on the participation of both North and South Vietnam in any military alliance. Finally, the agreement provided for the formation of an International Control Commission, with representatives from India, Canada and Poland, to supervise the implementation of the truce arrangements. In addition to the agreement, a Final Declaration, dated July 21, of the Geneva Conference provided for the holding of general elections throughout North and South Vietnam in July 1956 under the supervision of the International Control Commission with preliminary discussions to begin in July 1955.

The armistice agreement was reached over the objections of the State of Vietnam, which did not sign it. It vainly protested the manner in which the truce was arranged, as well as its terms, particularly those relating to the partitioning of the country. It demanded that the whole country be placed under the control of the United Nations until conditions warranted the holding of free general elections. It also objected to the Final Declaration, protesting that the French High Command arrogated to itself, without prior consultation with the State of Vietnam, the right to fix the date for elections.

The United States did not concur with the terms of the truce agreement or with the Final Declaration. In a unilateral statement issued on July 21, however, the United States representative declared that his country would refrain from the threat of or use of force to disturb the provisions of the agreement and of the Final Declaration and that it would view any renewal of aggression in violation of the agreement with grave concern as a threat to international peace and security. With regard to the provisions relating to the elections, the United States expressed its continuing determination to seek unification through free and fair elections, to be conducted under the supervision of the United Nations. It further reiterated its traditional position that all peoples are entitled to determine their own future and that it would not join in any arrangement which would hinder the realization of such a principle.

France then proceeded to complete the transfer of the remnants of its administrative and military control to the State of Vietnam with its capital at Saigon. The government of Ho Chi Minh, seated at Hanoi, moved steadily to achieve its program of communizing north of the seventeenth parallel. Despite the cease-fire agreement, a well-organized Viet Minh underground network was deliberately left behind in the South, especially in the jungle regions in the southern Mekong Delta and along the Cambodian and Laos border regions where French Union forces had not been able to establish effective control. This underground network formed the nucleus of subsequent Communist insurgency directed against the Saigon regime.

REPUBLIC OF VIETNAM

Shortly before the ending of the Geneva Conference, Bao Dai, as chief of state, called on Ngo Dinh Diem to form a new government. Under the premiership of Ngo Dinh Diem the new government was formed on July 7, 1954, but almost immediately it was confronted with the overwhelming problem of bringing order and stability to a country near social and economic collapse. Loyalties were confused, and the future was uncertain. Even in parts of Saigon the authority of the government was not recognized.

The first tasks of the new regime were to devise a workable political structure, revive the national economy, and resettle some 900,000 refugees from the Communist North. Moreover, the authorities were confronted with a series of conspiracies. The government itself was overtly challenged by such armed politicoreligious dissidents as the Cao Dai and the Hoa Hao sects, and a group of racketeer-gangsters called the Binh Xuyen (see ch. 26, Public Order and Safety).

By early October 1955, Prime Minister Ngo Dinh Diem effectively extended his authority in South Vietnam by defeating or adroitly outmaneuvering the armed units of the dissident sects and by crushing the Binh Xuyen bosses who had controlled 5,000 troops and much of the Saigon police. Meanwhile, the prime minister took steps to improve the efficiency and reliability of the government's armed forces, aided in part by economic and military assistance from the United States which began channeling its military aid directly to the Vietnamese Government beginning in January 1955 (see ch. 26, Public Order and Safety; ch. 27, The Armed Forces).

Feeling politically secure, Prime Minister Diem called a national referendum on October 23, 1955, to decide whether the country should become a republic under his own leadership as chief of state and president or whether Bao Dai should continue as chief of state. The Prime Minister reportedly won 98 percent of the votes, and on October

26 he proclaimed South Vietnam to be the Republic of Vietnam and became its first president. A constitution (written at his direction), bearing American and French precedents, was adopted in July 1956 and promulgated on October 26, 1956 (see ch. 13, The Governmental System).

No sooner had Ngo Dinh Diem consolidated his power than he had to cope with the Communist subversion and terrorist activities directed by the Hanoi regime, which had taken control of northern Vietnam in October 1954. Beginning in mid-1957 and especially since 1959, the Communist insurgency resulted in the serious curtailment of government programs for economic development, land reform, and other social welfare activities. The insurgent elements, popularly called the Viet Cong (abbreviation of Viet Nam Cong San—Vietnamese, Communists), have been operating under the direction and control of a self-styled National Front for Liberation of South Vietnam. It was created in December 1960 by the Hanoi regime, as the political arm of its subversive efforts in the South, so as to conceal its Communist identification and to give the impression that the insurgency was a genuinely popular nationalist movement.

Beginning in mid-1963 the government's difficulties were compounded by the outbreak of widespread civil disturbances, which were precipitated evidently by the defiant reactions of the Buddhist groups to what they regarded as the government's anti-Buddhist discrimination. Diem and his family were Catholics.

Other contributing factors were popular discontent arising from worsening living conditions, common suspicion of corruption among those in ruling positions, and frequent charges of dictatorial one-family rule brought against President Ngo Dinh Diem and his powerful brother, Nhu, political adviser. Another source of intense dissatisfaction with the government, especially on the part of urban intellectuals, was the government's systematic suppression of even the most moderate political opposition (see ch. 14, Political Dynamics).

The government's failure to cope with the mounting Buddhist crisis eventually culminated in the sudden overthrow of President Ngo Dinh Diem's regime on November 1, 1963, through a military coup d'etat executed by a group of key generals headed by Major General Duong Van Minh. The military promptly acted to grant religious freedom and proceeded to adopt a new constitution.

Nevertheless, the government continued to experience difficulties in almost all of its activities. These difficulties arose mainly from efforts to defeat the Communist insurgency as well as from apparent political disagreement among those in power and among contending political aspirants. By mid-1965 this political confusion had led to no less than seven abrupt changes in governmental leadership at the highest level (see ch. 14, Political Dynamics).

CHAPTER 4

POPULATION

The population in mid-1965 was estimated to be approximately 16.1 million. Of these persons, 10.6 million lived in the Region of South Vietnam, more than 5 million in the Region of Central Vietnam Lowlands and more than 600,000 in the Region of Central Vietnam Highlands (see ch. 2, Physical Environment). If the current annual growth rate, estimated to be up to 2 percent, continues, the population may double in less than 50 years. The population is relatively young, with a probable preponderance of females, as a result of their greater longevity and the loss of males during the Indochina War (1946–54) followed by antiguerrilla operations.

There are no data available reflecting distribution according to age and sex. Lacking official census results, demographic statistics have been computed from projections of a sampling of the population in 1960 and subsequent incomplete surveys by the Vietnamese National Institute of Statistics. Population losses and movements as a result of wartime conditions further inhibited the compilation of accurate government statistics. All figures, therefore, must be regarded as estimates lacking official verification.

Since the partition of 1954, South Vietnam controls approximately 66,000 of Vietnam's 127,000 square miles. Considering its size, the country as a whole is not densely populated—about 243 persons per square mile—but because of the uneven distribution of the inhabitants, local concentrations create a problem in some areas. Densities vary from more than 2,000 persons per square mile in portions of the Mekong Delta and in parts of the coastal strip of the Central Lowlands to only 13 persons per square mile on some of the plateaus of the Central Highlands.

The massive influx of refugees, concentrating into areas already overcrowded, has contributed to an imbalance in population distribution. Almost 1 million refugees arrived from North Vietnam soon after the end of the Indochina War in 1954, and since 1960 at least another million have fled from areas controlled by the Viet Cong or from areas exposed to antiguerrilla ground and air military operations. Thus, approximately one-eighth of the country's total population is composed of recently displaced persons.

The majority of the population is rural, although the number of city inhabitants has risen since the Indochina War. Most persons who have moved to the cities have been in search of physical safety rather than economic opportunities or diversion.

Involuntary mobility as a result of wartime conditions has imposed serious hardships on a basically sedentary society. Because of the observance of the Cult of the Ancestors, the Vietnamese are bound to their birthplaces, and to leave the family tombs and ancestral villages remains for most of them an extremely serious step. This has been an important reason for the limited success of government resettlement schemes designed to promote land cultivation and to relieve crowding in some areas. It also had a restrictive influence on the program of building fortified (strategic) hamlets which called for a regrouping of villagers in some areas (see ch. 8, Living Conditions; ch. 19, Agriculture).

Somewhat over 40 percent of the population is economically active—not including women and children working as unpaid helpers in agriculture and family-owned craftshops. Farmers and fishermen account for nearly 90 percent of the labor force. Industrial workers are employed mostly in Saigon and vicinity. Current information on the numbers of artisans and craftsmen following traditional trades is lacking. There is a shortage of skilled workers. Managerial expertise is also rare, although there is a fairly large government bureaucracy.

There have been no official attempts to change the predominantly agricultural character of the labor force. The creation of a reservoir of industrial manpower is dependent on a large-scale expansion of industry which is unlikely to occur under the unsettled conditions of the mid-1960's.

SIZE AND COMPOSITION

The mid-1965 population figure of 16.1 million was projected from a South Vietnamese government survey for 1960. The annual growth rate of between 2 percent is about the same as in the other countries of Southeast Asia. Incomplete surveys conducted in 1963–64 indicated that birth and death rates declined between 1961 and 1963 (both rates were higher among men than among women).

According to the most recent estimates, there were about 7.1 million males of a total population of 15.2 million in 1963. With respect to age, the population was basically a young one, with a large active force available for work and for the armed forces.

GENERAL CHARACTERISTICS

Distribution and Density

Because of striking contrasts between the physical features of the various regions, the population is unevenly distributed. Nearly 50 percent of the rural population lives in the Mekong Delta area in the southern part of the country, where tropical climate, abundant rainfall and fertile soil result in conditions eminently suitable for rice cultivation. The coastal strips and the small river basins of the Central Lowlands, where the main occupations are farming and fishing, are also thickly settled. The Central Highlands, an area of about 18,000 square miles, has a total population of approximately 600,000, although the area could support many more. Settlement there is deterred, however, by the inhospitable mountains of the Chaîne Annamitique and the fever-infested jungles and forests which cover most of the area. French efforts in the past and projects by postindependence governments to resettle some of the lowland population into this area have met only with limited success (see ch. 2, Physical Environment).

In the Mekong Delta Region the density varies between 750 and 2,000 persons per square mile in the area between the main channel of the Mekong River and Saigon, but in its southernmost portions it is sparsely settled.

Some areas of the Central Lowlands are comparable in density to that of the most populated parts of the delta areas: nearly 3 million people live on the fertile coastal strip between Mui Dieu and Vung Da Nang, an area of 12,350 square miles. On the other hand, the barren strip which extends along the coast for 100 miles northward from the Mekong Delta has the lowest population density of any lowland area.

Although only 10 percent of the population lives in the cities, not all of the remaining 90 percent may be regarded as having rural characteristics. Scattered throughout the 43 provinces are many small urban centers, including the provincial capitals, many of which had been classified as municipalities before the administrative reform of 1957 (see ch. 13, The Governmental System). Of the five major cities, Saigon, the capital, with almost 1.5 million inhabitants, accounts for 85 percent of the total urban population. Da Nang is the next most populous with 143,910 inhabitants, followed by Hue with 105,000, Da Lat with 56,760, and Vung Tau with 38,337.

Ethnic and Religious Characteristics

More than 80 percent of the people are ethnically Vietnamese. They perpetuate the dominant cultural tradition and exert a paramount influence on the national life. The numerically dominant Vietnamese, who have lived in the country since the beginnings of recorded history, are culturally and ethnically closed related to the Chinese. Nearly all Vietnamese have settled in the lowlands of the Mekong Delta, and in the river valleys and coastal portions of the Central Lowlands. They are mostly rice farmers, sedentary and soil-bound, and the rhythm of their life is regulated mainly by the rice calendar.

The Chinese represent the largest minority, estimated by various observers to number between 800,000 and 1.2 million in 1965. Two-thirds of these live in Cho Lon, the "Chinatown" of Saigon. Other sizable Chinese colonies are in the cities of Rach Gia, Soc Trang and Bac Lieu, all in the Mekong Delta. Engaged in the rice trade, milling, real estate, banking and various other forms of trade and commerce, the Chinese play an important role in the Vietnamese economy.

Since 1956 the government has passed various laws, designed to assimilate the Chinese and to break their hold on certain economic fields. Because of official efforts to assimilate the Chinese, Vietnamese statistics regarding the size of the Chinese community tend to be low. In 1964, for example, there were only 561,000 Chinese, including "Vietnamese of Chinese ancestry," according to the Ministry of Economy and Finance. The pace of the government-directed assimilation, however, has been a slow one, and, in general, the Chinese minority has retained its cultural distinctness and its traditional economic role (see ch. 5, Ethnic Groups and Languages; ch. 22, Domestic Trade).

The second largest minority group, the *montagnards* (mountain people), live in the highlands of the Chaîne Annamitique, spread over a territory about half the size of the country. They comprise more than 30 tribes, representing numerous social types, dialects and cultural patterns. Because of the relative inaccessibility of their settlements, their numbers have been difficult to determine, but many sources estimate that there are about 700,000 *montagnards*. Some estimates, however, far exceed this number. The size of individual tribes varies from under 1,000 to over 300,000.

Several *montagnard* groups inhabit the western fringes of the Chaîne Annamitique and extend into neighboring Laos and Cambodia. Others, including the Bahnar and Sedang, are restricted to Kontum Province. The Jarai are located somewhat further south in Pleiku Province. The Rhade and the Mnong live in the Darlac plateau region, still further south. Slash-and-burn farmers, hunters and gatherers, many *montagnard* groups live in virtual isolation in the deep rain forests. The Bahnar and Sedang, on the other hand, have considerable contact with their neighbors and with the people of the lowlands. Since the intensification of Viet Cong efforts to infiltrate the rural population, the government has shown marked concern with the improvement of the *montagnards*' economy and living standards (see ch. 5, Ethnic Groups and Languages; ch. 8, Living Conditions).

The Khmers (Cambodians), the third largest minority, number approximately 400,000. Concentrated in the southwestern portion of the country, they are nearly all farmers. Their language, customs and level of development differ little from those of the Vietnamese, and they are gradually becoming integrated with the host population.

Remnants of the formerly large population of Cham origin, numbering from 20,000 to 35,000, inhabit a small area near Phan Rang, a coastal town in the southern part of the Central Lowlands. Other minority groups include several thousand each of Indians and Pakistanis. There are also smaller numbers of Malays and Arabs who are mostly engaged in trade and moneylending in Saigon and its vicinity.

Reliable figures regarding the number of followers of religious denominations are not available. A majority, or approximately 80 to 85 percent of the population, is Buddhist. This includes persons who associate Buddhism with national independence and are, therefore, nominal adherents of that faith without practicing its tenets. Two major politicoreligious sects are the Buddhist-oriented Hoa Hao and the Cao Dai, a group representing a complex mixture of tenets drawn from Buddhist, Confucianist, Taoist, Christian and other sources, numbering approximately 2 million, are concentrated mainly in the area extending northwest of Saigon to the Cambodian border, particularly in the province of Tay Ninh. Hoa Hao adherents, numbering about 1.5 million, are clustered in An Giang, Vinh Long and Phong Dinh Provinces, in the southwestern portion of the Mekong Delta. There are also several thousand Moslems, Hindus and members of other religious majorities. Most of the *montagnards* follow various local animist beliefs, although Catholic and Protestant missionaries have been active among them and have converted several thousand to Christianity (see ch. 11, Religion).

Approximately 10 percent of the population is Catholic, but many are only nominal followers of Catholicism. Catholics accounted for more than half of the nearly 1 million refugees who came south from Communist-ruled Vietnam after 1954. They are also numerous among the new wave of refugees who fled from territories dominated by the Viet Cong following the increase in military activities in 1964–65.

There are some 200,000 Protestants, according to missionary sources, not including converted *montagnards*. Of the Protestants, 50,000 have been baptized; the rest are nominal adherents of that faith.

Mobility

After the partition of the country along the seventeenth parallel in 1954, over 900,000 refugees poured into South Vietnam from the Communist-ruled North. They and an estimated additional 120,000 military dependents were removed with the aid of French and United States shipping. The arrival of all these destitute people in an area devastated by war caused great administrative, economic and social difficulties.

The refugees were first sheltered in camps on the coast and thereafter gradually shifted to areas where they could become self-supporting. Since most of the refugees were Roman Catholics migrating in village units under the leadership of their local priests, resettlement in many instances was facilitated. For these and other refugees some 319 villages were set up which absorbed some 500,000 of their numbers. Most of the villages were for farmers, but 26 were for fishermen. The rest of the refugees moved to established towns and villages, or to the crowded Saigon-Cho Lon area, causing a sharp rise in the population of the capital. The single most important resettlement scheme was the Cai San project near Rach Gia on the Gulf of Siam where 100,000 refugees and 20,000 local inhabitants were placed on 270,000 acres of reclaimed land. In all, about 400,000 refugees were settled in the Mekong Delta area, 53,000 in the Central Lowlands and 64,000 in the Central Highlands.

To relieve crowded conditions in the coastal deltas of the Central Lowlands, the government, in 1956–57, launched a large-scale resettlement project to develop 3.7 million acres of uncultivated land in the highland plateaus along the Laotian and Cambodian borders. Under this project, some 100,000 farmers from the delta areas were moved to the plateaus to clear and farm the reclaimed forest land. At the same time, 25,000 *montagnards* were transferred from their villages to settlement centers to pursue sedentary agriculture instead of their customary slash-and-burn method. In the course of this project, over 210,000 persons were resettled in 147 centers carved from 220,000 acres of mountain wilderness.

The project, however, was only partially successful. A sizable number of the lowlanders, accustomed to rice farming and unwilling to adopt new agricultural methods required by the strange environment, returned to their former "homes." Such moves were also motivated by the lowlanders' fear of the mountains, which they believe to be inhabited by evil spirits and infested with fevers. Meanwhile, some shifting of the population also occurred in the southern part of the Mekong Delta as several thousand of families were settled on reclaimed land (see ch. 19, Agriculture).

Since 1964 some 700,000 or more refugees have fled Viet Cong strongholds and areas subjected to bombings by the South Vietnamese and United States air forces. Indications are that at the end of 1965 the number of refugees had reached approximately 1.5 million. In many cases, the Viet Cong reportedly have driven the refugees into government-controlled areas to aggravate problems of local administration and civilian morale. The situation is of increasing concern to governmental authorities, particularly those responsible for public welfare and internal security (see ch. 8, Living Conditions; ch. 26, Public Order and Safety).

Nearly half of the refugees who have arrived since 1964 are concentrated in the coastal cities of three provinces in the Central Lowlands: Quang Nam, Quang Ngai and Binh Dinh. In Quang Nam Province, the Da Nang municipal administration, in mid-1965, refused admission of some 60–70,000 refugees from neighboring provinces because food and shelter were lacking. In Quang Ngai, the provincial administration was unable to prevent the influx of about 80,000 refugees into the port city of Quang Ngai, despite the absence of accommodation facilities. Similarly, some 100,000 refugees pressed for admission to the city of Qui Nhon in Binh Dinh Province, but only 30,000 could be admitted.

Estimates in 1965 put the number of uncared for refugees between 100,000 and 376,000. Those who are temporarily resettled live in government refugee camps, nearly all of which are substandard as a result of overcrowding. Such camps are usually set up around district towns and provincial capitals, or at coastal points extending southward from the northernmost province of Quang Tri to as far as Nha Thrang in Khanh Hoa Province.

LABOR FORCE

Distribution

The labor force, estimated at 6.5 million persons in 1964, comprised 41 percent of the total population. The actual percentage, however, was probably higher, since unpaid family workers in agriculture and certain other occupations were almost certainly not included in this calculation. Of the total labor force, 84.2 percent were employed in agriculture, 3.7 percent in commerce, 3 percent in fishing, 2 percent in manufacturing and crafts, and the rest in transportation, services and construction.

A few details are available concerning the structure of the economically active people of Saigon in 1962. For example, from a total of 806,000 persons who were 14 years of age and older, 401,700 or 49.8 percent were employed. This represented 28.1 percent of Saigon's total population of 1.4 million in 1962. Men comprised the majority, or 70.6 percent of the city's working-aged population. Most of the workers (men and women) were between 20 and 39 years old. Their mean age was 36 years for men and 33 for women. The largest occupational category was that of artisans, craftsmen and industrial workers, accounting for over 33 percent. Salespeople accounted for over 26 percent of the working population. Women predominated in the sales field, which engaged 41 out of every 100 working women. It is likely that the number of economically active women increased between 1962 and 1965 because of the losses and casualties among the male population resulting from intensified military action against the Viet Cong.

Rural Labor

The great majority of the rural labor force—some 4,171,500 in 1961—work on small plots in the Mekong Delta and the smaller deltas farther north. The principal crop is irrigated rice, and every able-bodied member of the family contributes to the intensive hand labor involved. Some of the larger plantations which adopted modern farming methods have been receiving government subsidies, but by 1965 there had been no large-scale government efforts to introduce more efficient forms of farming on smaller holdings.

The majority of hired agricultural laborers work on rubber, coffee and tea plantations in the Central Highlands. In 1961 these plantations employed some 61,000 workers, of which 41,045 worked on rubber plantations. In view of the intensified military activities against the Viet Cong in 1964–65, the number of plantation workers has probably decreased.

Fishing is the prominent occupation along the long coast of the South China Sea and the Gulf of Siam. In 1961 about 191,000 persons were engaged in commercial fishing.

Industrial and Commercial Workers

According to 1961 estimates, the latest available, only 329,000 of 5.6 million employable workers were engaged in industry and commerce. Almost two-thirds, or 206,000, of these represented commercial workers, the rest were employed in the processing industries. Not included in these estimates is an unknown but probably large number of craftsmen and artisans, both urban and rural. Further information concerning the distribution of the industrial population is lacking.

Almost all factories of any size are in the Saigon area. In 1962 most of the city's 131,580 industrial workers and artisans worked in small to medium-sized enterprises. The manufacturing and the textile plants were the largest industrial employers, with 62,220 and 12,540 workers, respectively. By mid-1965 the growing textile industry employed about 80,000 persons throughout the entire country.

The nascent An Hoa-Nong Son industrial project (in Quang Nam Province) employed 850 workers in 1964. Eighty percent of the workers came from local villages and were also farmers. In 1965, however, practically all operations were at a halt because of military activities and floods (see ch. 20, Industry).

Government Workers

Although only 124,000 employees represent the government bureaucracy itself, the government is the largest employer with an approximate total of 486,000 persons on its payroll, not including employees of government-owned economic enterprises. Of these, about 210,000 are members of the armed forces, with another 72,000 in the paramilitary Regional Force and 80,000 in the local Popular Force units (see ch. 13, The Governmental System; ch. 28, The Armed Forces).

The majority of persons working in government offices are men, although in 1960 about 13,000 women also worked in government agencies. The number of women government workers has probably increased, since many are replacing the growing number of men who have been drafted.

In 1964 the Department of Education had a staff of 29,326, mostly schoolteachers. The Department of Public Works and the Department of National Defense employed 25,065 and 16,421, respectively. Employees of the Department of Rural Development number 6,799; those of the Department of Economy, 439; and those of the Department of Labor, 349. The Department of Interior, with some 31,640 employees (mostly security agents and policemen), had by far the largest staff of all government agencies in that same year. This last figure probably has more than doubled since the ascent of the Ky government in June 1965.

CHAPTER 5

ETHNIC GROUPS AND LANGUAGES

At least 85 percent of the 16.1 million people are ethnically Vietnamese. As a group, they exert a paramount influence on the national life through their control of political and economic affairs and their role as the perpetuators of the dominant cultural tradition. There is no ethnic boundary corresponding to the political division between North and South Vietnam. Ethnically the Vietnamese are one people, and a great many South Vietnamese have parents, sisters and brothers or more distant kinsmen in the North.

Among the remainder of the population the largest minorities are the Chinese and the various highland groups collectively known as *montagnards*. In addition, there are smaller numbers of Khmers and Chams, both of whom figure prominently in the population of neighboring Cambodia, as well as Indians, Pakistanis, Eurasians, French and other Europeans, and Americans.

A preponderance of the population is distributed over the fertile delta of the Mekong and along the narrow coastline to the north, adjoining the South China Sea. The inhabitants of the lowlands include nearly all of the Vietnamese proper and all non-Vietnamese except the *montagnards*, who live in the highlands out of direct contact with the bulk of the population and in partial isolation from each other. Most of the *montagnards* have little sense of identification with either South Vietnam or with their distant ethnic relatives in North Vietnam, Cambodia and Laos.

Vietnamese is the language of daily communication and the mother tongue of the ethnic majority. It is also spoken with varying degrees of fluency by many Chinese, and an increasing number of members of other non-Vietnamese minorities.

The non-Vietnamese minorities, of which the Chinese constitute the largest ethnically homogeneous group, use their own languages among themselves. The Chinese, numbering perhaps 1 million, speak mainly the Cantonese dialect, but those born in the country are usually also fluent in Vietnamese, and most members of the older generation acquire a fair knowledge of it. On the other hand, not many of the 350,000 to 400,000 Khmer-speaking Cambodians or the smaller number of

Chams, Indians, Pakistanis, French, Americans and other foreigners in the country speak the national language.

There are some 20 fairly distinct *montagnard* languages, little known among the Vietnamese population. Conversely, the spread of Vietnamese among *montagnards* has been hindered by physical isolation and cultural conservatism. Knowledge of the language is limited largely to the few who have left their native communities to work as plantation laborers or as traders in the lowlands. Many adult males, however, speak the language of at least one neighboring tribe.

French, which was the official language throughout the colonial period, is by far the best-known foreign language. Knowledge of French is widespread in the cities, where all persons who have completed secondary schooling read and speak it fluently and many less well-educated persons, including merchants, low-ranking civil servants and army veterans, have some familiarity with it. French is less well-known in the rural areas, but a number of *montagnards* learned at least its rudiments either in schools set up by the colonial administration or during service with the French army. In Saigon, English has become the second foreign language of the younger generation.

THE VIETNAMESE

The People

Like their forebears in Vietnam for well over 1,000 years, the more than 13 million ethnic Vietnamese in the country in the mid-1960's are predominantly villagers, skilled in the cultivation of rice and fishing. A minority live in urban centers, such as Saigon and Hue, where they are engaged in a variety of occupations and hold positions at all levels on the socioeconomic scale. The educated elite—composed of high government officials, military officers, professionals and wealthy landowners—consists almost exclusively of ethnic Vietnamese.

The majority of ethnic Vietnamese consider themselves Buddhists, but their religious beliefs and practices include Taoist and Confucian elements as well as remnants of an earlier belief in spirits and magic. A sizable and influential minority is Roman Catholic (see ch. 11, Religion).

The Vietnamese proper, although they show certain regional and local differences in customs and speech and include both city dwellers and villagers, retain a strong sense of ethnic identity. This rests on a common language and a shared heritage of historical culture rather than on a sense of physical or racial distinctiveness.

The commonest Vietnamese physical type is characterized by straight black hair, round head, broad face, high cheekbones, dark eyes with the Mongolian single fold of the eyelid, and brown skin which varies in shade from light to medium. The average height is small—61 or 62 inches for males—and the average weight is about 120 pounds.

Some South Vietnamese claim that refugees from the North can be recognized by their more Mongoloid, or Chinese, features—lighter skin color, higher cheekbones, more protruding jaws and heavier builds. However, most observers agree that such identification from physical characteristics alone cannot be made with any degree of accuracy.

The Language

Vietnamese is one of the many languages, dialects and subdialects spoken in the Indochinese peninsula. The relationships between these languages are not clear cut, and no single system of classification has been universally accepted.

The three major dialects of Vietnamese—northern, central and southern—differ from each other in vocabulary, pronunciation and tonal pattern. The dialects are mutually intelligible only within limits, the greatest divergences being found among villagers. Most persons say that they experience initial difficulty in understanding a dialect other than their own.

The structure of Vietnamese words is invariable. Verbs are not conjugated; nouns, pronouns and adjectives are not declined; number and gender do not exist. Grammatical distinctions are made through changes in word order and the use of certain words which serve as grammatical indicators. The basic components of Vietnamese words are single syllables, each of which expresses a distinct idea. There are, however, many compound words, formed by joining a pair of mono-syllables. The spoken language employs a system of tones in which distinctions in the meaning of particular words are made through the use of various levels of pitch.

Vietnamese was spoken before the Christian era by the Viets of the Red River Delta area. During more than 1,000 years of Chinese rule (111 B.C. to A.D. 938) its vocabulary was greatly enriched by the addition of many literary, philosophical and other terms, but it remained the medium of popular speech and was carried southward into the Mekong Delta area by the Viet conquerors in the seventeenth century (see ch. 3, Historical Setting).

Under French rule the Vietnamese language was once again influenced by exposure to the speech of a conquering people. The widespread use of French by the educated classes in the late nineteenth and early twentieth centuries caused minor changes in the grammatical structure of Vietnamese, adding some new technical, scientific and popular terms to its vocabulary. Most scientific and technical terms, however, have been borrowed from Chinese.

An important feature of Vietnamese is a system of personal pronouns and personal "classifiers" indicating status relationships. Age, education, personal achievement and official rank command respect, and this respect is displayed in speech as well as in conduct. Many subtleties and nuances are reflected in the choice of terms, and the use of the wrong form can cause offense.

Proper names are rarely used by Vietnamese in addressing one another, the traditional explanation being that to do so might call the attention of evil spirits to the person named. Fictive kin terms are commonly used, even with strangers. Thus, *anh* (elder brother) is used in addressing an older man. *Ba* (grandmother) is used in addressing or referring to an older woman, who, in speaking to her grandchild, will so refer to herself. A young man is politely addressed or referred to as *bac* (father's older brother), but the less esteemed Chinese and Indian are likely to be called *chu* (father's younger brother). Birth order, however, usually determines the referential term, for example, *chi hai* (second girl), *chi ba* (third girl), *chi bon* (fourth girl).

The Vietnamese learned writing from the Chinese some 2,000 years ago. The first scholars studied and wrote in Chinese. Later they devised a system of writing their own language which employed certain Chinese ideographs to represent Vietnamese sounds, while other ideographs continued to represent complete words, as in Chinese.

The Chinese character for "man," for example, was absorbed unchanged into Vietnamese as the Vietnamese word for "man" and so continued to be employed as an ideograph. Other Chinese characters, however, were divested of meaning and assigned a sound value as symbols in a phonetic script. This combined ideograph and phonetic system was known as *chu nom*.

Chu nom began to slip into disuse in the late sixteenth century, when Portuguese and French missionaries devised *quoc ngu*, a system of writing Vietnamese in Roman letters. With the compilation of a Portuguese-Vietnamese dictionary, Portuguese was for a time the only language for written communication with Europeans. By the nineteenth century *quoc ngu* had become the common method of writing. However, Chinese forms and ideographs continued to be used for religious and ceremonial purposes.

Quoc ngu uses various diacritical marks placed over or under letters to indicate particular vowel and consonant sounds and syllabic tone or pitch. Since most single syllables function as meaningful words, and many of these monosyllabic words were phonetically identical except for tone, the diacritical marks are an essential part of the written forms.

THE MONTAGNARDS

The term *montagnard*, which came into common usage under the French, refers to the long-settled inhabitants of South Vietnam's mountain region—an aggregate estimated to be more than 700,000 persons representing 40 or so distinct ethnic communities. These highland groups are also known, in allusion to their alleged backwardness, by the common Vietnamese term "Moi," meaning "savage," and the equally pejorative Laotian and Cambodian names, respectively, Kha and Phong or Phnong. An effort to play down ethnic differences between the highland and lowland populations is reflected in the official use, beginning in early 1966, of the expression "Nguoi Thuong," meaning literally "upland people."

The *montagnards* are distributed at varying altitudes throughout the Chaîne Annamitique, the mountain barrier which dominates South Vietnam from the Mekong Delta northward to the Demarcation Line. They are distributed over an area stretching inland from Hue on the north nearly to Bien Hoa on the south and from the lower spurs of the mountains on the east across the border into Cambodia and Laos on the west. The terrain is extremely rough, the land generally unproductive and much of it is covered with jungle growth, rain forest and savannahs (see ch. 2, Physical Environment). Lacquer, cinnamon and other forest products, ivory and rhinoceros horn are the chief resources of the region, which, throughout the country's history, has been a buffer zone in the struggles among Thai, Lao, Vietnamese and Western colonial powers. It has also furnished a rich hunting ground for slavers and a productive field for Christian missionary efforts.

Archaeological and documentary evidence regarding the early history of the *montagnards* is extremely scanty, but it is thought that their remotest ancestors included a dark-skinned and long-headed people who came into the area in ancient times. More certainly among their forebears was a later-arriving population which, in its short stature, light skin and wavy black hair, resembled a common modern Indonesian type. Successive invasions of Mongoloid peoples from China drove these earlier settlers into the highlands and pressed some of them southward down the central mountain chain. The physical mingling that took place during this process did not overwhelm the early *montagnards*, but it injected a strong Mongoloid increment in their physical makeup, just as it left a heritage of their traits in the lowland population.

The varying origins of the early *montagnard* arrivals are reflected in the extraordinary confusion of languages now encountered in the mountain region. These languages have not been completely studied. Not only are there more than a dozen languages and numerous dialects in use, but their distribution is not precisely known. They can, however, be rather loosely grouped into two major divisions: the large and complex Mon-Khmer family, distributed over most of the mountain region, and the smaller Malayo-Polynesian family, confined to southern parts of the mountain region. More than 15 distinct languages of Mon-Khmer origin, the best-known including Bahnar, Sedang, Mnong and Stieng, are spoken by some half a million persons. An additional 300,000 persons speak one or another of a number of Malayo-Polynesian languages, of which the most important are Rhade and Jarai.

Despite the complexity of languages, neighboring peoples are, in general, sufficiently familiar with one another's languages to communicate with relative ease. The sounds of basic words often are much alike, and, where verbal understanding fails, conventional sign language may be employed. Among the major groups, a number of persons speak either French or English with some fluency.

The distinction between one *montagnard* group and another is usually made on the basis of linguistic criteria. This system of classification, however, has certain limitations. First, although scholars have agreed on a broad framework of language families and language groups within those families, they have failed to reach a consensus regarding the classification of particular subgroups within that outline. There has been some controversy, for example, as to whether the Rengao constitute a group separate from either the Sedang or the Bahnar. Moreover, contrary to what might be expected, highlanders who speak the same language do not invariably share common thought and behavior patterns; for instance, sometimes there are differences in the economic practices and cultural observances between one Rhade, Sedang, or Bahnar village and another. A system of classification based on linguistic criteria alone fails to take account of these distinctions.

Social divisions throughout the mountain region are primarily local. Politically and economically the village is the unit of overriding importance, and identification between members of the same ethnic group living at a distance from one another is usually negligible. For the majority of South Vietnamese *montagnards*, knowledge of outsiders other than close neighbors has been extremely limited. Each village is a largely self-contained economic unit and handles its internal political affairs through the mechanism of an elected council of elders and headman. In the absence of hereditary chieftains whose political authority is acknowledged by the entire ethnic community and which derives from a kinship system, South Vietnam's *montagnards* cannot accurately be referred to as "tribes," although this is often done.

While the *montagnards* have not traditionally shown any degree of self-conscious unity, certain characteristic ways of thought and behavior have set them apart from the rest of the population. The typical *montagnard*, as seen by the lowlander, is a non-Vietnamese-speaking animist, dark skinned and clad in a loincloth, who lives in an isolated settlement deep in the mountains. He grows wet and dry rice and other crops by rudimentary techniques and occasionally stalks boar, wild goat or other prey with a crossbow. His life is governed by a myriad of taboos and rituals having to do with malevolent spirits, whom he greatly fears, and whose placation through sacrificial offerings is a major preoccupation. This image of the *montagnard* predominates in the lowlands, despite the fact that a few highlanders have acquired an education or a degree of technical competence; can speak French, English or Vietnamese; have been at least superficially converted to Christianity; and are serving in the South Vietnamese Army or special forces units.

Customs governing marriage and family life among the *montagnards* vary from group to group. Some communities are patrilineal, reckoning descent from the male line; others are matrilineal, reckoning descent from the female line; still others have a bilateral kinship system. In the bilateral society of the Bahnar, for example, the typical unmarried male lives in the communal or bachelor house, centrally situated among the so-called long houses which shelter the rest of the village population. Marriage arrangements may be initiated by the family of either the potential bride or groom. After marriage and before the birth of the first child, the groom spends a brief period of residence with his wife's parents and an equal period with his own before establishing an independent household. Later he may take an additional wife, who is established under the same roof. Personal possessions are inherited through the male line. Among the matrilineally organized Rhade, by contrast, women are the household heads, and family property is in the hands of the women. A certain judicial authority rests with the senior women, who hold title to the clan land by right of inheritance.

The religious beliefs and practices of the *montagnards* represent an admixture of magic, mythology and superstition. Their traditions are rich in legends, many of which have to do with the first appearance of human life on earth. Most *montagnard* groups worship an entire pantheon of spirits, of which some are good but most are evil. The evil spirits must be propitiated on numerous occasions—the building of a house, the birth of a child, the presence of an epidemic—with the celebration characteristically entailing the sacrifice of a buffalo and the drinking of rice wine.

Social and Political Integration

Before the coming of the French the *montagnards* lived largely in isolation from the lowland peoples. Contacts between the two groups were infrequent and peripheral, *montagnard* exposure to the dominant culture deriving almost solely from the commercial or political ambitions of lowland peoples. During the fifteenth century, for example, the Chams and the Khmers carried on a flourishing trade with each other across a route which passed over the Darlac Plateau. Later the imperial Vietnamese Government established a number of military installations in the *montagnard* areas bordering the lowlands. These bases served as trading outposts and offered protection against *montagnard* marauders for the local population, but had a negligible effect on the integration of *montagnards* into the national life.

With the expansion of French control in Southeast Asia during the late nineteenth century, contacts between the *montagnards* and the remainder of the population steadily increased. The French, interested in the highlands for plantation agriculture, gave the *montagnard* regions special status. They called these areas the Southern Montagnard Country (Pays Montagnard du Sud—PMS) and administered them separately from the rest of Vietnam. This status was retained under Emperor Bao Dai when Vietnam was granted semi-independence in 1949.

In some instances, the newly developing relationships were harmonious and, to varying degrees, mutually beneficial. The French and Vietnamese gained access to a largely unexploited territory, while the less isolated *montagnard* groups, on their part, were exposed to the goods and techniques of culturally more advanced societies. French administrators and Christian missionaries established schools, hospitals and leprosariums for *montagnard* use.

Often, however, the new contacts proved disruptive, giving rise to conflict between the *montagnard* communities and the outsiders, who were looked on as unwelcome interlopers. *Montagnards* asserted that Vietnamese merchants mulcted them, Vietnamese and French officials abused them, and most importantly, speculators of both nationalities were intent on usurping their traditional landholdings. A *montagnard* revolt against the French, lasting from 1931 to 1933, was followed by another in 1936, which continued until 1938. Eventually, the French were able to obtain what amounted to permanent rights to the use of some *montagnard* lands, particularly those of the Rhade and Jarai. These tracts have since been developed into large rubber, coffee and tea plantations.

After 1954 the Vietnamese Government incorporated the highland regions into the centralized governmental structure of the country, bringing the *montagnards* under direct Vietnamese administration. The aim of this policy was to integrate the *montagnards* socially, economically and politically into the framework of Vietnamese national life—an objective which was made urgent by the campaign of terrorism directed against them by Communist guerrillas. The government approached the problem by moving Vietnamese into the highlands from the overpopulated coast and by settling the seminomadic *montagnards* in the vicinity of the new communities where they would be exposed to Vietnamese influences and protected from guerrilla activity.

The resettlement program met with early resistance from the *montagnards*, who were reluctant to discard their traditional ways for life in the regroupment centers and also saw the influx of Vietnamese settlers as a threat to their ancestral lands. Moreover, the program was not always tactfully carried out, with the result that in some instances fear and antagonism were built up among the highlanders—a vulnerability which the Communists did not fail to exploit (see ch. 16, Public Information).

In late 1961 steps were taken to remedy the situation. Civil administrators were instructed to deal sympathetically with the *montagnards*, and the army's psychological warfare section was directed to promote friendly relations between them and the army personnel. Subsequently, the Civilian Irregular Defense Group, a paramilitary organization designed to win the loyalty of the *montagnards* and train them for combat against the Viet Cong, was incorporated into the armed forces (see ch. 27, The Armed Forces).

Latent opposition to Vietnamese dominance was suggested in mid-1964 by the formation of the Unified Front for the Liberation of Oppressed Races (Front Unifié pour la Libération des Races Opprimées—FULRO). Purporting to represent the Cham, Rhade, Jarai, Raglai, Bahnar, Sedang, Hre, Mnong, Stieng and other *montagnard* peoples, the stated purpose of the new organization was to obtain *montagnard* independence from the Vietnamese authorities. Later in the same year several hundred Rhade seized the radio station at Ban Me Thuot, capital of Darlac Province, demanding the establishment of an autonomous tribal state. United States Army officers headed off the revolt and arranged for the presentation of *montagnard* grievances to the authorities in Saigon. Among demands were title to their lands and the authority to settle internal disputes among themselves and in accordance with their own customary law.

Prime Minister Nguyen Khanh responded by promising greater recognition of *montagnard* status, social welfare benefits and inclusion of *montagnard* officers in the armed forces. Legislation covering many of these points was subsequently enacted, but had not yet been put into effect by September 1965, when new revolt threatened and had to be put down.

The *montagnard* population can be roughly sorted into two groups—those found in the northern half of the country's mountainous spine and those found principally in the southern part. The northern highland peoples all speak Mon-Khmer languages. The southern highland peoples include groups of Malayo-Polynesian as well as Mon-Khmer linguistic stock. Some of these groups extend across the border into eastern Laos and Cambodia, and some are related to groups in North Vietnam.

The Northern Mountain Region

The largest and, consequently, most important groups in the northern mountain region include the Katu, Sedang, Hre and Bahnar peoples. The Katu language belongs to the Katuic subgroup of the Mon-Khmer family; the languages of the others belong to the Bahnaric subgroup of the same family.

The Katu

Like the majority of South Vietnamese *montagnards*, the Katu (Kato, Ka–Tu) are a dark-skinned, muscular, seminomadic people, whose traditional relations with their neighbors have alternated between the formation of blood-oath alliances and the conduct of intermittent warfare in quest of food and slaves. The northernmost of the country's principal *montagnard* peoples, the Katu occupy an area extending from some 15 miles west of the coastal cities of Hoi An and Da Nang to the border of southern Laos. This sector is a particularly rugged area, thickly forested, with rocky slopes and precipitous peaks. As is the case with many highland peoples, little of their daily living habits is known; much of the available information comes from reports of missionaries or French military officers and is limited in scope. The Katu are said to number between 20,000 and 30,000.

Katu settlements are generally small and situated on high slopes because of the oppressive humidity at lower elevations. The few roads leading to them become impassable during the heavy rains. Houses, generally made of bamboo and wood and roofed with thatch, are usually arranged in a circle facing the bachelors' house, which is the focal point of village life. A residence for unmarried men and a gathering place for all, the bachelors' house is the site of all communal rituals, feasts and meetings.

In appearance, the Katu resemble other South Vietnamese *montagnards* in that they are generally of short or medium height and muscular. The men, most of whom are well built, range from 64 to 66 inches in height. Many Katu ornament the face, chest, arms, wrists and thighs with colorful tattoos.

The characteristic Katu weapon is a crossbow, made locally and used along with traps, in hunting. After a successful hunt the kill is salted and preserved in bamboo tubes, to be used as a supplement to the standard dietary fare. Rice, manioc and maize are the dietary staples along with wild fruits and roots gathered in the forest.

The Katu are patrilineal, and marriage follows the mutual consent of the parties and their parents to the arrangement and to the bride price. The extended family, consisting of a man and his wife, his male descendants and their wives and children, unmarried daughters and aged parents, is the typical household unit. A Katu may take more than one wife, but rarely does.

In general, Katu relations with their neighbors have been poor; reportedly, the Katu are still wont to kidnap intended victims for sacrificial offerings from nearby villages. Their principal contacts with lowlanders have occurred during occasional visits of Katu to market towns on the coast. Political loyalties formerly extended no higher than the village level. In the mid-1960's, however, it was reported that the Viet Cong had extensive control of the Katu, as they had over groups in the same general area. Some Katu had been sent to North Vietnam for military training.

The Sedang

The Sedang, also known as the Ha ndea (sometimes written Harh ndeang) or Xo-dang, are estimated to number between 60,000 to 80,000. They speak Sedang, a language which includes several dialects, but any Sedang can understand any other. No written form of the language has as yet been developed. The coming of the French and their establishment of special schools in Sedang territory resulted in the acquisition of French-speaking skills by some Sedang before 1954; since then, others have learned Vietnamese as a result of contact with government officials or dealing in lowland markets. Most Sedang, however, know only their own tongue.

The date of arrival of Sedang groups in the area northwest of Kontum, which they presently occupy, is unknown. Even in the modern period, they have been little studied, having had little to do with either the Vietnamese or the French until a few decades ago. Reportedly, there has been considerable contact between them and their Bahnar neighbors, not all of it friendly. They have intermittently engaged in feuding and in raiding contiguous territory and have jealously guarded their independence. Initial French efforts to gain a foothold in Sedang territory met with violent resistance. Since then movement through the area has been facilitated by the construction of Route 14, which is the principal north-south road in the Central Highlands region.

The Sedang are slash-and-burn cultivators of dry rice, but unlike some other *montagnard* groups, they also cultivate paddy in the bottomland where this is possible. Every member of the group has claim to some portion of the dry-rice harvest, which is cultivated collectively. The labor of a single family, however, goes into the farming of wet-rice paddy and kitchen gardens; hence, only its members share in the harvest. Fishing and hunting provide supplementary items for the diet.

Of special interest in respect to the Sedang economy are the iron deposits abounding in the area. Between rice-growing seasons many Sedang men engage in iron mining as a subsidiary occupation. The ore is extracted, molded and forged into various tools, such as hatchets, pickaxes, machetes and knives, for commercial sale.

Each long house, sheltering a number of nuclear families, has a ritual chieftain. She is responsible for cooking the rice, which, when grown according to traditional methods, is regarded as sacred. Rice may be cooked only in the half of the household in which she lives and must be carried to occupants of the other half from her hearth.

The Hre

The Hre are considered by some scholars as an independent group and by others as a subgroup of the Sedang, near whom they live. They occupy a sector of the northern mountain region, inland from the coastal city of Quang Ngai. Estimates of their number are at wide variation, reflecting lack of agreement among scholars as to whom should be included. The estimates range from 27,000 to more than 100,000, depending on what system of classification is used.

In recent years the government has forcibly resettled many of the Hre in lowland areas so as to cut off food supplies to the Viet Cong. The action aroused Hre resentment, apparently not so much because the people regretted having to leave their fields and villages as because the administration subsequently proved unable to provide protection against Viet Cong incursions in the newly settled area.

The Bahnar

The Bahnar live in the rugged mountains of southeastern Kontum, northern Pleiku and western Binh Dinh Provinces, south of the Hre area. Estimates of their number range from 70,000 to 200,000.

They may be divided, mainly on linguistic grounds, into seven major subgroups. The Alakong, Tolo and Bonom are settled mainly around An Khe; the Golar and To Sung are near Pleiku; and the Jo Long and Kontum, around Kontum. There are also some smaller subgroups—the Krem and the Kon Ko De near An Khe and the Ho Drong some 20 miles southeast of Kontum. On the fringes of Bahnar territory live the Rengao and the Krem, whom some scholars regard as Bahnar, others as closely related peoples.

These groups speak their own Bahnaran languages, which belong to the Mon-Khmer family. Bahnar, the principal Bahnaran language, was given a written form by Catholic missionaries during the French colonial period. The writing system employs romanized Vietnamese characters. Quite a few Bahnar elders understand French and speak it with a fair degree of fluency, but with a strong accent. Some speak English, too, serving as interpreters for United States Special Forces units.

Lean and well-muscled, the Bahnar have bronzed skin and short or medium-length dark hair. High cheekbones and broad noses are characteristic of many individuals. Average heights reported in one village ranged from 54 to 60 inches for men, 47 to 50 inches for women. Filing of teeth is commonplace, and many male adults bear the scars of self-inflicted wounds on the chest or thigh. Men wear a loincloth, sometimes adding a shirt, coat or shawl; women wear a knee-length skirt or sarong. Both sexes sometimes ornament themselves with a profusion of silver, copper or glass beads.

Neighboring Bahnar villages are generally grouped together in an administrative unit known as a *toring*, the residents of which share hunting, fishing and cultivation rights within the *toring* area. The Bahnar are dry-rice farmers but supplement their diet with cultivation of such secondary crops as millet, maize, pumpkins, eggplant and manioc. They also raise some buffalo, goats, pigs and chickens. The villagers exercise joint ownership over the domestic animals, which are offered as sacrifices when houses are built, crops are planted and birth, illness and death occur.

The usual settlement consists of a number of family dwellings, a communal house for bachelors, granaries and shelters for pigs and chickens. A tall gate with a thatched roof stands at the entranceway to the village; its barbed-wire doors are closed at night. Family dwellings, averaging 30 feet long, are roofed with thatch and set on pilings raising them some 6 feet off the ground as a protection against wild animals. The interior is reached by a ladder from the outside.

Living conditions are rigorous. Food is scarce and infant mortality high. Smallpox, sleeping sickness and other epidemic diseases strike the village from time to time, and, on occasion, a man or woman is attacked and fatally injured by a wild animal. Such disasters are generally regarded as the work of malevolent "spirits of the dead," who are greatly feared. Relief from fear and deprivation is generally found in drinking bouts, during which unrefined rice wine is drunk through bamboo tubes.

Social organization is based on the village. Each village elects a group of elders, who in turn select the headman, or *kra*. A political superstructure was imposed by the French so that now the *kra* usually acts as a liaison with the central government. Because of their location, Bahnar villages are especially susceptible to attack from the Viet Cong, and some have gone over to the Viet Cong side. In 1963, in a move intended to cut off Viet Cong food sources, a number of Bahnar villagers were resettled near Pleiku, where the people have since cleared land, dug wells and constructed housing.

Relations with neighboring peoples vary in character from hostile to friendly. In the past, Bahnar marauding bands made frequent incursions into contiguous areas to secure food and other goods; on the other hand some Bahnar men have contracted marriage with Jarai and Chan peoples, which have created kin ties among these groups. Also the Bahnar were one of the *montagnard* groups noted for their friendly and cooperative manner toward Christian missionaries and French administrators during the French colonial period.

The Southern Mountain Region

The southern mountain region includes *montagnard* groups of both the major linguistic stocks. Among the principal groups are the Stieng, Mnong, Kil, Sre and Ma, whose languages are of Mon-Khmer origin, and the Jarai, Rhade, Raglai and Bih groups, whose languages belong to the Malayo-Polynesian family. A number of the latter groups have been strongly influenced by the ancient Cham civilization.

The Stieng

The Stieng, sometimes known as the Budnip, are one of the smallest ethnic groups in the southern mountain region. Numbering about 20,000, they occupy Quang Duc, Phuoc Long and Binh Long Provinces on South Vietnam's western border. Stieng are also found in Cambodia, where their numbers are even greater.

Most of the group speak Stieng as their only language, although a few Stieng speak French as a result of having worked on foreign-owned rubber plantations, and some can speak Vietnamese. Stieng itself is one of the Stiengan languages of the Bahnaric subgroup of the Mon-Khmer family. It is thus linguistically related most closely to the languages of the Mnong, Kil, Sre and Ma, who inhabit other sectors of the southern mountain region.

The territory on which the Stieng are settled is less remote from lowland areas of habitation than that of many *montagnard* groups. Traversing it are National Route 13, running north and south near the Cambodian frontier, and Route 14, running southwest to northeast in the east across the mountains. Dense jungle and flat grasslands characterize much of the area. Because Viet Cong infiltrators cross over Stieng territory, many Stieng villages, for security reasons, have been forcibly resettled in the lowlands. This action aroused appreciable resentment among the Stieng, who apparently, like many other *montagnard* groups, are largely indifferent to the outcome of the current guerrilla action and want only to be left alone.

The Stieng, who have a patrilineal kinship system, handle their own affairs at the village level, each local community recognizing the authority of its own headman and council of elders.

The Kil, Sre and Ma

On a linguistic basis the Kil, Sre and Ma may be grouped, together with a number of smaller ethnic communities found in the same general area, under the collective label Koho. Their language and its various dialects are part of the Stiengan subgrouping of Mon-Khmer stock. The groups show less cultural than linguistic homogeneity, however, and differences in economic practices and social behavior among them are of interest.

The Sre, for example, unlike most other Mon-Khmer groups, apparently have a matrilineal kinship system. Women, whose prerogative it is to choose the marital partner, hold title to all family property. Numbering an estimated 30,000 in 1959, the Sre live in the vicinity of Djiring, some 30 miles southwest of Da Lat. In contrast to the slash-and-burn cultivation of dry rice practiced by most *montagnards*, the Sre are wet-rice cultivators who grow rice in paddy fields in the valley bottoms, using a buffalo and plow.

The Ma (Cau Ma), numbering about 30,000 and located about 60 miles west of Da Lat on the banks of the upper Song Dong Nai, practice both wet- and dry-rice cultivation. They also hunt game, which abounds in the valley. The fact that some Ma occupy dispersed farmsteads, rather than live in more compact settlement, distinguishes them from other groups. Their sociopolitical organization features an elite of prosperous families, from whom the village chiefs are drawn. Feuding and raiding were characteristics of Ma life in earlier centuries, with prisoners of war adopted as slaves in the family of the captors. Some Ma still hold slaves.

The Kil (Chil, Cil, Mnong Kil), estimated as numbering about 10,000, occupy a tract northeast of Da Lat, where they engage in slash-and-burn cultivation.

The Mnong

The Mnong are a seminomadic people, who inhabit the mountains, densely forested area between Ban Me Thuot and Da Lat. They include various subgroups which have little or nothing to do with each other but speak dialects of the same Mon-Khmer language. Among these subgroups, for instance, are the Mnong Bunor in the western part of the Mnong area, who have close contact with the Stieng; the Mnong Rlam, who occupy a swampy sector to the east; and also to the east, the Mnong Gar, who live to the south of Lac Thien basin. Until recently the Mnong engaged much of the time in feuding and raiding, and they still maintain a reputation for unfriendliness to outsiders.

Mnong villages vary in plan with each group. Long houses, providing shelter for several related or friendly nuclear families, may be ranged in a triangle, along a central path or at random. The houses themselves vary in construction, as to the type of roof, placement of the door and use of pilings.

The Mnong peoples collectively number about 40,000. They are seminomadic agriculturalists, who practice dry-rice cultivation in the uplands or, as in the case of the Mnong Rlam, utilize streambeds and lakeshores for irrigated rice growth. Their principal contacts with outsiders occur through commercial exchanges. Their religious life is largely concerned with the control exerted over their destiny by a pantheon of spirits; they attribute all untoward happenings to the work of spirits or sorcerers, called *caak*. Religious life finds its ultimate expression, as among other *montagnards*, in the ritual sacrifice of the buffalo.

Mnong Gar villages are established and abandoned at frequent intervals, the people never remaining in one place for long. Upland rice is cultivated in fields chosen by divination. The areas are cleared, cultivated and used for 1 year only. Settlements are sometimes deserted, too, after having been nearly wiped out by an epidemic or when it is thought the spirits have decreed a change.

Different clans are represented in each village. Clan membership gives the individual his place in the group as a whole, but the nuclear family is the basic economic, ceremonial and property-holding unit in the village. Descent is matrilineal, and newlywed couples generally live with the wife's family.

The Jarai

Much of the southern mountain region is occupied by hill peoples of Malayo-Polynesian linguistic stock. Little is known of their ancient history; but their speech and behavior reveals that they have been strongly influenced by the once-powerful kingdom of Champa, to which they lived in close proximity. Among the Chamized hill peoples, the largest and most important are the Jarai and the Rhade, whose languages and cultures are closely related.

About 200,000 Jarai (Djarai) live for the most part in the Darlac plateau in the southern part of the Central Highlands. Their subdivisions remain uncertain, although A-rap (Arap), Hdrung (Hodrung) and Hbau (Habau) are those most frequently reported. Mixed groups of Haroi and M'dhur have developed as a result of contact between Jarai and Rhade. The Haroi show a high degree of assimilation to Jarai culture; the M'dhur largely resemble the Rhade.

Physically, the Jarai are said to be well built, taller in some instances than other *montagnards*, light brown to almost black in skin color, with broad noses. Those on the northern fringe of Jarai territory are becoming assimilated to the Bahnar in culture, but, in general, the Jarai maintain traditional patterns of social and political organization. The Jarai have a matrilineal kinship system; after marriage the husband goes to live at the house of his wife. There is generally one extended family to a long house, consisting of related women, their husbands, children and unmarried male kin. Children take the mother's family name, and women own the house, gongs, jars, animals and other valuables representing the family wealth. After the death of the mother the daughters inherit the family goods. Land, too, is reportedly owned by individual families, rather than collectively, by the group, as is true among other *montagnards*.

Although in the past certain sorcerers have at times gained control over a number of neighboring villages, there is at present no political organization higher than that of the group of elders and the village headman. The Jarai have had, until recently, only limited contacts with the Vietnamese, and few speak the language. Many, Jarai, however, speak French.

The Rhade

To the south of the Jarai are the Rhade, whose numerical strength, relative sophistication and strategic location across a Viet Cong supply line gives them first-rank importance among *montagnard* peoples. The Rhade are centered around Ban Me Thuot, capital of Darlac Province. They are, however, dispersed over a wide area, including the neighboring provinces of Quang Duc, Khanh Hoa and Phu Yen, as well as portions of eastern Cambodia. Estimates of their strength range from 100,000 to 150,000.

Rhade participation in public affairs have been more extensive than that of other *montagnard* groups. The community includes a number of individuals who have acquired education and administrative or technical competence, and it has provided leadership and initiative in the *montagnard* autonomy movement. Y. Bham, a Rhade, is a former government official and currently president of the Unified Front for the Liberation of Oppressed Races (Front Unifié pour la Libération des Races Opprimées—FULRO), the independence movement of certain *montagnard* groups (see ch. 14, Political Dynamics; ch. 27, Subversive Potential).

Internally, the Rhade are divided into numerous subgroups, including the Kpa, M'dur, A'dham, K'tul, Epan, Blo, K'ah, K'drao and H'wing. Within each of these subgroups the population is organized into matrilineal lineages. These consist of individuals descended through the female line from a common ancestress three of four generations removed. Groups of lineages form clans related through still more remote female ancestors. Marriage between members of the same clan is forbidden. This negative regulation of marriage is a primary function of the clans. Clan members also gather on ceremonial occasions and may assist one another in housebuilding and other large undertakings. Each clan has a name and its own taboos associated with hunting or eating certain animals.

Land is owned by the clans, each of which has one or more large ancestral tracts. A clan representative, whose duties are hereditary, administers each tract according to tradition and customary law.

This representative is always the eldest woman of the senior line, who is designated *po lan* (proprietor) of the land, to which she holds title. The *po lan* has no right to sell the land unless the notables representing the entire group give their consent. The matrilineal system notwithstanding, men have an important sociopolitical role. A man, usually the husband of one of the elder women, is household head of each long house.

The animistic religion of the Rhade centers on a belief in spirits or supernatural powers associated with forests, water, ricefields, tombs, and other manmade and natural objects and living things. Their ceremonies and fertility rites include sacrifice of fowl, buffalo and oxen, which are offered to the spirits for protection, prosperity and health. The Rhade have recourse to sorcerers for the magical cure of illness, and omens based on dreams and taboos importantly influence conduct.

The typical Rhade settlement consists of small clusters of long houses, built on pilings and generally located near a good water source. Some villages have as many as 70 long houses. The orientation of the houses is almost invariably north-south, but may vary depending on the terrain in some areas. Each house shelters a senior woman, her husband, her daughters and their husbands and the grandchildren together with unmarried sons. The interior is divided into small compartments, each sheltering one nuclear family.

The Raglai

The Raglai (Orang Glai) are a smaller group than the Rhade, but, like them, are of Malayo-Polynesian stock and have a matrilineal kinship system. They are said to number about 40,000. Divided into three subgroups, the Afflai, the Tring and the Lre, they are found principally in two areas, one lying inland from the coastal city of Nha Trang, the other between Da Lat and the coastal city of Phan Rang. The population in the latter sector has reportedly been heavily influenced by the Cham.

Raglai settlement patterns are distinct from those of most other *montagnards* in that individual families generally occupy single homesteads rather than group together in a compact settlement. Houses are usually separated from one another by 500 to 700 yards. Married couples live in the community in which the wife's kinsmen are found, and women have title to all family property.

The Bih

Some scholars identify the Bih as a separate and distinct people, others classify them on a linguistic basis as a Rhade subgroup. Numbering well under 40,000, they are settled in the vicinity of the lower Krong Kno River, not far from Ban Me Thout. They have long been influenced by the neighboring Mnongs, a larger and more powerful people of Mon-Khmer stock.

Others

In addition to the long-settled groups already mentioned, there are a number of *montagnard* people who are recent refugees from North Vietnam. Among the principal of these are the Mnong, with a total population of over 180,000, of whom an estimated 10,000 now live in South Vietnam. In the South they have settled mainly around Ban Me Thout and Pleiku. Information on Mnong patterns of living is scanty, but they apparently follow generally the same customs and practices as other *montagnard* groups in the area. They are patrilineal, and only men can own property.

Another people, the Nung, who are concentrated in the highlands of North Vietnam near the Chinese border, have moved into the South in considerable numbers. Usually considered a Tai subgroup, the Nung have a patrilineal kinship system. Children bear the father's name, and the father has title to all family property. The Nung have made an important name for themselves as professional soldiers. President Ngo Dinh Diem employed Nung elements in the Vietnamese army to help overcome the dissident Cao Dai and Hoa Hao sect in March and April 1955 (see ch. 11, Religion). In the mid-1960's, Nung troops were aiding United States forces in South Vietnam in their operations against the Viet Cong.

THE CHINESE

The People

The Chinese, who are South Vietnam's largest minority, began to arrive in Indochina in the third century B.C. or earlier. They came as conquerors, but during the thousand years (second century B.C. to the tenth century A.D.) that the local population was ruled directly by China, Chinese culture traits were peacefully diffused through the society by education and intermarriage. The Viets became to an evident degree culturally Chinese; they were not, however, completely absorbed by the alien tradition. Many Chinese, moreover, became increasingly Vietnamese in outlook and behavior. Chinese appeared in the Cochin China area for the first time in the late seventeenth century. Full-scale immigration began, however, only in the nineteenth century (see ch. 3, Historical Setting).

In Vietnam overseas Chinese were organized into a number of associations, membership in which was based on place of origin in China. The principal function of these associations, called *congregations* by the French or *bang* by the Vietnamese, was to facilitate the assimilation of the migrant into local Chinese society, principally by providing economic assistance. Originally, seven *congregations* existed, but in 1885 these were merged into five groups, including the Cantonese group (the largest), the Fukienese group, the Hainanese group, the Teochiu group and the Hakka group.

Political difficulties in China and economic opportunities in the well-established Chinese communities of Vietnam increased migration in modern times. More than 400,000 are estimated to have immigrated from China after the Japanese invasion of China in 1937. In the mid-1960's the number of Chinese in South Vietnam was generally accepted as about 1 million. The figures are uncertain, however.

A further difficulty is the uncertainty surrounding the ethnic identity of second-generation or part Chinese, one of whose parents is Vietnamese. In an unknown number of instances such persons are educated as Vietnamese, marry ethnic Vietnamese, bear Vietnamese names and live entirely outside the Chinese community. More importantly, the matter of determining the precise number of Chinese is affected by legal considerations. Under the French the Chinese were permitted to retain Chinese citizenship and to appeal to China for protection of their special rights—a privilege which was complicated by Communist conquest of mainland China and the removal to Taiwan of the Chinese Nationalist Government. In September 1956, however, under the late President Ngo Dinh Diem, South Vietnam enacted a decree making all Chinese born in the country Vietnamese citizens if at least one parent was also born in Vietnam. Defined on a legal basis, the size of the Chinese community thus would be substantially smaller than the generally accepted figure of 1 million.

The partitioning of Vietnam had found the Chinese minority concentrated almost entirely in the urban centers of South Vietnam, mainly in Cho Lon. Their commercial importance, which had long been out of proportion to their numbers, had grown during the colonial period to a near monopoly of all but the largest business enterprises, which were in the hands of the French. Until 1956 they controlled 90 percent of the retail trade and played a leading role in rice brokerage, lumbering and the transport of goods between inland points and the seaports. They also shared with the Indians and Pakistanis, and with some of the wealthier Vietnamese, a prominent position in moneylending in the cities as well as the rural areas.

At the same time the nationality regulation was imposed, however, a decree was enacted which forbade any foreigner to engage in any one of 11 occupations, all of which were mainly pursued by Chinese. The impact of the occupational restriction was initially softened by the fact that Chinese who were married to Vietnamese women were permitted to continue to operate their businesses in their wives' names. However, a number of Chinese left the country rather than accept Vietnamese citizenship. The *congregations*, which by August 1948 had been officially renamed the Chinese Regional Administrative Groups, and through which the Chinese enjoyed extensive powers of self-government, were abolished in 1960. The Chinese schools were also brought under goverenment control and required to teach the Vietnamese language.

Within several years all but a few thousand individuals had complied with the citizenship formalities. Some outside observers felt that, in nominally accepting citizenship, the Chinese community had probably gained more than it had lost; it was able to continue its important role in the economic life of the country and still had ample opportunity to perpetuate its cultural identity.

In the mid-1960's, Chinese Regional Administrative Groups, which on paper no longer existed, were, in practice, actually operative. They continued to perform important integrating functions in commerce and trade and in the maintenance of Chinese cultural traditions. Chinese once again engaged in almost all businesses and occupations as well, although they were found in only token numbers in the armed services and the government.

In respect to the rice trade, almost exclusively dominated by the Chinese, some dealings with the Viet Cong occurred in Communist-controlled areas, but there was no formal evidence of any Chinese connivance with the Viet Cong. Nevertheless, some Vietnamese may hold Chinese merchants responsible for rising rice prices, thereby widening the gap between the two ethnic communities.

The Language

Until the French conquest in the late seventeenth century, Chinese was the language of administration and scholarship. Knowledge of the language was a mark of high social status and a prerequisite for government office or local recognition. As a literary language, however, its preeminence was challenged from the fourteenth century onwards by Vietnamese, which became the medium for a growing popular literature.

In the modern period, Chinese—mainly in its south Chinese variants—has been important chiefly as the spoken language of the largest ethnic minority. The Chinese have their own schools and social and fraternal organizations. They also have their own newspapers (see ch. 16, Public Information).

Immigration after World War II was thought to have considerably enlarged the size of the Chinese community, sizable segments of which had come originally from Kwangtung, Fukien and other provinces in South China. Information concerning the composition of the Chinese population in 1966, in terms of local origins, is lacking.

KHMERS AND CHAMS

The indigenous minorities of the lowlands—the Khmers and Chams—have, like the *montagnards*, been in the country for centuries. Also like the *montagnards*, they tend to be regarded by the Vietnamese as being less advanced than themselves. The poverty-stricken villages of the Chams in particular invite this judgment, even though the Chams are the descendants of a people who developed a high civilization and ruled an empire which lasted for 1,500 years. The Khmers are of the same stock as the dominant population of Cambodia. More prosperous than the Chams, they are the rural representatives of another ancient culture.

The Khmers

The extension of Vietnamese control over the Mekong Delta area in the eighteenth century brought a sizable Khmer population under Vietnamese rule. Since then, some have been assimilated, but the majority remain distinctively Khmer in language and culture.

Estimated to number between 350,000 and 400,000, the Khmers are concentrated northwest of Saigon around Tay Ninh, southwest of Saigon around Phu Vinh (formerly Tra Vinh) and in An Xuyen Province. During the Indochina War and since, an unknown number have abandoned their lands and fled to Cambodia to escape the fighting and terrorism in South Vietnam.

The Khmers tend to be slightly taller than the Vietnamese and somewhat darker and to have less Mongoloid eyes and, not infrequently, wavy hair. The traditional dress of both sexes is a tight jacket buttoned down the front and a sort of skirt with the lower end brought forward between the legs and tucked in a belt at the waist. Their Hinayana Buddhism, which also prevails in Cambodia, contrasts with the Mahayana Buddhism of the majority of the Vietnamese.

The government requires the Khmers, like all minority groups, to accept Vietnamese citizenship or register as aliens, and, apparently, a considerable number retain their alien status. As a group the Khmers have remained relatively isolated from the Vietnamese majority. They have not been militant about the preservation of their cultural identity, however, and, unlike the Chinese, they have established neither schools nor newspapers of their own.

The Chams

The Chams, estimated in 1955 at about 35,000, are scattered in villages in the less desirable places on the central lowland coast near Phan Rang and Hoa Da and around Tay Ninh and Chau Phu northwest of Saigon near the Cambodian border. Some are also found across the border in Cambodia. They have little knowledge of the former greatness of their civilization, of which all that remains are the ruined towers of their once-prosperous coastal cities. The typical Cham village is a collection of straw huts on low pilings surrounded by a palisade. The treeless village enclosure—it is thought to be harmful to live in the shade of trees—contrasts with the greenery of Vietnamese villages. Most Cham men dress like the Vietnamese. Women wear a knee-length, tight sleeved, loose-fitting tunic over a longer petticoat. They often wrap their heads in silk scarves.

Most of the Chams adhere to their ancient Brahmanist religion; the remainder are Moslems. Both groups have reinterpreted the orthodox precepts and practices of their faiths and have added beliefs and rituals of their own. Cham priests and *mullahs* (Islamic religious leaders), who are usually illiterate, occupy an important place in the community (see ch. 11, Religion). Descent and inheritance are through the female line, and women play an important part in religious and secular affairs. Marriage to outsiders is strongly disapproved.

The Khmers constitute an important linguistic minority. They speak Khmer (also called Cambodian), the principal eastern language of the Mon-Khmer family, which is also represented in Burma and India. The language is written in a system of characters devised in southern India in the sixth century A.D. Attempts to introduce a romanized alphabet have never been successful. Two types of scripts are used—cuneiform, which employs wedge-shaped symbols, and cursives. The Chams speak their own language, which belongs to the Malayo-Polynesian family.

OTHER MINORITIES

Other ethnic minorities in South Vietnam in the mid-1960's were the Eurasians and various foreign communities, including the French and other Europeans, Americans, Indians and Pakistanis.

In mid-1965 the French numbered about 17,000, including many French nationals of Vietnamese and Vietnamese-European ancestry. Among this group were some French businessmen who had left the area in 1954 and later returned, along with commercial representatives from Japan, Germany and the United States.

The prestige of French culture continues to be high and many warm friendships exist between Vietnamese and Frenchmen. The Vietnamese, however, look back on the colonial period with nationalistic indignation, and they remember with bitterness the hardship and suffering so many of them endured during the Indochina War.

With France gone, the Republic of Vietnam turned for support to the United States. Various agencies of the United States Government and private contracting firms were represented in the country, mainly in Saigon. Their number had increased to about 9,000 by early 1962, as United States economic and military aid was expanded to meet the challenge of a mounting Communist guerrilla offensive from North Vietnam. No information on the numbers of civilian personnel in the country in early 1966 was available, but the combined strength of United States military forces reportedly was 200,000.

French is the most commonly known foreign language. Nearly everyone who attended school before 1954 has some ability to speak and write the language. During the colonial period, in all but a few schools, French was either the language of instruction or was taught as an optional course from the primary level on. Persons who completed a secondary or higher education speak the language fluently and have a sound mastery of its literature. Some French speakers acquired knowledge of the language in the army, government service or business.

Although less widely used than before, French still has considerable importance as a foreign language. The government provides French translation of many of its official publications, and French newspapers circulate in Saigon and other cities. French is taught in Vietnamese secondary schools starting with the seventh grade and remains the language of instruction at all levels in private French schools (see ch. 9, Education).

English is the most important second language after French. Some government publications are accompanied by English as well as French translations, and many young people study English in the secondary schools, where it has been taught since 1954; in universities; or in the English-language school conducted by the Vietnamese-American Association (see ch. 16, Public Information). French cultural influence remains strong, however, and it is unlikely that English will rival French as the most widely known European language in the country in the foreseeable future.

Knowledge of other foreign languages is limited. Before 1954 a few specially trained functionaries knew Russian. The number of persons who could speak and read that language in early 1966 was unknown.

CHAPTER 6

SOCIAL STRUCTURE

For centuries a relatively static and conservative society, Vietnam during the past 100 years has experienced the successive impacts of colonialism and nationalism and is now undergoing a severe period of Communist insurgency. During the French period, when Tonkin (North Vietnam) and Annam (Central Vietnam) were French protectorates and Cochin China (South Vietnam) was a colony of France, the urban elements of the society began to be oriented toward modernization. This meant, in essence, French education, technological development and an expansion of private enterprise in many fields. The traditional elite was replaced by a new upper class based on wealth and French education and strong in the traditions of French liberalism and individualism. Rural society, however, was largely unaffected, and rural social structure remained for the most part unchanged.

After the collapse of the colonial regime the struggle for national status divided Vietnam into two separate political entities—South Vietnam and North Vietnam. At the time of the separation the two societies still had much in common. While the North was more industrialized than the South, both regions were basically agrarian in character and had known a similar experience under French rule. Since then, however, each society has been led by people committed to different political, economic and social philosophies who are moving social change along divergent lines.

In South Vietnam the structure of society remained for a while much the same as it had been under the French except that the ruling elite was no longer an alien one. Three classes could still be distinguished: a small upper class, made up of those in the upper ranks of government service, persons in the professions, owners of large estates and businesses, and religious leaders; an equally small and largely urban middle class, consisting mainly of self-employed and salaried persons with some education; and a lower class, of vast size in comparison with the other two groups, made up of the remainder of the population. It consisted mainly of farmers and fishermen concentrated in a rural environment, wage workers—city and country, shopkeepers and individuals in personal service occupations.

In the early 1960's the impact of the American military presence and of the expanded Communist guerrilla activity was making itself

felt at critical points in the traditional social system. Physical mobility of the population was at unprecedented levels, causing the weak-
ening of emotional ties to distant kin and to ancestral landholdings.
Refugee families from North Vietnam had been resettled in rural and
urban communities in the mid-1950's; village families fleeing from
counterinsurgency operational areas were moving into Saigon and
coastal towns or into temporary reception centers.

In these circumstances, most people lived a spartan existence, but
a few found themselves prosperous as never before. In a society where
inherited social standing, landownership or tenure in a government
position with a fixed salary had once been the identifying attributes
of upper-class life, acquired wealth and demonstrated political abili-
ties were becoming means of access to membership in the national elite.
With this modification, the composition of the upper class remained
unchanged.

HISTORICAL BACKGROUND

Before the French

At the time the French arrived, Vietnam was an agrarian society,
stratified according to wealth in land, ruled by an emperor and his
royal family, and governed by an intellectual elite organized in a civil
bureaucracy. Except for the emperor and his royal family, there were
no permanent hereditary statuses. An older, feudal nobility, originally deriving its position from large land grants from the emperors
and enjoying hereditary titles, powers and privileges, had already been
abolished and replaced by an honorary nobility which received, for
special services rendered to the court, only small, token grants of land.
Their titles bore no power or privilege and, moreover, in each generation were successively downgraded through five ranks until, in the
sixth generation, they were lost entirely. Anyone, whether of royal
or common extraction, could receive a title. Collectively, this nobility
had no special interests in common and did not form in any sense a
class; their titles might give them prestige in their own communities,
but their status in the country at large depended on their wealth as
landowners.

The royal family itself was a restricted group, being limited to the
emperor's household and lineage. Families related by blood or marriage to the royal family had no formal prerogatives because of this
fact, and the further they were removed genealogically from the
emperor's line of descent, the more tenuous became their claim even to
royal blood. Thus, although thousands of persons claiming royal
blood surrounded the court and although for reasons of descent they
might consider themselves socially superior to commoners, in fact their
real weight in the society depended more on other attributes—mainly
wealth in land or status in the governmental bureaucracy.

Apart from the royal family, the true social and political elite of Vietnam was formed by a corps of highly select classical scholars. Following the Chinese model, candidates were recruited solely on the basis of competitive examinations which were open to all but whose standards were rigorously controlled. Once a person passed the examination, he became an accredited scholar and was then eligible for appointment as an official in the imperial service. All important posts, whether civil or military, were filled by classical scholars.

The examinations for entry into the mandarinate dealt in substance only with classical literature and philosophy, and the mandarin newly appointed to an official post had little or no training in the profession of administration. Since, however, the administrative system itself was not highly technical but, rather, political, a mandarin could readily learn the details as he gained experience. His authority in office rested on two factors—his status as a scholar and his relationship to the emperor.

According to the occupational ranking of the society, the intellectual stood highest on the scale, followed in order by the farmer, the artisan and the merchant. The authority of learning was unquestioned, so much so that the most successful emperors rested their qualifications to rule on their intellectual achievements rather than military victories or the circumstances of their birth. Also, the mandarins in the imperial service were not simply functionaries in a bureaucratic hierarchy; they were the personal appointees and representatives of the emperor. Wherever they went, they were the delegates of imperial power and shared the aura of divinity which surrounded the emperor himself.

In theory the mandarinate was not a closed social group. People of common as well as royal blood, from poor as well as rich families, were permitted to apply for the examinations. Once a man had achieved the status of mandarin, he could not automatically pass it on to his son; the son of a mandarin could become a mandarin himself only by passing the same examination in his turn. In practice, however, the mandarinate became almost a self-perpetuating caste of professional governors, largely because the son of a mandarin was best able to obtain the training necessary to pass the examinations. Education, the key to such achievement, tended to be a monopoly of the mandarins themselves. In this self-perpetuating process mandarin family married mandarin family, and through a common interest in the prestige and wealth derived from imperial service, the mandarinate emerged as the most cohesive as well as the most powerful social group in Vietnam.

While social eminence and political power were thus highly concentrated in the hands of the mandarinate, economic power based on land was more widely diffused. The demise of the hereditary feudal nobility had been accompanied by the breaking up of their vast holdings and the redistribution of the smaller parcels to other groups in the society. Families of royal blood who were in favor with the court received shares, as did many families of the mandarinate, but much of the land went to families outside the bounds of royalty or government. The wealthier of these commoner families formed a kind of landed gentry who lived in rural towns and villages and wielded political power in their own communities.

Where large landholdings were common, many landowners acted as landlords and rented their land out to tenant farmers. Where landholdings tended to be on a smaller scale, the landlord was much less in evidence than the small peasant proprietor. In any case, the larger holdings were large only when measured against the average holdings of these peasants who, with the tenant farmers, made up the vast majority of the population.

French Period

The arrival of the French in Cochin China, Annam and Tonkin changed the political and economic structures of those areas and led consequently to changes in the social structure. Political subjugation, the introduction of French education, the beginnings of modern industrialization in Tonkin, the stimulation of urbanization and the growth, mainly in Annam and Cochin China, of commercial agriculture all made their impact felt on critical parts of the social system.

The French Rulers

The most important social change was the introduction of a foreign governing class. There had been a few French missionaries in the area since the sixteenth century, and the French had had a hand in establishing the Nguyen dynasty in the eighteenth century, but the 1860's brought the French in as governors. First taking possession of Cochin China as a colony, the French soon extended their power to Annam and Tonkin, which were made protectorates. In 1887 these political units, together with Cambodia and later Laos, were formed into the Indochinese Union. The colony of Cochin China was administered by a governor assisted by French civil servants and a French-educated Vietnamese bureaucracy. Vietnamese tribunals were replaced by French courts. In the protectorates of Tonkin and Annam the indigenous administration was largely retained, but over all was the French resident-superior in each protectorate plus a French resident in each province.

With the establishment of this new foreign ruling class, the power of the royal family began to decline. The emperor remained on the throne, but, at the royal court in Hue, French administrators were assigned to each ministry. The emperor's dominion over Cochin China and, in practice, over Tonkin was lost; he became in effect an appointed and, usually obedient, servant of the French. If the emperor rebelled, he was replaced by another member of the royal family. The size of the powers and the functions of the mandarinate were pared down considerably. Qualifying examinations for entrance to the mandarinate were held for the last time in Annam in 1922.

The New Intellectual Elite

In place of the old mandarinate a new intellectual elite began to merge. Emphasis was on achievement in science, history, geography, French and other modern subjects rather than in the Chinese classics. This transformation came about partly because of French desires and efforts but mainly, it seems, out of the efforts and desires of the Vietnamese people themselves. Impressed by the power of the French, by the Japanese defeat of Russia and by what many Vietnamese saw in Europe during World War I, Vietnamese demands for modern and higher education increased over the years. By 1920, even in conservative Hue, well-to-do families refused to marry their daughters to the sons of distinguished mandarin families unless the young men had acquired a modern, French-type education.

The old Confucian village schools were transformed into schools imparting modern education and teaching French and Vietnamese (in romanized script) rather than Chinese characters. Some of those who successfully acquired higher education at home or abroad entered government service as administrators, while many others were absorbed as doctors, engineers and teachers into the greatly expanded government role in the fields of health, public works and education. Still others took up professions outside of government, such as law, medicine and journalism.

This new intellectual elite was composed mainly of Vietnamese from Tonkin and Annam rather than from Cochin China, a fact which was to be of great significance in the subsequent history of the country. The regional bias in the new elite's composition came about principally because during the French period the only institution of Western higher education in Vietnam was in Hanoi.

New Economic Groups

The French period also saw the emergence of a new group of wealthy Vietnamese landowners who possessed riches far in excess of that which the well-to-do segment of the older society had enjoyed. This group came into existence as a result of French development of vast new tracts of land in Cochin China. A few of these large holdings were retained by French companies or citizens, but most came into the hands of Vietnamese from Annam and Tonkin; in the 1950's, holdings of over 100 hectares (approximately 247 acres) were in the hands of about 2,000 Vietnamese landlords and 430 French citizens. Cochin China had become one of the areas with highest concentration of large landholdings in the whole of Asia.

The new group of large, absentee landowners were not only wealthier than the local landlords and peasants of Annam and Tonkin, but also more urban. They lived mainly in Hanoi and Hue, in distinct contrast to their less rich counterparts who tended to stay on their lands in the rural areas. In the city they took on a modern Western orientation, which further separated them from rural society. A few of them invested in light industry and thereby became the first modern Vietnamese industrialists. A still smaller number invested some of their income in medium-sized trading activities.

Other kinds of new economic groups appeared in the urban areas. The French undertakings in both the governmental and private sectors created a demand for secretaries, clerks, cashiers, interpreters and translators, minor officials and supervisors of laborers. Vietnamese in these cocupations tended to form a modern white-collar group, based on French or French-influenced education and training and salaries which placed them well above the economic level of most manual workers.

French investment in mining, transportation and industry in Vietnam brought into being a modern Vietnamese working class. The nucleus of this class was formed between 1890 and 1919 in the mines, textile mills and cement factories in the north and in the match, tobacco, and other factories elsewhere in the country. At most of the natural resources, as well as a large supply of labor, were located in the north, it was there rather than in the south that modern industrial development was concentrated, and Hanoi and Haiphong became the leading industrial centers. During World War I almost 50,000 Vietnamese workers were recruited for work in factories in France. At first the workers were not conscious of differing from peasants and considered such work as temporary and to be abandoned as soon as possible for return to village life. By the 1930's they had become more conscious of themselves as a distinct group with problems and interests of their own.

Large-scale French and Vietnamese development of such crops as rubber, rice, coffee and tea, mainly in Cochin China gave rise to a group of agricultural and plantation wage workers. The labor supply for the rice and other plantations of the south had to be brought in from the crowded north, and between 1919 and 1934, 104,000 Vietnamese laborers were brought to Saigon from the north.

The Chinese

Besides altering the structure of Vietnamese society, the French takeover in Vietnam led to a tremendous expansion of the Chinese population in the country, especially in the south. When the French arrived they found the country's limited foreign and domestic trade already in the hands of the Chinese. The French lifting of the traditional ban on rice exports and the consequent upsurge in foreign trade brought new waves of Chinese merchants and shopkeepers to Vietnam at the end of the nineteenth century, and the Chinese population reached an estimated 57,000 by 1889. Vietnam's growing economy attracted even more Chinese at the beginning of the twentieth century. The French called on Chinese labor for the development of the road and railroad system and for industrial expansion.

Such a rapid growth in the Chinese population occurred as a result of the development of agriculture and industry under the French that by 1931 there were 217,000 Chinese in the country, of whom 171,000 were in Cochin China, 35,000 in Tonkin and 11,000 in Annam. They were active in almost every branch of the economy: trade, light industry, crafts and finance. Practically every village in Cochin China came to have its Chinese shopkeeper.

Deeply involved in the rice trade, the Chinese entered the rice-milling industry and established a monopoly in that field. The first modern rice-husking factory in Vietnam was built in 1878 by Chinese businessmen, and by World War I there were 11 modern rice mills in Cochin China, all concentrated in the Chinese city of Cho Lon and owned by Chinese.

The Chinese also were involved in sugar refining, manufacturing, coconut and peanut oil production, and the lumber and shipbuilding industries. Many Chinese began their careers in Vietnam as laborers on the French rubber plantations of Cochin China and eventually started their own tea and pepper plantations which supplied most of the needs of the local market. In addition, some Chinese started rice plantations, and many Chinese gardeners in the suburbs of Saigon became suppliers of the fresh vegetables consumed in that city. Many Chinese restaurants and hotels also sprang up in the urban areas.

SOCIETY IN THE MID-1960'S

The society of the mid-1960's differed from that which existed during the French period in the absence of a foreign ruling elite and in the decline of the Vietnamese nobility. The French governors had departed, and the subsequent changeover from a monarchy to a republic had left the king, the royalty and the nobility as obsolete institutions. The society, however, continued to be based upon the primarily agricultural economy which developed during the French period, and it remained characterized by division into similar classes.

The urban upper class was differentiated from the remainder of the population by its wealth, its advanced and, for the most part, French education, and the concentration of its male members in high-ranking positions in the military service and in the government. Also in the cities were an emergent middle class, still relatively small in size, and a somewhat larger urban lower class, made up largely of unskilled wage workers. In the villages there was a wide range in wealth and status, from very wealthy landowners to landless tenant farmers and part-time wage laborers.

The Urban Upper Class

The urban upper class consists of the principal government officials, including Cabinet members and other top administrators and their aides, high-ranking military officers, leading Catholic and Buddhist religious figures, nationally renowned scholars, professional persons and members of families engaged in banking and finance. Its members, concentrated in and near Saigon and Hue, constitute probably no more than 2 percent of the total population. Many of these families belong to, or have ties with, the group of large landholders which evolved in Cochin China toward the end of the French period. The majority, however, trace their origin to Tonkin and consider themselves, particularly those from Hanoi, to be culturally superior to other Vietnamese. Upper-class urban society freely admits foreign diplomats to its company, but excludes other non-Vietnamese.

Most urban upper-class South Vietnamese retain a strong personal interest in France and French culture. Among this group there are many individuals who have been at least partially educated in France and who have sons or daughters residing in that country. A significant number hold dual citizenship, the proportion, as to be expected, being higher among persons born in the former colony of Cochin China than in the former protectorates of Annam or Tonkin. Wealthier families have generally adopted a sophisticated mode of life copied from former French colonial officials and businessmen. They own late-model French or American cars which are driven by chauffeurs, and they tend to be concentrated in the French quarter of the city; they live in spacious, French style villas. Modern appliances, such as refrigerators and radios, are commonplace in their homes, as are Western foods and beverages. The men have adopted Western clothes, usually wearing white sharkskin suits for official functions. The women generally retain the national dress, although in Saigon some wear Parisian fashions with appropriate Western accessories and hair styles.

Education is of great importance to this group. The leading intellectuals are principally the products of French schools and universities, and the most acceptable higher education is one acquired in France. Virtually all of the men and many of the women speak French, frequently with greater ease and fluency than they speak Vietnamese. A rapidly increasing number, too, speak English as well. Private education is the accepted pattern, with boys expected to pursue higher education and take a degree. Medicine, in particular, and law have been the preferred fields of study in the past, but there is increasing interest in other fields. Girls want at least the equivalent of a bachelor's degree.

The Urban Middle Class

The small, almost exclusively urban middle class includes civil servants and lower-ranking officers in the armed forces, commercial employees, schoolteachers, shopowners and managers, small merchants and farm and factory managers. While most persons in this group are not employers of labor, neither do they themselves work with their hands, an activity which they consider degrading.

The Vietnamese middle class is not as close to the pattern of living introduced by the old French ruling class as the Vietnamese urban upper class, but not so far removed as the lower class. The men wear Western clothes, although ties and suit coats are reserved for important occasions. Girls and younger women, while retaining basic Vietnamese dress, are turning to short haircuts, nail polish and Western accessories. Many stylish young office girls still retain the conical straw hat, but the trend is definitely toward its abandonment, in imitation of the prevailing upper-class practice. The majority of the middle class live in the single-family wood or concrete dwelling units of Saigon, or in the suburbs. Most depend on their own bicycles or motor bicycles or on public transportation. A few own motor scooters, and even fewer own French cars. Most of their dwellings have electricity, and many have prominently displayed radios and refrigerators. Some may employ one or two domestic servants, but in most families it is the women of the family who perform household tasks.

Members of the urban middle class have at least completed primary grades and may even have had some secondary schooling. Most of those who work outside the home speak French, and increasing numbers are acquiring a knowledge of English.

Emotionally, middle-class individuals of the older generation customarily remain tied to the village of their forebears, to which, when possible, they return each year for Tet, the Vietnamese New Year.

The Urban Lower Class

The urban lower class is made up mainly of unskilled, largely uneducated, wageworkers or petty tradesmen, including taxi drivers, peddlers, fortunetellers, stevedores and domestic servants. Their mode of living is Vietnamese rather than European. The men have adopted Western-style dress for work, but favor traditional Vietnamese trousers and wooden clogs for home-wear. Unskilled laborers and lower-class women wear the conical straw hat and cotton trousers of their rural counterparts.

The members of the lowest level of urban society live in crude dwellings of straw or on boats. Most of the dwellings have neither electricity nor plumbing; their roofs and walls are of thatch, their floors of dirt. Such dwellings are built on land belonging to the government or to absentee landowners. With the exception of the domestic servants, who may partake to a limited extent of the diet of their employers, the diet of the lower-class Vietnamese is strictly the traditional one, based mainly on rice and fish sauce. For most, the means of transportation are buses and, occasionally, bicycles or motor- or bicycle-driven rickshaws.

Adult, urban lower-class Vietnamese are, for the most part, illiterate. Their children are exposed to primary education, but secondary education is rare, particularly for girls. Generally speaking, the children do not proceed far enough in school to acquire an elementary knowledge of French or English, and most adults of this class know only Vietnamese unless they have worked as domestics in close contact with Europeans.

Village Society

The sociopolitical elite of village society consists of the wealthiest landowners, who derive their wealth primarily by leasing or subleasing the lands which they own or rent. If they work any land themselves, the labor is done by hired hands who plant, irrigate and harvest under their supervision. In the slack season they may engage in entrepreneurial activities, investing their surplus wealth in moneylending, rice merchandising, rice milling and similar ventures.

In the past many persons in this group were the most politically active in the village. Members of the village council were drawn from its ranks as were the chief officials of the Cult committees (see ch. 11, Religion). By the mid-1960's, however, the interest of qualified villagers in seeking such positions had greatly declined.

These families differ from their urban counterparts mainly in their patterns of living and their outlook. Men of this class wear Western-style clothes when serving as members of the village council; they don white shirts, light trousers and, perhaps, shoes while on routine duty and wear suits and ties when receiving a government official from outside the village. At other times, however, they much prefer to wear Vietnamese dress—loose-fitting trousers, long-sleeved collarless shirts of white cotton or silk, and wooden clogs. Many older men of these families have not taken to Western-style haircuts and continue to wear their hair long and tied in a bun at the back.

Wealthy villagers live in solidly built houses of wood-tile or masonry-tile. Although most well-to-do homes have some Western furnishings, traditional furniture—including expensive, highly polished hardwood slabs which serve as beds—is predominant.

The most important room in the house is that containing the altar of the ancestors; anniversaries of their death are observed with elaborate ritual and feasting. Weddings and funerals are also elaborate affairs; the more prosperous families hire a professional funeral service to provide trappings, coffin bearers and musicians. Long before the death of an elderly member of a prosperous family, tombs are constructed and coffins purchased and placed on display in the main room of the house. Status demands that their family burial grounds have tombs of concrete or cement. The rich also support financially the rituals associated with the village cults, like the Cult of the Guardian Spirit, and they are the major contributors to the construction of village pagodas (see ch. 11, Religion).

Of all the villagers, the well-to-do are the most mobile. A few rely on motorscooters, motorbicycles and motorcycles, but most depend on bicycles.

The less prosperous families differ from the elite in being less of an entrepreneurial group. They own or rent enough land to maintain themselves on a level well above subsistance, but do not acquire a surplus large enough to invest in other economic endeavors. They do most of the work in their own fields, hiring some laborers, if needed, at planting or harvesting. A few supplement their income as artisans, but they never hire themselves out as laborers except under the direst of circumstances.

Because of the pressure of work in their own fields and their more modest economic circumstances, members of this group do not assume as many official and Cult responsibilities as do the wealthy villagers. They participate in rituals and feasts on a moderate scale, and in the village organizations they hold positions which are honorific in character, demanding little time or outlay of money. As a result of their peripheral position in the official life of a village, they have no need for Western dress and content themselves with traditional, loose-fitting clothes and wooden clogs for special occasions. Only the young men are likely to have a pair of Western trousers and a shirt and perhaps a pair of shoes. When in the fields, old and young alike wear the traditional dress of the peasant: black cotton shorts and shirt and a conical hat.

Members of this group usually live in houses of wood-thatch or wood-tile construction. Like the rich villagers, they customarily have hardwood slabs for beds, but seldom Western furnishings. Radios are rarely found in their homes. Few own any motorized forms of transportation and must depend upon bicycles, which together with lack of leisure and money, limit their physical mobility.

The lowest level of village society consists of a vast number of small peasant proprietors and tenant farmers. Forced to spend all of their time earning a living, they generally participate little in village affairs though it is possible for some to achieve the status of hamlet chief or receive one of the honorific titles in the lower echelons of the Cult committee. Because they do not cultivate enough land to support their families, most of them must work as part-time laborers, and their wives and children do much of the fieldwork. Their children frequently go to school long enough to learn the rudiments of reading and writing and then have to leave to help support the family. This group also includes a wide range of supplemental service occupations: artisans, practitioners of oriental medicine, small tradesmen and others.

CHAPTER 7

FAMILY

By late 1965 the Vietnamese family had experienced more than two decades of severe stress and hardship as a result of the Japanese occupation, the Indochina War and its aftermath, and the expanding military operations of the 1960's. After partition of the country in 1954, more than 900,000 refugees fled into South Vietnam from Communist-ruled North Vietnam. This number was more than equaled during 1964 and 1965 by South Vietnamese peasants fleeing from Viet Cong strongholds or from areas subjected to bombings by Vietnamese or United States aircraft in their anti-Communist operations. As a result, the population includes millions who have been uprooted from places where they had family ties dating back hundreds, in some cases, thousands of years. In the process individual members sometimes had been separated and resettled at places so far apart that they could not convene for the rites and celebrations which traditionally reinforced family solidarity. The network of family ties had been further disrupted by deaths and separation arising directly out of military action and by the fact that in some instances political loyalties set one kinsman against another.

Despite these occurrences much of the traditional family system persists. To varying degrees in different sectors of the country and among different social classes, the lineage—a group of people tracing descent from a common ancestor—still represents the chief source of social identity for the individual. Nearly all South Vietnamese still feel that the family has first claim on their loyalties and that the interests of each individual are subordinate to those of his common descent group.

Basically similar principles appear in the traditional family system throughout the country, developed as the consequence of a common cultural heritage which evolved centuries ago in the Red River Delta region (see ch. 3, Historical Setting). Extensive differences in details of actual practice, however, distinguish the indigenous family of southern South Vietnam (formerly known as Cochin China) from that found in the coastal villages of the Central Lowlands (formerly part of Annam).

THE VIETNAMESE FAMILY

In the traditional social order the individual was less an independent being than a member of a corporate family group which included not only living members but, in a spiritual sense, a long line of ancestors as well. Emphasis was on group rather than on individual interests. Family functions extended into many areas of behavior that in more complex societies are regulated chiefly by other institutions—economic, educational and religious.

Throughout his life the individual was caught up with the activities of a multitude of relatives. Members of the same household lived together, worked together and, on frequent occasions, met together with a wider circle of kinsmen for marriages, funerals, lunar New Year celebrations and rituals marking the anniversaries of an ancestor's death. A man looked first to his kinsman for help and counsel in times of personal crisis and to the interests of these same kinsmen in making decisions for himself or members of his household. Special reverence accorded to ancestral spirits derived from the notion that, after death, the spirits of the departed retained their influence in the world of the living. Honoring one's forebears and ensuring one's own immortality by maintaining the lineage were all-important.

In the mid-1960's individual Vietnamese families approximated this centuries-old pattern to varying degrees. The truest image, perhaps, could be found among families living in the villages of the Coastal Lowlands region, since this was an area that had once been a part of Annam, where the Vietnamese cultural heritage was homogenous and deeply rooted. The most significant departure from the pattern, on the other hand, was doubtless to be found in Saigon, a cosmopolitan city, where the intermingling of peoples with differing ideas and values had been greatest.

The Patrilineage

The traditional kinship system emphasizes the paternal, as against the maternal, line of descent. Individuals are identified primarily by their connections through the father and the father's male bloodline, and kin groups larger than the family—clans and lineages—are formed by kinsmen who trace their relationship to each other in this manner. It is through these patrilineal descent groups that both men and women inherit property and men inherit their primary obligations for maintaining the ancestory observances.

Clans and lineages are by definition exclusive in the sense that a man or a woman can belong only to the father's clan and lineage, not to the mother's. It is customary for husband and wife to come from different lineages, but ordinarily no strong sense of divided allegiance develops within the family. The married woman honors her husband's ancestors, and after her death it is in his family rather than her own that her soul is venerated. It is the husband's clan and lineage which tend to establish the family's social identity and standing, and his rights and obligations tend to determine the family's fortunes.

The patrilineal common descent group (*toc*) consists of all the descendants in the male line of a common male ancestor. South Vietnamese of the Central Lowlands and refugees from North Vietnam reckon descent from the fifth, or infrequently the seventh, ascending generation. On the other hand, South Vietnamese of the Mekong Delta region, where the patrilineage is less strong, ordinarily count only through the third ascending generation. Each lineage is divided into a number of branches or segments which are ranked in accordance with the senior line of descent. Thus, a lineage typically is composed of persons related in the direct line of descent from eldest son to eldest son, and several collateral branches composed of persons related through younger sons. Within each generation, and within each family, individuals are ranked by age. Traditionally, either the eldest male of the senior branch, or the eldest male in the patrilineage, acts as the *truong toc*, or lineage head. In the southern part of the country, however, a family council composed of all adult members, male and female, may elect as *truong toc* the man whom it considers most competent.

The term *ho* is applied to the kin group consisting of relatives, living or dead, who descended from the same ancestor. Persons in the same kin group bear the same lineage name. There are only a limited number of lineage names in use, perhaps no more than a few hundred throughout the entire country. One of the most common is Nguyen. Thus, many different kin groups have the same lineage or family name, but many individuals bearing that name are not of the same *ho*. Marriage to someone of the same surname, while no longer considered incestuous, is still something to be avoided.

The duties of the *truong toc* revolve mainly around continuation of the Cult of the Ancestors and include carrying out the main Cult rituals, keeping up the family tombs and maintaining the genealogy book (*gia pha*). He must also assume responsibility for managing income from the land legally dedicated to the support of the Cult of the Ancestors, where one exists. Besides this, he serves the living; he is generally looked to as counselor and arbiter in family affairs, particularly those involving marriage, divorce, adoption and guardianship. The *truong toc* is normally succeeded by his eldest son, though, if he has no son, leadership of the clan can pass to a collateral branch.

The Household

The traditional and still widely preferred family type is the extended family, three generations in depth, consisting of a senior couple, a married son with his wife and children, and the senior couple's unmarried children, all living under the same roof. Sometimes two married brothers live with their parents, but this often leads to such tension that it is generally held preferable for a second married son to move into separate quarters. In the southern part of the country it is often the youngest son (rather than the eldest), or even a married daughter, who lives with the senior couple. All members of the household live under the nominal authority of the oldest male, and all contribute to the income of the family. While this extended type of family is most characteristic of rural areas, where it operates as a unit of production, a substantial number of households in Saigon and smaller urban areas shelter extended family groups. Among the educated, urbanized group, however, the nuclear family, consisting of parents and their children, is more common than the extended family.

Sometimes a household will include, besides the so-called wife of the first rank, a second or third wife as well as her children. More often, however, additional wives are established by their husbands in separate households or may continue to live as they had before the marriage, in a house of their own or with their parents. Polygamy, widespread in Tonkin and Annam and fairly common in Cochin China during the French colonial period, has been legally outlawed in South Vietnam since 1959. Marriages contracted before this date, however, retain legal recognition, and wives and children enjoy the same rights as the first family. Moreover, the effects of the law are seen mainly in Saigon and other urban centers; in rural areas customary practices are continued.

In Annam, during the late colonial period, residence after marriage was almost invariably patrilocal (see Glossary), with the bride moving to join her husband's community. Only rarely did matrilocal (see Glossary) residence occur and then only for some compelling reason, if, for example, the bride's parents, without a son of their own, had adopted the groom as their heir. In Cochin China dispersal of family groups was more commonplace; nevertheless those who left the village generally tended to move only within an area which permitted their relatively easy return for Cult celebrations. In the modern period this situation still pertained to some degree, but in some areas deteriorating security conditions had uprooted and separated many families.

The Cult of the Ancestors

Central to the entire Vietnamese family system is the Cult of the Ancestors, the observance of which is a major preoccupation in life. The individual marries to have children and has children in order to assure his own immortality. Members of the common descent group, who remain together and venerate their forebears with strict adherence to prescribed ritual, rest serene in the belief that the souls of their ancestors in the other world are receiving proper spiritual nourishment and that after death they in turn will not lack such nourishment. To allow one's ancestors to have to beg nourishment from souls properly cared for by their descendants is not only shameful but dangerous, for, unless venerated in the expected manner, the soul becomes restless and is likely to exert an unfavorable influence on the world of the living.

Important elements of the Cult are an ancestral home, a piece of land legally designated for the support of the ancestors (*huong hoa*) and a senior male in the direct line of descent to assume the obligation for celebrations. Ownership of a piece of land which can be dedicated to the support of the Cult is, however, only a dream for most farmers who are landless, and rites of veneration are necessarily modest.

Where land has been set aside as *huong hoa* it is regarded as the joint property belonging to all members of the lineage, but it is held in usufruct by the *truong toc*, who is responsible for maintaining the rituals associated with the Cult. If the income exceeds the amount required for honoring the ancestors, the *truong toc* may keep it for himself, but is obliged at death to pass it on to the designated heir. If he fails to fulfill his duties, he can be removed by vote of a family council. An obligation ends when the property is materially destroyed, when the land is expropriated or when no male descendant exists. Two other types of Cultual estates are less important; land dedicated to the support of celebrations commemorating the death of a single person, known as *ky-dien;* and a foundation created for the benefit of either a family, a village or a pagoda, known as a *han-dien*. Rights and duties of the beneficiary are determined in the deed.

The anniversary of an ancestor's death is celebrated each year, the degree of importance attached to the observance depending on the rank of the deceased in the family. A representative of each family in the lineage is expected to be present. This includes, at a minimum, the male head of each household and sometimes, but not necessarily, his wife and their children. Presence at the celebration is demanded even when it requires travel from a distant place. The day before the anniversary a short speech is delivered before the principal altar to the god of the house, who is told to inform the ancestor of the rites to be performed the following day in his honor. On the anniversary date religious rites are performed before the altar, with sacrifical offerings made both to the god of the house and to the ancestor. The lavishness of the offering varies with family income but at a minimum includes an offering of betel nuts and leaves, alcohol, tea and incense. Substantial sacrifices include glutinous rice (used only for ceremonial occasions), roast pork or chicken and fresh fruits—all of which are placed on the small altar to honor the god of the house and on the principal altar to honor the ancestor of the highest rank.

The Marriage Contract

Marriage is viewed primarily as a social contract rather than a personal relationship, a reflection of the pervasiveness of family connections and obligations in the social order and the stress laid on the continuation of the lineage. The essential elements of the marriage contract are the intervention of an intermediary and the matching of horoscopes, the agreement of the parties and the presence of witnesses at the formal proposal and acceptance. Arrangements are concluded through a ritual exchange of visits which allow the parties to assess one another before a final commitment is made. Once the engagement is complete, the bride-price is agreed upon, and the prospective groom is expected to perform actual or token service to his future parents-in-law as a demonstration of good character.

In the selection of a wife, beauty may be an important consideration for the son, but his parents will place much more emphasis on the girl's character, her ability to perform household tasks and the social reputation and medical history of her family. Ideally, she should be docile, respectful, sincere, generous, polite and self-effacing. She should be a good housekeeper, skilled in the kitchen, and enjoy obvious good health. For a girl's family also, character and family background are important considerations in accepting or selecting a son-in-law. A family would prefer to find a rich husband for a daughter, but a man with only daughters may select a poor boy of good character who is willing to forsake his father's family and assume the responsibility for maintaining the Cult of the Ancestors of his father-in-law. In many areas a match in which the girl is 2 years older than the boy, or the boy 1 year older than the girl, is regarded as the most auspicious from the horoscopic point of view.

The actual age at which marriage occurs usually reflects the prosperity of the parents. In a Mekong Delta village, for example, children of relatively prosperous families tend to marry young—in middle or late adolescence, but postponement of marriage for economic reasons well beyond these ages is commonplace. In the Central Lowlands, on the other hand, some families have arranged the marriage of sons as young as 6 years of age to an adolescent girl in order to gain an additional worker in the fields.

The principal piece of legislation regulating marriage is the Decree Law of July 1964 on Marriage, Descent and Community Property, which supersedes the Code of the Family of January 1959. Like the 1959 Code, it is designed to equalize the mutual rights and obligations of the spouses, in contradistinction to previous law in which the legal status of women in marriage was subordinate to that of men.

Catholic influence was strongly evident in the Code of the Family of January 1959. Polygamy and concubinage were outlawed; separation was made extremely difficult; and divorce was made impossible except in instances of presidential intervention. Equal responsibility was placed on both spouses for the fulfillment of marriage obligations and the rearing of children. Husbands had the right to choose the family place of residence, and, in lieu of special covenants, a system of community property was established under which all property and revenues of husband and wife belonged to them jointly and were to be so administered. At the same time the law tended to reinforce the rule of parents, grandparents and the head of the lineage as formal validators of marriage, divorce or adoption and to support the tradition of the Cult of the Ancestors. The consent of parents or grandparents was required in the marriage or the adoption of a minor, and they or, in default of them, the head of the lineage had the right to oppose the marriage of a descendant or ward.

The Decree Law of July 1964 is similar in spirit and letter to the previous family law except that the sanctity of marriage is less assiduously cherished. Divorce or separation, for example, are permitted after 2 years of marriage on grounds of adultery, cruelty, abandonment or a criminal act on the part of the spouse. Concubinage, which was specifically prohibited under the 1959 law, is not mentioned, and adultery is no longer punishable by fines or imprisonment.

The law requires civil marriage for all. This entails the public posting of banns for 10 days before the performance of the ceremony, which takes place in the office of the civil registrar and is celebrated by him in the presence of two witnesses. Following the rites, the marriage is recorded in the civil register. Apparently, civil marriages are usual among the educated, urban group, but are rare among the rural peasantry. On the other hand, great significance is attached by villagers to the religious ritual, which ordinarily takes place before the ancestral altar in the residence of the bride and is celebrated by an elderly male relative or friend of the bride's family.

Customary Ceremonies

Betrothal and marriage formalities, other than among Catholic familes, follow a basically similar pattern throughout the country, deriving from the shared cultural heritage developed centuries ago in the Confucian centers of Hanoi and Hue. In general, however, the

111

people of the Central Lowlands and refugees from North Vietnam pay stricter attention to the minute details of the prescribed ritual than do those of the Mekong Delta region, where cultural influences are mixed.

The procedure begins with the selection of a possible bride, chosen by the young man's parents or, as is increasingly the case, by the young man himself. The girl under consideration may be someone from the same village whom they have known since her childhood. On the other hand, she may be a stranger, seen only once or twice, at a meeting arranged by a professional intermediary. In the latter circumstance it is important that the meeting be set on the pretext of some other business, so as to avoid hurting the pride of the girl should she be deemed unsuitable.

The young man's choice made, the intermediary visits the girl's family to broach the subject of marriage and to compare the horoscopes of the two persons to determine the suitability of the match. If the girl or her family disapproves, negotiations are broken off abruptly with some excuse made so as not to offend the young man's family.

If the contact made through the intermediary looks promising, the young man and his parents make a ritual visit to the girl's residence. The visit, known as the *coi mat* (lit., "show the face"), is arranged for a day considered auspicious by the astrologer. The young man and his parents arrive, carrying gifts of rice alcohol, fruit and flowers, and, after greetings exchanged outside the house, are invited indoors and given refreshments before the ancestral altar. The visitors take the opportunity to observe the girl's home, her family and the girl herself, whom the parents may never have seen. If they are pleased, they will invite the girl's parents to their home. Once this visit has been made and the outlook still seems favorable, the two families fix a date, with reference to the horoscope, on which the engagement will be announced.

The traditional betrothal ceremony is not so much concerned with making news of the engagement known to, and distributing gifts among, the living members of each lineage as with informing the ancestors of the event. In the first phase, the groom's parents solemnly present themselves before the family altar and make a ritual address telling of the coming event and asking the ancestors for their protection. This done, they and the groom depart for the bride's house laden with gifts, including a roast pig, glutinous rice, alcohol, betel, tea and small cakes. The bride's father greets them and ushers them into the house before the ancestral altar, on which he immediately places the offerings they have brought. All participants in turn make their obeisances before the altar. Afterwards, a feast is served, and the bride distributes small gift boxes containing cakes, tea and betel leaves. To each is attached a small card announcing the engagement.

Where as the traditional betrothal gift may be any piece of jewelry or valuable article, in the southern part of the country it has become customary for the groom to give the bride a pair of gold earrings as a symbol of their troth. These are presented at an engagement party, which, unlike the strictly family gathering common in the Central Lowlands, is a festive occasion in which a wide circle of friends as well as relatives are invited. Sometime after the engagement celebration arrangements for the dowry are completed.

The wedding is usually performed a few months later, on a date determined by an astrologer. In a traditional ceremony on the appointed day a formal procession moves from the groom's house to that of the bride. Places in the procession are assigned according to protocol, with the lead taken by two elder male members of the lineage, one of whom bears a container of incense, the other a box of betel. The remaining members assume their positions in proper order, and the cortege proceeds to the home of the young girl, where the elders set their burdens on the ancestral altar. Tea is provided to the assembled company, and the ritual of informing the ancestors is begun. The father of the bride, or an elder male relative, addresses the ancestors, burning some incense on the altar and informing them that the young man has come to claim his bride. The fiance then bows low before the altar three times, as does his bride after him. Next, the couple kneels before the bride's parents and in turn before all her elder relatives. Gift-giving and feasting by the guests follow the rites.

Afterwards, the entire party moves in procession to the house of the groom where, after tea has been passed, his father performs a ritual before the main altar informing the ancestors of what has taken place. The newly married couple then make their obeisances before the altar and in turn before the groom's parents, his grandparents and all his elder kinsmen. Meanwhile, an intermediary, standing before a smaller altar outside the house, performs the ritual of informing the god of love. Like the larger altar, the smaller one is set with offerings of chicken, glutinous rice, alcohol, betel and tea. After the ceremonies, a lavish feast, representing a great financial outlay for the groom's family, is provided for the assembled group.

Consummation of the wedding may not occur for several nights, owing partly to the reluctance the bride will often show. After intercourse has taken place, it is customary in some rural areas for the bride to return to her family, there to wait until her husband calls for her. When he comes, he carries a roast pig. If the pig is whole, all is well, and she returns to her new house with her husband; if, however, one of the pig's ears has been cut off, it means that the bride has been found not to be a virgin, hence is not acceptable as a wife.

In her new home the bride must please not only her husband but also his family, and girls tend to enter marriage with an often-justified fear of the mother-in-law. They have been told repeatedly that the shortcomings and ineptitudes which a mother overlooks or forgives will not be tolerated by a mother-in-law. The husband's sisters quite often make life unbearable for the newcomer, and, if she fails to please them, the mother-in-law is likely to take the side of her daughters. Even if a girl dislikes her mother-in-law, she may find herself competing with another daughter-in-law for her favor, but she probably cannot complain or appeal to her father-in-law, for he usually adopts a passive attitude, considering such matters his wife's business. The bride who has difficulty may go home and complain to her own parents, but they are likely to tell her that this is a phase through which a woman must pass before she becomes full mistress of her own household. Her husband may be distressed by her trouble, but she generally cannot count upon him to do anything about it, for he himself has no right to question his mother's actions.

The problem is apt to be most acute for the wife of the eldest son, for she is most likely to have to live in the household of her husband's parents and have the burden of the household management placed upon her by the mother-in-law. The girl who marries a younger brother usually lives in a separate household with her husband.

Funerals, like other customary ceremonies in which the members of the kin group participate, are an occasion for reinforcing lineage solidarity. In the Vietnamese tradition old age is a time to be passed in the bosom of one's family. There is no sending the old off to live by themselves. If they are invalid and need to be nursed and waited on, this is to be done at home. Much of the time of the elderly whose family circumstances permit it is spent in visiting or receiving friends. There are also ceremonies to attend and prepare for. Thought will also be given to the hiring of an expert geomancer, to choose the exact location of one's tomb, and to the purchase of one's coffin. When death comes, the traditional mourning rites are followed, their elaborateness depending upon the wealth and social position of the family of the deceased. It is usual for kinfolk, neighbors and friends to come, bringing offerings of money, food and, perhaps, rice alcohol to the bereaved household, and to kowtow in honor of the deceased.

Status of Men and Women

Great respect is given to men, especially to older men, and particularly to the head of the lineage, who traditionally made all the important decisions for every member of the family. In the modern period family decisions, such as the choice of occupation or marital partner, are generally made by the head of the individual household, with the concurrence of the wife and perhaps the grandparents.

Where decisions are made in this manner, unquestioned obedience on the part of the younger generation is demanded and received.

Throughout her marriage a woman is expected to be dutiful and respectful toward both her husband and his parents. In some areas when a young bride is brought home by her new husband, the mother-in-law places a brazier containing burning coals at the threshold, the bride being expected to step over, rather than walk around it, as a demonstration of her submissiveness. The wife is expected to become an integral part of her husband's family, to care for him and their children and to perform all household duties.

Nonetheless, a wife retains her own identity as an individual, and, with the passage of time, her role in family affairs increases. Many Vietnamese wives are in fact extremely powerful and exercise a strong formative influence on their husband's opinions and actions. Women also play an important role in the nation's economy and are particularly prominent in retail trade of all kinds. The village woman assumes a great deal of responsibility for cultivation of the family paddy fields, sometimes working harder than the men. The educated urban wife is accepted as an intellectual equal by her husband, entering into literary discussions with him and listening as he recites poetry; a few own agricultural estates, factories and other businesses. Both she and her village counterpart typically manage the family income. Ideally, relations between marriage partners are characterized by unfailing politeness and courtesy. A good husband and wife, the Vietnamese say, always treat each other as guests.

Mothers take pains to protect the reputation of daughters of marriageable age. Female premarital chastity is expected, and a girl of blemished reputation brings disgrace upon the entire family. Married women, too, are supposed to conduct themselves modestly, spending their time with their husbands and children and scrupulously avoiding any appearance of extramarital flirtations.

People nominally subscribe to the ideal of premarital and marital chastity for males as well as females, but many men in fact take wide license in this sphere. The Decree Law of July 1964, like the Family Law of January 1959 which it superseded, forbids concubinage and polygamy, both of which before the mid-century were widely practiced. Even now in rural areas people are inclined to shrug off the law as something meant only for the people in Saigon.

Children

Normal interest in having children is strongly reinforced by Confucian tradition, which makes it imperative to produce a male heir who will continue the family line. The husband and wife with numerous offspring are envied. Children are needed as family workers, but, more importantly, if there are sons among them it is more or less

115

assured that the lineage will be perpetuated and the Cult of the Ancestors maintained. Conversely, parents without a male heir are generally regarded as most unfortunate. The preference for sons over daughters, however, is somewhat less pronounced in the Mekong Delta area than in the Central Lowlands, where the patrilineage has retained more of its traditional character. Barren wives, who formerly could be divorced or supplanted by another wife because of their failure to produce, seek to overcome their condition by performing ceremonial ablutions at home followed by prayers, offered prostrate before the altar, at the pagoda. Adoption of a male heir by couples with no son of their own is common, the preferred candidate being a son of the husband's younger brother.

A wide range of taboos used to be observed by expectant parents to ensure successful delivery, to protect the unborn infant from malicious influences and to avoid bringing misfortune to others. Husband and wife were expected to refrain from sexual relations from the sixth, or sometimes an earlier, month of pregnancy. The wife herself remained at home as much as possible, stayed away from shrines and other sacred places where she might inadvertently arouse the wrath of resident spirits, and observed certain food taboos. Several months before the birth, a special bed was prepared for her and set up in a relatively private part of the house, which was designated by an astrologer as the place where she would be best protected from draughts of wind which might carry evil spirits. An altar was erected to the honor of the dozen goddesses who allegedly preside at birth, the attending midwife seeing to it that incense burned there constantly. Following the birth the midwife placed a brazier containing a smoldering wood fire under the bed in the belief that this would replace the mother's body heat lost at birth. Although some of these customs have been gradually disappearing, prenatal and natal practices, like other aspects of South Vietnamese life, continue to reflect a preoccupation with solicitation of good spirits and the avoidance of evil ones.

Following the birth of a child, which is a happy event calling for celebration, the baby's relatives gather for several ceremonies. Of these, the so-called fete of the first-month birthday and the first-year birthday are the most important. On each occasion offerings are made to the ancestors, and feasting takes place. At the first birthday celebration it is customary for the guests to bring money, confectionery or other gifts for the child. Another feature of this occasion is the placing of a child on a mat, where he is surrounded by an array of useful and symbolic articles, including a paint brush, flowers, household utensils and paper. The first object he touches is believed to suggest his future occupational choice.

Naming of the child is done in accordance with certain customs. A Vietnamese name ordinarily has three parts, the lineage name (*ho*), the middle name and the personal name, given, in the Chinese manner, in that order. Occasionally, in the Central Lowlands area the middle name is omitted. In all, there are no more than 200 or 300 *ho* designations in use, most of them the names of royal dynasties or feudal lords who once ruled over the country. Examples of this type include Dinh, Le, Tran and, the most common *ho* of all, Nguyen (see ch. 3, Historical Setting). Useful middle names are "Van" for males, "Thi" for females.

The significance of a given name varies; it may represent the child's rank among his siblings as does Nguyen Van Ba (Ba—third born) or suggest a desirable attribute as does Nguyen Van Manh (Manh—the brave). Sometimes the three parts of the name collectively express a single idea, as does Nguyen Hao Dan (Nguyen—who loves letters and culture; Hao—who loves Dang, the hillock where Confucius taught), which indicates that its bearer is a man of intellect and sophistication. In frequent instances when a first-born son has died, the second is given an undesirable name as a protective device to ward off malevolent spirits.

When the child reaches 3 or 4 years of age, he enters a new phase. From this age boys and girls are raised differently, and a small boy is limited more and more to the company of his own sex. Boys soon conclude that they are superior to girls, an impression which the family confirms rather than dispels; when children are introduced to guests, for example, the boys are brought out first.

Early childhood is a relatively free and unrestrained period of life, during which time the child enjoys considerable attention and affection. Rural children are allowed the run of their village, eating more or less when they like. Toilet training is casual. Nevertheless, the parents, fearful that the child might be harmed or carried off by a wicked spirit, take pains to warn him to avoid the road and certain sacred or taboo spots. He is usually given a talisman, such as a bracelet or earring, to wear. This is thought to be effective in keeping evil forces away.

As children grow older, however, they find increasing demands on their time and less and less opportunity for play. Many attend school for a few years, and both boys and girls, as soon as they are physically able, are expected to help in the cultivation of rice, which furnishes so large a part of the family food supply.

Mutually supporting forces are brought to bear in training the child. The main responsibility rests with the parents, but uncles and aunts, as well as older brothers and sisters, also command respect. When the child goes to school, teachers play a part in teaching him proper attitudes and behavior, and parents and teachers uphold each other's views. Training indoctrinates the child in his duty toward his parents, among which filial piety traditionally is of overriding importance. It also involves, at least for girls of educated families, instruction in manners—how to sit properly, how to respond to an introduction.

Regardless of their social origins, all children are expected to be polite to their parents and older persons and solicitous of their welfare, to show them respect through proper manner and forms of address, and to carry out prescribed tradition with respect to funeral practices and the observation of mourning. After the death of their parents it is incumbent upon surviving children, and their children in turn, to honor their memory through the maintenance of the Cult.

Children's Day, an occasion for lavishing attention on the young, is enjoyed by everyone. Coming in the middle of autumn, it is celebrated with a colorful lantern parade. Cakes, fruits of the season and other gifts are given to the youngsters, who visit from house to house.

The Catholic Family

Information on Catholic family life, especially among urban populations, is fragmentary. Data collected in one Mekong Delta village, however, provides tentative evidence that Catholic and Buddhist families share many similarities in behavior. Every Catholic household, for instance, has its counterpart of the ancestral altar, set with the usual candles, incense burners and flowers, but displaying Christian sacred and ritualistic articles rather than family photographs. Parents and children assemble before the altar each evening for recitation of the rosary.

In the village studied, marriages among Catholic families were ordinarily arranged, with the formalities of the official request for a marriage and the engagement performed in accordance with traditional Vietnamese customs. A bride-price is paid to relatives of the bride. Reading of the banns takes place 3 weeks before the wedding, which is performed in the church. It is followed by a feast at the groom's house, during which the couple pray before the family shrine and kowtow before their kin.

Extensive differences in the details of funeral practices distinguish the behavior of Catholic villagers from that of other residents of the community. When a Catholic dies, the man who is considered to be head of the Catholic community in the area informs the priest, who is called in to administer last rites. The body may be taken to the church for the funeral ceremony, but most families are unable to afford this expense and have the rites conducted by the priest in their own homes before the family altar. Burial takes place in consecrated ground just outside the village.

THE FAMILY UNDER WARTIME CONDITIONS

Events of the past two decades have brought grievous personal losses and led to tragic internal rifts within many Vietnamese families. During and after the Indochina War over 900,000 refugees from North Vietnam, mainly Catholics, fled to the South, and an unknown number moved to the North. Prisoners were exchanged, and in the South, an attempt was made to settle the refugee families on a permanent basis without separating kin. Separations were often necessary, however, either for economic reasons or because older persons could not stand the hardships of life in the new villages being established by refugee groups.

The expanding military operations of the 1960's found thousands of officers and soldiers in the South Vietnamese army who had a father, brother, sister or son fighting with the Viet Cong or holding a post in the North Vietnamese administration. In extreme cases divergent political loyalties split the members of a single household, giving rise to a situation where a family may have one son in the South Vietnamese army, another in the Viet Cong.

Throughout the country, and especially in those areas where guerrilla activities are most constant, the fighting is a family affair. Few young Vietnamese children have had the opportunity to know the simple pleasures of childhood. From a young age many have been forced to come face to face with the enemy and with death, learning to walk quietly, to remain silent with strangers and to accept bombings, assassinations, tortures and kidnapings as a familiar part of life. Women and children are sometime victims of guerrilla terrorist operations and, in some instances, follow the fighting men close to the actual scene of operations. Some women actually join the fighting.

The years of military operations and refugee movements have tended in many parts of the country to break up the extended family units and to reinforce the bonds uniting the nuclear family. The major preoccupation of the ordinary farmer is to earn a livelihood and to protect his immediate family, holding his household together at any cost.

THE NON-VIETNAMESE FAMILY

The Chinese family, in its broad outlines, is much like that of the Vietnamese family, whose formation it greatly influences. It is comparatively more strongly organized, however, and it has not been as immediately affected by the strain of prevailing conditions as the Vietnamese family. Traditionally considered to be the keystone of society, the family is strongly patrilineal, with descent and inheritance coming through the male line. The father is the center of authority, and, after marriage, sons—at least the eldest—establish residence in their father's household. Marriages traditionally are arranged by the parents with the aid of intermediaries who determine the suitability of the partners to one another and arrange the details of the contract. The wife is in a subordinate position and is expected to devote herself to household affairs and care of the children. Related families are linked together in lineages, whose sense of group solidarity is reinforced through ancestor veneration. Ancestral shrines and tablets are found in every typical home.

The traditional pattern has undergone varying degrees of modification within individual families. Mixed Chinese-Vietnamese marriages tend to be more lax in observance of traditional patterns. Vietnamese wives of ethnic Chinese often take an important part in a family-owned enterprise, upholding the Vietnamese woman's reputation as a shrewd, practical business partner.

Family systems of other minority groups differ, sometimes sharply, from that of the dominant Vietnamese population (see ch. 5, Ethnic Groups and Languages). Among the Rhade, for example, the most important of the *montagnard* peoples, the organization of kin groups and the character of marriage varies considerably from Vietnamese tradition. The principal differences are that descent is matrilineal; matrilineal long-house groups provide the basis for social organization; marriage within the lineage, even within certain groupings of lineages, is forbidden; inheritance is through women, and after marriage the couple live with the wife's parents. Other points of difference include the fact that initiation of marriage proposals are by the girl's family; a dowry is paid by them to the groom; marriages are traditionally regarded as indissoluble; and only one marriage is contracted at a time. Great formality is observed by sons-in-law toward their wives' mothers.

CHAPTER 8

LIVING CONDITIONS

Early in the 1960's living conditions were better than in many other parts of Southeast Asia. Although the Viet Cong (see Glossary) had been operating in the country since 1954, in most places food and shelter could be obtained without difficulty. The government was playing a key role in welfare activities, assisted by important supplementary and advisory functions of the United States Operations Mission (USOM). International voluntary agencies and philanthropic organizations were also extending considerable material aid, and some had dispatched volunteer workers experienced in agriculture, public health and education.

With such assistance, progress was being made in the building of schools and health stations, in modernizing teaching equipment and in improving agricultural production. In some areas villagers had benefited by improved living conditions offered to them in the so-called strategic hamlets (renamed "new-life" hamlets in 1964) and by community self-help projects conducted by voluntary agency workers in remote regions including those inhabited by *montagnards*.

By 1965 living conditions had deteriorated as a result of intensified military operations by the Communist guerrillas and counteraction by the South Vietnamese and United States forces. The scope of the welfare projects being carried on by the government with the assistance of USOM and other agencies had also been greatly restricted. The major adverse factor was the lack of physical security in some parts of the country, especially in the rural areas. More than 1 million persons had been uprooted by Viet Cong terrorism, and military activities. Some families had returned to their native villages after a respite in the fighting only to have to take flight again when the village once more became a combat area. The massive influx of refugees into the cities had aggravated crowded housing conditions and imposed additional burdens on already overtaxed public utilities. Saigon, where the annual rate of population growth exceeded 4 percent before the arrival of the refugees, was particularly affected; its tenements were overcrowded and its slums proliferated.

Because of Viet Cong guerrilla action, some supply routes were blocked or destroyed, hampering distribution and creating temporary shortages in rice and other essential commodities in the areas north of Saigon, including Phu Bon and Kontum Provinces, and in the cities of Ban Me Thuot and Da Lat. In several provinces the lack of building materials delayed badly needed reconstruction jobs. Middle- and low-income groups were gravely affected by the mounting inflation which had not yet been brought under control. Rising prices and the lack of consumer goods created dissatisfaction and unrest among the population in some areas.

In early 1966 the principal welfare efforts of the government, USOM and the international voluntary agencies were aimed at the resettlement and rehabilitation of refugees. Some 700,000 refugees were accommodated in large camps, located mostly near the major coastal cities, and were provided with the necessities of life. Because of logistical and transportation difficulties, however, many refugees lacked adequate supplies of food, medicine and clothing. The severe shortage of refugee administrators and welfare workers, moreover, has severely impeded the progress in the permanent resettlement and rehabilitation of displaced persons.

A large proportion of the population was debilitated by chronic ailments, and in 1965 the life expectancy of an individual was only 35 years. The major diseases—notably intestinal infections, tuberculosis, malaria and bubonic plague—are caused mainly by the lack of sanitation facilities and ignorance of health practices. Although significant improvements had been made in the field of preventive medicine, especially in antimalarial spraying and vaccination for smallpox, wartime conditions prevented the systematic followup of these measures.

With only a few hundred trained physicians in the country, the majority of people were treated by practitioners of Oriental medicine. Western medicines have gained much popularity mainly because of the observable efficacy of antibiotics. The widespread use of these drugs without proper medical supervision has, however, favored the development of drug-resistant strains of bacteria which have caused problems in the treatment of some diseases, including dysentery and bubonic plague.

The severe shortage of medical personnel and facilities has been aggravated by the increased demand for such services as a result of military operations. Since the early 1960's, United States and other Free World physicians and nurses have been working as volunteers in the country to alleviate this shortage and to improve local medical training.

The Viet Cong has seriously restricted practically all programs and efforts designed to improve health conditions. Rural well-digging teams have been attacked and their equipment destroyed, so that in many areas their work could proceed only on a limited scope. The work of malaria-eradication teams has encountered popular resistance in many areas where Viet Cong propagandists have told the population that their dwellings were sprayed with American-made poison gas. Similar propaganda has hampered inoculation campaigns. Many rural health stations have been destroyed and their staffs killed, kidnaped or threatened.

PUBLIC HEALTH

Diet

One of the most varied diets in the world is provided by the country's tropical climate, luxuriant vegetation, expansive areas of rich alluvial soil, a long seacoast and many inland waterways abounding in fish.

The principal food is rice supplemented by fish and vegetables. Fish and occasional meals of poultry and pork are the chief source of animal protein. The average daily per capita calorie intake of 2,490 in 1964 compared favorably with that of other countries of Southeast Asia. Despite these natural advantages, nutritional deficiency diseases caused by dietary imbalance occur in several areas. Beriberi is not infrequent among the urban poor since they consume mainly polished rice. Kwashiorkor, a fatty degeneration of liver tissue, caused mainly by an excessive intake of carbohydrates and insufficient protein, is often found among the rural and urban poor. The lack of vitamins A and B is reflected by the prevalence, in some areas, of keratomalacia, an eye disease characterized by an ulceration of the cornea, and stomatitis, an inflammation of oral tissue.

To some extent, the traditional Vietnamese cuisine reflects Chinese influence in the choice of foods and methods of preparation. Considerable ceremonial importance is attached to the preparation of rice. A woman's domestic proficiency is believed to be reflected in her ability to prepare it properly and in adequate quantities. Soup is an important part of every meal. It is also consumed as a snack at any time of the day or night. A staple condiment is *nuoc mam*, a pungent sauce made of fish preserved in brine. It is inexpensive and provides a good source of protein.

City dwellers of all classes eat three meals daily—in the early morning, at noon and at sundown. The noon meal is generally the most substantial one and is followed by a siesta. The diet of the wealthier urban dweller tends to be more varied than that of those who are less well off; some have developed a taste for French cooking, although most continue to prefer indigenous dishes. Ice cream and soft drinks between meals have attained a certain popularity, but they are luxuries which the average person can rarely afford.

In rural areas the number of meals varies, depending on the availabilty of food and the work season. A common pattern during the period of intense agricultural activity is a heavy meal at breakfast, which is generally taken at dawn; lunch at 10 a.m.; and dinner at 5 p.m. The meals may include rice, a fish and vegetable soup, fried shrimp, fish stewed in sauce, scented leaves or bean sprouts. Another variation may be rice, fish and pork cooked in *nuoc mam*, salted fish, shredded banana stalk blended with cucumber and scented leaves, and red pepper. The food is eaten from individual bowls with chopsticks—never with the fingers. The family sits in a circle on floormats or on a large camp bed, and a bowl with chopsticks is set before each family member. All dishes are served at the same time, and the meat is cut up in advance. On hot days the family gathers for meals in the beaten earth yard in front of the house.

In the cities the family usually gathers around a table. Urban workers, construction laborers or taxi drivers generally go to a corner restaurant at lunch time. For relatively little money they can get a simple but tasty meal consisting of a liberal serving of rice, an omelet with *nuoc mam*, fried shrimp and preserved cucumber. The meal, usually taken squatting on the ground, is followed by hot tea brewed in a large earthen vessel over a wood fire and is accompanied by cigarettes or by a water pipe. Between meals a worker may purchase a bowl of soup from a vendor. For the morning and late evening the choice is generally rice soup with hog intestines, liver and stomach or a clear meat broth with rice. The urban workers' home diet consists of rice with salted fish or fish cooked in *nuoc mam*, bindweed (a species of morning-glory), shrimp, soya cheese and very small amounts of meat, usually fat pork.

Wine and liquor are occasionally consumed by the upper class. Rice alcohol, on the other hand, is often served at meals and feasts, particularly in the countryside. It is made of fermented glutinous rice and is sometimes flavored with lotus or chrysanthemum flowers. Although home-distilling of rice liquor is illegal, most villagers patronize a distiller who caters to their needs. The visits of friends are often accompanied by drinking rice liquor served with snacks.

Sanitation

Polluted water supplies in Saigon as well as in the smaller cities and rural areas create ideal breeding grounds for enteric and other waterborne diseases. Not even the largest cities have drinking water which is considered safe at the source, since these supplies are being contaminated through infiltration of ground water into leaking or porous pipelines.

In Saigon water is chronically scarce. During the dry season the city water is usualy shut off between midnight and 6 a.m. The water supply, provided by 39 wells in 1963, was not only unsafe but insufficient, permitting a daily consumption of less than about 5.5 gallons per person. Excessive amounts of iron in the water further deteriorate its quality. In some areas of the city, sand and activated charcoal filters have been added to the system, but these are frequently out of order or must be bypassed to expedite operation.

In the early 1960's the Metropolitan Water Bureau began a major expansion and improvement of the water supply system. The new supply will be drawn from a dam and a filtration plant located at the confluence of the Song Dong Nai and the Saigon River, about 18 miles north of Saigon. A network of new pipes, water mains and piping stations will transmit the water to Saigon, at the capacity rate of about 55 gallons per person per day. Financed by a $17.5 million development loan from the United States Agency for International Development (AID), the project is scheduled for completion in 1966. Other cities benefited from the AID-sponsored "65 Cities Water Program." In 1963 and 1964, 52 water supply facilities were completed in 28 cities with a total population of 820,000.

A well-digging program in the rural areas has also been organized by USOM. In 1964 a total of 745 wells were dug in various villages and hamlets and several storage cisterns were built, the latter mainly in the Mekong Delta area. Tank trucks were dispatched to some areas to provide emergency water supplies to refugees. Viet Cong terrorism has severely handicapped the program, however. Supplies cannot be easily delivered over routes threatened by the Viet Cong, and in many instances operators have been attacked. Some supply trucks have been confiscated, completed cisterns blown up and other equipment destroyed by the Communist guerrillas.

Sewage- and waste-disposal methods are rudimentary. Sewer lines and flush toilets are found only in some of the cities. Even there, a large majority of the population is without plumbing facilities, and untreated sewage is discharged into the various canals and rivers without any purification. The few septic tanks are at the homes of the wealthy. During high tide the openings of the sewage networks become flooded, and large areas become inundated with sewage. In the poor sections of town and in the proliferating slum settlements open ditches are used as communal toilets, representing a grave and continuous health hazard. The entire situation has been aggravated by the massive influx of refugees.

Garbage-collection systems exist in Saigon and other major urban centers. Garbage and waste are put out for collection in uncovered containers and are transported in open vehicles, attracting rats and flies. There is little supervision or control of sanitary practices in markets, slaughterhouses and restaurants. Standards of cleanliness in such places are highest in Saigon and other main centers and lowest in the small towns. In the rural areas dishes and eating utensils are generally cleaned with sand and stagnant water.

Efforts to improve rural sanitation have included the construction of simple pit privies and the distribution of concrete slabs for such privies to thousands of villagers. Rural health education is needed as much as material assistance, however. The old ways of doing things have the sanction of generations of practice, and, lacking an understanding of the elementary principles of hygiene, people see no reason to change. Night soil is not generally used for fertilizer, although this practice may have been introduced in some areas by refugees from the North.

Diseases

Malaria, tuberculosis, intestinal diseases and parasitic infections are endemic and represent leading causes of illness and death. Bubonic plague has become a serious threat since 1963. Many victims of the various endemic diseases are young people and infants. In 1963 the national average for infant mortality was estimated at 36.2 per 1,000 live births, but it is probable that this figure is underestimated since statistics from rural areas are at best sporadic. In Saigon, where health statistics are maintained with greater regularity and accuracy, the infant mortality rate for 1963 was 83 per 1,000 live births. Complications following childbirth are very common, and about 8 percent of the infants born in hospitals do not survive.

Malaria has long been a serious disease problem, particularly in the Mekong Delta area and in the Central Highlands. In the colonial period and during the early years of independence it was a leading cause of illness and death. The environs of An Khe and Pleiku in the Central Highlands, and the provinces of Long An, Hau Nghia, Tay Ninh, Binh Duong, Phuoc Long and Lam Dong have the highest malaria incidence rates. The disease occurs throughout the year but shows a major peak in January, February and March, except in the Delta area, where no variation occurs. An intensive malaria-eradication program was begun in 1958. Large areas were sprayed, and by the early 1960's the malaria incidence around Saigon and in the Mekong Delta dropped to a low level. In the Central Highlands, however, where large areas had not been reached by mobile spraying teams, the incidence remained high.

Since 1961 the Viet Cong has conducted a campaign to undermine the malaria eradication program by means of propaganda and terrorist tactics. Its agent spread the rumor among villagers that poisoning resulted from the use of DDT. They also captured, intimidated and killed technicians and other persons assigned to carry out the program. As a result, villagers became increasingly reluctant to cooperate in eradication procedures. The malaria-infested Central Highlands have become a particularly high-risk area for spraying teams. Convinced by Viet Cong propaganda that DDT spreads death, the *montagnards* have killed or abducted many health workers.

Intensified military operations since 1964 have further reduced the effectiveness of malaria eradication work, since spraying teams have been unable to reach many places. Morever, the appearance of a drug-resistant malarial parasite (*Plasmodium falciparum*) has become a matter of growing concern. In 1964 and 1965 a significant number of drug-resistant cases were noted, particularly in the Bien Hoa area northeast of Saigon and the Plei Me area in the Central Highlands. Civilians and United States military troops who have routinely taken antimalarial drugs, notably chloroquine and primaquine, were among those affected. Spraying and malaria surveillance activities have been initiated by United States Army medical units in these areas as well as in the environs of Da Nang, Qui Nhon, Chu Lai and Phu Bai, all in the northern section of the Central Lowlands.

Tuberculosis, like malaria, is frequent and is a leading cause of illness and death. Pulmonary tuberculosis is the most common type. While more cases have been reported in the cities than in the rural areas, medical authorities point out that this may be due to the better facilities available in the cities for detection and diagnosis rather than to a higher incidence rate. According to a report of the World Health Organization (WHO), 60 percent of the population of Saigon was infected in 1963. The WHO and the United Nations Children's Fund (UNICEF) have initiated a program of drug therapy and preventive vaccination by means of BCG (the bacillus of Calmette and Guérin), notably in Saigon, to help reduce the incidence of this disease.

Enteric diseases, including amoebic and bacillary dysentery, intestinal parasites (hookworm, tapeworm and roundworm) and typhoid fever are endemic throughout the country. Diarrheas and fevers caused by intestinal parasites are the chief causes of mortality among young children. Adults who have been cured are almost certain to be reinfected because of poor sanitary practices. Food poisoning and infectious hepatitis are common because of inadequate food refrigeration. Since antibiotics have become widely available, self-medication for these conditions is commonly practiced in many areas. This has favored the development of drug-resistant bacteria, and many antibiotics are no longer effective for enteric diseases.

Cholera occurred in epidemic proportions in the spring of 1964. More than 15,000 cases with 700 deaths were reported between January and May of that year. Successful control of the outbreak and a relatively low death toll was largely the result of massive United States aid. More than $1.8 million worth of intravenous fluids were provided and administered by Vietnamese and United States medical personnel and USOM technicians. At the same time, immunization campaigns were organized in various provinces. This effort was seriously hampered in several areas as a result of Viet Cong propaganda. In a Mekong Delta hamlet, for example, people refused to take the injections since the Viet Cong told them that "the needle would kill." After witnessing the inoculation of their hamlet chief they finally agreed to be immunized but refused booster injections some weeks later since the Viet Cong had convinced them in the meantime that the injections cause "slow agonizing death that might not come for 3 years."

The incidence of bubonic plague has increased significantly since 1962. Accurate statistics are lacking, but cases reported in 1965 exceeded 3,000 (as compared to 32 in 1962). Many more went unreported. In the cool, damp provinces of the Central Highlands, notably in Kontum, Pleiku, Darlac, Tuyen Duc and Quang Duc, the disease has been endemic. In 1965 outbreaks were also noted in Tay Minh, Long An, Gia Dinh, Bien Hoa, Phuoc Tuy, Long Khanh, Binh Thuan, Khanh Hoa, Binh Dinh, Quang Ngai and in Saigon. In addition to the climatic and topographic factors, inadequate sanitation, including the absence of garbage disposal, has given rise to a massive rat and flea population which favors the spread of the disease. Many of the epidemics occurred when grain invaded by disease-carrying rats was shipped from Saigon and other coastal cities to non-infected areas. Such limited measures as were in effect to reduce the number of rodents and insects had to be suspended when many areas became inaccessible as a result of wartime conditions. Preventive measures were also hampered by a general shortage of insecticides and by the lack of a sufficient number of public health technicians. Vaccines and drugs, however, are dispensed in some of the outlying areas and in Saigon.

Trachoma is widespread, particularly in the northern part of the country. Most of the cases are of a mild, chronic nature, although an estimated 30 percent of those afflicted suffer partial loss of vision. In 1962, USOM began the training of trachoma-prevention teams.

Leprosy is greatly feared, and it is thought that the approximately 15,000 lepers registered in 1962 represent only a minor portion of the total number of persons afflicted with the disease. Tetanus and rabies occur frequently in both adults and children. As yet, no mass vaccination programs have been initiated for either disease. Smallpox occurs in epidemic form about every 3 to 4 years, although the general incidence has been reduced as a result of vaccinations. Smallpox control has become part of the national health program, and the vaccines dispensed are manufactured locally in the laboratories of the Institute Pasteur in Saigon, Nha Trang and Da Lat. Measles, whooping cough, mumps and other communicable children's diseases are prevalent and, most of the time, are unrecognized and unreported.

Respiratory diseases—of which the most common are pneumonia, bronchitis and influenza—and venereal diseases are common throughout the country. Skin diseases, including various types of ulcers, fungus infections and scabies, are common and constitute an outstanding medical problem, especially among refugees.

Medical Services and Facilities

The first Western-type medical services in Indochina were introduced by European and American missionaries before 1800. These efforts were later supported and augmented by the French colonial authorities. The French organized a public health service; constructed and maintained a network of hospitals, clinics and sanitariums; and established a school of medicine at the University of Hanoi. Western-trained Vietnamese doctors became predominant in the colonial health service, since French physicians were generally reluctant to serve in Indochina.

After independence a Department of Public Health was organized which coordinated the functions of a number of administrative sections in charge of various aspects of public health. In 1965 the Department of Health was under the minister of social and cultural affairs. Headed by a secretary of health, it included a Directorate General of Health and Hospitals, which supervised the Service of Health, the Service of Preventive Medicine, the Service of Environmental Sanitation, and the Service of Procurement and Supply of Pharmaceutical Products. Special departments were in charge of rural health and of the malaria eradication program.

Each province had a provincial medical officer, responsible for all government health facilities and programs in his province. Below him were the district health officers, in charge of dispensaries and infirmaries. At the lowest level were the village health workers, responsible for the village health stations. In theory, each province provided a hospital and public health services; each district had its infirmaries and dispensaries, and each village a health station. In many cases, however, facilities as well as personnel existed only on paper. Many dispensaries and health stations were still in the planning stage or were destroyed as a result of military activities. Moreover, there was a severe shortage of properly trained specialists to fill public health posts on the operating level.

Physicians and Paramedical Personnel

The country has one of the most severe doctor shortages in Southeast Asia. Of approximately 800 practicing physicians, some 500 serve in the army, and another 150 are in private practice in Saigon. Thus about 150 doctors, or 1 for about every 100,000 persons, are available for the rest of the country. Military operations have made the need for doctors even more acute. Seventy-five percent of the persons reporting for medical treatment in 1965 were civilian war casualties. Most of the high-ranking physicians, notably chiefs of hospitals or medical school department heads, are French trained. A few practicing physicians have had several years of residency in the United States. Because of the general lack of modern equipment, trained physicians must rely mainly on clinical diagnosis without supportive laboratory findings.

United States and other foreign physicians and surgeons have been serving in many areas of the country since 1963 to help alleviate the shortage of medical personnel. Several United States surgical teams, consisting of 2 or 3 surgeons and supporting paramedical staff, were working in some of the provincial hospitals, notably in Can Tho in the Mekong Delta, and in Da Nang and Nha Trang in the Central Lowlands. Medical surgical teams have also been dispatched by a number of countries, such as Australia, Italy, Korea, New Zealand, the Philippines, and France. In 1965, 19 such teams with 50 physicians and 150 medical assistants were operating in field hospitals throughout the country.

Also in 1965, the American Medical Association, through Project Vietnam and the AID-assisted People-to-People Health Foundation of Health Opportunity for People Everywhere (HOPE), began the recruitment of volunteer doctors in the United States for a 3-month to 1-year period of service in Vietnam. Under the program it is planned to have 20 United States doctors in the country at all times for a period of 3 years. Some of them are to be assigned to provincial hospitals which have been equipped with AID assistance. The Medical International Cooperation Organization (MEDICO) has also supplied medical specialists, including plastic surgeons, to help care for civilian and military casualties.

Medical training is offered in a 7-year course at the Medical School of the University of Saigon. The bulk of the training consists of lectures with only a little clinical and laboratory work because of the lack of facilities and equipment. Promising medical students may apply for military sponsorship which offers additional training at the Military Medical School and provides a regular army commission upon the successful completion of studies.

An expansion of the University of Saigon Medical School's laboratory and building facilities, underwritten by a $4.5 million AID grant, was completed in 1965. The project also called for an updating of the curriculum and teaching practices with the help of American medical educators. Evening classes on special subjects for Vietnamese physicians and fifth- or sixth-year medical students were also offered by American physicians. Some of these courses enabled students to pass examinations which qualified them for residency in the United

States. The school enrolls each year approximately 300 medical students, of whom only about 50 eventually graduate, a number far below the needs of the country.

A Faculty of Medicine was added to the University of Hue in 1961. It functions as an extension of the University of Freiburg, West Germany, but additional sponsors include Canada, New Zealand and other member countries of the Colombo Plan.

Special programs initiated by MEDICO were offered by American physicians at the Saigon and Hue medical schools and at various civilian and military hospitals. In early 1966 these programs provided training in orthopedics, gynecology, plastic surgery, general surgery and anesthesiology.

To support governmental efforts to fight epidemics, the United States Army Medical Research Team has sponsored a short-term program in virology and entomology to train Vietnamese scientists at the laboratories of the Southeast Asia Treaty Organization (SEATO) in Bangkok. A school for medical technologists, the first of its kind in the country, was opened in Saigon in 1963.

The Pasteur Institute, with branches as Saigon, Da Lat and Nha Trang, has facilities for research in microbiology and related fields and produces vaccines and serums. Other facilities at Saigon include the Malaria Eradication Center, sponsored by USOM and WHO, the National Cancer Institute and the Microbiological Institute.

Nurses are trained in two schools of nursing operating in conjunction with the medical schools of the Universities of Saigon and Hue, respectively. The schools offer a 3-year program taught by nursing instructors, 80 percent of whom received training in the United States. Graduates are assigned to provincial hospitals where they, in turn, instruct assistant nurses in a 1-year program. American nursing advisers, under contract with USOM, are assigned to some of the provincial hospitals to upgrade the training of nurses and midwives. Many of the nursing school graduates are men; in 1965 women were in the majority for the first time.

The number of nurses and midwives, 3,100 and 1,213, respectively, in 1965, was far below the needs of the country. Volunteer nurses from the United States, recruited by AID, were expected to arrive in 1966 to help fill the urgent demands.

Because of the shortage of doctors, nurses and midwives handle 90 percent of the births, even in hospitals affiliated with the two medical schools.

Other paramedical personnel, including village health workers, sanitary agents and persons staffing district dispensaries, numbered approximately 5,000 in 1965. These specialists are trained at provincial hospitals in giving first aid and dispensing simple medicines. Their short-term courses are sometimes limited to 2 weeks.

Other Practitioners

In contrast to the small number of Western-trained doctors, there are about 4,600 practitioners of Chinese traditional medicine (*ong lang*), 600 of whom live in Saigon. A majority of the people are treated by these so-called Chinese doctors, who may be of either Vietnamese or Chinese origin. Because they represent deep-rooted cultural values and social traditions, Chinese practitioners have retained great prestige which accounts for their relatively peaceful coexistence with Vietnamese practitioners of Western medicine, despite fundamental differences in basic concepts and methodology. The progress and growing prestige of Western medicine in the country, however, has prompted them to form professional organizations.

Facilities

Civilian and military hospitals in 1965 totaled 120, with 34,000 beds. Of these, 101, with an estimated 25,000 beds, served the needs of the civilian population. Most of the hospitals are public and provide free care to patients. In Saigon-Cho Lon there were 11 public hospitals with 4,917 beds, 4 private hospitals with 809 beds, and a number of small private clinics. One of the government facilities was a 250-bed childrens' hospital, including an outpatient center. In each of the provinces there was at least 1 hospital. Facilities for the care of the mentally ill are provided at the Cho Quan Hospital in Saigon, Hue Central Hospital in Thua Tien Province, and the Nguyen Van Hoai Hospital in Bien Hoa Province. These facilities, however, accommodate only a few of the 400,000 persons known to be mentally ill in 1965.

With only about 1½ beds per 1,000 population, hospital facilities, especially those in the provinces, are severely overloaded. Most provincial hospitals were built in the late 1800's and are in very bad state of repair, often handicapped by shortages of water and electricity.

Projects to improve existing hospital facilities and to establish new ones have been launched by AID, by various American nongovernment organizations and by the Military Public Health Assistance Project (MILPHAP) of the United States Army in Vietnam. Surgical units have been built and equipped by AID in 28 of the provincial hospitals. The Quang Ngai provincial hospital, headed by two MEDICO physicians, has been enlarged to a 250-bed unit, and its facilities have been modernized with MEDICO support. Project HOPE sent a hospital ship and established an orthopedic clinic near Saigon; CONCERN, another medical project similar to HOPE, has staffed and equipped a small hospital near Da Lat. The MILPHAP plans to set up or expand existing hospitals in all of the country's 43 provinces by July 1967.

In addition, there are about 255 district dispensaries and some 4,000 village and hamlet health stations. The dispensaries consist of an infirmary and maternity unit, provide basic diagnosis and treatment and refer the more complex cases to provincial hospitals. Village health stations give first aid, dispense basic medications and, where possible, offer advice on hygiene and sanitation. The present number of district dispensaries and village health stations is inadequate, particularly in view of the increasing demand for health services, as a result of wartime conditions. Governmental efforts to increase the number of these facilities are supported by AID funds and personnel.

Medical Civic Action Program (MEDCAP) teams of the United States Army Medical Service operate in rural areas to help improve local sanitation and render basic health services. Concentrating in areas with heavy civilian casualty rates or in those stricken by epidemics, MEDCAP teams are popular with the villagers. Their short stay in each area, however, limits health services to quick, on-the-spot treatments.

Popular Beliefs and Practices

Traditional medical practices and beliefs are widespread. Chinese or Oriental medicine is practiced not only among the unlettered villagers but also among educated urban families. Students of Chinese medicine in Vietnam have pointed out that some of its aspects and therapeutic practices have been adjusted in the course of centuries to suit the native physical constitutions. To cure disease, Chinese practitioners employ a considerable pharmacopeia of herbs, some of which have proven therapeutic values. In addition, a number of manipulative techniques are used, such as cupping, cauterizing and acupuncture.

Popular beliefs attributing the cause of disease to the entry of evil spirits into the body are common, particularly among the *montagnards*. Some believe that when a spirit has entered the body it can be induced to depart by sorcerers or village priests employing formulas and traditional rites. Others hope to keep the spirit away by wearing charms or offering sacrifices and petitions. Firecrackers are used to frighten timid spirits, imitation paper money to bribe greedy ones and politeness to mollify those who are angry. According to another set of beliefs, attributed to Cambodian and Cham influences, illness can be caused by a sorcerer who possesses something belonging to the victim—a picture, a piece of clothing, a lock of hair or even his name. The sorcerer need not be a highly skilled craftsman, since nearly anyone in the community is considered capable of inflicting injury or even death in this manner.

Popular beliefs have not interfered with the general acceptance of modern medical treatment. Such acceptance is based mostly on the effective performances of Western drugs, notably the antibiotics, and on striking surgical results. On the other hand, efforts to gain popular acceptance of such aspects of Western medicine as sanitation, personal hygiene and disease prevention have met with little success. Reliance on Western medicine is greatest in the cities, but rural people are tending more and more to take advantage of such modern medical help as is available to them. In doing so they are apt to view it as an additional curative aid rather than a substitute for the traditional remedies. In the villages many persons trained in Western medical techniques are also versed in Oriental practices.

On the other hand, traditional beliefs, mostly those deriving from Chinese medicine, have significantly shaped the less enthusiastic attitudes toward Western medicine. For example, it is often believed that Western medicine is unsuitable for the Vietnamese constitution since Western drugs are "hot" and have a dehydrating effect on the humor and on the blood. Many also feel that Western medical therapy and techniques are effective in acute illnesses and surgical emergencies but fail to restore vigor. The belief that good medicine has restorative as well as curative powers has led many persons to take antibiotic and sulpha drugs on a long-term basis. This practice has often caused serious toxic reactions and, in some cases, death. Many people tend to be critical of the Western doctor although his efforts are generally appreciated. Failure of the Western-trained practitioner are promptly blamed on the general unsuitability of Western medicine for the Vietnamese, while the unsuccessful ministrations of the *ong lang* are accepted fatalistically.

Popular beliefs often interfere with diagnostic and preventive procedures. A person who is afraid that he will become ill if someone— possibly a sorcerer—acquires something belonging to him is likely to refuse to allow a blood sample to be taken. Also, the traditional contempt and stigma attached to venereal diseases often prevents examination and treatment of those afflicted.

STANDARDS OF LIVING

In the villages family members contribute to total household earnings by working in the rice paddies, fashioning handicraft articles at home or performing outside labor for cash. In areas where only a single crop of rice is grown, for example, many men take outside jobs in construction work during the off season. Rural income is low by United States standards, but the differential is narrow between the great majority of rural families and the few who are relatively well to do. The housing, diet and other material comforts of the rural upper class is often only slightly superior to those of the average farmer. Some differences reflecting social or economic stratification are apparent in clothing. Rural schoolteachers or civic officials usually wear Western-style shoes, trousers and shirts.

Because the rural economy is only partly modernized, cash income is not the only measure of rural living standards. The majority of village families raise all or most of their own food and build their own houses from locally available and inexpensive materials. In the Mekong Delta, where about two-thirds of the population lives, the land is productive and responds quickly to cultivation. In other areas the increasing use of fertilizers and other aids for the increase and improvement of crops help to raise the farmer's cash profits and living standards. On the other hand, they have been hard hit by taxes collected, in cash or kind, by Viet Cong guerrillas. Moreover, military operations and Viet Cong terrorism have caused many families to abandon their villages, losing whatever small possessions they had.

In the Central Highlands, among the *montagnards*, the living standard tends to be much lower. Meager corn and rice crops are supplemented by hunting and fishing. In some areas ironwork, pottery and forest products are offered in barter to obtain salt, jars, medicines and other basic necessities. Since 1962 the government has initiated various programs to improve the economic and social level of the *montagnards*, but extremely precarious security conditions in the area have blocked much of the progress.

Families in the middle- and lower-income brackets experienced increasing difficulties during the early 1960's. In 1965 the government struggled to prevent runaway inflation. In spite of government control on wages and prices, however, the cost of living steadily mounted. In Saigon, the price of rice rose 68 percent between January and November 1965; pork was up 75 percent, shrimp, 50, *nuoc mam*, 30; and charcoal, about 55 percent. In some branches of industry wages rose along with the prices—in the construction industry, for example, as much as 120 percent. In other sectors of the economy, however, and in the Civil Service wages have remained static in the presence of soaring living costs. Adding to the difficulties of everyday life were the periodic shortages of basic consumer goods, resulting from the activities of Viet Cong terrorists who disrupted transportation on some roads and confiscated shipments.

Hoarding and black-marketing have become widespread, further raising the prices of essential items, including milk, rice and construction materials. The presence of the Americans has often brought at least temporary prosperity to the small lower-middle-class entrepreneur. Vendors and owners of small foodshops and bars near American military installations have done a thriving business, and many persons have been hired in service occupations by American employers.

Western movies and modern theater performances have become typical aspects of urban life. They are popular mainly with middle- or lower-middle-class youngsters and young adults who have also enthusiastically embraced soccer, tennis and other Western sports.

Games of chance are popular among all classes. The prospect of winning a million piasters on a 10-piaster lottery ticket appears equally attractive to the wealthy businessman's wife and to pedicab drivers. More than 3 million tickets are sold every week. The profits are used by the Directorate of Reconstruction for housing and other welfare projects and for public works. The tickets are usually sold in market areas by peddlers, most of whom are women. In obtaining the lottery tickets, the peddlers have to pay various intermediaries and are therefore forced to charge more than the official price. In some provinces, notably in Gia Dinh, measures have been initiated to check profiteering in the sale of lottery tickets.

Public utilities are insufficient everywhere to meet the needs of the population. In Saigon the rapid increase in the number of residents since the late 1950's quadrupled the load on public utilities, particularly water and electricity. In 1964 and 1965 the increased demands on electrical supply facilities necessitated the cutting off of electrical current for several hours each day. Most provincial towns have some electricity, but the major portion of rural areas is without current. The progress of United States-assisted electrification projects has been slow because of deteriorated security in the countryside.

The living conditions of more than a million refugees are substandard compared to those in their native villages. Seeking the safety of the cities, the refugees have been accommodated in camps equipped with the most rudimentary types of shelter. In the fall of 1965, there was a total of some 200 camps, housing approximately 680,000 to 700,000 refugees, mostly near the major cities along the coast northeast of Saigon. In camps which are considered well-equipped, people live in long, cement-floored, aluminum-roofed sheds, partitioned by heavy straw matting into 8- by 10-feet living areas. There is no electricity, and charcoal hearths are used for cooking. Still greater hardships awaited those who were barred by local authorities from entering the cities because of the lack of facilities to accommodate them. The difficulties in providing food and basic sanitary facilities have been overpowering in many cases, in spite of major efforts by the Vietnamese Government, USOM and international voluntary agencies. Although no major epidemics were noted in 1964 and 1965, exhaustion, various forms of physical deprivations and poor sanitation kept the incidence of disease high in refugee camps.

Housing

The wealthy residents of Saigon live in spacious villas solidly built of stone or brick and equipped with running water, electricity and sanitary facilities. Housing of this caliber commands a high monthly rent, in some instances 25,000 piasters (for the value of piaster, see Glossary), plus about 10 percent for utilities.

Middle- and lower-middle-class families live in multiunit structures. The individual units have one or two stories and often combine shops and living quarters. In the one-story structures the living room is in the back, and the front space is occupied by the shop. The two-story units have one or two living rooms upstairs and a smaller one on the ground floor behind the shop area. Also on the ground floor is another smaller room which may have kitchen furnishings, a small toilet and, sometimes, a shower. Some middle-class tenants may also have a small refrigerator, a sewing machine and some upholstered seats. Many tenants rely on kerosene and gasoline lamps for lighting and on charcoal braziers for heating. Water is drawn from nearby rivers or canals or from street-corner hydrants.

In 1963, 90 percent of the inhabitants of Saigon lived in small houses, of masonry, frame or thatch construction. The typical dwelling is a wooden structure of two rooms with a tin roof and walls made of straw or board. Often the lodgings form long, extremely narrow streets along a canal or river. These are broken up by an occasional small open space, resembling a square, where peddlers, fortunetellers and itinerant food vendors conduct their business. The wares of the food vendors are much in demand, since most lodgings have no cooking stoves. Water is obtained from communal faucets, each of which serves about 100 to 200 families. Public toilets are built over open ditches or canals, the surfaces of which are covered with litter and sewage.

Along the crowded riverbanks and canal banks, many low-income families live in boathouses, which are made of temporary building materials and lack any kind of facilities. The river or canal serves as a universal source of water except for drinking.

Rent on working-class housing is not high by local standards, even in Saigon. The major burden on the family is "key money," a sum equivalent to about one-third of the value of the house which is demanded of a new tenant at the time he moves in. It is, in effect, a deposit which is returned in part or in its entirety when the renter leaves.

With the exception of the few solidly built masonry or frame houses of the well to do, village dwellings resemble those of the urban working-class. They are small, dirt-floored thatch structures. Furnishings consist for the most part of a simple ancestral altar—the focal point of the main room—a few tables, chairs and hardwood planks which serve as beds.

Although the Vietnamese are frugal, a comparatively rich array of furniture and household goods may be displayed in the houses of the most prosperous villagers. These may include heavy pieces of hardwood furniture intricately carved and inlaid with mother-of-pearl, solid brass candelabra, bowls and similar items representing an accumulation of many years. There may also be more recent acquisitions, such as radios, French china and pressure lamps. Perhaps the most striking symbol of prosperity in the villages is a motor scooter.

Furnishings of urban homes of the middle- and upper-middle class show a marked Western influence. The traditional heavy wooden armchairs have been replaced by comfortable upholstered seats. The old furnishings which have been retained are used mostly for decorative purposes.

Clothing

Simple, light clothing is generally worn in the hot climate. The basic outer garments of traditional dress for both men and women are loose-fitting trousers and a long-sleeved collarless shirt. Those worn by peasants are usually made of cotton fabric, which was overpriced and in short supply in many areas in 1965. For ceremonial occasions the women wear long tunics of black or white cotton. Wooden clogs are worn with traditional attire, although many peasants go barefoot a good deal of the time as a matter of preference or economy. While purchases of wearing apparel are kept to a minimum in most households, even poor families try to buy at least one new set of clothing for each person at least once a year—usually at the time of the New Year's celebration (Tet).

Much about a person's social and financial position is revealed by the manner of dress. In the cities men wear Western business suits; those in the middle- and lower-income brackets, Western-style slacks, shorts and open-necked shirts. The traditional black silk tunic is worn only rarely, mostly on ceremonial occasions. Middle-class women wear the Vietnamese tight fitting tunic (*cai ao*) with full trousers, and sandal-like shoes with high heels. The conical hat is still worn by many women, even by those who wear Western clothing. In the villages prosperous men appear in public in slacks and shirts, but usually wear Vietnamese garments at home. The latter are made of silk or satin; if they are of cotton, the color is white—never the black garb of poor peasants.

WELFARE EFFORTS

During the French rule social assistance by the government began to assume importance, along with family and village charity, as means by which welfare was provided. The colonial administration extended education, inaugurated vaccination programs and built hospitals, clinics and medical research institutions. Its activities were supported by contributions from French-Vietnamese Catholic sources. These efforts were mainly confined to the cities, however, and accordingly benefited only a small fraction of the population.

After 1954 the Government of the Republic of Vietnam took over the administration of welfare institutions, which had been established in the South by the colonial administration. It continued their operation and, with material aid and technical assistance from the United

States, pressed vigorously to improve living conditions, particularly in the rural areas. As in the past, nongovernmental organizations, including various international relief groups, private American philanthropic agencies, religious orders and lay groups, also engaged in various charitable activities. Other forms of social assistance were left to the village and family.

In 1966 the administration of welfare programs at the national level was the responsibility of the secretary of social welfare under the Ministry of Social and Cultural Affairs. On the local level such programs were administered by district chiefs and province chiefs. Social security benefits, including sickness and maternity, work injury and family allowances, are applicable only to wage earners and are hanlded by the secretary of labor under the minister of social and cultural affairs (see ch. 21, Labor).

Rural Welfare

Since independence, official policy has stressed the provision of economic and physical security and the extension of social services in the villages. A land-reform program was initiated, and agricultural credit was extended. A major road- and canal-building program was launched with the assistance of USOM to link isolated villages with provincial centers. A program to establish district dispensaries and village health stations and to purify rural water supplies was launched. Army units of the United States and South Vietnam have contributed to these and other public projects in rural areas by providing assistance in roadbuilding, well-digging, construction of irrigation ditches and assisting in the evacuation of refugees from combat areas.

To promote rural welfare and security, the Strategic Hamlet Program was launched in 1962. Renamed the New Life Hamlet Program in 1964, it called for the establishment of small, fortified rural settlements for local defense against Communist guerrillas. Schoolrooms, communication posts and health stations were built in the hamlets. The residents received fertilizers, insecticides and various other forms of assistance to improve crops and livestock.

Because of heavy stress on military aspects and the forced relocation of many farmers in the process of setting up hamlets, the program had suffered some setbacks by 1963. A new policy was launched in 1964; placing primary emphasis on social and economic welfare, it has gained growing support among farmers and brought tangible improvements of living standards in many hamlets. Part of the new policy was a "hamlet self-help program" calling for the building of marketplaces, access roads, fishing ponds, wells, small bridges, the digging of wells and the planting of fruit trees. Material for these projects, including cement, tools, grains and cash, were provided by USOM.

By 1965 the government had achieved limited success in easing certain longstanding problems of the villagers. Progress, however, was seriously jeopardized by Viet Cong activity and by the country-wide destruction in the wake of intensified military activities. Hamlets were burned down or fell into Communist hands. In extensive areas villages were still without schools and medical facilities and lacked means of communication with provincial centers through which they could summon help in case of guerrilla attacks.

Women and Youth

Women have a more prominent place in public life in South Vietnam than their counterparts in many other Asian countries. They have been active in welfare, education, journalism, the professions and government. Some of them even took part in anti-Viet Cong military actions, following their husbands into combat areas.

Official efforts since 1963 have stressed the enlistment of assistance by youth organizations in public and welfare projects. The Voluntary Youth Association, largest of the groups, and the Boy Scout Association have been active in rural development work and cultural projects. In December 1965 the National Youth Commission was established under the secretary for youth, under the minister of war and reconstruction. The Commission's objective is to train youth cadres which will assist the government in maintaining public order and enforcing public morality.

A number of welfare efforts are concerned with young children. In the large cities dispensaries, nurseries and kindergartens are maintained for the children of working-class families. Plans were underway in 1966 to build an additional 20 kindergartens and 15 orphanages. A private charity group, Association of Friends of Go Vap Orphans, also maintains a number of orphanages and kindergartens for children of all religions. A Welcome Center for Children Victims of the Viet Cong is operated by the Goodwill Women's Association in Saigon for children injured in combat areas and those who have been orphaned as a result of wartime conditions. In November 1965 the government granted 300,000 piasters to the Unified Buddhist Church of Vietnam in Khanh Hoa Province to build an orphanage and 500,000 piasters to the Binh Dinh chapter of the same organization for similar purposes. At the same time, 110,000 piasters have been granted to the Buddhist Social Service to organize outdoor activities and a handicraft program for youths.

UNICEF sends wheat and milk shipments to national disaster areas or to areas where food is short as a result of military operations and also helps maintain maternity and child health centers. Other foreign voluntary agencies active in child welfare are Coordinated

American Relief Everywhere (CARE), Catholic Relief Services, the Mennonite Central Committee and Foster Parents Plan, Inc.

Widows and orphans of soldiers killed in action are entitled to cash benefits equaling 12 months' military pay. Many of these payments, however, are delayed for months because of complicated bureaucratic procedures. Acting upon numerous complaints by survivors, Prime Minister Ky in October 1965 ordered the immediate settlement of outstanding claims.

Refugees

One of the largest and most successful welfare efforts undertaken by the Vietnamese Government after independence was the resettlement of nearly 1 million persons who had fled North Vietnam between August 1954 and May 1955. The task was accomplished through the joint efforts of the government, USOM, the Catholic Auxiliary Resettlement Committee and Catholic Relief Services of the National Catholic Welfare Conference. Although by the early 1960's some refugees with special problems, such as the aged and the physically handicapped, still required public assistance, most were reasonably self-sufficient. Scattered in some 300 villages, mostly in the southern part of the country, they were earning an adequate living as farmers, weavers, tradesmen or fishermen. By 1966, however, many had left the countryside and moved to Saigon.

Because of the intensification of military activities against Communist guerrillas since 1964, the government has been again confronted with the formidable task of resettling and rehabilitating another million or more refugees. By early 1966 most of them had been temporarily accommodated in refugee camps where they were given food, supplies and a daily cash allowance. Only a fraction of them, however, have been permanently resettled. In December 1965 the secretary of social welfare granted more than 6.2 million piasters for refugee relief. Another 2 million piasters were earmarked for the construction and repair of welfare facilities for the benefit of refugees throughout the country. The largest sums went to the provinces of Quang Ngai, Binh Duong and Kien Hoa, where refugee populations are the largest. The sums granted to provinces for their relief are supplemented at intervals by cash grants distributed among refugee families.

The USOM and foreign voluntary agencies have donated large supplies of food, clothing, medicine, building materials and cash donations to supplement the government's efforts in refugee care. In October 1965 alone, the United States shipped 50,000 blankets, 50 tons of clothing, 700,000 tons of bulgur (parched crushed) wheat and 175,000 sheets of aluminum roofing. Further help has been forthcoming by shipments of canned food, medicine and clothing from some 17 voluntary agencies, including the Lutheran World Relief, Voluntary Foreign Aid, Catholic Relief Services, CARE and Church World Service.

Despite foreign aid, problems have emerged in the task of refugee administration and care. Essential supplies have failed to reach many camps because of the destruction or blocking of transportation facilities. Delays in the distribution of food, clothing, medicines and cash allowances and the lack of trained personnel have aroused dissatisfaction among many refugees in the camps. To fill the acute need for more personnel qualified in refugee administration work, AID, through USOM-Vietnam, has launched a major recruiting program for specialists in this field.

SOCIAL PROBLEMS

Public morality received a good deal of attention during the regime of President Ngo Dinh Diem, largely owing to the concern of Madame Nhu. In 1959 she sponsored the Family Code which ended concubinage, polygamy and arbitrary divorce rights for husbands. She presented another bill to the National Assembly prohibiting boxing, cockfights, sorcery, beauty contests, erotic dances, the cabaret dancer trade, the sale of alcoholic beverages and tobacco to minors, the use of contraceptives and the advocacy of birth control. It became a law in May 1962. Many provisions of both laws have been revoked since 1963—notably those dealing with divorce rights of husbands and illegalizing prostitution. Continued official concern with public morals is reflected in a law passed in 1963 prohibiting certain Western dances. The cabaret dancer trade, although often publicly denounced by government officials and religious leaders, apparently continues in some quarters.

The government also has voiced its disapproval at the rise of juvenile delinquency. Reporting the increase of arrests of juvenile delinquents from 1,413 in 1964 to 1,225 in the first half of 1965, the director general of the National Police blamed parental neglect, poor schooling and the misconduct of some servicemen who, he said, have assisted young people to get arms.

Alcoholism is not a major problem, but a number of persons in the cities and, to a lesser extent, in the countryside, are addicted to opium. Opium dens operate in Saigon and other major cities, but information is not available on the effectiveness of police measures controlling such establishments.

Venereal diseases have increased and have caused growing concern to civilian and military health authorities. Because prostitution is no longer outlawed, it has become possible in many cases to identify and treat carriers, but the systematic examination and treatment is hampered by the shortage of medical personnel.

CHAPTER 9

EDUCATION

The country has worked vigorously since independence to expand its educational system. Between 1955 and 1965 the number of elementary school pupils more than trebled, and the number of students in public secondary schools more than doubled. The lack of facilities, however, still presents serious problems on all school levels. The enforcement of the law prescribing compulsory and free education for children between 6 and 11 years of age is dependent upon the completion of 12,000 additional elementary school classrooms. In early 1966 the secretary of education expressed the hope that these facilities would be available within 5 years. At the secondary level, not only is the classroom shortage critical, but many families are unable to pay the required amounts for tuition and books. For both reasons, the number of secondary school students—although greatly increased—represents less than 10 percent of the children in this age group.

There is also an acute shortage of teachers at all levels. The large-scale departure of French academic personnel after 1954 and the continued lack of properly trained Vietnamese teachers seriously threaten to undermine educational standards.

The deterioration of security throughout the country, especially since early in 1965, as a result of military operations, has led to a grave decline in school attendance. Viet Cong terrorists have systematically burned down school buildings, particularly in the rural areas, and kidnaped, killed or threatened hundreds of teachers. As a consequence, the number of school dropouts has soared, and teachers have refused to accept posts in the dangerous areas.

The aims of education are closely linked with national goals. Although structural organization of the school system remains patterned after that of France, and French standards of instruction are maintained, the orientation of the curricula has become truly Vietnamese. New emphasis has been placed on the teaching of the Vietnamese language and literature, particularly on the secondary level. Teachers and university professors are encouraged to inspire their students to respect traditional Vietnamese values and to work for national unity.

Educational policies since 1954 also reflect official concern regarding the nation's lack of a trained elite, qualified administrators and technical specialists. Systematic efforts have been made to give the bulk of school-age youth at least an elementary education, to raise literacy levels among the adult population and to expand the ranks of skilled industrial workers. The government hopes to extend universal free education to cover at least 4 years of secondary schooling. A major reform is in the planning stage to replace the highly academic, essentially college-preparatory, secondary curriculum with a differentiated program adapted to the needs of the respective geographic areas (urban, rural, coastal and highland).

Since the ascent of Prime Minister Air Vice Marshal Nguyen Cao Ky in June 1965, the government has called for a further readjustment of the educational system, including the rewriting of textbooks, and the training of high school and university students in "revolutionary principles." The government of Prime Minister Ky has also stressed the enforcement of regulations designed to limit the number of students attending universities abroad to those enrolled in courses essential to the national economy which are not offered at Vietnamese universities.

The United States has made significant contributions to Vietnamese education in terms of funds, supplies and consultant services. Between 1955 and 1966, the United States contributed a total of $17,412,000 to help meet the country's educational needs. Intensive United States involvement in Vietnamese education is reflected in many schools by the growing reliance on modern visual teaching aids and testing methods and by an increasing emphasis on teaching by demonstration. English, moreover, has gained currency as a second language in governmental administration and in university-level instruction.

HISTORICAL BACKGROUND

Confucian Scholarship

The educational system in the pre-French period bore the imprint of nearly 10 centuries (111 B.C. to A.D. 939) of Chinese rule and cultural influence. Confucianism, with its emphasis on learning and filial devotion, was a central force in a social order which gave highest place to the scholar. Education provided the principal means by which a young man might move upwards in the social scale.

The aims of education were in keeping with the political and social structure of the society. The immediate purpose of formal training was to prepare young men for the examinations through which they might enter the mandarinate (see ch. 3, Historical Setting). The more esoteric purpose of education related to the cultivation of high moral character, especially an appreciation of the wisdom of the ancient sages of China and of Confucian principles.

144

With the exception of the Imperial College and a few other government schools in Hue, education was neither financed nor closely controlled by the government. Instruction was given in the homes of scholars, in the pagodas, or in a community building made available by the village council. Theoretically, anyone might attend and there was no age limit for schooling, but enrollment was small and the sons of the mandarins had more opportunity to acquire an education than had those of the uneducated.

The program of study centered on the Confucian classics. Some courses on Chinese history, Vietnamese history, ancient poetry and military tactics were also taught. The language of instruction was Chinese. Although the Chinese influence in culture and education was strong, Buddhist studies gradually began to gain ground under the guidance of several learned priests. By the time Vietnam first gained its independence from the Chinese, Buddhism enjoyed high prestige in learned circles and the sons of many noble families were instructed by Buddhist priests.

Formal training culminated in a series of rigorous competitive examinations. In the system which prevailed in the late eighteenth and early nineteenth centuries, candidates for scholarly rank were examined first in the provinces; then, if successful, in the capital at Hue; and finally, at the highest level, in the Imperial Palace. These examinations took place every 3 years. Successful candidates, depending on which of the examinations they passed, became low-, middle- and high-ranking government officials. Those who passed the court examination at the Imperial Palace were called "Doctors of the First Class." Theirs was considered the supreme achievement, and it gave them and their families special privileges and emoluments.

French Colonial Period

The introduction of Western learning and the abolition of the mandarinate in the early and middle years of French colonial rule (1868–1954) paved the way for the decline of Confucian education. Having lost much of its value in a slowly modernizing society administered by a Western power, traditional education faded out in Cochin China in the last quarter of the nineteenth century, when the mandarinate was completely abolished. The same process occurred somewhat later in Tonkin and Annam. The late mandarinate examinations were held in Tonkin in 1915 and in Annam in 1918.

In the meantime formal French education had been developing rapidly. Traditional schools were gradually replaced by new state and missionary schools whose programs of study and methods of instruction were similar to those prevailing in institutions in France and which prepared Vietnamese youth to serve in the lower ranks of the colonial administration. All classes were taught in French.

In 1917 the French authorities organized a standard system of French education in Indochina (including Vietnam, Cambodia and Laos), providing for a uniform syllabus for all schools and for highly selective examination given at the end of each cycle of studies.

Elementary education, which covered a 6-year period for children aged 6 to 12, was subdivided into two 3-year cycles, the first leading to a certificate of elementary studies and the second to a certificate of primary studies. Secondary education was given in the *lycées* and *collèges* in the cities. This program included a 4-year cycle, leading to a diploma, and a second cycle of 2 years (after 1927, 3 years) which ended in an examination for the *baccalauréat*.

Holders of the *baccalauréat* were eligible for admission to the University of Hanoi, which had been established by the French administration in 1917. By the late 1930's, the University comprised schools of medicine and pharmacy, pedagogy, fine arts, agriculture and commerce. The teaching staff of the University was entirely French.

Although elementary education was theoretically compulsory in Cochin China after 1927, most children received no schooling. In 1938, for example, in all Indochina there were only 406,669 pupils attending elementary schools, representing possibly less than 1 in 5 children in that age group. The number of students enrolled for secondary and university education was proportionately far smaller. The Roman Catholic Church, the Chinese community and the village councils—mainly in Annam—also played an important role in education during this period. In the late 1930's, out of a total private-school enrollment of about 60,000 students, Roman Catholic mission schools accommodated about 36,000 pupils in 650 institutions.

THE SCHOOL SYSTEM

Administrative Organization

After the establishment of the Republic in 1955, government activities in the field of education were the responsibility of a Ministry of Education. In the course of a reorganization in January 1964, the Ministry's five principal branches were regrouped under Directorates of Research, Higher Education, General Education, Technical and Vocational Education and Cultural Affairs. The National Center of Scientific Research and the Atomic Energy Agency were placed under the supervision of the Ministry. The former Cultural Office of the Ministry of Information and the liaison officer of the United Nations Educational, Scientific and Cultural Organization (UNESCO) were attached to the Directorate of Cultural Affairs. Later during that year two consultative bodies were established to assist the minister in drafting and coordinating reforms designed to meet the most urgent needs in education: the Commission for the Improvement of Education, composed of the 24 department heads of the Ministry; and the National Education Council, including 36 members elected by teachers and school administrators of the various provinces.

Under the government of Prime Minister Ky, the Ministry of Social and Cultural Affairs became the principal agency in charge of education. The Ministry coordinates the activities of the secretaries of education, health, social welfare and labor who head their respective departments. In December 1965, Tran Ngoc Ninh, former minister of education, held the post of minister of social and cultural affairs and that of secretary of education.

For school inspection purposes, the country is divided into five zones, all placed under the authority of a chief inspector, assisted by associate inspectors in charge of the different levels of education. The inspectors represent the authority through which school principals are responsible to the Ministry in matters of administration and curricula. School principals report to local authorities solely on matters pertaining to minor details of administration. Private schools are subject to supervision by the Ministry, and only a few receive financial subsidies from the government. In addition to public and private schools, there are about 100 so-called semiofficial schools which are supported by the government but are directed by a board of administration, usually chaired by the mayor of the locality or by the provincial governor.

Elementary and Secondary Education

Elementary education, intended for boys and girls aged 6 to 11, extends over a 5-year period, beginning with grade 5 and ending with grade 1. A minimum of 3 years of elementary education is compulsory, and legal decrees provide for sanctions against school principals failing to report absentees and dropouts and against parents whose children are absent for more than 15 days within a month. In 1965, however, compulsory elementary education, limited to 3 years, was enforced only in those areas where facilities were available.

After the fifth year of elementary school, students take an examination leading to the certificate of primary studies (certificat d'études primaires). In certain rural areas where schools are lacking, special classes in reading, writing and other elementary subjects are held for children and youths aged 6 to 18 in community halls, pagodas or any other available space. In 1963 there were 42,577 students in these "fundamental education courses."

The curriculum of elementary schools emphasizes Vietnamese language, national history, geography and civics in the early grades. Moral education, general science, arithmetic and drawing are given in the upper gardes. Teaching is largely by rote, and students are asked to memorize large portions of the subject matter. Each school period lasts 25 to 30 minutes. Classes normally meet for a total of 25 hours per week; on Mondays, Tuesdays, Thursdays and Fridays for a full day and on Wednesdays and Saturday mornings. The school year for elementary students lasts about 9 months and is divided into two semesters, with 3 months of summer vacation and a holiday of 10 days at Tet (lunar New Year).

In 1964 elementary education was provided in 4,625 public schools which accommodated 1,214,621 students. Some 22,041 teachers were employed in these institutions. In addition, there were 2,900 private elementary schools with 339,442 students. Enrollment increases have led to acute overcrowding in the schools, especially in Saigon and other cities. To provide for everyone, some schools have had to accommodate several shifts per day, operating from 6:30 a.m. to 7:00 p.m.

The creation of a Textbook Translation and Publication Service in the Department of Education marked an important advance in elementary education. This service supplies students with textbooks in Vietnamese and books and reviews translated from foreign languages, such as French, English and Chinese. In 1964 over 140,000 free textbooks were distributed among rural elementary schools and some 68,000 were sent to *montagnard* schoolchildren in the Central Highlands. The short supply of textbooks still continues to handicap teaching, however. To alleviate this shortage, the United States Agency for International Development in 1965 distributed some 7 million elementary school texts, some in *montagnard* languages. The books ranged from primers to simple texts in hygiene, history and mathematics. Additional textbooks were provided by other countries of the free world. Over 1 million copies were sent by Australia and some 500,000 copies by the Republic of China (Nationalist China).

Special emphasis has been placed on the building of schools in strategic hamlets, later called "new life" hamlets. By June 1963, of a total of such 1,320 classrooms planned, 973 were completed. The program has received substantial aid from the United States, mainly in the form of building materials, classroom supplies, teaching aids and salary support for teachers.

The progress of rural school expansion in general and of the new life hamlet school program in particular has suffered serious setbacks because of Viet Cong violence. Protesting against the official curriculum including the daily practice of saluting the flag and singing the national anthem, the Viet Cong, in 1959, began the systematic burning of schools and kidnaping of teachers in the rural areas, mainly in the southernmost provinces of Ba Xuyen and An Xuyen. By 1961 terroristic acts against rural schools were frequent throughout the country and also affected some urban schools. Between 1959 and 1961, 636 schools, serving more than 18,000 students, were burned down or closed. By 1962, 32 teachers had been killed, and more than 260 had been kidnaped or were missing. Enrollment in elementary schools dropped by approximately 80,000 as a result of Viet Cong terrorism.

As in France, secondary education continues over a 7-year period and consists of an initial 4-year cycle and a later 3-year cycle. The first cycle, from the seventh to the fourth class, includes work in Vietnamese history and geography; Chinese, English and French; civics; physics; chemistry and mathematics. It leads to the examination for the certificate of studies for the first cycle (*brevet d'études du premier cycle*).

Pupils who pass with distinction the examination given at the end of the first cycle can be admitted to the second cycle (from the third to first class) which ends in the examinations for the *baccalauréat*, first and second parts. Students concentrate in one of four chosen fields—modern languages, classical languages, mathematics or experimental sciences. The *baccalauréat* examination takes place twice a year, in May and July. Those who pass qualify for admission to institutions of higher education in Vietnam and abroad. Because the examinations are difficult and highly selective, candidates who fail may repeat the examinations at a later date. In 1964 only about 22 percent of the candidates passed the first part of the *baccalauréat*, and only some 32 percent passed the second part.

Like elementary education, secondary education has greatly expanded since 1955. In 1964 there were 112,129 students in 140 public secondary schools—more than twice the number attending in 1955. Of the students enrolled in 1964, 79,566 were in the first cycle and 32,563 were in the second cycle.

Secondary education is largely in private hands. In 1964, of a total of 590 secondary schools, 450 were private. The student body in private institutions totaled 179,836, as compared to the 112,129 students in public secondary schools. The majority of the students (151,911) in the private secondary schools were enrolled in the first cycle and the remainder in the second cycle.

Secondary education suffers from a severe lack of facilities and teachers. Classrooms are so overcrowded that 65 students to a room are not unusual. In Gia Dinh Province (surrounding Saigon), the construction of 35 secondary-school classrooms to accommodate 1,750 students was in progress in 1965; another 400 were in the planning stage. Of the existing public secondary schools, one each is located in the 43 provincial capitals, the rest are in Saigon and other major cities.

Vocational Training

The technical and vocational education program has undergone substantial expansion since independence. In 1964 vocational and technical training was provided at 22 institutions on the secondary level and 4 at the higher level. The total enrollment on the two levels was

5,902. Another 735 students received basic instruction in various skills at 9 training workshops on the elementary school level. American teachers and technicians were attached to many vocational schools.

The largest and best equipped technical and vocational institutions on the secondary level are the technical schools at Hue, Nha Trang, Da Nang, Qui Nhon, Ban Me Thuot, and Vinh Long; the Lycée Technique Cao Thang in Saigon; and the Polytechnic School of the Phu Tho National Technical Center near Saigon. Courses are offered in carpentry, ironworking and boilermaking, as well as in automobile and diesel mechanics. At the schools of applied arts in Bien Hoa and Binh Duong, instruction is available in furniture design, ceramics and in the graphic arts.

Secondary level vocational courses last 4 years and lead to a vocational training certificate (*certificate d'aptitude professionelle*). Graduates of the technical school at Hue receive the certificate of industrial training (*brevet d'enseignement industriel*) after completing 2 years of general academic work followed by 2 years of specialization in a technical field. Students at the schools of applied arts combine academic work with vocational training and, upon completion of the 4-year course, become eligible for the certificate of applied arts (*certificat d'études d'arts appliques*).

Vocational training in agriculture is given at the schools of agriculture, forestry and animal husbandry at Saigon, Can Tho, and Hue. The 3-year course includes academic and technical subjects and field practice in agriculture. Students may concentrate on a specialization subject for another year to become eligible for advanced training.

Advanced vocational courses covering 3 years' work are open to holders of one of the vocational farming certificates or to graduates of the first cycle of academic secondary schools. They are available in such schools as the technical colleges in Hue and Saigon, and at the Phu Tho National Technical Center near Saigon. The mathematics course of the technical colleges leads to the *baccalauréat technique*, which is regarded as equivalent to the general education *baccalauréat*. Other institutions offering advanced professional training on the secondary level are the schools of fine arts at Gia Dinh and Hue, the national schools of music and dramatics at Saigon and Hue, and the School of Maritime Navigation. Technical education beyond the secondary level is offered at the School of Public Works, the School of Electrical Engineering and the National School of Industrial Engineering. All three are part of the National Technical Center at Phu Tho which was established by the government with assistance from the United States and France in 1957. Students wishing to enroll in any of the vocational schools on the postsecondary level must hold the technical or academic *baccalauréat* with a major in mathematics or science. Also on the postsecondary level is a 2-year course for training teachers of vocational subjects, added in 1963.

Agricultural education on the university level is offered at the National College of Agriculture, Forestry and Animal Husbandry at Blao, about 50 miles northeast of Saigon. The 3-year program leads to the equivalent of a university degree.

Specialized postsecondary training is given at the National Institute of Administration in Saigon, connected with the Office of the Prime Minister. Designed to train a reserve of competent servants for top-level administrative posts in national and local government, the Institute offers a 3-year course in public administration, economics and finance. The third year is spent in on-the-job training in government offices. In 1964 special courses in English were offered to senior civil servants at the English Language Laboratory of the Ministry of Education.

Teachers and Teacher Training

In 1964 the national need was officially estimated at 3,500 teachers annually, but between 1960 and 1963 the number of normal-school graduates was only about 1,200 each year. Many teaching positions were left vacant by persons called to military service; some were filled by substitute instructors who usually lacked professional training. In 1964 about 60 percent of the practicing teachers were inadequately trained. The decline of public safety in the countryside since 1960 has become a serious deterrant to prospective teachers. Those who are offered positions in rural schools are reluctant to accept them, and many who accept soon request transfer to a city.

Training for teachers of elementary schools is offered at normal schools in Saigon, Ban Me Thuot, Vinh Long, Qui Nhon, and a Fundamental Education Center at Khanh Hau, southwest of Saigon. The schools are open to graduates of the first cycle of secondary schools, and offer a full 3-year course or a concentrated 1-year program. Another normal school for teachers in *montagnard* areas was under construction in 1964. An In-Service Center was opened during the same year, offering eight 1-month sessions to improve the skills of practicing teachers.

In the 1963–64 school year, 2,038 students were enrolled at normal schools. Some 5,500 hamlet school teachers were also trained in special 90-day courses during this period.

Secondary schoolteachers are trained at the universities at Saigon, Hue and Da Lat, in courses lasting 3 years. Nearly 300 students were graduated from the faculties of education at the Universities of Saigon and Hue in 1961. In 1963–64 a total of 1,224 persons were enrolled in secondary teacher training. In 1964 two new colleges for the education of secondary school teachers were planned, each with a secondary school attached for practice teaching. These colleges will specialize in the training of teachers in the fields of business education, home economics and industrial arts.

A considerable portion of aid from the United States has been devoted to the improvement of teached training. Particular emphasis has been placed on improving student testing methods and on teaching science and English. Thirty-eight new science laboratories have been equipped to serve as partial workshops for science teachers. A truck has been equipped as a mobile science laboratory to acquaint teachers in rural areas with modern teaching methods in science. Two language laboratories have been built, and a third was under construction in 1964 for prospective English teachers and for students of English.

Another language laboratory, under the Department of Education, served as an inservice-training center for more than 500 practicing teachers of English in secondary schools. Visual materials and other teaching supplies are also provided by the United States and by various international voluntary agencies. Under a contract with Southern Illinois University, teachers of technical subjects are trained in a 2-year course at the Phu Tho Polytechnic School of the Phu Tho National Technical Center. Some 187 prospective elementary, secondary and vocational schoolteachers studied at various institutions in the United States in 1964.

The scarcity of qualified teaching personnel for institutions of higher learning is even more acute than the shortage of elementary and secondary schoolteachers. Only a small number of Vietnamese have reached this level of training through study abroad. Thus, many positions on university faculties are held by foreign professors lecturing in French or English. Although both languages have gained currency in the county, some lectures are not wholly successful because of the language barrier.

Private Schools

In 1964, 28 percent of all elementary school pupils and over 62 percent of pupils on the secondary level attended private schools. Of the various private schools organized by foreigners, the French schools are the most popular. Since the majority of the elite are graduates of French schools, a French education continues to be highly valued. The French schools have proportionally more qualified teachers, and a degree from a French school is generally regarded as preferable to an equivalent degree from a Vietnamese institution.

The most important French schools in Vietnam are the Jean Jacques Rousseau Lycée for boys and the Marie Curie Lycée for girls, both at Saigon. The Lycée Yersin at Da Lat and the Colleges of Da Nang and Nha Trang admit both boys and girls. Admission to these schools is made on the basis of entrance examinations. Other private schools that follow a French curriculum include a moderate number of institutions operated by religious and a few maintained by private Vietnamese individuals or groups.

At the French schools the majority of the teaching staff are French; Vietnamese teachers are employed only to teach the Vietnamese language. The curriculum is similar to that of schools in France, although Vietnamese students are required to study Vietnamese 4 hours per week.

Besides the French schools there are also a number of other private schools operated by the Chinese and the Khmer ethnic minorities. Although under the supervision of the Department of Education, they enjoy considerable autonomy in matters of internal administration. In accordance with governmental efforts to assimilate national minorities, the teaching of Vietnamese language, history and literature has been made compulsory since 1956.

The Chinese schools, located mostly in the southern portion of the country, are operated by "congregations" (*bang*) (see Glossary). The curriculum includes Chinese cultural and religious subjects and language. In 1963 there were 175 Chinese primary schools with 50,135 students and 16 secondary schools with 5,635 students. More than 100 of the primary schools and 12 of the secondary schools are in the Saigon-Cho Lon area (see ch. 5, Ethnic Groups and Languages).

In the Khmer schools, pupils receive mainly religious instruction in the precepts of Hinayana Buddhism (see ch. 11, Religion). Before 1954 there were some 200 Khmer schools, with over 7,000 students. Later data regarding the number of these schools are not available, but they apparently have declined, and only a few are left in areas with predominantly Khmer population.

Special Schools and Courses

A countrywide literacy campaign was launched in 1956 under the direction of the Office of Private and Popular Education. The United States Operations Mission (USOM) and other foreign educators and advisers have assisted importantly in the planning and implementation of the campaign. Between 1956 and 1962 some 1.6 million persons between 13 to 50 years of age were taught reading and writing. In 1962, 1.5 million piasters (for value of the piaster, see Glossary) were earmarked for 236 special literacy centers for *montagnards*. In 1963, 42,577 persons were enrolled in more than 5,000 literacy centers conducting day and night classes throughout the country. Contributions by the United States to the literacy campaigns by 1962 exceeded 8 million piasters. The United States also financed the publication of 343,000 primers.

In conjunction with the literacy campaign, a committee was established to set up and direct adult-education courses for neoliterates in every district, town and village. In 1963 more than 3,000 courses in history, geography, civics and composition were offered to 69,329 neoliterates attending classes held in the late morning or in the evening. Village halls, pagodas, churches, factories, various organizations' headquarters and school buildings are used for this purpose. School supplies are distributed free.

The Popular Cultural Association, a private organization, has played an important role in adult education. Established in 1954, the Association maintained popular polytechnical institutes in various cities. In addition to health and vocational education courses, these institutes offer classes in Chinese, Japanese, Italian, French, English and Spanish. More than 50,000 persons have attended the institutes.

Foreign-language training for adults is also given by the Department of Education through its English Language Laboratory, the Modern Languages School in Saigon and also by the Vietnamese-American Association. Attendance of the Ministry's English Language Laboratory is limited to teachers of English and to civil servants. The Modern Languages School, where French, English, Japanese, German and Spanish are taught, is open to the general public.

Higher Education

Domestic

The number of university students increased from 16,835 in 1962 to 20,834 in 1964. Higher education is provided in four universities, of which the largest and most important is the University of Saigon. Organized in 1955, the University includes on its staff many former members of the faculty of the University of Hanoi, most of whom had fled to the South after the signing of the Geneva Agreement in 1954. In 1963 enrollment at the University of Saigon was about 14,854, distributed among the Faculties of Law, Letters (languages, literature, history, geography, sociology, psychology), Medicine (including dentistry), Pharmacology, Education, Science and the Higher School of Architecture. Since 1959 the University has been the recipient of considerable United States financial aid to expand its physical facilities, notably those of the Science Faculty and the School of Medicine, to add to its scientific equipment.

Established in 1957, the University of Hue has Faculties of Law, Letters, Science, Education and Medicine, as well as an Institute of Sinology (study of Chinese culture and language) and a Higher School of Fine Arts. With an enrollment of 2,491 in 1963, it is much smaller than the University of Saigon.

Both of these universities are administered by a rector appointed by the Chief of State. Under the rectors are the deans of the faculties, who are also members of the teaching staff. University administration generally tends to be decentralized, and a considerable degree of autonomy is accorded to the respective faculties.

154

The University of Da Lat was established in 1957 by the Catholic bishops of Vietnam. Financed by the Catholic Church of Vietnam, it is composed of Faculties of Letters, Science and Education. The latter plays an important part in the training of teaching personnel for the large number of Catholic schools and in the higher education of the Catholic clergy. The University also receives substantial financial support from the Société Vietnamienne d'Assistance á l'Enseignement Superieur (Vietnamese Society for the Assistance to Higher Education), an organization of businessmen in industry and commerce, founded in 1957.

Van Hanh University in Saigon was established in 1964. Devoted mainly to higher studies in Buddhism, it is sponsored by the Unified Vietnamese Buddhist Congregation. In addition to its Faculty of Buddhist Studies, the University in 1965 also established a Faculty of Letters and Human Sciences and a School of Social Work. Its enrollment during that year totaled 600. In conjunction with the intensified organizational activities of Buddhist political and religious groups during 1965 the physical plant and the library of the University were expanded, and added emphasis was placed on the recruitment of a high caliber teaching staff.

Holders of the *baccalauréat* are admitted to most of the faculties of the universities without further examination. The faculties of education, however, select their students on the basis of an entrance examination. Students in education receive a government grant during the whole period of study in return for which they are required to teach at the state secondary schools for 10 years following graduation to reimburse the state for the cost of their education.

The duration of the course of study in institutions of higher learning varies according to the faculty. The course in the Faculty of Science and the Faculty of Letters at the University of Saigon, for example, covers 4 years. Examinations are given at the end of each year, and certificates are awarded to those who pass. Successful completion of 4 years' work earn the student a license (approximately equivalent to a master's degree). The Ph. D. requires an additional 3 to 4 years. The course in medicine covers 7 years' work; architecture, 6; dentistry and pharmacy, 5; law and education, 3. Although the humanities and law still figure prominently as major fields of study, science is rapidly gaining popularity. In 1964 science courses enrolled the largest number of students at the universities of Hue and Da Lat. At the University of Saigon, science was the second most popular course after literature.

As in the French universities, class attendance is not always required, and the method of teaching consists mainly of lecturing. Because of the lack of library facilities and equipment, students rarely have an opportunity to pursue research. Officially, classes are conducted in Vietnamese rather than in French, a practice which was adopted in the Faculties of Law, Education and Letters in 1955. In the Faculties of Medicine, Pharmacology and Science, where most courses are taught by foreigners or by Vietnamese trained abroad, the language of lecturing is still French, and, to an increasing extent, English. The teaching of these subjects in Vietnamese is dependent on the availability of adequately trained Vietnamese academic personnel and on the development of scientific terminology in Vietnamese, both of which are likely to take a number of years to achieve.

Partly because of the French tradition for rigorous standards in learning, the academic level of Vietnamese universities is high. Many university professors have studied at French and other Western institutions of higher learning, and in many cases have won academic distinction abroad. During the 1960's most Vietnamese university degrees were still given full credit in France. French academicians generally were readily available to accept appointments to Vietnamese universities, although this has been less so since the intensification of military operations during the 1960's. At the end of 1965 there was still a shortage of university lecturers in science subjects, despite a moderate flow of visiting professors from the United States, France, Australia and Western Germany.

Abroad

Since independence many Vietnamese students have received higher academic education or technical training abroad through government or foreign scholarships provided by the United States, France and other countries. Students may also seek higher education abroad at their own expense, provided that the subjects to be pursued are not taught in South Vietnam and that the applicants are not of military age.

In 1964, 399 South Vietnamese students were enrolled in colleges and universities in the United States. Most of these majored in the social sciences and engineering. The largest number of Vietnamese students is generally found in France, although the 1,522 enrolled at French universities in 1964 represented a figure lower than usual. It reflected the general decrease in the number of South Vietnamese students abroad as a result of the state of emergency in the country.

EDUCATION AND SOCIETY

Education is held in high regard by all segments of the society. The traditional reverence of the scholar in ancient Vietnam and the admiration and emulation of the "intellectual"—the product of the French school system—have both contributed to the general respect for learning. Scholarship for its own sake, however, has become a thing of the past. To most Vietnamese, urban as well as rural, education represents the essential steppingstone to profitable jobs and social prestige.

Formerly, the upper-class Vietnamese valued learning for itself as well as an essential adjunct to power and prestige, but they have become increasingly aware that wealth and political connections are also prerequisities for power. Although it is general practice among the children of the upper class to take advantage of the educational opportunities which they consider their birthright, few if any continue the tradition of the gentleman-scholar.

The financially less well-off in both the cities and the rural areas show an equally strong desire to secure educational advantages for their children, but the lack of money often presents an insurmountable obstacle to education beyond the elementary level. Although the cost of tuition and books is low compared to similar costs in the United States, it is still beyond the means of most. Sons and daughters of prosperous businessmen, high-ranking government officials, bankers and lawyers represent the bulk of the student body in secondary schools and universities.

Official efforts have been made to increase the number of government scholarships, but relatively few students have benefited by them. Geographic factors further restrict educational opportunities beyond the elementary level; most secondary schools and institutions of higher learning are located in or near urban centers and are, therefore, inaccessible to the majority of the population. Those who live in the cities have the advantage of physical proximity to school facilities. In some cases, relations with highly placed government officials permit members of the small urban middle class—merchants, office clerks, low-level civil servants—to obtain scholarships.

In the villages only a very few are able to attend school beyond the elementary grades. Where schools are lacking altogether the parents make every effort to have their children tutored at least in the rudiments of reading and writing, since the illiterate is generally regarded with pity and contempt. Among the *montagnards*, on the other hand, education is usually limited to the initiation of boys and girls into the performance of various manual tasks upon reaching a certain age. Many *montagnard* tribes regard the study of reading and writing with suspicion, and their response to government literacy drives often has been poor. Adding to the difficulties is the absence of a written alphabet in many *montagnard* dialects.

Those who seek education look forward to the prestige and financial reward of a civil service job or of a professional practice in law or medicine. Many are also becoming aware of the opportunities open to graduates of studies in science. Among the formal proofs of education, the *baccalauréat* of the upper cycle of academic secondary schools is the most highly valued, next to university degrees. It has become an indispensable status symbol for being considered an "intellectual" by others and by oneself. For many, the *baccalauréat* itself has become a goal, regardless of its practical relevance to obtaining future jobs.

In spite of the severely limited scope of school facilities on the secondary and higher levels in relation to the school-age population, the further expansion of these facilities without corresponding economic progress appears to be of questionable value. Already during the mid-1960's, the *baccalauréat* and often even the university degree failed to bring its holder the hoped for job and prestige. This was particularly true of university graduates. In 1955 the government had no particular difficulty in placing the few hundred graduates of the University of Saigon. In 1962 there were some 2,400 university graduates, many of whom looked for jobs in vain. Disillusioned and restless, they and similar others from the universities of Hue and Da Lat continued to swell the numbers of an "intellectual proletariat," which had since been causing increasing concern to the government (see ch. 14, Political Dynamics).

As the sole supervisory and regulatory agency of schools and curricula, the government plays a prominent role in education. University rectors are appointed by the Chief of State, and university professors are regarded as government employees. Criticism of government policies from university lecturing platforms is, therefore, rarely heard. Students, on the other hand, have become increasingly vocal in political matters (see ch. 14, Political Dynamics).

Under the regime of President Ngo Dinh Diem, Catholic influence in the private school sector was considerable. By 1965, however, this influence had diminished, and Buddhists were playing an increasingly important role in school management. Since 1963 the agencies concerned with education have encouraged and supported the establishment of Parent-Teacher Associations. Except for sporadic fundraising drives by some of these associations in Saigon for additional classroom space, the official appeal has met with apathy. Although the shortcomings of the school system are frequent topics among families concerned with the future of their children, active public interest in education and in community-based plans for its improvement is as yet not evident.

CHAPTER 10

ARTISTIC AND INTELLECTUAL EXPRESSION

A thousand years of Chinese rule, ending in the tenth century A.D., left a cultural tradition that the Vietnamese were eager to preserve. Despite the subsequent influence of the European culture of France and the latent effect of Western education on traditional values, Vietnamese art forms basically continue to reflect the Chinese heritage with a strong Confucian influence running through the whole fabric of artistic and intellectual life. Combined with this fundamental Confucianism, recognizable in the emphasis on hierarchy and duty, there are elements of two other great Asian religions: the Buddhist belief in the spirit world, the reward of good and punishment of evil and the reincarnation of the soul and the Taoist tendency to accommodate to nature. Underlying these influences are traces of even more ancient aspects of Vietnamese character: a strong love of independence and a note of realism—or even pessimism and cynicism— about life (see ch. 12, Social Values).

Writers and poets have always enjoyed high standing in Vietnamese society; painters and sculptors, looked on as craftsmen, have ranked lower. But most degrading, until recent times, was the role of actor or musician. Earning their livelihood by traveling through the countryside, these performers were seen as little better than vagrants in a conservative agrarian society in which the highest obligation of the individual was to cling to his family and local group. Recently, the theater has become the most popular art form; actors and musicians have gained in stature, and in the cities their popularity approaches that of their counterparts in the United States.

The stage, once restrictedly the province of men, now includes actresses. Although some of the heroines of earlier Vietnamese literature were accomplished musicians, only recently have girls been permitted to learn music. Several women concert artists and composers have won high praise in Vietnam and France. Dancing is not a traditionally popular art form in Vietnam, although ritual dances are used in some religious ceremonies and once formed part of the state ceremonials around the emperor.

LITERATURE AND SCHOLARSHIP

Under the emperors, Vietnam was acutely conscious of its heritage of literature and scholarship. Writers and poets, particularly, were held in high regard. Nearly every village of any size had its own Temple of Literature, dedicated to the cult of Confucius and maintained by the scholars (see ch. 9, Education; ch. 11, Religion). The center of this cult was the imperial court, which maintained a national Temple of Literature and there enshrined the names of leading scholars. The last three emperors of independent Vietnam—Minh Mang, Thieu Tri and Tu Duc, who reigned in the nineteenth century—were themselves outstanding scholars, and for many centuries the imperial government was the chief patron of literature, learning and art (see ch. 11, Religion).

Temples of Literature still exist in many villages as public monuments, but the national cult of Confucius no longer functions. The institutions the French introduced in its place, however helped to salvage much of the old heritage. The most outstanding of these was the Ecole Française d'Extreme-Orient (EFEO), centered in Hanoi. This government-financed institution, through its French and Vietnamese scholars, for decades carried on research in East Asian antiquities and did excellent work in studying and preserving the relics and architectural monuments of Vietnam's past. Largely through its work, knowledge of the ancient Kingdom of Champa (which was conquered and absorbed into Vietnam in the fifteenth century) was revived, and critical study of Vietnamese history was stimulated. Many old Vietnamese manuscripts in Chinese characters were collected and preserved in its libraries.

After the settlement at Geneva in 1954, under special arrangement with the Communist regime of North Vietnam, the EFEO remained for a time in Hanoi under French direction, as did several other French schools. Conflict with the Communist regime forced the removal of EFEO headquarters to Paris; a branch office was established in Saigon.

The first written Vietnamese literature, dating from the 1,000-year period of Chinese rule (111 B.C. to A.D. 938), was composed in Chinese characters and based on Chinese literature. Subsequently, a new form of writing, called *chu nom*, was adopted. It continued to employ Chinese ideographs but made some of them stand for sounds rather than complete words, so that certain Vietnamese words could be written phonetically. The script was well developed by the fourteenth century, and after the Chinese withdrawal it was proclaimed the basis of the new Vietnamese literature. Chinese continued, nonetheless, to be the language of scholars, and Vietnamese writers produced large quantities of literature in both languages. Literary production was stimulated by the adoption of the Chinese system of examinations for all officials, under which the candidate was required to have mastered the great bulk of Chinese and Vietnamese literature.

Vietnam lagged behind China in introducing the printing press for general use, one result being that early Vietnamese literature remained mostly in manuscript form and was thus subject to deterioration in a tropical climate and to damage by insects, humidity and fire. A new era began with the arrival of the Europeans. Their initiative in devising the *quoc ngu*, a Roman-letter script, and the more extensive use they made of the printing press stimulated the growth of popular literature and encouraged efforts to reduce illiteracy.

Poetry was among the most admired of the scholarly accomplishments, and the Vietnamese have retained a special gift for this medium. The high popularity of poetry at all levels is reflected in the frequent appearance of poems in practically all kinds of newspapers and magazines. Although the long narrative poem is common, most poetry is short and pithy, characterized by a special proficiency at expressing several different meanings in a short phrase of few syllables.

Modern Western influence on Vietnamese literature stems from the translation into Vietnamese of European works during the colonial period. These works—particularly the novel, which became a popular literary form—had great influence on Vietnamese writers. They also brought about an important change in Vietnamese poetry, which retained its vitality and gained new breadth and a greater freedom from Chinese models and traditions.

The rising tide of nationalism was reflected in new forms of literature, ranging from propagandistic tracts to historical dramas and novels. Revolutionary themes became increasingly popular but were usually disguised by being placed in a historical framework.

A number of novels written before World War II by various members of the Tu Luc (self-strength) group, whose leader, Nguyen Tuong Tam, used the pen name Nhat Linh, are still widely read. Nguyen Tuong Tam is also notable for his leadership of the Viet Nam Quoc Dan Dang (Vietnam Nationalist Party) (see Glossary) and most especially for his part in the Buddhist crisis of 1963 which precipitated the downfall of President Diem. In July 1963 he committed suicide, leaving a note which pled for cessation of Buddhist suppression. A popular figure among the students, Nguyen Tuong Tam's suicide brought these groups into active alignment with the Buddhists (see ch. 14, Political Dynamics).

Particularly popular among the many Vietnamese who flooded the market with historical dramas, especially after World War II, are Luu Quang Thuan and Hoang Cong Kanh. The best known twentieth-century historian is Tran Trong Kim, who became Bao Dia's premier after the declaration of independence in March 1945.

The most famous and influential of all Vietnamese literary master-pieces is the long (over 3,000 lines) narrative poem, *Kim Van Kieu*. Written by Nguyen Du (1765–1820), this story of unhappy love and undeviating loyalty shows a deep psychological insight as well as a beauty of imagery and style that have won it lasting popularity. There are few Vietnamese who cannot recite some verses from this great work.

Romantic sentimentality, a theme sometimes found in Vietnamese literature and lore, reflects a contemplative mood somewhat at variance with Vietnamese everyday character. Although preoccupation with the supernatural world of spirits and genii, both good and evil, permeates the popular literature, much of Vietnamese literature is concerned with life here and now; genii may interrupt the action from time to time, however. Rarely do vague metaphysical or abstract ideas predominate. Even though the Vietnamese like to see good win over bad, they display in their folklore a high regard for craftiness, subtlety and successful lying—especially when these are used to combat the brute force they abhor. Accustomed to yielding to force, they nonetheless ridicule it, particularly when it is accompanied by what they regard as stupidity. Although one very often finds in Vietnamese literature a strong admiration for the scholar, there is also an occasional voice of resentment on behalf of the poor rice farmer who toils forever in the rice fields while the scholar sits and reads. Filial piety is another constantly recurring theme and, together with devotion between wife and husband, one of the most admired.

THE THEATER

The most popular art form of the Vietnamese people is the theater, which expresses their history, traditions, cultural heritage and moral values. The three main types of theatrical performance are the traditional *hat boi* (Sino-Vietnamese theater) the *cai luong* (reformed theater); and the *kich* (modern theater).

Hat boi, the Vietnamese adaptation of Chinese theater, can be traced to the eleventh century, when Chinese teachers trained Vietnamese to perform Chinese plays before the court and the nobility. Presented to the general public in the thirteenth century, the plays became very popular and, in the process, acquired Vietnamese characteristics. In *hat boi* theatrical performances no scenery is used and properties are few. Actors' makeup, gestures and costumes, however, compensate for the barren stage. Facial makeup identifies the characters, various skin colors representing different human qualities and the type of eyebrow, eye shape, and mouth indicative of the special traits of the role. From the detailed makeup the audience can identify the characters as they enter the stage. Gestures are stylized, and their meaning is familiar to the audience. Costumes are both Vietnamese and Chinese, the colorful and elaborate dress worn at the Vietnamese imperial court. Plots are drawn from Vietnamese and Chinese history and are arranged in a series of episodes, each play built on a set of tunes to fit the dramatic situation. Lines are sung or chanted. Plays promote the five Confucian virtues of humanity, loyalty, courtesy, wisdom and justice and all have a happy ending. *Hat boi* has declined in popularity as fewer and fewer Vietnamese study Chinese and as familiarity with the conventions of the stylized theater declines, but it remains the formal entertainment for traditional ceremonies.

The *cai luong*, which is most popular, is usually a comedy of manners, but the dialogue is interspersed with songs accompanied by orchestras, as in European operetta. The *cai luong* originated with the ritual music societies of the medieval imperial court. The primary purpose of the societies was the entertainment of the emperor and other members of the court. Originally they consisted of instrumentalists who performed a type of chamber music, but singers and actors were added as songs and dialogue were introduced. Court performers in time became public performers, and Vietnamese folk tunes and folk poetry were incorporated into the plays. Continuing to develop since the seventeenth century, the *cai luong* play is regarded as the contemporary Vietnamese theater. It is concerned with telling a story which deals with anger, joy, love and happiness and consists of dialogue, poetry, songs, both Oriental and Western, and, sometimes, dancing. The *cai luong* play is characterized by sentimentality, and the sweetness of the performer's voice is more important than acting ability. In 1966 the eight major theatrical companies were *cai luong* companies, and every night in Saigon, *cai luong* performances were given in the four major playhouses. *Cai luong* companies were also very active in the provinces.

The *kich*, modeled after the modern French comedy, is not greatly enjoyed by the Vietnamese, who are unaccustomed to a play without singing or music and who dislike lengthy prose discourse. The *kich*, however, is used extensively for entertainment in the countryside by the Psychological Warfare Division of the South Vietnamese Army and on radio broadcasts. Some theater groups see potentialities in it. Several playwrights are writing dramatic plays in Western style, and they are produced by various theatrical troupes even though they must be included in a variety show to attract patrons.

MUSIC

Music is an important part of the theater, and many dramas are, in effect, Chinese-style opera. To the Western ear the music, based on a five-tone rather than an eight-tone scale, at first seems harsh, discordant and monotonous and the singing, grotesque. The principal musical instruments, borrowed for the most part from the Chinese, are: various types of string instruments (some similar to guitars and mandolins, but played with a bow); a wide variety of percussion instruments, including tambourines, castanets, drums, cymbals and gongs; and a smaller variety of wind instruments, limited largely to flutes and woodwinds.

Western influence has led to the introduction of such instruments as the piano and violin, and Western music has been increasing in popularity in recent years. A notable example of the Western influence is seen in the works of Louise Thai Thi Lan, whose compositions include a symphony, *La Symphonie du Tet* (The Symphony of the New Year), as well as many sonatas and smaller music pieces, including many composed for children. Also indicative of the trend is the Saigon Symphony Orchestra, an organization which harmoniously blends some of the traditional string instruments with Western-style instruments.

Music teaching has become quite common in all major cities and is included in the high school curriculum. In recent years the Hawaiian guitar has become a fad, and guitars can be found even in modest homes. Pianos, however, are still a rarity and are seen only in the homes of the very wealthy.

Nearly all Vietnamese love to sing—an urge that normally expresses itself in their working chants, which seem to be a legacy from very remote antiquity. Workers carrying a load to market often sing rhythmically, and chants—coming alternately from the men and women—frequently are heard in the fields. The words are often meaningless, and the tune is usually sad and in a minor key.

In recent years, due to French and Catholic educational influences, group and choir singing have become widespread. The Communists, and also the Saigon authorities, have made mass singing one of their best psychological weapons. Troops sing on the march, and military bands are appreciated. A whole new generation of marching songs—sometimes based on French melodies, sometimes on Vietnamese themes, but always according to a generally Western rhythm—has been developed.

THE PLASTIC ARTS

Painting

Of the two main schools of painting, one is influenced by the European Renaissance and modern French art and applies European techniques to traditional themes; the other gives an Oriental touch to paintings styled after the European masters. Chinese-style painting was divided originally into two classes. The higher was the art of the scholar, whose great skill in calligraphy was often turned to painting impressionistic nature scenes. The lower was on the level of the craftsmen, who produced the stereotyped ancestor paintings on silk, boxes, screens, enamelware or lacquerware, often in slavish imitation of traditional patterns. These old art forms nearly became extinct after the French conquest, but managed to survive.

Painting on silk still retains its popularity, and the production of lacquerware murals is a flourishing business. Practically all well-to-do Vietnamese homes are adorned with scrolls inscribed with a Vietnamese motto expressed in Chinese characters. Produced by Vietnamese craftsmen specializing in the art of lettering, the scrolls are valued both for their beauty of design and the poetic nature of the text.

Architecture

Vietnam's finest architecture is found in its imperial palaces, mandarin residences, temples, pagodas and tombs—sometimes in wood, sometimes in stone, but nearly always elaborately carved and painted. In general, these structures are modeled after those of the people, differing in their more spacious dimensions. Some temples, rebuilt over and over in nearly identical form, represent very ancient styles. Whatever the origin of the architecture or the influences that have modified it, South Vietnamese proudly assert that it still preserves its own originality. Pillared porches, great peak gables, gracefully sweeping eaves and corners with dragon peaks are featured. Vertical lines are rarely accentuated, and Vietnamese architecture blends well with the natural surroundings, an impression fortified by careful landscaping.

Since French colonial architecture took little account of the native building style, the more modern sections of most Vietnamese cities look like small towns in southern France. More recently, Saigon has begun to construct city blocks with buildings of six or seven stories, and it will eventually lose its distinctly French air.

Sculpture

Sculpture and the other plastic arts until recently have had mainly a religious motif and have been highly stylized. Both wood and stone have been used in carving symbolic religious images, altars and furniture in the Chinese style; only occasionally does the ancient Indonesian or early Vietnamese influence show. As in architecture, style has changed little with time. Some modern artists still employ themes introduced by the Chinese over 1,000 years ago. The temples and tombs abound with statues of rich imagery representing mythical or real animals, genii and the figures of both legendary and recorded history. Often these figures are richly encrusted with stone, ivory or metals or are colorfully painted.

Immediately after the arrival of the French, there was a rapid decline in the number and quality of sculptors and carvers, who had ranked only as craftsmen and depended chiefly upon the royal family and the mandarinate for patronage. To prevent the traditional skills from becoming extinct, the French established arts and craft training centers and arranged for the sale of their products.

Other Arts and Crafts

Of the crafts, lacquerware probably has the highest standards. Vietnamese lacquerware, first developed in the fifteenth century and more modest in appearance than that of Japan or China, is usually inlaid with ivory, horn or mother-of-pearl. Carved lacquerware is rare and usually is in low relief. Originally used chiefly for decorating pagodas, it now is used on panels, screens, furniture, jewel boxes and similar articles. Ivory carving is a flourishing trade, based until recently on elephant tusks from Central Vietnam. Carving of tortoise shells and carving of buffalo bones are two other important crafts.

Vietnamese manual dexterity is fully displayed in the jewelry produced by their craftsmen. Silver, brass and copper are commonly used as settings for ivory, jade and gems. Needlework is also an important form of commercial art, as is the weaving of reeds and bamboo into mats, baskets and panels. Enameled china and porcelain provide another minor art form. It is perhaps in the minor arts that true Vietnamese taste is best revealed; however, cheap, Western machine-made products have had a deadening effect upon these once lively artistic traditions.

CURRENT DEVELOPMENTS AND TRENDS

Since independence, artistic and intellectual endeavor in South Vietnam has been largely initiated and financed by the government and is subject to a large measure of official control. The atmosphere of crisis created by the Communist threat in the countryside and the preoccupation with political, economic and military problems have temporarily diminished interest in poetry, the novel and literary criticism, while heightening that in textbooks and technical treatises. All books circulating in the country are subject to strict government censorship, and the importation of many foreign works—especially those dealing with the Vietnamese political situation—is forbidden.

Substantial United States assistance has been given to the government of South Vietnam in the fields of the graphic arts and crafts, music, motion pictures and the publication of textbooks. Among the more active Vietnamese government agencies in this sphere are those dealing with education and public information in the Ministry of Social and Cultural Affairs.

The government of South Vietnam has established various centers for the arts and crafts, some of which are designed to spur the production of handicrafts for sale abroad. The government also sends abroad traveling art and handicraft exhibits, one of which toured the United States in 1959. The government has also established schools of music and fine arts in Saigon and Hue and sponsors such cultural activities as concerts by the Saigon Symphony Orchestra (see ch. 9, Education).

In the literary field, a number of promising novelists and short-story writers, including Binh Nguyen Loc, Loan Quoc Sy and Vo Phien, are active. A small group of writers, called Sang Tao (creation), is attempting a new literature patterned on similar movements in France since World War II.

The literary monthly *France-Asie* has carried the work of a number of Vietnamese authors. Formerly published in Saigon and subsequently in Tokyo in a combined English-French edition, *France-Asie* has a large following in Vietnam, France and elsewhere. The magazine is owned by a French company and has both Frenchmen and Vietnamese on its editorial staff.

Since 1954, American cultural influence in Vietnam has risen steadily. Aside from United States economic aid and military assistance, there has been an influx of American educators and an intensification of the activities of the United States Information Agency (see ch. 16, Public Information).

Although the use of English has increased since independence, it is unlikely that French literature will soon lose its influence on educated Vietnamese thinking. The Vietnamese decisively rejected French political domination, but it was through French intellectual culture that they were introduced to the thought of the Western world. In French culture they found many characteristics of sharpness, elegance of style, wit and a common liking for casuistry and carefully built argumentation over fine points which paralleled features in their own tradition. Even though these common feelings and values have often made for angry confrontation between the Vietnamese and the French, they also constitute a lasting bond—as one Vietnamese leader put it, "We sometimes hate each other so deeply only because we understand each other so well."

CHAPTER 11

RELIGION

The majority of South Vietnam's 16.1 million inhabitants identify themselves as adherents of Buddhism, one of the world's great religions. Buddhism, founded about 500 B.C., emerged in northern India as an offshoot of the prevailing Hindu faith. Its founder, the monk Gautama, had decried the formalism of Hinduism as it was being interpreted by the priestly caste of Brahmins and challenged their claim to prescriptive rights in showing the way to salvation. After a quest for enlightenment, he arrived at what he felt to be the true path to the spiritual goal of salvation—the so-called Middle Path of commonsense and moderation. Open to all classes and conditions of men, the Middle Path rested its hope on the belief that a man could achieve deliverance by conducting his life on a middle course, avoiding the extremes of sensuality or an uncompromising asceticism.

In succeeding centuries, two principal forms or branches arose within Buddhism: Theravada (sometimes called Hinayana) and Mahayana. The predominant majority of South Vietnam's estimated 11.3 million to 12.8 million Buddhists are Mahayana Buddhists. The Theravada minority, numbering about 2 million, is made up largely of ethnic Cambodians living in the Mekong Delta region. In all, some 16 Buddhist sects are represented.

Two religious movements indigenous to the Mekong Delta, both founded in this century, enjoy important followings. The Cao Dai, the older of the two, is represented in the rural sectors of the southern Delta region. A self-styled reformed Buddhist sect, Cao Dai is in fact a synthesis of different beliefs drawing on a wide range of ethical teachings and writings, including those of Confucius, Jesus and Victor Hugo. It has 1 million to 2 million adherents, distributed among the main body of believers and numerous dissident splinter groups. The Hoa Hao, like the Cao Dai, also identifies itself as a reformed Buddhist sect but unlike it has in fact preserved a distinctive Buddhist coloration. Concentrated especially in the area between the Mekong River and the Song Hua Giang, the Hoa Hao has an estimated membership of about 1 million.

Catholicism was introduced to Vietnam by European missionaries in the sixteenth century and since the late nineteenth century has played an important role in the country's political life. Catholic-sponsored educational institutions had a large part in transmitting Western culture to the country. In early 1966, Catholics numbered 1.5 million persons, or 10 percent of the population, but their religious influence was not commensurate, partly because Catholicism precluded veneration of ancestors, a cornerstone of Vietnamese cultural tradition. In some cases, economic or political factors played a role in conversions.

Other organized religions represented in the country in tiny minorities include Christianity in its Protestant form, Hinduism, Islam and the Bahai faith, a religion which emerged out of one of the main branches of Islam in the mid-nineteenth century. Islam has its body of faithful among the remnants of the Cham population who number some 35,000 and are found in the central coastal region. Protestantism, introduced in the early twentieth century, has made little headway, having won fewer than 10,000 converts.

Beyond the realm of organized religion lies an equally important influence on Vietnamese life and thought, that of Confucianism, the ethical system originating in China in the teachings of the moral philosopher Confucius (551–479 B.C.) and his followers. Confucianism is present, in human, economic and social terms, throughout Vietnamese society, among all persons of Vietnamese ancestry, no matter what their professed religion. Until the late nineteenth century, Confucian values, learned in the home and from exposure to the Chinese classics, were universally held, supporting the traditional family structure and ideals of government (see ch. 7, Family; ch. 12, Social Values; ch. 17, Political Values and Attitudes). In the modern period changes in traditional attitudes and values are being brought about as a result of Westernization and the pressing conditions of life; nevertheless nearly everyone, including young persons educated abroad, continues, in one degree or another, to feel the impact of the country's Confucian heritage.

Similarily, but on another level, the animist beliefs in good and evil spirits, both animate and inanimate, which antedate the organized faiths, also permeate the society. The existence of such beliefs since ancient times is revealed in centuries-old legends, in which the underlying assumption is that all phenomena and forces in the universe— heaven and earth, rain and wind, mountains and rivers—are controlled by spirits upon whose good will man depends. Early Vietnamese peoples apparently also believed that the souls of the dead reappeared in a new incarnation. These souls, if propitiated, would provide humans with protection; if ignored, they would send sickness and death. Such indigenous concepts later came under the influence of Buddhist, Confucian and Taoist ideas introduced from China, to form with them the complex melange of beliefs and ceremonies which characterizes Vietnamese religion at the popular level today.

Persons who regard themselves as Buddhists, collectively comprising the great majority of South Vietnam's population, are found at all social levels, in all occupation groups, in all regions and in city and countryside alike. The Buddhist population, taken to include all persons who do not identify themselves as adherents of some other faith, includes an estimated 70 to 80 percent of the population. Buddhist spokesmen have stated that individuals who participate in Buddhist religious life by attending rituals at the pagoda represent only a minority of this group. Estimates of the number of those who join in Buddhist rituals outside the home range from 2 million to less than 6 million persons; the remainder of the Buddhist community is inactive and basically secular.

In general, devout and strongly traditionalist Buddhists are found in greater numbers in the five northern provinces (formerly Central Vietnam) than in the south. Hue, in the northern province of Thua Thien, was for centuries the imperial capital and a seat of classical Chinese culture and learning. The Buddhist revival movement of the mid-twentieth century an effort to purify the faith by ridding it of adulterating elements borrowed from other beliefs and to strengthen it through systematic organization, has been most successful in this area. Monks from the northern provinces have played a significant leadership role in the revival movement.

In the southern portion of the country, advocates of traditional culture and Confucian ethics are fewer and less vocal. The area, by contrast to the northern provinces, was long a frontier region, receiving the overflow of people from Central and North Vietnam. After the imposition of French colonial rule it accommodated relatively easily to the foreign presence, and, as a local elite developed, its members tended to emulate the French way of life. Many of them adopted, superficially at least, the Roman Catholic religious faith of their rulers.

The Catholic population of the country is made up of native Catholics and refugees from North Vietnam, in approximately equal numbers. Native Catholics in both the northern provinces and the delta region are settled mainly in or around urban areas and in the countryside of the coastal area where the first Catholic missionaries landed. As a result of efforts by Catholic educational missionaries in the highland regions some *montagnards*, too, accepted the faith. Refugees from North Vietnam, of whom about 700,000 entered the country at the time of the signing of the Geneva Agreement in 1954, have been established in various sectors of the country, including some resettlement areas in the highlands.

For over four centuries the Catholic Church in Vietnam has found itself alternatively opposed and supported by the government. During the precolonial period Vietnamese rulers in all three historic divisions of the country (North, Central and South) frequently banned the faith and persecuted its missionaries. The colonial administrators, however, reversed the fortunes of the missionary community, which under French rule enjoyed privileged status. Catholic priests collaborated closely with the colonial authorities, and Catholic churches, schools, convents and higher educational institutions in Vietnam flourished. Under former President Ngo Dinh Diem, himself a Catholic, the position of the Church and its adherents was further enhanced.

With the rise of important Catholics to top positions in government and the influx of refugees from the North in 1954 which suddenly doubled the Catholic population, Buddhist monks began, despite the essential passivity of the religion, to organize for greater strength. Buddhist organizations, under the supervision of a central authority, were systematically expanded throughout the country, and in the absence of political organization at the village level, the religious bodies took on the functions of a political party.

Buddhist leaders, representing themselves as the most authentic spokesmen for the majority of Vietnamese, including especially the rural population, asserted that a passive attitude was no longer appropriate and that secular means would need to be employed to help people realize their aims. As stated by a young Saigon monk: "In the past the monks have not dealt in business and politics, but when the government is not giving people what they want, it is time for the monks to step in." Political activities of the type in which the Vietnamese monks came to engage presented no conflict with their essentially passive faith, as the doctrine of nonviolence denounces killing but not the sacrifice of one's own life for a just cause.

RELIGIOUS HISTORY

The inhabitants of the first Vietnamese kingdom, established by legend in what is now North Vietnam, saw themselves as existing in intimate association with the supernatural world. They shared a common animistic belief in a host of powerful spirits and genii controlling all phenomena and forces in the universe and supposedly inhabiting rivers, mountains, rocky glens, trees and other natural features. Religious activity centered on the propitiation of these spirits through various sacrificial ceremonies. Such ceremonies were mainly concerned with the agricultural cycle, marking the seasons important to production, chiefly spring and fall.

Confucianism, Buddhism and Taoism, a religion and philosophy founded in China in the sixth century B.C., were introduced into the Red River Delta following the Chinese conquest in 111 B.C. During the next millennium, Vietnamese intellectuals were exposed to Confucian and Taoist thought through the study of Chinese classical literature, but neither body of teachings at that time established a broad base of popular support. Mahayana Buddhism, on the other hand, appears to have been initially more acceptable to the Vietnamese than either the rationalism of Confucianism or the individualistic mysticism of Taoism. Under Chinese rule, monks, civil servants and merchants spread the Buddhist faith through the Red River Delta and the region to the south where it became a major influence on developing Vietnamese culture.

In the early Christian centuries, several main trends were distinguishable within the common body of Buddhist thought. The Chinese monk Mou Po, who lived in the second century A.D. and is credited with being the first propagator of Buddism in Vietnam, represented the point of view of the Rationalist sects (in Chinese T'ien-T'ai) who believe that reason and knowledge provide the true path to salvation. This school has minimal influence in South Vietnam today. In the sixth century A.D., however, the Dhyana school (in Chinese, Ch'an; in Japanese, Zen), teaching the contemplative path to salvation rather than the path of reason, was organized. The influence of the Dhyana school is still pervasive and powerful in South Vietnam.

In the newly independent Dai Co Viet (Great Viet State) Buddhism further expanded its base of support among the common people, among whom it merged with indigenous beliefs and practices to become the dominant popular faith. At the same time, Buddhist influence on political affairs increased. A Buddhist hierarchy was established, whose most outstanding scholars served the throne in important advisory capacities. The Ly dynasty (A.D. 1009–1225) represented a high point in the history of Vietnamese Buddhism, during which it became accepted as the state religion. The first Ly king was an ardent Buddhist, who abdicated the throne in his later years and spent the remainder of his life as a monk. His successor, Ly Thai-ton (A.D. 1028–1054), was equally devout, and under him, Buddhism enjoyed unprecedented royal patronage. The crown made lavish gifts to the pagodas, and with this accumulated wealth some pagodas developed into vast feudal domains. The Buddhist clergy was exempted from taxation and military service, and its most scholarly members advised the king on political and military matters.

The later Ly rulers and the early kings of the Tran dynasty (A.D. 1225–1440) encouraged Confucianism and Taoism along with Buddhism, and in this period these three systems flourished alongside one another. Confucian temples were built and frequented by members of the court, and after 1075 government officials were recruited by public examinations in Confucian classics. Confucian scholar-officials, known collectively as the mandarinate, won renown both as learned men and outstanding administrators.

After the Chinese interregnum, Confucianism assumed a preeminent position at the court, which it held until the consolidation of French colonial rule in the late nineteenth century. The Le and Nguyen dynasties promulgated and enforced several laws intended to curtail the growth of the Buddhist and Taoist priesthood. Under the Le dynasty Buddhists and Taoists had to pass an examination in their religion before they could enter the priesthood: a law of the Nguyen dynasty required that they qualify for a license from the Ministry of Rites. For a period in the fifteenth century the Buddhist clergy was placed under surveillance, and it was forbidden to construct new pagodas, except with special permission. In time, the formerly high intellectual standards of the Buddhist monks degenerated. By the sixteenth century few of them were represented among the intellectual elite; most were poorly educated and knew little of the faith they espoused.

The secondary position of Buddhism in the ruling circles by no means meant, however, that the religion had lost its popular support. Although no longer a state religion, the object of court ceremonies or the subject of scholarly treatises by learned officials, Buddhism nevertheless was deeply entrenched among the people. Merged with Taoism, which had degenerated in Vietnam to a system of magic, and with indigenous beliefs and practices, it enveloped the daily lives of the villagers.

Christianity was introduced by Portuguese, French and Spanish Catholic missionaries in the sixteenth and seventeenth centuries. Portuguese Dominicans arrived in the Mekong Delta (which at that time was not yet under Vietnamese control) in A.D. 1550 and in Quang Nam Province in central Vietnam in the 1580's. During the next century, French Jesuits became increasingly active; efforts at propagating the faith produced a substantial number of converts and the nucleus of an indigenous clergy. By 1685 it was estimated that there were 800,000 Catholics in Vietnam, of whom 200,000 were in the north and 600,000 in the center and south. Credited with establishing a solid base for the spread of Catholicism in Vietnam was a prominent figure of this era, the Jesuit Father Alexander de Rhodes, who studied Vietnamese history and culture, traveled widely and invented a Roman letter script for the Vietnamese language. In 1659 he returned to Paris to found the Société des Missions Etrangères (Society of Foreign Missions) which sent increasing numbers of clergymen to Vietnam.

The eighteenth century was a time of indiscriminate persecution of Catholic missionaries and converts by Confucian officials who associated Catholicism with imperial expansion and resented efforts to graft an alien religious tradition onto their own integrated and highly stable society. Many Catholics were imprisoned or killed. Emperor Gia Long (A.D. 1802–1820), who, like his predecessors, regarded the new religion as potentially corruptive of local authority, nevertheless tolerated the faith out of gratitude to a Catholic bishop who had helped him secure the throne. Persecution began, however, with the reign of his successor and continued until France conquered Vietnam.

Under the French, the teaching of Catholicism again became completely free, and members of the priesthood received strong support from the colonial administrators. A Vietnamese clergy was developed, and preaching education and charitable works were launched on a large-scale basis.

In the first half of the twentieth century, two indigenous religious movements developed in the Mekong Delta region of South Vietnam, the Cao Dai and the Hoa Hao. Le Van Trung, a one-time colonial official, laid the doctrinal foundations of the Cao Dai faith and established a priestly hierarchy modeled on Roman Catholic lines. A capable organizer, he increased the number of adherents to over 20,000 within a single year, with membership eventually reaching between 1 million and 2 million. The Hoa Hao was formed in the 1930's. Its founder was Huynh Phu So, son of a village notable in Chau Doc Province in the western delta. Huynh Phu So attracted large followings, and the number of his followers grew rapidly to over 1 million adherents. Both the Cao Dai and the Hoa Hao quickly took on a political coloration, mixing anticolonialism with religious tenets (see ch. 14, Political Dynamics).

During the 1920's, a Buddhist revival, begun in republican China, spread southward to Vietnam, where it gained a considerable number of supporters, predominantly among the intellectual elite. Regional Buddhist associations were established in South, Central and North Vietnam in 1931, 1932 and 1934, respectively. World War II put a moratorium on expansion, but in 1958, despite the effect of the Indochina War, then in progress, the interrupted activities were resumed. Hanoi was the focal point of revivalist activity, and the clergy launched a number of welfare and charitable efforts, including the establishment of an orphanage, a private college and a center for rehabilitation of paraplegics.

Under President Diem, who acceded to power in South Vietnam in mid-1954, the Catholic community came to enjoy even stronger support from the government than it had had under French rule. Catholic administrators, many of them refugees from North Vietnam, filled key positions in the army, police and civil service. Catholics allegedly also were given special benefits of other types such as in respect to the obtainment of visas and of permission to stage public ceremonies. Meantime, the size of the Catholic community was expanding enormously, largely because of the massive influx of refugees from the North, and also because some educated South Vietnamese saw conversion as a path to posts in the civil bureaucracy and the military.

The Buddhist response to growing Catholic strength was to organize. The purpose in organizing, as declared by the Buddhist hierarchy and leading laymen, was to further scholarly interest in Buddhist teachings and to promote stricter discipline and standards among the priesthood. Presumably, however, the Buddhist leadership sought also to assert itself more effectively in the nation's secular affairs. The framework for a cohesive national organization emerged in 1955, with the formation of the General Buddhist Association (also known as the Buddhist Association of Vietnam) representing six of the country's 16 Mahayana sects. With headquarters after 1958 at Xa Loi Pagoda in Saigon, the group at first concerned itself publicly with theological and charitable affairs alone. In the early 1960's, however, growing resentment against the Catholic-oriented administration brought the organization and its leading spokesmen increasingly into the political arena (see ch. 14, Political Dynamics).

THE FAITHS

The greatest single influence on traditional Vietnamese social institutions, overshadowing that of any organized religion, has been that of Confucianism. One of the basic assumptions relating to the nature of life experience which is shared, though not necessarily expressed in words, by nearly all Vietnamese derives from Confucian teachings. The concept is that of universal order, in which the processes of heaven and earth are viewed as displaying a fundamental regularity and harmony of operation. The sun, the moon, the stars and the four seasons as well as all human relationships between individuals and within the family, the state and the society are controlled by natural principles. In their fundamental makeup, human beings, too, are completely in harmony with this arranged natural order. Not all persons, however, are equally able to control their passions and bring their inner selves into accord with it.

The structure of Confucian society was based on the notion that the particular individual in closest harmony with the natural principles, or order, was entrusted by heaven with the responsibility of governing mankind. He was regarded as the son of heaven, the emperor. Morally superior men, who were better able than common men to conform to the natural principles, helped the ruler to govern the people. They were subordinate to the will of the emperor as he in turn was subordinate to the will of heaven. As scholar-officials, they made up the highest ranking social class, followed in order by farmers, artisans and merchants.

Confucian doctrine and the state and family rites which developed in connection with it had religious aspects, but their focus was on the secular ethics of individual conduct and social relationships. Confucian scholarship and public ritual in which sacrifices were offered to heaven were the province of the emperor and the scholar-officials, and only they were permitted to perform the rites. Confucian precepts, however, molded the values of the simplest villager, and every family head performed the rites honoring his ancestors.

Holding up the patriarchal family as the ideal human institution, the Confucianists framed their morality in terms of the duties and obligations of child to parent, wife to husband, younger brother to elder brother and of all to the father as the senior representative of the family group; the welfare and continuity of the family group was held to be more important than the interests of any individual member. The veneration of ancestors symbolized in the rites before the ancestral altar affirmed the conception of the family as a supremely valued continuum of all its members—deceased, living and yet to be born. The Confucian scholars extended the familial model to comprehend the nation as a whole, with the emperor as father and the mandarins and the people, respectively, as superior and common men. The virtues which were regarded as necessary for the harmonious functioning of this hierarchy were benevolent love, righteousness, propriety, wisdom and faithfulness.

Mastery of the Confucian classics, demonstrated in a series of rigorous examinations, was the prerequisite to a place in the imperial bureaucracy. The rites performed by the emperor and his officials symbolically reinforced the Confucian teaching of a hierarchically arranged natural order, the harmony of which was to be maintained by the example of those above and the loyalty and obedience of those below.

The high ideals of Confucianism undoubtedly found expression in the conduct of many scholar-officials, and Confucian precepts strongly influenced the family life, personal relationships and attitudes of the illiterate mass of the people toward authority. Confucianism, however, had little to offer in the spiritual realm. Moreover, its rarefied ethical precepts often constituted little more than a verbal screen for behavior that departed widely from the formal ideal.

The advent of colonial rule in the nineteenth century destroyed the mandarinate by reducing the scholar-officials to the status of subordinate agents of the French administrators. Divested of its prestige as the ideology of a ruling elite, Confucianism also declined, a process hastened by the competition of new ideals and values from the West. The Confucian curricula and the mandarinal examinations were abandoned in South Vietnam in the late nineteenth century and in North and Central Vietnam between 1915 and 1918. Advanced Confucian studies thereafter were left to the interest of a small number of individual scholars.

Despite the decline in its significance as a formal intellectual tradition, Confucianism in the mid-twentieth century remains a pervasive force in the country's cultural heritage. Confucian precepts continue to influence, in one degree or another, the thought and behavior of all ethnic Vietnamese. Advocates of a return to traditional culture and education, moreover, comprise a respected and influential, though not numerically predominant, segment of society.

Within the traditional Confucian social framework, the individual found no conflict in accepting the personal solace and hope proferred by Buddhism. Besides this, uneducated persons and even, in varying degrees Confucian-educated persons sought explanations and solutions to problems beyond their control in Taoist divination and magic, and in good and bad spiritual entities and forces.

Taoism, founded in China in the sixth century B.C. by Lao Tzu, began as a system of speculative philosophy centering on the notion of man's oneness with the universe. Its metaphysical preoccupation, based on principles which made passivity the objective of human existence, contrasted with the Confucian emphasis on the practical ordering of social relations. Later some Taoist scholars lost all touch with the thought of the Chinese founder of the faith, and Taoism in Vietnam degenerated into a system of magic. Taoist sorcerers assert that the world of the supernatural is populated by both good and evil spirits with whom they are able to communicate. In touch with the spirit world through meditation or occultism, they claim to be able to cure illness or alleviate misfortune.

Attaining the favor of good spirits and avoiding the malice of evil ones is a continuing preoccupation in Vietnamese life, characteristic of group as well as individual behavior. A multiplicity of local and regional cults exists, each devoted to the veneration of a protective deity or collection of deities associated with the well-being of a particular community. An important cult is that of founders of the crafts.

Artisans of all types honor the so-called patron saint of their craft, who may be either the originator of the art or the first person to teach it to the people of a particular village or area. Guardian spirits preside over various occupations. Boatbuilders, for example, make offerings to their local guardian spirit in the ceremonies of "The Squaring of the Wood," when the first blow of the adz is struck; "The Joining of the Mortises," when the three pieces of the keel are joined; and "The Placing of the Beam," when the supports for the main mast are put in place.

Villages, especially those in Central Vietnam, almost always have their own special deity, known as the Guardian Spirit of the Village, whose veneration is a focal point of community religious activity. To

the villagers, the Guardian Spirit symbolizes their cultural unique-
ness as well as their future hopes. He is a majestic figure of power, a
spiritual bond that makes the village a cohesive unit. In most instances the Guardian Spirit was originally named centuries ago by the
emperor. The choice usually fell on someone who in his lifetime had
been a highly respected local dignitary, but some of the spirits wor-
shiped in the communal temple of particular villages are legendary
figures; others are celebrated national heroes or heroines, village
fathers, children who died at a young age or victims of violence.

The imperial document naming the Guardian Spirit is deposited in
the inner sanctuary of the communal temple on the principal alter of
the temple, dedicated to the Guardian Spirit. Images or tablets of
the spirit, along with ritual articles, also are placed here. This room
is usually closed to the public. Standing outside are altars dedicated
to other spirits (such as the god of the soil), also revered by the whole
community.

The spirit world of Vietnamese peasant belief is peopled with a
great variety of supernatural beings, most of them malevolent, and
with a host of wandering souls of criminals, spinsters and the victims
of accidents. Vietnamese villagers believe, for example, in a general
category of entities which can be called spirits of nature. All are
associated with topographic features, insects, birds or animals. The
peasant believes that spirits reside in many rock formations, especially
those of peculiar shape in grottoes or in front of temples, or rocks
in river rapids or along the seashores which present particularly great
hazards to vessels. Several varieties of trees, including the fig, are
believed to be inhabited by the souls of young girls who like to appear
on earth and torment young men. The dangerous entities are to be
avoided, placated or otherwise circumvented, and the benevolent ones
may be venerated or appealed to for help.

Another spirit of nature is the Goddess of the Five Elements—
metal, wood, fire, water and earth—who likes to start fires to show
her power. In addition, there are spirits of mountains, rivers, stars,
sun and moon, clouds, rain, wind, thunder, graves and tombs. Coastal
dwellers worship the whale as their special protector; in a similar
manner forest dwellers venerate the tiger.

Buddhism

Buddhism, the predominant organized religion in the country during the modern period, exists in conjunction with these widely held
animistic beliefs. According to Buddhist teaching, every person must
suffer the miseries of life through a series of incarnations, accumulating in successive lives sufficient merit by virtuous conduct to end the
cycle of birth, death and rebirth. This state is called nirvana, or

endless serenity. To achieve this one must eliminate life and everything having roots in life. This is achieved by following the Noble Eightfold Path, which is the essence of the Buddhist concept of right behavior.

The Eightfold Path consists of: Right Views, or sincerity in leading a religious life; Right Thought, or honesty in judgment; Right Speech, or sincerity in speech; Right Conduct, or sincerity in work; Right Livelihood, or sincerity in making a living; Right Effort, or sincerity in aspiration; Right Mindfulness, or sincerity in memory; and Right Concentration, or sincerity in meditation. Buddhist morality is based on the Middle Path of commonsense and moderation—the repudiation of desire conducive to an essential passive attitude toward worldly things.

The doctrinal distinction between Mahayana Buddhism, which predominates in South Vietnam, and Theravada Buddhism, followed chiefly by the Khmer (ethnic Cambodian) minority, rests on their respective views of Gautama Buddha. The Theravada Buddhists regard him as the one Buddha and a great teacher, although not divine. The Mahayanists, on the other hand, teach that he was only one of many "Enlightened Ones" who are deemed manifestations of the fundamental divine power of the universe. Persons who have attained the highest stage of enlightenment as described by Buddha but who choose to remain with their fellow men to be of service to them are known as Bodhisattvas.

Few Vietnamese outside the clergy are acquainted with or care about Buddhism's elaborate cosmology. What appeals to them is Mahayana ritual and imagery, although even these play a limited role in popular religious life. The formalities of Mahayana Buddhism fit more easily into the patterns of indigenous Vietnamese beliefs and practices than do those of Theravada Buddhism; the Mahayana Buddhist saints and supernatural beings are treated in much the same way as are the animist spirits.

The principal schools of thought represented in South Vietnamese Mahayana Buddhism are the Pure Land School and the Dhyana school or School of Meditation (in Chinese, Ch'an; in Japanese, Zen). The School of Meditation, as its name implies, seeks immediate insight, or enlightenment, through contemplation, in contrast to the Pure Land School, in which faith is believed to be sufficient for salvation.

Most persons in North Vietnam and in the northern provinces of South Vietnam are follows of the School of Meditation, which has enjoyed a predominant position in Vietnam for over 1,000 years. Whether or not it retains that preeminence in South Vietnam is debatable, although the strongest evidence points to the conclusion that the Pure Land School is now numerically the largest. A synthesis of the two schools was started in South Vietnam in the 1940's but remains relatively unimportant. Half a dozen or so other minor Mahayana schools exert influence over small numbers of believers.

Theravada Buddhism in South Vietnam is principally represented by the Disciplinary School (Luat Tong). Minor schools are Buddhist Nihilism (Thanh Thuc Tong) and the Realistic School (Cau Xa Tong). These schools of thought, like those representing the Mahayana tradition, are affiliated with the Unified Buddhist Church of Vietnam (Giao Hoi Phat Giao Vietnam Thang Nhat). A minority of schools, including notably a splinter group of the Pure Land group sect, Luc Hoa Tong, remain independent. Some 500 Theravada temples are distributed primarily in the southern Mekong Delta region. Of these temples, about 20 percent have religious schools attached to them in which Buddhist education is offered in Pali, the sacred language of the faith.

In the past, Buddhist temples in Vietnam, which like China was without hierarchical organization, were completely autonomous institutions. Their establishment and administration were entirely by local individuals or the community. The formation of the General Buddhist Association in 1955, the first unified Buddhist organization at the national level, however, signaled the start of efforts to centralize control of village temples and link them in a meaningful way with the highest ranking church authority.

In the post-Ngo period, the Buddhists, building from the groundwork laid in the previous decade, developed an impressive organization. A Buddhist Reunification Congress, convened at Xa Loi Pagoda, Saigon, in late December 1963, resulted in the formation early the following year of the Unified Buddhist Church of Vietnam. Representing the mainstream of the Buddhist movement in the country, the organization eventually gained the support of all major sects and declared itself the regional affiliate for South Vietnam of the World Buddhism Association.

According to the original constitution, later revised, the Unified Buddhist Church has two main branches: the High Council of the Buddhist Hierarchy, known also as the Supreme Council of Vietnamese Sangha (the Monastic or Priestly Order) and the Institute for the Execution of Dharma (The Law of Truth), known also as the High Council for the Execution of Dharma and more commonly as the Buddhist Institute for Secular Affairs. The High Council is composed of eight or more bonzes, of whom at least four must be over 60 years of age. Candidates for chairman are chosen from among the latter group. The chairman is elected by his fellow council members for a 4-year term and may not succeed himself. He is assisted by a deputy superior bonze who must come from a different sect than does the superior bonze. As the preeminent ecclesiastical authority, the High Council serves as a doctrinal advisory group to the Institute for the Execution of Dharma and is responsible for all matters concerning the clergy.

The chairman of the High Council, a post held in mid-1966 by the former president of the General Buddhist Association, the Venerable Thich Tinh Khiet, is the highest ranking dignitary of the church. Immediately under him is the Superior Bonze, who in mid-1966 was the Venerable Thich Toi Than, a prominent member of the Theravada Buddhist community with headquarters at Ky Vien Ty Pagoda in Saigon. Of the other High Council positions, the most powerful is that of secretary general, held by the Venerable Thich Tri Quang, politically prominent Buddhist leader and head of the Buddhist Association of Central Vietnam (see ch. 14, Political Dynamics).

The Buddhist Institute for Secular Affairs originally controlled all activities of the Unified Buddhist Church except those under the jurisdiction of the High Council, but after April 1966 political activities became the sole concern of the newly created Vietnam Buddhist Force (see ch. 14, Political Dynamics). The Institute, headed by the Venerable Thich Tam Chau, former chairman of the Intersect Committee for the Defense of Buddhism, includes both religious and lay representatives among its ranking officials. The principal functions of the organization are reflected in the titles of its six general commissions: the General Commission for Religious Personnel, concerned with clerical affairs; Faith Expansion, concerned with propagation and missions; Rites, concerned with legislation, social affairs and education; Finance and Reconstruction, concerned with construction, budget and finance; Lay Affairs concerned especially with occupation and other special groups; and Youth, concerned with students and youth.

An additional and major responsibility of the Institute for the Execution of Dharma is the expansion of Buddhism among the population, especially its rural segment. An elaborate hierarchy of regional and local associations has been established for this purpose. Ecclesiastically, the country is divided into seven regional units (*mien*), each headed by an eminent bonze, with subordinate provincial, district and village units. Urban subdivisions comparable to the village units are called zones. The *mien* organizations at Hue and Qui Nhon cover the northern provinces; those at Ban Me Thuot, Nha Trang and Chau Phu cover the Central Highlands, the coastal lowlands of central Vietnam and the delta area, respectively. Two *miens* are centered in the capital city, one covering the Saigon area, the other concerned with North Vietnamese Buddhists wherever located. Each provincial Buddhist association is administered by a provincial representative assisted by a committee of seven persons, including monks and lay people. Similarly, village and city zones are served by small com mittees of monks and laymen whose members are elected by their colleagues for 2-year terms.

Efforts by the church to associate itself with special elements of the population were well along by mid-1966. For example, organizations called Buddhist Families, offering programs for children and adolescents aged 8 through 17, were generally operative throughout the country. Patterned after the Boy and Girl Scout movements, the Buddhist Families are uniformed groups, subdivided by age and sex. Each unit is associated with a particular pagoda, and its members are given religious education. They also perform social services, drills and honorary guard duties at religious events.

Other Buddhist youth groups have shown varying degrees of success. The Buddhist School Youth of Vietnam, for instance, is by far the largest in membership, but it lacks a well-defined program of activities. Efforts to mobilize support for Buddhism among the adult population were reflected in the establishment of organizations aimed especially at intellectuals and members of the armed forces.

Special training for the clergy is provided in a number of institutions affiliated with the Unified Buddhist Church. The Buddhist Academy at An Quang Pagoda in Saigon provides a secondary education for some 180 monks; the Khuong Viet Buddhist Training Center' with headquarters at Thanh Minh Pagoda in Saigon, provides primary and secondary Buddhist education for priests and nuns and, in addition, offers instruction in elementary studies for laymen. Higher training of Buddhist monks up to the licentiate level is also offered at the Buddhist Academy in Nha Trang, which was established in 1956 and has an enrollment of about 40 persons.

Lay and clerical persons both are enrolled at the Institute for Higher Buddhist Studies in Saigon, an affiliate of the Institute for Execution of Dharma. Established in March 1964, the institution, with several hundred students, conducts a teaching program at the postsecondary school level with special attention to subjects of Buddhist interest. Buddhist authorities plan to expand this school into a university.

South Vietnam already has one Buddhist university, Van Hanh University, opened in February 1965. Unlike other Buddhist universities in Southeast Asia, it offers courses in the humanities as well as in Buddhist studies, including history and geography, letters, philosophy and human sciences. Early in 1966 classes were being held on a temporary basis in two Saigon temples, while funds were being raised for the procurement of grounds and the construction of buildings for a complete campus. Exclusively for lay youth is the Quang Trung Judo School in Saigon; opened in April 1964, it trains some 3,000 youth, including several hundred girls' in the art of self-defense.

Mobilization of popular support for Buddhist causes is additionally sought through the temple schools and through the distribution of extensive literature published by the Buddhist press. Included are several weekly and monthly reviews, among the best known of which are *Chanh Dau* (Right Path), semiofficial newspaper of the Unified Buddhist Church, and *To Quang* (Compassion), a monthly published by the Institute for the Execution of Dharma.

Educational opportunities are slowly raising the training standards of the Vietnamese Buddhist clergy, most of whom come from humble backgrounds and have had little formal instruction. Village monks, although they recite the appropriate litanies, are rarely learned in the sacred literature of the faith they profess.

A leading Buddhist spokesman states that the hierarchy is stratified into five levels. In descending order of rank these are: Hoa Thuong (Supreme), Thuong Thoa (Honorable), Dai Dui (Reverend), They (Teacher) and Cau (Novice). Training, especially in rural areas, has traditionally been casual and informal. Village monks usually received their instruction in prayers, ritual and doctrine from another monk in the same locality, sometimes a relative; a few went on to further studies in a nearby pagoda.

The several programs recently established by the Unified Buddhist Church, providing higher education and advanced training in Buddhist study for members of the priesthood, represent an attempt to raise standards among its members. A few leading bonzes are highly intellectual and sophisticated persons, cognizant of political and social developments throughout the world. In addition to bonzes, there are Buddhist laymen, sometimes called "lay monks," who differ from other members of the laity in that they observe 5 of the 10 monastic interdictions (against killing, alcohol, smoking, sexual pleasures and stealing) and who may perform rites in the absence of a bona fide bonze.

South Vietnamese monks, who unlike those in neighboring countries do not beg for food, generally wear gray garments; maroon robes usually indicate that the wearer is a North Vietnamese refugee. Saffron robes are frequently reserved for more formal occasions.

The Cao Dai

Between 1 and 2 million South Vietnamese belong to the Dai Dao Tam Ky Pho Do, or Third Amnesty of God, popularly known as the Cao Dai. Cao Dai doctrine draws heavily on Buddhism, Taoism and Confucianism as well as on the moral teachings of Jesus. Its ritual shows the strong influence of Vietnamese folk religion, and it has adopted some organizational features from the Catholic Church, with the addition of female cardinals. Its adherents are most numerous in the section of the Mekong Delta between the Mekong and the Song Hau Giang Rivers.

The center of the Cao Dai faith is in the city of Tay Ninh, 60 miles northwest of Saigon, seat of its cathedral and its administrative organization. The cathedral expresses the background of the sect in its structure and decor: its church towers are European in inspiration; the open sweep of its floor suggests a mosque, and its wall decorations of plaster cobras and dragons are reminiscent of a Buddhist pagoda. Statues of Confucius, Jesus, Buddha, Lao-tzu, Brahma, Siva and Vishnu are prominently displayed. According to its founder:

> We do not believe that there is only one true and uniquely sanctifying belief. The Creator has scattered the seeds of truth over the centuries and over the continents of the earth. Jesus or Buddha or Lao-tzu, their message is at bottom only a form of the great divine truth. In their depths all religions come together.

Dominating the great nave of the cathedral is a single staring eye— "the eye of God"—the supreme symbol of the religion. Ceremonies are held several times daily in the cathedral. During the midnight ceremony the spirits are questioned and, according to the believers, God speaks to them through a medium.

The Cao Dai claims several spiritual "fathers" who are believed to give guidance to the sect through a medium. Three of these spiritual guides are Sun Yat-sen, who overthrew the reign of the emperors in China and founded the Chinese Republic; Trang Thinh, a Vietnamese diviner, whose prophecies about the future are still highly regarded in Vietnam; and Victor Hugo, the French writer and poet.

The central organization of the Cao Dai consists of three main bureaus. The first, the Executive Corps (Cuu Trung Dai), controls the temporal administration. The head of this bureau is held to be the Giao Tong, or "pope"—not a living person, but the sanctified spirit of the Vietnamese philosopher Ly Thai Bach. The bureau in charge of religious affairs, called the Legislative Body (Hiep Thien Dai), is headed by the highest ranking living member of the sect, the Superior Ho Phap. The third bureau, the Charity Corps (Co-quan Phoc Thien), is a welfare agency charged with caring for the poor and invalid of the sect.

From the close of World War II, until mid-1955, the Cao Dai played an important role in South Vietnam's political affairs. It literally constituted a state within a state, administering and controlling a sizable area northwest of Saigon and maintaining its own army, which received support first from the Japanese and then from the French. In the spring and summer of 1955 the political power of the Cao Dai was broken (along with that of the Hoa Hao, a smaller politicoreligious sect, and that of the Binh Xuyen, a political and racketeering organization, by the national government under the leadership of President Diem through a combination of negotiations and force. In

February 1956 the Superior of the Cao Dai, Pham Cong Tac, fled to Cambodia, and South Vietnamese troops took over Tay Ninh.

With the surrender of its armies and the death of Pham Cong Tac after his flight to Cambodia, the sect lost most of its temporal power, but none of its religious fervor. In South Vietnam the sect supports, at least outwardly, the national government. In Cambodia across the border, the sect has an unknown number of adherents in the Vietnamese minority and constitutes a dissident group which is inclined to cooperate with the Communist-sponsored self-styled National Front for the Liberation of South Vietnam.

The Hoa Hao

The Hoa Hao movement, essentially a variant of Theravada Buddhism, was founded in 1939 by Huynh Phu So. He impressed people with his sincerity and zeal, and stories spread of miraculous cures he performed with simple herbs and acupuncture—a Chinese medical technique for curing illness, by which the skin is pierced with needles.

Huynh Phu So set forth his religious ideas—first preached on village street corners and canal intersections—in his book *Sam Gian* (Oracles and Prayers). His basic theme stressed the importance of internal faith and the unimportance of external experience. "It is better," he wrote, "to pray with a pure heart before the family altar than to perform elaborate ceremonies in a pagoda, clad in the robes of an unworthy priest."

Huynh Phu So approved of prayers and offerings only to Buddha, ancestors and national heroes. Every member of the sect was expected to pray four times a day. Although the ancestors were venerated, Huynh Phu So particularly disapproved of elaborate and expensive funerals.

In the chaos following the Japanese surrender, Huynh Phu So led his followers into politics, forming the Social Democratic Party, usually called the Dan Xa (see ch. 14, Political Dynamics). In April 1947 he was ambushed and killed by the Viet Minh, and his remains were scattered. No leader of equal stature emerged in the sect after Huynh Phu So's death. Consequently, the extensive area southwest of Saigon, where the Hoa Hao were concentrated, broke up into a number of so-called Hoa Hao "baronies," ruled like feudal states.

In the spring of 1955 the central government in Saigon asserted its control over the entire area, using military force. Several of the Hoa Hao leaders were outlawed, and the most powerful of them, Ba Cut, arrested in April 1956, was tried and executed in July.

Catholicism

Catholicism, which many Vietnamese associate with imperial expansion and resent as an alien Western religion, established a solid position in the country under French rule and capitalized on its gains under President Diem. The French encouraged Catholicism as a balance to Buddhism. During their administration and most of the decade thereafter, Catholicism added to its following, expanded its hierarchy, and engaged in numerous teaching, health and charitable programs.

Under President Ngo, Catholics in general had an advantage over non-Catholics in obtaining government positions. In addition, opportunties for education were relatively more accessible to Catholics, through the mission-operated schools. In 1957, at the instigation of the President's brother, the archbishop of Hue, a new university under Catholic direction was established in Da Lat. In 1959, in Saigon Cathedral, Vietnam was dedicated to the Heart of the Immaculate Virgin, a gesture which symbolically placed South Vietnam among the Catholic countries of the world.

Official estimates, published in 1966, gave the Roman Catholic population of the country as 1,560,000 persons, of whom about half are refugees from North Vietnam. The refugees are, for the most part, poorly educated peasants who in North Vietnam had lived in exclusively Catholic villages where their contacts with non-Catholic Vietnamese had been rare. In South Vietnam they again found themselves largely isolated from the rest of the population, having been placed at first in hastily created resettlement centers and later moved to permanent refugee villages, usually in the Central Highlands.

Catholics born in South Vietnam live mainly in the cities and the coastal areas of the northern provinces. The Saigon Catholic community is upper-middle class and is well represented in the civil service, the liberal professions and the armed forces. An estimated 25 percent of the country's educated elite are Catholics. Catholics of the northern provinces are a heavily outnumbered minority and, reportedly, have reverted to a self-effacing role.

The country is divided ecclesiastically into 13 dioceses, with some 700 local parishes, each headed by a priest. Over all is a papal delegate stationed in Hue. Several religious orders with branches throughout the country carry out welfare activities. In early 1966 there were more than 1,700 priests, 4,000 nuns and 625 seminarists. Some 265,000 primary-level students and 133,000 high school students were in Catholic-run schools, while the University of Da Lat had an enrollment of 1,300. Several small Catholic newspapers are published, of which one had a circulation of approximately 15,000 (see ch. 9, Education). The Catholic Church operated 26 hospitals, 7 leprosariums, 55 orphanages and 19 resthouses.

Other

American Protestant missions have operated in the country since 1911, at first in the Mekong Delta region. Not until 1929 did the court permit Protestant missionaries to preach in the northern provinces, which at that time were part of the French Protectorate of Annam. Protestant evangelists have concentrated their efforts especially on the *montagnards* in the Central Highlands region. Baptist and Seventh Day Adventist missions are, however, found in several cities. Some Protestant students are being sent to the United States for advanced theological training. Approximately 2,000 North Vietnamese Protestant refugees are grouped in three separate Protestant refugee villages.

Other faiths represented by small communities of believers in South Vietnam are Hinduism, Islam, and the Bahai. Of these, Islam, with between 30,000 and 40,000 followers, principally among the Chams, is probably numerically the largest. Hinduism has adherents among the Indian moneylenders in Saigon and other major towns.

PRACTICES

Certain characteristics of religious behavior are shared by most of the people. Nearly every ethnic Vietnamese (excepting perhaps some converts to Christianity) retains some of the Confucian general respect for order and harmony. Solemn national sacrifices in Confucian temples are no longer held, but most Vietnamese families continue to observe family rites in honor of their own ancestors.

In addition, most Vietnamese, whatever their professed religion, place of residence, type of education or level of sophistication, are influenced at one time or another, by magic, fortunetelling and geomancy (the discovery of hidden knowledge through interpretation of figures or lines). Diviners and other specialists in the occult are in popular demand, diagnosing supernatural causes of illness, establishing lucky dates for personal undertakings, or predicting the future. They are most frequently resorted to by villagers and the urban poor.

Many Vietnamese believe that individual destiny is guided by a particular star, and that the positioning of this star in the heavens on his birth date predisposes him to good or ill fortune at certain times. By consulting his horoscope, he can make the most of auspicious periods and avoid disaster during inauspicious periods. Traditionally, it was most unusual for any couple to marry without consulting an astrologer, who not only determined whether the potential partners were suitably matched on the basis of their individual horoscopes but fixed the date of the ceremony.

188

Before building a house, some Vietnamese employ a geomancer to choose the site, hoping to avoid disturbing any potentially vengeful spirits. Selecting the proper site for family tombs is equally important.

The Family

Family religious observances take place in the home, or in the family temple if there is one. Most families have both an ancestral altar and an altar dedicated to Buddha placed in a prominent place in the main room of the house. There may also be smaller altars to lesser deities, such as the God of the Hearth. The ancestral altar is set with incense burners, candlesticks, trays and bowl stands, together with the ancestral tablets, which in traditional households are of the past four generations. Those of the fifth generation have been buried. Cao Dai, Hoa Hao and Catholic households also contain family altars honoring their own deities.

The chief of the extended family, or, in the immediate family, the head of the household, is responsible for seeing that the ancestors are properly venerated. The rites are performed on feast days and the anniversary of the death of each ancestor. They consist of invoking the spirit of the particular individual being honored and making sacrificial offerings of betel, wine and incense. Besides the individual anniversaries, sacrifices are offered to all the ancestors in general on other days, the most important of which is Tet, the New Year celebration. Besides this, whenever there is an occasion of family joy or sorrow—a wedding, an anniversary, success in examination, a promotion or a funeral—the ancestors are informed.

In traditional households, there are several occasions for family rituals other than in connection with the Cult of the Ancestors. Whenever a celebration takes place, the family is always careful to make an offering to the God of the Hearth. Prayers and sacrifices are also made to the God of the Hearth when misfortune falls upon the household. The Kitchen God is another lesser deity, honored on the twenty-third day of the last lunar month, the day when, according to legend, he reports to heaven on the good and bad deeds of all mankind.

The devout Buddhist family gathers for thrice-daily rituals held before the Buddhist altar. These rites consist of burning incense, kowtowing, reciting prayers and making offerings of food and tea. Similarily, in Catholic homes members gather each evening to recite the rosary before the family shrine.

Village

The *dinah*, or communal temple, is the focal point of village religious activity, and it is here that the village offers sacrifices to its

Guardian Spirit and to the God of the Soil. Four main village celebrations are held each year: Cau An (Wish for Peace), a ritual calling on the Guardian Spirit of the village to bring peace and prosperity; Ha Dien (Descent to the Fields) and Thuong Dien (Ascent from the Fields), celebrations honoring the Spirit of Agriculture and the Village Guardian Spirit; and Chap Mieu (Appreciation at the Temple), festivities marking the end of the harvest. Catholic villagers do not participate in rituals associated with the cults of the Guardian Spirit, but usually appoint an individual to attend and represent them.

Veneration of Buddha is not a village function; nevertheless, nearly every village has a *chau* (Buddhist temple). In some instances the *chau* has been built by a group of villagers, in others, by a bonze, who recruits other bonzes and nuns to live there. Wealthy persons can earn merit by donating a temple to the village or accumulate it through gifts to existing temples.

Rites in the temple are held at daily, monthly and annual intervals, but only the three great annual rituals—the beginning of the new year, the midyear festival and the end of the year, draw many of the village residents. In their daily rituals, performed morning, noon and evening, the bonzes light ceremonial lamps, ring bells, sound wooden clappers and recite prayers. The faithful take offerings of flowers, incense and food to the temple, praying there for help and protection. Besides the ceremonies the bonze conducts in the temple, he sometimes goes to private homes to offer prayers, as, for instance, when someone in the family is ill. In case of death, he is usually invited to perform rites of expiation or purification.

CHAPTER 12

SOCIAL VALUES

Vietnamese social values derive most conspicuously from the ethics taught by the Chinese philosopher Confucious (551–479 B.C.) and his followers. A number of other cultural and religious traditions, including the essentially alien secular tradition of the West, have had some influence at various times on the thought and behavior of the people. Nonetheless, Confucian precepts are deeply embedded in the social and political institutions of the country, and today probably no ethnic Vietnamese, whatever his education or professed religion, fails to feel to one degree or another the impact of this Confucian heritage. Confucian values are not shared, however, by the culturally distinct ethnic minorities in the Highlands (see ch. 5, Ethnic Groups and Languages).

Buddhism, the predominant organized religion in the country, has had a lesser but still significant role as a source of social values. Buddhist teachings and those who espoused them have importantly affected the national life, manifesting their influence in artistic, social and political affairs. In South Vietnam today most of the people, whether or not they actively participate in Buddhist rituals, identify themselves as adherents of the faith, and such Buddhist values as compromise, charity and avoidance of injury to others are widely upheld.

Western secular values, introduced since the late nineteenth century, have some currency among upper- and middle-class professionals, businessmen and civil administrators, including members of the Roman Catholic minority. In particular, they are likely to be held by persons who have studied or lived abroad in France, other European countries or the United States. Changes in the attitudes and values of Vietnamese educated in foreign-operated schools in their own country are also taking place. By comparison with the orientation of the former group, however, the modification of values has been gradual and of limited scale.

As a group the inhabitants of the northern provinces of the country (formerly Annam or Central Vietnam) are more engaged with traditional Confucian values than are those of the southern provinces (formerly Cochin China). In many instances, the northerners tend to distrust their southern compatriots as persons who adapt too readily to foreign influences and who, in their eagerness for wealth, show disrespect for simple and austere Confucian virtues. This attitude, generally shared by refugees from North Vietnam, is intimately bound up with the historical development of the country (see ch. 3, Historical Setting).

For most South Vietnamese in the mid-1960's, choices of action and attitude in general were determined by expediency rather than by moral dictates (see ch. 17, Political Values and Attitudes). In the climate of insecurity brought on by two decades of war and political instability, actual behavior tended to depart to some extent from the ideal behavior advocated by Confucianism, which stresses loyalty, generosity and sacrifice among a wide circle of kinsmen and close friends. The matter of survival was an immediate, overriding concern, and the welfare of those persons to whom one had the closest, most intimate ties took priority over all other considerations.

PERPETUATION OF THE FAMILY

In accordance with his Confucian heritage, a Vietnamese identifies himself almost exclusively as a member of a particular family rather than of a community, occupation group or other informal association. The strongest bond in the society has always been that of family loyalty, and the members of the kin group have been mutually responsible to and for one another. Attachments between kinsmen have been, both in the ideal and in everyday practice, deeper, stronger and more extensive than in Western societies. Family loyalty and filial piety have held the society intact for over 2,000 years, through periods of war, foreign domination and national disaster.

The family is thought of as consisting not of its living members alone but of past and future generations as well. The living members are the link between their ancestors, to whom they owe an unending duty, and their unborn progeny. A man's duty toward his forebears consists of honoring their memories on feast days, on the anniversaries of their deaths and on all occasions of family joy or sorrow. He is expected to maintain their graves and to offer sacrifices of food and incense to them on the family altar at appropriate times. Land dedicated to the Cult of the Ancestors is set aside by each family, and the revenue from it is used to pay the expenses involved. By fulfilling his obligation to his ancestors, a man assures himself that he in turn will be well treated after his own death and will not be condemned to eternity as a wandering spirit without food and care from anyone.

One of the chief dreads of the Vietnamese peasant is that his family will disintegrate, leave its ancestral home and fail to carry out its duty to the ancestors. It is for this reason that he tries to remain near the graves of his forebears, even in military operational areas, and will leave only under extreme duress. If the family is separated, its members are generally inclined to make a considerable effort to reunite for Tet, the lunar New Year celebration.

Families bound by traditional values set a high premium on having at least one male heir to carry on the Cult of the Ancestors. The more male heirs, the better. When a couple has been married some years and still there is no son born to them, they will often adopt a young boy, preferably a nephew or cousin. Polygamy, until recently an accepted and commonplace practice, helped to assure that there would be a male heir to carry on the family line. Polygamy has been outlawed, but, in many instances, it is still customary for a man to take a second "wife," to whom he is not officially married, or to live temporarily with different women. Having many children is often mentioned as one of the elements of a good life.

In the context of a morality which holds that the welfare and continuity of the family group are more important than the interests of any individual member, traditionally oriented Vietnamese emphasize strongly the difference in the social roles of men and women. In principle, the head of the family has absolute authority in the household; when he dies, his sons become heads of their own households, with the same rights and duties previously held by their father. A wife must obey her husband and her mother-in-law; a daughter, her parents, especially her father. Girls, accordingly, are given a more confined upbringing than boys, but both boys and girls are strictly disciplined and constantly reminded of the importance of obedience to their elders.

In traditional households the women are still overwhelmingly concerned with household and child-rearing tasks, but within the home they are usually influential, often dominant. Despite the cultural emphasis on obedience and docility in women, they are not regarded as the frail sex. They are often highly self-reliant and strong-willed. In the countryside and in urban lower-class neighborhoods, many women, through circumstances beyond control, live alone with their children and are their sole support. Some follow their husbands to defense outposts manned by government troops in areas of military operations, and a few have been extremely effective guerrilla fighters. Some upper- and middle-class women who have been exposed to Western values, choose to break with tradition and strike out on their own in some profession or business enterprise. Women control an important share of the nation's economy, and a few participate in political affairs.

HARMONY IN INTERPERSONAL RELATIONSHIPS

Most Vietnamese place a high value on maintaining harmony in their social relationships. Both the Confucian doctrine of the Golden Mean and the so-called Middle Path of Buddhism dispose the individual toward flexibility and a readiness to compromise. He calls this "bending like the bamboo."

From early childhood he is taught that whatever serves to enhance harmony is good and that an insistence on absolutes is to be avoided at all costs. He learns that it is important to bring himself into harmony not only in the social realm but also with his physical environment and the spirits inhabiting it. Harmony is to be sought not only with one's own family but also in dealings with all other persons.

This emphasis on compromise and avoidance of injury to others was manifested conspicuously during and after the so-called Buddhist crisis of 1963 (see ch. 14, Political Dynamics). From the beginning of the organized movement by the Buddhists to oust President Ngo Dinh Diem, spokesmen of the moderate Buddhist line repeatedly reiterated the importance of compromise and nonviolence in bringing about their desired goal. Decrying more direct and aggressive methods, they employed various techniques of noncooperation and nonviolent resistance, including marches, fasts, strikes and, ultimately, suicide by fire.

The value set on harmony in interpersonal relations is expressed in everyday situations through the use of delicacy, tact, politeness and gentleness in dealing with others. When an arrangement is to be made between two individuals or interested groups, for example, it is customary to hire an intermediary to conduct the negotiations, so as to minimize the possibilities for friction. An intermediary is usually employed, for instance, when a marriage is to be arranged between a potential bride and bridegroom who are unknown to one another. The intermediary makes preliminary soundings, sometimes arranging for the potential bridegroom, and perhaps his parents, to see his girl without her knowledge. By avoiding a face-to-face confrontation until both parties have agreed to the contract, either possible partner, if he so desires, can ease out of the situation gracefully with no offense to the other.

Ideally, the same attitude should be carried over into marriage. A Vietnamese proverb states: "The good husband and wife always treat each other with the same courtesy and etiquette extended to a guest." Similarly, in the interest of harmony in social relationships the Vietnamese are prone to refrain from litigation and formal processes for settling differences; they prefer to work things out informally.

To avoid offending others, Vietnamese are careful to behave modestly. Bragging and boasting are strongly disapproved. Parents, for example, when hearing their child praised for doing something well usually reply proudly with the customary polite expression, "He has really done so little."

Notions of ideal character in men and women reflect the same concern with harmony in dealing with others. Firmness, gentleness, patience and tactfulness are stressed as desirable attributes in men; obedience, gentleness, generosity and delicateness denote exemplary character in women.

Because of the value placed on harmonious relations, a person, if offended by someone of equal or superior social status, will make an extreme effort to maintain his equanimity and to avoid revealing resentment or anger. In other circumstances, however, the same pattern of behavior may not hold. Rival wives and jealous sisters and cousins, for example, quarrel frequently. Often the reunion of a large family group becomes an occasion for backbiting and exchange of malicious gossip among the women.

Concern for harmony in interpersonal relations is manifested characteristically in an indirect approach to issues and ideas. The Vietnamese generally equates directness with rudeness, considering subtlety more pleasant for all concerned. He prefers to tell a pleasant lie rather than a truth that hurts. In responding to a question, he is motivated by the desire to satisfy or please the person who inquires and thus replies in the affirmative whether in actuality he means "yes," "no" or "perhaps."

DISCIPLINE

Vietnamese culture, reflecting its Buddhist heritage, places a high premium on the disciplined acceptance of things as they are. Life is hard, especially for the peasant, and insecure for all, yet complaints are rarely heard. The peasant who sees his rice crop destroyed, his village burned, his child wounded, typically behaves with notable patience and forbearance. He sets about to rebuild his life as best he can. Stoicism is a major value. Casualties resulting from military operations, no matter how severely wounded, seldom betray any sign of physical suffering or discomfort.

Self-control also demands restraint in conduct; well-bred Vietnamese keep their voices low and conduct conversations quietly. They respect those who show themselves to be gentle and amiable, polite and courteous in dealings with others, and passionate, uncontrolled displays of feeling are strongly disapproved. From childhood the members of traditionally oriented families are taught the importance of discipline and of willing submission to parental authority, and their upbringing is extremely strict. Unquestioning obedience is demanded; offenses are promptly and rigorously punished.

TRENDS

Under the combined impact of French colonial rule and French culture, the traditional social order, based on the Confucian ethical code, and the system of values supporting it, rapidly began to crumble. As the governing intellectual elite, or mandarinate, became subordinate to alien French governors and reduced in power, so the prestige of the traditional Confucian scholar waned. Patriots returned from abroad, convinced that the defeat of their country lay in the classical Confucian scorn of technical and scientific knowledge, advocated the abandonment of traditional education for the teaching of sciences in the schools, and urged the people to modernize their thinking and living. Concurrently, the French, through the medium of local schools, sought to inculcate French learning and culture. The final blow to Confucian education occurred at about the time of World War I, when the French "reform" of the civil service examinations required European rather than Confucian learning. The Vietnamese responded by avidly turning to the French schools.

These changes impinged largely on the urban centers and involved mainly the foreign-educated elite who had at one time or another lived abroad; but the tendency to reexamine the old values was noticeable among all social groups except the most conservative advocates of classical culture and learning. The decline in traditionalism spread to the villages as well. The mandarins, who provided the link between the villages and the central government, were the intellectual leaders of the traditional order as well as administrators. As they became increasingly self-seeking, their behavior undermined the peasants' respect for the mandarinate and the precepts it had formerly exemplified. The French further accelerated the process of decline by introducing external controls into village affairs which disrupted customary relationships. Increased taxation drove the peasant to orient himself to a cash economy.

Since World War II and the departure of the French, the traditions of individualism and liberalism, as imparted by French education, have continued to flourish among some members of the upper and middle classes. During this period, however, the insecurity and uncertainties precipitated by two decades of political and military strife have been more important than formal educational processes as an impetus for reappraisal of traditional values. The tendency to question the appropriateness of age-old values became widespread in an atmosphere of terror, death and destruction which instilled in the general population a growing, and eventually almost exclusive, preoccupation with the matter of physical survival.

In the mid-1960's the Vietnamese society was moving away from its former emphasis on family loyalty and toward a more individualistic standard. Political and economic conditions no longer supported the notion of a large group of kinsmen living under one roof or within the same small village and recognizing a complex set of mutual obligations and responsibilities. To put the interests of one's immediate family first in all circumstances was no longer dishonorable.

Similarly, concern for the welfare of future generations of the family lessened. Whereas people formerly had been motivated to work hard and make sacrifices in the hope of transmitting a modicum of advantage to their descendants, the focus has changed to considerations having to do with the immediate present. Parents labored for the well-being safety of their children and strove to provide them with the best education possible rather than for the ultimate benefit of the family members yet unborn.

In the modern period the Vietnamese, always pragmatic in his approach to life despite his concern with spirits and the supernatural world, has become even more practical in his outlook. While focusing on survival, he hopes for a better life, social and legal justice, more land, more material comforts and better schools for his children. He is willing to accept aid supplementing his own efforts toward these goals, and, with characteristic flexibility and adaptability, he appears ready to take it from whatever source he believes will provide him the most benefits.

SECTION II. POLITICAL

CHAPTER 13

THE GOVERNMENTAL SYSTEM

In early 1966 the character, structure and direction of the entire governmental system were affected by the exigencies of the counterinsurgency efforts. The government of Prime Minister Nguyen Cao Ky and his military associates was being challenged by Communist subversive forces operating throughout the country, more so in the rural than in urban areas. It was frequently asserted by some Vietnamese that the country was ruled by "two governments"—the Saigon government by day and the Communist-led insurgents (commonly referred to as the Viet Cong—see Glossary) by night.

National leaders seemed convinced that the outcome of the Viet Cong challenge would ultimately hinge on their ability to inspire the people with a sense of commitment to the regime in Saigon. Accordingly, they were attempting to prosecute successfully the counterinsurgency operations on the military front and at the same time preserve gains by extending economic and social benefits to every segment of the population through rural and urban self-help construction and pacification projects officially labeled the Revolutionary Development Program (formerly known as the Rural Reconstruction or Pacification Program).

Formal governmental authority emanated from the provisional constitution of June 19, 1965, prepared by a group of military leaders. Under this constitution the government, on June 24, 1965, proclaimed a "state of war" (equivalent to a state of national emergency, rather than a formal declaration of war on a foreign power). The proclamation authorized the application of "appropriate measures to defend the territory and to maintain public order and security."

The government was authoritarian and centralized. Executive and legislative powers were being exercised summarily by 10 generals having membership in what was commonly called the National Leadership Committee, and its executive arm, known as the War Cabinet, was headed by Prime Minister Ky. The authoritarian pattern appeared likely to continue so long as the gravity of Communist insurgency persisted.

In February 1966 there was an official announcement that an advisory council would be formed to draft a constitution which was to be ready by November 1966. According to the announcement, a national election would be held sometime during 1967 to prepare for the transfer of power to an elected government. The February plan was revised, however, because of civilian agitation in March and April 1966, for a prompt end of military rule. In mid-April the government issued a decree providing for the election of a constituent assembly in September (see ch. 14, Political Dynamics).

HISTORICAL DEVELOPMENT

Before the imposition of French control in the latter half of the nineteeth century, Vietnam was a unified state under a hereditary emperor, and its political system was based on traditional principles of government embodied in Confucian concepts introduced from China. These held government to be the concern of morally superior, benevolent civil officials. Their purpose was to maintain harmony in a hierarchical social order. The ruler, as emperor, presided over an elaborate bureaucracy of scholar-officials. Highly authoritarian, the government combined executive, legislative and judicial authority in the persons of its ranking officials, and it provided no formal limitation on the emperor's power.

When the French took control of Indochina, they retained much of the traditional system, superimposing upon it and its mandarin officials their own colonial administrators. The French colonial administration remained intact until near the end of World War II. In March 1945, with Japanese support, Emperor Bao Dai proclaimed Vietnam's independence and established a short-lived, ineffective national government with Trang Trong Kim as Prime Minister.

After the defeat of Japan, however, the well-organized, Communist-led Vietnam Independence League (Viet Nam Doc Lap Dong Minh), called the Viet Minh, under Ho Chi Minh assumed effective control in the north and in parts of the central and southern portions of the country. In August 1945, Bao Dai abdicated in favor of the Viet Minh, and the new Democratic Republic of Vietnam was proclaimed by Ho Chi Minh on September 2, 1945. The declaration was carefully phrased to imply that the regime had United States and Allied support. No mention was made of the Soviet Union, but many references were made to the spirit of the United States Declaration of Independence, to the French Revolution and to the United Nations Declaration at San Francisco.

Returning to Indochina, in September 1945, the French clashed almost immediately with the Ho Chi Minh regime which soon led the fight to force the French out. In 1949, after 3 years of inconclusive fighting, the French agreed to limited independence for Vietnam and established the State of Vietnam with Bao Dai as Chief of State. His French-supported regime, however, was in control only where French Union Forces were present. From 1949 to 1954 these areas of control were limited mostly to the few larger cities and towns, whereas the Viet Minh regime gained increasing support in the rural areas. It controlled large areas of the Mekong River Delta in the South, 60 percent or more of the rural countryside outside of Hanoi in the North, most of the Central Highlands and scattered areas of the Central Lowlands (see ch. 2, Physical Environment; ch. 3, Historical Setting).

With the end of hostilities, under the Geneva Agreement, signed on July 20, 1954, a provisional military Demarcation Line was fixed roughly along the seventeenth parallel. The Final Declaration of the Geneva Conference (July 21, 1954) stated that "the military Demarcation Line is provisional and should not in any way be interpreted as constituting a political or territorial boundary." To the north of the Demarcation Line the Ho Chi Minh regime established itself at Hanoi, whereas in the South an independent, sovereign, anti-Communist government emerged under the leadership of Bao Dai as Chief of State and Ngo Dinh Diem as Prime Minister. In the South the signing date of July 20, 1954, has since been regarded as "the saddest day in the history of Vietnam." It is known as "The Shameful Day." Its anniversary is officially observed as the "National Unity Day for the Liberation of North Vietnam."

THE NGO DINH DIEM REGIME

On October 26, 1955, Prime Minister Ngo Dinh Diem declared South Vietnam to be a republic under his presidency. One of his first official acts was to call for the election of a National Constituent Assembly. The Assembly, whose 123 members were elected in March 1956, appointed a 15-member commission to draft a constitution, which, with certain changes recommended by the President, was formally promulgated on October 26, 1956, the first anniversary of the proclamation of the republic.

In form, the Constitution drew from the example of the United States Constitution and, to a lesser extent, on French influences. It provided for separation of executive and legislative powers on American lines, but in practice the relative strength of the two branches was markedly different. There was no separate, autonomous judicial branch; the court system was under the supervision of the then Department of Justice, following the French precedent. The principle of separation of powers was, however, sufficiently circumscribed, with a stipulation that "the activities of the executive and legislative agencies must be brought into harmony." The harmony had to be in consonance with President Diem's conviction that a strong and efficient executive organization, capable of rapidly solving the complex and urgent problems, was "a guarantee of the democratic regime."

Under the 1956 Constitution the President was elected to a 5-year term by direct and secret vote based on universal franchise. He was designated Chief of State, Chief Executive of the Government and the Supreme Commander of the Armed Forces. He was vested with broad emergency powers to rule by decree between sessions of the National Assembly and, in case of war, internal disturbances or financial or economic crisis, to exercise extraordinary powers to institute any appropriate measures. There were certain constitutional checks on presidential powers, but such restraints, if imposed at all by the National Assembly, were perfunctory, since members of the Assembly themselves were largely progovernment.

The entire governmental system revolved around the Office of the President, in which President Diem's political adviser and brother, Ngo Dinh Nhu, played a key role as policymaker and supervisor of all governmental activities. Aided by highly personalized networks of political surveillance, the Ngo brothers ruled with iron hands, and their powers extended, formally as well as informally, down directly to the provinces, districts, villages and, even, hamlets. By late 1963 it appeared as if the whole system had been transformed into a personal concern of the Ngo family (see ch. 14, Political Dynamics). Meanwhile, the Communist campaign of terror and guerrilla activities systematically intensified, and conditions within the country continued to deteriorate.

President Diem's regime came to an abrupt end on November 1, 1963, when a group of generals successfully executed a coup d'etat (see ch. 14, Political Dynamics). The 1956 Constitution was replaced by the hastily drawn provisional constitutional charter of November 4, 1963. The charter vested all executive and legislative powers in a Revolutionary Military Committee, headed by Major General Duong Van Minh. Despite some structural changes the government's authoritarian control, exercised for the first time by the military, remained unchanged.

On July 2, 1964, the initial provisional charter was replaced by Provisional Charter No. 2, which, in turn, was supplanted by another charter, dated August 16, 1964. Both documents continued to stress the primacy of military leadership and executive powers, but the Charter of August 16 had to be withdrawn shortly after its promulgation because of popular criticisms that it would provide for a military dictatorship. Under the Charter of August 16 a Revolutionary Military Council was defined as "the supreme organization" of the nation, and Major General Nguyen Khanh, who had unseated Major General Duong Van Minh in January 1964, became its chairman, in addition to being the President and Commander in Chief of the Armed Forces (see ch. 14, Political Dynamics).

A new provisional constitution—the fourth since November 1963—was proclaimed on October 20, 1964, to provide for an orderly transfer of authority to a civilian government. The civilian leadership installed thereby, however, proved ineffective and in June 1965 handed over its authority to a group of military leaders headed by Air Vice Marshal Nguyen Cao Ky.

THE GOVERNMENT OF NGUYEN CAO KY

The Air Vice Marshal came to power, in fact, on June 9, 1965, after which the civilian leadership of Chief of State Phan Khac Suu and Prime Minister Phan Huy Quat resigned. On June 14 a group of generals, including Major General Nguyen Van Thieu and Brigadier General Nguyen Huu Co (both were promoted to lieutenant general in 1965), joined the Air Vice Marshal in establishing the National Leadership Committee—a 10-member military directorate. On the same day the Committee appointed Major General Thieu as its chairman, a position comparable to that of Chief of State. The new government was officially formed on June 19, when the Committee named Air Vice Marshal Ky as Prime Minister and proclaimed another provisional constitution—the fifth since November 1963.

Under the vaguely worded provisional constitution—officially called The Convention—authority is temporarily vested in the Congress of the Armed Forces of the Republic of Vietnam, pending the promulgation of a permanent constitution. The Congress is composed of all of the general officers of the armed forces, including the four corps commanders, the Commander of the Capital Military Region (Saigon) and all division commanders. The executive leadership of this Congress is vested in what is formally known as The Directorate, but is more popularly referred to as the National Leadership Committee (see fig. 9). The government in May convened an Election Law Drafting Committee and empowered it to prepare drafts of an election law and constituent assembly organization law. On the Committee's recommendation, the Directorate was enlarged on June 6 to include 10 civilian members to equal the 10 military members. They are Tran Van Do, Pham Buu Chuong, Phan Khoang, Nguyen Luu Vien, Tran Van An, retired Major General Van Thanh Cao, Nguyen Van Huyen, Vu Ngo Tran, Quang Huu Kim, and Huynh Van Nhiem.

Tentative Plans for Transfer of Power

Since their accession to power, the military leaders generally have maintained that their regime was only "temporary but necessary" and have stressed the need of measures which would pave the way for an

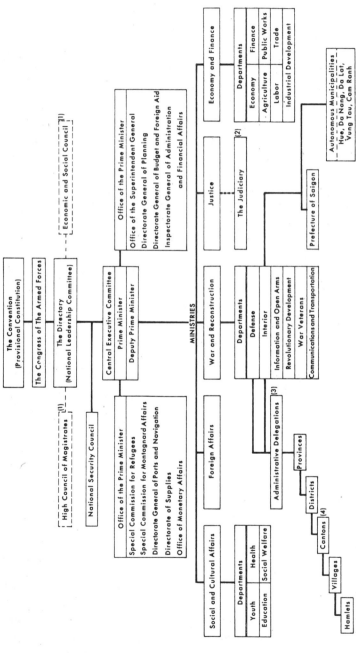

The Convention
(Provisional Constitution)

The Congress of The Armed Forces

The Directory
(National Leadership Committee)

High Council of Magistrates [1]

Economic and Social Council [1]

National Security Council

Central Executive Committee
Prime Minister
Deputy Prime Minister

Office of the Prime Minister
Special Commission for Refugees
Special Commission for Montagnard Affairs
Directorate General of Ports and Navigation
Directorate of Supplies
Office of Monetary Affairs

Office of the Prime Minister
Office of the Superintendent General
Directorate General of Planning
Directorate General of Budget and Foreign Aid
Inspectorate General of Administration
    and Financial Affairs

MINISTRIES

Social and Cultural Affairs

Departments
Youth   Health
Education   Social Welfare

Foreign Affairs

Administrative Delegations [3]

Provinces

Districts

Cantons [4]

Villages

Hamlets

War and Reconstruction

Departments
Defense
Interior
Information and Open Arms
Revolutionary Development
War Veterans
Communications and Transportation

Justice

The Judiciary [2]

Prefecture of Saigon

Economy and Finance

Departments
Economy   Finance
Agriculture   Public Works
Labor   Trade
Industrial Development

Autonomous Municipalities
Hue, Da Nang, Da Lat,
Vung Tau, Cam Ranh

(1) Not formed yet.
(2) The court system is administered by the Ministry of Justice.
(3) The military commanders of the four corps areas also head the four administrative delegations; military aspects of provincial administration are reported directly to the
     Secretary of State for Defense, whereas civil aspects are reported to the Secretary of State for the Interior.
(4) Not present in all districts.

Figure 9.   The Governmental System of South Vietnam, April 1966.

orderly transfer of power to an elected government. On January 15, 1966, Prime Minister Ky announced his government's plan for a return to a constitutional, broadly based government. In mid-April the Prime Minister convened the National Political Congress, in which all major non-Communist groupings were represented, to seek the views of all its members regarding steps to be taken to return to constitutional government. In accordance with the general consensus of the Congress, Chief of State Thieu convened an Election Law Drafting Committee on May 5 and empowered it to prepare drafts of an election law and constituent assembly organization law. After consultations with the government, the Committee's drafts were incorporated into decree laws promulgated on June 19.

The Central Government

The Directorate (National Leadership Committee)

The Convention entrusts The Directorate, responsible to the Congress of the Armed Forces, with the exercise of both executive and legislative powers and with "the direction of all the affairs of the nation." The Directorate's 10 members include: the Chairman, Secretary General, Prime Minister (also known as The Commissioner for the Executive or Chairman of the Central Executive Committee), Minister of War and Reconstruction (also known as Commissioner General for War and Reconstruction), the Chief of the Joint General Staff of the Armed Forces, the Commander of the Capital Military Region, and the four corps commanders (see ch. 27, The Armed Forces).

The Chairman of The Directorate, Lieutenant General Nguyen Van Thieu, functions as Chief of State and appoints, on recommendation by the Prime Minister, ambassadors and plenipotentiary ministers, rectors of universities, Cabinet ministers and subordinate secretaries of states, the prefect (mayor) of Saigon and all judges. In addition, he appoints and promotes all general officers, but in accordance with the decision on The Directory and on recommendation by the Minister of War and Reconstruction. The Chairman is also empowered to proclaim a state of emegency, martial law or a state of war (if the National Security Council so decides); he may also declare war, make peace or conclude international agreements if such decisions are made by the Congress of the Armed Forces. All legislative documents and measures of enforcement deriving from court judgments are issued in the Chairman's name. Finally, the Chairman enjoys the power on amnesty.

In case the Chairman is incapacitated, the Secretary General is to replace him, but a new Chairman must be named by the Congress of the Armed Forces within a 10-day period. The Secretary General's duties are to study and outline broad national policies, draft all legislative documents "in agreement with The Directorate" and to convene regular or extraordinary sessions of The Directorate.

The Prime Minister, as chief executive officer, wields extraordinary powers. He may propose draft-laws to The Directory for deliberation and promulgation, and he implements policies recommended by The Directory. He enjoys full powers to organize all executive agencies and to appoint and replace public officials. In his decisions affecting agencies of the provincial government and at the level of directorate general and higher in the central government, the Prime Minister must obtain prior consent from The Directory. This consent is also required for actions affecting the personnel of the rank of secretary of state (deputy Cabinet minister in large departments) or higher.

National Security Council and other Councils

The National Security Council is composed of the Chairman (acting as presiding officer) of The Directory, the Secretary General of The Directory, the Prime Minister, Minister of War and Reconstruction (also designated as Deputy Prime Minister since October 1965) and the Chief of the Joint General Staff. The Council is empowered to recommend to The Directory measures on national security and others relating to the proclamation of a state of emergency, martial law or war. Since the statutory members of the Council also hold key positions in The Directory, the Council's recommendations are virtually assured of endorsement and for all practical purposes can be regarded as policy decisions.

The Convention provides for two advisory bodies, the Economic and Social Council and the High Council of Magistrates. The Economic and Social Council has broad advisory responsibilities in relation to economic and social problems and policies. The High Council of Magistrates has the responsibility of "safeguarding the independence of the judiciary." In early 1966 these two councils were not yet established.

Central Executive Committee (The War Cabinet)

The Central Executive Committee, headed by the Prime Minister, is also known as the War Cabinet or "Super Cabinet." Its statutory membership includes only five ministers representing the portfolios of War and Reconstruction, Economy and Finance, Social and Cultural Affairs, Foreign Affairs, and Justice, but in actual official practice the heads of all departments subordinate to the ministers are also regarded as "Cabinet members." The Committee exercises broad coordinating and supervisory powers over various executive departments and agencies and functions as the initiator of major governmental policies.

Each of the five ministers is sometimes called Commissioner General but is officially designated as a minister. Except for the Ministries of Foreign Affairs and Justice, each of the remaining three ministers is in charge of four or more departments of ministerial status. All departments (also frequently referred to as ministries) are headed by secretaries of state of ministerial rank who are commonly, though not officially, called "ministers." The relationship of the three ministers to their respective departments is largely limited to coordination, and, hence, the making of decisions affecting various departmental activities are left, as a rule, to the departmental heads concerned. In early 1966 the Minister of War and Reconstruction, in addition to being the Deputy Prime Minister, was concurrently the Secretary of Defense; similarly, the Minister of Social and Cultural Affairs was the Secretary of Education, and the Minister of Economy and Finance was also the Secretary of Economy.

The most important and powerful unit of the government is the Ministry of War and Reconstruction because of its primary responsibility for the prosecution of counterinsurgency efforts. Four of its six departments are directly involved in other national security measures: the Department of Defense is concerned with both operational and administrative control of the military establishment; Information and Open Arms, with psychological warfare; Interior, with control of all government agencies in the field and of the national police forces; and Revolutionary Development, with socioeconomic efforts in rural and urban areas.

The Department of Revolutionary Development (formerly the Department of Rural Reconstruction) is concerned with activities commonly known as the pacification or rural reconstruction program, which is designed to improve the material well-being mainly of the rural people and also to generate the spirit of collective self-help efforts in their local communities. As a result, the program forms a crucial link in the overall governmental efforts against Communist insurgency throughout the country (see ch. 14, Political Dynamics).

The Judiciary

The court system is supervised, administratively, by the Ministry of Justice. All judges are appointed and do not have security of tenure. The judicial organization is defined, not by the Constitution, but by statute. Decisions relating to the appointment, promotion, transfer, demotion or dismissal of judges are made by The Directory and administered through the Ministry. As a result, judicial integrity and independence have been frequently questioned by the Vietnamese themselves; some judges are known to have been generally indisposed to make decisions unfavorable to the government.

Unlike other governmental branches, the judiciary, except for the military courts, has remained virtually unchanged since 1955 (see ch. 27, The Armed Forces). The number of courts required to administer justice is, by Western standards, relatively small, because the

Vietnamese on the whole are not inclined to excessive litigation. They tend to settle disputes out of court whenever possible.

Before 1954, French citizens were tried under French law. With the transfer of power in that year, the Vietnamese courts acquired full jurisdiction over all cases involving any person residing in the country. The official language of the courts is Vietnamese, although French continues to be used as the second language of legal discourse.

Derived from the French model, the judicial organization is based on the dual system of jurisdiction, each with a separate hierarchy of courts. Civil and criminal cases are heard by what are commonly called judiciary courts, and litigations arising from disputes between a private citizen and the public authorities are handled by the administrative court. Any violation of public order and national security comes under the jurisdiction of military courts (see ch. 27, The Armed Forces).

On the judiciary side the lowest courts are the ordinary Courts of the Peace (or Justices of the Peace), which usually consist of a single magistrate (justice of the peace) assisted by a court clerk. Frequently, a district chief acts as the magistrate. Five in number in late 1962, they try minor civil cases and petty criminal offenses. The Courts of the Peace with Extended Jurisdiction, of which there were 20 distributed throughout the provinces in 1962, exercise control over the Courts of the Peace. Presided over by a single magistrate, these courts have jurisdiction over civil and commercial cases and over all but the most serious felonies.

There are seven Courts of First Instance. On the same hierarchical level with the Courts of the Peace with Extended Jurisdiction, each consists of a presiding judge, an examining magistrate and at least three assistant judges. They have unlimited criminal, civil and commercial jurisdiction.

Appeals from the Courts of the Peace are made to the Courts of the First Instance. Appeals from cases tried ordinally by Courts of the Peace with Extended Jurisdiction or Courts of First Instance are heard by the Courts of Appeal, of which there are two, one in Saigon and the other in Hue. These courts are divided into two chambers, civil and criminal. Appeals in civil cases are heard by a panel of three judges; those in criminal cases are heard by three judges and two citizens acting as assessors. In addition, the Courts of Appeal exercise judicial control over the lower courts in their territories.

The highest judicial authority is the Court of Cassation (Supreme Court) in Saigon. It hears appeals from the decisions of the military courts and the lower courts. Decisions of the military courts affecting national security, however, cannot be heard by the Court of Cassation. If in its opinion the law has been violated in judicial proceedings, the Court may reverse the decisions of the lower judges and transfer the case to another court at the same level. Only in cases where a lower court fails to concur with the highest court's opinion does the latter render a final decision.

In addition, there are a number of special courts which are established wherever necessary. By the end of 1961 labor courts had been set up in eight cities; they have separate jurisdiction over labor disputes in public or private enterprise in their respective areas. In places where there is no labor court, a Court of First Instance or Court of the Peace with Extended Jurisdiction may render judgment in labor disputes. Workers involved in disputes are entitled to counsel without fee. In 1957 agrarian reform courts were created to settle disputes arising from the government's Agrarian Reform Policy, and by 1961 four were in operation (see ch. 19, Agriculture). Four Juvenile Courts were established in 1958 to deal with offenders under 18 years of age. Those in Hue and Saigon also function as courts of appeal in juvenile cases. In 1961 six juvenile tribunals were operating.

In February 1966 the government set up a Special Court to deal with cases involving bribery, corruption, misappropriation of public funds and economic offenses such as hoarding, smuggling, profiteering, illegal transfer of moneys, violation of customs regulations and market-cornering practices. Seated in Saigon and to be operative until the end of the state of war, the Special Court has territorial jurisdiction over the whole country but may organize local hearings in the provinces. The Court is empowered to try both civilians and military personnel. It consists of a presiding judge, two assistant judges, a prosecutor and one or more assistant prosecutors. Court procedures are the same as those of military field courts (see ch. 27, The Armed Forces). Defendants are brought before it without preliminary investigation by warrants issued directly by the Prime Minister. Sentences may range from imprisonment at hard labor to death by a firing squad (see ch. 26, Public Order and Safety).

On the administrative side the highest judicial authority is represented by the Council of State in Saigon. The Council hears appeals from decisions of the Administrative Court. The Administrative Court, situated in Saigon, has competence over the whole country as a court of first instance. Cases involving disputes between private citizens and the government or between government agencies themselves are tried by the Administrative Court. The Council of State has additional competence over the Court of Pensions which specializes in the settlement of disputes over pensions paid to the war-wounded. The Council also functions as an advisory body on legal affairs, rendering legal opinions to the government whenever requested by the latter.

CIVIL SERVICE

The civil service system covers only those agencies which are supported by the national budget. The employees of autonomous municipalities (except Saigon) and of provinces, both of which are supported by local budgets, are under the jurisdiction of their respective authorities. Civil servants are divided into career (permanent) and noncareer (temporary) categories; functionally, they are classified into administrative and technical cadre systems, respectively. The civil service function is attached to and controlled by the Office of the Prime Minister. In late 1964 there were about 133,900 civil servants, of whom 33 percent (43,000) were permanent. About 18,600 career employees were stationed in Saigon, and the remaining 24,400 were attached to the field service of the national government.

Modeled initially on the French system, the civil service was established by the Bao Dai regime. In 1949, when the State of Vietnam set up its own system of administration, staffed by Vietnamese nationals, it found itself seriously handicapped by a lack of trained and experienced administrative personnel, the French having previously reserved to themselves most of the high- and middle-level positions of administrative and managerial responsibilities.

Training schools in public administration were established in Hanoi and Saigon, and in 1953 the National Administration School (Ecole Nationale d'Administration—ENAD) was established at Da Lat and began offering a 2-year program. Its students were recruited from recent high school graduates and civil servants with 2 years or more of practical experience. Students spent 1½ years in study at the school and 6 months working in the field with a local administrative body. The curriculum of ENAD preserved the French emphasis on legalistic-oriented administration; instruction was given in both French and Vietnamese.

In 1955 the National Administration School, renamed the National Institute of Administration, was moved to Saigon and brought under the control of the then office of the presidency. Through the United States foreign aid program, American advisers worked with faculty members of the Institute until 1962. Under American influence the school was oriented away from the heavy stress on law and toward practical training in public administration. The training of administrative cadres was the primary responsibility of the National Institute of Administration, whereas technical cadres were trained in specialized schools maintained by the various departments concerned.

Civil servants are recruited through competitive entry examinations and are assigned to either the administrative or the technical corps. Except for certain supervisory positions, they are not recruited for specific jobs with fixed duties and responsibilities. Within each system there are no specific standards for job classification, and, hence, job assignments are likely to be determined by the personnel needs of various agencies at any given moment; to a large degree, political connections play an important part. Recruits are required to serve probationary periods and may be subjected to another examination before being given full career status. Positions requiring highly specialized skills, administrative or technical, are filled usually through contractual arrangements, renewable on a yearly basis. In late 1964 there were only 1,970 "contract" employees.

One of the major problems affecting the efficiency of the civil service continues to be the preoccupation of administrative personnel with restrictive form and procedure. Inherited from the French colonial administrative service, this legalistic orientation has evoked criticism, because it allegedly tends to make many civil servants reluctant to take initiative and assume responsibility. This tendency, combined with a disinclination to delegate authority to subordinates, has been blamed for frequent administrative bottlenecks at the higher levels of bureaucracy. Under emphasis on form and procedure is also said to have hampered developmental efforts by stifling the flexibility and initiative needed to cope effectively with varying local conditions.

Since the military takeover in 1963 the morale of the civil servants has appreciably improved. Increasing stress is placed on merit rather than on political reliability as the basic criterion for promotion. Officials are no longer sent to remote provincial or district outposts because of questionable political loyalty. The weekly political indoctrination sessions sponsored by the Diem regime for all bureaucrats have been discontinued, and the civil servants are generally secure from excessive political interference, although they are permitted to engage in political activities within certain statutory limitations. Moreover, officials may resign from their posts with relative ease. This situation is in sharp contrast to the days of the Diem regime when officials could not resign unless they had "legitimate" reasons; often, political manipulation was needed to leave governmental service.

FIELD ADMINISTRATION

South Vietnam is administratively divided into provinces (see fig. 10). These in turn are subdivided into districts, cantons (being gradually abolished), villages and hamlets. Six cities (Saigon, Hue, Da Nang, Da Lat, Vung Tau and Cam Ranh) have separate status as autonomous municipalities with administrative powers similar to those of the provinces. Except for the mayor of Saigon, who is appointed by the Chief of State, the mayors of the autonomous municipalities are appointed by the Prime Minister. All field administrative activities are supervised, in civil matters, by the Department of Interior.

The provinces (43 in early 1966) are grouped into four administrative regions, which are also coterminus with the four military corps areas. Officially designated as Central Vietnam Lowlands (I Corps), Central Vietnam Highlands (II Corps), South Vietnam-East (III Corps) and South Vietnam-West (IV Corps), these regions are each headed by a delegate appointed by and responsible directly to the Prime Minister. Within his area the delegate exercises supervisory and coordinating authority in civil matters over the field offices of the central government and over the province chiefs. In early 1966 the four corps commanders were serving also as delegates in their respective military areas, thus combining both civil and military functions.

Provincial Government

The central government relies on the provincial administration to carry out national policy at the local level. Province chiefs maintain close contact with the authorities in Saigon. In mid-1965 all but three were military officers. Three main channels of contact are customarily employed: with the Prime Minister and members of his office; with the regional delegate who represents the Prime Minister as his regional inspector and as his civil as well as military assistant; and with the various departments and agencies, particularly the Department of Interior, which is directly responsible for the supervision of all administrative affairs in the provinces.

The province chief (governor) is appointed by the Prime Minister and is answerable to both the Prime Minister and to the Secretary of State for the Interior. He exercises all general administrative powers as well as budgetary and fiscal powers within his area. Specifically, he is responsible for the enforcement of national laws and for the maintenance of security, but, in recognition of the diversified cultural attitudes and ethnic composition of the provinces, he is given wide latitude in adapting the application of the laws to local conditions (see ch. 5, Ethnic Groups and Languages). He can also make recommendations regarding military matters to the Prime Minister and to the Minister of Defense. In addition, the chief has supervisory and coordinating authority over services of the central government agencies operating within his jurisdiction and oversees the administration of district, canton and village affairs (see ch. 26, Public Order and Safety; ch. 27, The Armed Forces).

The province chief may be either a civil official or a military officer. He is assisted by two deputies: a civilian deputy chief for administrative affairs and a military deputy chief for political affairs (see ch. 27, The Armed Forces).

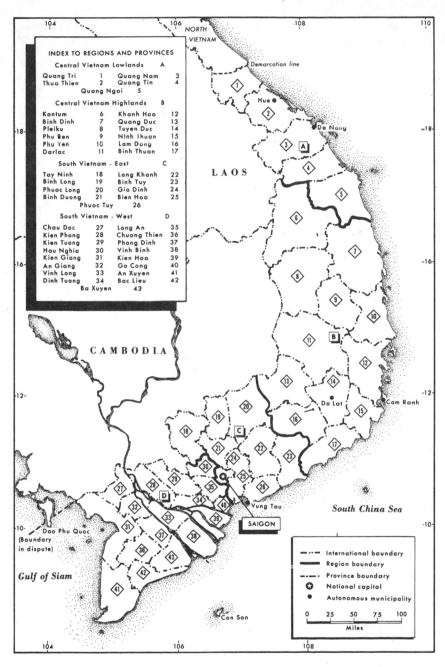

INDEX TO REGIONS AND PROVINCES

Central Vietnam Lowlands   A

Quang Tri	1	Quang Nam	3
Thua Thien	2	Quang Tin	4
	Quang Ngai	5	

Central Vietnam Highlands   B

Kontum	6	Khanh Hoa	12
Binh Dinh	7	Quang Duc	13
Pleiku	8	Tuyen Duc	14
Phu Bon	9	Ninh Thuan	15
Phu Yen	10	Lam Dong	16
Darlac	11	Binh Thuan	17

South Vietnam - East   C

Tay Ninh	18	Long Khanh	22
Binh Long	19	Binh Tuy	23
Phuoc Long	20	Gia Dinh	24
Binh Duong	21	Bien Hoa	25
	Phuoc Tuy	26	

South Vietnam - West   D

Chau Doc	27	Long An	35
Kien Phong	28	Chuong Thien	36
Kien Tuong	29	Phong Dinh	37
Hau Nghia	30	Vinh Binh	38
Kien Giang	31	Kien Hoa	39
An Giang	32	Go Cong	40
Vinh Long	33	An Xuyen	41
Dinh Tuong	34	Bac Lieu	42
	Ba Xuyen	43	

International boundary
Region boundary
Province boundary
National capital
Autonomous municipality

0   25   50   75   100
Miles

Figure 10.   Administrative Divisions of South Vietnam, April 1966.

213

In performing his duties, the chief is advised by a provincial council, an elective body of 6 to 15 members. As created in April 1965 (elections took place in the following month but only in secure areas), the council is empowered to debate and advise on the budget draft and to review the entire range of actions carried out by the province chief, but only "within the framework of policy and courses of action of the government." It has no legislative authority. A council member may communicate directly with the Prime Minister and other Cabinet members to express his views on provincial matters.

Districts

To the majority of Vietnamese outside the few urban centers, the district administration is the most concrete symbol and embodiment of governmental authority. The people tend to judge the character and performance of the central government by the success or failure of the district officials. District administrations (241 in February 1966) are each headed by a chief (civil or military), appointed by the Prime Minister on the nomination of the provincial chief. In mid-1965 all but three were military officers, most of them captains or lower ranks. In the governmental hierarchy the district chief is the lowest official appointed directly by the Prime Minister.

The district chief spends much of his time in the field, maintaining direct contact with village officials, local notables and the peasants. His duties are manifold. He is responsible for the maintenance of law and local security and for the coordination of activities of the various governmental services operating in his area. He collects vital statistics and administers programs dealing with public health, schools, agricultural extension, civic action, public works, etc. In addition, he supervises the administration activities of cantons (where they exist), villages and hamlets. Judicially, the district chief may act as coroner and as assistant to the public prosecutor of the province and may also adjudicate minor civil and criminal cases.

Village Administration

The village is the lowest formal link of the central government with the rural population and is the basic administrative unit in the governmental system. There were some 2,558 villages in August 1965. They are subdivided into hamlets or settlement areas, totaling some 15,000 in early 1966. The cantons (319 in early 1962), serving as intermediaries between districts and villages, are being eliminated gradually. Where they still exist, they are under the direction of chiefs appointed by provincial chiefs and function as auxiliary administrative arms of the district chiefs.

Traditionally, the Vietnamese village functioned as a nearly autonomous administrative unit. From the first century A.D. onward villages governed themselves, provided that the demands of the central authorities were met for tax collections and manpower for military service and public works (see ch. 3, Historical Setting). Village chiefs were usually chosen from among the senior men of the village by the local people, and each community maintained its own traditions and customs. Each village saw to its own internal order and security and its few public services.

A decisive break with the past occurred in October 1956 when a presidential decree provided for the appointment of village councilors by the province chief, thereby injecting direct government control into the traditionally self-governing community. The purpose of this ordinance was to eliminate the influence of subversive elements, many of whom had risen to positions of local leadership in areas controlled by the Viet Minh during the Indochina War.

The village administrative structure, as of mid-1965, was based on a decree issued in May 1964, which provides for a village administrative committee (formerly village council), composed of a chairman, vice chairman and, usually, four staff members. Each staff member is in charge of one of the following functions: economy and finance; security and police; information and propaganda; and youth and civil defense. The committee is assisted by a village people's council, an elective body of 5 to 11 nonsalaried members, each representing a constituency corresponding to a hamlet.

The chief responsibility of the council, which meets once a month, is to "discuss and decide" communal matters such as the budget plan and village developmental programs. The council functions more or less as an auxiliary to the village administrative committee. It may be dissolved by the province chief if there is evidence of subversive activities by more than half of the council members—a measure designed to remove Viet Cong influence from the local community. A councilor may be dismissed individually on similar grounds, without dissolution of the council.

A village may be divided into varying numbers of hamlets. Each hamlet usually has a locally elected chief and deputy chief. An assistant, appointed by the district chief, is in charge of youth and civil defense matters. The deputy chief is normally responsible for information and propaganda.

CHAPTER 14

POLITICAL DYNAMICS

Since 1960 the counterinsurgency efforts of successive Saigon regimes have overshadowed all nonmilitary matters. After the downfall of President Ngo Dinh Diem, in the absence of any effective civilian alternative, the armed forces both waged the war and sought to maintain political order.

South Vietnam continued to be plagued by insecurity, persistent dissensions among non-Communist forces and the apparent lack of firm allegiance to Saigon of nearly half of the people. Additional complicating factors were the rapidly rising cost of living and growing indications of war weariness on the part of the people. Saigon military leaders were confronted, therefore, with the need to carry out nonmilitary efforts to defeat the Viet Cong on political, social and economic fronts.

Prime Minister Nguyen Cao Ky, as had his predecessors, affirmed that, to accomplish the two tasks, the formation of a broadly repre-sensative government under an elected civilian leadership was needed. In February 1966 he offered plans to transfer power through con-stitutional processes no later than 1967. Militant civilian pressures, as manifested in the Buddhist-inspired political disturbances of March and April 1966 at Saigon, Hue and Da Nang, however, led to the government's decision to advance the timetable and to hold an election for a constitution-drafting assembly in September 1966.

In early 1966 the armed forces, the Buddhists and the Catholics constituted the Big Three of the non-Communist forces. Political turbulence since November 1963 had resulted in part from the lack of agreement on fundamentals and in part from the unbalanced position of influence among the three elements. Political peace and cooperation between the two religious groups in particular were regarded in Saigon as a pivotal factor in governmental stability. In early 1966 the Viet Cong movement represented the only organized and disciplined mass following on a national scale. The insurgents' strength was greater in the rural than in the urban areas.

Non-Communist political activities were largely urban based, and the number of those who were actually involved in political manifestations of one kind or another was small. Political parties proliferated, but none of them had any appreciable mass base.

Organizational discipline was weak, and leaders were lacking in stature Programmatic statements issued by parties had little popular appeal. Closely related to the irrelevancy of political principles in politics was the people's indifference toward the so-called ideological aspects of the North-South conflict.

An age-old popular tendency to mistrust nearly everything connected with the ruling authorities still persisted. Moreover, continual exposure to violence and insecurity made many people adopt a prudent attitude of noninvolvement with either the Viet Cong or the Saigon government, unless their physical safety was directly affected. Under these circumstances most of the people continued to rely on personalized relationship as the basis for political, economic and social activities. Family connections, regional or religious identification, professional background or school ties figured prominently.

Under President Diem, the country was in the hands of a single family which allowed no legal political opposition. After the downfall of the regime in November 1963, street demonstrations, hunger strikes or the tactics of self-immolation by fire became the means through which various demands and grievances could be channeled to the ruling authorities. Coups and countercoups became familiar instruments of changing government. Moreover, the government often found itself unable to carry out announced policies and programs because of the unpredictably changing political scene. As a separate political entity (as opposed to the historic entity of the whole of Vietnam) South Vietnam has existed for only 12 years, and during most of this period it has been concerned with the effort to survive the Communist threat. It has no tradition of representative government and is constantly plagued by Communist insurgency, so that the efforts of government leaders to develop a viable political order through constitutional processes continue to be slow and painful.

THE NGO DINH DIEM REGIME (1955–63)

Grave armed insurrections by dissident groups against the central government during the first 2 years of independence apparently led President Ngo Dinh Diem to believe that any political or social organization not under his control represented a threat to him and to the nation (see ch. 3, Historical Setting; ch. 26, Public Order and Safety). To consolidate his control, he relied heavily on his brothers.

The most influential was Ngo Dinh Nhu, who, as political adviser to the President, had a firm grip over all channels of governmental control and of mass mobilization within and outside the government. Nhu's wife, Madame Nhu (nee: Tran Le Xuan), also played an influential role as the unofficial First Lady at the Presidential Palace. Nhu's power was limited mainly to the southern region of the republic. The northern half was ruled by another brother, Ngo Dinh Can, commonly referred to as the unofficial governor of Central Vietnam because he had held no official position in the government. Two other brothers, Thuc (the archbishop of Hue and dean of the Catholic episcopacy) and Luyen (ambassador to Great Britain), helped the President but played secondary roles to Nhu and Can.

President Diem also utilized the Army, police and civil bureaucracy to reinforce his control. Inclined to be suspicious of the southerners (the inhabitants of former Cochin China) and Buddhists, he filled key positions in these establishments with personally reliable figures—many of them Roman Catholic refugees originating from north of the seventeenth parallel. Politically loyal persons were also given special benefits in nongovernmental sectors. Some aspiring and ambitious persons adopted Catholicism, hoping in this way to gain access to choice positions in government.

To ensure loyalty within and outside the government, the Diem regime had at its disposal several organizations tightly controlled by Ngo Dinh Nhu, and Ngo Dinh Can. For example, there was a semi-secret, elite organization called the Revolutionary Personalist Labor Party (Can Lao Nhan Vi Cach Mang Dang), popularly called the Can Lao. Organized by a group of intellectuals and labor leaders under Ngo Dinh Nhu after Diem came to power, the Can Lao claimed membership of some 20,000 selectively recruited persons holding key positions in the armed forces and civil service. The Can Lao, seeking no mass following, did not compete in elections.

Apart from functioning as a political intelligence network, the Can Lao also played a leading role in inculcating its members with the political ideas of President Diem and his brother, Nhu, which were officially labeled as Personalism (Nhan-vi). Conceived as an all-embracing doctrinal alternative to Marxism, Personalism was derived from a movement, started in Paris by the late Emanuel Mounier, editor of *Esprit*, which had attracted a number of Catholic intellectuals in France. Through it, President Diem sought to find a middle ground between capitalist individualism and Communist collectivism, both of which, he said, "have inflicted great damage on man."

The government also used the National Revolutionary Civil Servant's League (Lien Doan Cong Chuc Cach Mang Quoc Gia), created in mid-1955. It included in its membership nearly all civil servants. The League was to conduct "study sessions" for civil servants, to acquaint them with Personalism, government policies and anti-Communist strategy and tactics.

To get broad popular support, the regime used the National Revolutionary Movement (Phong Trao Cach Mang Quoc Gia)—the official party of the government. The movement was formally established in October 1954 under the honorary leadership of President Diem, but its actual control was in the hands of Ngo Dinh Nhu and Ngo Dinh Can.

As the dominant party in the National Assembly, it was the only one which had a semblance of a national following. Under official sponsorship, it organized meetings in every village to instruct the citizens in their civic duties and engender enthusiasm for the government. The movement worked closely with a number of auxiliary groups, including the Republican Youth Movement and the Vietnamese Women's Solidarity Movement (founded and led by Madame Nhu).

There were, in addition, a number of secret police and political intelligence services. Probably the most powerful (and most feared by the people) was the Social and Political Research Service (So Nghien Cuu Xa Hoi Chinh Tri), which was placed directly under the presidency and headed by a close associate of Ngo Dinh Nhu. A primary responsibility of this agency was to conduct surveillance over all politicians, government officials, military officers, professionals, businessmen and intellectuals and to manipulate political, social and student groups for governmental advantages.

The Diem regime by 1959 was well on the way toward firm governmental control. The President had successfully established his claim to national leadership, but his initial popularity declined as his dependence on his family increased and as this dependence led to a monopoly of power by the family.

All political and social organizations, loyal as well as in opposition, were subject to a high degree of official control. No political party could be formed unless officially approved, and any newspaper suspected of being in sympathy with opposition views or critical of the government invariably provoked official retaliation. Because of the government's tendency to regard all political dissenters as conspiratorial, nearly all opposition elements were forced to operate in semilegal conditions.

The opposition forces themselves were, however, factionally divided, financially weak and lacking mass following—a legacy of the pre-1954 pattern of political activities among non-Communist nationalists. South Vietnam became a virtual one-family and one-party state.

When Communist insurgency increased after mid-1959, President Diem tended to suspect and distrust even the moderate non-Communist opposition. On April 26, 1960, a group of 18 elder politicians and civic leaders who had held many secret meetings at Saigon's Caravelle Hotel (hence known as the Caravelle Group) issued the Manifesto of the Eighteen. They called upon the President "to liberalize the regime, promote democracy, guarantee minimum civil rights and recognize the opposition so as to permit citizens to express themselves without fear, thus removing grievances and resentments, opposition to which now constitutes for the people their sole reason for existence."

The Manifesto had no tangible effect, and one of the 18 members, Phan Khac Suu (later a chief of state), joined the paratroopers' coup of November 1960. The abortive coup attempt, led by Colonel Nguyen Chanh Thi and joined also by Phan Quang Dan, who had been a principal opposition leader, was successful for a few hours, but the rebel force was outmaneuvered by Ngo Dinh Nhu and his loyal troops. Colonel Thi and his associates fled to Cambodia and did not return to Saigon until after President Diem's downfall in November 1963. After this incident the repressive actions of Nhu and his wife increased considerably, thereby further reinforcing the unpopularity of the Diem regime.

The government, however, had far less success with the Communists, who, beginning in mid-1959, stepped up campaigns of terror, assassination and subversion, and used propaganda to capitalize on a long list of accumulated peasant grievances. They sought to present themselves as nationalists, concealing their Communist identity.

In order to coordinate and direct the insurgency under a non-Communist label, the Hanoi regime established in December 1960 somewhere in the south, the so-called National Front for the Liberation of South Vietnam (Mat Tran Dan Toc Giai-phong Mien-Nam). Another function of the organization was to neutralize politically all non-Communist elements. The Saigon government attempted to counter the insurgency mainly through military means, tending to neglect economic and social aspirations of the people. The urban orientation of the officials made them, in many cases, indifferent to the basic needs of the peasantry.

By October 1961, President Diem declared that his regime was confronted with "a real war waged by an enemy who attacks us with regular units fully and heavily equipped. . . ." He proclaimed a state of emergency and on October 24 lodged formal charges of aggression against North Vietnam with the International Control Commission, requesting that the Commission conduct an investigation into the role of the Hanoi regime in its efforts to conquer the South.

By the end of 1961 the government was harassed by about 20,000 guerrillas, as against an estimated 6,000 to 7,000 in 1960. Between 1959 and the end of 1961 some 636 rural schools had to be closed because the safety of the students and their teachers could not be assured. Moreover, many local officials were reported to have been killed by the Communists—about 4,000 of them during one 12-month period alone—causing near paralysis in government activities in some areas. Meanwhile, the Communists established a rival administrative structure in their areas of control, collective taxes, running their own schools and even issuing currency.

The government's attitude toward the question of a more liberal political system was expressed by a senior presidential adviser who, in November 1961, said "When we must make war against the Communists there is no possibility of democracy." An indication of popular discontent with the regime was the bombing and strafing of the Presidential Palace by two fighter pilots in February 1962. During the same month the Venerable Thich Tinh Khiet, titular leader of the Buddhist movement in South Vietnam, submitted to President Diem a letter urging the government to cease "religious discrimination activities" against the Buddhist community.

Nevertheless, except for occasional complaints by exiled opposition elements in Paris or Cambodia, internal non-Communist political forces were rendered virtually inoperative. The first opposition against the regime came from the Buddhist group, which had by far the greatest potential for mass following.

THE BUDDHIST UPRISING

The Buddhist crisis was touched off on May 7, 1963 (the fourteenth day of the fourth lunar month, celebrated in Vietnam as the anniversary of the Buddha's birthday). The disturbance broke out at Hue in Central Vietnam, the center of Vietnamese Buddhism and also the seat of Roman Catholic Archbishop Ngo Dinh Thuc, President Diem's elder brother and the most powerful voice in South Vietnam's Catholic community. Politically, Hue was also the seat of Ngo Dinh Can, who had ruled Central Vietnam, often independently of Saigon.

The crisis was precipitated by the government order forbidding the flying of the Buddhist flag. Buddhist followers who had gathered at Hue's Tu Dam Pagoda on May 7 were aroused by the government's order, and the next day they staged protest demonstrations to demand religious equality. At this rally Thich Tri Quang, militant leader of the Buddhist movement in Central Vietnam, declared their demand to be "legitimate." His recorded speech, to be rebroadcast that evening on Radio Hue, was, however, canceled by the authorities. Thereupon, some 10,000 persons defied the local security authorities, who countered by firing into the crowds.

The shooting resulted in the death of nine demonstrators. The authorities blamed Communist terrorists, but the Buddhists held the government troops responsible. On May 9, Thich Tam Chau, a relatively moderate leader of the Buddhist movement in the southern zone of the Republic, appealed to all Buddhists to join in protest against the government. The next day a group of Buddhist leaders, including Thich Tri Quang, called upon the government, in a five-point manifesto, to withdraw the order forbidding the flying of the Buddhist flag, to grant Buddhism equal status and privileges accorded the Catholic Church, to punish officers responsible for the Hue incident and compensate the victims thereof, to allow freedom of worship to the Buddhists and to stop harassing Buddhist faithful. Two weeks later the Buddhist leadership disavowed any political ambition by declaring that they were not advocating the overthrow of the government and that they had "no yearning nor desire to struggle for power."

The government announced on June 1 the dismissal of three senior officials involved in the Hue shooting incident, but this step failed to satisfy the Buddhists. The Buddhist cause was strengthened on June 11 by the self-immolation by fire of an elderly monk, Thich Quang Duc, on a Saigon street. On this date representatives from both sides tentatively reached a compromise agreement whereby the government promised vaguely to satisfy the Buddhist demands.

Thich Tinh Khiet, on behalf of the Buddhist community, expressed the view that the agreement would "inaugurate a new era and that no misunderstanding, no erroneous action from whatever quarter will occur again." The agreement failed to improve the situation, in part because of subsequent government charges that some of the Buddhist leaders were associated with the Communists and in part because of the government's delaying tactics. Moreover, measures reflecting increasingly anti-Buddhist attitudes on the part of Ngo Dinh Nhu and Madame Nhu served to widen the breach between the two sides.

The relation between the government and the Buddhists deteriorated beyond repair after August 20 and 21, when, under the direction of Ngo Dinh Nhu, several hundred armed police and troops raided a number of pagodas in Saigon and Hue, arresting nearly 1,000 monks, nuns and laymen. Three monks, including Thich Tri Quang, evaded the authorities and were granted asylum by the United States Embassy in Saigon. This raid, which resulted in the inactivation of most of the leading Buddhist elements, also occasioned the emergence of student groups as a politically significant force. Despite the proclamation of martial law after the raid, the student groups continued antigovernment demonstrations in major cities; during the final week of August alone some 1,400 students were arrested by the authorities. In early September, 2,400 additional students were detained.

The Buddhist struggle, especially after the raids of August 21, attracted widespread sympathy in South Vietnam and abroad. On August 22, Saigon's Foreign Minister Vu Van Mau, a Buddhist, and Ambassador to the United States Tran Van Chuong (father of Madame Nhu) resigned in protest against the government. The United States Department of State issued a statement deploring "serious repressive measures against the Vietnamese Buddhist leaders." Cambodia broke off diplomatic relations with Saigon on August 27. The Roman Catholic Archbishop of Saigon, Monsignor Paul Nguyen Van Binh, appealed to the government for religious toleration. At the United Nations on September 4 the representatives of 14 Afro-Asian nations formally requested a debate concerning the question of "The Violation of Human Rights in South Vietnam" at the forthcoming session of the General Assembly. On October 24 a 6-nation United Nations Fact Finding Mission arrived in Saigon.

The Buddhist crisis also aroused many military leaders, some of whom had been used and discarded by the Ngo family. The officers in general were concerned over deteriorating security and were especially disturbed by Ngo Dinh Nhu's attempt to shift the responsibility for the August raid to the military establishment. In addition, they appeared to have been alarmed over Nhu's reported disclosure in mid-October 1963 that he had been probing the possibility of direct negotiations with the Hanoi regime.

THE NOVEMBER 1963 COUP AND ITS AFTERMATH

Military Rule

On November 1, 1963, a group of senior generals led by Major Generals Duong Van Minh, Tran Van Don and Le Van Kim carried out a coup d'etat against the regime with the aid of troops supplied by Major General Ton That Dinh, then commander of the III Corps and military governor of Saigon. President Diem and his brother, Nhu, fled the Palace but were captured after taking sanctuary in a Catholic church in Cho Lon. The next day, while en route under guard to the General Staff Headquarters, they were killed by army officers. Their death ended the Ngo family's 9 years of rule.

The coup leaders eschewed political ambitions, pledged a relentless anti-Communist drive and on November 2 installed as prime minister Nguyen Ngoc Tho, a Buddhist who had served as vice president since 1955. They also suspended the 1956 constitution and dissolved the National Assembly. An interim civilian-military Cabinet was formed on November 4, and a 24-member Revolutionary Military Council, with authority to exercise executive and legislative powers, was established under the chairmanship of Major General Duong Van Minh.

The Revolutionary Military Council in turn announced programs to establish a "disciplined democratic political structure," to guarantee the freedom of religious worship for all, to recognize all non-Communist political parties "within the framework of national security," and to transfer governing powers to an elected government "when the situation permits." The Council also announced the creation of a 60-member Council of Notables to draft a new contitution.

Furthermore, the Council initiated a series of measures designed to liberalize much of the repressive practices instituted by the Diem regime, including the disbanding of all political and social organizations that had been controlled by the Ngo family. Political prisoners were released, but, at the same time, several hundred persons regarded as leading collaborators of the former regime were arrested for investigation. The Council's attempt to shift personnel of the top command structure of the military was, however, blocked by internal resistance and rivalry.

The Buddhist leaders, despite their major role in the anti-Ngo Dinh Diem struggle, did not participate directly in the decision-making process of the government. Instead, their new strategy was to develop a cohesive national organization, presumably to assert themselves more effectively in public affairs. On January 3, 1964, they formed a Unified Buddhist Church of Vietnam (Giao Hoi Phat Giao Vietnam Thong Nhat) under the nominal leadership of the aged Thich Tink Khiet; in fact, the organization was led by Thich Tri Quang and Thich Tam Chau.

The regime of Major General Duong Van Minh was supplanted, in a coup carried out on January 30, 1964, by a group of younger generals headed by Major General Nguyen Khanh (see table 1). He declared that the previous regime had been "too slow to keep up with the progress of the revolution and to respond to the exigencies of the struggle against the Communists."

He installed himself as prime minister, induced Major General Minh to accept the ceremonial post of chief of state, pledged a more vigorous anti-Communist and antineutralist struggle and promised better living conditions. A new governing body, called the Military Revolutionary Council, was established under Khanh's chairmanship. In April, Prime Minister Khanh dissolved the Council of Notables and announced plans for the formation of a popularly elected constituent assembly within 4 to 6 months.

The January 1964 coup was coolly received by the public, probably because it ousted Major General Minh, who had been widely regarded, particularly by the Buddhists, as the nation's most capable and popular general. It was also evident that many people looked upon the coup merely as an offshoot of an ongoing intramilitary power struggle. As a result, the Khanh regime was not popular with the Buddhists, the urban intellectuals or the Catholics. The intellectuals pressed for the early establishment of a civilian government, and the government countered by banning a number of Saigon newspapers. The Buddhists complained that the "remnants of the old regime" continued to harass them in Central Vietnam. Meanwhile, the Catholics charged the regime with being pro-Buddhist, and in June 1964 some 35,000 Roman Catholics staged protest demonstrations in Saigon, Hue and Da Nang.

The Prime Minister proclaimed a state of emergency on August 7, press censorship was reimposed, strikes and public meetings were banned and the government was given additional investigative and detention powers. On August 16, Prime Minister Khanh proclaimed himself president under a new constitution written at his direction.

Table 1. Changes in the South Vietnamese Government Leadership, 1954–66

Date of change	Chief of state	Chief executive	Real source of power
1954:			
July 7	Bao Dai	Prime Minister Ngo Dinh Diem	Ngo Dinh Diem.
1955:			
October 23	President Ngo Dinh Diem	Ngo Dinh Diem	Ngo Dinh Diem, Ngo Dinh Nhu and Ngo Dinh Can.
1963:			
November 1	Major General Duong Van Minh	Prime Minister Nguyen Ngoc Tho.	Revolutionary Military Council, under Duong Van Minh.
1964:			
January 30	Major General Nguyen Khanh	Nguyen Khanh	Revolutionary Military Council, under Nguyen Khanh.
February 8	Major General Duong Van Minh.	Prime Minister Nguyen Khanh	Revolutionary Military Council.
August 16	President Nguyen Khanh		Do.
August 27		Acting Prime Minister Nguyen Xuan Oanh.	Provisional Leadership Committee (Khanh Minh and Tran Thien Khiem).
September 3 [1]	Major General Duong Van Minh.	Prime Minister Nguyen Khanh	Khanh, Minh and Khiem, until September 30, 1964.
October 26	Phan Khac Suu	Prime Minister Tran Van Huong.	Armed Forces Council (from December 18, 1964 to May 6, 1965) (Minh was dropped in November 1964).
1965:			
January 27	do	Acting Prime Minister Nguyen Xuan Oanh.	Armed Forces Council.
February 16 [1]	do	Prime Minister Phan Huy Quat.	Armed Forces Council (Khanh was ousted on February 21, 1965).
June 19 [2]	Major General Nguyen Van Thieu.	Prime Minister Nguyen Cao Ky.	The Directory (National Leadership Committee—10 generals).

[1] Attempted coups, on Sept. 13, 1964, and Feb. 19, 1965, respectively, failed.
[2] Actual takeover by Air Vice Marshal Nguyen Cao Ky on June 12; the formation of the Cabinet took place on June 19.

The new regime was almost immediately denounced by nearly all political groups as being worse than the Ngo Dinh Diem dictatorship. Massive antigovernment demonstrations were staged by Buddhists and students throughout the country; their demands included an early end to military rule, elections within 3 months, elimination from government of all persecutors of the Buddhists and the resignation of President Khanh. Under pressure, the Military Revolutionary Council announced on August 25 the resignation of President Khanh and the annulment of the August 16 constitution. Two days later, the Council established a three-man Provisional Leadership Committee composed of Major Generals Khanh, Duong Van Minh and Tran Thien Khiem (popular with the Catholics) and dissolved itself. Major General Khanh resumed the post of prime minister on September 3.

This compromise formula pleased neither of the two religious groups; the Buddhists continued to campaign for more thorough purging of the so-called Diemists—many of them Catholics. When Prime Minister Khanh appeared to be yielding to the Buddhist pressure, a group of Catholic officers staged an unsuccessful coup on September 13, presumably to minimize the' Buddhist influence. Prime Minister Khanh removed Lieutenant General Tran Thien Khiem from the Provisional Leadership Committee, sending him to Washington as ambassador to the United States. The attempted coup failed mainly because the Prime Minister was firmly supported by then Brigadier General Nguyen Cao Ky, the Air Force commander.

Civilian Rule

General elections to a constituent assembly, which had been promised in April 1964, were not held; instead, the Khanh regime appointed on September 26 a 17-member civilian High National Council, which represented various political groupings. A new constitution framed by the Council was promulgated on October 20, and 4 days later Phan Khac Suu was elected by the Council as provisional chief of state. Suu in turn appointed, on October 26, Tran Van Huong as prime minister, and an all-civilian 15-member Cabinet—drawn mostly from the ranks of the civil service—was installed on November 4, 1964. Although in form, at least, the principle of civil supremacy was assured, the exercise of actual power, remained in the hands of military leaders.

The Huong Cabinet was opposed by nearly all political groups as being unrepresentative. Buddhist and Catholic groups as well as many party politicians, including those on the High National Council, alleged that they had not been "consulted in advance" of the formation of the Cabinet. The Buddhists appeared to be especially displeased with Prime Minister Huong's announced intention to minimize the influence of religious groups on the government.

Buddhists and students once again resorted to street demonstrations. When tear gas was used by the police the Buddhists charged the regime with using the same repressive police tactics as did the Ngo Dinh Diem regime and called on the United States to withdraw its support from the Huong government. Prime Minister Huong implied that the Buddhists were infiltrated by the Communists and fortified his position by declaring martial law in Saigon, imposing press censorship, banning public meetings and closing all schools in the city. Moreover, in December 1964 the Huong regime helped form a rival organization called the General Association of Vietnamese Buddhists, apparently to undermine the influence of the Unified Buddhist Church, which carried by far the most powerful voice in the Buddhist community.

Prime Minister Huong's uncompromising posture was generally backed up by the military. On December 18 some 30 young generals organized themselves into an Armed Forces Council to regain tighter control over the civilian establishments and also to ensure a balance of power among themselves. Two days later the Armed Forces Council, chaired by Nguyen Khanh (who had been promoted to lieutenant general), announced the dissolution of the High National Council on the grounds that it had been "abused by counterrevolutionary elements." The so-called December 20 coup was widely interpreted in Saigon as a blow to civilian politicians and also as occasioning the arrival of the so-called Young Turk generals onto the center of political power.

Amid mounting Buddhist discontent with the government, Prime Minister Huong promised in late January 1965 to hold general elections to a 145-member national legislature in March 1965. The Buddhists, nonetheless, continued to press for the resignation of Prime Minister Huong, whom they described as a lackey of the United States ambassador in Saigon. Antigovernment demonstrations also assumed an anti-American character.

In efforts to contain mounting disorders, the Armed Forces Council, on January 27, 1965, dismissed Prime Minister Huong and, on February 16, appointed Phan Huy Quat as successor. The facade of continuing civilian administration was thus maintained, but the authors of real power were Lieutenant General Khanh and his military associates. The new Cabinet, which included representatives of nearly all political groups, was favorably received by the Buddhist elements. As a transitional legislature, the Armed Forces Council established a 20-member civilian-military National Legislative Council on February 17, under the chairmanship of Major General Phan Xuan Chieu.

On February 19, however, a group of militant Catholic officers who had been implicated in the anti-Khanh coup attempt of September 1964 rebelled once again against Lieutenant General Khanh, whom they denounced as a dictator. The coup attempt was crushed, but on February 21 the Armed Forces Council ousted Lieutenant General Khanh as chairman of the Council and as commander in chief of the armed forces. It appeared that Lieutenant General Khanh had become unpopular with many of the Council members reportedly because of his strong man tendencies.

The Armed Forces Council dissolved itself on May 6 after announcing that it had full confidence in the Quat government and that it had wanted to concentrate on the war efforts. Prime Minister Quat was, however, unpopular with the Catholics, allegedly because of his pro-Buddhist attitudes and policies. He had another difficulty with Chief of State Suu over divergent views on the constitutional powers affecting appointment of Cabinet members. On June 12, 1965, Suu and Quat formally relinquished their offices and invited the military to take over the government.

The Return of the Military

Two days later a National Leadership Committee, frequently called The Directorate, was formed under the chairmanship of Major General Nguyen Van Thieu as the supreme governing body. Major General Thieu, a Catholic convert from Buddhism, after noting that 8 months of civilian rule had hampered counterinsurgency efforts, pledged to return power to an elected civilian government as soon as the war was won and "corrupt elements" were eliminated.

A new "war Cabinet" of 14 civilian and 3 military officers was formed on June 19 under Air Vice Marshal Nguyen Cao Ky, as prime minister. The reinstitution of military rule was protested by the Buddhist, Catholic and student groups alike. In February 1966, Prime Minister Ky formally announced plans for the formation of a civilian government after an election to be held sometime in 1967 (see ch. 13, The Governmental System). Civilian elements, the Buddhists and Catholics in particular, acted in concert in mid-March 1966 to demand the end of military rule.

Civil-military strife was touched off on March 10, 1966, when Prime Minister Ky relieved Lieutenant General Nguyen Chanh Thi of the command of the I Corps (comprising the five northern provinces) and from The Directorate "for reasons of health." General Thi had been widely regarded in Saigon as the Prime Minister's chief rival within the military power structure and reportedly had often resisted or delayed the execution of orders from the central government which he did not endorse. His removal almost immediately aroused anti-Saigon feelings among many people of the five northern provinces, especially in Hue and Da Nang. Also, the General, a Buddhist, was a close friend of Thich Tri Quang, the leader of the militant wing of the Buddhist movement. He was also said to be the only general in the nation having any measure of popular political support, and, in addition, he enjoyed the personal loyalty of many military officers and civil officials in the northern area.

The combination of these factors precipitated a state of political tumult in the northern area. Buddhist leaders instigated a series of antigovernment demonstrations, in which students, civil servants, urban workers, police officers and large numbers of the military participated. In Hue and Da Nang dissidents formed the so-called Popular Force Struggling for Revolution, more commonly known as the "Struggle Force." Anti-Saigon demonstrations at times became overtly anti-American. By the end of March it became evident that the central government had lost effective control in the northern provinces. Saigon itself became the scene of antigovernmental disturbances in which the Catholics also played a leading part.

In an effort to prevent further political chaos, Prime Minister Ky summoned a National Political Congress in early April to recommend appropriate procedures for establishing an elected civilian government. Some 170 delegates were invited to attend the Congress. Buddhist and Catholic groups initially boycotted the Congress, but later each sent two "observers."

The Congress submitted a 10-point list of recommendations to the government. One accepted was the Buddhist demand that the participants in Hue and Da Nang demonstrations should not be punished by the government. Prime Minister Ky announced that he would accept the findings of the Congress, and Chief of State Thieu on April 14 announced a decree that general elections for a constituent assembly would be held within 3 to 5 months.

Thereupon, moderate Buddhist leaders in Saigon ordered all antigovernmental demonstrations suspended but vowed "to adopt an appropriate attitude and action" if the government acted in bad faith. The dissidents in Hue and Da Nang, under the Struggle Force, however, continued to demand the resignation of Prime Minister Ky and pledged to maintain their militant vigilance "until Vietnam has a government elected by the people."

MAJOR POLITICAL PROBLEMS

Insurgency and Rural Uplift

In the early 1960's no stratum or segment of the population, urban or rural, was free from Viet Cong terrorism. In the countryside, the backbone of Viet Cong strength, thousands of local government officials were subjected to intimidation, assassination and kidnaping.

230

In some instances officials, fearful of Viet Cong vengeance, refrained from taking effective action.

Saigon itself was not immune to occasional Viet Cong raids. Successive regimes in Saigon were seriously handicapped in satisfying the social, educational and economic needs of the rural population. The task was further complicated by the Viet Cong strategy of economically and physically isolating towns and cities from the rural areas. In nearly half of its territory, the Saigon regime barely functioned as an effective government. The greater part of the country was controlled by government authorities during the day and by the Viet Cong at night.

Over the years the Saigon leaders had generally acted on the assumption that internal security could be realized largely through military efforts. As a result, much of the government's efforts and resources were diverted to battlefronts, and little consideration was given to the welfare of the economically distressed people, especially in the rural areas. The Diem regime's attempts to weaken Viet Cong influence among villagers through the *agroville* program in early 1959 (reorganized and modified as the Strategic Hamlet Program in March 1962) proved ineffective (see ch. 19, Agriculture). These programs, initiated mainly to deny Viet Cong agents the food, money, intelligence and recruits that they had been obtaining from the peasants, had little to offer the villagers who had been relocated or uprooted, often forcibly, from their ancestral lands. Because of its unpopular reception, Prime Minister Khanh overhauled the Strategic Hamlet Program and renamed it the New Life Hamlet Program.

By late 1965 it had become evident that the problem could not be effectively solved unless the people themselves had confidence in the government and were willing to fight for their homes and villages against the Viet Cong. To restore security and bring the benefits of governmental services to the countryside. Prime Minister Ky in February 1966 initiated a new rural reconstruction program. He called it the Revolutionary Development Program and gave it top priority as one of the three major governmental objectives for 1966.

Administered by the Department of Revolutionary Development, under the Ministry of War and Reconstruction, this program in mid-1966 was being carried out by some 23,000 revolutionary development cadres, largely of village origin. After training at Vung Tau for a period of up to 13 weeks in information dissemination techniques, military skills, political matters, public health, civic affairs, intelligence work, economic development and census taking, they were assigned to selected villages in teams consisting of 59 to 80 armed men. Operating only in militarily secure areas, each team was expected to stay in one village for about 13 weeks, with the ultimate aim of winning the trust and affection of villagers. The team's functions included initiating locally needed welfare and developmental projects, establishing local paramilitary defense, making a list of local grievances for corrective action and issuing identification cards to the villagers.

Unlike the earlier *agroville* and Strategic Hamlet Programs, the new program did not attempt to relocate villagers. In essence, these revolutionary development teams were attempting to defeat the Viet Cong agents in their own practice of building the basis of popular support of the village level by befriending the peasants. Their mission was to convince the villagers that the Saigon regime recognized their grievances as legitimate and was ready and willing to respond to them; another important objective was to spread the notion that the Saigon regime had more to offer than the Viet Cong in terms of peace, spiritual and material welfare and social justice.

There were signs in 1966 that the Revolutionary Development Program, operating in only 980 hamlets (out of some 15,000), might cut into the Viet Cong capability to exploit rural areas as the bases of their operation. Formidable problems remain to be solved, however, including red tape in the bureaucracy, the continuing need for experienced specialists, governmental instability in Saigon and the problem of checking the rapidly rising living costs (see ch. 8, Living Conditions; ch. 13, The Governmental System; ch. 18, Character and Structure of the Economy).

Political Disunity

In the early 1960's, there was little evidence that the major political groups were ready to work together in the task of nation-building. Among non-Communist elements a common ground for concerted political action appeared to be lacking, and at times, the threat to national survival itself seemed to be of secondary importance. In fact, the reason for the nation's own existence appeared to be unclear and unintelligible to many. Nonetheless, the body politic somehow demonstrated the capacity to survive one crisis after another, without suffering total disintegration.

Because colonial Vietnam was ruled as three regional entities— Tonkin, Annam and Cochin China—the people of each region had no single identifiable focus of allegiance except the common awareness of being Vietnamese and the accompanying desire for independence. Combined with partisan sentiments for their respective regions, people living in the former Annam could not readily reconcile themselves to accepting Saigon as their political and intellectual capital; those of former Annam, along with those of former Tonkin, tended to regard the people of former Cochin China unpolished and lacking in drive and vigor (see ch. 12, Social Values).

President Diem's regime came to be identified mainly as a government by northerners and Catholics; other major political forces of the nation seldom had any opportunity to work together in competitive harmony. Therefore, South Vietnamese exposure to free partisan politics began only after 1963, and then only in a limited way. It appeared likely that the process of resolving conflicting demands and of achieving agreement would be subjected to further stresses and tensions. Frictions between the Buddhists and Catholics, between civilian politicians and military leaders, between ethnic minorities and the Vietnamese, and among other groupings appeared likely to persist in years to come, whether in war or peace.

Disunity was also fostered by the popular tendency to distrust strangers and all ruling authorities and by the resultant inclination to remain indifferent and apathetic toward the nation's political life. Many Vietnamese are prone to assume that everyone acts out of selfish motives. Furthermore, more than two decades of wartime conditions and attendant human miseries have caused many Vietnamese to develop a prudent, opportunistic outlook. Because of the government's inability to provide protection from Communist terrorism in many areas, they tend to believe that their physical survival depends largely on their own efforts. In many cases, the people seem to prefer nonparticipation in activities involving political extremes, and to avoid being harassed by any outsiders, whether the Viet Cong or the government. Moreover, because of their deep-rooted seeing-is-believing attitude, most of the population tends to react against all political ideologies and slogans (see ch. 12, Social Values; ch. 17, Political Values and Attitudes).

Still another complicating factor is the South Vietnamese propensity to rely on highly personalized relationships in their social and political behavior. No organized sector of this society is free from the frequently divisive influence of this personalized social relationship. The civil service, the armed forces, political parties and organizations, labor unions, student organizations and even religious organizations tend to function on the basis of personality factors rather than on the basis of abstract political principles or a set of codes governing organizational life. Personal relationship is in turn conditioned by the cross-currents of regional origins, family connections, school ties and religious background.

In the early 1960's charges of irregularity among officials and also among businessmen were frequently raised. After his takeover in June 1965, Prime Minister Ky pledged relentless elimination of those whom he called "corrupt officials, horders and speculators." The Prime Minister declared these elements to be even "more dangerous than the Communists" and announced his intention to establish "a government of the poor, the hungry." He continued to warn, in his March 1966 speech to the nation, that dishonest elements should be regarded as "the nation's enemies because they have hindered a great deal the struggle of the people."

*MAJOR POLITICAL FORCES

The Armed Forces

Under the regime of Ngo Dinh Diem, the armed forces were sub-ordinate to civilian leadership and, despite their potential as a political force, elements of the military establishment as a group seldom sought an independent political role. Their political involvement, confined mainly to the officer corps, was carefully dictated by the President and his family, and many of the senior officers, a large proportion of them Catholics, derived their favored position from demonstrated personal loyalty to the Ngo family.

The dominant position of the armed forces after November 1963 was attributable to the absence of any alternative civilian groups with effective leadership and organization. Collectively, the officer corps drew its power and influence from control of the troops and the governmental administration down to the district level (see ch. 13, The Governmental System). Moreover, its political importance was enhanced by its leading role in the counterinsurgency efforts.

The officers on the whole have proven their unity in counterinsurgency operations, but their behavior in relation to other matters seemed to be less cohesive. The officer group is a mixture of diverse elements. Among them are Catholics and Buddhists as well as northerners and southerners. There are still others whose political activities cannot be explained in terms of either religious or regional background.

Latent mutual jealousy and suspicion between Buddhist and Catholic officers often affected adversely the solidarity of the officer corps. A desire to minimize the disruptive influence of religious factors on the military and also on the society in general, for example, appeared to be the main consideration in filling the membership of the 10-member Directory with five Buddhists and five Catholics; in addition, the question of regional balance was also taken into account in its makeup.

At times, however, religious considerations proved to be irrelevant. For example, Lieutenant General Nguyen Chanh Thi, former I Corps commander, had a number of Roman Catholic officers on his staff as did other Corps commanders. General Thi's successor, Major General Ton That Dinh, was also a Roman Catholic, but he was well received by the antigovernmental and anti-Catholic Buddist-inspired members of the Struggle Committee at Hue and Da Nang. Prime Minister Ky, whose resignation was demanded by a group of militant Buddhists, was himself a Buddhist.

The officer corps in general disliked any single man becoming too powerful or domineering. Prime Minister Ky repeatedly emphasized that he was merely a coequal among the 10 generals of The Directorate and that no one general could be singled out as more influential than another. Such public assertions were intended apparently to allay the common apprehension that no single political or religious group should be predominant.

In terms of political influence, the commanders of the four corps, the Capital Military Region and the Air Force were regarded in early 1966 as important. In most instances, support or lack of it from the III Corps, elements of which surround the capital area, and from the Air Force, was sufficient to prolong or shorten the life of a Saigon regime. The traditional popular belief that government is the function of civil officials has also been a factor contributing to the existing friction between military and civilian elements.

It appeared likely in early 1966 that the armed forces would remain an influential political force. They would go on playing the role of watchdog, political stabilizer or arbiter, as in June 1965 when the political deadlock between Chief of State Suu and Prime Minister Quat culminated in the military takeover.

Religious Groups

The Buddhists

Between 70 and 80 percent of the South Vietnamese population, or more than 11 million persons, are considered to be Buddhists, but only about half of them adhere closely to the precepts of that faith (see ch. 11, Religion). Political activists among them probably number no more than 2 million, but this numerical strength is sufficient to assure them a major role in national politics.

Buddhists are found on all levels of society, in all regions, in urban and rural areas, in the civil service and in the armed forces. They include party politicians, professionals, students, merchants, labor union members and peasants. Among them are nationalists, proponents of neutralism, anti-Communists and infiltrated Communists in Buddhist disguise. Geographically, they are divided into the so-called northern and southern groups of South Vietnam. In addition, they are divided into numerous sects (see ch. 11, Religion).

Given effective leadership, organizational discipline and unity, the Buddhists could readily convert their numerical superiority and cross-sectional representation into a powerful political movement. On a national scale, members of the hierarchy are probably in closer touch with the people than any other political group. At the village level, monks and nuns are accepted as an integral and natural part of the daily life. Usually, Buddhists are regarded as more Vietnamese than are Catholics, partly because Buddhism was not closely identified with the French administration, which had favored Catholicism as an instrument for political and cultural colonization. This negative attitude toward Catholicism was further reinforced during the unpopular, Catholic-oriented Diem regime.

The massive upsurge of Buddhist influence was the direct result of President Diem's policy of repressing organized political opposition. His downfall in November 1963 resulted in a political vacuum, and the Buddhists, who had been the only political group independent of the government, found themselves, along with military figures, at the forefront of national politics. Thereafter, the Buddhist hierarchy sought to portray itself as the guardian of 80 percent of the Vietnamese people, whom they claimed as the Buddhist faithful. The Buddhist leaders have repeatedly eschewed political ambitions and have asserted that they were not foreign-oriented. As early as May 25, 1963, a group of leaders, including Thich Thien Khiet, Thich Tam Chau and Thich Tri Quang, declared:

> Who has made the most sacrifices, who has made the most contributions to the fight against foreign invasion and for national revolution? Who has had more deaths on the battlefronts rather than sit tight at desk jobs and enjoy life in the cities? Who has been and is making most of this kind of contribution and yet never wanted to know about foreign aid nor had any desire to get to power? . . . Who are they, if not the Buddhist faithfuls, and Buddhist soldiers themselves?

Political developments since early 1964 indicate that, seemingly at least, the Buddhist leadership could often dictate the direction of government actions. Their opposition activities were responsible for General Khanh's relinquishing the presidency in late August 1964 and for the downfall of Prime Minister Huong in January 1965. Buddhist pressure in March and April 1966 also caused the government of Prime Minister Ky to agree to the transfer of power to an elected government earlier than it had originally intended. The standard Buddhist tactics included street demonstrations, hunger strikes and self-immolation by fire. The principal participants were mostly high school and college students, supplemented at times by adult sympathizers.

It was difficult in mid-1966 to ascertain the extent and depth of the Buddhists' real political potential. It was likely that, because Buddhist leaders are highly regarded in the country for their integrity and self-renunciation, many people willingly followed their leadership. On the other hand, it was equally possible that many of the street demonstrators took advantage of the Buddhist-instigated rallies as convenient forums for voicing their discontent with the ruling authorities without actually endorsing the Buddhist political posture.

Except for small numbers of monks and nuns genuinely motivated by doctrinal considerations, it became increasingly evident that most of the protestors were driven more by personal grievances than by religious motives. They appeared to be protesting, under Buddhist cover, as politically aroused, and sometimes exploited, individuals troubled by one or more of the problems involving the rising cost of living, physical insecurity, intense but formless nationalist sentiments, war weariness, uncertain political future, regional feelings or recurring frictions between Buddhist and Catholic groups.

The Buddhists' role in antigovernmental activities often reflected the society's social and economic tensions. There is no tradition of loyal opposition. In the absence of popularly based political parties and free information media, efforts to change government leadership tended to be made through conspiratorial maneuvers, and attempts to convey political messages to the leaders took extremist forms.

In early 1966 the dominant Buddhist organization was the Unified Buddhist Church of Vietnam under the titular leadership of Thich Thien Khiet (see ch. 11, Religion). Established in January 1964 the Unified Buddhist Church carried on its political activities through the Institute for the Execution of Dharma (Vien Hoa Dao), more commonly known as the Buddhist Institute for Secular Affairs, headed by Thich Tam Chau.

After April 1966 the political activities became the exclusive concern of a newly created Vietnam Buddhist Force (Luc Luong Phat Giao Vietnam) but subject to overall control by the Vien Hoa Dao. The Vietnam Buddhist Force, directed by a steering body called the Buddhist Forces Leadership Committee, was set up to coordinate and centrally control all Buddhist-inspired political activities under the chairmanship of Thich Thien Minh, head of the Youth Department in the Vien Hoa Dao and the third most important leader within the Unified Buddhist Church. A protege of Thich Tri Quang, Thich Thien Minh played a leading role in the anti-Diem movement in late 1963. Next in command in the Vietnam Buddhist Force was Thich Ho Giac, head of the Lay Department in the Vien Hoa Dao.

In September 1964, Thich Ho Giac, as the publisher of the *Hai Trieu Am* (Echo of the Rising Tide), the official organ of the Vien Hoa Dao, called on the Viet Cong to lay down arms and indirectly criticized alleged United States interference in Saigon's internal affairs. He was reportedly censured by Thich Tam Chau for his stand.

The Vien Hoa Dao exerted its influence down to the village and hamlet level through its extensive territorial organization (see ch. 11, Religion). Taken together, this organization, with its regional, provincial, district, and village and city branches, constituted, for all practical purposes, a sort of shadow government parallel to that of the Saigon administration.

Buddhists based in Hue and Da Nang are regarded as more politically partisan, militant and nationalistic than Buddhists based in Saigon. In their attitudes and activities, the northerners, led by Thich Tri Quang, generally took a militant line, while the southerners, led by Thich Tam Chau, were more conciliatory. The northerners' attitude derives from Thich Tri Quang's personal influence, strong regional feeling in the five northern provinces, the severity of anti-

Buddhist discrimination under the Diem regime and the relatively more severe economic depression of the region (see. ch. 18, Character and Structure of the Economy).

Other prominent bonzes were Thich Phap Tri, Thich Tam Giac, Thich Minh Chau, Thich Quang Lien, Thich Huyen Quang and Thich Thien Hoa. Among leading laymen were Tran Quang Thuan, formerly chairman of the Buddhist Student Association and secretary of state for social affairs in Prime Minister Khanh's Cabinet, and Mai Tho Truyen, spokesman for the Buddhists of former Cochin China.

The Unified Buddhist Church declared that Vietnam should not become "one of the Sino-Russian satellites or a colony of the Western imperialists." It also repeatedly expressed the hope that a "fratricidal war in Vietnam" be brought to an end through "an honorable solution." The Buddhists firmly opposed any form of military rule and similarly displayed sensitivity to any signs of a Catholic political comeback. Toward the Communist insurgents, denounced by Buddhist leaders as antinational and atheistic, the Unified Buddhist Church demanded that they be disbanded and withdrawn to North Vietnam. On a more positive note, they asserted that the government should be managed by civilians representing all segments of the population and that all persons who had contributed to the downfall of the Diem regime be returned to active political life. The Buddhist leaders, however, seldom went beyond the generalities to touch on specifics.

The Catholics

The Roman Catholics, numbering about 1.5 million, or approximately 10.5 percent of the population, were the most important political group under the Diem regime. Although their dominant position was taken over by the Buddhists after November 1963, the Catholics continued in 1966 to constitute a highly influential group because of their cohesiveness and extensive representation in the officer corps of the armed forces, in the higher echelon of the civil service and among the liberal professional elements. The Catholic community, comprising some 700 parishes throughout the country, is, on the whole, better educated and more affluent than any other aspiring groups.

The Catholics, like the Buddhists, are divided into militant and moderate groups. The militant element, often called the northern group, is made up of about 700,000 refugees from Communist North Vietnam, mostly from the Red River Delta area. They are regarded as being more partisan, anti-Buddhist and anti-Communist than their southern compatriots, who are made up of those Catholics native to the former Annam and Cochin China regions. The northern group is led by Father Hoang Quynh, chairman of the Greater Unity Force (Luc Luong Dai Doan Ket), or Greater Solidarity Bloc as it is sometimes called, a lay organization which has provided the bulk of the Catholic activists since March 1965.

In mid-April 1966 this organization was rechristened the Vietnamese Catholic Citizens Bloc. Still led by Father Hoang Quynh, it claimed to represent all Catholics, regardless of regional origins, and its apparent purpose was to serve as a single political arm of the Roman Catholic Church in South Vietnam, presumably to counter the Unified Buddhist Church and its newly created political arm, the Vietnamese Buddhist Force.

The southern Catholics are led by the Archbishop of Saigon, Monsignor Paul Nguyen Van Binh, who is assisted by Father Ho Van Vui. The southern adherents of Catholicism were less favored by President Ngo than those originating in the former protectorate of Tonkin. As a result, the southern Catholics tended to sympathize with the Buddhist grievances against the Diem regime and generally took a more relaxed and conciliatory attitude toward the Buddhist-Catholic frictions.

In early 1966, Monsignor Binh, through the Liaison Office of the Archdiocese of Saigon, continued to exert a moderating influence upon the militant northerners. Despite occasional signs of internal friction between Monsignor Binh and Father Quynh, their united front vis-a-vis the Buddhist community was generally maintained.

Political developments since November 1963 indicated that governmental stability in Saigon would depend in part on the balance of power between the Catholics and the Buddhists or on governmental ability to accommodate the conflicting demands between the two religious groups. The post-Diem regimes generally attempted to cultivate the good will of both groups, but failed to please either of them, partly because of the suspicion between the two and partly because of the nearly one-sided upsurge of Buddhist influence. In their efforts to offset the Buddhist strength, therefore, the Catholics often sought to enlist the support of two other religious groups, the Cao Dai and the Hoa Hao (see ch. 11, Religion).

The Catholics, as a whole, regard themselves as more pro-Western and anti-Communist than the Buddhists. In principle, however, their political aspirations represented no appreciable departure from those of their adversaries. Catholic leaders generally stood for the goals of national unity, social revolution, peace, the development of new political forces and the establishment of a truly representative form of government. In addition, Catholic students publicly urged the United States to respect Vietnam's sovereignty. To achieve these goals, the Catholic leaders repeatedly emphasized that the choice of political means and its timing should exclude any form of compromise with the Viet Cong insurgents.

In actual political conduct the Catholics have been hypersensitive to any action that might result in Buddhist predominance in the government, civil or military, in war or peace. They have consistently alleged that any governmental yielding to Buddhist pressures would amount to a policy of anti-Catholic revenge and discrimination. This underlying fear largely accounts for their antigovernment demonstrations in the summer of 1964 against the alleged pro-Buddhist posture of Prime Minister Khanh. It also explains the two coup attempts of September 1964 and February 1965 by a group of pro-Catholic officers. Furthermore, the militant Catholic opposition was a prime factor in causing the resignation of Prime Minister Quat's civilian regime in June 1965.

In early 1966 it became evident that the Catholics were apprehensive about Prime Minister Ky's decision to hold elections in September 1966 instead of sometime in 1967 as initially announced—a turn of events for which the Catholic agitation was partially responsible. They feared that an electoral contest held at such an early date would give the Buddhists distinct advantages and believed that they needed more time to live down the effects of former political ties with the Diem regime.

The Cao Dai and the Hoa Hao

The Cao Dai and the Hoa Hao, commonly referred to as politicoreligious sects, are the other two politically significant religious groups (see ch. 11, Religion). Their adherents, predominantly peasants, are concentrated mainly in the areas northwest and southwest of Saigon. These sects together claim nearly half of the 6 million people in the Mekong Delta region. By mid-1954 they had a combined strength of 35,000 men under arms. Until late 1955 their political strength was derived from independent control of administrative machinery and private armies in their respective territories, which had constituted the so-called states within a state.

The political behavior of the sects was conditioned mainly by their nationalist-oriented, anti-Communist but autonomy-oriented sentiments. During World War II they collaborated with the Japanese occupation authorities against the French, who had suppressed the sects for their anticolonial activities. After the war, however, in return for arms and other assistance from the French, both sects fought the Communist-dominated Viet Minh to resist its increasing inroads into their respective domains. Their separatist sentiments culminated in their demands in 1948 for political independence, control of foreign relations and maintenance of their own national armies. The high point of their separatist behavior was the armed insurrection in 1955 against Prime Minister Diem to resist his efforts to bring them under his direct control.

After being militarily subdued by Prime Minister Diem's forces, both sects lost much of their former influence, and, outwardly at least, their leaders gave periodic expressions of allegiance to the Saigon regime. Some militantly dissident members, however, fled to Cambodia, and some reportedly joined the Viet Cong to continue their opposition to Saigon. After November 1963 this collaboration with the Communist insurgents reportedly was discontinued.

President Diem's successors came to recognize that the sects' separatist orientation had tended to serve as a barrier to Communist infiltration. Although a sizable number of Communist elements have been operating in parts of the Cao Dai and the Hoa Hao territories, the sects' adherents, on the whole, have been less receptive to Communist agitation and less subject to Viet Cong harassment than those in other areas of South Vietnam. Therefore, in order to win their loyalty, various Saigon regimes have appointed Cao Dai and the Hoa Hao representatives to Cabinets and to advisory councils; high provincial officials and district chiefs in their respective areas have been appointed mainly from among the followers of the sects. Sect adherents also have been allowed to defend their respective areas as members of the Regional or Popular Force troops.

In early 1966 their separatist sentiments were far less evident than formerly. Although they appeared to favor civilian rather than military rule, neither of the sects took overt action against the Saigon generals, nor did they side with the Buddhists or Catholics, apparently hoping to antagonize neither of them. This passive attitude could be explained in part by the absence of any mass following outside the sects' respective territories and in part by the lack of unity between the two sects, which have tended to be mistrustful of each other. Moreover, both sects have been troubled by acrimonious factional strife.

Nevertheless, the Cao Dai and the Hoa Hao leaders appeared likely to be represented sizably in an elected national legislature because of their close touch with the peasants. This possibility was contingent on the effectiveness of leadership and internal cohesion for both sects, the evidences of which were, in early 1966, not readily discernible.

Both sects regard themselves as political and religious minorities and, hence, with little chance of dominating the Saigon power structure. Therefore, in early 1966 indications were that they wanted to enhance their political position by employing one or more of the following three alternatives: to form a joint parliamentary working group to exact concessions from the dominant group; to form a "third force" with other marginal parties and groups; and to support, individually or jointly, either the Buddhist or the Catholic group, with the possible consequence of swaying the balance of power one way or another between them.

In early 1966 the spiritual leader of the Cao Dai was Cao Hoai Sang. Among active secular leaders were Le Trung Nghia, Le Van Tat, Tran Quang Vinh, Nguyen Thanh Phuong and Nguyen Hoang Bay. Among the more militant elements was Phan Duy Nhung, who in early 1965 had issued a peace manifesto calling for a neutral federation of North and South Vietnam and for withdrawal of the United States from the country as soon as peace was restored. He was arrested in 1965 on charges of serving communism and in mid-April 1966 was still under detention.

Among prominent Hoa Hao spiritual leaders was Luong Trong Tuong, president of the Hoa Hao Religious Institute, the governing body of the sect. In political circles Trinh Quoc Khanh, Phan Ba Cam, Nguyen Giac Ngo and Madame Cao Thi Nguyet were influential. Madame Cao Thi Nguyet is one of the three widows of Huynh Phu So, founder of the Hoa Hao faith who was murdered by the Communists in 1947. None of these Hoa Hao and Cai Dai leaders had any national stature.

The Students

After mid-1963 student participation in numerous politically inspired demonstrations and activities became a standard feature of South Vietnamese society. The politically active elements appeared to represent only a small part of the total student body. Evidently, they had not been directed and controlled by any single student or outside political organization, partly because they, like other political groups, were divided into a number of subgroupings based on religious, regional and political tendencies: Thus, it proved to be difficult, and often meaningless, to separate the students' political activities from those being carried out by the older generation. In actuality, the students tended to play the part of action arms or instruments for the various religious groups and parties, none of which before 1963 had had any trained reserves of cadres for political purposes.

The most politically active students were those who had been associated with Buddhist and Catholic groups. They were at the forefront of all the antigovernmental demonstrations sponsored by either of the two religious groups. Often Buddhist-Catholic clashes in the streets, as in the summer of 1964, involved students affiliated with the respective faiths. The political importance of these youths was officially recognized, for example, by Prime Minister Ky's invitation to them in April 1966 to send group representatives to the 170-member National Political Congress. Two of the student leaders figured prominently in Congress activities: Le Dinh Thai, as deputy secretary general of the executive committee; and Le Dinh Thong, as a drafter of the Congress' 10-point list of recommendations.

The students as a group are idealistic rather than practical in their political orientations; they are intensely nationalist and extremely sensitive to any signs of foreign domination or interference in Saigon's internal affairs; some believe that the threat of Communist China must be eliminated before peace can be restored.

They prefer an elected civilian leadership, desire an early end to the war and tend to regard themselves as the genuine watchdogs of government and society. Compared to the older generation, they appear to have greater self-confidence in their ability to win over the Communist insurgents. They are inclined to believe that the Viet Cong are first nationalist-oriented Vietnamese and only secondarily misguided conspirators. Moreover, they seem to believe that when elements of compulsion and terror are eliminated from Viet Cong-controlled areas, the people in them will be less susceptible to Communist manipulation and control.

Labor Unions

Labor unions, which claim the membership of close to half a million, seldom sought an independent role under President Diem, partly because of strict official supervision. Until 1962 most of the unions supported the Diem regime in return for government subsidies. Union members are largely urban based and, hence, are more susceptible to worsening living conditions than the rural population (see ch. 8, Living Conditions). Moreover, because political protest activities take place mainly in urban areas, the proven ability of the unions to bring many members to the streets on a short notice could become an important factor to be reckoned with by various political groups, especially the Buddhists and Catholics.

In early 1966 two of the more influential labor organizations were the Vietnamese Confederation of Labor (formerly the Vietnamese Confederation of Christian Labor) and the Confederation of Unions of workers of Vietnam (also known as the Vietnamese Workers Syndicate Confederation). Of the two, the former was the larger and better organized and was led by Tran Quoc Buu, a Roman Catholic, who had been implicated in the anti-Khanh coup attempt of September 1964, which was staged by a group of pro-Catholic military officers; its leaders regarded themselves as more anti-Communist than those of the Confederation of Unions of Workers of Vietnam (see ch. 21, Labor). Although Catholic and Buddhist influences were apparent in these and other unions, none of them were exclusively identified with any religious or political groups. Despite recurring official hints that some of the unions had been infiltrated by the Communists, there were few overt indications, up to early 1966, that any of the unions had been utilized for subversive purposes.

Ethnic Minorities

South Vietnam's minorities, especially the ethnically diverse *montagnards* of the Central Highlands and the predominantly urban-based Chinese, are significant elements of the body politic: the former, because of their strategic geographical position and separatist sentiments; the latter, because they have considerable influence over the nation's economy. Neither of these two minorities has been effectively assimilated into national life, but outwardly at least they express allegiance to the Saigon government. Similarly, the Khmers (400,-000) and the Chams (35,000) of the lowlands have remained alien enclaves in the Vietnamese society around them (see ch. 5, Ethnic Groups and Languages).

The Montagnards

The 700,000 *montagnards*, ethnically distinct from the Vietnamese and divided by language and custom into 40 or more groups, are not a cohesive entity. They are, however, traditionally hostile toward the Vietnamese. Moreover, they are exposed to Viet Cong efforts to gain their favor for the purpose of exploiting the sparsely settled Central Highlands, in which they live, for use as infiltration routes and as sanctuaries. Under these circumstances, accompanied by increasing outside influences which they historically have resented, the *montagnards* are beginning to acquire a political awareness and a sense of unity heretofore unknown among them (see ch. 5, Ethnic Groups and Languages).

The *montagnards*' traditional hostility was further aggravated in 1954 by President Diem's action terminating the special status they had enjoyed under the French and bringing their homelands under Saigon's direct control. Thereby, Vietnamese law superseded customary law, and Vietnamese administrators were appointed to the highland districts. Other activities of President Diem's government added to *montagnard* resentment and resulted in an uprising of the Bahnar, Jarai, Rhade and Koho against the South Vietnamese Government in 1958. It was quickly suppressed, and seven leaders were jailed. Five were released in 1962 but two, Y Bham of the Rhade and Paul Nur of the Bahnar, were kept in prison until after November 1963 (see ch. 5, Ethnic Groups and Languages).

Realizing the importance of winning the loyalty of the *montagnards*, the Diem regime in 1961 initiated a more liberal policy. At the same time, the United States Special Forces advisers began the selection and training of *montagnards* for service in counterpart South Vietnamese units. These United States advisers demonstrated an ability to work with the *montagnards* but were unable to transfer the trust placed in them by the *montagnards* to the South Vietnamese officers who were assigned by the Saigon regime to command these small units. Hostility aggravated by this action on the part of the government was further heightened by the *montagnards'* knowledge that certain Rhade, Jarai, Bahnar and Hre, who had been induced to fight with the Viet Cong, were permitted to do so in units officered by fellow tribesmen (see ch. 5, Ethnic Groups and Languages; ch. 27, The Armed Forces).

Tensions between the *montagnards* and the South Vietnamese mounted. On August 1, 1964, Y Bham, the Rhade leader, announced the formation of a Unified Front for the Liberation of Oppressed Races (Front Unifié pour la Libération des Races Opprimées—FULRO), claiming to represent the Khmers and Chams as well as the *montagnards*. The announcement accused the South Vietnamese of systematically suppressing and mistreating the minorities and declared liberation from the "Vietnamese yoke" to be the purpose of the Front. In Darlac Province, on September 20, 1964, *montagnards* of the local defense groups, including Special Forces in five camps, revolted, killed their South Vietnamese officers, raised their own flag (red, green and black with three yellow stars) and occupied the radio station in Ban Me Thuot, the provincial capital, whence they broadcast a demand for an autonomous tribal state. Simultaneously, Y Bham issued a declaration accusing the South Vietnamese of practicing "extermination" of the minorities.

Major General Nguyen Khanh, then prime minister, hurried to Ban Me Thuot to put down the revolt. He was prevailed on by United States advisers not to use force to retake the rebel camps and, after a week of negotiations with tribal leaders and the rebels, the camps were turned over peacefully to the South Vietnamese. Prime Minister Khanh refused to consider autonomy for the seven highland provinces where the *montagnards* are in the majority but agreed to "give consideration to their just aspirations" for equality.

Important concessions were promised. Villages were to be given title to an area four times as large as the land they actually occupied. Tribal customs and courts were to be restored. Highlanders were to be given preferential treatment when they sought admission to South Vietnamese high schools, the Thu Duc Infantry School and the Da Lat Military Academy. Tribal languages were to be taught at the primary school level, with Vietnamese being introduced gradually at higher levels (see ch. 5, Ethnic Groups and Languages).

Meanwhile Y Bham had disappeared into the jungle, but in March 1965 he appeared in Phnom Penh, Cambodia, as guest of Prince Sihanouk (Chief of State) at an official dinner. During a speech at this dinner, Y Bham praised the Cambodians for their help to his people and attacked the Saigon government. Later, however, he expressed satisfaction to Prime Minister Khanh for his promised concessions, but demanded the right to fly the FULRO flag at *montagnard* camps and to organize a 50,000-man highlander army under its own officers. He also wanted United States aid to be channeled directly to the highlanders without passing through South Vietnamese intermediaries.

Desultory consultations were held between FULRO representatives and the Saigon government; FULRO groups continued to operate in the highlands, much to the displeasure of the II Corps commander, who branded them as rebels. On July 22, 1965, Chief of State Thieu promulgated Decree No. 6–65, which reorganized the tribal customs courts and defined their jurisdiction, and on July 27, accompanied by Prime Minister Ky, he visited Pleiku to open a *montagnard* center for the training of local security forces.

The promised restoration of tribal courts and other concessions to the *montagnards*, however, went unimplemented, and, on September 10 and 11, 1965, 400 tribesmen in Special Forces camps near Ban Me Thuot revolted but were disarmed by South Vietnamese marines. Chief of State Thieu made a hurried visit to the highlands to "convince the *montagnards* that they were full-fledged citizens . . . and that the South Vietnamese government was trying to eliminate the social injustices that may have existed."

After this revolt was suppressed, Prime Minister Ky visited Ban Me Thuot, where the tribesmen reaffirmed their loyalty to the South Vietnamese Government. The Prime Minister promised the highlanders that the government would reassign all military and administrative personnel of *montagnard* origin to services relating to the tribal population and would facilitate the admission of their youths into the National Institute of Administration, the Thu Duc Infantry School and the Nha Trang Non-Commissioned Officers' School. Action was taken immediately by the government to set up an office in Ban Me Thuot called La Direction Spéciale des Affaires Montagnards (Special Department for Montagnard Affairs). Although this office was headed by a South Vietnamese, his superior in Saigon was Paul Nur, a *montagnard*.

Unrest among the *montagnards* recurred on December 17, 1965, when FULRO sympathizers rose in the three provinces of Phu Bon, Darlac and Quang Duc. In Quang Duc they temporarily occupied the provincial capital, Gia Nghia; in Darlac they took over for a short time two Special Forces camps; in Phu Bon, they killed some 30 South Vietnamese, including a district chief. As in the previous September, the revolt was short lived. On this occasion, however, a military tribunal tried 20 leaders of the rebellion, charging them variously with treason, murder and attempted murder. Four were ordered executed by firing squad; others received sentences ranging from 5 years of hard labor to life imprisonment. Four were acquitted.

By February 1966 the FULRO-led dissident activities in the highlands were reported to be gaining momentum, but no new rebellious actions had occurred through April. Meanwhile, in March the Special Commissioner for Montagnard Affairs in Saigon, Paul Nur—the first *montagnard* to attain the status of a top government official—appealed to the highlanders to seek "closer unity with the lowland people and to give up any suspicion in order to help realize a new Vietnamese society, in which all racial groups will merge into a single national entity." He stated that the present government's policy was based on principles of racial equality and solidarity and on respect for *montagnard* ways and customs, and he promised them measures to improve their welfare. Labeling FULRO as a group of dissidents, he asserted that "once the aspirations of the *montagnards* are realized, there will be no reason for the FULRO movement to exist." Moreover, he stressed that his office was planning to improve programs aimed at increasing security among the highlanders (see ch. 26, Public Order and Safety).

The value of winning *montagnard* loyalty or support has been equally recognized by the Communist-controlled, self-styled National Front for the Liberation of South Vietnam (NFLSV), which also has a program stressing autonomy for the tribal areas. Y Binh Aleo, a Rhade, is a vice chairman of the Central Committee of the Front and its Presidium, as well as chairman of the Executive Committee of the so-called Highland People's Autonomy Movement.

The Chinese

The Chinese have long played a central role in business, almost completely dominating commercial enterprises. This role, while indispensable to the economy, has incurred Vietnamese resentment, and this in turn has reinforced the tendency of this able and energetic group to remain apart. The country not only suffers from the resultant tensions, but it is denied the contribution the Chinese could make outside the narrow economic realm. President Diem initiated a long-range program designed gradually to integrate them into Vietnamese society. He tempered the measures which required them to accept Vietnamese citizenship and which restricted their business activities. These governmental efforts were, however, generally resisted by the Chinese, who resorted to moderate economic boycotts, which, nevertheless, proved to be disquieting enough to cause the Diem regime to adopt a more conciliatory approach.

Politically, the Chinese have rarely sought an active partnership with any of the Saigon governments, nor with any of the various political forces. On the whole, they appear to be hostile to the Communist regime in their homeland and to recognize that their future is linked with that of a non-Communist and probusiness regime in Saigon. There are indications, however, that some of the younger members of the community sympathize with Communist China rather than with the Nationalist regime of Taiwan, and this group constitutes a potential source of support for the Viet Cong.

The overriding concern of the Chinese community has been with their business and commercial interests, which in their view give them collective strength against outside pressure. In mid-1966 attempts by the South Vietnamese authorities to penetrate the protective wall built around the community's economic base of power had been less than successful. The Chinese tendency to act cohesively against outside interference was partly illustrated in March 1966 when the government of Prime Minister Ky executed a Chinese businessman after finding him guilty of "economic crimes." The Chinese reacted by staging a sort of economic disobedience campaign which disrupted the nation's commercial activities for about 3 weeks. Some of the merchants have been suspected of paying "taxes" to the Viet Cong to secure freedom of movement throughout the country.

The most influential organization among the Chinese appears to be the General Chamber of Commerce, acting as the principal intermediary between them and the Saigon government. Leading figures of this body apparently carry authoritative voices in matters affecting the community.

The Peasants

Nearly 80 percent of the South Vietnamese are peasants, traditionally uninterested in political matters outside their immediate area. The peasants, by force of circumstances beyond their control, have involuntarily played a crucial role in the nation's political life.

During the anti-French struggles spearheaded by the Viet Minh, the peasantry comprised the main component of the independence movement. Later, in Saigon's struggle against the Viet Cong insurgents, the peasants provided most of the combatants for both sides in this conflict. Moreover, the success or failure of the government's counterinsurgency operations are often directly affected by the extent of villagers' cooperation with either of the opposing forces. Thus, both Saigon and the Viet Cong have come to regard the peasantry as a decisive factor in determining the political future of the country.

The peasants have had no independent national organization or leader of any national stature to represent them in the urban-oriented Saigon government. Probably the segment of the population most neglected by the government, many peasants have been susceptible, especially during the past decade, to the Communist efforts to gain their favor and to turn them against the Saigon authorities. Since most of the Viet Cong agents were posing as nationalists and were native to the villages in which they were operating, they have in many areas encountered little or no resistance from the peasants.

Official neglect and unconcern thus inadvertently contributed, initially at least, toward increasing Communist influence in the rural areas. To arrest this trend, successive Saigon governments have instituted extensive measures intended for rural uplift, variously known as pacification, civic action, rural reconstruction or, more recently, as the Revolutionary Development Program.

The peasants' aspirations and needs are usually expressed in terms of land ownership, education and improved opportunities for their offspring, better houses to live in, adequate water for their rice paddies, availability of seeds and fertilizer, rent reduction and, in most cases, a desire for peace. They have a deep-seated conviction that these ends will have to be achieved mainly through their own efforts, partly because of their longstanding distrust of governing authorities (see ch. 17, Political Values and Attitudes). In recent years, however, they have been led to expect help in the fulfillment of these needs, at least in part, because of the competitive promises being made to them by both Viet Cong and government sources.

Peasants, like many other South Vietnamese, have shown little interest in abstract philosophical principles or political ideologies which have had little or no relevance to village life. Their mistrust, or evasion wherever possible, of governing authorities has been proverbial and has tended to insulate them from outside influences. As a result, the Viet Cong and the Saigon regime have found themselves constantly groping for means to penetrate the villagers' psychological barriers.

Depending upon circumstances, peasant reaction to the Viet Cong or to the Saigon authorities usually took the form of willing support, fatalistic acquiescence, evasion or opportunistic noninvolvement. On the whole, conscious support came from small numbers living in areas securely controlled by either the Viet Cong or the government, where the risk of reprisals from the opposing side was relatively absent. The bulk of those who acquiesced in Viet Cong rule apparently did so because of the ever-present threat to their life and property; some of them appeared reluctant to leave their ancestral land and to face an uncertain future elsewhere. Still others, if they lived a long distance from the nearest government-controlled area, apparently preferred to remain under Viet Cong control. Wherever opportunity presented itself, hundreds of thousands of villagers fled to adjoining areas not under exclusive Viet Cong control, but without overtly committing themselves to Saigon. It is estimated that over 1 million refugees have fled from Viet Cong-controlled areas since January 1965.

For the majority of the peasants, however, the standard behavior was one of opportunistic noninvolvement—ever ready to switch sides or give outward gestures of support to either side, if such action seemed necessary for survival. Many of them inhabit the so-called twilight zones, or contested areas.

The Viet Cong Insurgents

The Communist insurgency continued in mid-1966 to be the most pervasive political factor confronting the Saigon government. The insurgents, known under the generic label of Viet Cong, were operating within the framework of the self-styled National Front for the Liberation of South Vietnam.

The Communist Hanoi regime announced, in January 1961, that the so-called National Front had been established on December 1960 in the South by "various forces opposing the fascist Ngo Dinh Diem regime." The announcement, which came 4 months after the ruling Lao Dong Party in Hanoi declared its intention to "liberate" the South, also exhorted the South Vietnamese to set up a "broad national united front directed against the United States-Diem clique."

The National Front claims that it is a South Vietnamese nationalist rather than a Hanoi-inspired Communist-front organization and that it is the only genuine representative of the South Vietnamese people. It avoids references to communism in all of its public pronouncements. Its avowed political and military aim is the overthrow of all pro-Western regimes in Saigon and the establishment of what it calls a neutral South Vietnam free of all alliances. In the early 1960's, the National Front claimed that it controlled 75 percent of South Vietnamese territory and more than 70 percent of its population and that it was the sole legitimate voice of the South Vietnamese people.

In early 1966 the Viet Cong, predominantly rural based, seemed to constitute only a minor segment of the population, confined mainly to remote, sparsely settled areas not controlled by the Cao Dai and the Hoa Hao sects, Catholic priests or governmental authorities. Buddhist leaders continued to warn their followers against Viet Cong efforts to exploit and undermine their religious faith. Viet Cong influence among the 3 million urban dwellers was less evident than among the peasants, partly because of the relative safety of cities from Communist terrorism and partly because of suspicion of all crusaders. The Viet Cong's call for general strikes in cities on two different occasions in late 1965 had no tangible effect. The greatest problem faced by the Viet Cong was that of justifying the need for continuing insurgency and still more sacrifices (see ch. 27, The Armed Forces).

Superficially, the high command of the Front is its 49-member Central Committee and a more selectively constituted Presidium. In early 1966 they were both headed nominally by Nguyen Huu Tho, a former Saigon lawyer who called himself a socialist. His executive deputy was Huynh Tan Phat, carrying the title of deputy chairman of the Presidium and secretary general of the Central Committee. Directly subordinate to the Central Committee were a number of administrative commissions dealing with such functions as military affairs, foreign relations, information, culture, education, health, economic affairs and communications. The Commission for Foreign Relations was headed by Tran Buu Kiem, and its chief roving ambassador was Nguyen Van Hieu.

Most of these commissions had their provincial, district, and village counterparts. For military purposes the Front divided South Vietnam into five regions and one special zone for the Saigon area; nominally, the commanding authority over the military establishment emanated from the Front's Commission for Military Affairs. For external propaganda activities, the Viet Cong high command relied on the so-called Liberation News Agency and its Liberation Radio and nine permanent missions (accorded semidiplomatic status) established at Algiers, Budapest, Cairo, Djakarta, East Berlin, Havana, Moscow, Peking and Prague. Another mission was also expected to be set up in Pyongyang, North Korea. The official organ of the Front was called *Giai Phong* (Liberation) (see ch. 16, Public Information).

In fact, however, both in political and in military matters, the ultimate power of leadership and control within the Viet Cong movement has been vested in and exercised by the Front's so-called Vietnamese People's Revolutionary Party (Dang Nhan Dan Cach Man Viet Nam), one of the least known aspects of the Communist insurgency, probably even to some of the Viet Cong operatives themselves.

Inaugurated in January 1962 by representatives of Marxist-Leninists in South Vietnam and joining the Front allegedly on a voluntary basis, this openly Communist party came to constitute the supreme political and military directorate of the Viet Cong insurgency and, hence, the authentic politicomilitary instrument of Hanoi's Workers' Party of Vietnam (Dang Lao Dong Viet Nam—contracted as the Lao Dong Party). This fact was brought to light in May 1962 in a captured Viet Cong document from the Ba Xuyen provincial committee of the Lao Dong Party in the Mekong Delta to the party's district committees concerning the formation of the People's Revolutionary Party. The instruction, dated December 7, 1961, reads in part:

> The People's Revolutionary Party has only the appearance of an independent existence; actually, our party is nothing but the Lao Dong Party of Vietnam (Viet-Minh Communist Party), unified from North to South, under the direction of the central executive committe of the party, the chief of which is President Ho. . . . During these explanations, take care to keep this strictly secret, especially in South Vietnam, so that the enemy does not perceive our purpose. . . . Do not put these explanations in party bulletins. . . .

Another Viet Cong document seized in Chuong Thien Province, also in the delta region, in November 1964 stated that ". . . we should realize that our country is one country, that the Vietnamese People's Revolutionary Party and the Vietnam Lao Dong Party are one party. . . . There is nothing different between the two parties."

The leader of the People's Revolutionary Party, variously known as Nguyen Van Cuc or Mei Ku (in Chinese), is thought to be a secret member of the Lao Dong's Central Committee. Supreme military authority in South Vietnam, subject to the political control of the Lao Dong Party (Hanoi) and the People's Revolutionary Party, is said to be exercised by Tran Nam Trung, the "representative" of the so-called Liberation Army and as a deputy chairman of the Presidium of the National Front for Liberation.

Tentative indications are that Tran Nam Trung may be in charge of the Military Committee of the People's Revolutionary Party, which is known to the Saigon authorities also as the Central Office for South Vietnam. Several Viet Cong prisoners reportedly have suggested that he was actually Lieutenant General Tran Van Tra, a deputy chief of staff of the North Vietnamese army and an alternate member of the Lao Dong's Central Committee. Another source asserted in February 1966 that Nguyen Chi Thanh, one of Hanoi's two four-star generals, possibly was the military commander in the South. He is a member of the Political Bureau and of the Secretariat of the Lao Dong Party.

PARTY POLITICS

Political parties have never played a significant role, either as a training ground for future leaders or as a process for articulating the political needs of the citizenry. Under President Diem the only legal parties were those unequivocally progovernment, and their existence was permitted mainly to lend a multiparty facade to an otherwise one-party state dominated by a single family. After November 1963 successive governments encouraged the resumption of partisan activities but barred those advocating neutralism or communism.

By April 1966 there were no less than 60 registered political parties, but none of them had as yet functioned as a party in the Western sense of the word. In fact, an influential Saigon daily newspaper commented, in December 1965 that ". . . political parties have done nothing praiseworthy since the 1963 revolution. . . ." In early 1966 parties which existed more than in name were the two nationalist and anti-Communist organizations, the Vietnamese Nationalist Party and the Nationalist Party of Greater Vietnam, and those organized by the Cao Dai and the Hoa Hao sects.

Features common to nearly all of the parties were the lack of any appreciable mass appeal, frailty of party structure, nondescript programs, factionalism stemming from personal differences, and the urban origins of most of the party leaders. In terms of potential, parties as a whole, as then constituted, were given little chance by Saigon political circles of exerting any significant influence, unless they were supported by major religious groups. Indications in early 1966 were that both Buddhist and Catholic groups preferred to remain unattached to any outside political organizations. On the other hand, there were also some indications that parties might emerge as potential rallying points for many political activists if the religious elements failed in their own efforts.

Vietnamese Nationalist Party

The Vietnamese Nationalist Party (Viet Nam Quoc Dan Dang—VNQDD) was first established at Canton in 1925 to oppose Ho Chi Minh's Communist group (see ch. 3, Historical Setting). Although inactive during the Diem regime, this party emerged after 1963 as a major organization standing for anticommunism, antineutralism, national reconstruction and democratic socialism.

The VNQDD in early 1965 was composed of four factional groups divided along religious and regional lines. The largest of these claimed about 95,000 members, most of them Buddhists living in the Mekong Delta region. It was led by Nguyen Hoa Hiep and Tran Van Tuyen. The second component, numbering about 50,000, was based mainly in the province of Quang Ngai and, to a lesser extent, in Quang Nam and Quang Tin. Also predominantly Buddhist, this faction, let by Nguyen Dinh Bach and Bui Hoanh (chief of Quang Ngai Province), was reportedly under the political influence of Buddhist militant Thich Tri Quang. The third element, led by Le Hung, was made up of about 10,000 Roman Catholic refugees from the North who had formerly constituted the northern chapter of the VNQDD. The fourth element, numbering less than 1,000, consisted also of refugees from the North.

Nationalist Party of Greater Vietnam (Dai Viet)

The Nationalist Party of Greater Vietnam (Dai Viet Quoc Dan Dang—DVQDD), usually known as the Dai Viet, was established at Hanoi in 1939 by a group of pro-Japanese, anti-Communist nationalists, initially under the name of Dai Viet Nationalist Alliance (Dai Viet Quoc Gia Lien Mien). Outlawed by the Communist Hanoi regime in 1946, the Dai Viet shifted its base of operations to the South. After November 1963 it was revived by Phan Thong Thao and Nguyen Ton Hoan; the latter served as a deputy prime minister under General Khanh. The party has been firmly committed to anticommunism and national independence. Claiming a membership of some 20,000, the Dai Viet derived most of its supporters from the Hue and Quang Tri areas of Central Vietnam.

In early 1965 the party was divided into three major factions. Prominent party figures included Ha Thuc Ky, Nguyen Ngoc Huy, Tran Van Xuan, Dang Van Sung and Phan Huy Quat. A faction under the latter two leaders published the *Saigon Post*, an English-language daily, and the *Chinh Luan* (Right Opinion), an influential Vietnamese-language daily (see ch. 16, Public Information).

Among the younger members of the Dai Viet, Catholic influences appeared to be strong. In the antigovernmental coup attempts of September 1964 and February 1965, for example, the principal participants were Catholic and pro-Catholic officers affiliated with the Dai Viet. The September 13 attempt was made a week after Nguyen Ton Hoan, then party leader, was forced into exile by General Khanh.

Other Parties

Other lesser known but potentially significant parties were those identified exclusively with either the Cao Dai or the Hoa Hao sects. In 1965 the Cao Dai sect carried out its political activities mainly through the Vietnam National Restoration Association (Vietnam Phuc Quoc Hoi), established first in 1943. Under the Diem regime, the Association—then known as the National Restoration League—constituted one of the progovernment showcase parties. After November 1963 the League was reconstitued as the Association by those who had refused to support the Diem regime. Divided into at least two competing factions, the Association's leading figures included Nguyen Thanh Phuong and Nguyen Hoang Bay. Those who had supported the Diem regime formed a separate rival organization called the War Veterans Association.

The Social Democratic Party (Dan Chu Xa Hoi Dang)—abbreviated as the Dan Xa—is a political outlet for the Hoa Hao sect, established in 1945. After the sect was crushed by President Diem's forces in 1955, certain progovernment Hoa Hao elements continued to operate under the Dan Xa label. Reconstituted after 1963, the Dan Xa (with its swastika symbol) was lead, in early 1966, by Phan Ba Cam. The Dan Xa was opposed by the Vietnam Social Democratic Party (Vietnam Dan Chu Xa Hoi Dang) under Trinh Quoc Khanh. The Trinh Quoc Khanh group (with a flag bearing three stars) continued to ridicule the Dan Xa group for its former pro-Diem posture, and, in fact, Khanh's followers raided the Dan Xa's head office in September 1964.

In addition, there were scores of so-called parties or "forces." Information regarding their leadership, political orientations and membership was unavailable in mid-1966. Among those organizations often in the news were the Democratic Youth Force, headed by Nguyen Thanh Tung and claiming a membership of 110,000; the Duy Dan Party; the National Revolutionary Force; National Unification Force; Democratic Forces Alliances; National Self-Determination Front; United Struggle Force; Solidarity Movement; People's Coalition; Anti-Communist Bloc, etc.

254

ELECTORAL PROCESS

The electoral process became a subject of lively political debate after mid-April 1966 when Chief of State Thieu decreed that a constituent assembly would be chosen by ballot within 3 to 5 months. In mid-April it was difficult to determine what kind of an electoral procedure would be worked out and who would be involved in preparing the procedure.

Under President Diem's rule, elections, when permitted, served only to lend a stamp of legitimacy to the government. Because origanized political opposition was not tolerated by his regime, elections played no positive role in political life. Moreover, the Communist insurgency and the resultant lack of security in many areas made it difficult for many rural people to vote for fear of Viet Cong reprisals.

The first general elections in South Vietnam took place in March 1956 for the 123-member National Constituent Assembly, which in October 1956 was sworn in as the National Assembly. The next elections for this Assembly were in August 1959, at the end of its 3-year term. In April 1961, President Diem, at the end of his 5-year term, was returned to office by an election. The second National Assembly was elected in 1963 instead of 1962 because of the intensification of Viet Cong insurgency. All of these elections were carried out under strictly worded codes prepared by the National Assembly and approved by President Diem. The suffrage was universal, and all South Vietnamese citizens over 18 years of age were eligible to vote. Candidates opposing those favored by the government faced formidable odds, and few were ever elected.

After November 1963 successive Saigon governments promised to hold national elections for a constituent assembly, but by mid-1966 none had been held. In May 1965, however, local elections took place to form 44 provincial councils and 5 municipal councils. Some 441 councilmen were chosen out of a total of 1,002 candidates who for the most part ran as independents, using no party label. Each candidate was identified with voting symbols, such as an elephant, plow, ox or lotus. To eliminate the danger of Viet Cong infiltration or influence, all campaign speeches were censored, and press publicity was restricted.

Of an estimated 9.5 million people under "government control" (out of some 15 million), roughly 4.5 million were regarded as eligible voters over 18 years of age. Approximately 73 percent of the voting population, or 3.4 million, cast ballots. In mid-1966 the Saigon government estimated that about 5 million people would be eligible to vote out of a total population of 10.5 million "under the government."

CHAPTER 15

FOREIGN RELATIONS

The Geneva Agreement on Vietnam, which the State of Vietnam (under Bao Dai and Ngo Dinh Diem) had rejected as "shameful," had the consequence of indefinitely partitioning the country into two parts, although the Demarcation Line drawn along the seventeenth parallel was intended only as a provisional military measure. The settlement of a political future for the country as a whole was left by the Geneva Conference to the Vietnamese themselves to decide through "free general elections by secret ballot" as provided for under the Final Declaration of the Geneva Conference (see ch. 3, Historical Setting).

This settlement, which was to take place in mid-1956, failed to materialize because of differences between two major political forces; by early 1956, two mutually exclusive political systems, Communist to the north of the seventeenth parallel and non-Communist to the south, had developed. As a result, the provisional Demarcation Line came to constitute a territorial boundary between the Communist North and the free South.

The problem of Vietnam was further complicated by the political and moral alignment of the two regimes with opposing power blocs in the cold war; therefore, internal developments in Vietnam and external factors affecting the broader aspect of East-West confrontation tended to interact. The North-South conflict in early 1966 approached the proportions of a full-fledged war without any formal declaration by either side.

The government of South Vietnam consistently refused to have any form of relations with North Vietnam or with any other Communist states. Prime Minister Nguyen Cao Ky, like all his predecessors, saw his country as a frontline in the Free World's battle against communism. The massive aid provided by the United States, within the framework of the Southeast Asia Treaty Organization (SEATO), was accepted as its contribution toward the maintenance of the Republic of Vietnam as a free and independent entity. The treaty establishing SEATO and its accompanying Protocol came to figure prominently in shaping the subsequent South Vietnamese-United States relations. For example, on February 19, 1966, United States Secretary of State Dean Rusk, in a statement before the Senate Foreign

Relations Committee regarding the legal basis of the United States commitment in South Vietnam, reiterated that "it is this fundamental SEATO obligation that has from the outset guided our actions in South Vietnam."

Since the late 1950's, in response to intensifying Communist insurgency activities, Saigon has asked for and received increased United States military and economic aid and a pledge to help the country. In early 1966 the government was reluctant to approve of any negotiated cease-fire unless there were effective measures to ensure the withdrawal of all Communist elements from the South and the continued stay of the United States forces in the South until such time as conditions warranted their departure. It also opposed the neutralization of Vietnam or any international attempt to form a coalition government with the Communists. Similarly, it categorically refused to recognize the so-called National Front for the Liberation of South Vietnam as a legitimate group worthy of representing any part of the South Vietnamese population.

Saigon has sought to cultivate friendly relations with many non-Communist nations in Western Europe, Africa and, particularly, Asia. It has been supported by some 33 nations, providing aid in varying types and quantities, but all on a much smaller scale than that of the United States. It has actively participated in international organizations, associations and conferences.

AFTERMATH OF THE GENEVA CONFERENCE

Under the Geneva Agreement on Vietnam, signed on July 20, 1954, between the French High Command and Ho Chi Minh's People's Army High Command, a demarcation line was fixed roughly along the seventeenth parallel. The Agreement also provided for the withdrawal of the forces of the People's Army of Vietnam (under Ho Chi Minh) to the north of the line and the French Union Forces to the south. Furthermore, it set up an International Control Commission composed of representatives from Canada, India and Poland. Finally, under the provisions of the Final Declaration of the Geneva Conference, the northern and southern parts were to have reunified following an election in July 1956, to be supervised by the International Control Commission.

In the spring of 1955, North Vietnam, supported by Communist China, the Soviet Union and India, stated that it was ready to begin discussions on elections with the government of South Vietnam. The Hanoi regime urged Great Britain and the Soviet Union, which were cochairmen of the Geneva Conference, to uphold the Final Declaration. In July Ngo Dinh Diem, then prime minister of South Vietnam, stated that his government was not bound by the Geneva Agreement, which it had not signed. He insisted that a prerequisite to elections had to be cessation of North Vietnamese violations of the Geneva Agreement and satisfactory evidence that the northern leaders would not subordinate Vietnamese interests to foreign Communist interests.

The United States agreed that the situation in North Vietnam precluded the possibility of free elections. Great Britain, which had at first urged the South Vietnamese to participate in election preparations, suggested to the Soviet Union in the spring of 1956 that the preservation of peace was more important than the election issue. The Soviet Union tacitly agreed. After the Soviet-British talks in London in April 1956, notes were sent to the authorities in Hanoi and Saigon urging them to keep the peace, to cooperate with the International Control Commission, and to advise when it would be possible to hold elections. The elections were never held, and, for practical purposes, the military Demarcation Line became the political or territorial boundary between the Democratic Republic of Vietnam (Hanoi) and the Republic of Vietnam (Saigon).

After the Geneva Conference the International Control Commission, under the chairmanship of India, began to function. The Indian and Polish members consistently showed most concern about South Vietnamese unfriendliness to the Commission; the Canadian members, on the other hand, issued a number of minority reports calling attention to North Vietnamese obstruction of refugee movement to the South and to the refusal of the North Vietnamese authorities to permit the Commission to establish contact with groups wishing to go to the South. In February 1965 the Canadian delegate refused to sign a report submitted by the Polish and Indian members protesting the United States bombings on North Vietnam and suggesting that this action violated the Geneva Agreement. The same month North Vietnam requested the Commission to withdraw to Hanoi its observers posted on its border with Communist China.

RELATIONS BETWEEN SOUTH AND NORTH VIETNAM

In 1966, Saigon maintained no diplomatic, trade or cultural relations with Hanoi. Beginning in the late 1950's, a de facto state of war existed between the two Vietnams, although the respective regimes continued to stress the goal of reunifying the country through peaceful means. With the intensification, since 1958, of subversion and armed activity in the South, the prospect for a peaceful reunification became increasingly dim. In early 1966 the South Vietnamese Government suspected the sincerity of Hanoi's call for peace and avowed that peace would never be attained so long as Communist elements were not "exterminated." Nevertheless, Prime Minister Ky continued to affirm his government's desire for peace and has maintained that it would carry on military operations only to counteract, in self-defense, Hanoi's acts of aggression.

The fundamental principles governing Saigon's relations with North Vietnam were enunciated on June 23, 1965, and on the same day they were endorsed in Washington by Secretary of State Dean Rusk. These principles are: that the Communists must stop military and subversive activities and observe the 1954 Geneva Agreement under international law; that they must disband all puppet organizations in the South, such as the National Front for the Liberation of South Vietnam, the Liberation radio station, the People's Revolutionary Party, and withdraw troops, political and military cadres illegally sent into the South; that the people of South Vietnam must be left alone to settle their own affairs according to democratic principles and without any outside interference whatsoever; that, when Communist aggression ends, the government of the Republic of Vietnam will be ready to ask friendly countries to withdraw their military forces from the South, reserving, however, the right to adopt all necessary measures to maintain peace and order throughout the territory of the South and the right to call on friendly countries to reextend their assistance in case the Communists renew their aggression or threaten to commit aggression; and that the independence and freedom of the people of South Vietnam must be guaranteed effectively. Saigon has also stipulated elsewhere that it would "reject any international solution which has not received the agreement of the government and people of Vietnam."

North Vietnam's proposals for peace were first put forward in a four-point formula on April 8, 1965, presumably in answer to President Johnson's offer of unconditional discussions on Vietnam which was announced on April 7 in his speech at Johns Hopkins University. The Hanoi proposals were made public on April 12 and were formally endorsed by Communist China on April 20 and the Soviet Union on April 29.

Specifically the proposals are: that the basic national rights of the Vietnamese people—peace, independence, sovereignty, unity and territorial integrity—must be recognized; that, according to the Geneva Agreement, the United States must withdraw from South Vietnam its troops, military personnel, and weapons of all kinds and, in addition, must dismantle its military bases there and cancel its military alliance with South Vietnam; that the United States must also stop intervention and aggression in the South and cease all acts of war and other hostile acts violating the integrity and sovereignty of North Vietnam; that, pending the peaceful reunification of Vietnam and while Vietnam is still temporarily divided into two parts, the military provisions of the 1954 Geneva Agreement on Vietnam must be strictly respected; that the two zones must refrain from joining any military alliance with a foreign country; that no foreign military bases, troops or military personnel be permitted in either zone; that the internal affairs of South Vietnam must be settled by the South Vietnamese people themselves, in accordance with the program of the National Liberation Front of South Vietnam without any foreign interference; and that the peaceful reunification of Vietnam is to be realized by the Vietnamese people of the two zones without any foreign interference.

Hanoi's April peace conditions closely paralleled those which were proclaimed earlier on March 22, 1965, by the National Front for the Liberation of South Vietnam, the political mouthpiece and military arm of the Hanoi regime operating in the South. The National Front's terms are: that the United States and its allies must stop aggression in the South and North; that all troops, weapons and war equipment of the United States and its satellites must be withdrawn from South Vietnam; that Vietnamese internal affairs must be handed over to the Vietnamese for self-determination; that intervention by any imperialist country must be prohibited; and that the National Front for the Liberation of South Vietnam "as the sole legitimate representative of the South Vietnamese people" must have a decisive voice concerning the South Vietnamese problem.

RELATIONS WITH THE WEST

The United States

Relations with the United States have always been friendly. Formal relations with the United States began in February 1950 when Washington accorded diplomatic recognition to the government of the State of Vietnam under Chief of State Bao Dai, seated in Saigon, and raised the status of its consulate general there to that of a legation. In December 1950 the Bao Dai regime became the beneficiary of the United States military aid which was channeled through France. Later, under an agreement with Washington signed in September 1951, United States economic aid was sent directly to South Vietnam, bypassing France. Nevertheless, until mid-1954, the United States had played only a secondary role in Saigon's foreign relations (see ch. 3, Historic Setting).

After the conclusion of the Geneva Conference in July 1954, relations with the United States entered a new phase in which France's former dominance was gradually replaced by that of the United States. In September 1954 the United States took the lead in the establishment of a collective defense system known as the Southeast Asia Treaty Organization, under the Southeast Asia Collective Defense Treaty. Composed of the United States, Great Britain, France, Australia, New Zealand, Thailand, Pakistan and the Philippines, SEATO was designed to guarantee the security not only of the member nations but also, under Article IV, Paragraph 1, of the Treaty, to extend military protection to certain states in the treaty area to be unanimously designated by member states. In a Protocol to the Treaty, SEATO named the State of Vietnam, Laos and Cambodia, as "protocol states" to which provisions of Article IV and Article III (concerning assistance in the development of economic measures) were to be applicable. South Vietnam is not a member of SEATO, however, because it is prohibited by the Geneva Agreement from joining any military alliance. Moreover, in order to preserve the integrity of the territory and political independence of the designated states, the Treaty stipulates that no action on these states should be taken "except at the invitation or with the consent of the government concerned."

The Communist threat from the North became a source of concern to the government of South Vietnam and to the United States as well. In May 1957 a joint statement was issued in Washington by President Diem and President Eisenhower, affirming the common desires of the two nations for closer cooperation in working for South Vietnam's freedom and independence. The two presidents also noted that the Republic of Vietnam was covered by Article IV of the SEATO Treaty and agreed that "aggression or subversion threatening the political independence of the Republic of Vietnam would be considered as endangering peace and stability"—a position explicitly enunciated by the United States in its unilateral declaration at Geneva in 1954 (see ch. 3, Historical Setting).

By 1961 the campaign of guerrilla warfare, terror and subversion, supported by the Communist Hanoi regime, had intensified. Vice President Johnson, while on a visit to Saigon in May, reiterated the United States pledge to honor its commitments in the area and declared that additional military and economic assistance would be provided in order to help South Vietnam counter the Communist insurgency. In December of the same year President Diem's request for still more aid from the United States was granted by President Kennedy.

Relations with the United States since August 1964 have become closer than ever before. In early August, when two United States destroyers were attacked by North Vietnamese gunboats in international waters in the Gulf of Tonkin, the United States Congress passed the "Southeast Asia Resolution" which reaffirmed that the United States was prepared, as the President determined, to take all necessary steps, including the use of armed forces, to assist any SEATO member or protocol state requesting assistance in defense of its freedom.

The governments of South Vietnam and the United States jointly carried out, through mutual agreement, retaliatory attacks on February 7, 1965, against targets in North Vietnam. On February 27 a comprehensive report detailing "the massive evidence of North Vietnamese aggression" against the South was released by the United States. The evidence was jointly analyzed by experts from both countries.

South Vietnam has been assured repeatedly by the United States of its determination to help the country defend itself against any threat from the Communist North. Since 1954 the United States foreign policy objective in relation to South Vietnam has remained constant, and on April 7, 1965, President Johnson continued to reaffirm the United States position. On this date, in addition to offering to the Communist sides "unconditional discussions" for a peaceful settlement of the war in Vietnam, the President declared:

> Our objective is the independence of South Viet-Nam and its freedom from attack. We want nothing for ourselves—only that the people of South Viet-Nam be allowed to guide their own country in their own way. We will do everything necessary to reach that objective, and we will do only what is absolutely necessary.

South Vietnamese leaders generally welcomed the United States military and economic commitments as essential to countering the Communist challenge. They requested still greater assistance from Washington. Probably the most emphatic United States declaration of intent to help South Vietnam was enunciated at the United States-South Vietnamese summit conference held in early February 1966 at Honolulu, where President Johnson met with Vietnamese Chief of State Nguyen Van Thieu and Prime Minister Ky for 3 days. They discussed and exchanged views on a wide range of South Vietnamese problems, and in a joint communique the two governments renewed their pledges: to defend against Communist aggression; to bring about social revolution; to achieve the goal of free self-government; to attack the problems of hunger, ignorance and disease; and to commit themselves to the unending quest for peace. On his return to Saigon from Honolulu, Prime Minister Ky declared that "today we bring back the full assistance of the United States in our fight against oppression and against poverty."

In March 1966 the United States military strength in South Vietnam totaled approximately 215,000, and appeared likely to increase. In contrast, the United States had maintained only about 770 military advisers in the country in January 1961. On the nonmilitary, nongovernmental side, a number of voluntary agencies from the United States, including the Lutheran World Relief, Voluntary Foreign Aid, Catholic Relief Services, Cooperative for American Remittances to Everywhere, Incorporated (CARE), Church World Service and International Voluntary Service, have contributed foods, medicine and clothing (see ch. 8, Living Conditions).

France

During the period when South Vietnam remained within the French Union as the State of Vietnam, French political influence and economic controls aroused a strong anti-French feeling among many groups. After the end of the Indochina War, this sentiment was heightened by the continued presence of the French Union Forces, the continuance of nominal French command of the South Vietnamese armed forces, and by the fact that France had retained a mission in North Vietnam.

By mid-1956 the South Vietnamese Government had succeeded in negotiating the elimination of most of France's special privileges in the country, and relations improved. France, nevertheless, retained its role as a leading supplier and customer, and the government encouraged French business (see ch. 23, Foreign Economic Relations).

In August 1963, French President de Gaulle publicly called for the reunification of Vietnam, on a basis of neutrality and independence of all foreign intervention. The government of President Diem did not officially react to this proposal. In November 1963, France renewed its appeal to the military government which had supplanted the Diem regime, but this appeal was categorically rejected. Relations with Paris became extremely strained during January 1964 after the French recognition of Communist China. The Saigon leaders regarded the French action as less than friendly in light of their frequently announced position that Communist China had been actively supporting the North Vietnamese aggression against the South.

South Vietnam, moreover reacted negatively to many of France's subsequent pronouncements pertaining to the country. On a nongovernmental level, in July 1964, some 200 Saigon students stormed the French Embassy smashing furniture and equipment; other anti-French student demonstrations included the burning of an effigy of President de Gaulle. On an official level, the South Vietnamese Government, on May 5, 1965, suspended a daily 2-hour broadcast on French culture by Radio Saigon and also expelled the chief of the Agence France Presse from the country. The government's action was in part to manifest its avowed dissatisfaction with the lack of French support for Saigon's cause at the SEATO Council of Ministers meetings of 1964 and 1965. South Vietnam was especially irritated in May 1965 when France sent only an "observer" to the SEATO meeting in London and refused to sign SEATO's May 5 communique condemning the Communist aggression on the South.

The government of Prime Minister Nguyen Cao Ky, on June 24, 1965, formally severed diplomatic relations with France on the ground that "the de Gaulle government has persistently assisted our enemies."

Relations with France continued at the consular, cultural and economic levels without adversely affecting the 17,000 French citizens living in the country. Despite policy differences, France continued to provide South Vietnam with some 600 educators, medical and technical personnel.

Other Western Nations

In its de facto state of war with the Communist North, South Vietnam has been supported by Great Britain. Saigon has favorably regarded London's condemnation of Hanoi's aggressive policies against the South. In addition to its moral support of the South Vietnamese struggle against Communist aggression, Great Britain has sent some dozen technicians and advisers to the country and has provided facilities for a few of the educational institutions and the equivalent of $140,000 worth of construction equipment. Limitations in material aid have been imposed mainly by its own involvement elsewhere in Southeast Asia and by strong opposition in Parliament by members of the ruling British Labor Party itself.

In early 1966 some South Vietnamese government leaders felt uneasy about British Prime Minister Wilson's advocacy of a negotiated settlement, envisaging a neutral South Vietnam free from foreign interference. This apprehension was accentuated by the knowledge that more than 40 percent of the shipping in and out of Haiphong in North Vietnam was in British vessels under Hong Kong registry. Some Saigon newspapers had asserted that Great Britain, the Soviet Union and France are "international appeasers" who are "putting pressure on the United States to convene an international conference to seek a solution for Vietnam" on the basis of neutrality.

Saigon has friendly relations with Australia and New Zealand— both members of SEATO—whose geographical position makes events in South Vietnam and other parts of Southeast Asia of special concern to them. Australia was one of the first countries with which the Republic of Vietnam established diplomatic relations, and in September 1957, President Diem made a state visit to Australia. Many South Vietnamese students are enrolled in Australian universities.

In 1965, Australian support of Saigon was described by the Canberra regime as that of an "active junior partner" of the United States in Vietnam. This aid consisted of the combat force of some 1,400 infantrymen with logistic support, including 100 jungle warfare advisers and 6 transport aircraft with crews, and 2 medical teams. Other contributions included 1 million textbooks, 3,300 tons of roofing, 6 windmills, 15,750 sets of handtools, 400 radios, 16,000 blankets and 14,000 cases of milk. In addition, in March 1966, Prime Minister Harold Holt announced that Australian combat forces in South Vietnam would be tripled in the next few months.

Relations with New Zealand are cordial. New Zealand has furnished an artillery battery and a tank unit, totaling about 150 men, in addition to combat engineers, a surgical team, and science building costing the equivalent of $200,000. Its support of Saigon is, however, limited by sharp domestic political controversy regarding the government's decision to give combat aid to South Vietnam. In 1965 the government favored a negotiated peace and reunification through elections.

Relations with Canada, a member of the International Control Commission, are also friendly. Canada has provided $850,000 worth of flour and butter, a science building costing $170,000 and 130 scholarships. A Canadian survey team assigned to the Mekong River Project (see Glossary) within the framework of the Colombo Plan is provided local currency by the South Vietnamese Government.

Diplomatic relations with other Western countries include the Federal Republic of Germany (West Germany), Italy, Spain, the Netherlands, Belgium, Denmark and Sweden. Most of them have given some form of nonmilitary aid to South Vietnam. Nations contributing material support were: West Germany (medical support, the equivalent of $20 million in credits for economic development, 23 technicians and instructors and promise for a 3,000-ton hospital ship being outfitted in early 1966); Italy (a 9-man surgical team and science scholarships); Spain (a medical team, 800 pounds of medicine and blankets); the Netherlands (two surgical teams, one dredge and some antibiotics); Denmark (medical supplies); Belgium (medicines); Austria (blankets and medicines); Ireland (the equivalent of $2,800 in cash); Greece (medical supplies); and Luxembourg (plasma and blood transfusion equipment). Switzerland has sent microscopes to the University of Saigon.

RELATIONS WITH ASIAN NATIONS

Cambodia

Relations between the Vietnamese and Cambodians have been antagonistic for centuries. Among the issues which have troubled mutual relations since 1954 are the Cambodian rights of navigation on the Mekong River, conflicting claims to offshore islands in the Gulf of Siam (the largest of which is Dao Phu Quoc currently in Saigon's possession), the status of Cambodians in South Vietnam and of Vietnamese in Cambodia, and poorly defined borders between the two countries, which give rise to frequent border violations.

Reactions of both countries to these disputes are compounded by their divergent attitudes toward the issues of the cold war. Cambodia professes a neutralist policy which, in Saigon's view, is oriented toward the Communist side. Saigon maintains that this attitude makes political neutrality impossible, and it accuses the Cambodians of aiding the North Vietnamese Communist infiltrators and their counterparts in the South by allowing them to use Cambodian territory as a sanctuary from which to attack South Vietnam.

The question of minority rights has been aggravated by repeated mutual accusations of mistreatment of the Cambodians and Vietnamese minorities in each country. Moreover, formal relations have been further strained by South Vietnam's assertion that Cambodia has often given asylum to dissident South Vietnamese political elements and refuge to the Vietnamese Communist insurgents. In turn, Cambodia has charged that South Vietnam, along with Thailand, had been aiding and abetting an anti-Sihanouk, pro-Western dissident movement known as the Khmer Serei (Free Khmer).

The two countries attempted to improve relations in January 1962 by opening talks on the question of border disputes. This effort failed, however, because of a Cambodian claim that some of its border villages had been attacked by South Vietnamese troops. Another complicating factor was that, despite Saigon's request for extradition, Cambodia had granted political asylum to a South Vietnamese air force pilot, who had bombed President Diem's palace in February 1962.

Deteriorating relations finally culminated in the severance of diplomatic ties by Cambodia in August 1963; Prince Sihanouk justified his action on the ground that, in addition to continued border violations, Buddhists and the Cambodian minority in South Vietnam had been mistreated by President Diem's government.

The downfall of the Diem regime in November 1963 aroused hopes in both countries for improved relations. Prince Sihanouk proposed to restore diplomatic ties if Saigon agreed to recognize Cambodian sovereignty over the disputed islands, respect Cambodian neutrality, stop supporting the Free Khmer movement, and protect the rights of Khmers in South Vietnam. He also suggested the creation of a neutral confederation of both Cambodia and South Vietnam.

South Vietnam responded by sending an exploratory mission to Phnom Penh, and eventually the two sides initiated bilateral talks on border issues. The meeting, however, was again called off by Cambodia on March 23, 1964, following a South Vietnamese incursion against the village of Chantra, 75 miles west of Saigon and 4 miles inside Cambodian territory. This action was taken despite the Saigon government's formal apology for the incident and promise to compensate for damages.

In May 1964, Cambodian charges of aggression were brought before an emergency meeting of the United Nations Security Council. South Vietnam countered by suggesting that further border incidents might be averted if the two countries would agree to the initiation of effective bilateral measures designed to deny the Viet Cong the use of Cambodian territory as a sanctuary.

Relations with Prince Sihanouk's government steadily became worse during the remainder of 1964 because of recurring border troubles. Moreover, subsequent developments in Cambodia further irritated the South Vietnamese Government. In March 1965, Phnom Penh was the scene of the so-called Indochinese People's Conference, attended mostly by representatives from the Communist-controlled National Front for the Liberation of South Vietnam, Communist North Vietnam and pro-Communist Laotian elements. Saigon boycotted the Conference at which Prince Sihanouk declared his "sincere and complete solidarity" with the self-styled National Front for the Liberation of South Vietnam.

During the conference Prince Sihanouk disclosed that "the Front and other brothers" had expressed their intention to intervene on Cambodia's behalf if his country were attacked by "the forces of the Americans and their lackeys." In the same month he also declared that he would extend full political support to North Vietnam and the Viet Cong in their conflict against the United States, a position he has since reiterated repeatedly. Other aggravating factors were Cambodia's severance of diplomatic relations with the United States in May and its support of North Vietnam's four-point peace policy in June.

Laos

Diplomatic relations with Laos were established in 1956, and by 1960 several Laotian government missions had been to Saigon and trade, transit, payments, immigration and other accords had been concluded between the two nations. Beginning in mid-1959, South Vietnam became deeply disturbed about the onset of internal conflict in that country, involving a three-way struggle for power among anti-Communist, Communist and neutralist forces. Saigon supported the pro-Western government of Prince Boun Oum and strongly opposed the formation of a neutralist regime, which it felt would lead to a Communist takeover.

South Vietnam, apprehensive regarding its own security, has been alert to developments in Laos, whose frontiers are contiguous with both North and South Vietnam. Saigon government leaders have consistently maintained that the Communist North is using Laotian territory as a transit and infiltration route to South Vietnam. Thus, at the 14-nation Geneva Conference on Laos—attended from May 1961 to July 1962 by South Vietnam, Laos, North Vietnam, Burma, Thailand, Cambodia, Communist China, India, France, the United Kingdom, the Soviet Union, Poland, Canada and the United States—the Saigon delegation strongly pressed for the inclusion in any Laotian settlement of a clause prohibiting the use of that country's territory for aggressive purposes.

In July 1962 the 14-nation conference formally declared the "neutrality" of Laos and created a coalition government of anti-Communist, Communist and neutralist forces. The Saigon regime remained deeply concerned because Communist troops and supplies continued to pass through Laos en route to the South on the so-called Ho Chi Minh Trail. Dissatisfaction with Laos intensified in November 1962, when the coalition government permitted Hanoi to establish an embassy in Vientiane; South Vietnam reacted by breaking off diplomatic relations. By mid-1965, however, relations with Vientiane had much improved and were formally restored, mainly because of Laotian governmental efforts to interdict Communist supply lines winding through two of its south-central provinces bordering both North and South Vietnam. In 1965, Laos contributed the equivalent of about $4,200 in cash for flood relief in South Vietnam.

Thailand

The long history of friendly relations between Vietnam and Thailand and the need for solidarity to safeguard security were stressed during President Diem's visit to Thailand in 1957 and that of Thai Foreign Minister Thanat Khoman to South Vietnam in 1959. Thailand, a member of SEATO, has been especially concerned about the threat to its security posed by Communist activities in both South Vietnam and Laos. Ambassadors were exchanged between the two countries soon after the Republic of Vietnam was proclaimed. South Vietnam was, in 1966, serving with Thailand, as well as with Laos and Cambodia, on the United Nations Mekong Project Committee (see ch. 20, Industry).

The problem of Vietnamese who had sought refuge in Thailand during the Indochina War strained relations between the two countries in 1959. In August of that year the Thai Red Cross Council and the North Vietnamese Red Cross Committee signed an agreement for repatriation to the North of those refugees expressing the desire to go there. South Vietnam protested, stating that the enforced regroupment of both Communist and nationalist refugees in one area had obstructed the free choice of the nationalists, who were subject to coercion by Communist agents. Thailand answered that South Vietnam had previously refused to accept the Vietnamese and that the Thai were not to blame for the consequences. The fact that the King and Queen of Thailand visited Saigon in December 1959 indicates that this dispute did not seriously disrupt friendly relations between the two countries.

The close relationship between South Vietnam and Thailand has been fostered by Cambodia's hostility toward both and its friendship with Communist China; increased aggression on the part of the Viet Cong has also strengthened the ties uniting them. Prime Minister

Ky paid an official visit to Thailand from August 20 to August 22, 1965, reportedly to promote a new anti-Communist Southeast Asian alliance based primarily on economic cooperation. At the conclusion of his visit, Thailand agreed to train more South Vietnamese pilots and provide additional medical units. Thai aid to South Vietnam also includes aviation crews, cement and roofing materials. More substantial aid seems unlikely, however, as Thailand also has to cope with its own increasing Communist threat and other domestic problems.

Republic of China

There has been some friction between the Republic of Vietnam and the Republic of China (Nationalist China) arising from the treatment of the Chinese minority in South Vietnam and from conflicting claims over islands in the South China Sea, particularly the Paracel Islands some 200 miles east of Hue. These tensions have been eased, however, by common interests growing out of the similar problems they face as a result of the Communist threat to their territories.

Diplomatic relations were established between the two countries in December 1955 and received their severest test from 1956 to 1958. In August 1956 the Republic of Vietnam issued a nationality decree requiring all Chinese born in Vietnam to become Vietnamese citizens without option. A decree in September, also aimed at the Chinese, prohibited aliens from engaging in 11 lines of trade (see ch. 4, Population; ch. 5, Ethnic Groups and Languages). The Chinese Government made representations to South Vietnam, requesting moderation of these regulations. Vietnamese rejection of the requests strained relations between the two countries. Later the decrees were somewhat modified in application, and tension eased in 1958. South Vietnam's more relaxed policy toward its Chinese minority was no doubt due in part to a recognition of the important role of the Chinese in Vietnam's economic life, but it also came about through awareness of the fact that a serious split between South Vietnam and the Republic of China could only benefit the Communists.

The visit of President Diem to Taiwan in January 1960 was preceded by an information campaign by both governments stressing the common Vietnamese-Chinese cultural heritage. A Vietnam-China Cultural Association was also formed.

Since the increased tempo of the war in South Vietnam, relations between Saigon and Taipei have been even closer. Nationalist China has expressed readiness to send troops to South Vietnam. Taipei has sent 124 technicians, engineer specialists and instructors, in addition to assistance in agriculture, education, psychological warfare and electric power. Chinese newspapers in Saigon have urged overseas Chinese to enlist in the South Vietnamese army.

Prime Minister Ky made a state visit to Nationalist China from August 15 to August 18, 1965, to promote an anti-Communist Southeast Asian alliance. A joint communique was issued affirming closer Saigon-Taipei cooperation in military, economic, commercial and cultural spheres. Nationalist China also agreed to increase aid to South Vietnam for economic development.

Republic of Korea

South Vietnam regards South Korea as probably the most reliable Asian ally. In September 1957, President Diem visited Seoul, and the two countries reaffirmed their common dedication to the anti-Communist cause and stressed the importance of cultural cooperation. In a joint communique issued at Seoul in November 1965, at the end of Prime Minister Ky's visit there, the two nations pledged to strengthen their political and economic ties and expand technical cooperation and trade relations.

By mid-February 1966, South Vietnam had received more military aid from South Korea than from any other country except the United States. The Korean contribution included 17,200 men (a combat division of 15,000 and an engineer unit of 2,200), one Landing Ship, Tank (LST), two Landing Ships, Material (LSM), about 100 technicians, 10 transport pilots, 20 karate experts, a mobile surgical unit of 130 men, and two construction firms to dredge the Saigon harbor. In addition, Seoul announced a plan in February—in response to Saigon's request—to dispatch shortly 20,000 more combatants.

Japan

Diplomatic and commercial relations were established with Japan shortly after the Republic of Vietnam was formed, and by 1957, Japan had become one of its leading trade partners. On May 13, 1959, the two countries concluded a war reparations agreement as well as arrangements for Japanese loans to South Vietnam for economic development projects.

Resentment at Japan's actions in Vietnam during World War II seems to have subsided, and Japan is admired for the high level of its economic development and technical competence. South Vietnam looks to Japan for technical as well as economic assistance in its efforts to introduce new crafts and industries.

By the end of 1965, Japan had sent 90 technicians and instructors, aided South Vietnam in bridge construction and electric power projects, and furnished 20,000 radio transistors and 25 ambulances. In addition, it supplied the equivalent of $55 million in World War II reparations. Japanese aid, however, is likely to be limited, for not only does the Japanese Constitution prohibit the sending of troops, but many press and political elements sympathize with the Communist-controlled insurgents, in spite of the governing Liberal-Democratic Party's pro-United States policies.

The Philippines and Malaysia

The Republic of Vietnam has diplomatic, commercial and cultural relations with the Philippines and Malaysia (known as the Federation of Malaya until September 1963), and both have received South Vietnamese state visits. Having contended with Communist guerrillas, they share with South Vietnam a postwar experience of conflict with a Communist foe. South Vietnam takes every opportunity to foster a unified anti-Communist front in its relations with these countries. In the fall of 1965, Prime Minister Ky visited Malaysia to discuss its participation in an anti-Communist Southeast Asian alliance.

The Philippines has sent two civic action teams and a psychological warfare detachment to South Vietnam. Because of internal political disagreement, the Manila government deferred action on sending a 2,500-man detachment to South Vietnam. In August 1965 the minister of war and reconstruction, then Brigadier General Nguyen Huu Co, headed a 17-member delegation, which visited the Philippines to discuss and seek more aid from Manila.

South Vietnam shares Malaysia's concern with the Communist danger in Southeast Asia. Malaya's Prime Minister Tunku Abdul Rahman's mission to South Vietnam in 1958 was his first visit to a foreign country after Malaya's independence, and the two heads of state expressed "complete identity of views." Malaya's prime minister paid a second visit to the country late in 1961 when the two chiefs of state conferred on the Communist threat to South Vietnam. Subsequently, Malaysia sent advisers to give the South Vietnamese the benefit of its successful experience against Communist insurgency. During 1965, Malaysia, despite its conflict with Indonesia, was training more than 2,000 Vietnamese counterinsurgency troops. In mid-August, Saigon recognized Singapore as an independent state and sent a congratulatory cable to the prime minister of Singapore, Lee Kuan Yew.

Other Asian Nations

Relations with Indonesia have been less than cordial because of that country's formal recognition of the Communist-controlled National Front for the Liberation of South Vietnam and avowed friendship with Communist North Vietnam and Cambodia. The self-styled National Front for the Liberation of South Vietnam maintains a mission in Djakarta. Saigon has been further irritated by Indonesia's opposition, along with North Vietnam, Cambodia, Communist China and

North Korea, to the anti-Communist struggles of the South Vietnamese people. Deteriorating ties culminated in Saigon's severance of diplomatic relations with President Sukarno's government in August 1964, when Indonesia announced its decision to exchange ambassadors with the Hanoi regime and South Vietnam withdrew its consulate general from Djakarta.

Saigon has been apprehensive regarding India's general stand on the Vietnamese situation. In its role as chairman of the International Control Commission since 1954, India has frequently joined with Poland in criticizing South Vietnam for alleged violations of the terms of the Geneva Agreement. In 1955, Saigon was the scene of mass demonstrations against India and Poland. In 1957, President Diem made an effort to ameliorate relations with India, and during a state visit to New Delhi, he and Prime Minister Nehru noted India's important contribution through the International Control Commission toward maintaining peace in Southeast Asia. In 1962, India voted with Canada in upholding the position that the problem of internal security in the South was a proper question for the International Control Commission to investigate. Saigon, however, had reservations about India's support of Poland in condemning the United States airstrikes on North Vietnam as "violations of the Geneva Agreement" and also about India's advocacy of a Geneva-type conference aimed at the political solution of the Vietnamese question. In 1965, India contributed some medical supplies to South Vietnam and the equivalent of $15,000 in flood relief.

South Vietnam has no formal diplomatic relations with Pakistan, which has followed a policy of noninvolvement in Vietnam. Neither Saigon nor Hanoi is formally recognized by Pakistan. Apart from contributing the equivalent of $10,000 in flood relief to South Vietnam, Pakistan has made no positive gestures on Saigon's behalf. Pakistan, although a member of SEATO, did not fully endorse the organization's declaration of May 5, 1965, which condemned the Communist aggression against the South.

RELATIONS WITH AFRICA, THE MIDDLE EAST AND LATIN AMERICA

The Republic of Vietnam has sought to develop friendly relations with the new states of Africa. It has been particularly successful in those parts of West Africa which, like itself, were formerly under French rule. One Vietnamese ambassador, in many cases, is accredited to several African capitals.

In March 1965 an embassy was established in Addis Ababa, Ethiopia. Diplomatic relations also have been established with Niger, Senegal, Tunisia and Morocco. The Ministry of Foreign Affairs has announced that the creation of the mission in Ethiopia was a "necessary step in the defense of" Saigon's interests, as Addis Ababa was centrally located in Africa. The South Vietnamese mission reportedly hopes eventually to have contact with representatives from all African states and to follow the political events and conferences in the various countries.

In the Middle East, South Vietnam has diplomatic missions in Turkey and Lebanon. A trade agreement was signed with the United Arab Republic (UAR) in 1960, and in 1961 a South Vietnamese goodwill mission in Cairo discussed economic and cultural relations with President Gamal Abdel Nasser. In general, however, the UAR fully backs Hanoi. Algeria has received a permanent mission of the so-called National Front for the Liberation of South Vietnam. In June 1965, however, the South Vietnamese Government sent a message of congratulations to the Algerian minister of defense, Colonel Houari Boumedienne, after he had ousted President Ahmed Ben Bella from office in a military coup. Turkey supplied some medicines; other contributing countries were: Iran (1,000 tons of petroleum products and a medical team); and Israel (medical supplies).

The Vietnamese Ambassador to the United States is also accredited to Brazil, Argentina and Mexico. Token noncombatant aid has been given by Brazil (coffee and medical supplies); Ecuador (medical supplies); Guatemala (15,000 doses of typhoid vaccine); Honduras (medical supplies); and Venezuela (500 tons of rice).

VIETNAM AND ASIAN REGIONALISM

The need for Asian unity has been a major theme in the speeches of the country's leaders. South Vietnam is a member of the Asian subgroups of the United Nations and its Specialized Agencies as well as of the Organization of Asian News Agencies, the Eastern Regional Organization for Public Administration and other Asian groups established for special purposes. In the past the country has not, however, pressed for the establishment of an Asian regional grouping dedicated to broader purposes, and in mid-1966 no such framework existed. In August 1965, Prime Minister Ky made trips to Taiwan and Thailand to promote a new anti-Communist Southeast Asian alliance based on economic cooperation. He emphasized that a better life, more freedom and social justice among the Southeast Asian non-Communist nations are necessary to rid the area of Communist influence. The prime minister also pointed out that a military alliance was not of prime importance because of the United States commitment. Discussions of this alliance reportedly were continued in his visits to South Korea in November 1965.

The development of a regional grouping of the non-Communist Asian nations has been hindered by a number of factors: the divergent attitude toward the issues of alignment and neutralism; poor communication between countries; production of competitive rather than complementary products; strength of nationalist sentiment; and ethnic, religious and cultural differences. South Vietnam has rejected Cambodia's proposal for a federation of Indochinese states.

SOUTH VIETNAM AND INTERNATIONAL ORGANIZATIONS

South Vietnam actively participates in international organizations and conferences of all kinds. Although a Soviet veto in 1952 barred its membership in the United Nations, the Republic of Vietnam maintains an observer at United Nations Headquarters in New York. In early 1966, South Vietnam, unlike Hanoi, was generally in favor of enlisting the support of the United Nations in the settlement of the Vietnamese question.

South Vietnam is a member of a large number of United Nations organizations, including the Economic Commission for Asia and the Far East (ECAFE); United Nations Children's Fund (UNICEF), as a member of the executive board; United Nations Educational, Scientific and Cultural Organization (UNESCO); Food and Agriculture Organization (FAO); World Health Organization (WHO); International Labor Organization (ILO), as a member of the executive board; International Telecommunications Union (ITU); Universal Postal Union (UPU); International Civil Aviation Organization (ICAO); International Bank for Reconstruction and Development (IBRD); International Monetary Fund (IMF); International Atomic Energy Agency (IAEA), as a member of the board of governors; World Meteorological Organization (WMO); and International Development Association (IDA).

South Vietnam is a member of the Colombo Plan for the Cooperative Economic Development in South and Southeast Asia. This organization coordinates the aid of Western nations and Japan to the Asian countries. Although South Vietnam receives technical assistance, equipment and scholarships from the Colombo Plan members, the international political status conferred by association with the Colombo Plan nations is of equal importance to South Vietnam. The first international conference held in South Vietnam after its independence was the Colombo Plan Conference of 1957.

South Vietnam is a member of numerous other international organizations. Important among these are the International Institute of Administrative Sciences, the International Union of Official Travel Organizations and the International Union for Health Education.

In April 1965, Saigon cabled to the president and secretary general of the World Peace Conference in Stockholm protesting that South Vietnam was not invited to the meeting to be held in July 1965. Moreover, it questioned and criticized the presence at the Conference of the delegation from the National Front for the Liberation of South Vietnam. The government also expressed displeasure at being refused an invitation to the proposed Afro-Asian Conference, then scheduled to be held at the end of June 1965 in Algiers. Saigon protested against this slight, claiming that as a participant in the Bandung Conference of 1955, it had a right to be invited.

FOREIGN POLICY FORMULATION

Under the Provisional Convention of June 19, 1965, the chairman of The Directory (National Leadership Committee) "performs all functions relating to the representation of the Republic of Vietnam at home and abroad" (see ch. 13, The Governmental System). Upon the decision of the Congress of Armed Forces, the chairman of The Directory declares war, makes peace and concludes international agreements. The chairman of The Directory, after suggestion by the prime minister and consultation with the War Cabinet, appoints ambassadors and plenipotentiary ministers. Lastly, the chairman of The Directory, on the recommendation of the prime minister, also appoints the minister of foreign affairs (see ch. 13, The Governmental System).

In early 1966 leading figures who participated in foreign policy-making were the prime minister, minister of war and reconstruction, and the minister of foreign affairs. When the policy pertained to a specific matter, such as economic relations or international health problems, other Cabinet ministers were called in.

Because of intensification of the counterinsurgency effort in the early 1960's and the government's increasing preoccupation with the more immediate problems of military strategy and internal security, the function of foreign relations tended to be relegated to secondary importance. The government of Prime Minister Ky noted, however, that this "passive" approach to foreign relations, coupled with the lack of trained and experienced personnel, had caused many foreign nations to misunderstand the aspirations of the South Vietnamese.

As a result, in June 1965, the government announced its decision to improve and energize the diplomatic establishment and the conduct of foreign relations by coping with the four most urgent tasks: reappraisal of all diplomatic personnel by the use of tests; establishment of centers of diplomatic activity in South America, the Middle East, Africa and in the vicinity of the United Nations Headquarters; dissemination, in French and English, of all documents, photographs and films needed to make the case of South Vietnam better known abroad; and inducement of Vietnamese residents abroad to support and participate in the present struggle within the country. In August 1965, Prime Minister Ky expressed the hope that, by replacing "inefficient" personnel with more dedicated and competent foreign service officers, the diplomatic establishment might be able to rid itself of what he described as a "resort place" image.

ATTITUDES TOWARD OTHER PEOPLE

French

France is no longer the object of the nationalist indignation that it once was, and even the bitterness engendered during the Indochina War seems to have largely subsided. The Vietnamese, on the whole, continue to blame France for the colonial regime and the manner in which it was administered, but educated persons generally express admiration for French culture.

The French in South Vietnam have been forced to relinquish their holdings in riceland, but they still control most of the rubber plantations. Despite the severance of diplomatic relations with France by Saigon in June 1965, the Vietnamese attitude toward the French community of about 17,000 appears to be good.

Chinese

The Chinese are admired for their culture, which has strongly influenced Vietnam, and for their commercial acumen. They are resented for the same reasons. Chinese resistance to assimilation tends to offend nationalist feeling, and a great many Vietnamese have had the experience of dealing with the Chinese moneylender, rice buyer or merchant on the latter's own terms. The rise of an aggressive Communist regime in China also gives special urgency in the South— and perhaps only to a lesser degree in the North—to the questions of the loyalty of the Chinese community. This question of loyalty probably explains the extremely aggressive policy toward North Vietnam and Communist China taken by the Chinese newspapers in Saigon. The editorials continuously advocate bombing raids on Hanoi and Peking, as well as urge overseas Chinese to enlist in the South Vietnamese Army.

Other Asian Peoples

The defeat of Russia by Japan in 1905 won Vietnamese admiration as an Asian victory over a Western power. Japan's industrial achievements also excited the imagination of Vietnamese nationalist, many of whom found refuge in Japan before World War II. Japan's actions in the final months of World War II, when it took over the administration of the country from the French, exacerbated some Vietnamese feelings, and the conduct of Japanese troops roused anger. In the South the attitude toward Japan has become friendly, particularly since the settlement of World War II reparations with the

Republic of Vietnam and the opening of markets in Japan for South Vietnamese products.

Laos and Cambodia are looked upon by many South Vietnamese as troublesome countries whose people are regarded by them as indolent and lacking in enterprise and culture. Thailand is somewhat more respected.

The small number of Indians and Pakistanis in South Vietnam are generally unpopular, as most are unassimilated foreign moneylenders and small shopkeepers. The government has never been happy with India's vocal neutralism and its recognition of the regime in the North.

Americans

The attitude of many South Vietnamese toward the American people has been on the whole friendly. In educated Vietnamese circles, however, there has been some adoption of French feelings of cultural superiority over Americans. Moreover, because of their historic suspicion of all foreigners, some Vietnamese regard Americans as partly responsible for transforming their country into a pawn in the conflict between East and West. The corollary of such an attitude has been the persistent Vietnamese desire to remain free from all foreign influences, political or ideological, especially from Communist China, the Soviet Union or France.

Communist propaganda from Hanoi and from the Communist-controlled National Front for the Liberation of South Vietnam relentlessly attacks United States involvement in South Vietnam as "imperialist" or "neocolonial" intervention, and those Vietnamese in the South who are dissatisfied with or disaffected by the conduct of the government tend, to one degree or another, to be susceptible to these charges. The government of South Vietnam itself has been sensitive to any suggestion, Communist or non-Communist, that Saigon is a "lackey" of the United States. Thus, in public statements, South Vietnamese government leaders have continually stressed their country's independence vis-a-vis the United States. Most recently, for example, upon his return from a summit conference with President Johnson at Honolulu in February 1966, Prime Minister Ky especially emphasized that the meeting had been conducted on the basis of "genuine equality."

In early 1966 trust in the United States and friendliness toward Americans seemed to be steadily growing, as the Vietnamese gradually came to realize that the United States entertained no colonial designs on their country. Awareness of the gravity of the Communist threat, which in their view is directed and supported by Communist China through the agency of the Hanoi regime, also played a large role in shaping their friendly attitude.

As the war intensified after 1965, many of the Saigon newspapers expressed fear, particularly in early 1966, that the United States would bring about a negotiated settlement which might eventually compromise the integrity and independence of the Republic of Vietnam. On the other hand, it also appeared that the increasing United States military and economic aid, in direct proportion to the Communist escalation of insurgency, tended to allay such apprehensions.

CHAPTER 16

PUBLIC INFORMATION

In mid-1966 modern methods of public communication were only beginning to reach outside the cities and larger towns. Newspapers, magazines and books circulated mainly among the urban minority whose members also made up the bulk of radio and motion picture audiences. An increasing number of radio receivers in the villages were bringing more country people within the orbit of the developing broadcasting system. The radio had become by far the most important among formal communications media, reaching between 60 and 75 percent of the population. The average peasant, however, continued to depend primarily on the announcements of local officials and on personal contacts for news of the world outside his community.

Wartime conditions and political unrest significantly impeded the official efforts that had been made since 1963 to expand the scope and technical facilities of communications media. Military operations prevented or slowed down the building of additional broadcasting stations in certain areas. Activities of mobile film units were curtailed in the rural communities threatened by Viet Cong insurgents, although there is an estimated monthly rural audience of 1.5 million. Some broadcasting station, including Da Lat, were damaged during the civil disturbances in the spring of 1966.

Newsprint shortages and cuts in electric power interfered with the regular publication of newspapers. Because of unsettled conditions in the countryside and the lack of transportation, newspapers could not be distributed regularly outside the major cities, and rural readers depended mainly on official government news bulletins.

Radio and press served more as instruments for the spread of the government's political views than as channels of objective information. The governments which followed the coup against President Ngo Dinh Diem implicitly recognized freedom of expression, but official controls working through a variety of devices, including censorship, narrowly restricted the public expression of private opinions in newspapers, other publications and radio. All newspapers were subject to censorship, and those criticizing government policies or top-ranking government officials were subject to closure or suspension. The government also regulated newspaper's content by instructing editors to give prominent coverage to government press releases and by prohibiting the printing of news stories dealing with certain topics.

The broadcasting system is a semi-autonomous corporation guided by the government and is the principal means for the distribution of government-controlled news and political commentaries. The technical facilities of broadcasting stations were modernized and, wherever possible, additional ones were installed with substantial financial and technical aid from the United States. Thousands of inexpensive transistor radio sets were imported, also with United States aid.

The number of newspapers had increased notably since 1963. Although many had been sponsored by groups opposing government policies, strict censorship had prevented criticism of the government. Protests by newspaper publishers and journalists against the close surveillance of the press had grown in intensity since 1965.

Television was launched with United States assistance, in February 1966. During early 1966 its operation remained limited to telecasts from specially equipped aircraft and reached only the Saigon metropolitan area. When the Saigon ground-based facility was to become operational in late October, the aircraft was to be moved to the Can Tho area until airborne transmissions could be replaced by a ground station in Can Tho. Two other ground stations were planned in the I and II corps area.

The government expanded the scope of information services and programs which aimed to explain its policies and to enlist popular support for the struggle against the Viet Cong (see Glossary). The programs were intended mainly for the population of the South but also reached North Vietnam through radio broadcasts and leaflet-drops. Film shows, lectures, rallies, allegorical drama shows and recitals reached many villages and hamlets, including those of the *montagnards* in the Central Highlands.

A special program, entitled "Open Arms" (Chieu Hoi), was designed to encourage defection among members of the Viet Cong. Started in 1963, "Open Arms" provided retraining and reorientation for former Viet Cong members. Because of the importance attached to this program, a section, named after it, was added to the former Department of Psychological Warfare, which was then renamed the Ministry of Information and Open Arms.

The Communists were sending subversive propaganda into South Vietnam from North Vietnam by radio, and clandestinely within the country through the Viet Cong and its political arm, the so-called National Front for the Liberation of South Vietnam. Newspapers and other publications, printed by the National Front, were passed from hand to hand in Viet Cong-controlled areas. The Front also operated at least one radio station, called Liberation Radio, the broadcasts of which could be heard in many parts of the country.

Viet Cong agitation and propaganda teams were active in the countryside, attempting to exploit current issues which they believed to be of popular concern. The basic propaganda theme in mid-1966 identified the Hanoi regime as the champion of Vietnamese independence and welfare, and condemned Prime Minister Nguyan Cao Ky and his government as "willing agents" of an "imperialist" United States.

GOVERNMENT AND FREEDOM OF THE PRESS

Background

The first newspapers and magazines printed in South Vietnam, which appeared during the 1880's, were intended mainly for members of the colonial administration and their families. Vietnamese periodicals and newspapers, first published in the late 1890's, were closely supervised by the colonial authorities. The founders of most of the early newspapers were Vietnamese who chafed at this French control, and their violent criticisms soon brought on strict censorship.

By 1954, when independence was achieved, government regulation and supervision of the press had long been a feature of national life. During the reign of Emperor Bao Dai, Prime Minister Tran Van Huu reinstated a French decree providing for precensorship of the press to discourage criticism of his government.

The policy of close government control was continued under President Diem. Although freedom of the press was nominally guaranteed in the Constitution of 1956, it was never achieved. Newspapers were subject to strict screening, before and after publication, by government officials; newsprint supplies were owned and allocated by the government; and the distribution of newspapers was handled by the Thong Nhat Company, a government-subsidized enterprise.

The legal basis for the government's control was a presidential ordinance, promulgated in February 1956, providing penalties for publishing or circulating material which "could be exploited by subversive elements" or which might threaten security and public order in some other way. The same ordinance prohibited the publication of obscene and slanderous material.

Precensorship was legally reinstituted in a decree promulgated in 1957, requiring newspapers to deposit two copies of each issue before publication with the Ministry of Information. Other restrictions included reduction of newsprint allocations, threats of suspension and the buying up of daily press runs by government agents. In some instances, newspaper offices were attacked by mobs, allegedly venting their resentment over the newspaper's criticism of the regime. In the presence of the official policies and actions, the press rarely dealt with governmental or political issues. Some editorials on minor political issues and criticism of low-level officials were tolerated and sometimes even encouraged by government leadership.

Government-Press Relations Since 1963

The military regimes which followed the coup against President Ngo announced the intention to remove the restrictive practices of the preceding era. By mid-December 1964, some 23 dailies were published as compared to 15 in 1963. Many of those published before 1964 changed their names to disassociate themselves from the Diem era. The Ministry of Information was flooded with additional applications, but not all such applications were followed by the publication of a newspaper.

Strong antigovernment criticism appearing in the new dailies, and in some of the old ones, caused the governments of Prime Ministers Duong Van Minh, Nguyen-Khanh and Tran Van Huong to decree restrictive measures, including censorship and the reduction of newsprint quotas. The government of Minh adopted no new decrees dealing with the press but warned that the Ministry of Information would observe newspapers closely and that those which published anything "contrary to the spirit of the revolution" would be closed.

Decrees passed during the early months of Prime Minister Khanh's government reflected official efforts to provide standards for publishing and for the organization of the press. At the same time, however, several newspapers were closed or suspended, and draft copies of dailies and weeklies had to be submitted to the Ministry of Information 1 hour before release.

A decree announced on February 19, 1964, set forth the conditions under which newspapers and periodicals could be published. It required a 200,000-piaster deposit (for value of the piaster, see Glossary) from publishers who were not professional journalists, and one-half of this sum from professional journalist publishers. It also defined the conditions under which newspapers could be sued for endangering state security and for publishing libel and obscenity.

The organization of the press was regulated by a legal decree promulgated on April 30, 1964, which called for the establishment of a nine-member press council to be elected from a general press assembly that would include the publishers and editors of all newspapers. The council was to act as a liaison between press and government, establish criteria for the training of journalists and for the issuance of press cards, and was empowered to issue reprimands to newspapers and to recommend their suspension. The press council was established in May; it was still in existence in mid-1966, but no data were available regarding its functions.

The Provisional Charter issued on October 20, 1964, by the government of Prime Minister Tran Van Huong, recognized the freedom of the press but warned that it "may not be abused in order to make false accusations, slander, violate public morale and order, or to make propaganda for communism and neutralism." Article 16 of the same document, however, declared a state of emergency and the suspension of guarantees. The promulgation of the Charter was followed by intensified censorship and a reduction of newsprint allocations, but both measures were relaxed following the protests of newspaper publishers.

The antagonism between Prime Minister Tran Van Huong and Buddhist leaders in December 1964 marked a new period of strain between government and press. Three newspapers, *Song* (Life), the pro-Buddhist *Noi That* (Let's Speak the Truth) and the anti-Buddhist *Su That* (Great Truth), started publication without licenses and were subsequently confiscated.

Since the establishment of the government of Prime Minister Ky, the friction between press and government has been a steady under-current of national life. Late in June 1965 the government, through Dinh Trinh Chinh, secretary of state for psychological warfare, announced the closing of all Vietnamese-language newspapers for a 1-month period. The purpose of the move was, according to Secretary Chinh, to "clean up the press" and to consider qualitative improvements in newspaper content. Because of the vigorous protests of newspaper publishers, the measure was only partially implemented: of a total of 36 dailies, 23 were allowed to resume publication after a 3-day suspension.

The government, however, has kept close watch over newspapers. Suspension or closure of dailies and weeklies which have allegedly violated laws prohibiting the printing of matters harmful to national security has occurred frequently. Because of extensive censorship, many newspapers have appeared late, with large blank spaces.

Newspaper editors, moreover, are periodically exhorted to print more government releases and news items originating with the government-owned domestic news agency, Vietnam Presse. Each day the Secretary of State for Information and Open Arms releases a list of topics about which no news stories may be published. Among such topics in 1965 were the demonstrations in the United States against the war in Vietnam, the release of South Vietnamese prisoners by the Viet Cong and some strike news. The government has also shown growing sensitivity to press coverage of the war.

This attitude has been shared by the United States Military Assistance Command for Vietnam (MACV) which, until January 1966, had briefed all newspapermen on military actions of United States as well as Vietnamese units. In July 1965 the MACV requested the news correspondents to observe rules of voluntary censorship in reporting military operations. According to these rules, newsmen would abstain from reporting casualties, troop movements and the identification of military units engaged in combat except in general terms. After January 1966 the same rule was applied to daily briefings of newsmen held by Vietnamese government officials on the actions of Vietnamese units.

Press criticism directed against the government and against the intervention of the United States in the Vietnam war has brought forth official warnings of suspension and closure. In December 1965 several newspapers were confiscated, including *Sinh Vien Hue* (Student Union of Hue), a publication of the pro-Buddhist students of the University of Hue.

Censorship measures were further tightened in the early spring of 1966. Newspaper publishers requested a meeting with Dinh Trinh Chinh to discuss what they called the "rigid and illogical" nature of these measures, but their request was not granted. Protest against censorship was one of the factors in the political unrest beginning in March 1966. In a resolution addressed to Secretary Chinh the Association of Vietnamese Publishers protested against the continued censorship and the attitude of the Director of the Press in the Department of Information and Open Arms toward certain newspaper publishers. Students of the National Institute of Administration and students of the Faculties of Medicine and Pharmacology of the University of Saigon declared their support of the publishers' resolution.

INFORMATION MEDIA

The Ministry of Information and Open Arms, in April 1966, was in charge of the control and coordination of communications media and of government information programs. The Department is subordinated to the Ministry of War and Reconstruction and is headed by a secretary, who, in addition to his official title of secretary of state for information and open arms is often referred to as psychological warfare secretary or information minister.

The Press

Since 1963 the number of daily and weekly newspapers has been extremely fluid. At the end of 1965, for example, there were 10 Vietnamese newspapers, 2 English newspapers and 1 Chinese newspaper among those considered most influential (see table 2). Almost every month, however, newspapers are suspended, closed or discontinue publication for financial reasons, while new ones begin to publish. In April 1966, there were 23 Vietnamese, 2 English, 2 French and 10 Chinese dailies published in Saigon; these, however, represented only a fraction of the more than 60 dailies and weeklies published throughout the country. In contrast to the constantly changing number of

Vietnamese-language newspapers, the number of those published in French, English and Chinese tends to remain steady.

After the end of the Diem regime, progovernment newspapers no longer received official subsidies. Compelled to look for other sources of revenue, publishers turned to former politicians or politicoreligious groups, although the solvency of such persons and groups had not always been durable. Newspapers linked to political or religious sponsors tended to oppose government policies. The swift official

Table 2. Major Newspapers of South Vietnam, 1965

Title	Language and circulation *	Publisher	Remarks
Chinh Luan (Right Opinion)	Vietnamese 40,000	Dang Van Sung	Nonpartisan, anti-Communist; has the highest circulation.
Dan Chu (Democracy)	Vietnamese 20,000	Vu Ngoc Cac	Nonpartisan, anti-Communist; appeals to intellectuals.
Dan Chu Moi (New Democracy)	Vietnamese 25,000	Ha Thanh Tho	Nonpartisan; supports the government.
Dan Chung (The Mass)	Vietnamese 25,000	Tran Nguyen Anh	Nonpartisan; supports the government.
Ngay Nay (Today)	Vietnamese 22,000	Hieu Chan	Pro-Buddhist.
Tu Do (Freedom)	Vietnamese 25,000	Pham Viet Tuyen	Nonpartisan; supports the United States.
Xay Dung (Construction)	Vietnamese 15,000	Father Nguyen Quan Lam	Pro-Catholic.
Tin Sang (Morning News)	Vietnamese 20,000	Do Cuong Duy	Represents Buddhist political views.
Lap Truong (Standpoint)	Vietnamese n.a.	Ton That Hanh	Weekly; mouthpiece of the antigovernment dissident groups in Hue and Da Nang.
Chanh Dau (Right Path)	Vietnamese n.a.	Ngo Huu Dat	Semiofficial organ of the Unified Buddhist Church.
Yuen Tung (Far East)	Chinese 16,000	Chu Min Yee	Oldest and most influential Chinese newspaper.
Saigon Daily News	English 4,000	Nguyen Van Tuoi	Independent; pro-Western.
Saigon Post	English 6,000	Tran Ly Thich	Independent; pro-Western.

n.a.—not available.
* Estimated.

repercussions which followed antigovernment press articles explained the brief lifespan of many daily and weekly publications.

For Vietnamese-language newspapers, the average circulation is approximately 19,000 to 20,000, about 7,000 for Chinese newspapers and lower for English- and French-language newspapers. Circulation figures are often exaggerated. Data pertaining to actual circulation, financial status and names of persons or groups supporting a newspaper are considered secret by publishers and are not divulged to outsiders.

Sales in Saigon represent a substantial portion of the total circulation. In the capital and in the larger cities, many people read more than one newspaper. On a countrywide basis, on the other hand, average readership per newspaper copy is as high as 50 in some areas.

Despite their instability, newspapers since 1963 have become more varied in type and highly competitive. In an effort to maintain or increase circulation figures, most newspapers show a propensity for sensationalism and banner headlines, and devote considerable space to serialized novels and cinema gossip.

The average newspaper is made up of 4 to 6 pages. Because of economic shortages, paper, printing and pictures are of poor quality. The staff of reporters and feature writers is small, sometimes consisting of not more than 10 or 12 persons. Although formal training in journalism is offered at the university level, many newspapermen learn the trade on the job and never acquire a degree.

The leading professional associations for journalists are the South Vietnamese Journalists Union and the Federation of Journalists. Publishers are represented by the Newspaper Publishers Association. The Press Council, formed in 1964, includes both publishers and journalists. In March 1966 the Journalists Union offered a 3-month course in journalism, taught by teachers from the United States and Canada. The course received technical and financial assistance from the International Federation of Journalists and the American Newspaper Guild.

Probably the most influential newspapers are the *Chinh Luan* (Right Opinion) and *Dan Chu* (Democracy). Both are nonpartisan and anti-Communist. *Chinh Luan's* estimated circulation of 20,000 is the highest among Vietnamese-language newspapers. *Dan Chu*, with a circulation of about 10,000, appeals mainly to intellectuals. *Dan Chung* (The Mass), with an estimated circulation of 6,000, is nonpartisan and tends to support the government. The nationalist *Ngay Nay* (Today) generally favors the Buddhist cause and has a circulation of about 22,000. *Tu Do* (Freedom), with an estimated circulation of 12,000, is noted for its support of the United States.

Catholic and Buddhist political points of view are reflected in several newspapers. The daily *Xay Dung* (Construction) has an estimated circulation of 12,000 and is generally regarded as the semiofficial Catholic newspaper. The daily *Tin Sang* (Morning News) represents the views of the Buddhist political movement. *Tu Quang* (Compassion), a monthly review, is the lay publication of the Buddhist Institute for the Execution of the Dharma. The weekly *Duoc Tue* (Torch of Intelligence) is an organ of the Refugee Buddhist Church. Its former publisher, Thich Duc Nghiep, was a Buddhist spokesman to the foreign press. *Chanh Dau* (Right Path), founded in November 1964, is the semiofficial newspaper of the Unified Buddhist Church of Vietnam.

The Chinese-language *Yuen Tung* (Far East) has a circulation of 16,000. The oldest and most widely read among the Chinese newspapers it was first published in 1939. The English-language *Saigon Daily News* and *Saigon Post*, both founded in 1963, have circulations of 4,000 and 6,000, respectively, and have extensive foreign news coverage, although war stories and domestic events are generally featured on the front page. Crimes are reported in detail, frequently with pictures and names of the persons involved. The *Saigon Daily News* carries features by United States syndicated columnists and Western-style political cartoons and comics.

Some periodical journals are published by scientific or professional groups, but their circulations are very small. Popular periodicals include the English-language *Vietnam Illustrated*, published by the *Saigon Post*, and the *Vietnam Combat et Edifie* (Vietnam Fights and Builds), published in French and in English. The Vietnamese-English *Lu'a Thieng* (Sacred Flame) is the illustrated periodical of the Buddhist movement.

Because the circulation of commercially published dailies and weeklies is limited to Saigon and the major provincial cities, newspaper needs of the rural population are met by provincial newspapers published by the Vietnam Information Service (VIS) or by the Province Chief. Published weekly or biweekly, provincial newspapers serve the information need of the rural areas.

Publishing

Saigon is the center for the publication of books and pamphlets as well as newspapers and periodicals. It is the seat of the country's largest printing facility, the National Printing Plant, which is owned and operated by the government. Established with financial and technical assistance from the United States, the National Printing Plant is equipped with machines for various types of printing. Additional printing facilities are operated by the Vietnamese Army Psychological Warfare Directorate, the Department of Agriculture and the Joint United States Public Affairs Office (JUSPAO). In addition, there are a few private publishing and printing firms, most of which lack modern printing and binding equipment.

News Agencies

The government owns the only domestic news agency, Vietnam Presse, which supplies much of the local and national news and most of the foreign news to the domestic press. Vietnam Presse subscribes to the services of Agence France Presse (AFP), Reuters, Associated Press (AP), United Press International (UPI) and others. It also maintains its own correspondents abroad. Morning and evening editions of Vietnam Presse daily bulletins and a weekly bulletin feature domestic and foreign news. In December 1965, Nguyen Ngoc Linh, director of Vietnam Presse, announced the government's plan for the building of a 14-story press center in Saigon.

Radio

The government-owned National Broadcasting System of Vietnam (Vo Tuyen Viet Nam—VTVN) operates under the supervision of the Ministry of Information and Open Arms. A decree promulgated in October 1965 provided for the autonomous operation of Radio Vietnam under a director general by January 1966. Information is lacking, however, regarding the implementation of this decree.

In January 1966 the country's broadcasting system consisted of a main station in Saigon and regional stations in the cities of Ban Me Thuot, Da Lat, Hue, Nha Trang, Quang Ngai, Qui Nhon, Can Tho and Da Nang. Provincial stations operate in Quang Nam, Phu Yen, Dinh Tuong, Long An and Kien Tuong Provinces (see table 3). The stations broadcast on shortwaves and mediumwaves, on transmitters ranging in power from 1 to 55 kilowatts. The basic shortwave program relay system has been improved since 1963 and will be further strengthened by the addition of new antennas. Twenty-five additional broadcasting sets are to be installed, mainly in the Mekong Delta, to improve broadcasting coverage of that area. Parts of the military troposcatter system (broadcasts based on the scattering of radio waves from the weather-zone, approximately 50,000 feet above the earth) have also been made available to Radio Vietnam to facilitate program relay.

By early 1966, however, the broadcasting system consisted mainly of shortwave and some low-powered mediumwave transmitters which were neither powerful nor numerous enough to function as a network. Plans had been made to build additional mediumwave transmitters and to increase the power of existing ones so that the system may be transformed into an actual mediumwave network.

Sites of the broadcasting stations operating in 1966 were selected with the view of serving the most densely populated areas, but in

Table 3. The National Broadcasting System of South Vietnam, 1965–66

Station	Frequency (in kilocycles)	Remarks [1]
Radio Saigon (located at Phu Tho and Quan Tra).	Channel A 870 (50 kilowatts) 9775 6116 4810 Channel B 7260 610 (20 kilowatts) Channel C 1090 9754 Channel D n.a.	Has a total of 30 transmitters.
Regional Stations:		
Radio Ban Me Thuot.	690 (55 kilowatts) 4810 1090	New 55 kilowatt transmitter has a radial range of 200 kilometers by day and 500 kilometers by night.[2]
Radio Can Tho	780	Formerly in Ba Xuyen.
Radio Da Lat	6116 7140 1440	
Radio Da Nang	1090 7265	New since January 1966.
Radio Nha Trang.	9720 970	
Radio Hue	9670 650 7205 1490	Voice of Freedom broadcasts intended for North Vietnam on 9670 kilocycles and 650 kilocycles.
Radio Quang Ngai.	800 890	New since 1963.
Radio Qui Nhon	1253	New since 1963.
Provincial Stations:		
Radio Quang Nam (located at Hoi An).	n.a.	
Radio Phu Yen (located at Tuy Hoa).	n.a.	
Radio Dinh Tuong.	n.a.	
Radio Long An (located at Tan An).	n.a.	
Radio Kien Tuong.	n.a.	

n.a.—not available.
[1] Technical data incomplete. Broadcasts are on mediumwave and shortwave, on transmitters ranging in power from ½ to 55 kilowatts.
[2] 1 kilometer equals 0.62 miles.

mid-1966 only about 60 to 75 percent of the population could be reached by radio broadcasts. A more complete broadcast coverage depended upon the establishment of additional stations and further technical improvements to link the system into a network. Most of the broadcasts were on shortwaves, since the country's geographical features are not favorable to mediumwave emissions. Atmospheric conditions, on the other hand, often interfere with the reception of shortwave relay broadcasts. In spite of technical shortcomings and operational difficulties, the radio far exceeds the importance of newspapers as a medium of communication.

The Saigon station (situated at Phu Tho, in the outskirts of the capital) broadcasts on three shortwave and six mediumwave bands on transmitters ranging in power from 1 to 25 kilowatts on the shortwave and from 1 to 10 kilowatts on the mediumwave band.

Radio Hue has a combined 20-kilowatt mediumwave and shortwave transmitter; plans have been made for the installation of an alternate mediumwave transmitter. The combined transmitter operates on 9670 and 650 kilocycles.

The Quang Ngai and Qui Nhon regional stations have been added to the network since 1963, and the facilities of the Nha Trang and Da Lat stations have been modernized. The Da Nang regional station was inaugurated in January 1966. It is powered by a 10-kilowatt transmitter, which broadcasts on 1090 kilocycles, and by an additional 5-kilowatt transmitter.

The Ban Me Thuot station was being modernized in 1965 and 1966 with equipment supplied by Australia. Its new 55-kilowatt transmitter represents a more than fivefold increase of the station's previous broadcasting power.

In the course of the political disturbances in March and April 1966, following the dismissal of I Corps Commander Lieutenant General Nguyen Chanh Thi, the radio stations of Hue and Da Nang were taken over by rebel forces and broadcast antigovernment programs.

In 1964 the country's radio stations broadcast a total of over 120 hours per day, mostly in Vietnamese. Radio Saigon broadcasts also in Chinese, French, English, Cambodian and Thai. The daily hours of broadcast for regional stations vary between 4 and 12 hours a day.

Since 1965 the government has encouraged local radio stations to devote as much program time as possible to relay broadcasts from Saigon. In February 1966 more than 60 percent of the programs of some regional stations, including Can Tho and Da Nang, consisted of rebroadcasts from Saigon. Special broadcasts in *montagnard* dialects have been introduced by Radio Da Lat and Radio Ban Me Thuot. The programs intended for *montagnards* are entitled: "News," "Common Knowledge" (featuring reports and talks on reconstruction programs, hygiene, agriculture and history), "Music" and "Drama."

Radio Saigon broadcasts on four channels, of which Channel A has been on a 24-hour schedule since January 1966. News, press reviews and talks on current political topics predominate in the program which is beamed on 870, 9755, 6116 and 4810 kilocycles. In early 1966 several new features were added to the program of Radio Saigon, including an educational program, a children's hour and a drama show. Channel B (on 7260 and 610 kilocycles) features programs in Chinese dialects (Cantonese and Mandarin). The French-sponsored Channel C broadcasts music, French cultural programs and language lessons on 1090 and 9754 kilocycles. Radio Hue is on the air for 16 hours a day, mainly with "Voice of Freedom" programs intended for North Vietnam. An estimated 420,000 private radio receivers were in use in 1964. Approximately two-thirds of the privately owned sets were located in Saigon-Cho Lon; the rest were in the countryside mainly in provincial district towns.

The government estimates the number of radio receivers in 1966 at 800,000. Since 1965, 125,000 transistor sets have been put on sale for prices ranging from 800 to 1,000 piasters. Government rural credit cooperatives handle the commercial distribution of sets in the rural areas. In addition, USOM has supplied more than 5,700 community receiving and listening sets, and some 10,000 hamlet receivers.

Most urban owners of radio receivers tune in every day for news, broadcasts of traditional drama, or Western music. The large majority of rural listeners prefer traditional music and classical drama (*tuong cai luong*) to political programs and newscasts. A growing interest in agricultural information programs has been noted in some areas. Rural radio owners tune in for about 2 hours a day, mostly in the morning. During harvesting and planting time, however, radio listening time drops off sharply. A limited survey in April 1964 among rural radio listeners indicated that they would favor a reduction of broadcasting time devoted to modern and Western music and would welcome additional broadcasts of traditional drama, poetry and music. Only students and teachers have expressed a preference for modern music and news commentaries.

Television

Television, first introduced in February 1966, has been operating on a provisional system of airborne telecasting. Signals are transmitted from specially equipped aircraft, while circling above Saigon, to receivers on the ground. Two channels are in operation: one, presented by the government, carries programs of information, education and entertainment; the other, used by the United States Armed Forces, features programs in English. During the initial phase, the Vietnamese channel operated 1 hour a day; the United States Army channel, 3 hours a day.

The first television showing, presented on February 7, 1966, on sets installed at various public places, was hampered by technical difficulties which the government hopes to correct when ground stations are installed. The United States has pledged to distribute 2,500 television receiving sets; 500 of these had been installed by February 1966.

Films

The importance of motion pictures as channels of information has been increasing. Mobile units of the United States Information Service, the Vietnam Information Service and Vietnamese Army Psychological Warfare battalions have reached a growing number of rural residents, but the scope of operations for mobile film units has been curtailed because of wartime conditions.

The USIS supplies about 70 percent of the films shown in rural areas. In 1964 more than 10,000 of the USIS prints were shown, representing about 800 titles. Most of the technical equipment required for film showings in rural areas was also supplied by USIS. More than 600 of a total of 800 16-millimeter projectors which were in use in rural areas in 1964 were made available by USIS and USOM. These agencies also furnished accessory equipment needed by mobile film units, including generators, tape recorders, loudspeakers and vehicles.

Throughout the country, there are about 156 cinemas with a total seating capacity of 65,000. Of these, some 100, with a seating capacity of 35,000, are in Saigon. Most full-length feature films are imported from Nationalist China, the United States, India, Japan and France. Since 1965 interest in French films has been slackening in favor of those produced in the United States.

There are five local firms equipped to produce full-length feature films. Because of the high price of raw film and operational difficulties incident to wartime conditions, the domestic production of feature films came to a halt in 1964.

The Motion Picture Directorate of the Ministry of Information and Open Arms produces 35- and 16-millimeter newsreels at a rate of 52 10-minute newsreels a year, in addition to various documentary films. These are supplemented by documentaries and biweekly "news magazine" films furnished by USIS. Other documentaries and short features are produced by the Vietnamese Army Psychological Warfare Directorate.

Informal Communication Channels

The traditional reliance on oral transmission of information is reinforced by suspicion of the reliability of the radio and press, and people tend to give more credence to hearsay information than to information received through more formal channels. Rumors and reports originate in diverse settings, ranging from government offices in Saigon to the marketplace, where they are picked up and passed on by members of the armed forces, pedicab drivers, traveling food vendors and others whose activities bring them into contact with new listeners.

In the countryside, people look to village elders and officials, members of the military services and religious leaders for information. Countrywomen who sell produce in the markets of towns near their villages are also important links in the chain of person-to-person communication. News and gossip are also passed on at the village community center (*dinh*), where people gather in the evening and carry home what they have heard to friends and neighbors.

GOVERNMENT INFORMATION ACTIVITIES

The government makes extensive use of formal and informal communications media to solicit public support for its policies. In 1965–66 more than two-thirds of the daily broadcasting time of the government-owned radio was devoted to news, news analysis and political commentaries. Other means of spreading information about government policies and plans range from the distribution of handbills to the dispatching of specially trained psychological warfare teams to the countryside.

Government officials stress current policy themes in speeches delivered in the course of personal visits. Prime Minister Nguyen Cao Ky made several such visits in 1965 and 1966, speaking in military camps, hospitals, hamlets and to members of various civic groups. The Prime Minister, moreover, encouraged persons from all walks of life to address themselves to him in personal letters regarding problems and difficulties encountered when dealing with government officials and agencies.

The basic themes the government seeks to develop are those of nationalism, elimination of "social injustice," defense against Viet Cong terrorism and the denunciation of communism and neutralism. The principal agency for the dissemination of government information is the Ministry of Information and Open Arms and its provincial organization, The Vietnam Information Service. The VIS supports the Provincial Phychological Operations Committee. The programs and activities of the Department of Information and Open Arms are complemented by the psychological warfare battalions of the South Vietnamese Army. Government information programs receive material and consultative support from the Joint United States Public Affairs Office.

The rural areas are special targets for the official information programs. In these areas the government relies heavily on the use of informal channels to reach peasants, who, by threats or inducements, have come under the influence of the Viet Cong. In 1965 the Department of Information and Open Arms dispatched some 7,450 psychological warfare workers to the villages in the Mekong Delta area. Traveling in teams of 100, the workers spent several nights in each village or hamlet, studied the peasants' needs and assisted in reconstruction projects. Using speech and song they explained the purpose of new government programs, interpreted political developments, countered Communist propaganda and encouraged the farmers to participate in the defense of villages and hamlets.

Cultural troupes of signing minstrels and musicians are dispatched by the VIS to remote villages, including those in the Highlands inhabited by *montagnards*. Through musical and dramatic allegories the entertainers denounce the misdeeds of the Viet Cong and extoll the joys of life during peacetime. The presentation is followed by a more direct exhortative message on the need to support the government in its fight for peace, delivered by the local chief of the Psychological Operations Committee. Sometimes the minstrels perform in conjunction with film showings presented by mobile VIS units. The films feature color travelogues, market scenes, agricultural information and newsreels showing United States military power. Other means aimed at regaining the loyalty of dissident peasants are local improvements benefiting agriculture, health and education (see ch. 8, Living Conditions).

The government's major effort in this field is the "Open Arms" (Chieu Hoi) program administered and directed by the Department of Information and Open Arms. The program is designed to encourage members of the Viet Cong to desert, return to their former homes and assist in the counterinsurgency activities. Leaflets urging the Communists to defect are scattered over Viet Cong-controlled territory by Vietnamese and United States aircraft. Messages offering incentives and encouragement to those who turn themselves in to Open Arm stations located throughout the countryside are transmitted from helicopters equipped with loudspeakers. The returnees are given full amnesty and are placed in one of 200 camps which are maintained for them. In the camps they receive food and clothing and attend political reeducation courses. After 4 to 6 weeks and sometimes longer they are released and usually return to their native villages. Others join the South Vietnamese Army or participate in psychological warfare campaigns to induce other Viet Cong members to defect.

According to official reports, the number of Viet Cong defectors has steadily increased since 1965. In that year, almost 45,000 Viet Cong insurgents defected, more than double the number for the previous year. Among them were tax collectors, village officials and some soldiers from the regular North Vietnamese army.

In 1966 foreign information activities of South Vietnam were conducted on a limited scale. The government's major effort had been to strengthen the facilities for broadcasting to foreign countries. Broadcasts intended for North Vietnam and for neighboring Cambodia, Laos and Thailand are transmitted mainly from stations close to peripheral areas, notably Hue and Quang Tri. Radio Hue's "Voice of Freedom" broadcasts, intended mainly for North Vietnam, are transmitted for 16 hours daily. One channel of Radio Saigon, operated by the South Vietnamese Army, also broadcasts "Voice of Freedom" programs. Information officers assigned to embassies of South Vietnam distribute newsletters, brochures and other printed material to interested individuals and groups.

North Vietnam is also reached by leaflets and pamphlets dropped by South Vietnamese and United States aircraft. In 1965 the leaflets stressed the North Vietnamese Government's complicity with Communist China in the economic exploitation of the country, in return for Chinese-made weapons, and contrasted economic and social progress in the South with the dire conditions prevailing in North Vietnam.

COMMUNIST INFORMATION ACTIVITIES

North Vietnam carriers out a major part of its propaganda against South Vietnam through the so-called National Front for the Liberation of South Vietnam (NFLSV) to which it gives direction and material support. The propaganda channels at the disposal of the Front are the Liberation News Agency, Liberation Radio and the South Vietnam Liberation Motion Picture Company (see ch. 14, Political Dynamics).

In 1965 the Liberation News Agency (LNA) claimed to publish some 40 national and regional newspapers and 17 periodicals. *Nhan Dan* (The People), best known among the newspapers, is an organ of the People's Revolutionary Party, a dominant member of the Front. The LNA also publishes an extensive daily bulletin dealing with NFLSV activities and various pamphlets. Some of the newspapers and other publications are printed in the Viet Cong-controlled zones and are passed from hand to hand.

The Front's clandestine broadcasting facility, Liberation Radio, broadcasts 56 hours weekly in Vietnamese and 3½ hours per week each in Mandarin, Cantonese and Cambodian. A 15-minute weekly broadcast in English is intended for United States servicemen. Liberation Radio broadcast a week of special 2-hour programs daily from December 15 to December 22, 1965, commemorating the fifth anniversary of the establishment of the Front. In 1966 the total number of weekly broadcasting hours on Liberation Radio was increased to 67.

Propaganda films and newsreels are shown by mobile units of the so-called South Vietnam Liberation Motion Picture Company in Viet Cong-controlled areas.

In addition to the formal media utilized by the Front, members of the Viet Cong engage in propaganda activities which are adapted to local conditions. Trained in the tactics of combined political and military warfare, they distribute mimeographed handbills, song sheets, banners, printed tracts and crudely lettered signs in the villages. They are also instrumental in dispatching agitation and propaganda teams, delivering speeches and calling for demonstrations on public address systems and loudspeakers. Often the Viet Cong present themselves to the villagers as peasants who, in indignation at the alleged abuses of a "corrupt regime," are fighting for a better life for the farmer and for the true independence of the country. Resentments of the population, whether manifested against the conduct of local officials, living costs or United States military operations in the area, are thoroughly exploited. In its dealings with the *montagnards* the Viet Cong has employed both coercion and inducements. In an effort to gain their confidence and cooperation Viet Cong agents have moved in to live with *montagnard* groups, learned their languages, married local women and promised the highlanders autonomy under North Vietnamese rule.

Direct Communist propaganda from North Vietnam reaches the country mainly through broadcasts. Radio Hanoi's "Voice of Vietnam," transmitted on shortwave and mediumwave, broadcasts several programs which are intended mainly for South Vietnam. At the end of 1965 the weekly number of broadcasting hours in Vietnamese by Radio Hanoi totaled 67 hours and 15 minutes. Included in these programs was a thrice-weekly half-hour "Program for Southern Youth and Students," and 12 hours and 15 minutes of weekly transmissions in *montagnard* languages, notably in Jarai and Rhade. Little is known about the effectiveness of Hanoi's radio propaganda in the South. It appears, however, that it has considerable influence on the attitudes of Viet Cong insurgents regarding conditions in North Vietnam and the war in the South. Weekly broadcasting output in English totaled 14 hours and included two daily 15-minute propaganda programs aimed for United States servicemen in South Vietnam.

Radio Moscow broadcasts 21 hours a week in Vietnamese. Radio Peking's Vietnamese-language broadcasts increased from 28 hours a week in 1964 to 31½ hours in 1965.

In 1965 and 1966, Communist propaganda continued to play upon nationalist feelings by constant repetition that the United States represented "imperialist aggression" and was the "real enemy of the Vietnamese people." Because of the intensified military activity, the

United States was no longer referred to as a "paper tiger" in the propaganda vocabulary of the Viet Cong. Extensive use was made, on the other hand, of atrocity themes in connection with United States military operations. Another basic propaganda theme has been the defamation of the South Vietnamese Government as a puppet of the United States which lacks popular support. At the same time, the Front is extolled as a patriotic and truly representative popular movement. Because Communist appeals dealing with peace, independence, patriotism and national liberation have been relatively ineffective, Front and Viet Cong propaganda agencies in 1966 turned increasingly to the exploitation of everyday issues. Almost daily, they referred to conscription, house evictions, economic shortages, the rising living costs and similar issues, which they regard as sources of popular concern in South Vietnam.

Ancillary propaganda campaigns generally took the form of face-to-face agitation by members of the Viet Cong encouraging the rural population to join the guerrilla movement or to support its operations through donations of food and the purchase of Viet Cong war bonds. The Viet Cong also issued threats and warnings against reading leaflets disseminated by the South Vietnamese Government and listening to Saigon broadcasts.

UNITED STATES AND OTHER WESTERN INFORMATION ACTIVITIES

The United States leads the non-Communist nations in providing information activities in South Vietnam. The United States program is carried out chiefly by the Joint United States Public Affairs Office (JUSPAO), an interagency organization created in May 1965 which incorporates USIS Vietnam, the Communications Media Division of the United States Agency for International Development, and specialists from the Military Assistance Command Vietnam. The JUSPAO field representatives are based at the headquarters of the four military regions and at 38 provincial locations covering all 44 provinces.

American Cultural Centers are maintained by JUSPAO at Can Tho, Da Lat and Da Nang. Vietnamese-American Associations operate in Saigon, Cho Lon, Da Nang, Nha Trang, Da Lat and Can Tho. The Centers and Associations inform the South Vietnamese people about the United States through books, films, periodicals, tape recordings and other channels. The JUSPAO cooperates with and supports activities of the VIS in its provincial branches and provides printed material, records and films for showings in the provinces by VIS mobile units.

The JUSPAO distributes the *American Cultural Journal* in Vietnamese, a scholarly quarterly journal intended for intellectuals, *World*

Today, a Chinese-language periodical published every other week, *Free World*, a monthly magazine designed for high school level readers, and another monthly, *Quest*, also intended for youthful readers, and *Rural Spirit*, a monthly magazine designed for a peasant audience.

The Voice of America broadcasts Vietnamese-language programs 5½ hours daily, including Sunday. The programs feature news, interviews and musical entertainment.

Information activities of France and the United Kingdom have been considerably reduced since 1962. France maintains no official representative, although some information concerning France is available to the South Vietnamese through the Alliance Française, a cultural organization which still operates.

The British Council, similar to the Alliance Française, functions with a small membership in Saigon. Information concerning the United Kingdom is available from the press officer assigned to the British Embassy.

CHAPTER 17

POLITICAL VALUES AND ATTITUDES

The struggle for independence from French rule served to unite many different political groups and elements of the population in a common cause and reinforced the older sense of national unity based on ethnic, linguistic and historical ties. Since independence, however, official efforts to evoke the same patriotic sentiments from among the population proved to be less successful, and the divisive patterns of political orientation are frequently manifest (see ch. 14, Political Dynamics).

In the rural areas, where nearly 80 percent of the people live, family and village loyalties affect attitudes toward the Saigon government. Urban dwellers are on the whole more politically motivated than the peasantry, but because of the lack of orderly means of expressing themselves effectively, many remain indifferent toward the government (see ch. 14, Political Dynamics).

Political values, if definable at all, are largely traditional in content. Principles and related political practices originating in the West have not taken root and exert little influence on the political scene. Moreover, because of the prolonged conflict between government forces and the Viet Cong, the political attitudes of most people are strongly conditioned by physical security considerations. Having been continually subjected to wartime conditions and accompanying tensions and stresses, the people have come to regard flexible adjustments to unpredictable and changing situations as the best guarantee of physical survival. As a result, overt expressions of allegiance to either the Saigon regime or the Viet Cong are often likely to be ephemeral and, hence, cannot be taken for granted as proof of positive commitment.

VALUE ORIENTATIONS

In broad outlines two types of value patterns, the traditional and Western, are discernible. Fusion or integration of the two elements into a workable arrangement geared to the South Vietnamese society is yet to take place.

Traditionally, Vietnamese beliefs concerning the ideal political order were shaped by the Confucian philosophy of government. Essentially, according to this philosophy, the ruling class was to be virtuous and benevolent toward the people. If officials conducted themselves in an exemplary manner, it was believed that the people would unquestioningly obey them. This view was epitomized in a popular saying: "If the water is clean upstream, it will be likewise downstream." Thus, the quality of government, whether good or bad, was attributed mainly to the moral quality of the officials.

Because of this background, many people are inclined to assert that the emergence of a truly dedicated and capable national leadership, preferably civilian, would significantly stimulate popular enthusiasm for the central government. This emphasis on personality factors has led to the underdevelopment of political norms based on impersonal, formal institutional relationships or on abstract ideological considerations. Political tensions in South Vietnam, therefore, are often less the results of differences stemming from political beliefs than of personal clashes between and among political leaders themselves (see ch. 14, Political Dynamics).

Exposure to Western political values is of more recent origin. Moreover, during the past several decades, only a few educated Vietnamese became familiar with the Western concepts of individual rights, political freedom and representation and of accountability for public officials.

These educated elements, most of them urban in origin, came to play the leading role in the nation's public affairs, but they were unable to transform the Western values into a way of political life combining Vietnamese and Western features. This is partly because the contact between the traditional and Western value system was largely on a theoretical level without the benefit of actual experimentation. Under President Diem's authoritarian rule, the constitutional system, which was patterned after Western models, seldom functioned as initially conceived. Coupled with the disruptive impact of Viet Cong insurgency on nearly all facets of national life, the applicability of the Western political values and practices to South Vietnam came to be questioned by even the most educated and articulate political elements of the country (see ch. 13, The Governmental System: ch. 14, Political Dynamics).

Another factor of significant political consequence is the popular concept of suppleness and flexibility. Although it has a traditional basis deriving from the Confusion notion of social harmony and aversion to extremist attitudes, it has been reinforced by the distressing events of the past two decades (see ch. 12, Social Values). Over the years the importance of flexible adaptation to shifting political and other conditions has taken on the character of a virtue or a value. Some South Vietnamese tend to regard this flexibility almost as a national tradition; for example, they attribute their country's survival from foreign domination to their ancestors' political suppleness and cultural eclecticism. They assert that, combined with their forefathers' military prowess, it was Vietnam's calculated flexibility, in relation to the dominant powers, which enabled the country to preserve its common heritage—bowing before superior power in the manner of bamboos bending with the wind but rebelling against it wherever possible (see ch. 3, Historical Setting).

PATRIOTISM AND UNIFICATION

Patriotic sentiment among a small number of politically articulate South Vietnamese, young and old, is strong enough to cause a general dissatisfaction with the existing partition of the country. In early 1966, however, this feeling was not powerful enough to evoke a spontaneous movement for immediate reunification. Refugees from the North, many of them Catholics with members of their family left behind in the North, were nostalgic for the region of their origin; but very few, if any, expressed wish for unification under a Communist regime or on terms which might lead to a Communist takeover. Relatively small groups of militant students and young Buddhists, however, were known to favor some sort of neutralist solution (see ch. 14, Political Dynamics).

Officially, the Saigon government's highest political goal continued to be national reunification to be brought about by the freely expressed will of the people throughout North and South Vietnam. The government, in periodic formal statements, has sought to inspire patriotic sentiment in favor of reunification. Because of the grave threat posed by Viet Cong insurgency, however, governmental leaders became increasingly concerned with the immediate problem of national survival. Coupled with the growing popular awareness that both North and South Vietnam are committed to mutually exclusive systems of political and social order, reunification as a symbolic concept for patriotism has lost much of its original meaning.

LOYALTY AND NATIONAL SYMBOLS

For the vast majority of the population, their allegiance, as in the centuries past, is directed to the family and, to a lesser degree, the village. Traditionally, the small world of each village composed of varying numbers of tightly knit kinship groups was economically self-sufficient, and, politically, its members followed the age-old custom of village self-administration (see ch. 6, Social Structure; ch. 13, The Governmental System).

Beginning in 1956 village administration was subjected to direct control of the central government, partly as a means of instilling in the people a sense of loyalty toward the nation and partly as a means of effectively extending governmental authority into the heretofore isolated rural communities. An increasing number of peasants and urban dwellers have become conscious of their status as citizens of South Vietnam with accompanying duties toward the Saigon regime. Nonetheless, for much of the population, the concept of nationhood in the abstract and loyalty to it are still in an incipient state.

National symbols are slowly but steadily gaining in effectiveness as stimulants for forging a sense of national identity and patriotism. This is especially the case among students who have experienced the daily practice of singing the national anthem and saluting the flag. The flag of the Republic of Vietnam is a solid yellow rectangle with three horizontal red stripes across the center. The yellow background is the symbolic color of the former imperial dynasty and of the Buddhist faith; the red stripes represent the union of the country's traditional regions (ky): North, Central and South Vietnam.

The national coat of arms is a triangular shield with bamboo reeds (representing resiliency and strength) in the background. The word VIET-NAM is inscribed on a banner which is superimposed on the reeds; at one end it encircles a writing brush, symbol of the scholar, and at the other end, a sword, symbol of the military. This design, shortly after the founding of the Republic in 1955, replaced a dragon signifying the mythical national origin.

South Vietnam's national anthem, composed initially as a patriotic college song by a Hanoi student in 1943, gained wide popularity throughout the country after World War II. It was officially adopted by the State of Vietnam in 1949 and continues to be the official anthem of the Republic. The text of the anthem, entitled "Appeal to Youth" (Tieng Goi Thanh Nien), is as follows:

> Youth of Viet-Nam,
> This is the time we must liberate our country
> Let us all march forward and if need be, repay our nation with our lives
> So that our beloved Viet-Nam will forever remain free and secure
> Even if we should perish on the battlefield
> We should shed our blood to defend the honor of our country
> In the time of crisis we must defend our nation and,
> We, the youth of the nation, must remain firm and determined
> To fight for our country so that everywhere the good name of Viet-Nam
> will live for ever.
> My friends, let us close ranks under the banner
> My friends, let us rid our fatherland of all the destructive forces
> And live up to the glorious heritage of our Lac Hong origin.

Holidays are also a means of conveying a sense of national unity in symbolic form. The founding of the Republic in October 1955 and the promulgation of the Constitution a year later were celebrated on October 26 until 1963. Since President Ngo Dinh Diem's regime was overthrown on November 1 (1963), that date is celebrated as National Day (frequently referred to as Revolution Day). Premier Ky proclaimed in 1965 that the date on which the Geneva Agreement on Vietnam was signed, July 20, previously called "Shameful Day," be celebrated as "National Unity Day for the Liberation of North Vietnam."

The most important traditional holiday is Tet, or lunar New Year, on which the Vietnamese are reminded of their cultural heritage. This occasion, partly religious in character, brings all business to a complete halt for 3 or 4 days, always on the first day of the first month by the lunar calendar. Traditional usages are observed, obeisance is made to the ancestors; debts are paid and a fresh start is pledged for the new year. Another important holiday, the sixth day of the second lunar month commemorates the Trung sisters, who led a revolt against the ruling Chinese in A.D. 39.

National commemorative days, though not celebrated as holidays, honor certain Vietnamese patriots. One, on the twentieth day of the eighth lunar month, honors Marshal Tran Hung Dao, who defeated the armies of Kublai Khan in the thirteenth century; another, on the twenty-second day of the eighth lunar month, honors King Le Loi, who drove out the Chinese after their second occupation in the fifteenth century (see ch. 3, Historical Setting). The birthdays of Buddha and Christ are officially recognized as religious holidays. A commemorative celebration of Confucius' birthday also has been established by the government.

ATTITUDES TOWARD GOVERNMENT AND THE VIET CONG

The vast majority of the people have little notion and still less experience of representative government and related political processes. Members of an educated, urban minority, familiar with constitutional concepts and influenced by democratic ideals, are eager for a larger voice in national affairs. They are apt to be anti-Communist and to dominate politics and government. They believe, however, that mere promulgation of a constitution or creation of formal representative institutions cannot alone bring about a viable democratic political order. They see time and successful counterinsurgency efforts against the Viet Cong as preliminary essentials, but many of them believe that steps should be taken to broaden the base of popular support for the government in some as yet undetermined manner (see ch. 13, The Governmental System; ch. 14, Political Dynamics).

To a majority of the rural population, the national leadership represents the remote authority of a central government with which they are only indirectly concerned and know mainly through the provincial administration. For many, their only contact with the state is with its taxing power and security measures, which have sometimes been applied in peremptory fashion by military officers. Fully aware that such irritants and sources of resentment make for vulnerability to Viet Cong propaganda attacks, governmental leaders in 1966 were vigorously attempting to establish closer relations with the rural population. There were indications that some villagers were responding favorably to such efforts, but most of them still tended to prefer noninvolvement as the best means to insure their personal security.

During the past few years both the Viet Cong and the government have competitively exerted themselves to win over the peasants. The Viet Cong used terror and coercion while the government sought to extend effectively its educational, health and social welfare programs. Many of the rural people preferred, wherever possible, to stay outside of the conflict, the real nature of which was not readily comprehensible to them. Where a noncommital position was impossible, as when they were confronted with the armed authority of the competing contestants, many of them flexibly yielded to pressures. Some fled from the Viet Cong to areas under government control. Most of those who cooperate with the Communists appear to do so out of fear without genuinely endorsing or comprehending what the Communists preach (see ch. 26, Public Order and Safety).

SECTION III. ECONOMIC

CHAPTER 18

CHARACTER AND STRUCTURE OF THE ECONOMY

South Vietnam has an agrarian economy based largely on rice cultivation. Farming is the principal occupation of the people, and rice and rubber are the usual items of export. The next most important sector of the economy is trade, both domestic and foreign, which is centered on the Southeast Asia entrepôt of Saigon-Cho Lon. Industry, consisting mostly of food processing plants and factories producing consumer goods, though still small in size, is expanding but is hampered by a power shortage. Commercially exploitable natural resources are limited.

The economy is far from self-supporting and is heavily dependent on foreign aid. The United States is the foremost donor and has financed the development of the defense establishment and the reconstruction of roads, railroads, canals, ports and airfields heavily damaged or destroyed in the Indochina War. It has supported the currency, met the large deficit in the balance of payments and supplied the equipment and credit for the development of agriculture, industry, power and transportation. It also has provided funds for carrying out new projects in many other fields. As South Vietnam has come under increased Viet Cong (see Glossary) attack, United States aid has been expanded in order to continue past programs in support of the deteriorating economy and to finance additional activities designed to counter the insurgency.

Productivity and per capita income are generally low, even in Asian terms. Most of South Vietnam's 16.1 million people are farmers living in scattered villages and hamlets which are largely concentrated in the Mekong Delta, the most fertile area of the country, and along the coast in the flood plains of the Central Lowlands.

Of 7.6 million acres under cultivation, between 6.2 and 6.4 million are in irrigated rice which is grown in small plots called paddys. Annual rice production is estimated at 5 million tons. Tea and rubber plantations on the slopes of the Central Highlands are still mostly French owned. They cover some 350,000 acres and employed about 50,000 persons until Viet Cong activity and general intensification of the war by United States and South Vietnamese forces against the Communist insurgents caused plantations to lose their former immunity from damage through military operations. Faced with this situation, several rubber estates closed down. In the sparsely settled Central Highlands, where the area of fertile uncultivated land is estimated at 5 million acres, some 500,000 to 700,000 *montagnards* practice a shifting agriculture. In the villages along the 1,100-mile coast there are approximately 246,000 fishermen.

About 15 percent of the population lives in the cities, mainly in Saigon-Cho Lon, which has grown to almost 2 million. The metropolis is not only the capital of the country but also the major seaport and a road, rail and air center. Commerce and industry, including handicrafts, employed about 520,000 persons at the end of 1961, the latest year for which an estimate is available. Most of these enterprises are located in or near Saigon-Cho Lon, which is the focal point for all commercial and financial activity.

The internal transportation network which centers on Saigon is inadequate, and freight charges are high, the result of numerous disruptions caused by widespread Viet Cong sabotage operations concentrating on the destruction of bridges, uprooting of rail trackage and assassination or intimidation of technicians and specialists. Because of wartime conditions, roads and canals lack adequate maintenance and the supply of railway rolling stock, motor vehicles, boats and aircraft is insufficient. About 870 miles of railroad, largely inoperable, connects Saigon with the main coastal cities. The main rail line, terminating at Dong Ha near the seventeenth parallel, is the southern section of the railroad built by the French to link agrarian Cochin China in the south with Hanoi in the more industrialized Tonkin to the north.

Some 9,200 miles of highway, much of it unusuable because of Viet Cong action, were mostly French-built, either to facilitate delivery of produce to Saigon or for strategic purposes. Also oriented toward Saigon is the 2,500-mile network of waterways in the Mekong Delta which is estimated to carry 4 million tons of traffic per year in small sampans and on barges. Most urban centers have airfields built with United States aid; domestic flights to and from Tan Son Nhut Airport at Saigon are frequent but insufficient to meet the demand, since airplanes constitute the most practical means of movement from place to place within the country.

The people, with the possible exception of some of the *montagnard* groups, are accustomed to the use of money. The unit of currency is the piaster (for value of the piaster, see Glossary), directly supported by the United States since January 1, 1955. South Vietnam has a central bank and 14 commercial banks located in Saigon-Cho Lon with a few branches in other urban centers. The central bank holds the government's gold and foreign exchange reserves and has the exclusive right to issue currency. By the end of 1964 reserves had sunk to their lowest level since the partition of Vietnam, brought about by the Geneva Agreement of 1954, and currency issued was considerably beyond the legal limit established by the bank's charter.

The commercial banks are engaged almost entirely in financing foreign trade. Under French rule, foreign trade consisted of rice and rubber exports and imports of manufactured goods from France. After partition, however, rice exports dwindled, were sporadically prohibited as a result of shortages and finally ceased in 1965. Rubber exports also declined steadily. Imports of manufactured goods, on the other hand, have been maintained at a high level, averaging $250 million per year, through the Commercial Import Program, financed by United States aid. The United States has replaced France as the major supplier. The United States also meets the deficit in South Vietnam's balance of payments.

Government revenues are derived largely from customs duties and other associated indirect taxes. Direct taxes are assessed on land, income and business profits but have proved difficult to collect. Published data on revenues collected are incomplete and generally based on estimates. At no time have revenues financed more than a small part of government expenditures. Budgets are characteristically unbalanced, with the deficit being met by foreign aid. Published budgets are not reliable indicators of actual government expenditures as a result of omissions in compilation, reorganizations in government departments within the fiscal year and the shifting of funds from one use to another.

In 1965, as counterinsurgency efforts increased, Vietnamese budgetary expenditure rose considerably, totaling 51.3 billion piasters, nearly double that of 1964. The total deficit was estimated at 38 billion piasters, to be covered either by a United States aid contribution or by advances from the National Bank. In 1965 United States aid was more massive than ever, the total being estimated at $287 million. In addition, United States expenditure on military construction of roads, airbases, ports and other United States Army installations attained a rate of $1 million per day, creating an enormous need for raw materials, goods and labor.

The increasing magnitude of the United States presence was also accompanied by a steady rise in the cost of renting buildings for housing, business and military establishments. Wages doubled and tripled, but, as earnings increased, families sought to buy more and better food and clothing. At the same time, the Saigon port continued to be congested, and warehouse space was in short supply, resulting in long delays in unloading cargo. As both shortages and demand increased, a serious inflation developed, aggravated by hoarding and speculation. Within the year 1965, according to official statistics, the cost of living rose 58 percent in Saigon and 70 percent in Hue.

The economic benefits derived from the inflow of American money, credit and goods are confined mostly to the city dwellers, many of whom are recipients of unusually high wages and salaries paid out by contractors and businessmen competing in the tight labor market for various types of services. An inflationary stimulus to the economy is maintained by the increased income of merchants, shopkeepers, real estate owners, skilled and semiskilled workers, bar hostesses and others seeking lucrative returns from the greatly augmented cash flow. The rising wage and salary rate, however, is largely offset by mounting living costs. The excess of imports over exports, financed largely by United States aid, indicate that the country is living beyond its means. Dependence on foreign aid and frequent changes in government have hindered the long-range planning and the enforcement of measures needed to combat the inflationary forces.

At the same time that South Vietnam's towns and cities are enjoying the greatest prosperity in their history, the farmers, who make up the majority of the population, have lost ground economically. Unable to raise or deliver normal crops as a result of military activities, farmers grumble that rice prices are too low compared with other prices. Although the wholesale rice price has risen to a level 40 percent higher than usual, the farmer continues to feel that he is not getting his proper share of the price rise. Moreover, the government's ability to carry out the land reform plans essential for building up the agrarian economy to support an economically viable state of South Vietnam, are severely hampered because much of the land area involved is under Viet Cong control. Thousands have fled their ancestral villages to seek physical security.

To counter the inflation, the United States aid mission has imported rice and airlifted it to shortage areas in order to keep the price down. Another major step, in the hope of limiting the circulation of dollars in Vietnam, was the adoption by the Americans of a system of military payment currency or script which may be exchanged for piasters. The most important anti-inflationary effort, however, remains the Commercial Import Program, under which the United States buys goods with dollars and sells them in South Vietnam for piasters, maintaining a flow of goods to absorb excess spending power.

To combat the transportation shortage, the United States is importing eight coastal vessels to serve the main ports from Nha Trang north to Quang Tri 20 miles from the Demarcation Line. In addition, a fleet of over 200 motorized junks has been assembled to tranship supplies to the smaller ports and river hamlets that cannot handle the larger freighters. The Vietnamese Government has established special courts to try those accused of bribery, hoarding and speculation in goods and threatened to execute profiteers who make exorbitant gains from dealing in scarce commodities. An example was made of a Chinese merchant early in 1966.

Since partition the United States aid mission has made a concerted effort to diversify the economy and hasten its technical development. Some light industries have been established, and marked gains have been recorded in industrial production. Additional industrial installations are under construction or are planned. Various forms of assistance have been provided by the government for the development of industry and handicrafts. Important steps were the establishment of the Industrial Development Center and the Handicraft Development Center. A further stimulus to industrial growth was the government's foreign investment policy which gave foreign investors assurance against war risk, expropriation or possible nationalization and also offered incentives of various types. The government itself has either entirely or partially financed investment in industries, public utilities and transport facilities considered basic to development of the economy.

Gains were also made in the agricultural sector. These were attributed almost entirely to the government's program of land reform and land reclamation, a program designed to bring back into cultivation 2.5 million acres of abandoned riceland in the Mekong Delta and to extend cultivation in the Central Highlands. Land reform measures began in 1955 with the issuance of new land ordinances which established rent limits and provided security of tenure to tenants. Landowners were required to declare their uncultivated land, and, if they failed to bring their unused holdings into production, the properties were subject to government requisition for the settlement of refugees from North Vietnam. According to published reports during President Diem's regime, more than 500,000 refugees from the North were settled on such properties.

A presidential decree in 1956 limited individual ownership of ricelands to a maximum of 284 acres and provided that land in excess of this amount was to be purchased by the government for resale in small plots, preferably to tenants who were already working the land. By the end of 1962, when the program was declared complete, over 600,000 acres had been distributed to more than 100,000 farmers, mostly tenants. Further land reform programs were initiated by Prime Minister Nguyen Khanh in 1964 and by Prime Minister Nguyen Cao Ky in 1965. Under these programs the respective prime ministers distributed a few hundred land titles to tenant farmers; thousands of other land titles, including *montagnard* titles to their lands, are reportedly being processed.

Other factors resulting in increased crop production are better cultivation methods, improved water resources, the use of chemical fertilizers and pest control. New agricultural techniques and new varieties of crops have been introduced through agricultural extension services and local training centers. The average farmer had demonstrated his willingness to accept new ideas and technical innovations which would improve his livelihood, but by the close of 1961 security conditions in the countryside prevented extension agents from visiting many rural areas, and the benefits of experimental work could thereafter reach only a limited number of farmers.

Fishermen have benefited from the creation of government credit facilities and cooperatives which have made it possible for them to purchase modern gear and market their rapidly expanding catch. The availability of credit also stimulated the forest industries which supplied firewood, charcoal and bamboo until Viet Cong activities made transportation difficult. Exploitation of the forests, which cover, 30 percent of the country, is limited, however, as no adequate survey of timber resources has been made.

A Five-Year Plan for industrial development was announced in 1957 but was never formally adopted. A second Five-Year Plan, launched in 1962, was abandoned. In 1965 economic development was necessarily linked to counterinsurgency programs. The stated economic goals were to increase production, expand exports, provide import substitutes and develop skilled manpower. The rural development program announced in February 1966 involves the use of teams now undergoing training. Under the program, after the enemy has been cleared from an area, a team will enter a village, conduct a census, issue identification cards and weed out Viet Cong suspects. Other members of the team will start schools, provide medical services, help farmers with their crops, organize local government and help train village leaders. Goals for 1966 are modest. They call for clearing and holding 900 new hamlets, consolidating government control in 1,000 already cleared villages, building 2,251 new classrooms, 568 miles of road, 57 dams and 148 bridges, and digging 118 miles of canal. In February 1966 there were 33,838 trained men and women in the field, and by the end of the year another 20,000 were expected to be trained. At least 440,000 will be required to blanket every province.

A serious deficiency hampering development of all sectors of the economy has been the shortage of trained technical, professional, managerial and administrative personnel. Technical schools and colleges have been established; on-the-job training programs have been initiated, and Vietnamese students have been sent abroad for advanced study.

CHAPTER 19

AGRICULTURE

The country is predominantly agricultural. About 75 percent of the estimated total population of 16.1 million consists of farmers and their families, most of them engaged in the cultivation of rice. In normal years production is sufficient not only to feed the population but to make rice exports the major foreign exchange earner. In 1965, however, Viet Cong interdiction of the roads and waterways leading from the Mekong Delta, South Vietnam's rice bowl, to Saigon had resulted in serious shortages so that the capital city and the northern part of the country were being fed by imports of United States surplus foods. Cultivation and export of plantation crops such as rubber, tea and coffee continued, but protracted military action was causing a decline in output.

Agricultural production rose steadily after the close of the Indochina War in 1954. By 1959 crop levels in excess of those registered before World War II were being reported, and in subsequent years official statistics indicated only minor fluctuations from these high levels. Yet it is questionable if the rice production reported in 1959 could have been the same in 1964 when 600,000 persons were reported to have fled their homes in Viet Cong-controlled territory to become day laborers in Saigon, fishermen along the coast or unemployed in a refugee settlement.

A substantial portion of the increase in agricultural output which took place after 1954 was the direct result of restoring to cultivation land abandoned during the war years. Other factors included better methods of cultivation, improved water resources, use of chemical fertilizers in some areas and pest control. Agricultural development has been fostered by substantial foreign aid given by the United States Agency for International Development (AID) to finance a land reform program, the establishment of agricultural credit and various technical projects designed to increase production and introduce new crops.

By the 1960's, serious attention was being given to agricultural diversification in an effort to improve the living standard of the farmer. New agricultural techniques and new high-yielding varieties of staple food crops had been introduced through the agricultural extension service. In 1960 considerable success was reported, but by the close of 1961 security conditions in the countryside prevented government agricultural workers from visiting many of the rural areas, and the benefits of experimental work had reached only a limited number of farmers.

LAND UTILIZATION

Physical geography has largely determined the pattern of land utilization. The country may be divided roughly into three agricultural regions: the Mekong Delta, the coastal plains of the Central Lowlands and the Central Highlands portion of the Chaîne Annamitique (see ch. 2, Physical Environment). The principal farming areas are the alluvial Mekong River plain and the small deltas along the narrow coast of the Central Lowlands. In contrast, the Central Highlands area is sparsely settled and contains a large area of uncultivated fertile land, much of which is forested.

Of the total land area of approximately more than 42 million acres, a little more than 7.6 million are under intensive cultivation. In 1964 the total area producing wet rice was estimated to be between 6.2 and 6.4 million acres (see fig. 11). Included in this figure was over half a million acres where floating rice is cultivated in the waters of the rivers and streams which make up the many mouths of the Mekong. Rubber plantations on the southern slopes of the Central Highlands account for about 350,000 acres, and the remainder produce such crops as hard fibers, tea, coffee, sugarcane, fruits and vegetables. Hard fibers are produced in the Central Highlands; tea and coffee plantations are located on the Central Highlands slopes. Some sugarcane, fruits and vegetables are produced in every province. About 14 million acres are covered with forest.

The Mekong Delta is watered by rain and by the annual flooding of the Mekong River. The river's flow is relatively gentle, and its rise and fall are gradual. There have been destructive floods, but these are unusual. Since the Delta is extremely flat, with a slope of approximately 1:100,000, the chief problems are those of drainage and of tidal action which carries brackish water a considerable distance inland (see ch. 2, Physical Environment).

Surveys made in selected areas indicate a wide variety of soils in the Mekong Delta. Soils range from light, sandy loam to heavy clay, which is impossible to plow when dry. Most of it is slightly acid, generally lacking in phosphorus and low in essential organic material. The Mekong River deposits only a small amount of silt in the Delta. The best soils are found in the southwestern section; these are of more recent origin and have a high degree of natural fertility.

In the upper reaches of the Delta, soils tend to contain active alumina in toxic quantities. The condition is said to be most prevalent in the plains northwest of Saigon and in the Saigon area itself. These soils,

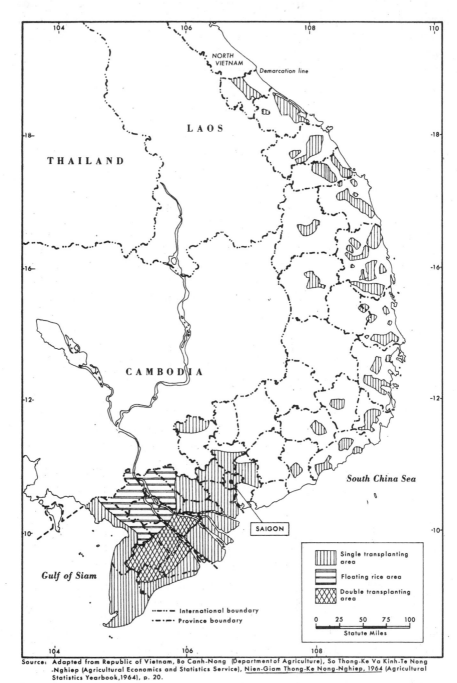

Single transplanting area

Floating rice area

Double transplanting area

International boundary
Province boundary

0   25   50   75   100
Statute Miles

Source: Adapted from Republic of Vietnam, Bo Canh-Nong (Department of Agriculture), So Thong-Ke Va Kinh-Te Nong
-Nghiep (Agricultural Economics and Statistics Service), <u>Nien-Giam Thong-Ke Nong-Nghiep, 1964</u> (Agricultural
Statistics Yearbook,1964), p. 20.

Figure 11.   Chief Areas of Wet-Rice Cultivation in South Vietnam, 1964–65.

with proper leaching, are suitable for growing rice which has a shallow root system. Subsoil water tends to be salty, particularly during the dry season. Although the use of chemical fertilizer was introduced by the French, few farmers have any understanding of its proper application in relation to the various soil types.

About 90 percent of the cultivable area of the Mekong Delta is planted to rice. The only other agricultural product of importance is copra, which is found in sandy areas along the coast near Truc Giang about 40 miles southwest of Saigon. Tobacco, corn, manioc and vegetables are produced, most for local consumption, on the riverbanks which are a few feet above the flooded rice paddies. In a few areas where irrigation is available in the dry season, corn is planted as a second crop after rice.

Cultivable land in the coastal region of the Central Lowlands is confined to the small deltas of the short rivers flowing out of the eastern slopes of the Chaîne Annamitique. Because of the position of these mountains in relation to the prevailing monsoon winds, there is considerable variation in climate and rainfall from Mui Dinh to the Hue plains bordering the seventeenth parallel (see ch. 2, Physical Environment). The total cultivable area does not exceed 1 million acres, most of which is used for wet rice cultivation. Because of the scarcity of good land, most fields are double cropped.

The most fertile land in the Central Lowlands is located north of Mui Dieu (formerly Cape Varella). South of the cape the climate is relatively dry, and all crops must be irrigated. The soil is generally sandy and of low fertility. North of Mui Dieu fertile loams are found in the deltas, but except in the limited areas of recent alluvial deposit the soil is generally poor. The best soil is found in Binh Dinh and Phu Yen Provinces where a modern irrigation system, built under the French colonial administration, is in operation.

The Central Highlands rise to the steep, densely forested area of the Chaîne Annamitique bordering the narrow eastern coast. The inland plateau, ranging in altitude from 2,000 to above 3,000 feet, slopes gently westward toward the drainage basin of the Mekong (see ch. 2, Physical Environment). The partially lateritic soils in this plateau area are of volcanic origin.

The western and southern slopes of the Central Highlands have large areas of uncultivated fertile land, estimated to amount to as much as 5 million acres. *Montagnards* who inhabit the area engage in shifting agriculture (also known as swidden), hunting and gathering. The *montagnards* grow rice, corn, manioc, other vegetables and tobacco. On the slopes of the Central Highlands are rubber, tea and coffee plantations. It has been demonstrated that various temperate-climate crops thrive in the area. Much of this land is in secondary forest or grassland (see ch. 2, Physical Environment).

LAND TENURE

There has been no cadastral survey, and most titles to land depend on oral tradition in the village or in the tribal group. Large plantations and estates, termed "concessions" by the French colonial government, are likely to have been surveyed (if only by eye) and registered at the Land Registry Office in Saigon. Since 1954 some land abandoned during the Indochina War and some reclaimable land have reportedly been surveyed in order to grant land titles to refugees from North Vietnam being relocated in the South. The titles to land distributed to tenants or landless farmers under President Ngo Dinh Diem's Ordinance No. 57 of October 22, 1956, have not been issued, because payments from the recipients have lagged, and sufficient staff is lacking to survey fields and process titles.

Traditional Tenure

In the first century A.D. the Viets, the forebears of the Vietnamese people, were already wet rice farmers as well as fishermen. They lived in compact villages in their homeland in the Red River Delta, and each village was governed by a council selected by the resident families. The wet ricefields were held in common by all the families in the village, a situation arising presumably from equal participation by all in building the bunds and dikes which made the paddy fields. Individual families held usufruct rights to particular plots which were reallocated every few years by the village council.

Throughout subsequent centuries, as, behind their conquering armies, the descendants of the Viets colonized the eastern rim of the Indochina peninsula, they clung tenaciously to the way of life and beliefs of their ancestors. They were interested solely in wet ricefields and, ignoring the highlands, they established their villages in the alluvial deltas along the coast. As in their homeland, the villages were governed by a village council, a custom honored by the emperors and continued with modifications to the present.

The push southward along the coast was underway by the fourteenth century, and by the end of the seventeenth century the descendants of the Viets (called Annamites by this time) had reached the Mekong Delta. In the early settlements the wet ricefields were communally held and periodically reallocated in accordance with ancient practice. As colonization spread farther south, however, in order to entice settlers, permanent and inheritable usufruct rights in specific fields were conferred on individual families as well as a right to a share in communal village lands which were still set aside for allocation by the village council. If the family line died out, the permanently assigned fields reverted to the village.

Colonization of the Mekong Delta was still in process at the time of the French conquest, and thereafter the traditional communal village lands were not set aside. A survey in 1931 showed that 25 percent of the ricelands in the narrow coastal strip of the Central Lowlands and 3 percent in the Mekong Delta were communal lands. Although subsequent developments under the French introduced new concepts of land tenure which deviated from the traditional pattern, nonetheless the Vietnamese peasantry still holds the conviction that every family has a right to a share of land and that communal lands should be reserved for the use of the poor, needy and landless.

Land in which a family had permanent usufruct rights was theoretically inalienable. The peasants, however, when in need of funds, might transfer the use of a portion or all of their land to persons with money to invest. In return for a sum of money, usually between 60 to 80 percent of the land's value, the lender took over possession of the property. After an agreed period, usually 3 years but sometimes much longer, the borrower could redeem the land by returning to the lender the sum of money originally received. In the nineteenth century, under Emperor Gia Long's legal code, it became possible for the lender to become the possessor of the land by paying the borrower, with his consent, the difference between the amount of the loan and the value of the land. In this manner numerous transfers of usufruct rights have taken place out of the normal channels of inheritance (see ch. 3, Historical Setting).

Another tradition which has not lapsed is the custom whereby the head of a well-to-do family declares a portion of the family fields to be dedicated to support the rituals and feasting associated with the Cult of the Ancestors. Ownership of such land is vested in all the adults of the patrilineage, reckoned from a male ancestor in the third ascending generation. The head of the patrilineage is charged with the proper management of the income of the designated lands. Although theoretically the designated fields can be alienated with the consent of all the adult members of the patrilineage, no such instance has been reported.

French Concessions

The French were primarily interested in developing the resources of their new territorities, and in that part of the Indochina peninsula which is now South Vietnam the major resource was uncultivated and undeveloped land. Large land grants (called concessions) for the cultivation of rice, rubber, tea and coffee were made to Frenchmen, Chinese and favored Vietnamese, on the condition that they would clear the land, build canals and make other improvements.

Until a decree issued in December 1913, concessions were granted under local regulations special to each of the component territories comprising French Indochina. The 1913 decree was the first in a series whereby the French administration sought to regularize and clarify the procedures for obtaining grants, the conditions to be met by the concessionaire and payments to be made for different types of concessions. The theme of all the decrees was land development. Titles were provisional and could be withdrawn if the improvements specified in the registration documents were not carried out.

Maintenance of native (*indigènes*) rights and the "reservation for the natives of sufficient land to meet their present and future needs" was provided in a 1926 decree. This decree also required that an applicant for a grant present proof that he had sufficient capital and equipment to develop the concession. A 2 percent tax was placed on the gross production of all concessions. A 1928 decree tied the grant of concessions to a program which "fixed the territory reserved to the natives, areas open and closed to colonization, and land reserved for reforestation." Under this decree, if the land grant was not developed within 5 years, it would be withdrawn. A clause of this decree reserved *montagnard* lands for their use only.

Land Reform After Independence

In 1954, at the end of the Indochina War, the countryside was devastated. Nearly 2.5 million acres of the most valuable riceland had been abandoned and was overgrown with brush and weeds. Irrigation and drainage facilities had fallen into disuse; canals and indispensable waterways were silted or overgrown and needed redredging.

About 2.5 percent of the landowners held roughly half of the cultivated land, and more than 80 percent of the land was cultivated by peasants owning no land at all. Most of the large landholdings were divided into small tenanted plots of 5 to 12 acres.

Conditions of tenancy were usually verbal, although sometimes recorded in written contracts, and were renewed from year to year. Before 1954 there were no regulations governing farm leases, rents or loans. The tenant had little protection from the landlord who could dispossess him without cause. Rentals were high, frequently as much as 50 percent of the crop. The tenant had to provide his own housing, tools, livestock, seed and hire extra help for planting or harvesting. Often without sufficient rice for food or seed at planting time, the peasant borrowed from the landlord or a local moneylender to cover his immediate needs. He frequently paid double the amount at the end of the harvest, and by the time his obligations were met, his share of the crop might be less than a third of the total harvest.

Large holdings and tenant farming predominated in the Mekong Delta, half of the cultivated land being occupied by properties of over 123.5 acres. Only 12 percent of the land was held by peasant proprietors with holdings of 12.4 acres or less. In no Delta province was the average size of a plot less than 2½ acres, and they increased in size to 24.7 acres in the west. The Delta had been the first part of Indochina to be conquered by the French, who in that sparsely settled region had parceled out extensive tracts for themselves and a few favored Vietnamese. As a result, subsequent Vietnamese settlers found it difficult to acquire land and were forced to become tenant farmers or agricultural laborers.

In the longer settled coastal plains of the Central Lowlands landholdings were small. Three-fourths of the farmers owned their land, with holdings averaging from 2 to 5 acres; not more than 50 individuals owned as much as 125 acres. In this part of the country communal or village landownership persisted. In some districts 50 to 70 percent of the cultivated land might be communal; in others, this form of ownership was almost absent. Inalienable village property, communal land was administered exclusively at the village level. It was rented to members of the village on terms which varied from one village to another, according to custom. Rents were paid directly to the village treasury and, in some villages, constituted the main source of public revenue.

The sparsely populated Central Highlands, an area of roughly 17,000 square miles, was considered to be almost exclusively in the private domain of the royal family before 1955. After World War I the area was not extensively exploited, but some rubber, coffee and tea plantations were established by the French and a few wealthy Vietnamese. These plantations caused unrest among the *montagnards*, who resented the invasion of their ancestral lands even though they themselves were left largely undisturbed. The *montagnards* belonged to different ethnic groups and had various systems of land tenure. In some groups land was the property of an extended kin group; in others it belonged to the small family (see ch. 6, Social Structure). After independence the Central Highlands were declared to be in the public domain. The rubber plantations, reportedly covering some 250,000 acres, and a few coffee and tea plantations continued to be largely French owned.

In the Mekong Delta, where the worst abuses of tenancy and landlordism prevailed, the Viet Minh found ready support in the villages during the years of the Indochina War. Throughout this period the Viet Minh forces lived off the land. Where they controlled the countryside, they imposed tax burdens in grain as heavy as the rentals formerly collected by the landlords. They did so not only by their power to coerce but also by convincing the peasants that they represented the cause of national liberation.

Though the Viet Minh had no specific land program, the landless were led to believe that the landlord's property would belong to them as soon as the French were defeated. Many landlords had fled and those who normally lived in Saigon did not dare to venture outside the city. Peasants were encouraged to take over abandoned land, and payment of rent, as distinguished from taxes, virtually ceased. Quasi-

320

military religious sects, such as the Hoa Hao and the Cao Dai, gained control over substantial areas of the Mekong Delta along the Cambodian border where, citing traditional concepts of land usage, they also encouraged peasants to occupy abandoned land without regard to legal titles. As a result of all these factors, a virtual land reform program had been carried out in this area before independence.

After independence the first phase of rural reform was the promulgation of a rent reduction and tenure security program. Ordinance No. 2 of January 1955 limited rents to no more than 25 percent of current average gross yield and assured tenants of security of tenure for a period of 3 to 5 years under a written contract. Ordinance No. 7 of February 1955 had a precedent in the precolonial tradition making land abandoned for 3 years subject to redistribution, reaching back to a fifteenth-century imperial decree which forbade landowners to leave land fallow under threat of confiscation.

Ordinance No. 7 required all landowners to declare their uncultivated land and their intentions respecting it. Those unable or unwilling to cultivate it were directed to lease it to a farmer who would do so. Farmers who brought back into use land which had fallen idle during the war years were given a written guarantee of tenure for a period of 8 years, the first 3 with reduced rent and the remainder on the same terms as established tenants. By June 30, 1959, there were 774,386 written land lease contracts, involving 4 million individuals, three-fourths of all tenants in South Vietnam. Of the 5 million acres of land covered by these written contracts, most of it located to the south and west of Saigon, about one-fourth had been abandoned land.

In 1955, spurred on by Ordinance No. 7, many owners brought their unused holdings back into production; others who failed to act found their properties taken over by the government for refugee resettlement. Altogether, more than 500,000 refugees from North Vietnam were resettled. A dramatic example of refugee resettlement is the Cai San project in the Mekong Delta. The Cai San area comprises some 270,000 acres between the southernmost branch of the Mekong, the Song Hau Giang, and the Gulf of Siam. In 1956 the greater part of this land was an overgrown wilderness of weeds and brush. Approximately 50,000 refugee families, each assigned a 3-hectare plot (7.41 acres) at a nominal price, have reclaimed the land, cleared the canals and begun harvesting good rice crops.

In addition to refugee resettlement, the government also established a land reclamation program in the Central Highlands. Possibly as many as 100,000 people were moved from the crowded coastal deltas of the Central Lowlands to the sparsely populated Highlands. They exchanged their half-hectare (1.23 acres) tenant holdings in the Lowlands for a gift of a plot of 2 to 3 hectares (4.9 to 7.4 acres) in the public domain of the Highlands. By 1960, 78 new villages were said to have been created.

Under the same program, approximately 25,000 *montagnards*, who tended to be isolated from the national administration and were thought to be vulnerable to Communist coercion and subversion, had also been resettled in new locations in the area. By 1965, however, it was reported that most of the people from the Central Lowlands had returned to their native villages and that their settlement in the Highlands had served to exacerbate the resentment of many *montagnards* toward the Vietnamese. The *montagnards* regarded the lands as their own, and written title to their lands was one of the demands which they made of the Vietnamese Government at the time of the revolt in November 1964 (see ch. 26, Public Order and Safety).

Another far-reaching decree dealing with land reform was President Diem's Ordinance No. 57 of October 22, 1956. It provided that no one might own more than 100 hectares (247 acres), plus an additional 15 hectares (37 acres) of riceland entailed for the expenses of the family ancestral cult. This cult land could not be sold. Land in excess of 100 hectares was to be purchased by the government for resale in plots equivalent to 5 to 12 acres in size. Incumbent tenants were allowed first option, followed by descendants of disabled soldiers or those who died in combat, refugees and those reclaiming their homes, the unemployed, small landowners having more than five children but less than 3 hectares (7.4 acres), and the landless.

The government was to pay the landlord 10 percent in cash and the balance of the purchase price in nontransferable government bonds bearing 3 percent interest and maturing over a period of 12 years. The landowners might gradually exchange their bonds for stocks in government-owned paper, glass, textile and other manufacturing industries. The purchaser could pay for the land in six annual installments, each approximately equal to a year's rent. When the application was approved the tenant received a temporary title, which was to become permanent when payments were completed; during the interim, final ownership rested with the government. The law did not apply to village communal land or to other than ricefields.

The land redistribution program was slow to start. Surveys had to be made, and surveyors and equipment were scarce, as were qualified administrative personnel. With United States aid these difficulties were gradually overcome. The Ordinance 57 program was launched finally by President Diem in 1957 and resulted in the expropriation of 1.7 million acres, most of it in the Mekong Delta south of Saigon. Of the total land subject to transfer, 1.1 million acres (of which 222,300 acres had been abandoned) were Vietnamese owned; about 654,000 acres (of which 323,570 acres had been abandoned) were French owned. This required that compensation be paid to some 2,500 owners, of whom 433 were French citizens.

The average price per hectare paid by the government for cultivated land was 7,000 piasters (for value of the piaster, see Glossary); that for idle land, about 1,000 piasters. To enable the Republic of Vietnam to pay for the French-owned land, the French Government granted South Vietnam 1,490 million francs (for value of the franc, see Glossary), plus an additional 400 million francs for the purchase of agricultural equipment. The administrative costs of the land transfer program, totaling $2.2 million, were covered largely by United States aid funds.

The benefits of the land reform program were minimized by the intensification of guerrilla warfare after 1959. Landlords gave up land to the government in areas so insecure that rents could not be collected, and tenants who had been farming such land free saw no reason why they should pay the government for it. In areas of greater security, even though the large landholdings of the past were eliminated, tenancy remained a problem. Progress of the program was dependent upon the efforts of provincial administrations, which varied from complete cooperation to outright rejection of the whole concept.

By the end of 1962, when President Diem declared the land reform program completed, 609,043 acres had been distributed to 115,381 farmers, mostly former tenants. Subsequently, about 900 acres were allocated, but over a million acres remained government owned Some of this land was used for the *agroville*, strategic hamlet and new life hamlet programs, but the province chiefs, whenever possible, continued to collect rent on most of this land on behalf of the government.

In March 1964, Prime Minister Major General Nguyen Khanh initiated a further land reform program which was estimated to apply to over 900,000 acres. Ricelands were not involved. Illegal squatters on government land were to receive ownership rights to a maximum of 10 hectares (24.7 acres) if they had cleared and cultivated the land. Areas over 10 hectares would be sold "either by friendly arrangement or by bid." Annual installment payments on land purchased from the government, including sales of land under Ordinance 57, were extended from 6 years to 12. To inaugurate this program, Prime Minister Khanh distributed about 200 titles.

The next effort toward land reform was made by Prime Minister Air Vice Marshal Nguyen Cao Ky in August 1965. First priority was given to the sale of the 650,000 acres in the Mekong Delta of former French-owned land which the government still held, and to the equitable division of village communal lands to tenant farmers. Peasants could purchase up to 24 acres of land under 12-year government financing. Land values were to be based on yield, and tenants were to have the first option to buy the lands they were farming. Only some 50,000 acres of the French-owned land were free of Viet Cong control, but distribution of titles to purchasers in this area was expected to begin immediately. *Montagnard* titles to their lands were also being prepared.

The second of Prime Minister Ky's programs dealt with the 750,000 acres of village communal lands which traditionally were rented to landless villagers. These lands were not included in the rent control provisions of former President Diem's land reform ordinances; meanwhile, rents had risen in level to more than 50 percent of the crop. When villagers could not pay, the land was put up for bids, and much of it was reported to have come into the hands of absentee landlords in Saigon. Under the new program, bidding was abolished on communal lands, rents were limited to 15 to 25 percent of the average yield, and a new distribution priority system was put into effect. Disabled war veterans and members of local militias had first priority, followed by those then on the land who were refugees from the Viet Cong. As with other land reform programs, it appears that progress will be hampered by lack of qualified technical and administrative personnel.

PRODUCTIVE ACTIVITIES

Farming

Farming, which engages about 75 percent of the people, is largely a family affair. Units are generally small and individually operated. Farm size, climate, topography and conditions of soil and water, which vary regionally, largely determine the pattern of farm life. With few exceptions methods have changed little over the centuries; horoscopy, taboos and sanctions play an important role in farming activities. Tools and equipment are, in general, locally made.

During the 5 hot months of the dry season, when there is little farmwork to do, the farmer may look for supplementary labor in a larger village center. Generally, however, his activities are confined to fishing, mending and repairing the dikes and houses and similar work, until the start of the rainy season and new crop planting begins. The average farmer probably accepts this subsistence pattern as part of the natural order of things, but he has shown himself ready to accept new ideas and technical innovations that will improve his livelihood.

Most of the farmers in the Mekong Delta produce only one rice crop a year, relying on rainfall and the annual flood in the Delta for the necessary water supply. This flood, which starts in June and reaches its first peak at the end of July and a second peak in September and October, establishes the agricultural cycle in the delta region. It begins in June with transplanting or direct sowing in the fields from

July to September. Most harvesting starts in December and continues through February. The average tenant unit is around 5 acres and the holding of peasant proprietors between 10 and 15 acres. Rice yields are high, from 1,000 to 1,500 pounds per acre for a single crop. Total production in the region is estimated at 4 million metric tons a year.

In addition to rice, farmers usually raise vegetables for family use and plant a few fruit trees, the commonest of which are papaya, banana, orange, guava, mango and jack fruit. Most farm families have a few ducks and chickens and a pig.

On the coastal plains of the Central Lowlands all of the arable land has been cultivated for centuries, and most of it is divided into many smallholdings. The average farm is in a small delta hemmed in on three sides by mountains. Most holdings do not exceed 5 acres, and they center around a plot of paddy land which is double cropped. Each farm family does most of its own work, which includes operating a paddle wheel to lift water into the fields during the growing season. In addition to rice, there is usually an acre or more of dry land and where manioc, beans, vegetables, some tobacco and a few fruit trees are grown. Ducks, chickens and various other types of fowl are kept for home consumption. In some areas where livestock breeding has improved, the sale of pigs for export to Hong Kong and elsewhere is an important source of income for the farmer.

The rice yield in this region is lower than in the Mekong Delta, about three-fourths of a ton per acre being obtained for each of the two annual crops, although where sufficient irrigation is available and adequate fertilizers are used, production is considerably higher. The annual harvest of about 1 million tons of paddy hardly covers local consumption, and rice is usually imported from the southern delta.

In the Central Highlands, shifting agriculture still predominates among the *montagnards* (see ch. 5, Ethnic Groups and Languages). In this process a thickly wooded area is selected several months before the rainy season begins. The trees and brush are cut and allowed to dry. The fields are then burned, and before wind or rain can dissipate the ash, the fields are raked, and rice, corn, manioc, other vegetables and a small quantity of tobacco are planted. This is done with digging sticks and hoes. When the fields are at a distance from an established village, temporary shelters are constructed in which the men of the village live until the crop matures. The crops are entirely dependent upon rainfall and subject to the depredations of birds, monkeys, wild pigs and rats from the surrounding jungle. A field is usally cultivated for 3 years and then left to fallow for 5 to 10 years while other fields are cleared and cultivated.

After 1956 the Central Highland plateaus, formerly limited to the shifting cultivation of the *montagnards* and some plantation production of rubber, tea and coffee, were opened to diversified farming. In this area, estimated to have 5 million acres of fertile land, an attempt was made to establish new villages of 100 to 500 families of army veterans and people from the Central Lowlands. Substantial American aid was given for the clearing and plowing of the newly cultivated land, and water was obtained by pumping from subartesian wells.

Rice Production

In terms of the number of people engaged in its cultivation—nearly three-fourths of the total rural population—rice production is the most important agricultural activity in the country. There are some 1,500 known varieties of rice and several distinct types of rice culture adapted to regional geographic differences. Although most rice is grown in lowland paddies which are flooded in the growth process (wet rice method), *montagnards* cultivate rice on upland fields which are dependent solely on rainfall (dry rice method). The rice may be classified into three main categories according to the period of growth from seeding to harvest—early-, medium- and late-maturing. The early-maturing varieties develop in as few as 120 days; the late varieties require 5 to 6 months to mature. In the Mekong Delta the late-maturing varieties are most common because of poor drainage does not permit sufficient control of the floodwaters to dry the fields between crops or allow for irrigation in the dry season to make double cropping possible.

In the region where the Mekong enters South Vietnam, drainage is very slow and the annual flood covers the area to a depth up to 10 or more feet. Floating rice, a subvariety of a late-maturing type, is grown in this area. The seed is sown in April and May when the soil is dry. While the floodwaters cover the field, the rice, which is not transplanted, grows with great rapidity and, supported by the water, reaches a tremendous length, with its tip just above the waterline. As the flood recedes the plants stretch out on the mud and two or three nodes on the plant produce new plants on which the rice flower develops and from which the crop is harvested. Considerably less labor is involved in this method of culture, but production levels are generally not as high as with other varieties because of competition from weeds and the irregularity of spacing.

Further south in the delta, in the provinces of Chuong Thien, Phong Dinh, Vinh Long and Ba Xuyen, where the floodwaters do not reach such a great depth but where drainage is still insufficient, the soil seldom completely dries out and double transplanting is practiced. During the normal dry season the area is covered with rank vegetation which must be removed. In July seedlings grown in the nursery are transplanted to a cleared area in clumps rather close together. Four to 6 weeks later they are separated and replanted with wider spacing. The practice of double transplanting, peculiar to the southern area, allows for weed control and checks excessively rank growth.

More than half of the riceland in the total Mekong area is transplanted only once. The usual practice is to germinate the seeds in a nursery plot approximately one-tenth the size of the field to be planted. When the seedlings are at least 8 inches high they are transplanted to allow for even spacing, which ensures higher yield.

As they have been for centuries, most of the ricefields throughout the country are plowed by a simple buffalo-drawn wooden plow with a metal cutting blade. In refugee centers, such as that at Cai San, where tractors are used for deep plowing during the dry season, weed control has been greatly improved and fertility increased. Where adequate drainage can be achieved and fresh irrigation water provided in the dry season, the cultivation of ricefields for another crop—such as corn, peanuts, soy beans or any other fast-growing crop—during the off season greatly improves the texture and fertility of soil in the ricefields.

Most of the ricefields in the deltas along the coast in the Central Lowlands are double cropped, using early- and medium-maturing varieties of rice. Unlike the Mekong Delta, the rice-growing areas of this region get the benefit of the northeast monsoon and usually have good irrigation systems. The growing season is from October or November to February or March. The early-maturing varieties are grown during the beginning of the rainy season and the medium-maturing varieties follow.

In the Central Highlands rice is the main subsistence crop of the *montagnards*. It is cultivated usually by their traditional dry, shifting cultivation method, although some groups appear to have been using wet-rice cultivation methods for a number of generations. Yields are low, and no estimates are available on annual production. Within the last 10 years, however, paddy ricefields have been developed in valley bottoms in some parts of the Highlands to increase the food supply of the *montagnards* and to train them in the more productive agricultural techniques. Such paddy fields of more than 169,000 acres produced 69,000 metric tons of rice in 1964.

Other Field Crops

Varied climatic and soil conditions of South Vietnam permit wide diversification of agricultural production, but until recent years the development of secondary crops has been haphazard. Corn, beans, peanuts, and a wide variety of tropical fruits, including citrus, papaya and bananas, have long been grown by the farmers for their own use and as a limited source of additional cash income by those living near larger villages and towns. Many farmers grow sweet potatoes which are an important supplement to their diet and are sometimes also fed to livestock, particularly pigs. The crop is customarily grown without the use of fertilizer.

Of South Vietnam's other food crops, one of the most important is corn. It is a dry-season crop, customarily planted in the fall and harvested in the early winter in areas where two crops of rice are not grown. Corn is raised for human consumption and is seldom fed to livestock. In those areas of the Mekong Delta where soil conditions are favorable and irrigation is available, corn provides a supplementary income for the farmer.

Vegetables, which are of great importance in the Vietnamese diet, are grown commercially in the cool climate of the Central Highlands plateau around Da Lat. Temperate climate vegetables may be grown there successfully, and government-sponsored cooperative programs increased productivity and expanded the variety of vegetables. By 1960, in addition to supplying Saigon-Cho Lon and other local markets, South Vietnam was able to export 1.25 million tons of fresh vegetables to Singapore. Beginning with 1961, the use of the road from Da Lat to Saigon became increasingly dangerous, and deliveries of vegetables from the plateau became so circumscribed that the overseas market was lost.

Several new crops have been introduced in the South since 1955. Cocoa seedlings, which have been distributed to farmers in the Mekong Delta and the Central Highlands, appear to do well. Avocado from the Philippines was introduced in various places in 1958; the first crops, harvested in 1961, were well received on the local market.

With the exception of a small quantity of jute, fiber plants were not grown on a commercial scale before the war. As a result of extensive experimental work since 1956 and assistance from the United States foreign aid program, three fiber crops are now produced in South Vietnam—kenaf, ramie and abacá. These fibers, together with peanuts, constitute the most important cash crops of the land development centers of the Central Highlands. Abacá, closely related to the banana and commonly known as Manila hemp, has been widely distributed to remote mountain villages in the Central Highlands in the effort to develop a cash crop for the *montagnards*.

Plantation Agriculture

Plantation agriculture, involving large-scale production of a single commodity for sale and usually for export, included before the Indochina War such products as rubber, sugar, tea, coffee and coconuts. Most of the plantations were financed and managed by the French, employing Vietnamese labor. Some were owned by a few wealthy Vietnamese. In 1961 over 55,000 persons were working on plantations.

Rubber

Rubber (*Hevea brasiliensis*) was first introduced from Malaya in 1897, and the first trees were tapped in 1905. Cultivation of the crop was developed on large plantations owned mostly by French companies which, in 1964, still accounted for more than 85 percent of the country's total rubber output. Most of the rubber plantations were located on the red and grey semilateritic soils of the southern slopes of the Central Highlands. After the Indochina War the planted area showed a steady increase to 352,642 acres in 1963; since then, as a result of Viet Cong harassment, new planting has been falling off. In 1965 two of the largest plantations were closed down. Production had reached a peak of 77,870 metric tons in 1962, but decreased to 74,200 metric tons in 1964. As the Viet Cong have disrupted rice deliveries to Saigon, the export of rubber has become South Vietnam's main source of foreign exchange.

Other Plantation Crops

Sugar production during the colonial period reached a peak in 1937 of 20,000 tons, most of which was produced in the southernmost slopes of the Central Highlands northeast of Saigon and in some of the coastal deltas. During the Indochina War many of the canefields were diverted to other food crops. Some fields were abandoned altogether, and by 1954 sugar production had fallen to 4,000 metric tons. By 1964, however, production on about 83,000 acres had risen to over a million metric tons—sufficient to meet over half of the country's rising requirements.

Tea is indigenous to the area where it is grown in the uplands. In 1964 it was being cultivated on approximately 23,800 acres, mostly located in the Central Highlands where the climate and soil are ideal. The bulk of the 5,000-ton crop was processed as green tea which the Vietnamese prefer, and the rest as black tea for export.

In 1964, 27,466 acres, located mainly in the Central Highlands, produced 3,420 metric tons of coffee. In 1962 over 100,000 acres of coconut palms, grown in the western provinces of the Mekong Delta, produced 168,528,000 nuts from which sufficient oil was derived to meet local needs. Most of the plantations, however, are located in that part of the Mekong Delta which the Viet Cong control, and since 1962 both areas planted and production have decreased.

Animal Husbandry

The neglect of livestock breeding during the Indochina War, combined with the slaughter of buffalo for food, reduced the number of buffalo by as much as 50 percent. Imports from Thailand and livestock breeding stations have improved the quality of local breeds. In 1964 the total number of buffalo was reported to be 800,000 as compared to 222,000 in 1954. The slaughter of buffaloes under 10 years of age has been prohibited since 1955.

Cattle in Vietnam are of two kinds—the Chinese yellow type, which resembles the small Jersey cow, and the large, long-legged, gaunt Indian type. The bulls of both breeds have pronounced humps at the shoulder. They are used as work animals as well as for meat. The quality of the cattle has been improved by importation of selected stock for crossbreeding purposes. Any large-scale increase in cattle herds is rendered unlikely by the inaccessibility of rangeland and difficulty in maintaining adequate pasturage during the long dry season. There were reported to be 1.2 million head in the country in 1964.

The production of pigs has been greatly increased in quantity and quality since 1955. Local stocks have been improved by the introduction of American boars. In 1960 live animals and meat ranked third in value in the export market. Deteriorating security conditions in 1961 interrupted communications between Saigon and the rural areas, resulting in a decline in deliveries. In 1964 it was estimated that the number of pigs totaled 3.7 million.

Ducks are an important source of income for many farmers, particularly in the delta area where small flocks are raised from ducklings. They are also raised commercially in large, roving flocks which feed along the innumerable waterways and glean the ricefields after harvest. Ducks were estimated to total 12.6 million in 1964. Fresh and preserved eggs are produced for both local consumption and export, and surplus ducks from big flocks are sold in the city markets. The export of duck feathers and down is an important source of income. In 1964 there were an estimated 22 million chickens in the country.

Forestry

Woodcutting for construction purposes, firewood and the manufacture of charcoal is the principal forest industry in Vietnam. About 30 percent of the country is forested, and some 2.5 million acres are covered with timber of commercial value. Four-fifths of the commercial stands are classed as hardwoods; the rest are mangrove, pine, bamboo and related species.

With few exceptions, forest land in South Vietnam is in the public domain and classified as "forest reserve." Timber-cutting rights are granted to applicants through issuance of a forest license by the Directorate of Forestry in the Secretariat of Rural Affairs. Terms vary according to the type of timber sought and the extent of the proposed exploitation. Prescribed fees are payable to the Directorate. All products and byproducts from protected forests are subject to taxation.

No adequate inventory or survey of virgin forests has been made, but it is from these forests that large logs are cut and hauled to the sawmills. In secondary forests, the original growth has largely disappeared, and only the most aggressive species have reappeared. More than half of the forested areas are of this secondary type which has only a limited quantity of commercially valuable species and whose main yield was fuel wood.

Bamboo, found in all parts of the country, is one of the most useful products of the forest. Because of its availability and the case with which it can be worked, it has an enormous variety of uses. Various species suitable for particular purposes are cultivated, including several varieties whose young shoots are edible.

Rattan (*may*) is a climbing palm that grows only in the dense, moist rain forests of the Central Highlands. It has exceptional tensile strength and is used for making heavy cables. It is easily bent in sharp curves and is employed in the local manufacture of furniture.

The mangrove forests in South Vietnam cover an area in excess of 1 million acres and stretch along the coast from Mui Bai Bung northeastward to Vung Tau. There are two types of mangrove. One is the initial growth which comes up in brackish water influenced by the ocean tides; it is characterized by a stilted tripod-type of root system. As silting builds up and saline deposits are leached out, a climax-type of growth of larger species replaces the original stand.

Several species of mangrove have high commercial values. Three species supply wood for a charcoal which is considered superior to that produced from wood obtained in the dryland forests. Small timber is also cut from the climax-type of mangrove forest for fishnet poles, pilings for home construction and small lumber. Leaves of the nipa palm, which grows in the tidal areas, are used for thatching and woven partitions and walls, and pigs are frequently fattened on the fruit. From the bark of the wood cut for charcoal and firewood, about 9,000 tons of tannic extracts are produced annually. A brown pigment used by the rural people for dyeing clothes is also derived from bark. In 1961 some 69,000 persons were reported to be engaged as woodcutters, charcoal producers and laborers in the mangrove forests.

Fishing

Fishing is an important occupation along the entire coastline. Over a thousand edible species of deep-sea fish are known, of which around 50 are of commercial value. Inshore areas yield large catches of shrimp, lobster and shellfish. Rivers and canals also supply a considerable amount of both salt- and fresh-water fish, but by far the largest commercial catch is from the sea.

In 1964 there were about 246,000 fishermen and 56,470 fishing boats, of which 9,710 were motorized. Total catch was established at 397,000 metric tons. Although some fish are exported, most are sold fresh on the local markets. From 50,000 to 60,000 tons of fish are used each year in the preparation of *nuoc mam*, a pungent salty sauce that is an important element in the Vietnamese diet. With the introduction of freezing facilities, shrimp culture is being developed, and shipments have been made to France and the United States.

Hunting and Gathering

In the Central Highlands the *montagnards* supplement their food supply by hunting and gathering. Among the game taken for food are the deer, wild boar, monkey, wild ox and many smaller species, including wildfowl. Hunting is done by individual stalking and trapping. Traps include various types of snares, pitfalls and deadfalls. Hunters employ bows and arrows, and a few are equipped with firearms.

The *montagnard* women gather bamboo shoots, wild fruits, roots, edible leaves, mint and saffron. Cinnamon is found in the forests of Quang Ngai and Quang Nam Provinces, and, although there is some cultivation of the cassia tree from which the aromatic bark is derived, the highest quality is found in the wild state. It is used locally for medicinal purposes, but the bulk of the product collected is shipped to Hong Kong and the United States for use as a seasoning.

SPECIAL GOVERNMENT PROGRAMS

Substantial foreign aid has made it possible for the government to establish a number of special programs to benefit farmers. The most important of these are those creating farm-credit organizations, cooperatives and various facilities for improved agricultural education.

Agricultural Credit and Cooperatives

The National Agricultural Credit Office was officially created by presidential decree in April 1957. Its initial capital consisted of assets transferred from already existing agricultural credit agencies which, because of duplication of effort, scattered administration and lack of trained personnel, had been ineffective. It was capitalized at 850 million piasters, of which 330 million piasters were provided by the national budget and the remainder allocated from United States aid funds. By 1965 its capitalization had been increased to 895 million piasters. Its policy was to grant small loans to farmers without collateral and to extend credit to cooperatives (see ch. 25, Banking and Currency).

Agricultural cooperatives existed during the colonial period, but since they were primarily for the purpose of facilitating the export of agricultural products, they were of little benefit to the Vietnamese farmer. Regulations established in 1954 governing cooperatives imposed such complex procedures that no effective leadership or organization was developed. Various rice-milling, fishing, tobacco, charcoal and forestry cooperatives were in operation before this time, but these had little support and only a precarious financial standing be- cause of insufficient capital and bad debts.

In 1959 the Commissariat for Cooperation and Agricultural Credit was created by presidential decree to coordinate and provide general direction in the area of farm credit and cooperatives without undue interference in the internal affairs of local organizations. In June 1960 there were reported to be 266 cooperatives with a total member- ship of 96,810 and a paid-in capital of 27,660,807 piasters. There were 40 rice cooperatives, 80 farm cooperatives of other types, 3 forestry cooperatives, 2 livestock cooperatives, 76 fishery cooperatives, 57 handi- craft cooperatives, 6 consumer cooperatives and 2 others. The Com- missariat was abolished in 1965, and the Directorate of Cooperatives which succeeded it reported 333 local cooperatives with 130,154 mem- bers and 6 unions of cooperatives consisting of 154 local cooperatives and farmers' associations.

Farmers' Associations (Hiep Hoi Nong Dan) were also authorized by presidential decree in 1958 and were, in part, designed to supple- ment cooperative organizations. Established with the assistance of Chinese Nationalist technicians of the Joint Commission for Rural Reconstruction from Taiwan, the associations were organized on vil- lage, district, provincial and national levels. In 1965 membership was reported to be 284,130 persons.

Insufficient capital and a lack, at district and village levels, of trained administrative personnel able to explain the purpose and bene- fits of cooperative action and to direct specific programs has limited the expansion of the cooperative movement. Another obstacle has been the farmer's distrust of all forms of outside authority which, when not feared, has often been resented as interference in village affairs. Furthermore, the government policy of promoting and directing co- operatives from above, without adequate explanation of the program to the people, has worked against it.

The villagers have traditionally cooperated with one another in certain tasks beyond the capacity of the single family or of special importance to the community, such as the repair of dikes, the gather- ing of the harvest or the thatching of a roof. The principle is not readily carried over, however, into work in which there is no estab- lished sanction for joint effort, and much education and demonstration will be needed to develop general enthusiasm for the cooperative movement.

Agrovilles, Strategic Hamlets and New Life Hamlets

Within the framework of rural development, President Diem in- augurated a program for the creation of *agrovilles* in the Mekong Delta. These new villages, of which there were 21 in 1961, brought together the inhabitants of scattered and isolated hamlets strung along the banks of the canals and waterways. They were created for the dual purpose of bringing urban benefits to rural areas and providing security for the villagers. The program was controversial, and no *agro-villes* were constructed after 1961. Criticism included charges of abuse of voluntary labor used in constructing the centers, claims that favoritism influenced the assignment of dwellings, and complaints of failure to provide promised facilities and services. Aside from such complaints, the program inevitably involved the problem of popular adjustment to a radically new pattern of community life.

As the Viet Cong redoubled their subversive activities in the countryside, the need to give protection to the villagers became imperative, and the policy of constructing strategic hamlets was initiated by President Diem in April 1962. The strategic hamlets were fortified centers provided with one or more guard towers, barbed wire fences or moats, bamboo stakes and minefields. The inhabitants of each hamlet coped with ordinary security problems with their own forces.

The hamlet program was based on the concept of community development, with participation by local citizens in proportion to their means. The central authorities contributed to this collective effort through assistance in terms of funds, equipment and personnel to give technical advice and guidance. The Diem government planned to construct about 16,000 hamlets, and by November 1963 about 9,000 (in which 8 million peasants were living) had been built. The government of Major General Duong Van Minh (November 1963 to August 1964) had no policy regarding the strategic hamlets, and the residents in many instances destroyed the defenses. In 1964 the government of Major General Nguyen Khanh (August 1964 to September 1964) adopted the policy of reconstructing the defenses of the hamlets which were rechristened "new life hamlets."

Agricultural Education and Extension Services

A serious difficulty facing the government has been the shortage of trained personnel to carry out programs for improved agricultural techniques and crop diversification. There was no reservoir of specialists to draw upon, since the tradition in well-to-do families was to send their sons to study the humanities, law or engineering rather than agricultural science.

Recognizing the need for agronomists able to explain modern methods in simple terms to the farmer, the government established a National College of Agriculture at Bao Loc (Quang Duc Province, northeast of Saigon) in 1955. A 4-year institution with a faculty of 17 and an enrollment of over 350, it has benefited from extensive foreign aid. Applications each year have far exceeded the number that could be accepted. There are also two vocational agricultural schools which are geared to take students with elementary education and give them 2 years of agricultural training. The courses include animal husbandry, agronomy and forestry.

Agricultural extension services have been made available in all the provinces of South Vietnam, and local training centers have been established. Proper application of fertilizers and insecticides, better methods of cultivation and improved techniques of animal husbandry are parts of the extension service program, which operates in conjunction with the rural cooperatives and the farmers' associations. Rural youth groups, called 4–T clubs (similar to 4–H clubs in the United States), have been organized and claim a membership of over 100,000. Where conditions are relatively secure, the 4–T clubs appear to be popular and have made significant contributions to improved agricultural productivity, particularly in the field of animal husbandry. Ten pilot agricultural experimental stations have been functioning for several years, conducting test demonstrations for the benefit of the farmers.

CHAPTER 20

INDUSTRY

In 1965, after 10 years of development with government encouragement and heavy infusions of foreign aid, industry was still small in scale and consisted mainly of light manufacturing and processing of local agricultural and forest products. More than half the establishments made consumer goods for domestic consumption. Plants were heavily concentrated in the secure area of metropolitan Saigon-Cho Lon. Inevitably the spread of the conflict had begun to undermine industrial activity. The country's only coal mine had discontinued production late in 1964, and it had not been resumed. The implementation of many industrial projects was being postponed until the political situation was clarified, but, nonetheless, expansion continued although at a slower pace.

South Vietnam is relatively poor in industrial resources. There is a vast hydroelectric potential, which, however, would require large sums for development. Agricultural raw materials and some ores offer opportunities for the development of light industries, but the country continues to lack sufficient fuel and power. Only the one coal deposit has been identified, and no oil deposits are known to exist.

By 1965, notwithstanding the difficulties, some progress had been made in creating an industrial base. Certain light industries were in operation, and others were in the planning stage. To make loans to industry, the Industrial Development Center (IDC) had been established by the government with funds derived from United States aid, and the government had attracted other foreign capital. The whole effort, however, was taking place under wartime conditions and during a time in which the Republic had to expend much of its energy and resources in defending itself against the mounting campaign of guerrilla attack, subversion and terror. The prospects for industrial development have been viewed as depending as much on mastering the Communist threat as on solving the economic and technical problems of industrial progress.

BACKGROUND

The extent and character of industry in the past was limited by traditional preferences for other pursuits on the part of the Vietnamese themselves and by French colonial development policies. So ingrained has been Vietnamese orientation to agriculture as a means of livelihood and to scholarship as the goal of education, that only since World War II has serious attention been given to other economic opportunities and has any esteem been accorded to technical and specialized administrative skills. Those Vietnamese with money usually lacked business experience, and most of them preferred to invest their capital in urban real estate. Industrial development was almost entirely the concern of the French.

French policy was guided by two major principles: the exploitation of those natural resources which provided raw materials for France; and the reservation of the Vietnamese domestic market for French manufactured goods. This resulted in the establishment of a few mining operations and some small processing industries producing items which were uneconomic to import from France or peculiar to Vietnamese culture.

France viewed the area of Tonkin, Annam and Cochin China—now North and South Vietnam—as an economic unit, and, since the southern part of this area was considered best suited for agricultural production, most industrial development was concentrated in Tonkin. In exchange for rice, the North supplied the South with coal, paper, cement, textiles and glass. Saigon-Cho Lon did have certain processing industries—mechanized mills for the husking and polishing of rice, plants for distillation of rice alcohol, sugar refineries and factories for the preliminary processing of rubber. There were also a few establishments for the production of matches, soap and cigarettes. The first electric powerplant was built at the end of the nineteenth century, but most producers had their own generators.

After 1954 the Republic of Vietnam found itself cut off from its customary northern source of coal and other minerals and certain manufactures. Steps were taken by the government to develop a number of hitherto unexploited natural resources, such as the Nong Son coal deposits (about 30 miles southwest of Da Nang), water power in the Central Highlands (the Da Nhim Project) and the phosphate deposits of the Paracel Islands (in the South China Sea, 240 miles east of Hue) and Spratly Island (375 miles southeast of Saigon).

To reduce the dependence on imported articles, government policy also aimed at the gradual development of small industries, such as sugar refining and the manufacture of pottery, glassware, household articles and fiber sacks. The disturbed condition of the country and the urgent need initially to increase agricultural production kept the industrial development program almost at a standstill for several years. By the 1960's, however, industry still played a minor role in the economy in comparison with agriculture, but industrial activity contrasted markedly with the stagnation of previous years.

A Five-Year Plan for industrial development was announced in 1957, but was never formally adopted. However, a list of plants to be completed by 1965 was released. Scheduled for completion be-.tween 1961 and 1964 were two paper mills; a spinning and weaving mill; four sugar mills; two cement plants; a rice-bag plant; four bicycle-tire plants; a soda plant (for the manufacture of sodium carbonate, hydrochloric acid and calcium carbide); a plant for the manufacture of prefabricated houses; an oil refinery; a fertilizer plant; and several pharmaceutical plants. By mid-1962 some of these plants were in operation and others were under construction. A second Five-Year Plan, launched in 1962, could not be followed up as a result of deteriorating security.

NATURAL RESOURCES AND DEVELOPMENT

Since the country has never been completely surveyed, the Republic of Vietnam in 1954 found itself without a clear knowledge of what its scanty natural resources were. In 1959 an agreement was concluded with the United States Operations Mission (USOM) for a geological survey of southwest Vietnam, and in 1961 an operational plan for a mineral survey of central Vietnam was signed with the United Nations Special Fund. As a result of the resurgence of Viet Cong activity beginning in 1960, neither survey has been carried out (see ch. 23, Foreign Economic Relations).

Fuel and Power

The only exploitable coal field is at Nong Son. This deposit, with estimated reserves of 3.5 million metric tons, was worked by the Chinese under the terms of a concession granted by the court of Hue in 1878. Operations, halted before World War II by exhaustion of surface beds and lack of capital, were resumed by the South Vietnamese Government in 1957. Production reached 104,000 metric tons in 1963, but operations had to be suspended in 1964 as a result of repeated Viet Cong attacks. Viet Cong disruption of the transport system had also made it increasingly difficult to move the coal from the mine to customers.

The coal at Nong Son is a somewhat sulfurous anthracite which must be washed before it is marketed. The deposit varies in thickness from a few inches to 60 feet. Coal must be transported on the Song Thu Bon to a transshipment point at Ky Lam just south of Da Nang on the South Vietnam National Railway. The United States Agency for International Development (AID) has invested over $2 million in improvements and technical assistance in order to expand production.

Coal outcrops have also been found in the Mekong Delta. The only other fuel is peat, which is present in the southwestern part of the country.   The deposit has not been prospected, but, on the basis of surface measurements, it is thought to exceed several million metric tons. Peat, however, is not well suited to most industrial uses.

The most important sources of electric power, around Saigon in particular, are diesel and thermal installations which rely on imported fuels costing $3 million annually.   Water is potentially an important source of power, but the sole hydroelectric plant serves a single factory in the Central Highlands.

In 1962, South Vietnam had an installed electric power capacity of 107,000 kilowatts and an annual production rate of 359 million kilowatt-hours, up from 212 million in 1956.   Eighty percent of the installed capacity was located in metropolitan Saigon-Cho Lon and its vicinity.   Residential use accounted for about half the power consumed, industry for one-third and various public facilities for the remainder.   Electric service was supplied principally by five privately owned companies; the four largest were French corporations, the fifth Vietnamese.

Steps have been taken to increase power facilities.   In January 1961 the National Office for Reequipment of Installations for Production and Distribution of Electric Power received a loan of $12.7 million from the United States Development Loan Fund (DLF) for the construction of a 33,000-kilowatt thermoelectric plant at Thu Duc (near Saigon) and related transmission and distribution facilities. This thermal plant will provide electric power to the Saigon-Cho Lon area.   Under a reparations agreement the Japanese are building a hydroelectric powerplant at Don Duong on the Da Nhim River, southeast of Da Lat.   Together, these plants are expected to meet most of South Vietnam's electric power requirements for the near future.

The Da Nhim Project, which is expected to cost $50 million, is being built in two phases.   Involved in the project was the construction of an earthen dam 1,585 yards long across the Da Nhim River.   The waters of the river have been backed up to create a lake containing 209 million cubic yards of water and covering an area of 3.7 square miles. The water falls 2,500 feet, producing enough power to turn four generator turbines..   Two 42,000-kilowatt generators have been installed, and a transmission line to Thu Duc has been completed.   Work on the second phase has begun.   On completion of the second phase, power capacity will be 160,000 kilowatts, sufficient to provide a yearly output of 800 million kilowatt-hours.

South Vietnam also has a potential source of power in the Mekong River.   The United Nations, through its Economic Commission for Asia and the Far East, has explored the river and proposed a comprehensive development program known as the Mekong River Project (see Glossary), which contemplates plans for navigation, large-scale irrigation, and an installed electric power capacity of between 10 million and 15 million kilowatts. The Republic would share in these benefits.

Minerals

Mineral deposits do not promise to be of more than moderate economic value. Before partition, gold, lead and copper were mined at Bong Mieu, and prospecting for copper ore was carried out at Duc Bo, both south of Da Nang. The copper seam at Duc Bo has been reopened, but no regular prospecting has yet followed. During World War II, the Japanese obtained substantial tonnages of high-grade iron ore around Phong Dien (near Hue). Other indications of iron have been found in Quang Ngai and Quang Tri Provinces. During the war the Japanese also mined molybdenite on a small scale at Song Pha in Binh Thuan Province, but the economic value of the deposits has not yet been investigated.

The white sands along almost the full length of the coast, which are reported to contain more than 99 percent silica, are being used as the raw material for a glassmaking industry. A privately financed project at Vinh Cam Ranh is excavating glass sand for export to Japan. Considerable deposits of limestone 3 miles southwest of Hue supply the Long Tho cement plant, and other deposits near the Cambodian border provide limestone for the cement plant at Ha Tien. Clay deposits are numerous and are the basis for a small ceramics industry.

MANUFACTURING

Manufacturing is very limited, but since 1958 some progress has been made in establishing light industries which complement agriculture and cater to the domestic market. The most promising results have been obtained in plants for the processing of local agricultural or forestry products, such as wallboard, sugar, paper, bicycle tires, or other local products, such as mineral waters, glass and cement. Construction of an oil refinery has been planned for a number of years.

In 1965 manufacturing facilities were still characteristically small. There were factories producing cotton cloth from imported yarn, foundries, machine shops, pulp mills and papermills, pottery and glassware plants, match factories, cigarette manufacturing plants, printing plants, leather-tanning establishments and plants manufacturing sandals, soap, brick and tile. Oxygen, acetylene, carbon dioxide and some other industrial chemicals were also manufactured. Important food industries were those producing sugar, beer, ice, alcohol, soft drinks and fish sauce.

Industry was concentrated in the Saigon-Cho Lon metropolitan area. The comparatively few manufacturing establishments elsewhere included some small pulp mills and papermills and assorted plants making ceramics, fish sauce and some other consumer goods. Production of all important manufactured goods rose steadily after 1957, and the trend was continuing in 1965. The biggest rise was in the production of textiles.

The conversion of food and industrial crops into products ready for consumption, or into a semifinished state, led all other industrial activities in a number of units. In size, such enterprises ranged from the artisan family to the modern mill. Since virtually the entire country produced rice, husking and other processes connected with rice were common activities. Rice milling was the principal food products industry. The large surpluses over the needs of the growers were processed by large mills, located chiefly in the port area of Saigon-Cho Lon. Most of the big rice mills were owned by Chinese and French businessmen, who also controlled virtually all of the rice marketing network.

Some rice was converted into alcohol for local consumption, the chief producer being the French Distilling Company of Indochina (Société Française des Distilleries de l'Indochine). The company also produced rum. A few other smaller distilleries were financed by French, Chinese and Vietnamese capital.

The making of cane sugar ranked second in the food-processing industry. The production of sugar more than tripled between 1955 and 1963. Under the colonial regime the highest annual production was 20,000 metric tons. During World War II and the Indochina War many plantations were abandoned, and the production of sugar fell drastically. In 1955, the first year of the Republic, about 7,000 metric tons were produced. By 1963 output had risen to 43,000 metric tons. The import of sugar continued, however, totaling over 54,000 metric tons in 1963.

Of the total production in 1963, 32,000 metric tons of raw sugar came from some 400 small sugar mills in the provinces of Binh Duong, Tay Ninh, Gia Dinh, Bien Hoa, Long An, Vinh Long, Quang Ngai and Quang Nam. Only in Quang Ngai was there a mill capable of producing white sugar. White sugar production was otherwise confined to the large refinery in the southern part of the country at Hiep Hoa, northwest of Saigon. This refinery was formerly owned by French interests, but it has been renovated and newly incorporated as a joint enterprise of the South Vietnamese Government and French capital. The enterprise also owned the Khanh Hoi sugar refinery, which has an annual capacity of between 20,000 and 30,000 metric tons. Plans have been announced at various times for the construction of at least 4 additional sugar refineries, but by the end of 1965 none of the plans had matured to the point of breaking ground.

Textiles were the oldest, most important and fastest growing consumer goods industry in the country. Textile production climbed from 14.8 million yards of cotton cloth in 1956 to almost 200 million yards in 1965. In the same period the number of looms (power and hand) for all textiles increased from 5,000 to over 20,000, most of the new ones being electrically operated. Projected further expansion should, within a few years, bring the country close to self-sufficiency. Still in 1965 most of the raw cotton was being imported and there was a need to increase domestic cotton cultivation.

Major producers were the Vietnam Cotton Mills, founded in 1955, the Vietnam Textile Company (VINATEXCO), officially opened in October 1959, and the Vietnamese-American Textile Company (VIMYTEX), which began operations in 1959 and expanded in March 1961. All were expanding their operations with government loans and assistance from the United States. Vietnam Cotton Mills has constructed a branch factory in Da Nang which is the first cotton mill to operate outside of the Saigon area. The Vietnam Synthetic Fabrics, Inc., established in June 1960, operates the first synthetic fabrics factory in the country. It is equipped with German-made knitting machines and looms and a dyeing complex from Japan. Using imported raw materials, it produces over 2.5 million yards of synthetic fabrics (nylon, Dacron and Orlon) per year.

By the end of 1965 pottery production equal to domestic requirements was assured by three modern plants, and pottery imports had been prohibited, except for some luxury items. Production of rubber and plastics by 1962 was estimated at 5,000 metric tons and included a great variety of items. A tire factory, owned by French interests, has a daily capacity of 4,000 tires and tubes, mostly for bicycles and motorscooters, and another, formed in 1960, produces 500,000 tires and 100,000 tubes per year. Glassware, by 1962, was being produced at a rate of 25,000 metric tons a year. Pencils and light bulbs were also being manufactured. In addition, there were assembly plants for motorscooters, sewing machines, portable radios and automobile and flashlight batteries. Some 60 laboratories were producing drugs and pharmaceuticals. Four of the largest were either subsidiaries of foreign firms or were licensed to produce foreign products in South Vietnam.

The paper industry consists of two firms. One company, the Donai Paper and Chemical Products Company, began operating in 1962. Its capital was provided by the West Orient Trading and Financial Trust, an Italian-Swiss company, and by the Vietnamese Government. The plant, with an initial production capacity of 9,000 metric tons of writing and packing paper per year, was located to the north of Saigon. The intention was to use imported raw materials only in the beginning, turning later to local wood, bamboo and rice-straw fibers. The second paper-manufacturing enterprise, a joint American-Vietnamese venture, will eventually produce 9,000 tons of paper and 6,000 tons of pulp. It was expected that the combined output of both plants would be sufficient to meet domestic requirements.

The Bien Hoa Lumber and Sawmills Company, which had a monthly production capacity of 2,000 cubic yards of finished timber, was purchased by the Republic in 1958 from its former French owners. A wood-paneling plant built by this company went into production in 1960, and in 1962 its output was 3,000 metric tons of paneling. The Republic of Vietnam and West Germany have agreed to collaborate in setting up a plywood factory. Equipment for the factory and technical aid will be provided by West Germany.

A few other small industries were engaged in processing local raw materials. The Vietnam Jute Society in Saigon was producing rice bags from jute and kenaf. Its capacity of 3 million bags per year was to be increased to 6 million bags with equipment bought from Ireland. Another rice-bag factory with a capacity of 3 million bags a year and using equipment from Italy started production during 1960 at Bien Hoa near Saigon. The Saigon Feather Mill Company, which has a worldwide market, processed about 1,800 metric tons of feathers a year, using the most up-to-date machinery. A small company for bottling mineral water was located at Vinh Hoa, and a condensed-milk-canning plant, in Saigon.

There were numerous brick and tile kilns throughout the country. Most were traditional village installations which converted delta clay into bricks and tiles. A plant at Saigon produced soil pipe and artificial stone which was used in a wide variety of construction projects. By 1962 the government had taken the first steps toward creating a cement industry designed to displace imports. The Long Tho cement plant, 3 miles southwest of Hue and near good limestone deposits, was acquired in 1959 from the French firm which owned it before World World War II. New machinery gave it a capacity of 20,000 metric tons of lime cement a year. By 1961 it was supplying one-fourth of the needs of central Vietnam. Another cement factory, capable of producing 160,000 to 200,000 metric tons annually was built at Ha Tien by French firms and with French insurance credit. It came into operation in 1964 and is under government management. Together with the Long Tho plant, it will supply the whole of the country's demand.

HANDICRAFTS

Craftsmen working in tin, pewter, copper, bronze, silver, gold, lacquer, wood, marble, tile, ceramics, cotton, jute, silk, ivory, tortoise shell and leather produce a wide variety of essential articles and luxury goods. Coppersmiths produce bells, trays, boxes, vases, Buddhist statues, bowls and containers of various shapes and sizes. Potters pride themselves on the traditional and classical designs with which they decorate glazed pots and bowls. Bien Hoa is renowned for its pottery. Woodworkers include sculptors, engravers and artisans, who inlay mother-of-pearl in wood. Objects decorated with inlay include altars for pagodas, temples, churches and homes; tables; chairs; beds; chests of drawers; screens; and panels. The lacquer industry manufactures all kinds of useful articles, including tables, boxes, trays or purely decorative objects, such as the gilt-lettered maxims written in parallel script and hung against a black background on each side of ancestral altars.

Embroidery is an old and advanced art in the area. Embroidered silks are often given on ceremonial occasions, and designs vary with the purpose of the gift. Fine brocaded silks continue to be woven, and this craft receives special encouragement from the government. Baskets are of all shapes and sizes and are made in close and open weave. Mats, window shades, parasols, hats and fans are also made. The main material, bamboo, is put to an almost endless number of other uses as well.

STRUCTURE AND OWNERSHIP OF INDUSTRY

Before 1954 practically all Vietnamese industry was privately owned. The handicrafts were almost exclusively in the hands of Vietnamese individuals and families. Machine-equipped enterprises belonged to the French and to the few Chinese who had the financial resources, the experience and the interest in business to succeed in this field. What Vietnamese capital there was went, for the most part, into real estate.

Since 1954, important economic changes have taken place. The end of French control brought restrictions on the transfer of profits to France and other measures which made business enterprise less attractive to the French than it had been. As a result, private ownership shifted from the French to the Chinese and Vietnamese. In the rapid liquidation of French business interests, it was more often the Chinese than the Vietnamese who acquired the properties the French put up for sale. Subsequently the Chinese were forced to accept Vietnamese citizenship to retain their holdings.

Although the declared policy of South Vietnam was to reserve areas of the economy for private enterprise, the government has acted to influence the type and character of new industries, especially where foreign private investment has been involved. For industries which it considered basic to the welfare of the country, the government has insisted that it hold at least 51 percent of the stock. It also is sole owner of some manufacturing plants. Its role has been explained as necessary for the development of needed industries which private enterprise was unwilling or unable to start, and the authorities have pointed to the shortage of private capital and the general lack of managerial experience in the industrial field as factors making their course of action imperative.

ROLE OF GOVERNMENT

Various forms of assistance have been provided by the government to promote industrial development. An important step was the establishment in late 1957 of the Industrial Development Center. Its objectives were to provide credit and technical assistance for the expansion and modernization of existing industries and to facilitate the establishment of new industries. Between late 1957 and May 1961 the Center had made available to local industries some 480 million piasters (for value of the piaster, see Glossary). Of this amount, 351 million piasters represented loans; the remainder was in direct investments. No reports have been made subsequently relating to the disposition of funds. An investment bank, Société Financière pour le Développement de l'Industrie au Viet-Nam (SOFIDIV), was created in November 1961 to take over the investment banking functions of the Industrial Development Center. It had, however, not come into operation by the end of 1965.

Although the government has encouraged the formation of cooperatives, most craft industry is organized on a family basis. A Handicraft Development Center, established in 1958, provided organizational and technical assistance and also extended long-term loans to craft enterprises. A Handicraft Sales Store located in Saigon was inaugurated in August 1959. Technical services for the project have been provided through contracts with American consulting firms. The program has expanded the domestic market for handicraft products and helped to create a foreign market which shows promise of becoming increasingly important. To supplement the inadequate private sources of industrial financing, the government-owned Commercial Credit Bank of Vietnam, which operates principally as a commercial bank, was authorized in 1958 to engage in investment banking (see ch. 25, Money and Banking).

A further stimulus to industrial growth was the government's foreign investment policy, which gave foreign investors assurance against war risk, expropriation or possible nationalization. Incentives were also offered in the form of exemption from taxes and guarantees concerning repatriation of industrial and commercial profits.

CHAPTER 21

LABOR

In 1966 only about 10 percent of the working population earned wages and salaries; the rest were self-employed agriculturists, craftsmen and petty vendors. In the small wage- and salary-earning sector most workers were employed in light industry and in commerce, although, after 1964, there was a slight increase in the number of persons employed in construction work on military installations.

The size and character of the labor force has not been altered significantly by the modest industrial progress which has been made since independence, and under wartime conditions, it seems unlikely that the industrial labor force will increase in size in the immediate future. Moreover, in 1966 there were not enough skilled workers to meet fully the military requirements of the country or the requirements of the industrial sector. The government, assisted by the United States Agency for International Development (AID), was exerting considerable efforts to increase the pool of skilled labor through technical and vocational education. Among the unskilled labor force, on the other hand, there was some unemployment and considerable underemployment.

Because of wartime conditions many local factories are prevented from working to capacity, and some have been forced to close down completely. Furthermore, wartime emergencies have aggravated the general instability of the labor force. As a result of military operations, thousands of workers have become refugees. In an effort to meet the adverse circumstances, rules relating to hours of work have been suspended, and strikes have been banned.

The slow development of industry and the prevalence of family-type craft enterprises tended to limit the potential scope of labor organization. Estimates reported by the press in 1966 of the claimed number of unionized workers in the wage- and salary-earning sector (not including civil service workers) ranged between 150,000 and 400,000. Of these, only some 70,000 were paying dues. More than 90 percent of labor union members were in the Vietnamese Confederation of Labor (Confédération Viêtnamienne du Travail—CVT), oldest of the three legally recognized labor union federations.

Because of the official trend to discourage the participation of organized labor in politics and because of the precarious economic situation of the large majority of unionized workers, labor unions had not attained great strength. They concentrated on welfare, health and educational programs and on aid in the resettlement of refugee workers rather than on involvement in politics. The political aloofness of labor unions, however, curtailed their effectiveness when bargaining for wage raises and social benefits.

During the 1960's labor unions were relatively successful in organizing significant numbers of industrial workers as well as agrarian wage earners and persons in service occupations. As against organizational gains, most unionized workers, steeped in family-oriented traditions, did not understand the aims of organized labor and advantages of union membership. Because wages in most labor categories were low compared to the steadily soaring cost of living, many workers had no funds available for union membership dues. Hence, in numerous instances, union management granted membership to workers who merely asserted that they were willing to accept union leadership and participate in union activities.

The government of Prime Minister Nguyen Cao Ky has been concerned about the possible role of labor in politics and its vulnerability to Viet Cong (see Glossary) infiltration. The government's cautious attitude toward organized labor has tended to prevail, although the leaders of major unions have reiterated their anti-Communist attitudes and have, in general, kept aloof from the political scene. Many unions, however, protested the Ky government's requirement for a police permit to hold union meetings and, since June 1965, the proscription of strikes. Although the law has not been repealed, the government has been lax in enforcing it.

A relatively new development since 1962 was the Buddhist interest in the labor movement. Buddhist labor groups have been organized in some areas designed to promote the welfare of workers and encourage the study of Buddhism among them.

Although the government has not favored their organizational and strike activities, it has helped unions to improve the training of labor representatives, taken steps to develop the machinery of arbitration and conciliation and supported union-sponsored welfare and educational programs. These programs also were the recipients of support and financial aid from the United States.

The relationship between employers and workers traditionally was paternalistic. Since most small enterprises of all kinds were family undertakings and usually completely staffed by relatives, paternalism was rooted in social conditions as well as in the ethical principles of Confucianism. The merchant and master artisan commonly housed and fed their employees and were generally responsible for employees' welfare. In return, employees owed the employer obedience and personal loyalty. Although the system has declined in the modern period with the growth of large-scale enterprises, wage labor and the introduction of Western concepts of individualism, paternalism still characterized many employer-employee relationships in 1966.

CHARACTERISTICS OF THE LABOR FORCE

The hostilities prevailing after 1946 forced thousands of rural workers to flee to the cities. Most of them entered service occupations or became petty vendors and cabdrivers. Some joined the industrial work force; others were unable to find work of any kind.

The number of rural migrants to the cities reached an alltime high after the intensification of military activities in 1964. Although unemployment statistics are lacking, officials in Saigon and in the coastal cities expressed concern over the growing number of jobless refugees. Skilled only in farming and in the traditional crafts, most of them could not find industrial employment. At the same time, however, the presence of United States military and civilian personnel increased the demand for cabdrivers, servants, petty entrepreneurs and entertainers and improved employment opportunities for unskilled workers from the countryside.

While unemployment posed problems in Saigon and in other cities, many rural areas were beset by labor shortages. Because of military conscription and the cityward migration, common laborers were increasingly difficult to find in some rural areas, particularly those near military installations or locations undergoing extensive reconstruction.

Among the urban labor force there is considerable mobility, even under relatively peaceful conditions. Many industrial workers live in the country and take on factory jobs only during the agricultural slack season. Others hope to accumulate a small sum of cash as petty vendors or servants and return to the ancestral homes as soon as possible (see ch. 7, Family; ch. 11, Religion).

Women represent an unknown but large proportion of the labor force. Vietnamese and *montagnard* women often perform the major portion of farm chores. In many rural areas, where selling and bargaining are regarded as unworthy of a man, artisan products are taken to market and sold by women. Women of all ages predominate among urban petty vendors. In the textile, food-processing and plastic products industries the majority of workers are women. Most women in the textile plants are under 20 years of age. The nascent communications equipment industry has employed a growing number of women and trained them in skills formerly reserved for men. Many of the large business enterprises, including export-import and real estate firms, are headed and managed by women; the wives of middle- and upper-level civil servants often pursue business activities in their spare time.

Traditional crafts, such as pottery, shoemaking, bronze working and silk weaving, are widely practiced in the countryside. Self-employed artisans concentrate in villages which are known for their specialized products.

In the small wage- and salary-earning sector, however, there is a severe shortage of skilled workers. Military conscription has further reduced their critically low numbers in the industrial sector. Factory owners have deplored the difficulty of continuing operations without skilled workers and complained about the loss of time involved in training women as replacements for jobs requiring skills. In the case of major construction projects the need has been partially met by the importation of skilled workers from Korea and the Philippines.

Government efforts to expand and improve vocational training facilities receive substantial support from AID, including financial contributions for the building of vocational training institutions, technical equipment and the assignment of teachers to vocational training schools. In 1966 some 21 institutions for the training of skilled workers and technicians operated in various parts of the country.

The largest and best equipped school was the National Technical Center at Phu Tho near Saigon which offers training in a wide variety of technical subjects and also trains instructors in these subjects. Tailoring, mechanics and carpentry are taught at training centers in Hue and Hoi An (15 miles south of Da Nang). Other vocational schools are located in Da Nang, Qui Nhon and Vinh Long. A new Training Center in Gia Dinh (5 miles north of Saigon) was opened in 1966. The army offers technical training courses to about 40 percent of its recruits. Officers receive training in transportation, communications and engineering. Many foreign contractors, including those from the United States, offer on-the-job training courses (see ch. 27, The Armed Forces).

There is a critical need for managerial and administrative workers and intermediate-level technicians. The National Institute of Administration in Saigon is the principal institution to train such personnel for the Civil Service. In 1964 the Institute planned to establish 21 provincial training centers (see ch. 9, Education).

Productivity in the industrial sector is low. Many workers are handicapped by chronic illness, malnutrition and inferior living conditions. Industrial workers are only one generation removed from the agricultural work pattern where periods of intensified physical effort (at planting and harvesting time) are followed by idleness. When employed in industrial plants, workers will often stay on the job for several months and then leave without apparent cause.

LABOR AND GOVERNMENT

The first Labor Code, based largely on French labor legislation, was issued under Emperor Bao Dai in 1952. This document, amended by subsequent ordinances, covers various aspects of employment for wage- and salary-earning workers. The most recent version of the Labor Code, which includes ordinances passed up to and including 1963, was published by the Ministry of Labor in 1965. In practice, the Code is supplemented by other legal sources. For example, certain provisions of the Agricultural Code of 1953 and those of the Collective Agreement Governing the Rubber Plantation Industry are frequently invoked to establish criteria for enforcement and to settle labor disputes.

Labor laws are administered by the Department of Labor under the Ministry of Economy and Finance. Headed by the secretary of state for labor (Nguyen Xuan Phong in 1966), the Department maintains an Inspectorate and operates the Vocational Training Office and the Employment Service with regional branch offices. The National Labor Advisory Committee acts in an advisory capacity to the government in matters concerning labor and labor relations. Members of the Committee include the inspector general of labor and representatives of several ministries and of employers and workers. The Manpower Directorate, established in 1964 to deal with manpower needs and problems, also includes representatives from other ministries. In 1966, however, most matters concerning manpower were handled by army authorities.

In 1965, 24 Labor Service Offices (also called Inspectorates) operated under the inspector general of labor. Most were situated in the provinces around Saigon. Each Labor Service Office is subdivided into branches dealing with workers' and employers' claims under the Labor Code, and each operates a placement service and an office of labor hygiene. The Labor Service Offices also help to organize local worker representation and employer organizations. In the absence of regional municipal inspectorates, matters concerning manpower and labor legislation are handled by the province chiefs.

Labor law enforcement is severely hampered by the lack of an adequate number of competent labor inspectors. In 1963 only 460 persons were charged with enforcing the Labor Code throughout the country. Training courses for 100 newly recruited labor inspectors were organized by the Department of Labor in March 1965. At the same time, inservice training was offered to some of those in the field. Both types of training were organized and supervised by the International Labor Organization (ILO). In 1965 the Department was granted 11 scholarships from the ILO to set up courses in labor administration and industrial relations.

The Department of Labor has also initiated a training program for shop stewards from enterprises employing more than 25 persons. Trainees received instruction in labor laws, workers' responsibilities and rights, industrial security and labor relations. In addition, the trainees were offered orientation in governmental labor policies and anti-Communist ideology. In 1966 graduates from the course totaled 316, of whom 234 were from Saigon, 62 from Gia Dinh and 20 from the western provinces.

Lack of adequate personnel hindered efficient operation of the government employment service and its local offices. Generally, only a fraction of the requests for placing unemployed workers were filled by these officers. Most of the workers placed possessed some skills and lived in the Saigon area.

Labor inspections in factories and on plantations were not frequent and rarely extended into enterprises outside the provinces near Saigon. Most inspections involved health facilities on rubber plantations. Some medical inspectations also took place in commercial and industrial enterprises of the capital, but only a few were checked for compliance with industrial safety standards. The number of inspections apparently rose in 1966. Labor Secretary Nguyen Xuan Phong in February 1966 reported that some 2,126 factory inspections had been made since the formation of the War Cabinet in June 1965.

While the enforcement of the Labor Code lagged, the government intensified its efforts to improve the general welfare of workers. A total of 20 million piasters (for value of the piaster, see Glossary) have been earmarked by the Department of Labor for workers' housing projects throughout the country. Part of these funds represents profits from the National Lottery (see ch. 8, Living Conditions). Railroad workers, dockers and fishermen will be the principal beneficiaries of the new low-cost housing. Some of the dwellings will be purchasable on a 10- to 20-year installment plan. In 1964, 400 dwelling units were made available for workers in Quang Nam (around Da Nang) and Gia Dinh Provinces. In September of the same year, 76 families moved into a workers' housing project in Hue. More than 150 low-cost housing units were allotted to low-income worker families in the town of Tan Quy Dong (southeast of Saigon) early in 1966.

Day-nurseries and low-cost cafeterias in urban slum areas and recreational and vacation centers in Da Nang, Cho Lon and Vung Tau were planned within the framework of government projects designed to improve workers' welfare. Government assistance was also extended to petty entrepreneurs in the form of favorable credit arrangements. Some 300 taxi and motorscooter drivers became owners of vehicles sold to them on credit.

WORKING CONDITIONS

Hiring and Dismissal

Provisions of the Labor Code require employers to list job openings with the nearest government employment office. Because of lack of personnel, however, the operations of these offices are confined to certain areas, and the scope of their activities is limited. In 1962 government employment offices placed some 4,000 job applicants, but data regarding their more recent activities is lacking. In practice, most employers hire friends or relatives of persons already working for them. Presentation by the applicant of his official identification card, issued by the government, and of written proof of a job previously held are considered sufficient for most employers. Agricultural employees, notably those working on rubber plantations, are hired on the basis of contracts running from 1 to 3 years.

Minors under 14 years of age may not be hired. There are also special laws providing that women and children under 18 may be examined by a medical officer to ensure that the work assigned them does not involve excessive physical demands. The law also prohibits boys under 16 years and women of any age from working below the ground.

The hiring of labor through a professional recruiter-supervisor (*cai*) has been customary for several centuries and was still practiced in 1966. The *cai* recruits the workers, supervises their work and pays their wages. The *cai* himself is hired and paid by the employer and, in addition, retains a share of the workers' wages. During periods of unemployment the *cai* sometimes feeds and houses the workers recruited by him.

Employers have generally appreciated the *cai's* services, since he has relieved them of many managerial chores in connection with the labor force. The *cai*, on the other hand, often demands an excessive share of the workers' wages and prevents them from voicing grievances. Because of lack of funds, workers from rural areas are often unable to return home and are forced to continue on jobs paying token wages and working under harsh conditions. The abuses of the *cai* system were especially serious among the dockworkers. A decree passed in August 1965 prescribed the conditions under which dockworkers may be hired and paid. It called for the establishment of the Dockers' Management Board, which represents labor, management and the government; determines the number of dockers authorized for each port; maintains a register of dockworkers and their employers in each port; and controls payment methods.

Applicants for civil service jobs are hired after passing competitive examinations. Educational prerequisites for perspective civil servants depend on the position applied for. The *baccalauréat* is required for high-level positions; completion of secondary school without a degree, for intermediate jobs; and completion of elementary school, for lower grade positions.

In the event of dismissal or resignation, notices must be given by employers and employees alike. The period of notice varies, depending on locality, on the trade or on the provisions of a collective agreement. Acts of theft, embezzlement, sabotage and the divulgence of industrial secrets constitute reasons for immediate dismissal. Workers who initiate or participate in "political demonstrations, propaganda or activity" at the place of employment are subject to dismissal without notice. Workers, employees and apprentices who have been drafted into the armed forces have reemployment rights upon completion of their military service.

After working for an enterprise or an employer for at least 2 years, workers are entitled to severance pay. The amount of such pay varies according to the period of employment or the type of industry or collective agreement covering the workers. In the wage-earning agricultural sector severance pay consists of 5 percent of the worker's earnings held back as a "forced saving" and matched by the employer by another 5 percent when the worker leaves.

Hours of Work and Wages

The Labor Code provides for an 8-hour workday and a 48-hour workweek. Under wartime conditions, however, rules applying to hours of work may be suspended, and in some cases this has been done. The weekly day of rest is rotated among employees in enterprises which handle spoilable materials and those in transportation, public works and hospitals. After 1 year of service employees are eligible for at least 15 days of annual leave. The 4-day celebration of the lunar New Year (Tet); National Day, on November 1; May Day; and the tenth day of the third lunar month are paid holidays.

There are no legal provisions for paid overtime work for employees in industry, mining and commerce. The rate of compensation for work done outside of working hours is usually established by collective or individual agreements between workers and employers. Agricultural workers receive time-and-a-half pay for work done after hours on weekdays and double pay for work performed on Sundays, in accordance with the provisions of the Agricultural Code.

The Labor Code provides for guaranteed minimum wages but sets different rates according to administrative regions, depending on economic and climatic conditions in the respective regions.

Decree No. 19 of February 1, 1964, represented the first revision of minimum daily wages on a nationwide basis since 1956. The provisions of the new decree, however, applied only to workers in industry, mining and commerce. An earlier decree (1963) provided for a small wage increase, applicable in the Saigon-Cho Lon area only.

The amounts of the 1964 wage increase were largest in the southern part of the country, notably in Binh Long, Kien Phong, Kinh Tuong, An Xuyen, Gia Dinh and Con Son Provinces (from 34.85 to 45 piasters). In Tay Ninh and Long An the difference between the old and the new wage rates was only a little over 3 piasters (from 38.95 to 42). In Central Vietnam the size of the wage increase ranged from 4 piasters (42 to 46) in Binh Thuan Province in the extreme southeastern part of the Central Highlands to 1 piaster (47 to 48) in Quang Tri Province, just south of the Demarcation Line. In the Highlands, notably in the provinces of Kontum and Pleiku and in the city of Da Lat, wages rose from 45 to 50 piasters. In Lam Dong Province the differential was only 2.40 piasters (from 44.60 to 47 piasters).

The Decree also provided that women and children doing equal work were to be paid the minimum for adult males and that supplementary benefits, such as family allowances, could not be included in computing minimum wages.

Earlier in 1964 a pay raise amounting to one-half of the take-home pay was ordered for civil servants. Family and cost-of-living allowances for lower level civil service workers were raised to the level applicable to top-grade civil service personnel. Earlier decrees sought to equalize salaries and benefits between higher and lower echelon civil service personnel. Governmental orders in July and December 1965 provided for a reduction in salary for government workers who earned in excess of 15,000 piasters per month. According to the decree passed in July 1965, high-level civil service officers were no longer entitled to special allowances for servants, water and electricity.

In practice, the minimum wage raise and the increase in civil service salaries were little more than official gestures and accomplished little to equalize the income with the rising cost of living. In the oil and textile industries and in banking, wages have been above the legal minimum since 1962. Higher-than-minimum rates prevailed in other occupational categories, as well as in the district towns and cities. At the end of 1964 many industrial enterprises granted a 5 to 20 percent cost-of-living allowance to their employees. On the other hand, employment at below minimum wages is widespread, especially among unskilled and occasional workers, because of the lack of personnel to enforce minimum wage legislation. Nevertheless, since 1966 the bargaining position of such workers has improved because of the increased employment opportunities near United States military bases and other installations. In Thua Thien Province (around Hue in the north), for example, common laborers were paid 100 piasters per day by American employers and 60 to 70 piasters per day by Vietnamese employers.

The upward trend in wages has barely kept pace with the cost of living, which rose by 56 percent between July 1965 and January 1966. Workers are frequently forced to resort to borrowing. Since most loans are available on short-term basis at usurious rates, borrowers are often compelled to take on another job at night to make ends meet.

Benefits

Employment-connected benefits are limited to the payment of family allowances and maternity subsidies. The laws operate in some parts of the country only and are not fully enforced. Maternity benefits call for up to 8 weeks' leave at half pay before and after confinement. Married workers with one or more children under 16 years of age are eligible for an allowance representing 6 percent of the base wage of their wage category for each of the first five children and 3 percent for the sixth and each additional child. For a dependent wife, 15 percent of the base wage is payable. Only a few enterprises comply with the law concerning the payment of family allowances. Employers who do pay the allowances tend to choose workers with small families, since the rates increase with the number of children.

The liability of employers for work-connected injuries and illnesses is established by law. Employers are required to pay for medical treatment, hospitalization, medications and appliances for workers who are injured or become ill on the job. Workers are also entitled to 50 percent of their earnings during temporary disability and to a lump sum of 1 year's earnings if they are totally disabled. In practice, these laws are only sporadically enforced, and workers often have to resort to court action to obtain indemnification if they are injured or become ill on the job.

Supplementing earlier legislation, a new decree was passed in October 1965. It sets forth provisions for the prevention and treatment of industrial accidents and occupational diseases and for the compensation of workers for loss of time due to such accidents and diseases.

There are no legal provisions for retirement pension plans for workers and employees except for those in the civil service. Under the terms of a collective agreement applicable to workers on rubber plantations, workers may opt for a lifetime annuity instead of a lump-sum severance pay upon retirement.

The absence of social security legislation is not generally regarded as a major shortcoming. Traditionally, the extended family group is expected to provide for the welfare of the aged and the infirm. Moreover, because of the short life expectancy (35 years), the number of potential beneficiaries of retirement plans would be low.

In practice, working conditions vary widely by industry and geographic area. Large modern enterprises, as well as the major rubber, tea and coffee plantations, however, offer working conditions well above the legal minima. Only few enterprises comply with the laws providing for family allowances, but sick leave is granted by most employers, although there are no legal requirements for it.

Working conditions are generally favorable for the approximately 80,000 textile workers. The Sukymen wool blanket factory near Saigon has dormitories, playgrounds, weekly movies, a medical office and cooperative stores. Other textile plants in the metropolitan area—including Visyfasa, with 600 workers; Vimytex, with over 2,000 workers; and the Dacotex factory—offer free meals, transportation and uniforms to workers. Medical care, recreational facilities and free meals are available to the workers of the Dainamco rubber-processing plant in Gia Dinh Province and to most of the 2,000 workers employed in the plastic products industry. Workers on the large rubber, tea and coffee plantations receive free housing or housing allowances and protective clothing and may purchase essential items at commissaries.

In spite of retirement pensions, cost-of-living supplements and family allowances, working conditions for civil service employees are regarded as below average. Most work in offices inadequately furnished and ventilated, at salaries which are low compared to those outside the government service. The pay raise granted them in 1964 was insufficient to cover the costs of the growing number of essential items which are available only on the black market. To help government workers obtain these items at prices they can afford to pay, the government has planned to establish supply centers for them similar to the post exchanges and commissaries available to American personnel.

For most industrial workers improvement of working conditions above the legal minima is not the main concern. Wages are considered far more important, and workers readily leave a comfortable and clean place of work for another employer who offers a few piasters more under less favorable working conditions.

FORCED LABOR

The practice of requiring people to contribute a certain number of days of work to communal projects each year has been carried on in Vietnam for centuries. Under the emperors who ruled before the coming of the French, masses of people were forcibly employed on various kinds of economic development projects, particularly water-control works. Temporary forced labor of this sort was required of all able-bodied males, but well-to-do persons avoided it by forfeiting a lump sum in cash.

French colonial authorities continued the practice of compulsory labor for public purposes with the corvée, a tax paid in a specified number of days of work on such programs as dike repair, construction of irrigation ditches and roadbuilding. During both world wars corvée units provided important support to the French army in France by building trenches and fortifying positions behind the frontlines. Some were employed in munitions factories.

A government decree in December 1964 ended the drafting of rural inhabitants to work without pay on community projects. The decree provided that persons must receive compensation for such work and that recruiting may take place only in cases of emergency for public or military needs.

THE LABOR MOVEMENT

Background

Article 23 of the Constitution adopted in 1956 provided that the "right to free trade unions and the right to strike are recognized and shall be exercised in conformity with the procedures and conditions prescribed by law." The same Article, however, withholds the right to strike from public officials or workers in activities "related to national defense, public security or the needs indispensable to the life of the community."

Although in the Constitution of 1956, Prime Minister Ngo Dinh Diem (1954–63) reiterated the provisions of the French-formulated Labor Code of 1952 concerning the freedom of labor organization, his regime was more concerned with controlling and regulating the labor unions than with promoting them. This attitude—reinforced by the fear that labor unions and workers were particularly vulnerable to Communist infiltration and subversion—persisted under the government of Prime Minister Major General Nguyen Khanh (January to October 1964). He, nevertheless, promulgated a decree in October 1964 which replaced the provisions of the early Constitution relating to labor and which contained much more specific and extensive provisions concerning the conditions under which unions may be organized and officially recognized.

According to one of the key provisions of the new law, a labor union could consider itself to be officially recognized if within 3 months of its application the government failed to respond to its application for recognition. If refused recognition, labor unions had the right to appeal the government's ruling. The law also provided that labor unions which failed to hold elections of officers would be dissolved. Labor representatives to the government or to international commissions were to be appointed from the ranks of the "most representative trade union organizations." As defined by the decree, the "most representative unions" were those which have the most members, collected dues regularly and conducted "important activities."

The law also forbade labor unions to conduct or to join political or religious activities and defined illegal strikes. The attitude of the Khanh government to the role of labor in general was reflected in a speech Prime Minister Khanh made to labor union leaders in which he declared that, while his government favored the trend of democratization in management, it expected labor to contribute "ideas and initiatives" rather than to share in the task of running the enterprises.

The Provisional Constitution promulgated by the government of Prime Minister Nguyen Cao Ky on June 19, 1965, contained no explicit provisions regarding the activities of organized labor although such activities were recognized by implication. However, an emergency decree proclaiming the state of war, issued by the Ky government a few days later (June 24, 1965), prohibited all strikes because of wartime conditions. Because of vigorous protests by organized labor, however, this measure was not fully enforced.

Official apprehension regarding possible disturbances perpetuated by unionized workers was heightened by the intensified propaganda efforts of the Viet Cong directed at the labor movement. Throughout 1965 broadcasts and leaflets by the Communist self-styled South Vietnam Liberation Federation of Trade Unions, the labor-arm of the so-called National Liberation Front, encouraged South Vietnamese workers to protest openly against the American presence and against the bombing raids. In October of the same year the Viet Cong issued a call for a general strike to observe the anniversary of the execution of a Viet Cong terrorist. Workers' response to this strike call, however, was negligible.

Labor Unions

The traditional labor organization was the *phuong*, a type of guild for the various crafts and trades. Each *phuong* had its own leader and its guarded spirit in whose honor annual rites were held. *Phuongs* also maintained apprenticeship systems, set standards and prices and marketed the products of artisans.

The *phuongs* are unrelated to the modern labor union movement in Vietnam which began in 1947 with the establishment of the Society for the Protection of the Rights of Workers, a local of the French Confederation of Christian Workers (Confédération Française des Travailleurs Chrétiens—CFTC). The Society professed adherence to Christian social ideals, strongly opposed French colonial rule and denounced communism. In 1952 the Society became the Vietnamese Confederation of Christian Labor (Confédération Viêtnamienne du Travail Chrétien—CVTC). Its organizational activities were directed mainly at workers in industry, agriculture, commerce and the liberal professions.

In 1966 there were 402 legally recognized labor unions organized by craft as well as by geographic area. There were three labor federations, each headed by a small group of men who had founded the federation and continued to manage it. High union officials were elected by indirect vote. Union representatives at the plant level, who presented grievances to the management and maintained liaison with union headquarters, were directly elected, but they themselves had no vote in the higher bodies.

The largest and most important labor union federation in 1966 was the Vietnamese Confederation of Labor (Confédération Viêtnamienne du Travail—CVT), known until 1964 as the CVTC. It had an estimated membership of 300,000, of whom an unknown but large proportion of the members were Buddhists. Reportedly about 20 percent of the CVT members were able to pay the dues of 10 piasters a month. Four labor union confederations and 380 individual unions were affiliated with the CVT. The Confederation was an affiliate of the International Federation of Christian Trade Unions (IFCTU) and of its Far Eastern branch, the Brotherhood of Asian Trade Unions.

The CVT's strongest affiliates were the Farm Workers Federation, with over 100,000 members; the Plantation Workers Federation, with about 25,000 members; the Federation of Railway Workers, with an estimated 3,000 members; and the Transport Workers Federation, with an estimated membership of 1,000. The Confederation of Weavers, a more recent (1964) CVT affiliate, had some 5,000 members, mostly in the Saigon-Cho Lon area. One of the largest dockworkers' unions, the 3,000-member Union of Saigon Harbor Workers, was another new CVT affiliate. The CVT also had strength among textile and hotel employees and among workers in the service trades.

President of the CVT since 1952 and reelected in 1964 was Tran Quoc Buu, who, in spite of criticism by some of the Confederation's affiliates, commanded the firm allegiance of its officials and its membership at large. After 1964 the CVT intensified its organizational efforts among rural workers where it had lost some strength during the early 1960's because of President Ngo Dinh Diem's programs designed to bring about rural reform.

The CVT has been noted for building up its social and educational services. In 1964 it operated 14 social welfare centers, 2 of which were organized in Saigon early that year. The centers were located in workers' districts and offered health education, elementary school courses and recreational activities. Because of intensified counter-insurgency efforts, only 13 such centers were reported in March 1965.

About 250 families of refugee workers benefited by CVT's resettlement projects for refugee workers in Phuoc Long Province, some 80 miles northeast of Saigon. This settlement, however, was disrupted in the winter of 1965 by Viet Cong attacks.

The CVT-affiliated railway and rubber plantation workers' unions were among the chief targets of Viet Cong terrorists. Many railway workers were killed or wounded in the course of duty, and plantation workers were often forced to leave their places of work because of Viet Cong harassment and coercion.

In 1964 and 1965 the CVT consistently sought government assistance to remedy problems which confronted its affiliates and workers in general. A resolution passed at the CVT National Convention in March 1964 asked the government to amend the Labor Code with a provision that dismissal for cause must be examined and agreed upon by labor unions and by representatives of the Department of Labor's local officials. The delegates also pleaded for the extension of the provisions of the Rubber Plantation Workers Collective Agreement to employees of other, smaller plantations. On behalf of the National Federation of Fishermen, the CVT asked for government assistance to establish fishing cooperatives for the purchase of equipment. Fishermen have long been faced with the hardship of having to pay exorbitant rent for equipment and having to sell their catch at lower than standard prices to persons from whom the equipment was rented.

A meeting of 25 CVT affiliated unions (including the textile, machine, plastic products and restaurant workers' unions) in October 1965 petitioned the government to stabilize community prices in order to narrow the gap between wages and the cost of living. The petition called for a 30 percent wage increase and for abolishment of discrimination against union members and their arbitrary dismissal. It also demanded the reestablishment of the right to strike.

The Confederation of Workers' Trade Unions of Vietnam (Confédération des Syndicats des Travailleurs Viêtnamiens—CSTV) was founded in 1952. In 1960 it had an estimated 60,000 members; half of these, however, withdrew to form an independent federation. When they failed to obtain government recognition, they affiliated with the CVT as a "special section."

In 1966 the CSTV claimed a membership of 30,000, but the actual number of members was probably much lower. Most lived in the Saigon-Cho Lon area where a number of CSTV unions had a large Chinese membership. Other members were plantation workers and rice farmers. Since 1963 the CSTV has strengthened its ties with the anti-Communist International Trade Secretariats (ITS) and through them with the International Confederation of Free Trade Unions (ICFTU).

The Vietnam Labor Union (Union Ouvriere du Viet Nam—UOV) was organized in 1953. Although it claimed over 40,000 members in 1966, official membership estimates in 1963 barely exceeded 1,000. An affiliate of the free-world ICFTU, the organization represented mostly civilian technicians formerly employed by the French army.

Leadership training continued to be one of the outstanding problems of the labor movement. Most leaders were not workingmen but members of the educated elite or young intellectuals, out of touch with the rank and file of workers. The prevailing view, with evident roots in the old order, seemed to be that only the educated man was qualified to lead. The workers themselves apparently accepted this traditional judgment.

There was a grave shortage of intermediate-level union officials, notably on the plant level, to present grievances to management, assist in collective bargaining and maintain liaison with the labor union's headquarters. In 1963 the CVT organized 13 training courses for 490 labor organizations throughout the country. The courses were subsidized by the International Confederation of Christian Labor and were designed to graduate labor union executives, shop stewards, union management experts and union propagandists.

Labor leader training programs have received official assistance from the government, AID and ILO. In 1965, AID offered 10 scholarships for study tours in the United States and 3 others for local training of potential union leaders and administrators. Under the Colombo Plan several scholarships were granted to unions for leadership training and for sending candidates on study tours to India and Israel and other countries.

International Affiliations

Official representatives of the three major labor federations and of employers associations have regularly attended conferences of the ILO since 1952. The country has been a signatory to ILO conventions dealing with labor inspections, with discrimination against labor union members and with the right of workers to organize and to bargain collectively. A seven-man delegation representing management, workers and the Ministry of Labor attended the ILO conference in Geneva in June and July 1964. The agenda included compensation for industrial accidents and the definition of the status of female labor. Many labor unions are affiliated with the International Trade Secretariats. For example, the Plantation workers Federation of Vietnam is affiliated with the International Federation of Plantation, Agricultural and Allied Workers; the Petroleum Workers of Vietnam, with the International Federation of Petroleum Workers; the Vietnam Union Telecommunication Workers, with the Postal, Telegraph and Telephone International Secretariat, the South Vietnamese Journalists Union, with the International Federation of Journalists; and the Vietnamese Transportation Union, with the International Transport Workers Union.

Vietnamese labor leaders and union representatives have made frequent visits and study tours to foreign countries since 1962. In March

1965, 10 union leaders visited the United States to study working conditions and union activities. In the following December, CVT Chairman Tran Quoc Buu attended the conference of the Brotherhood of Asian Trade Unions in Hong Kong. In the course of reciprocal visits by labor union representatives from the United States, a delegation representing the American Federation of Labor and the Congress of Industrial Organizations (AFL-CIO) visited Chairman Tran Quoc Buu in June 1964. The American delegation was taken on a tour of the CVT-affiliated Rubber Plantation Workers' Union in Phuoc Tuy Province (southeast of Saigon) and of CVT welfare centers in Saigon. The International Longshoremen's Association sent a delegation to Vietnam in the winter of 1965 to advise dockworkers in loading and unloading techniques. Although the CVT is an affiliate of the IFCTU, it also maintains contacts with the ICFTU and with labor unions of Western Germany.

EMPLOYERS' ORGANIZATIONS

In 1966 there were 88 legally recognized employers' organizations. Largest and best known were the General Confederation of Vietnamese Employers, established in 1953, and the Association of Employers of Vietnam (also called the Vietnam Association of Employers), established in 1960. Both are affiliated with the International Organization of Employers. Other major employers' organizations are the Association of Catholic Employers of Vietnam and the Rubber Planters and Transport Owners Association. Representatives of labor unions' employers' associations and the government, serving on national and regional consultative committees, take under consideration matters of mutual concern.

LABOR RELATIONS

Although worker representation in enterprises has been gradually gaining during the 1960's, employer paternalism has remained characteristic of labor relations. The concept of subordination to the employer is rooted in the Confucian tradition and is therefore regarded as a natural relationship by the Vietnamese worker. At the same time he expects the employer to treat him with courtesy and with respect for his human dignity. For example, a reprimand by the employer in private is accepted as a matter of course, but if given in front of fellow employees, it constitutes a loss of face and becomes a great personal calamity.

The Confucian tradition, making employers responsible for the welfare of workers, has been the source of a benevolent paternalism on the part of most employers. In the traditional small craft shops and in the small enterprises this attitude manifests itself mostly in courteous speech by the employer to the worker and by granting token material favors to the workers on religious holidays and family celebrations. It is not incompatible with the payment of substandard wages and with the presence of unhealthy working conditions. In fact, legal provisions concerning workers' welfare are often complied with only if enforced by Labor Department officials.

On the other hand, large, modern enterprises, under Vietnamese or foreign ownership, offer extensive welfare facilities and services, including medical care, low-rent housing and schooling. By early 1965 some 16,000 housing units intended for 40,000 workers had been built by private industrial enterprises and plantations. The same enterprises maintained 130 elementary schools for 13,500 pupils.

Settlement of Disputes

Only a few enterprises have formal procedures for the settlement of grievances submitted by individual workers. In many instances, labor union representatives or shop stewards present the grievances to management. Because of the extreme dearth of skilled workers, the latter are usually in a favorable negotiating position with their employers in the event of individual dispute over alleged injustices and rarely need a go-between. Workers may ask officials of the Department of Labor, or union representatives, to mediate in individual disputes with employers.

If settlement is not reached, the workers may file suit in one of the eight labor courts located in Saigon, Dinh Tuong (southwest of Saigon), Bien Hoa, Da Lat, Phong Dinh (near Can Tho, southwest of Saigon), Khanh Hoa (south of Saigon), Hue or Da Nang, respectively. The labor courts consist of a judge appointed by the Department of Labor, two workers' representatives and two employers' representatives. Judgments of the labor courts may be appealed at higher levels of the regular law courts (Court of Appeals or Supreme Court). In practice, nearly all individual disputes are settled on the local level. Department of Labor officials settled 75 percent of the individual disputes in 1962 and 939 disputes between June 1965 and February 1966.

An attempt for settlement on the local level must be made in the event of collective disputes. If no agreement can be reached between workers and management, Department of Labor inspectors mediate between workers and employers. If the parties fail to reach a settlement, an Arbitration Council is appointed by the Department of Labor, consisting of a judge and of employers' and workers' representatives. Rulings of the Arbitration Council are not binding, however, and may be appealed through local government channels. As in the case of individual conflicts, nearly all collective conflicts are settled on the local level. Between June 1965 and February 1966,

55 cases were settled through the mediation of the Department of Labor.

Both individual and collective grievances usually involve compensation claims for sickness or injury contracted on the job, dismissal without cause, wage raises, family allowances and, sometimes, employer discrimination against union members.

Collective Bargaining

Collective bargaining is not practiced on a large scale, but provisions of existing collective agreements are generally extended to nonunionized workers. Domestic and family workers, however, are not covered by the provisions of the agreements.

Collective agreements regulate working conditions for rubber plantation workers; oil, textile and bank workers; and workers in government-owned business firms, public transportation enterprises and electric power companies. The agreements must be approved by the government on the regional level or, if the enterprise operates in several regions, on the national level. Provisions usually cover wages, method of payment, bonuses, severance payments and conditions of dismissals.

The Rubber Plantation Workers' Agreement provides for periodic pay raises, and it deals with nearly all aspects of working conditions for approximately 40,000 unionized rubber plantation workers. Its provisions have been made applicable to several thousand nonunionized workers on other types of plantations. The Agreement has been promulgated as an official decree and has been invoked by labor inspectors throughout the country whenever disputes arose on plantations between management and workers. Renegotiations in 1963 provided for an 8 percent pay raise, for the continued payment of family allowances during illness and for the right of workers to appeal disciplinary measures. Another collective agreement, first negotiated in 1962 and applied throughout the country, is that of the bank employees of the Saigon-Cho Lon area. The Petroleum and Chemical Workers Union and the Shell Oil Company signed a collective agreement in March 1965.

Strikes

According to legal stipulations, all arbitration and mediation procedures must be exhausted before workers may resort to strike. These provisions have not always been adhered to, particularly since workers have become increasingly restive under the hardships of rising prices and low wages. Strikes have also been called to protest against governmental restrictions of workers' rights to demonstrate and against arbitrary dismissals. Viet Cong agitation among workers also contributed to some of the labor unrest in 1964 and 1965.

A general strike involving some 22,000 workers in transportation and in the electric power, oil and textile industries was called by the CVT on September 21 and 22, 1964, to protest Prime Minister Khanh's government emergency regulations, promulgated on August 24, of that year. The regulations prohibited strikes and restricted the rights of labor unions. The arbitrary lockout of many employees in a Saigon textile factory employing 2,000 brought about the work stoppage which was eventually settled by the government's recognition of the right to strike and the reinstatement of the dismissed employees.

Strike and strike threats in late 1964 involving cement workers in Ha Tien, dockworkers, bank employees and workers on rubber plantations and in the tobacco and glass industries were based principally on protraction of official procedures in handling labor union applications for legal recognition, failure to respond to organized labor's demands for more specific laws concerning relations of labor and management and on arbitrary dismissals.

Demands for wage raises precipitated most of the strikes during 1965. In spite of the ban on strikes announced in June of that year, dockworkers and cigarette factory workers in Saigon struck in July for an increase in wages. In September, Saigon water and electricity workers threatened to strike unless they were granted a 10 to 35 percent wage raise.

CHAPTER 22

DOMESTIC TRADE

Domestic trade provides a livelihood for the largest segment of the population after agriculture. Most enterprises are small; thousands consist of one individual. Wholesale trade in both domestic products and imports is dominated by the Chinese. They also own and operate most of the shops in Saigon-Cho Lon and in provincial cities and market towns, although increasing numbers of Vietnamese are becoming shopkeepers. In the villages the shopkeeper is usually a Vietnamese, the wife of a farmer. Each city and town has one or more marketplace; the majority of the stallkeepers are Vietnamese women, as are most of the peddlers and soft-drink vendors found in the city, town and village.

The buying and selling of rice and other surplus farm produce, livestock, poultry and poultry products, fish and fish products, charcoal, firewood, sugar, textiles, tools and household articles account for the bulk of internal trade. Surplus rice is usually sold by the farmer himself to a miller or to an intermediary for a Chinese dealer in Saigon-Cho Lon. Other farm and fishery produce is usually sold by a member of the producer's family directly to consumers or to dealers in the marketplace of a town, provincial city or Saigon-Cho Lon. Sugar, domestically manufactured consumer goods and tools are distributed by wholesalers in Saigon-Cho Lon to wholesalers and retailers in provincial centers, who in turn sell them to retailers in the market towns and villages of the province. Most imported foods and consumer goods are marketed in Saigon-Cho Lon, which is by far the largest trading center in the country. Some stocks of imported goods are shipped to Da Lat and Hue where many wealthy Vietnamese live.

During 1965, as the Viet Cong intensified their economic offensive against Saigon, the marketing system became seriously disrupted. The Viet Cong repeatedly cut the main roads leading to the capital and attacked barges on the canals and waterways throughout the Mekong Delta. Rice deliveries to Saigon became slow and uncertain, and prices soared. Hoarding and speculation added to the shortages which were alleviated by imports of rice from the United States. Distribution of goods from Saigon to rural areas was made equally difficult, especially in the mountainous areas to the north where emergency supplies had to be dropped by air. The north-south railway was rendered practically unusable, except for short intermittent stretches, and it took a major military operation to open the main road leading from the coast to the Central Highlands.

Toward the end of the year, as the areas under Vietnamese Government control were expanded, it was hoped that Viet Cong interdiction of rail, road and water transport would be gradually curtailed and orderly marketing resumed.

BACKGROUND

Before the French came, Vietnam was a country composed almost entirely of nearly self-sufficient villages. With each village devoted to virtually identical pursuits—mainly crop cultivation, fishing and subsidiary occupations such as local crafts—there was little need for commerce between villages. The few cities—Saigon, Hanoi and Hue—drew upon the surrounding countryside for their needs.

Under French colonial rule the development of exports—rice, rubber and other crops—and the importation of French manufactured goods greatly stimulated internal commerce. Further commercial activity was generated by the evolution of a pattern of trade within the territories of French Indochina whereby the agricultural surpluses of Cochin China were exchanged for the coal and manufactured goods of Tonkin. French and Chinese were preeminent in trade, largely excluding the Vietnamese.

Although the French dominated the export and import trade until after World War II, they became to a large extent dependent on the Chinese for the preliminary handling of local produce for export and for the local marketing of imported goods. The socially and economically well-organized Chinese quickly assumed the role of middleman between the Vietnamese producers and consumers and the French. The Chinese controlled the rice trade and most retailing and wholesaling, the main development of which began during the 1880's in the area then known as Cochin China.

In the latter part of the nineteenth century the French began constructing rail lines, and roads; waterways were improved and extended, and many new canals were dug. By 1910 short stretches of railroad were open for traffic, connecting Saigon with nearby centers and Hue with Quang Tri, 30 miles to the north, and with Da Nang, 50 miles to the south. After World War I networks of roads were built from Saigon into the Central Highlands. The famous coastal Mandarin Route from Saigon to Hanoi, originally constructed by the Annamese emperors, was made into a modern motor route. Other new roads connected Saigon with Cambodia and Laos. In 1936 the rail link between Saigon and Hanoi was completed, and this greatly facilitated trade between north and south.

The transportation system suffered greatly in World War II and even more so in the Indochina War which followed; it underwent, in fact, more destruction than any other physical element of the Vietnamese economy. Railway rolling stock was almost totally destroyed or seriously damaged, and most of the highways were left unusable as a result of military action and lack of maintenance. Boats and other obstacles were sunk in the navigable waterways, and silting closed many of the main river channels and harbors to large ships. The great majority of the junks which carried cargo on the rivers and along the seacoast were destroyed.

World War II also began the disruption of the marketing system which had developed during the colonial period. The rice and rubber of Cochin China and the coal of Tonkin were diverted to Japan, and imports declined drastically. The Indochina War and the destruction of the transport system brought to a standstill the movement of goods other than that within the local community. Commerce revived after the cessation of hostilities in 1954, but the partition into North and South Vietnam which took place soon afterwards abruptly shattered the French-evolved exchange of products between these two sections of Indochina, requiring a drastic readjustment in both economies (see ch. 23, Foreign Economic Relations).

WHOLESALE AND RETAIL TRADE

Trade in imported processed foods and manufactured consumer goods continues in unreduced volume. The largest concentration of consumers of imported goods is at Saigon-Cho Lon, although there is demand in other cities where Europeans and well-to-do Chinese and Vietnamese live. Basically, however, the bulk of domestic trade consists of the purchase and sale of agricultural products and locally made essential consumer goods. An appreciable part of this trade takes place at village or town markets where sales are made directly by producers to retailers or consumers. Most of the rice trade, however, moves through channels established by brokers, wholesalers and dealers (who in normal times are also exporters) centered in Saigon-Cho Lon.

Saigon-Cho Lon is the commercial center, and most of the export, import and wholesale houses are situated there. Almost all of the exporters, who are relatively few in number, deal in rice, since rubber, the other main export crop, is shipped directly from the plantations. Many of the approximately 1,000 import houses are small firms. Some—mainly the larger ones—add wholesaling and retailing to their activities and deal in a wide variety of goods. A number are exclusive distributors or sales agents for foreign companies—mainly European, American and Japanese. Importers, exporters, forwarding agents or shippers own most of the warehousing facilities.

Most of these firms are in Chinese hands, but some French concerns are still in business and the number of Vietnamese enterprises is increasing. The larger Chinese merchant houses commonly operate both as independents and as agents for European companies. They channel the produce of the rural areas into the cities for sale or export and, operating through a network of relatives, friends, and members of their "congregations" engaged in business in all parts of the country, provide outlets for imported goods (see ch. 5, Ethnic Groups and Languages). The broker who specializes in locally manufactured goods for domestic sale may receive a commission, as a manufacturer's representative, or may buy on his own account for retail merchandising.

All businesses, including wholesalers and retailers, are required to have licenses issued by the national government. The charge for a license varies according to size and type of business; in addition, there is a provincial surcharge and a further surcharge by the city, town or village. Stallkeepers in the market pay for the right to use a stall; this charge also varies with the type of business.

In Saigon-Cho Lon there are eight commercial banks which offer plentiful credit to reputable businesses of the metropolis. The Vietnamese Chamber of Commerce, the French Chamber of Commerce and the Chinese Chamber of Commerce are located in Saigon. Vietnamese chambers of commerce are also located in Hue and Da Nang.

The Marketing of Rice

The most important wholesale trade is in rice. Until the 1950's it was entirely in the hands of Chinese dealers located in Cho Lon who also owned most of the storage and shipping facilities. In close contact with their network of agents in the provinces, on the one hand, and the large French interests on the other, the Chinese figured significantly at every stage of the marketing process. Beginning with 1950, however, Chinese control diminished, especially after the issuance on September 6, 1956, of Ordinance No. 53, which closed to foreigners 11 occupations, including rice milling, dealing in cereals and the transport of merchandise. The Ordinance opened new entrepreneurial doors to the Vietnamese, who seized on the opportunity to develop rice mills and rice merchandising in the delta provinces. Although the Ordinance was enforced for little over a year, the expansion of Vietnamese participation in the provincial rice trade has continued.

Most of the domestic rice which enters wholesale channels is grown in the Delta where the harvest begins in September, rising to a peak in December and January. The farmer, with a surplus of rice to sell, once had no choice but to deal with an agent from a firm in Cho Lon. He now can continue that practice, or have his rice milled nearby for sale on the local market or shop around for the best price among local brokers. Once the rice is sold it is moved by barge or truck by the purchaser.

Most farmers sell their rice immediately after the harvest when the price usually has been between 50 and 55 piasters (for value of the piaster, see Glossary) per *gia* (44.1 pounds). Some sell throughout the year as they need cash. Only a small minority of the wealthiest farmers retain stocks for later sale when the price has generally risen to 70 to 80 piasters per *gia*. Farmers of the lowest economic level generally do not grow rice for sale but may sell their rice and buy a poorer quality for home consumption.

The condition of paddy is an important consideration in price. Rice which is properly dried and winnowed commands the highest price. The government has set prices for average quality but not for superior or inferior grades; thus, the broker has a wide price range in which to operate. He may be an agent of a large rice-trading company or he may buy on his own account. He may sell locally, ship to Cho Lon for marketing, or keep the rice in a storehouse in anticipation of higher prices. Because prices are lowest during the period immediately after the harvest, brokers customarily hold large supplies of rice off the market in order to take advantage of the subsequent price rise.

As the Viet Cong have expanded their activities in the Delta, they have introduced numerous obstructions to the movement of rice through normal channels to the provincial centers and to Cho Lon. In areas where they exercised effective control they levied a 40-percent tax in kind on the farmer's annual yield and charged dealers a 4 piaster per *gia* "circulation tax" for shipments by both barge and truck. Beginning early in 1965, the Viet Cong offered farmers 100 piasters per *gia* for the 60 percent of their harvest they were permitted to retain, topping the official givernment rate of 60 piasters per *gia*. Viet Cong roadblocks between Ca Mau and Can Tho and between Can Tho and Cho Lon, were increased. Attacks on barges on the canals and waterways of the Delta became commonplace. In order to discourage dealers from shipping rice to government-controlled centers, the "circulation tax" was steadily increased until, in June 1965, it reached 12 piasters per *gia*. Meanwhile, both deteriorating security and poor weather conditions having impaired the prospects of a good harvest, the farmers resorted to hoarding as a safety measure, further reducing rice sales.

By 1965 the government, faced with the necessity of purchasing annually some 400,000 to 500,000 tons of rice to feed the capital and the deficit areas to the north, and of providing the armed forces with 30,000 to 40,000 tons, had become the major customer of Cho Lon's 36 wholesale firms. In the first 6 months of the year, shipments to Saigon were so erratic and government stocks became so depleted that the authorities were forced to pay the dealers the exhorbitant rate of 840 piasters per 100 kilograms (220 pounds) as compared to the government's official rate of 600 piasters per 100 kilograms.

Shortly after becoming prime minister, Air Vice Marshal Nguyen Cao Ky moved to strengthen the position of the government vis-a-vis the rice dealers. On July 2, 1965, he issued a decree against speculation. Rice dealers were ordered to declare all their holdings and, when they declared only a mere 12,000 tons, the government threatened to confiscate all rice found to be held by the dealers over the tonnages reported by them. As an alternative the government offered to buy all available rice at 700 piasters per 100 kilograms. In the meantime, it had authorized the import of 50,000 tons from the United States under United States Public Law 480. As a result of these measures, some 50,000 tons of rice were procured from Cho Lon dealers, of which 15,000 tons was delivered from the provinces. A crisis was averted, but, despite the import of an additional 50,000 tons from the United States, as the year drew to a close, rice still remained in short supply. To break the semimonopoly of the 36 Cho Lon dealers on the distribution of rice, Prime Minister Ky proposed the development of rural marketing cooperatives and government backing for Vietnamese, rather than Chinese, rice dealers.

Retail Trade

Retail outlets vary from the Saigon department store and specialty shop selling luxury goods to the peddler with a few rice cakes, fruits or vegetables to sell. The typical retail enterprise, however, is the stall or small shop of the city, town or village marketplace. A village' market may boast of no more than a half dozen shops, while its counterpart in the city may be a great covered square with hundreds of stalls and stores. Saigon has, in addition to its large central market, some 27 others in different parts of the city.

Both the city shops and the open-air stands of the villages are usually family enterprises, generally not large enough to warrant the employment of outsiders. Most city shops are owned and operated by Chinese, although an increasing number of Vietnamese have been entering the field since 1945. In the villages, it is invariably the peasant's wife or daughter who markets the few pounds of rice, the occasional chicken, or the few eggs he has available for local sale. Regular vendors make their appearance at the village marketplace; others are peddlers who go from village to village selling their wares or exchanging them for local produce. In particular, this is the usual method whereby the wares of the potters, bronze workers, weavers and shoemakers are marketed. These artisans are concentrated in certain villages and are organized into a type of trade guild which functions as a cooperative. A guild member travels from marketplace to marketplace and village to village selling the artisans' products.

Among the *montagnards* who are predominantly self-sufficient there is little trade. The Katu, the Rhade, the Mnong and the Sedang are exceptional in this respect, trading with the Vietnamese and acting as middlemen with other ethnic groups among the hillmen. The Katu trade with the Vietnamese especially for highly valued iron and pots. The Rhade exchange cloth with the Mnong for their pigs and poultry. The Mnong also deal with the Chinese and Vietnamese, exchanging their own livestock, including buffalo, for much coveted salt and jars. The Sedang are quite unusual in the wide extent of their trading alliances among the minority groups of the highlands, dealing in local produce and Vietnamese goods.

Trade Practices

Shops are normally open from 9 to 12 and from 3 to 6, and holidays are numerous. There are several advertising firms in Saigon, but they are handicapped by the fact that advertising channels are only slightly developed. Newspaper circulation is limited, and commercial radio broadcasting is nonexistent. Motion-picture commercials are a favored means of reaching rural as well as urban audiences.

In Saigon some merchants on fashionable To-Do Street have adopted a fixed-price policy, and the government has licensed a number of food shops to sell rice at the price set by the government. Bargaining, however, remains the normal accompaniment of most retail transactions. The buyer is expected to reject the price first quoted and is likely to be thought incompetent if he does not do so. The haggling that follows may lead to noisy arguments but rarely to a real quarrel which, in such a situation, would bring discredit on both parties. Barter is virtually extinct.

TRANSPORT SERVICES

After the Indochina War transportation facilities were rehabilitated and modernized, greatly expanding the services of motor vehicles, rail and airlines. Nonetheless, the bulk of goods in domestic trade continued to move in sampans and junks on the inland waterways and in carts pulled along the dike roads by draft animals. After 1959 domestic air transport became increasingly important as Viet Cong activity closed major highways to public transportation and rendered inoperable much of the railroad.

The number of buses and other public carriers using the highways increased steadily from 1955 to 1959, in keeping with the rising imports of passenger cars, trucks and, especially, motorcycles and motorscooters. From 1959 to 1962 this increase continued in all categories, except passenger cars. By the end of 1962, the dropoff in passenger cars, due principally to wartime conditions, was about 7,000 leaving slightly less than 29,000 still in use. By the end of that same period, the number of trucks and buses had risen to 26,000 and motorcycles and motorscooters to almost 46,000. Most of the passenger cars taken off the roads were replaced by cycles and scooters, particularly in the urban areas.

Buslines are in operation in Saigon, and large interurban buses transport passengers and goods between the larger market towns and cities. Such operations are precarious, however, since the Viet Cong have been active in attempting to disrupt the economy by preventing the movement of foodstuffs into and goods out of major population centers. Transportation to and from local markets includes small buses, converted trucks, motorcycles, motorscooters, and bullock carts, and is also subject to harassment from the Viet Cong. Buslines are owned and operated by both the government and private concerns.

By the end of 1962 restoration and rehabilitation of the railroads had progressed to the point where service provided for over 2 million passengers and loadings of about 400,000 metric tons of freight. In that year, however, as a result of Viet Cong interference with railroad operations, night traffic ceased, and in 1965 the only portion that remained operable was a section between Da Nang and Nha Trang. To keep this part of the line open required considerable assistance from United States troops (see ch. 2, Physical Environment).

An estimated 10,000 craft—barges, sampans and junks—ply the waterways of the Mekong Delta. Some have motors, but most are powered by oars or sail. The Republic also has a merchant fleet consisting of 16 small craft with a total net tonnage of 5,896. Three of the vessels are government-owned; the others are owned by private individuals. The merchant fleet is used largely in the coastwise trade; virtually all South Vietnam's ocean shipping is carried by ships of foreign registry (see ch. 2, Physical Environment).

The main port of Saigon has an extensive area which is equipped with piers, warehouses, cranes and floating equipment. In 1962 the total tonnage entering and leaving the port amounted to 3,621,000 and 3,617,000 metric tons respectively, almost triple the amount of cargo handled in 1960. Other commercial ports, though of much less importance, are at Da Nang, Nha Trang and Qui Nhon. These ports are being dredged and improved by the United States, which is also developing a large port on Vinh Cam Ranh (see ch. 2, Physical Environment).

Air Vietnam (AVN) has continued to make progress and to expand its services. The number of domestic passengers carried on internal routes grew from 52,000 in 1959 to 534,000 in 1964. At the same time international traffic rose from about 30,000 passengers to almost 70,000. In 1964 under its expanded activities, AVN operated 18 flights a week from Saigon, to Da Nang and Hue, 14 flights to Da Lat, 12 to Ban Me Thuot and Nha Trang, 11 to Pleiku, 6 to Kontum, 3 to Can Tho, Ca Mau, Rach Gia and Phu Quoc, 2 to Phan Thiet. Outside the country, AVN flew 4 times a week to Phnom Penh, 3 times a week to Bangkok and Hong Kong and twice to Vientiane. Its fleet included six DC–3s, one DC–4, one DC–6, one DC–6B, two Cessnas and one Caravelle (see ch. 2, Physical Environment).

CHAPTER 23

FOREIGN ECONOMIC RELATIONS

In 1965 the Ky government, like its predecessor, the Khanh government, initiated extensive efforts to widen South Vietnam's foreign economic relations, especially among Asian nations. These endeavors were directed more toward obtaining aid and adherence in the war against the Viet Cong than toward the development of new trading partners. After partition South Vietnam had received massive foreign aid, mainly from the United States, to reconstruct and develop the economy. By 1965, as a result of protracted military action, the country was becoming even more dependent on foreign assistance. This had been widely sought with some success from a few European nations and Japan.

The prospect was for continued trade deficits which must be covered by foreign aid. Since partition, imports, mostly manufactured goods, have averaged in cost over $250 million a year. On the other hand, exports—mainly rice and rubber—have varied in value from $45 million in 1956 to $84 million in 1960, depending on the size of the rice crop and the world price for rubber. A fall in exports in 1964 was directly attributable to Viet Cong interdiction of rice shipments to Saigon and to other urban centers, necessitating rice imports and the prohibition of rice exports. France remained South Vietnam's major customer, but the United States had replaced France as chief supplier.

BACKGROUND

Before World War II

The foreign trade of Vietnam before World War II was determined by French policy, which regarded France's colonial territories as sources of raw materials and markets for French manufactured goods. French dominance of Vietnamese trade was assured by a special law of January 1892 which applied high tariffs to imports from other countries while imports from France remained duty free. Under the same law customs duties on Vietnamese exports to France were reduced; in 1928 they were removed by a tariff law which established a system of free trade within the French empire. These regulations remained in effect until early 1940 when, under pressure from the Japanese, a new tariff law was passed setting uniform duties on all goods regardless of country of origin.

During this period exports originating in Annam and Cochin China consisted chiefly of rice and rubber, with rice by far the most important commodity. By 1938 exports of rice from Cochin China—the only rice-exporting area—reached over 1 million metric tons a year. Plantation rubber, introduced after World War I, became an increasingly significant export, rising to almost 70,000 metric tons in 1939. Imports consisted principally of manufactured goods, of which textiles were the most important, followed by machinery and metals.

China, Japan and other countries of the Far East were also important trading partners of Vietnam before World War II, Hong Kong acting as collecting and distributing center for the Far Eastern trade. Rice was the most important shipment to China and to France; rubber, the major export to Japan. The United States was also an important buyer of rubber, taking 16,000 tons, or more than France, in 1937. In exchange the United States supplied petroleum products, machinery and machine tools.

Vietnam had an export surplus in its trade with the rest of the world before World War II. In 1939, although France was less important as a market for Vietnamese exports (it took about a third of the total) than as a supplier of Vietnamese imports (it supplied more than half), Vietnam had a surplus of export earnings over import payments in its trade with the franc area and with the United States. Outside the realm of merchandise trade heavy financial transactions were carried on with France, India and China. Capital from these countries moved into Vietnam, while personal and business remittances to them from Vietnam were substantial.

After World War II

Vietnam's pattern of foreign trade underwent a significant change between 1945 and 1954. Although France resumed its dominant position in the colony's external trade, the United States began to account for an increasingly large percentage of Vietnam's imports and exports. In contrast to the large trade surpluses before the war postwar trade returns revealed a deficit gap between export earnings and import payments.

The fall in export earnings resulted largely from a decline in production as a consequence of war devastation, while the rise in imports was in response to the increased demand generated by the presence of the French Union Forces. The gap was so great that, at least in the years 1952 through 1954, export proceeds were not sufficient to pay for more than 22 percent of Vietnam's import bills. Covering these heavy trade deficits was a substantial franc surplus (for value of the franc, see Glossary). This resulted from the heavy military outlay of the French Union Forces in Vietnam and the aid received from the United States and France (see ch. 3, Historical Setting). Vietnam was also receiving technical assistance under the Colombo Plan for Cooperative Economic Development in South and Southeast Asia and under United Nations programs, as well as welfare assistance from American and international voluntary and charitable organizations.

In January 1955 the United States began giving financial assistance directly to South Vietnam in dollars, whereas aid had previously been provided through France and in francs. Under the United States-financed commercial import program machinery was established for purchasing imports on a competitive basis from eligible countries of the Free World. The quadripartite arrangements with France, Laos and Cambodia—which previously governed Vietnam's economic relations with the other three and with the rest of the world—were dissolved and replaced by bilateral treaties. Laos and Cambodia were given freedom of navigation on the Mekong, their only practical outlet to the sea, and new conventions were to be negotiated fixing the conditions of passage on the river and through the port of Saigon.

South Vietnam remained temporarily in the franc area but, free to leave at will, severed this connection in December 1955, pegging the piaster to the United States dollar—a reflection of the new orientation of its foreign trade. A bilateral agreement with France retained preferential tariff treatment for the goods of both parties (see ch. 25, Banking and Currency).

PATTERN OF FOREIGN TRADE

South Vietnam aims ultimately to make major changes in the commodity composition of its trade with other countries, but because of unsettled conditions it must for the time being live with the commodity trade pattern of the past. Accordingly, since independence, it has produced and exported as much as possible of the same foodstuffs and raw materials that formerly accounted for most of the export trade. It was also still buying the same types of goods from foreign suppliers as before, although imports of petroleum and certain other items had risen as a result of military requirements and the fact that some of the commodities which used to come from the North had to be bought from foreign sources. The main change discernible in the foreign trade pattern after 11 years of independence was the more important trading role of the United States.

Since independence South Vietnam's foreign trade policy has been determined largely by the substantial United States aid available to cover its trade deficit and by the fact that customs duties on imports account for a significant part of government revenues. Thus, value of exports has little influence on level of imports, while loss of revenue must be taken into account if imports show a decline (see ch. 24, Public Finance). At the same time, a primary objective of foreign trade policy has been to ensure markets for rice and rubber. The danger of overdependence on these two exports has been recognized, and greater diversification is planned, along with an increase in local output of consumer goods, in order to reduce these imports in favor of capital goods.

Despite a decline in imports from France since 1957, it still remained South Vietnam's main customer in 1964 (see table 4). The United States, however, had replaced France as major supplier, followed by Nationalist China and Japan (see table 5).

France retains certain trading advantages in the Vietnamese market resulting from the close commercial contacts that were developed over the years between exporters in France and importers in Vietnam, as well as from the development of French tastes among many Vietnamese consumers and the maintenance and repair requirements of the large amount of French equipment in use. These advantages are outweighed, however, by the fact that French prices are, in many cases, not competitive with prices of goods from other areas, such as Germany and Japan, and by the emergence of the United States dollar as the main foreign exchange at South Vietnam's disposal.

Japan has won a much greater share of the South Vietnamese import market than it previously enjoyed. Many Japanese products have a price advantage—in terms of delivered prices if not on an f.o.b. basis—over merchandise from other important sources; they also have a special quality appeal for the Vietnamese consumer.

Table 4.   South Vietnam's Imports, by Country of Origin, 1957–64

[In millions of dollars]

Country	1957	1958	1959	1960	1961	1962	1963	1964
France	82. 7	58. 8	40. 6	51. 1	38. 8	35. 0	31. 4	18. 2
United States	65. 5	54. 9	58. 5	61. 2	68. 3	97. 2	107. 0	126. 3
Japan	61. 8	45. 0	47. 6	52. 7	59. 9	44. 6	27. 6	32. 1
Indonesia	15. 5	14. 5	15. 6	15. 5	15. 2	14. 2	18. 9	13. 2
West Germany	17. 9	13. 1	13. 2	13. 7	14. 7	10. 3	7. 1	8. 4
Nationalist China	8. 8	5. 6	6. 1	5. 0	14. 3	25. 0	37. 5	38. 3
United Kingdom	6. 4	6. 3	5. 9	6. 6	7. 6	4. 5	4. 3	4. 9
Italy	5. 4	5. 3	5. 2	8. 6	7. 3	4. 9	6. 4	8. 5
Other	24. 7	28. 6	31. 9	25. 9	29. 0	28. 8	46. 0	47. 9
Total	288. 7	232. 1	224. 6	240. 3	255. 1	264. 5	286. 2	297. 8

Source: Adapted from United States Operations Mission to Vietnam, Economic and Financial Planning Division, *Annual Statistical Bulletin*, No. 8, 1965, p. 65.

Table 5. *South Vietnam's Exports, by Country of Destination, 1957–64*

[In millions of dollars]

Country	1957	1958	1959	1960	1961	1962	1963	1964
France	40. 9	29. 7	23. 8	30. 6	25. 5	20. 4	18. 7	15. 5
United States	11. 0	5. 1	6. 4	3. 7	3. 6	1. 8	1. 1	2. 0
West Germany	1. 3	0. 8	11. 4	5. 8	7. 1	6. 0	6. 6	8. 4
Japan	3. 9	0. 6	1. 9	2. 4	1. 4	2. 9	4. 3	4. 3
Hong Kong	0. 9	0. 9	5. 3	7. 4	5. 7	3. 1	7. 0	2. 4
Singapore		6. 1	4. 6	5. 2	1. 7	2. 0	8. 0	2. 3
United Kingdom	0. 1	1. 2	2. 3	4. 7	8. 0	8. 8	5. 6	5. 1
Indonesia	0. 5	3. 4	0. 8	7. 0	4. 3		1. 1	2. 1
Other	22. 0	7. 4	18. 6	17. 7	12. 5	11. 6	24. 3	6. 3
Total	80. 5	55. 2	75. 1	84. 5	69. 8	56. 6	76. 7	48. 4

Source: Adapted from United States Operations Mission to Vietnam, Economic and Financial Planning Division, *Annual Statistical Bulletin*, No. 8, 1965, p. 59.

The government in Saigon has sought to expand South Vietnam's trade with countries of Western Europe other than France. Even before the cease-fire in 1954 Vietnam had negotiated trade agreements with Italy, West Germany and the Benelux countries (Belgium, the Netherlands, Luxembourg). These agreements were concluded within the framework of French trading arrangements with those countries. Transactions were recorded in French francs. Enjoying at that time a credit balance in its dealings with France, Vietnam could use these franc balances to pay for purchases from the other signatory countries in excess of what it could earn from exports to those markets.

Since 1955 South Vietnam's franc balance has shifted from credit to a debit position, and it has been using United States aid to pay for purchases abroad which are not compensated for by its own exports. Under the original provisions of the United States-South Vietnamese economic aid agreement, it was stipulated that United States aid dollars could be spent in part for such purchases if the prices of foreign products were competitive with those of similar products offered by American suppliers. In 1960, in order to lessen the flow of dollars out of the United States, the aid agreement was modified, and restrictions were placed on the use of aid funds to make purchases in certain developed countries. From 1956 through 1959, United States aid financed 85 percent of imports; in 1960, over 74 percent; and from a low of 55 percent in 1961 rose to 66 percent in 1965.

Both exports and imports require a license. Export licensing is designed to control foreign exchange transactions, to prevent the export of commodities in short supply and to enforce the embargo on trade with the Sino-Soviet block. Each year the government publishes a list of exports for which licenses will be granted. Most exports are subsidized by the government through the licensing system. Import licensing is maintained for the purpose of conserving the foreign exchange and channeling imports into lines of goods desired by the government. Licensing procedures vary with commodities and sources of financing; they are complex and are frequently changed. Evasion of export controls is reported to be widespread, especially on supply routes which pass through Viet Cong territory to Cambodia.

Exports

Rubber and rice constitute between 80 and 90 percent of exports. In addition, South Vietnam sells abroad limited quantities of beer, tea, duck feathers, scrap iron, hogs and fish. In 1960, the year South Vietnam's exports reached their highest peak, of a total valued at $84 million, rice shipments accounted for over $27 million and rubber shipments for $48 million. Rubber and rice exports declined in 1961 and in 1962 showed further sharp decreases. A marked improvement in rice shipments in 1963 raised the level of the export trade. In 1964, however, the trade year was catastrophic as rice sales fell to $5.4 million and rubber sales to $33.3 million of total exports valued at $48.5 million. Exports in 1965 are expected to reach an even lower level.

The decline in rice exports in 1961 and 1962 resulted from the suspension by the government, in July 1961, of rice sales abroad. The worst floods in a number of decades, coupled with heightened Viet Cong activity, had limited the availability of rice stocks in Saigon, and the suspension of exports was necessary to retain food needed domestically and preclude speculation accompanied by undue price rises in Saigon and other urban areas.

Rice exports were resumed in October 1962, the result of an excellent rice crop, and continued at a higher level throughout 1963, reaching a volume of 322,000 tons, valued at $35.7 million, for the year. In 1964 the rise in the prevailing insecurity and floods again caused a drastic fall in rice sales, a trend which became even more pronounced in 1965. Beginning with 1961 the value of rubber exports has decreased with each succeeding year. In 1961 and 1962 this resulted from a fall in the world price of rubber, but in 1963 and subsequent years the annual volume of rubber exports has been declining mainly as a result of disruption of transportation facilities by war.

In 1960 and 1961, South Vietnam sold about 75 percent of its rubber to France and the remainder to the United Kingdom and West Germany. By 1964 only 45 percent of Vietnamese rubber was being shipped to France. The United Kingdom and West Germany were still customers, but additional important purchasers were Italy,

Netherlands, Nationalist China and Spain. After 1954 rubber purchases by the United States, which had been a major buyer, began to decline and are no longer of significance. When rice is available for sale, major buyers are Malaysia, the Philippines and Indonesia.

Imports

Manufactured goods of all kinds make up the largest part of imports. Between 1957 and 1964 principal imports were textile fabrics, machinery, metal products, petroleum products, yarns and thread, milk and dairy products, pharmaceuticals, electrical equipment and motor vehicles (see table 6). Since 1957, when domestic industries began to get underway, there have been significant changes in the import pattern. Imports of fabrics, for example, in 1964 were only one-seventh of the 1957 figure, but imports of yarn and thread had almost doubled as a result of the textile mills which had come into production. With the opening of local laboratories, imports of pharmaceuticals have also declined. While imports of consumer goods decreased, imports of machinery and metals showed a steady increase as the industrialization program advanced.

Table 6. South Vietnam's Main Imports, 1957–64
[In millions of dollars]

	1957	1958	1959	1960	1961	1962	1963	1964
Textile fabrics_____	43. 5	36. 9	24. 4	24. 9	22. 9	12. 7	6. 2	6. 6
Machinery_____	18. 4	14. 2	17. 8	20. 5	21. 7	31. 6	24. 8	28. 3
Iron and steel mill products_____	16. 2	10. 9	12. 5	12. 3	18. 4	16. 4	30. 4	22. 6
Petroleum products__	15. 3	16. 1	17. 8	17. 2	17. 5	17. 7	19. 4	18. 4
Yarns and thread____	12. 2	10. 1	11. 2	17. 7	17. 2	15. 4	22. 0	21. 5
Milk and dairy products_____	8. 9	9. 2	9. 9	12. 0	12. 6	13. 1	12. 6	17. 4
Pharmaceuticals_____	16. 6	12. 4	12. 5	11. 6	12. 0	12. 5	10. 1	10. 9
Electrical equipment_	10. 4	7. 4	8. 0	10. 2	10. 8	14. 3	9. 6	12. 1
Motor vehicles*_____	229. 7	200. 2	162. 2	191. 7	162. 7	175. 5	161. 9	147. 0

*Figure also includes bicycles, motorscooters, tractors and parts.

Source: Adapted from United States Operations Mission to Vietnam, Economic and Financial Planning Division, Annual Statistical Bulletin, No. 8, 1965, p. 66.

Beginning in 1962 imports originating in the United States increased by 50 percent, resulting from the full implementation of the regulations concerning the use of United States economic aid credits. Nationalist China also benefited from these new regulations, and its sales to South Vietnam more than doubled at the same time that imports from Western European countries and Japan sharply decreased. In January 1964 a further decline in French imports followed the South Vietnamese Government's protest to France against the French policy of neutralizing South Vietnam. The protest was accompanied by a decision to discontinue imports from France except on special authorization and to cease issuing import licenses to French trading firms operating in the country. This measure was greatly modified in November of the same year, and France remains an important supplier of consumer goods. The United States, however, furnishes a major portion of metal products, machinery and appliances, automobiles and accessories, textile fabrics and pharmaceuticals, as well as almost all dairy products and wheat flour. Other suppliers are Japan, Indonesia (mainly petroleum products), West Germany, Italy, the United Kingdom, Nationalist China, South Korea and India.

FOREIGN AID AND LOANS

The total of expenditures by the United States for economic and military aid to South Vietnam from January 1, 1955, when the aid agreement was signed with the government through December 31, 1965, is not available. Data is available for the period 1955 through 1962, and the total of both economic and military aid is some $3.6 billion (see table 7). The sum given for military aid does not include aid given in kind, which provides the Vietnamese armed forces with fuel, spare parts and many other supplies and equipment purchased by the United States Department of Defense from its direct military assistance funds (see ch. 27, The Armed Forces). Expenditures for

Table 7. United States Expenditures for Ecomonics and Military Aid to South Vietnam, 1955–64

[In millions of dollars]

Year	Economic aid	Military aid	Total
1955	322. 4	(*)	322. 4
1956	210. 0	167. 3	377. 3
1957	282. 2	110. 5	392. 7
1958	179. 1	53. 2	232. 3
1959	200. 6	41. 7	242. 3
1960	169. 0	69. 6	238. 6
1961	132. 6	65. 0	197. 6
1962	110. 7	144. 0	254. 7
1963	133. 2	n.a.	n.a.
1964	159. 3	n.a.	n.a.
Total	1, 899. 1		

n.a.—not available.
*Military aid still being given to the French Union Forces.

economic aid from the beginning of 1955 through 1964 total $1,899.1 million. The rural construction program for expanding counterinsurgency activities while stepping up economic and social services to raise living standards, adopted in the spring of 1961, is expected to entail large increases in United States aid (see ch. 18, Character and Structure of the Economy; ch. 8, Living Conditions; ch. 13, The Governmental System).

More than 70 percent of the economic aid funds have been used to support the Commercial Import Program. Under this program money or credits are made available for the purchase abroad of commodities and equipment needed to enable the economy to operate. The piasters which importers pay for aid-financed imported goods are deposited at the National Bank in a special account called the "counterpart fund" (for value of the piaster, see Glossary). Customs levied on these imports are also deposited in the same account. The fund is jointly administered by the Republic of Vietnam and the United States. Periodically, allocations are made from the fund for development projects and in support of military requirements.

The United States has also provided project assistance—aid in the form of goods and services rendered directly to government agencies or to autonomous entities such as the state railroads—for the purpose of building or rebuilding some specific enterprise. Examples of such projects are the refugee resettlement program, the Industrial Development Center and the reconstruction of highways, bridges and the railroad. The United States also carries out extensive programs in public health and education. Technical assistance has been provided in the form of services and training. American, British, French, Italian, German, Dutch, Chinese, Australian, New Zealand and other foreign specialists are working in Vietnam. Many South Vietnamese students and officials are being given specialized training in Vietnam and abroad, mainly in the United States, the Philippines, Japan and Nationalist China.

In 1956 the United States Export-Import Bank lent South Vietnam $25 million for 40 years (at an interest rate of 3 percent if repayment was made in dollars and 4 percent if made in piasters) for the purchase of merchandise and to make subscription payments to the International Monetary Fund and to the International Bank for Reconstruction and Development. In 1958, the United States Export-Import Bank made an additional loan of $25 million under the same terms for the import of equipment. In 1958 the Bank opened a credit of $3.3 million, repayable in 32 years and carrying an interest rate of 3.5 percent, for the development of a telecommunications network.

The United States Development Loan Fund has made three loans to Vietnam; one of $9.7 million to the railroad for the purchase of rolling stock; one of $17.5 million to the Saigon metropolitan area to improve the water supply; and one of $12.7 million for the construction of a power plant at Thu Duc. All are long-term loans at 3½ percent interest.

France maintains an Economic and Technical Aid Mission in South Vietnam. It is financed by French credits of over 6 billion old (predevaluation) francs, of which more than 300 million are earmarked for technical assistance. Its economic assistance has included such projects as refugee aid, technical education, financial aid to enable the government to implement its land-reform program, the purchase of transportation and industrial equipment and the rehabilitation of irrigation works. Under the technical assistance program the Mission finances training courses in engineering, agronomy and town planning, and it also sends Vietnamese civil servants and technicians to France for advanced instruction. In 1960, France lent South Vietnam 7 billion old francs, repayable in 15 years, and granted a credit of 11 billion old francs, repayable in 5 years, for the purchase of capital equipment in France. Both carried an interest rate of 3 percent.

Under an agreement concluded in 1959, Japan agreed to pay $39 million over a 5-year period as war reparations to the South Vietnamese Government. Of this amount, $37 million is being used for the construction of a power-generating station on the Da Nhim near Da Lat and the remaining $2 million for an industrial center (see ch. 20, Industry). Japan also agreed to a loan for purchasing equipment and materials for a barrage to implement the Da Nhim Project and another credit of $9.1 million for the building of a urea plant. The loan for the Da Nhim Project was for 7 years and carried an interest rate of 5.75 percent.

In 1962 West Germany extended a long-term loan of DM50 million (about US$12.5 million) for the purchase of equipment for several industrial installations and, in 1963, agreed to grant a DM15 million credit for the purchase of drugs, fertilizers and insecticides in West Germany. The credit was to be repaid in 12 years at 3 percent interest. An additional loan of DM25 million was promised to South Vietnam in August 1964.

Foreign aid also includes technical aid under the Colombo Plan and the United Nations and assistance from various United States and international welfare groups. Under the Colombo Plan, Australia and Great Britain contribute the equivalent of over $1 million a year for scholarships for higher education, and Canada has undertaken to finance the aerial survey of the lower reaches of the Mekong at a cost of $500,000 as its contribution to the proposed Mekong River project (see ch. 2, Physical Environment). The United Nations Technical Assistance Administration maintains a group of specialists in South Vietnam and also finances fellowships and scholarships in statistics. The United Nations Special Fund has contributed over a quarter of a million dollars for the investigation of mineral resources in the Central Highlands (see ch. 20, Industry). American and international religious and charitable organizations are rendering valuable services in such fields as education, public health, distribution of United States surplus foods and various relief projects. They report expenditures in South Vietnam of over $4 million annually.

Additional sources of military aid and economic assistance were sought after the fall of the Ngo Dinh Diem government. In May 1964 it was announced in Washington that the United States and South Vietnam had appealed to 25 Free World countries to start or to increase military or economic aid. The following July, General Nguyen Khanh, then prime minister, asked 34 governments for increased aid to South Vietnam. In August 1964, with the United States acting as mediator, negotiations were reported to be in progress between South Vietnam and 35 foreign governments. As a result it was alleged that commitments totaling $100 million to start new aid programs or expand existing ones, had been undertaken by Australia, Canada, Nationalist China, West Germany, Italy, Japan, South Korea, New Zealand, Iran, the Philippines, Thailand and the United Kingdom. Also seeking a step up in aid and military assistance, beginning in August 1965, Prime Minister Nguyen Cao Ky made visits to Thailand, Nationalist China and South Korea.

BALANCE OF PAYMENTS

Ever since South Vietnam became an independent nation its national accounts have been balanced by substantial grants of foreign aid (see table 8). The larger part of the deficit, which must be met by financial resources outside the country, results from the excess of imports over exports. From 1955 through 1964 the value of each year's imports was from 3 to more than 6 times the value of exports. In some years the gap is closed slightly by an increase in exports but widens again with a gap in exports and an upswing in imports. The deficit in national accounts has been further aggravated by the outflow of funds for travel, investment and government expenditures abroad.

Grants-in-aid have been almost entirely from United States official sources, but these have been supplemented by comparatively small amounts from other donors. Initially, the annual amount of the United States grants was determined by the local currency requirements of the government. In 1961, however, the United States modified its approach and began to calculate requirements on the basis of South Vietnam's balance-of-payments deficit position.

On South Vietnam's capital account the trend in the outflow of private capital was not reversed until 1959 when the government's program of inducing investment in industry began to be effective. Net capital investment showed an upswing in 1960 but fell again in 1961

Table 8. *South Vietnam's Balance of Payments, 1958-64*

[In millions of dollars]

	1958	1959	1960	1961	1962	1963	1964
Current account:							
Imports	−182.2	−217.4	−235.6	−272.6	−268.6	−307.3	−319.8
Exports	+57.4	+61.8	+88.8	+71.7	+48.7	+83.3	+48.9
Invisibles	−23.3	−13.8	−7.7	−12.4	+1.8	+9.1	+20.4
Total goods and services	−148.1	−169.4	−154.5	−213.3	−218.1	−214.9	−250.5
Grants-in-aid	+172.8	+185.4	+188.6	+163.2	+165.0	+200.3	+192.5
Total current account	+24.7	+16.0	+34.1	−50.1	−53.1	−14.6	−58.0
Capital account:							
Private	+14.6	+8.6	+9.3	+8.9	+31.4	+36.1	+20.0
Official and bank	−33.7	−24.6	−39.8	+40.4	+22.0	−22.0	+38.1
Total capital account	−19.1	−16.0	−30.5	+49.3	+53.4	+14.1	+58.1
Errors and omissions	−5.6	---------	+3.6	−0.8	+0.3	−0.5	+0.1

Source: Adapted from United States Operations Mission to Vietnam, Economic and Financial Planning Division, *Annual Statistical Bulletin*, No. 8, 1965, p. 71.

as a result of unsettled conditions. Liabilities of both the government and commercial banks were greater than assets until 1961. This change in position was almost entirely due to heavy holdings of foreign exchange generated by the United States aid program.

CHAPTER 24

PUBLIC FINANCE

The system of public finance is still in the process of evolution and at the same time is confronted with difficulties ranging from continued military strife to widespread tax evasion. Revenues are largely derived from numerous indirect taxes, a reflection of the country's French colonial background, and the pattern of expenditures demonstrates the high cost of providing ordinary government services as well as maintaining a large armed force to defend the country. Annual budgets are characteristically unbalanced, with foreign aid meeting a major portion of government expenses. The United States supports the defense budget and various other government activities and supplies additional revenues through customs and other duties paid on imports largely derived from United States aid.

BACKGROUND

Before the arrival of the French the imperial government imposed direct taxation, chiefly the poll tax and the land tax. The poll tax was assessed on all persons listed in the registry of inhabitants of each village. Land taxes varied from dynasty to dynasty, but under the Nguyen emperors the land registry of each village indicated the area and boundaries of each field, with the names of the original and present owners. The imperial government left to the villages the collection of taxes for the national exchequer, as well as those for local purposes. It was the village as a unit, not its inhabitants as individuals, that paid taxes to the national treasury. The central authority had no contact with the villages as long as they stayed within the confines of their communities. The financial outlay of the national government and, therefore, the revenue demands imposed on the country as a whole were relatively low because of the delegation of public works and most other economic responsibilities to local authorities and the obligations of local government to pay the expenses of the military contingents they were expected to provide.

The responsibilities of the central government expanded in the colonial period, increasing the need for revenue. Beginning in 1890 the French introduced the land tax, the business license tax, a head tax, excise taxes, customs duties and a variety of consumption taxes. The first direct tax on income, a gross tax on dividends and interest paid by corporations at the source, dates from 1908. By 1938 the head tax had evolved from a tax on salaries, wages and pensions and into a general income tax with progressive rates. Finally, in 1941, a special tax on agricultural, commercial and industrial profits of both unincorporated and incorporated enterprises was added.

The French administration collected taxes and managed finances and also formulated, authorized and applied budgets. Vietnam as a whole did not exist until 1949, when it became an associated state within the French Union. Before that time funds were channeled through the separate establishments for the protectorates of Tonkin and Annam and the colony of Cochin China. Detailed regulations providing comprehensive financial procedures for all French Overseas Territories had been promulgated by the French Government in 1912, and in 1962 these were still in force with only minor changes in South Vietnam.

In 1949 conventions liquidating various French-administered financial interests were signed by the two states. Although the French retained control of customs, collection of some taxes and other financial matters until 1954, other responsibilities, including that for the preparation and administration of its own budget, were assumed by Vietnam in 1949.

After 1954 the Ngo Dinh Diem government introduced two major budgetary reforms in connection with government reorganization. The first was the abolition of the three autonomous regions into which South Vietnam was administratively divided. The tax collecting and budgetary functions of the abolished regions were transferred to the national government, thereby creating a national budget. The second fiscal reform was the introduction of the National Assembly into the budgetary process, in accordance with the provisions of the Constitution (see ch. 13, The Governmental System).

Early in his second term of office President Diem announced a program of fiscal reform. A commission was set up under the secretary of state for finance which was to make recommendations for simplifying the tax system, eliminating fraud and injustice and raising revenue. Certain of the commission's recommendations were incorporated in proposals made by a joint South Vietnamese-United States committee in 1961 and were adopted by the government later in the same year in a decree which provided for increases in the main indirect taxes. Certain other recommendations were reflected in a simplification of the foreign exchange system, which was, in effect, a devaluation of the piaster (see ch. 25, Banking and Currency; ch. 23, Foreign Economic Relations).

Tax administration in South Vietnam has been handicapped by the lack of an experienced body of career revenue officers. Under the French the Vietnamese occupied only the lower positions in the administrative hierarchy, and in the confusion of the years after World War II, they had little opportunity to gain experience. The exodus of the French administrators with the advent of independence left a gap which the South Vietnamese were in no position to fill. This situation was a factor in the important use which the newly established government of the Republic made of the indirect forms of taxation, since sales and excise taxes could be collected with greater ease and efficiency than direct taxation on individual incomes and business profits. The withdrawal of French capital, which resulted in a considerable shrinking of the income tax base, also greatly increased the burden on other sources of tax revenue.

The total expenditures and revenues of the government are not published. A major omission in published budgets is the total amounts spent on United States military and economic aid, although these grants provide the greater part of the government's revenue. Domestic sources of revenue, derived mostly from customs duties and excise taxes, cover only a portion of published expenditures. The resulting deficits are, however, covered by United States aid and smaller sums received from France and a few other countries.

The part played especially by the United States and France in keeping the Republic of Vietnam financially on its feet has been the target for criticism only from the Communist-bloc countries. To the South Vietnamese, who place responsibility for World War II and the Indochina War on the foreigner, it seems only natural and fair that the deficits which these conflicts have generated should be financed from foreign sources. It was, in fact, President Diem's ability to obtain financial and other forms of assistance that gave him much of his political strength. As prime minister, Major General Nguyen Khanh sought foreign financial assistance, as has Air Vice Marshal Nguyen Cao Ky as prime minister.

THE BUDGETARY PROCESS

Before 1962 the budget of the South Vietnamese Government consisted of one document which presented a comparison of current and estimated receipts by type and made a detailed exposition of expenditures by major government agency or single department. As required by the Constitution, it was submitted by the president to the National Assembly for approval and was published at the same time. Although the National Assembly voted each chapter and title separately, the budget total was treated as a lump sum appropriation, and the president was bound only by the total amount voted, which he allocated as he saw fit for utilization by government agencies and programs.

An innovation introduced in 1962 was the creation of the Special Budget for Security to include all expenditures of the national armed forces and the supplementary forces, including paramilitary organizations such as the Civil Guard (redesignated the popular Force in

1964), thus permitting flexibility in use of funds without relaxing strict control of government expenses. In the same year the government also established the Special Budget for Economic Development to finance industrial and agricultural development projects. The fourth budget maintained by the government was the Aid Projects Budget which incorporated funds to finance joint government-United States projects and counterinsurgency programs. From 1964 these four budgets were consolidated into the single National Budget, each special budget retaining its identity as a special section within the overall budget. Although most of the government's fiscal operations are enacted within the framework of the National Budget, additional activities are carried out under a number of extrabudgetary accounts.

The budget is prepared by the Directorate General of Budget and Foreign Aid in the Office of the Prime Minister, formerly the Office of the Presidency. Before the November 1, 1963, revolution, the Directorate General compiled the budget in accordance with instructions from the Presidency. Beginning in 1964, however, the Directorate General has cooperated with the relevant civilian and military agencies in working out mutual agreement on final estimates before preparing the National Budget. In the compilation of the Civil Budget each ministry or department and each province, in consultation with the relevant technical division or divisions of the United States aid mission, prepares its consolidated budget estimate, which is forwarded to the Directorate General of Budget and Foreign Aid. After review and analysis and the holding of hearings on each estimate the Directorate General purposes the final amount of the National Budget, including the subsidy in support of the provincial budgets. The National Budget is then presented to the prime minister who discusses it with the Cabinet. After Cabinet approval the National Budget is promulgated by the National Leadership Committee with the formal sanction of the chief of state.

Procedures differ with regard to other budgets. The National Security Budget is developed in discussions between the Department of Defense and the United States Military Assistance Advisory Group (MAAG) which determines priorities and those items which the MAAG considers the most crucial to United States objectives. The United States generally finances the latter, and such items do not appear in the National Budget. That part of the National Security Budget included in the National Budget usually covers only salaries of .Vietnamese Government agency employees and the pay of the South Vietnamese armed forces and paramilitary organizations.

To compile the national Rural Reconstruction Budget, each province prepares a budget estimate in collaboration with provincial technical services, including United States advisory personnel. The estimates are forwarded to the Directorate General of Rural Reconstruction in the Ministry of War and Reconstruction. The Directorate General of Rural Reconstruction reviews and coordinates provincial estimates, clearing items with pertinent ministries, departments and United States aid officials. After clearance a document consolidating the provincial estimates is presented to the Central Rural Reconstruction Council for approval of programs and budgetary allocations. When the budget has been approved, the Directorate General of Rural Reconstruction is notified and in turn notifies each of the provinces with regard to its rural reconstruction budget.

GOVERNMENT EXPENDITURES

Budgeted government expenditures have been published for each year beginning with 1957. Meaningful analysis is, however, difficult, since extrabudgetary expenditures from various Vietnamese government accounts and by foreign donors play a large part in financing government activities. These include amounts spent by the United States and France on military and economic aid and the expenditures of certain autonomous agencies, such as the railroad administration. In addition, functions and staffs have been shifted between agencies from one fiscal year to the next and within the same fiscal year. Furthermore, funds allocated to a particular function may appear in the budgets of numerous agencies or in different parts of the budget. Funds in support of education, for instance, are itemized as expenditures of both the Ministry of Education and of agencies under the Office of the Prime Minister; they are also listed as allocations to the provinces under the aid projects budget or the Rural Reconstruction Budget.

Despite omissions the budgeted government expenditures reflect the large amounts being spent on security maintenance and territorial protection. Each year the largest portion of annual expenditure has been allocated to defense, an average of 40 percent beginning with 1958 through 1961, rising to over 50 percent in 1962, 1963 and 1964, and to 55 percent in 1965 (see table 9). This vast expansion is a result of the United States decision to increase its support of the government's efforts to overcome the Communist insurgents in South Vietnam (see ch. 26, Public Order and Safety; ch. 27, The Armed Forces).

Study of the budgeted expenditures also indicates that, despite heavy defense costs, the funds devoted to community development in rural areas, investments in sugar, textile and paper industries and land development and reform more than quadrupled between 1957 and 1965. During the same period expenditures for reconstruction, maintenance and expansion of roads, railroads, airfields, canals, ports, telecommunications and other public works have risen steadily, as have those for education and public health. Expenditures for other items have been kept to a minimum.

Table 9. Budgeted Expenditures of the Government of South Vietnam, 1959-65

[In millions of piasters [1]]

	1959	1960	1961	1962	1963	1964	1965
Chief of State, Prime Minister's Office, councils and agencies under the Prime Minister's Office [2]	885	876	616	607	127	1,605	1,184
Ministry of Information and Youth and Sports [3]	169	143	442	[4] 549	348	314	684
Ministry of Finance [5]	407	393	397	403	456	488	507
Ministry of Interior [6]	2,246	2,042	852	934	1,633	2,566	3,233
Ministry of Foreign Affairs	129	102	106	125	144	191	216
Ministry of Justice	113	112	109	110	110	125	142
Ministry of Education [7]	811	846	912	1,169	1,326	1,497	2,547
Ministry of Health, Labor and Social Welfare [8]	550	425	427	476	562	896	1,304
Ministry of Economy and Agriculture [9]	328	306	340	328	364	480	525
Ministry of Public Works [10]	1,147	1,399	1,257	1,296	1,373	1,345	1,478
General expenditures	2,494	2,772	2,768	3,080	1,784	2,070	2,460
Dissolved agencies [11]					1,273	174	
Ministry of Armed Forces [12]	5,997	5,798	8,374	[13] 12,105	[13] 14,050	19,357	25,700
Economic development				1,500	1,500	2,209	1,834
Aid projects					2,000	3,793	4,756
Total	15,276	15,214	16,600	22,682	27,050	37,110	46,570

[1] For value of the piaster, see Glossary.

[2] Before June 1965 it included the National Assembly and read "Premier's Office, Agencies under Premier's Office"; before 1964 it read "National Assembly, Presidency, Vice Presidency Agencies under Presidency."

[3] The Department of Information and Youth existed in 1957 and 1958; in 1959 it became the Department of Information, and youth affairs became the responsibility of an agency directly under the Presidency; during the 1961 fiscal year the Department of Information became a directorate general under the Presidency; in 1962 it was transferred to the newly created Department of Civic Action; between June 1965 and February 1966 it was the Department of Psychological Warfare, along with the Department of Youth in the Ministry of War and Reconstruction; in February 1966 the name was changed to the Department of Information and Open Arms.

[4] Referred to in that year as the Department of Civic Action.

[5] In June 1965, became the Department of Finance in the Ministry of Economy and Finance.

[6] In June 1965, became the Department of Interior in the Ministry of War and Reconstruction.

[7] In June 1965, became the Department of Education in the Ministry of Social and Cultural Affairs.

[8] In June 1965, became the Department of Health, Social Welfare and Labor in the Ministry of Social and Cultural Affairs.

[9] In 1962 the Department of Agriculture was incorporated with the Department of Land and Land Affairs to form a new Department of Rural Affairs; in June 1965 it became a department in the Ministry of War and Reconstruction.

[10] In June 1965, became the Department of Public Works and Communications in the Ministry of War and Reconstruction.

[11] A certain number of offices abolished subsequent to the events of Nov. 1, 1963, are grouped under the heading of Dissolved Agencies.

[12] Previously, the Department of National Defense; in June 1965, became the Department of Defense in the Ministry of War and Reconstruction.

[13] Referred to in these years as the "Special Budget for Security."

Source: Adapted from United States Operations Mission to Vietnam, Economic and Financial Planning Division, *Annual Statistical Bulletin*, No. 8, 1965, p. 48.

SOURCES OF REVENUE

Next to the United States economic assistance, the most important sources of government income have been tax revenues derived primarily from indirect taxes, customs duties and excise taxes (see table 10). The tax system was simplified as a result of fiscal reforms effective on January 1, 1962. A number of import taxes were abolished, and an "economic development and national defense surtax" was imposed on all imports in the amount of 25 piasters (for value of the piaster, see Glossary) per United States dollar of value. The customs tariff was revised for numerous items; selected categories of equipment and raw material directly contributing to development were wholly exempt from import duty, and an "austerity tax" was established on all luxuries and on commodities directly competitive with local production. Other taxes were revised or overhauled, including the business license tax, the excise tax on petroleum products (which was replaced by a consumption tax), the income tax on salaries and the tax on income from stocks and corporate shares. Before the 1962 tax reform numerous indirect taxes were the major single source of tax revenue, but after 1962 customs duties took first place.

Indirect taxes are of many types. They include a tax on all production activities from the rice harvest and the fish catch to mining and industry; on consumption of food and drink in resturants, bars and nightclubs; on the sale of petroleum, oil and lubricants; on theatricals, musicals and sports matches; and on the use of automobiles and other motor vehicles. Customs duties are charged on both imports and exports. An additional "austerity tax" is applied to a frequently revised list of imported luxuries and an "equalization tax" to similar commodities of diverse origin. Excise taxes are imposed on the sale of alcohol, beer, carbonated drinks, tobacco, cigars and cigarettes. Charges are made for the registration of legal documents and for many business documents attesting to purchase and sale. Direct taxes are imposed on all profits regardless of source; on salaries, wages, pensions and rents; on income; and on land.

The prevailing state of insecurity makes the collection of revenue from land taxes difficult. Inexperience in fiscal administration and tax evasion contribute to the difficulties of tax collection. A survey made by United States experts in 1964 showed that nonpayment of taxes varied from 5 to more than 70 percent and that, in 53 percent of the cases, the rate was higher in the urban areas than in the rural areas. It was also found that nonpayment had increased from 44 percent in 1960 to 74 percent in 1964.

Table 10. *Revenues of the Government of South Vietnam, 1959-65*

[In millions of piasters*]

Source of revenue	1959	1960	1961	1962	1963	1964	1965
Direct taxes	769	820	860	1,101	1,188	1,206	1,074
Indirect taxes	3,176	3,271	3,772	1,749	1,814	2,235	2,372
Customs duties	2,406	2,181	2,915	4,287	4,396	4,680	5,350
Excise taxes	1,447	1,478	1,655	1,379	1,345	1,620	1,860
Receipts from registration fees, government properties and stamp duties	517	600	600	635	635	850	905
Receipts from the Department of Public Works and Communications and other administrative agencies and public enterprises	527	590	633	642	730	788	1,021
Miscellaneous revenues	949	1,477	2,002	1,622	1,862	1,436	988
Contribution from United States aid	5,051	4,515	4,163	7,145	9,620	7,800	11,000
National Bank of Vietnam advances	434	282	------	1,580	5,460	16,495	22,000
Total	15,276	15,214	16,600	20,140	27,050	37,110	46,570

*For value of the piaster, see Glossary.

Source: Adapted from United States Operations Mission to Vietnam, Economic and Financial Planning Division, *Annual Statistical Bulletin*, No. 8, 1965, p. 48.

PUBLIC DEBT

The public debt, at the end of 1964, stood at 24.76 billion piasters as compared to 10.68 billion in 1960. It consisted in part of South Vietnam's inheritance of 8.33 billion piasters of the debt of the Indochinese treasury—a note issue which the National Bank assumed at its inception on January 1, 1955—and advances of 2.35 billion piasters which the Institute of Issue of the Associated States made to Vietnam prior to its achievement of full independence. The remainder consists of advances from the National Bank to cover budgetary deficits.

The foreign debt, on December 31, 1963, amounted to $153.4 million: $43.2 million represented various United States Government loans, payable in dollars at 3 percent interest with maturities ranging from 15 to 30 years; $50 million consisted of two 40-year United States Government loans repayable in piasters at 4 percent interest; $0.5 million represented a 6-year United States Government loan repayable in piasters at 6 percent interest; and $59.75 million comprised medium-term and long-term loans from France, West Germany and Japan.

France had granted a 15-year loan of 7 billion old (predevaluation) francs (for value of the franc, see Glossary) at 3 percent interest for financing the An Hoa-Nong Son electrochemical complex and a 5-year export-insurance credit line of 11 billion old francs at 3 percent interest plus 2 percent commission for financing imports of equipment and machinery for various industrial projects, including the Ha Tien cement plant. West Germany had granted two loans: DM50 million (about $12.5 million) for 17 years (also for financing the An Hoa-Nong Son complex) and DM15 million credit ($3.75 million) for 12 years at 3 percent interest for the purchase of German consumer goods. Japan had extended a 7-year $7.5 million loan at 5¾ percent interest for financing the Da Nhim Dam Project (see ch. 20, Industry).

CHAPTER 25

BANKING AND CURRENCY

Money in the form of coins has been in use in Vietnam for centuries, and except perhaps in the more remote *montagnard* villages of the highlands, most exchanges of goods and services take place through the medium of money. There is some barter in the countryside, but even the rural economy is monetized. The farmer sells for cash what rice he does not keep for home consumption, and in need he borrows against his crop. Wage labor is common in the villages, most farmers supplementing their income by seasonal employment on the farms of more prosperous neighbors and in various enterprises in nearby towns.

A banking system has existed in Vietnam since the latter part of the nineteenth century. It was, and still is, almost entirely confined to serving the business community in the urban centers. South Vietnam has a government-owned central bank, and, in addition, there are a number of privately-owned commercial banks—most of them founded during the colonial period—which are mainly engaged in serving the export-import trade. Most people keep their savings in the form of cash, gold or rice, and the popular attitude toward saving has compounded the difficulty faced by the government in accumulating sufficient capital to finance reconstruction and economic development.

BACKGROUND

Before World War II the currency was the Indochina piaster, linked directly with the French franc. The piaster, issued by the Bank of Indochina, which was owned by French private financial interests, was the first currency used in Vietnam to have nationwide acceptance and uniform value. There were a few commercial banks, largely French and Chinese, and several government organizations which provided low-interest loans. Most Vietnamese who needed to borrow, however, dealt with local moneylenders.

World War II brought about a major change in the country's monetary situation. The Vichy French authorities, who remained in control at Japanese sufferance, issued a large quantity of completely unsecured paper piasters. There was little merchandise on which to spend them, and the result was acute inflation.

The return of the French administration in 1946, after its expulsion the year before by the Japanese, found the Indochinese piaster thoroughly depreciated. Shops were bare of consumer goods, and much capital equipment had either been removed by Japanese occupation forces or destroyed by Allied bombing. In an attempt to stimulate the dislocated economy, the official value of the piaster was raised from 10 francs to 17 francs (1 franc equaled US$0.02), thus increasing its purchasing power on the French market and stimulating French imports. The position of the piaster in relation to the franc was further bolstered by the extensive military expenditure of the French Government in the country during the Indochina War and by the influx of nearly 250,000 members of the French Expeditionary Forces who spent a good part of their pay and allowances on goods and services available on the local market.

Outside the franc area, the market value of the piaster was closer to its prewar level. In Hong Kong, for example, it did not command the official rate of 21 piasters to US$1, but sold on the free market at the rate of 65 piasters to US$1. This disparity enabled financial operators to more than double their money by buying piasters with dollars on the free market and converting them into francs in Vietnam at the official rate, with the French treasury taking the loss.

Upon the attainment of self-government in 1949, the three states of former French Indochina—Vietnam, Laos and Cambodia—together with the French Government, established the Bank of Issue of the Associated States which assumed the issuing authority of the Bank of Indochina. The piasters of the Bank of Indochina were left in circulation, and a new piaster was issued at the same unrealistic rate of exchange with the franc.

The French administration did not impose control as a brake on currency manipulation until 1952. Exchange controls were followed by a devaluation of the piaster in 1953 which narrowed the gap between the official and the open-market rates. Following the Geneva Agreement in 1954 the Bank of Issue of the Associated States was formally dissolved. Its assets were divided among the three participating states to enable their new central banks to start functioning. In December 1954 the Republic of Vietnam notified France of its intention to withdraw from the franc zone, but did not formally take the step until 1959. On January 1, 1955, the South Vietnamese Government issued its own independent piaster through its newly established central bank, the National Bank. From that date, the piaster was directly supported by the United States. The new piaster, set at the official rate of US$0.02857, was exchanged at par for piasters in circulation issued by the Bank of Indochina and the Bank of Issue of the Associated States.

THE BANKING SYSTEM

The banking system consists of the National Bank, a few governmental financial institutions, 14 private commercial banks and a savings bank. The banks are concentrated in Saigon-Cho Lon and serve the business community almost exclusively. Otherwise the traditional money markets provided by the moneylender, the merchant and the prosperous farmer prevail. The authorities are seeking to extend the activities of modern banking institutions, both governmental and private.

The National Bank has most of the powers and functions usually attributed to a central bank. The scope of its authority is greater than the Bank of Indochina and the Bank of Issue of the Associated States which it replaced in January 1955. It has the exclusive right to issue notes and coins and is responsible for safeguarding the value of the currency, acting as agent of the government in foreign exchange control and advising the government on economic and financial matters. The National Bank is authorized to discount, rediscount, buy, sell, or make advances on negotiable instruments; to sell National Treasury bonds and securities for the government; to control the formation of new banks and changes in banking establishments; and to exercise supervision over commercial banks. Credit controls are exercised by establishing the reserve requirements of the commercial banks and the rediscount rates and by limiting the volume of certain types of loans.

The National Bank has a legal reserve requirement of 33 percent against its outstanding note issue. In December 1964 reserves in the form of gold, United States dollars and French francs had sunk to $141 million from a high of $216 million in 1960. Currency in circulation, on the other hand, had risen steadily from 6.78 billion piasters (for value of piasters see Glossary) in 1955 to 19 billion piasters by the end of December 1964, an amount substantially in excess of the legal limit.

Under regulations effective in 1964 commercial banks were required to maintain on deposit with the National Bank reserves of 10 percent of the amount of their deposit liabilities. As a measure of credit control, this requirement may be raised as high as 35 percent. In general, the commercial banks keep more on deposit with the National Bank than the required reserves.

The National Bank is concerned, not only with monetary control, but with the general development of the banking sector of the community. In December 1956 it entered the field of commercial banking through the establishment of the Commercial Credit Bank of Vietnam. Initially a deposit bank dealing in short-term transactions, it was authorized in July 1958 to deal in long- and medium-term credit.

By mid-1962 the Commercial Credit Bank was one of the largest in the country in volume of business.

Two institutions, the National Agricultural Credit Office and the Industrial Development Center, have been established by the government to serve credit needs which the private banks have been reluctant or unable to meet. The National Agricultural Credit Office was created by presidential decree in April 1957 as an autonomous public institution. It took over the assets and liabilities of certain other agencies, principally the Popular Agricultural Credit and the National Company for Agricultural Credit, Artisans and Cooperatives. By the end of December 1964 it had one interprovincial agency, 40 provincial agencies, 17 interdistrict agencies and 34 agencies at district level. The National Agricultural Credit Office is capitalized at 895 million piasters, of which 628 million piasters were allocated from United States aid funds, the remainder from the national budget (see ch. 19, Agriculture; ch. 20, Industry).

The National Agricultural Credit Office grants small loans to farmers. Short-term loans for annual crop production are from 6 to 18 months, medium-term loans from 18 months to 5 years and long-term loans from 5 to 15 years for capital invested by cooperatives, plantation owners and well-established farmers. Interest rates charged are 1 percent per month for short-term loans, 8 percent year year for medium-term loans and 6 percent per year for long-term loans. Legally established cooperatives are charged 5 percent per year, and farmers' associations at district level are charged 9 percent. By the end of December 1964 the National Agricultural Credit Office loans had totaled 4,976.6 million piasters, of which 4,235.7 million had been short-term loans to farmers. Aid to rubber planters, a project also controlled by the National Agricultural Credit Office but terminated in 1961, amounted to 315.8 million piasters loaned to 26 Vietnamese and 10 French planters (see ch. 19, Agriculture).

In June 1964 the Pacification Fund was created within the National Agricultural Credit Office with a capital of 300 million piasters granted from the national budget. Loans under this program were intended to support animal husbandry, fisheries and the use of fertilizer. On December 18, 1964, 92 million piasters were withdrawn from this fund to establish a special fund exclusively for the relief of flood victims in 12 provinces in the Central Highlands and Central Lowlands. Loans from the Pacification Fund were issued under simplified procedures, and loans in kind for chemical fertilizers were free of interest. Under the flood-relief program, farmers and fishermen were specifically stated to be eligible and loans also bore no interest. At the end of 1964, Pacification Fund loans amounted to 117.1 million piasters.

The Industrial Development Center was established in 1957 as an autonomous government agency. It replaced the National Investment Fund which had been created in 1955 to provide financial assistance for small industries and for the development of new industries in cooperation with private industrial capital. The National Investment Fund, however, had been endowed solely with local currency and had received no support from United States aid. It thus lacked a source of foreign funds to purchase capital goods and equipment. The Industrial Development Center, on the other hand, was given an initial grant of $6 million from the United States in addition to 100 million piasters from the Vietnamese Government (see ch. 23, Foreign Economic Relations). All loans require the approval of its board of directors. Loans are for 7 or 8 years, and interest rates are generally 6.5 to 8 percent per year. From inception to the end of 1964 the Industrial Development Center expended 1.4 million piasters of which 38 percent was equity investment. During this period it assisted or established 718 industrial establishments (see ch. 20, Industry).

At some time in the future the loan functions of the Industrial Development Center will be largely taken over by a new investment bank, the Financial Company for the Development of Industry in Vietnam (Société Financière pour le Développement de l'Industrie and Viet-Nam—SOFIDIV). Half of the initial capital of 400 million piasters is being subscribed by 10 local commercial banks— Vietnamese, French, British and Chinese. The remainder is to to be made available by the United States Agency for International Development (AID). SOFIDIV's objectives, broader than those of the Industrial Development Center, will be to encourage private enterprise, foreign investment and the creation of new industries through offering long-term loans and direct financial participation. The SOFIDIV will administer the newly created Vietnam American Private Enterprise Development Fund, which will be maintained by government repayments in piasters of United States Mutual Security Loans which have come to maturity.

Fourteen commercial banks were in operation at the end of 1965: Viet-Nam Thuong-Tin (Commercial Credit Bank of Vietnam), Viet-Nam Ngan-Hang (Bank of Vietnam), Tin-Nghia Ngan-Hang (Trust and Loyalty Bank), Viet-Nam Cong-Thuong Ngan-Hang (Commercial and Industrial Bank of Vietnam), Banque Française de l'Asie (French Bank of Asia), Banque Nationale pour le Commerce et l'Industrie (National Bank for Commerce and Industry), Banque Franco-Chinoise pour le Commerce et l'Industrie (French-Chinese Bank for Commerce and Industry), The Chartered Bank, The Hong Kong and Shanghai Banking Corporation, Bank of China, Bank of Communications, Bank of East-Asia, The Bangkok Bank, Ltd., and the Bank of Tokyo, Ltd. Ten of them are branches of foreign banks—French, British, Nationalist Chinese, Japanese and Thai. Leading banks in the United States have correspondent relations with some of them, and two United States banks—the Bank of America and Chase Manhattan—have filed applications with the government to open branches. In addition to the government-owned Commercial Credit Bank of Vietnam, there are three other South Vietnamese-owned banks—the Bank of Vietnam, the Commercial and Industrial Bank of Vietnam and the Trust and Loyalty Bank. The 14 banks operate 36 offices, 27 in Saigon-Cho Lon and 9 in the provinces. The Commercial Credit Bank of Vietnam has branches in Can Tho, Long Xuyen, Ba Xuyen, Rach Giá, Phan Thiet, Nha Trang, and Da Nang; the Commercial and Industrial Bank of Vietnam at Da Nang; and the French-Chinese Bank for Commerce and Industry at Khanh Hung.

The country's only savings bank is the Savings Bank of Saigon, founded in 1887. It is governed by a board of administrators, the chairman of which is prefect of Saigon. The board is formally subject to the control of the treasurer general of Vietnam. The minimum savings deposit is 10 piasters and the rate of interest is fixed at 1.5 percent a year. In December 1964 deposits totaled 166.5 million piasters, almost 2 million piasters more than in 1960.

OTHER CREDIT INSTITUTIONS

There are a number of other credit institutions in South Vietnam outside of the formal banking system. In December 1955 the government abolished all private pawnshops, which charged very high rates of interest, and replaced them with a greatly expanded system of pawnshops of its own.

The major source of credit in terms of number of borrowers, however, remains the private moneylenders. People continue to turn to the moneylender, notwithstanding his often usurious charges, both because he is a familiar figure and because his services can be had without the red tape connected with the government institutions.

Mutual aid societies are also of some importance. The most common type is the *giap*, a term once applied to an administrative subdivision of the village but now signifying an association of men or women who have banded together for financial self-help. The organization's funds and other assets come from the contributions and bequests of its members. In addition to its insurance and benevolent functions, the *giap* is a vehicle for ceremonial and social activity.

Another type of association, the *ho* ("family" and, by extension, "cooperation" or "mutual association"), is often formed by women and combines speculation with mutual assistance. There are various types of *ho*. The *ho hieu*, or filial piety associations, are somewhat like burial insurance societies in the United States. Other *ho* help the peasant with the purchase of seed and agricultural implements.

Another form of mutual aid society is the *bang* of the Chinese community. A charitable and mutual aid association for its established members, the *bang* also provides the newly arrived Chinese with food and shelter until he finds employment, lends him money and gives him advice. The Vietnamese authorities have found it a convenient channel through which to deal with local Chinese groups.

CURRENCY AND FOREIGN EXCHANGE

The Vietnamese piaster (called *dong* in Vietnamese, but referred to as piaster in all other languages) consists of 100 Vietnamese cents, but inflation in recent years has driven coins out of circulation. The piaster circulates in the form of notes printed by the Security Banknote Company of the United States in denominations of 1, 2, 5, 10, 20, 50, 100, 200, and 500 and 1-piaster coins made of an alloy of copper and nickel.

The money supply increased from 6.78 billion piasters in 1955 to 23.7 billion early in 1964. It rose steadily in subsequent months to 28.6 billion piasters in August, the sharp rise resulting from a 2 billion piaster increase in the note issue during that month. By the end of 1964 the money supply had fallen to 27.4 billion piasters as notes were withdrawn from circulation.

The official exchange rate, established in May 1953, is 35 piasters to US$1. The exchange system was modified in January 1962, and a new rate was established which, in effect, devalued the piaster. Technically, the official rate continued to stand, but a premium of 25 piasters to US$1 on purchases of foreign exchange and a tax of 25 piasters to US$1 on piaster sales introduced an effective rate of 60 piasters to US$1. The rate was made applicable to all trade transactions and certain transfers of funds. As established in 1953, a controlled rate of 73.5 piasters to US$1 applied to other specified transfers of funds.

The highly complex and variable structure of administered multiple exchange rates remained unchanged. The rates varied from commodity to commodity and also by category of importer. Certain preferred capital goods imported on government account were accorded the official rate, and other commodities, including luxuries, were imported by private persons at much higher rates. The free market rate in Hong Kong ranged, during 1964, from 130 to 180 piasters to US$1, in comparison with a range between 80 to 105 piasters to US$1 in 1961.

In August 1965 the United States military and civilian personnel were no longer paid in United States dollars but in Military Payment Certificates (MPC) or "scrip." MPC could be used by United States personnel only to purchase goods in United States Army canteens, clubs, or commissaries in Vietnam or to purchase piasters through United States disbursing officers at the rate of 118 piasters to US$1.

SECTION IV. NATIONAL SECURITY

CHAPTER 26

PUBLIC ORDER AND SAFETY

Since the emergence of the Republic of Vietnam as a state in 1955 the Communist campaign against it has greatly magnified and aggravated the problems of public order and safety. The growth of the internal Viet Cong into an aggressive military force brought new problems associated with an expanding war effort. The large increase in military support facilities and installations created more targets for the Viet Cong.

At the same time the influx of refugees as well as bona fide jobseekers into the principal towns and cities produced conditions which caused sharp rises in the ordinary crime and vice rates. In addition, the greatly inflated economy, primed by the inpouring of foreign aid and personnel, encouraged the appearance of speculators, hoarders, black-marketeers, tax evaders and other war profiteers. To counteract the actions of these undesirable elements, a Special Court was activated by special decree in early 1966 to deal specifically with these crimes.

By 1966 the Viet Cong controlled or moved freely over large areas of the country, and other members of their organization operated clandestinely in the principal towns and cities. In addition to organized armed action, they used terrorist tactics involving assassination, sabotage, kidnaping, robbery, arson, intimidation and blackmail.

The role of maintaining public order and safety assigned to the principal enforcement agencies (National Police, Regional Forces and Popular Forces) continued to be an increasingly important one, and, with extended United States aid, they developed and enlarged counterinsurgency programs to complement those of the military (see ch. 27, The Armed Forces).

Although the operations of the public order and safety forces bear some resemblance to military operations in their execution and purpose, they have retained their basic defensive concept of providing protection and service to the country and its people. The law enforcement agencies attack by force only in a very restricted sense and in special situations.

THE POLICE SYSTEM

Development

At the beginning of World War II large cities, such as Saigon, had municipal police departments administered by the mayor for the municipal council. The National Security Police, modeled after the French Sûreté Nationale, were responsible for maintaining public order in the outlying areas. Ordinary police functions were performed by men recruited from the local population. They had their own officers, but these were closely supervised by their French superiors. The development of uniform police procedures was hindered by frequent changes of the French supervisors who were transferred to other foreign stations or to France after a short tour of duty.

When the Japanese in 1941 occupied the southern part of what is now South Vietnam (then called Cochin China), they permitted the old French police organization to continue to function under the Vichy French administration. After the fall of Vichy France in 1945, a short-lived nationalist regime was established under the former emperor, Bao Dai, who retained the existing police organizations. This regime was tolerated by the Japanese, but as Japan's position in the area deteriorated, Communist Viet Minh (see Glossary) forces in the North, led by Ho Chi Minh, increasingly took control. In August 1945, Bao Dai abdicated in favor of a Viet Minh government. In September the British, who, at the Potsdam Conference in July of 1945, had been designated to accept the Japanese surrender in the southern portion of the country, arrived in the area and exercised police powers until the French Expeditionary Force arrived a short time later (see ch. 3, Historical Setting).

This turbulent period, with its successive changes in the application of law enforcement authority, was accompanied by much disorder. Many records, including criminal files, were lost or destroyed. Moreover, Communists infiltrated into many key positions in government agencies, including the military and the police.

Reinstalled in Vietnam, the French were confronted with a widespread and growing sentiment for independence and an active Communist movement which knew how to exploit it. French efforts to impose strict controls, especially in the urban centers, contributed to the intensity of the rising nationalist sentiment. The Communists consolidated their control in the North in 1946, and in 1949, when France recognized Vietnam's independence within the French Union, ex-Emperor Bao Dai returned from voluntary exile in France to assume office as Chief of State.

Some police powers were acquired by the Bao Dai government, but these proved to be more nominal than real. For one thing, the French continued to maintain a police apparatus of their own. For another, many Vietnamese, though potentially capable, lacked experience in responsible positions; others were unsuited for their jobs. Criminal and subversive elements took advantage of the opportunities which the situation provided.

By June 1954, when the Indochina War ended with the establishment of a military Demarcation Line which had the effect of partitioning the country, the police had ceased to be effective, even in the cities, and the villages were virtually controlled by the Viet Minh forces. In Saigon, control of both the Municipal Police and the Security Police had been turned over by Bao Dai to the Binh Xuyen, a political and racketeering organization which had agreed to carry out police functions in return for a monopoly on gambling, opium traffic and prostitution in the metropolitan areas. The group also collected fees for visas, licenses and permits of various kinds. It also profited from the control of imports and the sale of rice, fish and pork.

Two strong politicoreligious sects, the Cao Dai and the Hoa Hao, controlled large areas of the countryside, maintaining their own police and security forces. The Cao Dai operated in Tay Ninh and neighboring provinces north and northwest of Saigon; the Hoa Hao was dominant in the provinces southwest of Saigon. Both of these groups are so-called reformed Buddhist movements (see ch. 11, Religion).

By the summer of 1954 the Binh Xuyen organization, supported by the French and Bao Dai, then in Paris, threatened to take control of all government functions. The state of public order deteriorated further, particularly in Saigon where there was a concentration of the agents, sympathizers and hangers-on of the contending groups—all of them hostile to government efforts to make its police powers effective. Another source of tension was the presence of the French Expeditionary Force with its European, Indian, Algerian, Moroccan and other African troops.

In June 1954, Bao Dai appointed Ngo Dinh Diem as prime minister, vesting him with full military and police powers. The new prime minister set about to win the loyalty of certain army battalions and of the Cao Dai and Hoa Hao leaders and troops, and in this he achieved some success. A few leaders of the sects and of the Binh Xuyen, however, were uncooperative. Prime Minister Diem's position was strengthened when he was elected president in October 1955, replacing Bao Dai as Chief of State of South Vietnam, which he proclaimed a republic.

By April 1956 the Binh Xuyen had been defeated as an organized armed insurgent force, and dissident remnants of the Cao Dai and Hoa Hao were also crushed or forced into exile. These victories, followed in mid-1956 by the trial and execution of the Hoa Hao leader, Ba Cut, helped to restore considerable confidence in the effectiveness of the government's police and other law enforcement agencies. Meanwhile, arrangements were made to acquire the services of a police advisory group from Michigan State University to replace the French advisers, whose contracts were due to expire in 1956. In 1959 this group was replaced by personnel operating under the Public Safety Division of the United States Agency for International Development as part of the United States Operations Mission (USOM).

Organization

From the time of its establishment as an independent state until June 27, 1962, when President Diem signed a decree integrating all the then-existing police agencies into a single national police organization, South Vietnam depended upon a multiplicity of law enforcement groups with overlapping responsibilities. Before 1962 ordinary police functions had been performed mainly by the National Security Police, the Municipal Police and a paramilitary group known as the Civil Guard. All three forces were under the Secretary of State for Interior until 1960 when the Civil Guard was transferred to the Department of National Defense. Along with its transfer went a change to a strict military posture. The National Security Police and the Municipal Police were responsible to the Director General of Police and Security Services who reported to the Department of Interior. In addition, there was a directorate of police and security in each of the headquarters of the three regions into which the country had been divided. Each province also had a local chief of police and a security service. All the larger cities, such as Saigon, Hue, Da Lat and Da Nang, had municipal police forces.

With the signing of the integrating decree in 1962, all of these various law enforcement units were consolidated into a single police agency, called the Directorate General of National Police, under the direction of the Director General of National Police, responsible directly to the Department of Interior. As of early 1966 the Directorate General was composed of the headquarters proper, six regional directorates and a municipal directorate which included the police within the Saigon metropolitan area and the surrounding province of Gia Dinh. The regional directorates' headquarters were located at Hue, Nha Trang, Ban Me Thuot, Bien Hoa, My Tho and Can Tho. They were charged with the supervision of the police units located within the provinces making up the region, as well as the municipal police forces in the larger towns such as Hue, Da Nang, Nha Trang, Cam Ranh, Da Lat and Vung Tau. Each province had a police chief who was responsible for the police activities within his province and also supervised the police organized in the various districts of the province.

The strength of public order and safety forces has increased substantially since 1963, when the National Police numbered 21,000, keeping pace with the general increase of insurgency within the country. In early 1966 the National Police totaled about 52,000, and plans were in existence to increase this total to about 72,000. Of the 52,000 total, about 6,000 were allocated to the Directorate General proper, and approximately 14,000 were assigned to the Saigon Municipal Directorate. The six regional directorates varied in strength from about 3,000 to 7,000, depending on the number of provinces and of large population centers located within each.

Responsibilities

Directorate General

The headquarters of the Director General of National Police is located in Saigon, where he maintains a staff consisting of a deputy director and four assistant directors, one each for administration, intelligence, telecommunications and operations. Operating also at the assistant director level are the chiefs of the two major police counterinsurgency organizations, the National Police Field Forces and the Resources Control Service. Directly under control of the Director General is the Internal Activities Division, which deals with headquarters security, public information and inspections. It also contains the Internal Affairs Branch, which investigates alleged irregularities and complaints within the entire police organization.

The Assistant Director for Administration is responsible for general supervision and administrative control over personnel services, logistic support services, fiscal affairs, training, a crime laboratory and the identification and record service, which furnishes technical and scientific support for crime detection throughout the country. The Assistant Director for Intelligence is generally concerned with affairs relating to national security, including counterintelligence and countersubversive activities. The Assistant Director for Telecommunciations supervises the countrywide communications service provided for the National Police and conducts a cryptographic bureau to fulfill police requirements. National Police communications are operated independently, but they are an integral part of the Combined Security Telecommunication Directorate which provides, operates and maintains facilities, systems and services for various government civil security agencies.

The Assistant Director for Operations is responsible for the supervision of the activities of the Judicial Police, Administrative Police, Rehabilitation Service, Immigration Service, Uniform and Traffic Police Service and Order Police.

The Judicial Police is the investigative arm of the National Police. Under Vietnamese law, investigation privileges are not given to all police, but to a limited number who conduct thorough and detailed investigations of criminal offenses and prepare cases for trial.

The Administrative Police perform functions derived from French practice, only a few of which are found in the American police system. These functions include assisting in the supervision of price regulations, the issuance of passports, visas, identity cards, radio licenses and weapons permits. They also make clearance checks on applicants for government positions.

The Rehabilitation Service is a relatively small group which is concerned only with those police matters relating to the incarceration of prisoners while in the custody of the National Police. The prison system is the primary responsibility of a separate Rehabilitation Directorate under the Department of Interior which assumes full control of prisoners who have been turned over to them to await trial or have been convicted and sentenced.

The Immigration Service of the National Police is responsible for all exit and entry matters, including those dealing with residence permits. It is also charged with the maintenance of supervisory control of foreigners for the purpose of extending or revoking resident permits as may be necessary.

The Uniform and Traffic Police Service deals exclusively with those problems relating to the uniformed municipal police. It assists in all matters involved in basic law enforcement, such as traffic control, patrolling, guarding of public property, investigation of ordinary crimes and the enforcement of local ordinances.

The Order Police, formerly known as Combat Police, represent a centrally controlled force whose various elements are strategically located throughout the country. They number about 500 and are organized and lightly equipped along military lines. Their primary mission is to assist in the quelling of riots and civil disturbances, but they are also used in protecting visiting dignitaries, reinforcing municipal police and assisting in large-scale search and security activities and the exploitation of intelligence collected by other elements of the National Police.

The National Police Field Forces represent a relatively new and major police advancement in counterinsurgency work. This quasimilitary group was organized in 1962 as part of the Combat Police to help cope with the growing police problems brought on by the intensification of the Communist insurgency. Reorganized and separated from the Combat Police in 1965, these forces are planned to have an eventual strength of about 15,000. The mission of the National Police Field Forces is similar to that of the Order Police, but, in addition, they help local authorities consolidate government control in areas cleared of Viet Cong by regular army troops. These company-sized units are assigned to a province with the mission of detaching roving elements to various cleared villages for a temporary period of time to assist the rural police in firmly reorganizing the security of the villages and reestablishing law and order. In early 1966 six companies of the Field Forces had completed training and were employed in the field.

The second major police effort in the field of counterinsurgency, the Resources Control Program, also was initiated in 1962. It was created as a defensive security measure to regulate the movement of people and goods and thereby restrict the flow of information and supplies to the Viet Cong. This system of controls has operated with considerable success in the Saigon and northern Mekong Delta areas, and appropriate elements of the system are being expanded throughout the country, consistent with the availability of police resources. The general program is based on several contributory programs—the National Identity Card Program, the Family Census Program, the National Checkpoint Program and the Police River Control Program. Each of these subprograms is centrally controlled, but operations are decentralized to the greatest practicable extent.

The National Identity Card Program consists of issuing identification cards to each of the nearly 8 million persons in the country who are 18 years of age and over. Printed on specially prepared paper for protective purposes, the card is laminated in plastic under heat and pressure and contains a photograph, two fingerprints and a physical description of the individual to whom it is issued. By early 1966 nearly 7½ million of these cards had been issued.

The Family Census Program was initiated in 1963 as an independent security measure and incorporated into the Resources Control Program approximately 1 year later. This subprogram consists of registering in a family booklet all pertinent data relative to all members of a particular family. A group photograph of the entire family is also included. Mobile processing teams have been utilized in this project, and over 1.5 million families had been registered through 1965.

As of early spring 1966 the National Checkpoint and the River Control Programs operated from a series of mobile and fixed control points strategically placed on land and in the offshore waters surrounding the major port and transshipment areas. Along extensive waterways a system of mother ships was employed, the ships serving as base points and extending the range of the smaller assigned patrol craft.

In carrying out their normal police duties, all elements of the National Police work in close cooperation with other governmental agencies which have limited police powers. One of the most important of these is the Directorate of Customs Service, which is part of the Ministry of Finance. This Directorate is responsible for smuggling and narcotics control, registration and inspection of commercial shipping, and border control. All of these responsibilities are closely allied with the mission of the National Police in the overall national effort to maintain security and public order.

Regional Directorates

Each of the six regional directorates operates a scaled-down version of the headquarters of the Directorate General which furnishes supporting services and supervises police activities in the provinces within the region. It is headed by a Director who is assisted by a Deputy Director, a Chief for Administration, a Chief of Uniform Police and a Chief of Special Police. The Chief for Administration is responsible for personnel, supply, training, and document and laboratory services. The Chief of Uniform Police is responsible for judicial, traffic immigration, order and security police functions. The Special Police department concerns itself primarily with counterintelligence, countersubversive and counterinsurgency problems.

Saigon Municipal Directorate

The Saigon Municipal Directorate is the largest within the police system and performs the most varied and complex functions. Essentially, it serves in the role of a large reinforced Municipal Police department for the metropolitan area of Saigon, while at the same time discharging the many special tasks assigned to it as the principal operating arm of the Directorate General. It is organized into a headquarters, eight precincts, the Harbor Police, the Airport Police, the Traffic Police and the Gia Dinh provincial police. The normal uniformed Saigon city police force numbers about 10,000 and is charged with the maintenance of law and order within its eight precincts. Heavy emphasis is placed on antiterrorist security measures and control of black-market operations, vice and crimes of violence.

The Harbor Police are engaged in general law enforcement, and criminal investigation in the port area, performing passport checks on arriving ships, issuing passes for port workers and conducting security patrol of the Saigon railroad station and port installations. They also participate in the Resources Control Program with their harbor craft, concentrating on the control of the movement of contraband goods. The Airport Police, relatively small in number, have the primary duty of operating the civilian security controls at Tan Son Nhut international airport just outside Saigon.

Traffic of all types in the Saigon area multiplied manyfold in 1965 with the expansion of port and governmental activities, and slightly more than 700 Traffic Police are now assigned to cope with it. Like the Harbor Police they collaborate in the Resources Control Program and have contributed considerably to the success of that work. The police of Gia Dinh Province are utilized to a great extent in maintaining a general security belt around the Saigon area and its expanding environs.

416

Training

The general rapid expansion of the National Police has been accompanied by the development of an appreciable number of comprehensive training programs with the assistance of United States advisers. In 1966 these programs included courses in basic police work, command and leadership techniques, firearms and such technical subjects as photography, fingerprint classification, riot control procedures, communications, countersubversion and counterinsurgency. The principal training centers, including the National Police College, are situated in and around Saigon, Da Lat and Vung Tau, and each regional directorate operates a police school at its headquarters location. In early 1966 the total trainee capacity of the system was slightly greater than 5,000, and the annual output exceeded 20,000. More than 80,000 police officers and Regional Force personnel have been trained under these programs. All police recruits attend a standard 12-week basic course before being assigned to duty.

Improvements in training have been accompanied by equal advancement in the equipment furnished to the National Police. By the end of 1965, weapons types in use had been reduced in number from 36 to 7; weapons maintenance and repair services had been modernized; and an up-to-date system of storage and distribution had been put into effect. The reduction in the variety of weapons also simplified the stocking of ammunition and spare parts. Similar improvements were also made in the fields of transportation and specialized police equipment.

The National Police have a complicated rank and grade structure which reflects a primary division between the three functional categories: command, administration and operations. It is patterned basically after the French system and has two definite groups which can be compared to officers and enlisted men. The titles of rank are also a French heritage, but the great amount of United States assistance provided by the USOM Public Safety Division has introduced American equivalents, which are gaining in use.

Because of their national character and the nature of their work, the police are a visible symbol of the government and are in a position to influence public attitudes to an appreciable degree. This factor has been weighted heavily in the development of police counterinsurgency programs since 1963. Training programs also stress the "public servant" image of the police and have the goal of continually improving the "people-oriented" character of the police through increased efficiency and competence.

ROLE OF THE ARMY AND PARAMILITARY UNITS

In the years immediately following the end of the Indochina War in 1954, the Communist insurgents deliberately left behind in South

Vietnam were relatively weak and only sporadically active. The government, during this period, continued to utilize the National Gendarmerie that had been inherited from the French and organized two additional paramilitary groups, the Regional Force and the Popular Force, for the primary purpose of relieving army units of internal security duties. With the substantial increase in Communist insurgency after 1963, these paramilitary groups, except for the National Gendarmerie, were reorganized, modernized and strengthened in order to meet the growing Viet Cong threat.

Gendarmerie

The Gendarmerie was established by the French as a relatively small, uniformed, well-trained police organization, charged with civilian as well as military investigative functions. It was equipped by the army and operated throughout the country as an agency of the Department of Defense. Apparently because its highly specialized functions could be performed equally well within other existing organizations, the Gendarmerie was disestablished on January 1, 1965, 900 of its approximate 1,200 personnel being absorbed by the National Police and the remaining 300 being assigned to the Military Police.

Regional Force

The Regional Force is a national paramilitary group organized to provide internal security at the province level. Activated in 1955 under the Department of Interior, as the Civil Guard, it was transferred to the Department of Defense in 1960 and redesignated in 1964. Since that time it has grown in strength from 80,000 to about 119,000 men. It is a uniformed, lightly armed force, centrally administered by national and regional headquarters, but normally under operational control of the province chief. When employed jointly with units of the regular armed forces, however, it comes under operational control of the military commander.

Although organized into squads, platoons, companies and battalions, the company is the basic combat unit employed in offensive security operations. Included in its overall counterinsurgency mission is the collection of information, participation in civic action programs and the futherance of confidence of the rural population in the central government.

Popular Force

Similar in general purpose to the Regional Force, but operating at the village and hamlet level, the Popular Force is a more static village defense organization. Recruited in villages, the men in this force are not uniformed and are less well armed. They are organized into squads, platoons and companies, with the squad the basic unit used for employment, usually in local offensive and counterattack roles. Operational control is exercised through sector and subsector headquarters. As in the case of Regional Force, units of the Popular Force come under the operational control of the military commander when employed jointly with units of the regular armed forces.

The Popular Force is an outgrowth of the Self-Defense Corps which was created in 1956 as an adjunct to the regular security forces. In 1964 it had a strength of about 90,000; at that time it was combined with other local defense organizations, and by early 1966 it had grown to a strength of approximately 140,000. It receives extensive assistance from the United States Military Assistance Command Vietnam (MACV).

CRIMINAL COURTS AND PROCEDURES

Courts

Persons accused of criminal offenses generally are tried in one of three types of courts, depending on the nature and seriousness of the charge: a Court of First Instance, a Court of the Peace with Extended Jurisdiction or a Court of the Peace. There are also special military tribunals which have jurisdiction not only over military offenders but also over apprehended Communists and all persons regarded as a threat to national security. Also, in February 1966, the government activated a Special Court for the duration of the war to deal with crimes relating to war profiteering and corruption. Seated in Saigon, this court has territorial jurisdiction throughout the country and is empowered to try both civilian and military personnel. It is composed of a presiding judge, two assistant judges, a prosecutor and one or more assistant prosecutors. It may impose sentences ranging from imprisonment to the death penalty (see ch. 13, The Governmental System; ch. 27, The Armed Forces).

There are seven Courts of First Instance in South Vietnam, and they sit in Saigon, My Tho, Vinh Long, Bien Hoa, Hue, Da Nang and Nha Trang. Courts of First Instance have jurisdiction over civil, commercial and criminal cases, including felonies and misdemeanors. They are also authorized to rehear cases previously tried in a Court of the Peace with Extended Jurisdiction or in an ordinary Court of the Peace. A Court of First Instance is composed of a presiding judge, at least three assistant judges and an examining magistrate. The examining magistrate makes preliminary investigations and prepares the evidence for presentation by the prosecutor at the trial. A prosecuting attorney—not a member of the court—represents the state in pressing the charges against the accused. The prosecuting attorney or his deputy must be present at all sessions trying a criminal or civil case. In criminal cases he is responsible for carrying out the court's decisions.

There are 20 Courts of the Peace with Extended Jurisdiction. Each of these appears to exercise judicial control over the Courts of the Peace within a specific territory. The Courts of the Peace with Extended Jurisdiction have jurisdiction over civil and commercial cases, including labor disputes and litigation over work accidents, and also over felonies and misdemeanors. The latter jurisdiction, however, seems to overlap with that of the Courts of the First Instance. In practice, the Courts of the Peace with Extended Jurisdiction appear to hear misdemeanor cases and cases involving the less serious felonies, while serious criminal cases of national or regional interest are normally placed before a Court of the First Instance.

A Court of the Peace with Extended Jurisdiction is ordinarily composed of one magistrate who functions in the triple capacities of presiding judge, examining magistrate and prosecuting attorney. He is assisted by a court clerk. For criminal cases two assistant judges from a Court of First Instance or two justices of the peace may be added.

Courts of the Peace, each consisting of a justice of the peace and a court clerk, are the lowest courts in the judicial system. Besides trying minor civil cases and cases involving petty penal offenses, they are authorized to conciliate disputes brought before them by local citizens. When a misdemeanor or a felony comes to his attention, the justice of the peace makes a preliminary inquiry into the case and forwards his report, together with the complaints, charges and other data pertaining to the case, to the prosecuting attorney of the Court of First Instance or to the magistrate of the Court of the Peace with Extended Jurisdiction, depending upon which has competence. Appeals to decisions rendered by a justice of the peace in a Court of the Peace are heard by the court having jurisdiction over him.

Criminal Laws

The legal code consists of a body of decrees, legislation and court rulings, some of which date from the colonial period. Juridical concepts and practice combine indigenous Vietnamese, traditional Chinese and French elements. In the absence of a uniform code of criminal law, judges, particularly those in the lowest courts, often mete out sentences which vary greatly for the same offense and which reflect nonlegal considerations, such as the social status or national or ethnic origin of the offender.

Formerly even those convicted of serious crimes could pay a fine in lieu of other punishment, and, since the law tended to be moralizing and general rather than prescriptive and specific and the discretionary powers of magistrates were great, it was often difficult to distinguish a fine from a bribe. This tradition has been discountenanced in modern times, but the attitudes associated with it have proved to be persistent, and charges of venality in the court system are common. A complete review of legal codes and procedures was undertaken in late 1955. In 1958 the Department of Justice published the Reformed Rural Code, the Civil Procedure and the Explanatory Background of the Civil Law. By early 1966, however, a uniform body of criminal law apparently still had not been adopted, although study reportedly was begun in 1962.

The organization of the courts suggests that four general categories of criminal offenses are recognized: petty offenses, misdemeanors, felonies and crimes against the state. Important legislation passed by the National Assembly in 1959 fixed penalties for various crimes against the state, such as sabotage, loss or damage of public property and assassination of public officials. To try persons charged with offenses which had been defined by these laws, special military tribunals were created. There is no press coverage of such trials, and it appears that they are often held in secret.

Rural Justice

In the villages of the lowlands and in the mountain regions many disputes and petty offenses are dealt with informally by family heads and local leaders. Under existing conditions such customary proceedings seem to have at least the tacit approval of the authorities, although they are not entered in the records of the formal court system.

Lowland Village Justice

In the lowland villages the district chiefs have limited judicial powers. When using their authority to gather evidence and to bring offenders to court, they function as assistants to the prosecuting attorney. They are not authorized to hold trials of any kind, but they may arrest anyone caught in a criminal act, interrogate witnesses and prepare an official statement for the prosecuting attorney. When a serious crime has been committed, the district chief makes a personal investigation on the scene and informs the prosecuting attorney of the facts. Where public safety or morals are involved, the provincial governor must also be informed. Village chiefs are authorized to mediate disputes between villagers, but criminal offenders are customarily turned over to the police for investigation to determine what further action is to be taken.

Most disputes in lowland villages are settled informally by hamlet chiefs or village councils. Differences between members of the same family are probably most often settled within the family to avoid the disgrace attached to airing family troubles in public. Angry villagers seeking a settlement of their differences commonly take their cases first to the heads of the families involved or to the hamlet chief. If settlement cannot be agreed upon, they then may go to the village council, which serves as an informal court for petty offenses or minor litigations.

The limited information available indicates that most complaints or infractions arise from quarrels within or between families, disputes over property ownership or damage, defaults in debts or services, altercations over the use of land or irrigation water, jealousy and marital infidelity.

The informal judicial role of the village council is an important means of preserving tranquility. Moreover, hearing cases enables the council to keep closely in touch with village attitudes and activities. Procedures are extremely informal, with no ritual and seemingly with no particular person in charge. The contending parties on entering the village hall may begin telling their stories to the first councilman they meet. Onlookers may interject statements, and the councilman may make suggestions for settlement or refer the disputants to the police chief, who, though without specific legal authority, also acts as adjudicator in village quarrels.

In serious disputes the entire council may meet and listen to the complaints of the parties. After questioning them the council may ask the hamlet chief to investigate further, delegate the case to him for settlement or itself try to effect a reconciliation. It may also require indemnity for loss or damage, levy fines or impose other sanctions, such as contributions of labor to village projects. Unresolved cases are forwarded to the district chief for further consideration.

A threat to refer a case to the district chief, who may place it before a court, often brings a settlement. Village justice, which costs nothing, generally seems to be administered effectively, and villagers prefer its relatively mild operation to the expense and possible severity of the regular courts.

Montagnard Justice

Among the *montagnards* in the highland areas customary law and the manner of settling disputes varies among the different ethnic groups. It appears, however, that everywhere the local council of elders combines juridical with governing functions.

So-called Highland Customs Courts, some of which may even dispose of felonies, were reactivated in early 1966 in the provincial capitals of the Central Highlands. These courts apparently were closed in 1963, toward the end of President Ngo's regime, in accordance with its policy of intensifying centralized control of the country.

The president of one such court was reportedly a member of the dominant ethnic group in the province. He was assisted by several other representatives of his group and by a court clerk. The court convened on certain days each month to hear disputes between *montagnards*. Altercations between families about property were said to be common, but the most frequent and troublesome cases apparently involved marital infidelity. Vietnamese who came to this region from urban areas reportedly regarded the justice meted out by the customary courts as unusually harsh. Information pertaining to incidence of crime and penalties imposed is not available.

THE PENAL SYSTEM

The prison system, referred to as the Rehabilitation Directorate, is headed by the Director General of Rehabilitation Centers, who is directly responsible to the Secretary of State for Interior. The headquarters of the directorate is located in Saigon and is responsible for the overall administration, security, the selection and training of staff personnel and the rehabilitation of prisoners to include vocational training.

Forty-one prison centers are scattered throughout the country, 34 of which are under control of the provinces. Seven centers, including the major one, Chi Hoa, in Saigon and the prison island of Con Son (about 140 miles south of Saigon), are centrally controlled by the Directorate General. In addition, municipal jails and village police centers also serve as places for the detention of light offenders and persons awaiting trial. Prison installations and facilities, with only a few newer additions, consist almost entirely of those inherited from the French. With USOM Public Safety Division assistance, plans have been developed for an expansion and modernization program for the entire system.

In early 1966 the prison population had been reduced to a total of about 16,000 after a steady decline from a previous high of 30,000 in 1963. Most of this reduction resulted from the emphasis placed on the rehabilitation and reeducation of "political" (Viet Cong) prisoners, who make up the single largest category of detainees. Prisoners are transferred from one center to another, depending upon length of sentence or crowded conditions. The policy in the past has been to send to the Con Son island prison all political prisoners who have been sentenced to over 3 years and have that much time left to serve. Convicted criminals with sentences of 5 years or more are also sent to Con Son, but may be maintained in the prison serving the province of their origin, if conditions permit.

The Chief of State has the power to mitigate sentences and grant pardons. In exercising this power, he has been generally guided by the recommendations of the Pardon Commission, of which the Secretary of State for Justice is the presiding officer. Announcements of amnesty and executive clemency are usually made on national holidays and other memorable occasions.

CRIMES AND PUNISHMENT

Treason and other major offenses against the State, particularly those directly affecting national security, are regarded as the most serious crimes. The greatly expanded wartime conditions within the country since 1963 have brought a great increase in those crimes directly related to this expansion: speculating, hoarding, black-marketeering, smuggling, desertion, forgery of documents, draft evasion, and corruption among officials and war suppliers. Crimes against the state are commonly given wide publicity, as are convictions resulting from corruption and war profiteering. Infractions against persons are treated more nearly as general news items and receive limited press notice.

Crime statistics are lacking, but the offenses having an economic background apparently have increased with the war effort in far greater proportion to crimes of violence. Petty offenses and misdemeanors are quite common, and their rates are usually directly related to population increases caused by war dislocation.

Types of Punishment

The most common punishments are fines, imprisonment and confinement at hard labor. Information is scanty regarding the penalties attaching to various offenses and the maximum punishments that different courts may impose. The death sentence is still applied in accordance with the French criminal code and is carried out with the guillotine. Death sentences imposed by the Special Court dealing with war profiteering and corruption are carried out by firing squads.

Political Offenses and Punishments

A presidential ordinance of January 1956, still believed to be in effect, provided that persons regarded as "dangerous to national defense and common security" could be imprisoned or compelled to reside at a specific place under police supervision. The application of this ordinance, which contained no provisions for hearings, in cases involving mass demonstrations or other civil disturbances has resulted on occasion in numerous arrests and detentions. Ringleaders or suspected troublemakers have been effectively divorced from their base of strength by being placed in "forced residence" in selected provinces or towns or by being exiled from the country for periods of time.

Another decree of the same year authorized heavy fines and prison sentences up to 5 years for persons convicted of publishing statements which could endanger security and public order; journals or newspapers in which such statements were printed could also be suspended. The provisions of this latter decree were reinforced by the government of Prime Minister Ky on June 24, 1965, when it promulgated a series of State-of-War (National Emergency) regulations. These regulations specifically prohibited the distribution of books, newspapers, leaflets and other publications, photographs or documents harmful to national security. On the date of promulgation the Secretary for Psychological Warfare suspended 36 South Vietnamese newspapers for 3 days for violating these regulations (see ch. 16, Public Information).

Criminal Offenses

Gambling and other offenses not regarded as involving moral turpitude are generally punished with no more than a fine. Vice is more severely dealt with, and such offenses as opium smoking, prostitution, embezzlement and robbery are apt to bring prison sentences. Murder and aggravated assault are among the most serious crimes and may be punished with sentences ranging from 5 years' imprisonment to death. Crimes against the state, as defined in Law Number 10 of May 1959, call for the severest punishments. In furtherance of an effort to reduce crimes against the public interests, Chief of State Nguyen Van Thieu, in June 1965, announced that a forced-labor camp was being opened on Cu Lao Re (an island in the South China Sea, 75 miles southeast of Da Nang) for black-marketeers, corrupt officials and lesser criminals.

The death penalty and confiscation of property are prescribed for persons guilty of murder, poisoning or abduction of public officials, or of sabotaging (by explosives or fire) public buildings, dwellings, storehouses, factories, churches, temples or pagodas. The same sanctions apply to persons guilty of willfully damaging: air, land or water transport facilities; mining installations, communications and power systems; agricultural crops, cattle or machinery; dikes, dams, bridges, canals or port facilities.

Life imprisonment with forced labor and confiscation of property (all or part) is decreed for those convicted of interrupting transportation on land, air or water by terrorism or intimidation, threatening assassination, abduction or arson (burning of dwellings or crops); disruption of public markets; and plundering. Membership in any group plotting against the state is also a crime. If persons involved in such groups help to bring the principals to justice before authorities begin action on the case, they may be given reduced sentences or immunity from prosecution in return.

Smuggling and Black-Marketing

Smuggling and black-marketing in normal times reduce internal revenue collections and thus indirectly retard development of the national economy. As serious as the peacetime effects of these illegal actions are, their effects under the wartime stress experienced by South

Vietnam in early 1966 were extraordinarily serious in terms of inflation, war suppiles diverted to the Viet Cong and huge losses in needed revenue. Both kinds of activity are difficult and costly to control. The opportunities for black-marketing are as broad as the scope of trade itself and are even more dangerously enlarged with the influx of massive foreign aid into South Vietnam. Smugglers have the same advantages as those exploited by the Viet Cong in their general infiltration tactics—a long coastline almost impossible to police and land frontiers which are relatively inaccessible, sparsely settled and overgrown with dense tropical cover.

Opium, most of it apparently produced in Laos and Cambodia, is historically the most important item of the smuggling trade. The drug is introduced into the country on foot, in land vehicles, by airplane and by coastal craft. The main distributing point for retailers in South Vietnam is Saigon. A greater variety and volume in smuggled goods has also been brought about by the intensified Viet Cong insurgency. The most important of these items are gold, watches, cigarettes, medicines and foodstuffs.

CHAPTER 27

THE ARMED FORCES

The Armed Forces of South Vietnam were actively engaged in early 1966 in countrywide warfare against strong Communist-led and -controlled insurgent forces. The extensive military aid rendered by the United States had resulted in noticeable modification of much of the French heritage of the South Vietnamese forces as they had developed and expanded in the previous few years. While appreciable progress was made in improving the overall framework and posture of the military forces on the field of battle and off, limitations still existed, and the government was striving to overcome them through improved and more effective training and administrative procedures.

South Vietnam in early 1966 maintained a military establishment of approximately 585,000 officers and men, almost equally divided between the regular armed forces (Army, Navy and Air Force) and the paramilitary forces composed of three well-developed groups. Within the regular forces the Army of the Republic of Vietnam (commonly referred to as ARVN, or the Army—see Glossary), predominated, with an estimated strength of nearly 264,000. Naval strength (including Marines) was about 25,000, and the Air Force totaled slightly more than 11,000. The paramilitary groups, which supplemented the regular forces, included the Regional Force (formerly Civil Guard) of about 120,000 men, the Popular Force (formerly Self-Defense Corps) of approximately 140,000 and the Civilian Irregular Defense Group of nearly 25,000. These paramilitary organizations were utilized almost exclusively for regional security, static defense and special counterinsurgency operations. All components have been provided equipment supplied by the United States. Since 1954 training in the regular forces, with the assistance of United States advisers, has closely followed United States military concepts adapted to accommodate specific Vietnamese capabilities and modified to meet the country's needs in its prolonged struggle to defeat the Communist insurgency within its borders.

Throughout the history of Vietnam the people have regarded their precolonial warriors with great respect, second only to that accorded to their scholars, because of their part in the centuries-long struggle for independence from the Chinese. The people also supported the military expansion against their neighbors to the South, the Chams and the Khmers (Cambodians), in the seventeenth and eighteenth centuries. National holidays commemorate military leaders' successes, and lyric poetry praising war, honor, loyalty and Confucian morality has always been a favorite literary form (see ch. 3, Historical Setting).

The Army of the Republic of Vietnam in 1966 was a relatively young army, with an increasing number of combat-seasoned officers and men. Many general officers were still in their forties and had held a variety of assignments in operation field units. A large proportion of the officers had received commissions after attending Da Lat Military Academy, had been commissioned from officer candidate schools or had received battlefield commissions. Educational requirements were being revised in order that more combat-experienced soldiers and noncommissioned officers could qualify for officer training. Most of the enlisted men were youths who had enlisted or had been drafted after 1957 and who had only limited experience in counterinsurgency action against the Viet Cong (a condensed form of the term Viet Nam Cong San—meaning Vietnamese Communists—see Glossary).

Since 1954 the Army has gradually developed from a rudimentary force serving within the French Union Forces into a regular military establishment, well-organized, cohesive and reflecting a broad, nationally based character. The necessity of dealing with increasing Viet Cong activity over the past 6 years has done much to increase battle worthiness, but it has also served to deprive the military forces of the training time necessary to improve their all-round effectiveness. The introduction of United States combat troops in 1965, to help check the increasing counterinsurgency effort, has contributed to a spirit of mounting general confidence within the Army and within the country.

BACKGROUND

The Vietnamese pride themselves on the courage and fighting ability of their men, and they look back on a long history of bloody wars, generally defensive but sometimes offensive in character. In the tenth century they expelled the Chinese who had ruled them for nearly 1,000 years and thereafter, except for a later brief period of reasserted Chinese occupation, resisted both Chinese and Mongol invasions (see ch. 3, Historical Setting).

The first Vietnamese military academy was established in the mid-thirteenth century. The government at that time had a dual hierarchy of civil and military mandarins under the emperor. Many generals distinguished themselves in successful defensive actions against stronger enemy forces. Vietnamese historians take special pride in their country's forces which stopped the formidable Mongol army of Kublai Khan in 1285.

During the seventeenth and eighteenth centuries the Vietnamese engaged in intermittent wars with the Chams and the Khmers, their neighbors to the south, who occupied most of the southern part of what is now South Vietnam. Eventually, the Vietnamese decisively defeated the Chams, occupied their lands and all but exterminated them. The Khmers were also subdued, and Vietnamese control was extended throughout the Mekong Delta.

A cult of military heroes eventually developed; their exploits are celebrated in song and story, and temples have been erected in their memory. These celebrated events include heroic defeats as well as great victories, as in the case of the Trung sisters who led a revolt against the Chinese in the first century A.D. and chose suicide rather than surrender (see ch. 3, Historical Setting). The episode has long been a source of inspiration to Vietnamese artists and writers, and it is commemorated annually as an example of self-sacrificing devotion to country.

Throughout most of the long period of French colonial rule the Vietnamese served primarily as indigenous auxiliaries within the French Union Forces. These organizations were mixed with French units and performed general field and garrison duties. This subordinate status of the Vietnamese military remained essentially unchanged during the greater part of World War II since, by agreement, the Japanese permitted the French to continue to exercise control over the country during that period. Although the Japanese took over full control in March 1945, French authority was restored in September of the same year after the surrender of the Japanese.

Meanwhile, the Viet Minh (see Glossary), under Communist leader Ho Chi Minh, gained control of the nationalist movement and sought to establish a so-called independent Vietnamese government. When the French returned to power, they were unwilling to grant independence to Vietnam outside the French Union, and continued Vietnamese resistance led to the Indochina War. The growing demands of that war caused the French, in 1949, to alter their previous policy of not permitting independent indigenous forces and to form the first Vietnamese regular military units under French officers and noncommissioned officers.

By the close of the war, in 1954, the Vietnamese army had grown to an appreciable force of well over 200,000, but it had little or no artillery, armor, communications or other support troops. It was weak in staff and command positions above the rank of major, and its morale and prestige had been adversely affected by having participated in a losing war.

After Vietnam was declared a republic in 1955, French cadres were withdrawn, but French advisers remained until 1957, when they were replaced by those from the United States. Since 1955 the Army has continued its progressive development into a competent fighting force despite the harassment and interference to training caused by the Viet Cong insurgency.

ECONOMIC IMPACT

Manpower

Early in 1966 the strength of the military establishment was approximately 585,000, or about 3.6 percent of the total population. This included those on duty with the paramilitary forces as well as those in the Army, Navy, Marine Corps and Air Force. Further increases in both the regular and paramilitary forces have been forecast as a result of the upsurge in Viet Cong activity. It is estimated that there were approximately 4,371,000 fit males between the ages of 15 and 49 in South Vietnam as of January 1, 1965. About one-half of this total were regarded as fit for military service. Each year about 140,000 males reach military age. This manpower base is sufficient to keep units up to their authorized strength. A source of general reserve manpower exists in those individuals who have served on active duty with elements of the armed forces and have since been demobilized. The government in 1965 initiated a census of males in this category between the ages of 20 and 45.

Military Budget

The struggle against the Communist insurgency imposes a burden of military expenditure which the country's economy can carry only with extensive foreign aid. Since its emergence as a national entity in 1954, South Vietnam's yearly contribution toward the development and maintenance of its military establishment has been well under 20 percent of the actual cost, and the percentage has decreased with rising costs as the security forces have been enlarged and strengthened (see ch. 23, Foreign Economic Relations; ch. 24, Public Finance).

The funds allocated for defense in the annual budget remained fairly constant from 1958 to 1962 when they mounted sharply because of a substantial increase in the armed forces. After 1962 military expenditures rose steadily from this higher plateau and by the end of 1965 were expected to have doubled the 1962 rate. In relation to the total budget, the portion allocated for defense declined from 44 percent in 1958 to less than 39 percent in 1961, but, as an indication of growing concern over the security situation, it increased to approximately 50 percent in 1962 and continued to mount through 1965. Forecasts for fiscal year 1966 indicate that close to 63 percent of the total national budget will be earmarked for defense.

In 1965 the military budget amounted to approximately 25.7 billion piasters (for value of the piaster, see Glossary). The United States aid program, however, provided about 70.35 billion additional piasters, exclusive of the cost of such materiel as weapons, vehicles, aircraft, naval craft and ammunition, which was also acquired under the air program. Including the cost of these items, the South Vietnamese Government actually paid for about 10 percent of the national defense costs. Meanwhile, the allocation to the military establishment was larger, by far, than for any other single governmental agency.

Military expenditures have not roused any significant popular criticism, although the subject is exploited overtly and clandestinely by Communist propagandists. The human and material sacrifices required to counter Viet Cong aggression are felt keenly among the rural population, but few people are in a position to reflect on the division and expenditures of government revenue.

MISSION AND ORGANIZATION

Mission

The dual mission of the armed forces is to defend the nation's sovereignty and to eliminate the Communist insurgency within the national territory. Since the withdrawal of the French Union Forces from Vietnam in June 1956, the principal task of the military has been the internal one of ending threats to the security of the state—first from armed religious sects and lawless groups and currently from the Viet Cong (see ch. 26, Public Order and Safety).

The Army, as the major component of the armed forces, is expected to exert the main effort in offensive operations against the Viet Cong and at the same time to act as a ready reserve in support of the operations of the local Regional Force and the Popular Force against insurgent forces. In addition, elements of the Army perform many important noncombat functions, most of them indirectly related to the improvement of internal security. Most district, provincial and regional chiefs are army officers, and many others are on temporary duty with government civilian agencies. The Army also participates in many aspects of various civic action projects and provides considerable assistance in the overall rural reconstruction program (see ch. 13, The Governmental System).

The official mission of the Regional Force is to enforce the law and maintain public order and security in rural areas. It is also responsible for assisting other components of the armed forces in the reestablishment of internal security throughout the national territory.

The local Popular Front groups are charged with helping the authorities in the villages and other administrative units in which they are organized to maintain public order and security. They guard against sabotage and terrorist activities and protect public works. They are also used on emergency relief missions to local areas stricken by fire, flood and devastating storms. Despite their wide range of responsibilities their police powers are limited to the apprehension of offenders and turning them over to the police (see ch. 26, Public Order and Safety).

The Civilian Irregular Defense Group has the broad mission of preserving national security through territorial border surveillance. These units are also employed in other special operations.

The general mission of the Navy is to provide for the security of the sea approaches to the country and for the protection of the inland waterways in the Mekong Delta. It may also be called upon to furnish water transportation for Army personnel and materiel. It is charged with maintaining a marine group capable of conducting operations either alone or in conjunction with Army forces. The Navy also is responsible for maintaining coastal and inland waterway counterinsurgency patrols and to assist, when called upon, custom officials or internal security authorities operating against smugglers or others engaged in illegal activities.

The Air Force, besides providing close air support for ground troops, has additional missions which include: attacking guerrilla groups and installations; transporting ground forces and their supplies; airlifting airborne troops; aerial reconnaissance; and search and rescue operations.

High Command

Pending the promulgation of a permanent constitution, supreme command of the armed forces, as a part of the national sovereignty, was vested temporarily in a Congress of the Armed Forces under the provisional government established on June 19, 1965. The Congress of the Armed Forces, in turn, delegated to a National Leadership Committee the exercise of all power and authority over the affairs of the nation, including military (see ch. 13, The Governmental System).

The Chairman of the National Leadership Committee acts as Chief of State and, upon recommendation of the Minister of War and Reconstruction and with the approval of the Committee, appoints and promotes all general officers. The Chairman is also empowered to award decorations and grant amnesty, and, based on the approval of the Congress of the Armed Forces, he also has the authority to declare war, make peace and conclude international agreements. A National Security Council was created to assist and advise the Chief of State in carrying out his duties concerning states of emergency, martial law or actual law in parts or in the whole of the national territory.

The position and title of Commander in Chief of the Armed Forces was not established within the provisional government, but the military authority commonly associated with that office is apparently discharged by the Minister of War and Reconstruction within the complex of the Central Executive Committee (Cabinet). Air Vice

Marshal Nguyen Cao Ky, as Chairman of the Central Executive Committee, acts as Prime Minister and has retained the position of Commander of the Air Force. The Minister of War and Reconstruction, Lieutenant General Nguyen Huu Co, concurrently holds the position of Secretary of Defense and in October 1965 was designated Deputy Prime Minister. Upon this latter appointment he was relieved of the post of Chief of the Joint General Staff, an office which in practice also included the functions of Commander of the Army (see fig. 12).

The Minister of War and Reconstruction has an extensive staff organization through which he directs the defense establishment and pacification efforts of the government. With concurrent control of the office of Secretary of Defense, he has direct control of all aspects of military activities, both administrative and operational.

Directly subordinate to the Minister of War and Reconstruction (and Secretary of Defense) is the Chairman of the Joint General Staff, with a Chief of Staff through whom he directs the commanders of the Air Force, the Navy and the Marine Corps, as well as the commanders of the principal field commands, installations and facilities. The so-called Joint General Staff is in fact an Army general staff composed almost entirely of Army officers who also perform staff functions for the Navy and Air Force. As in the case of the Commander in Chief of the Armed Forces, the title and position of Commander of the Army is nonexistent. The responsibilities of such an office are included for all intents and purposes within those of the Chief of the Joint General Staff.

The Joint General Staff is organized along United States Army staff lines, adjusted and modified to meet the particular requirements of the South Vietnamese Armed Forces. There are four deputy chiefs of staff who have supervisory responsibility over the general staff divisions and offices. The Deputy Chief of Staff, Personnel, supervises J–1 (personnel) as well as the Staff Judge Advocate and the Adjutant General; the Deputy Chief of Staff, Logistics, is responsible for the Logistics Division and the Technical Services; the Deputy Chief of Staff, Operations, directs J–2 (intelligence), J–3 (operations), J–5 (plans) and J–6 (communications); and the Deputy Chief of Staff, Political Warfare, supervises the work of the Political Warfare Division.

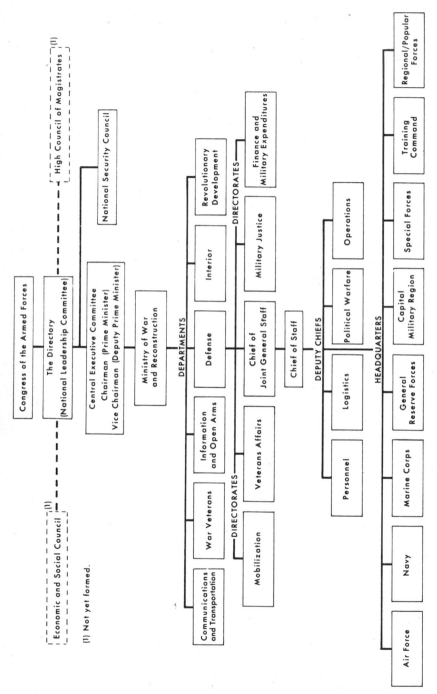

Figure 12. High Command of the South Vietnamese Armed Forces, 1966

Economic and Social Council (1)

High Council of Magistrates (1)

(1) Not yet formed.

Congress of the Armed Forces

The Directory (National Leadership Committee)

Central Executive Committee Chairman (Prime Minister) Vice Chairman (Deputy Prime Minister)

National Security Council

Ministry of War and Reconstruction

DEPARTMENTS

Communications and Transportation

War Veterans

Information and Open Arms

Defense

Interior

Revolutionary Development

DIRECTORATES

Mobilization

Veterans Affairs

Chief of Joint General Staff

Military Justice

DIRECTORATES

Finance and Military Expenditures

Chief of Staff

DEPUTY CHIEFS

Personnel

Logistics

Political Warfare

Operations

HEADQUARTERS

Air Force

Navy

Marine Corps

General Reserve Forces

Capital Military Region

Special Forces

Training Command

Regional/Popular Forces

434

FIELD COMMAND

Army

Direct channels operate between the Joint General Staff and field commands. This centralized chain of command extends from the Chief of the Joint General Staff through the Chief of Staff to corps commanders. From corps level it passes to commanders responsible for the conduct of tactical operations who may be either division commanders or commanders of specially designated forces (see fig. 13).

Territorially, the country is organized into four corps areas and a Capital Military Region, for purposes of command, administration and logistics. Each corps area embraces several provinces and has two or more divisions assigned to it. The Capital Military Region includes the Saigon-Cho Lon metropolitan area and the surrounding Gia Dinh Province. The corps areas function as tactical military zones, and corps commanders are responsible for the conduct of all security operations against the Viet Cong within their respective zones.

At the end of 1965, corps designations, with the location of corps with their headquarters and areas of responsibilities, were as follows: I Corps, Da Nang—northernmost provinces; II Corps, Pleiku—the central provinces; III Corps, Saigon—provinces between the central provinces and the Mekong Delta, except for the Capital Military Region; and IV Corps, Can Tho—Mekong Delta. The Army's 10 divisions are allocated to corps areas generally in proportion to the density of population and the intensity of Viet Cong insurgency activities in the areas. As of late 1965, I Corps and II Corps each had two divisions; III Corps and IV Corps, in the densely populated southern portions of the country, each had three divisions.

The corps areas are divided into divisional tactical zones, each generally comprising several civil provinces. Most civil provinces are headed by military officers who serve concurrently as commanders of troops within their provinces and, in such capacity, are subordinate to their respective division commanders for the conduct of security operations. When special security measures dictate, certain areas within provinces are designated for intensified counterinsurgency operations. Two such sectors, Zones "C" and "D," have been so designated in the III Corps area because of the heavy concentration of Viet Cong elements located there.

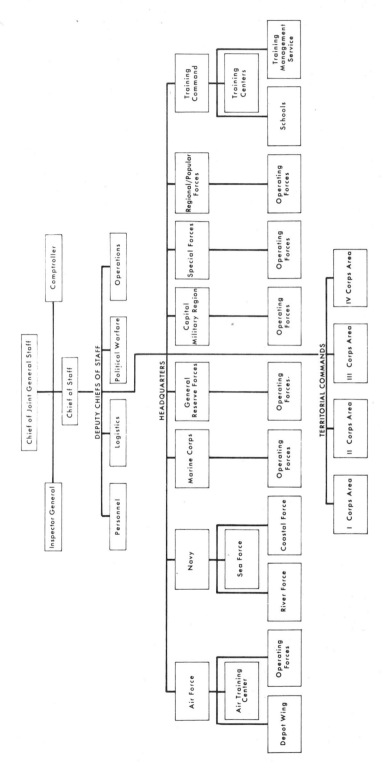

Figure 13. Field Command of the South Vietnamese Armed Forces, 1966.

Navy

The Navy, under a Chief of Naval Operations, is composed of Operating Forces and the Shore Establishments. The Operating Forces include the Sea Force, the River Force, the Coastal Force and the Marine Corps. The Sea Force consists of three squadrons (patrol, amphibious and minesweeping) and includes various types of small ships, such as escort vessels, patrol boats, minesweepers and shallow-draft landing craft. The River Force is divided into a number of River Assault Groups, a River Escort Group and a River Transport Group. This force is assigned light armed and armored patrol boats, as well as LCVPs (landing craft, vehicles, personnel). The Coastal Force is a former paramilitary group (Junk Force) which was incorporated into the Navy in 1965 and operates more than 400 junks in 28 divisions. It is charged primarily with the surveillance of intracoastal shipping.

The Marine Corps, composed principally of a marine group with headquarters in Saigon, is organized into several battalions with infantry, artillery and support elements; these are similar to units of the United States Marine Corps. The Shore Establishments include the Naval Headquarters, Supply Center, and Shipyard, all in Saigon, and the principal naval training center at Nha Trang.

Air Force

The Air Force is organized into five tactical wings and a depot wing. Operating units include transport, helicopter, tactical and liaison squadrons distributed among the major air bases throughout the country, including Saigon, Nha Trang, Ban Me Thuot, Bien Hoa and Pleiku. The principal air training center is at Nha Trang. Air Force Headquarters, with supporting staff elements, is in Saigon.

POSITION OF THE MILITARY IN GOVERNMENT

The overthrow of President Ngo Dinh Diem by a military coup in 1963 projected the military into a position of overall political control which it has continued to maintain, although no less than seven abrupt changes in governmental leadership have taken place since that time. The previous constitutional position of the armed forces, subordinate to the authority of a civilian president, was initially set aside by the military coup of 1963. Since June 1965 supreme authority has been vested in a Congress of the Armed Forces of South Vietnam (see ch. 13, The Governmental System; ch. 14, Political Dynamics).

The Vietnamese have long preferred civilians as a source of national leadership, and they feel that they have had good leaders in the historical past. Since the creation of South Vietnam as a republic in 1955 it has been beset with political, economic, social and security problems which have increasingly threatened its national survival. The extent of dissatisfaction with President Diem's regime and the intensification of the Communist insurgency brought the intervention of the military.

Before the seizure of power in 1963 none of the military leaders of the country played an important part in the formulation of national policy. Under President Diem the military forces were an instrument of rule, but they played almost no part in formulating that rule. Since taking over governmental control the military have taken little part in civilian political activities and movements and, as a group, have succeeded in retaining their collective strength and unity. With the passage of time this corporate unity may be subject to dilution through the reemergence of general political activity.

FOREIGN INFLUENCE

Late in 1954 the South Vietnamese Government requested the United States to undertake training functions on an equal basis with the French. By 1957 all French training missions had been withdrawn, and a United States Military Assistance Advisory Group (MAAG) took over the major task of training the Vietnamese forces and substituting United States methods for French ones. The training mission increased steadily in size from about 800 in 1960 to about 2,000 in 1961; to nearly 11,000 in 1962; to approximately 15,000 in 1963; and reached more than 23,000 in 1964. The number decreased in 1965 to about 5,000 when the United States assumed a more direct combat role in aiding South Vietnam. The great interest and continued determination of the United States was expressed in 1962 when the United States Military Assistance Command for Vietnam (MACV) was formed in order to deal more effectively with the problems of increased military support.

In 1965, with South Vietnam critically involved in an evermounting struggle, the United States initiated direct participation in the war against the Viet Cong with combat troops, in addition to supplying advisers. United States troop strength increased to more than 160,000 in 1965 and had almost reached 230,000 by early 1966. In addition, major United States naval forces were deployed off the coast in a direct support combat role. Extensive United States Air Force elements were moved to South Vietnam, and others were assigned long-range bombing missions against Communist targets in North and South Vietnam.

Direct United States combat troop presence has fortified the United States influence imparted by the American advisers operating at all command and staff echelons of all components of the South Vietnamese forces. Also, over the past few years, a sizable number of Vietnamese officers and men have attended military schools in the United

States or have been sent on orientation visits to American military installations.

Aside from the United States, which is carrying the main burden of support for South Vietnam, foreign influence of a far less significant degree has resulted from the assistance of some 32 other nations. These nations have contributed various amounts of military and civilian aid in one form or another. Australia, New Zealand and South Korea have contributed limited numbers of field troops, and a small unit is likely to be made available by the Philippine Government. Other assistance has included aviation crews, police and counterinsurgency instructors, surgical teams, and various forms of noncombat aid (see ch. 15, Foreign Relations).

South Vietnam has no military alliances with other nations, but, although it is not a member of the Southeast Asia Treaty Organization (SEATO), it receives protection as a protocol state under Article IV as a result of military aggression by North Vietnam (see ch. 15, Foreign Relations).

INSURGENCY

The end of the Indochina War in 1954 left Communist North Vietnam with a highly developed composite politicomilitary organization, under the direction of Ho Chi Minh, capable of waging war both as a guerrilla underground force and as a conventional land army. This organization was then deployed throughout Vietnam, with about 90,000 military troops occupying portions of South Vietnam. With the signing of the Geneva Agreement in 1954, which partitioned the country, most of these troops were regrouped and evacuated to North Vietnam. Ho Chi Minh left many thousands of specially selected men (variously estimated from 5,000 to 10,000) and numerous caches of arms and equipment behind in hideouts in the remote jungles of the Mekong Delta and the mountainous region north of Saigon. When the government of the newly formed Republic of Vietnam refused to participate in the referendum, those men known as the Viet Cong, served as the nucleus of military and subversive efforts to overthrow the government.

During 1956 and 1957 the Viet Cong elements devoted most of their time to recruiting and expanding their bases throughout South Vietnam. Many South Vietnamese Communists who had withdrawn with the North Vietnamese forces in 1954 and had completed instruction courses in subversive tactics returned to the South to take up responsible positions in the Communist movement. Military units were strengthened in manpower and equipment, and strong efforts were made to exploit the unrest and confusion which accompanied the establishment of the new government of South Vietnam.

Having received substantial increases in men and materiel in 1958, the Viet Cong embarked on a new campaign of terror and intimidation.

Their strength mounted to about 12,000, and with relatively small units they increased the tempo of guerrilla harassment, sabotage and intimidation of additional areas of the country. By 1960 the Viet Cong began attacking in company-sized units and, on occasion, in groups of up to several battalions in strength. Meanwhile, reinforcements infiltrated from the North in increasing numbers, and more local recruits were obtained.

By 1962 the Viet Cong numbered more than 75,000 and were divided into three main categories: full-time guerrillas, part-time guerrillas and village activists. The full-time guerrillas, organized into companies and battalions, numbered over 18,000 and constituted the hardcore of the Viet Cong forces; the part-time guerrillas, approximating 40,000 in strength, were organized on a district basis into platoons or company-sized units. They were provided with small arms, grenades, landmines and explosive charges and received some training while assembled in hideouts or guarding cached supplies.

The village activists, also with an approximate strength of 17,000, were, in effect, an active reserve in the villages. Working at their regular occupations during the day, they participated in night missions on the orders of the area guerrilla leader. Their usual arms were knives and machetes, but a village group on occasion possessed several submachine guns as well as rifles, grenades and landmines. Viet Cong of this latter type played an important role, identifying lucrative military targets, procuring recruits and food supplies and furnishing information on the vulnerability of village defenses as well as the activities of local government officials and security forces.

These three groups have become known as main force units, local units and guerrillas and have steadily intensified the campaign of Communist aggression by stepping up the number of armed attacks and increasing terrorism and sabotage despite vigorous governmental countermeasures.

Between 1963 and 1965 the armed conflict in South Vietnam reached new high levels of intensity. Internal political difficulties in the country's government gave the Viet Cong opportunities which it exploited. Increasingly, it enlarged its scope of activity on a broad basis. In 1964 alone, 436 hamlet chiefs and other government officials were killed outright, and 1,131 were kidnapped. More than 1,350 civilians were killed in bombings and other acts of terror, and at least 8,400 civilians were kidnapped by the Viet Cong. This level of activity continued well into 1965.

By the end of 1963 total Viet Cong personnel in South Vietnam rose to about 30,000, exclusive of local irregulars and part-time guerrillas. Since that time, the figure has steadily mounted. Military infiltration from the North continued in growing numbers, and the flow of weapons from North Vietnam and Communist China increased, particularly those of larger caliber. The hardcore Viet Cong force in early 1966 was estimated to be close to·90,000, reportedly including between 12 and 15 regiments of the regular People's Army of North Vietnam. The number of irregulars, including sympathizers and Communist party workers supporting the hard core troops, probably had reached 150,000 or more.

QUALITY OF MANPOWER

The average South Vietnamese soldier has given a good account of himself in battle over the years. Exhibiting many basic soldierly qualities, he has always responded to good leadership with determination and courage. He is a peasant, accustomed to hard work, inured to hardship, highly realistic and possessed of a well-developed sense of field craft. As an individual, he is hospitable, human and moderately aggressive. As a result, he is fairly fatalistic about war, accepts pain and death with a high degree of patience and endurance and responds to adversity with self-discipline. On the other hand, he shows little initiative in unexpected contingencies and relies to a great extent on leadership.

Despite his many favorable qualities the average South Vietnamese soldier possesses some physical limitations. By United States standards he is small—only slightly more than 5 feet tall and weighing about 120 pounds. Accordingly, he is, comparatively, somewhat less strong and finds some difficulty in using many items of United States equipment. The introduction of the light United States Army AR–15 "Armalite" rifle, however, did much to alleviate this situation in the field of individual weapons. On the whole, the strong individual qualities of the South Vietnamese soldier far outweigh his weak ones.

CONSCRIPTION

The Military Mobilization Ordinance of 1953, which prescribed the military service obligation in wartime for all male citizens between 18 and 33 years of age, is the basis for all subsequent conscription programs. The first of these programs was initiated in 1957 and established compulsory peacetime military service for all males 20 and 21 years of age. Under this program all individuals served a total of 12 months, which included 4 months devoted to basic training and 8 months of duty in units. In January 1959 the service period was extended to 18 months and in July 1961, to 24 months.

This 1957 program has been subject to further changes and modifications, largely in accord with the country's expanding ·needs to counteract the long-term Communist insurgency with which it has been confronted. In 1964 the term of service was lengthened and applied on a graduated scale between the regular and the paramilitary forces.

The maximum term was prescribed for those members of the paramilitary forces who served closest to their home villages.

A further modification by special decree in August 1965 made all males between the ages of 18 and 37 subject to military draft. Considerable opposition to this decree was voiced, principally by students, university professors and civil servants. To lessen the impact on these groups, which were heavily affected, the government has allowed certain personnel to be drafted "in place," subject to later call, and has permitted others to return to their former occupations after a 4-month training course at the Infantry School.

The Viet Cong have been using every means to disrupt conscription in South Vietnam. They conduct intensive recruitment for their own units, utilizing numerous techniques, including false promise, intimidation and terror. Their propaganda campaigns urging draft evasion are both subtle and direct, and in certain areas they have employed carefully executed civic action programs to sway the loyalties of the youthful peasant population.

TRAINING

The increased tempo of military action against the Viet Cong and the gradual expansion of the armed forces have caused the establishment of a comprehensive system of training installations and military schools. These installations and facilities are improving steadily and are turning out increasing numbers of trained officers and skilled technicians available to the armed forces. American advisers and instructors have introduced United States training methods and have assisted in the development of special counterinsurgency doctrine and techniques.

Although the intensification of Viet Cong activity has placed heavy emphasis on counterinsurgency training, technical skills have not been neglected, and after completing basic training about 40 percent of the conscripts are enrolled in technical courses. Army, Navy and Air Force units receive intensive training in the operation and maintenance of equipment received from the United States. While their training is primarily within their own service, combined training is conducted in preparation for joint actions against the Viet Cong.

The Command and General Staff College, which was organized in 1956 at Saigon, is the highest institution in the military educational system. Its course for field-grade officers offers instruction in staff and command techniques, in combined operations and in general academic subjects. The course for selected company-grade officers provides training in staff procedures. Short refresher courses are available to selected officers in the grades of colonel and lieutenant colonel to keep them abreast of important changes in policy and acquaint them with the employment of new weapons.

442

The National Military Academy was established by the French in 1948 at Hue and moved to Da Lat in 1950. Originally a 3-year institution, its program was extended to 4 years in 1961. In August 1962, however, because of the shortage of junior officers in field units, the government placed the Academy on a wartime basis and reduced its curriculum to 2 years. The first United States advisers were assigned to the academy in 1955, and since that time much has been accomplished in converting the school into a true academy that can produce officers with a sound, if limited, basic college education and a broad knowledge of military subjects.

The Thu Duc Officers' Candidate School was established in the mid-1950's to prepare students for reserve commissions. The installation was expanded progressively with the addition of special courses in artillery, engineering, ordnance, transportation and signal communications, and by 1958 it had graduated almost 3,300 reserve officers. Branch schools developed out of these special courses, and the combined schools became known as the Thu Duc Military Schools Complex. Increased military needs have caused further expansion, and the development of additional facilities for more diversified training at the Complex, which has become one of the most important military training institutions in the country. The Complex provides theoretical instruction and practical training for officers and enlisted men in the use of equipment and the handling of units in their respective services.

The Air Force Training Center at Nha Trang conducts basic training courses for pilots, observers, mechanics and other specialists. A limited amount of on-the-job training in various technical specialties is also performed at some of the major airbases throughout the country.

Aside from practical shipboard training, naval personnel receive most of their basic and intermediate training at the main Naval Training Center located at Nha Trang. In addition to the Naval Officers' Candidate School, the Center conducts basic technical training courses for naval specialists and for potential petty officers. The Navy also operates a training center at Saigon, primarily for on-the-job training of ship and boat crews.

The Armed Forces Language School was established in 1956 as an English-language school, and its courses are designed to give officers and enlisted men a working knowledge of English before they enter foreign military courses or engage in advanced training with United States military units.

The Logistics Management School and the Psychological Warfare School train personnel in these two important specialties in courses of varying lengths. Logistics management is a comparatively new doctrine which is taking on increasing importance in South Vietnam, and much of the instruction has been devised by United States advisers. Psychological Warfare has long been recognized at all levels as a most important ingredient in the type of insurgent warfare faced by the South Vietnamese. In recognition of this fact and of the rising need for more personnel trained in this specialty, the intelligence training, a part of the former Intelligence and Psychological Warfare Schools' curriculum, was transferred to a school of its own, permitting the scheduling of additional classes at both facilities.

The Military Medical School, an adjunct of the University of Saigon, has modern, up-to-date facilities and conducts a comprehensive program of medical instruction with a capable staff of instructors. Of the 13 courses taught durng the 1964 calendar year, only one was offered to medical officers. This course, lasting 26 weeks, dealt with the techniques of field surgery, and it qualified graduates as unit surgeons. Three other courses ranging from 4 to 12 weeks in duration, offered orientation to medical students and enlisted men in general medical subjects. The remaining 9 courses trained enlisted technicians as general medical attendants, aid men and litter bearers, or as medical specialists in the fields of general medicine, dentistry, anesthesiology and laboratory and X-ray techniques.

The Military Medical School is also responsible for the conduct and supervision of a program designed to procure doctors, dentists and pharmacists for the armed forces. Each year a 3-day competitive examination is given at the school to select medical, dental and pharmacy students for direct commissions.

Students selected under this program are commissioned and receive regular military pay in accordance with their rank while they continue their studies at the Faculty of Medicine. Upon graduation they are required to pay back each year of training under the program with 2 years of active duty. Since medical students study for 6 years, a student could enter the program in his first year of study and be given the rank of student officer. At the end of his first year he would progress to second lieutenant, and at the end of his third year he would be promoted to first lieutenant. He would continue as a first lieutenant and, after 3 additional years, graduate and enter on active duty with a 12-year obligation. Similar rank progression takes place for pharmacy and dental students, but their course of study lasts for 4 and 5 years, respectively..

The Quang Trung Military Center near Saigon is a major training facility for all conscripts and enlistees. Short courses, lasting about 2 months, are given in basic military subjects relating to military combat, after which the majority are sent to combat units. About 40 percent are selected for further training in branch or technical courses.

LOGISTICS

Within the Joint General Staff the Deputy Chief of Joint Staff, Logistics, exercises overall staff supervision of the logistic support system. The Army maintains a logistical command in each of the four corps areas, which supports all units and facilities throughout the corps area. Each logistical command operates a number of forward field depots from which supplies are distributed to using units. The five Technical Services (Signal, Ordnance/Chemical, Quartermaster, Engineer and Medical) operate base depots which serve as central distribution points for issue of technical service items to field depots. The Technical Services also provide common-item support to all elements of the Army, Navy, Marine Corps and Air Force.

The receipt, storage and issue of supplies follows a pattern similar to that employed by United States forces. The supply system is seriously affected, however, by Viet Cong interdiction of a large portion of the available ground transportation, requiring the extensive use of helicopters to alleviate the situation. An additional complicating factor is the increased difficulties being experienced by the United States in bringing in heavily expanded quantities of military aid. In early 1966 new port areas under development since mid-1965 still lacked deepwater piers and warehouse space, causing long delays in unloading cargoes and subjecting supplies to deterioration from open beach storage.

The armed forces in general are equipped with United States equipment. Actual armament in all services approximated that utilized by corresponding United States military units. This equipment is of modern design and has been furnished in considerable quantities. Maintenance of equipment is a continuing problem, and emphasis is being placed on the training of more maintenance personnel.

The Chief Surgeon, Vietnam Armed Forces, is responsible for medical care in all three of the military services. All hospitals in the armed forces are Army facilities; the other services operate only dispensaries. The Regional and Popular Forces retain only limited patient-holding capacities, in small attached medical sections.

The military medical program includes general, station and field hospitals and is being expanded to cope with casualties which have increased with the intensification of the war effort against the Viet Cong. Thirteen station hospitals are located throughout the country, and four field hospitals are serving strategic areas in which major counterinsurgency operations are taking place. For battlefield evacuation, heavy use is made of helicopters because of the inaccessibility of many operational areas and the insecurity or inadequacy of the road network.

Indicative of the role the Army plays in the program of rebuilding the country is the participation of military personnel under the

Medical Civic Action Program (see ch. 8, Living Conditions). These medical teams have been very effective in convincing the rural population of the governments' interest in their welfare.

PERSONNEL SERVICES AND SUPPORT

Ranks

The structures of rank in the Army, Navy and Air Force broadly resemble those of the corresponding French forces, but since 1962 increasing numbers of changes based on the United States systems have been introduced (see figs. 14, 15, and 16). The normal duties and responsibilities of officers and enlisted men in the various ranks and grades parallel those in the United States Forces. There are no warrant officer grades, and only a few active-duty officers occupy senior general officer ranks as high as lieutentant general. Being the predominant service element, the Army has more senior officers on duty in both command and staff positions. Because of its limited size, the Navy is commanded by a captain. The command of the Air Force was retained by Major General Nguyen Coa Ky when he assumed the position of prime minister in 1965. General Ky also enjoys the title of air vice marshall, an honorary distinction awarded him in 1964.

Vietnamese Title	Translation	United States Equivalent	Rank Insignia
OFFICERS			
Thuong Tuong	Superior General	General of the Army	[1]
Dai Tuong	Senior General	General	[1]
Trung Tuong	Intermediate General	Lieutenant General	[1]
Thieu Tuong	Junior General	Major General	[1]
Chuan Tuong	Sub General	Brigadier General	[1]
Dai Ta	Senior Grade Superior Officer	Colonel	[2]
Trung Ta	Intermediate Grade Superior Officer	Lieutenant Colonel	[2]
Thieu Ta	Junior Grade Superior Officer	Major	[2]
Dai Uy	Senior Grade Junior Officer	Captain	[3]
Trung Uy	Intermediate Grade Junior Officer	First Lieutenant	[3]
Thieu Uy	Junior Grade Junior Officer	Second Lieutenant	[3]
Chuan Uy	Student Officer	None (Cadet Military Academy)	[4]
Sinh Vien Si Quan	Student Officer Candidate	None (Officer Candidate)	[5]
ENLISTED MEN			
Thuong Si Nhat [6]	Senior Grade Superior NCO	Sergeant Major	[7]
Thuong Si [6]	Superior Grade NCO	First Sergeant	[8]
Trung Si Nhat [6]	Senior Grade NCO	Sergeant First Class	[9]
Trung Si [6]	Intermediate Grade NCO	Sergeant	[10]
Ha Si Nhat [6]	Junior Grade NCO	Corporal	[11]
Ha Si [6]	Low Grade NCO	Private First Class	[12]
Binh Nhat	Private First Class	Private	[13]
Binh Nhi	Private Second Class	Recruit	NONE
Trung Dinh	Able Bodied Man	None (Conscript)	NONE

(1) Silver stars.
(2) Silver plum blossoms
(3) Gold plum blossoms.
(4) Gold disc with raised letter in gold.
(5) Gold disc with raised letter in red.
(6) "Si," the Vietnamese term for "student," is also applied to NCO's.

(7) Gold disc.
(8) Silver disc.
(9) Three silver chevrons.
(10) One silver chevron.
(11) One silver, two gold chevrons.
(12) Two gold chevrons.
(13) One gold chevron

Figure 14. Ranks and Insignia of the South Vietnamese Army, 1966.

447

Vietnamese Title	Translation	United States Equivalent	Rank Insignia
OFFICERS			
Do Doc	Senior Admiral	Admiral	 (1)
Pho Do Doc	Intermediate Admiral	Vice Admiral	 (1)
De Doc	Junior Admiral	Rear Admiral	 (1)
Pho De Doc	Sub Admiral	Commodore	 (1)
Hai Quan Dai Ta	Senior Grade Superior Naval Officer	Captain	 (2)
Hai Quan Trung Ta	Intermediate Grade Superior Naval Officer	Commander	 (2)
Hai Quan Thieu Ta	Junior Grade Superior Naval Officer	Lieutenant Commander	 (2)
Hai Quan Dai Uy	Senior Grade Junior Naval Officer	Lieutenant	 (2)
Hai Quan Trung Uy	Intermediate Grade Junior Naval Officer	Lieutenant Junior Grade	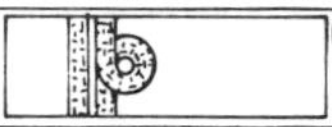 (2)
Hai Quan Thieu Uy	Junior Grade Junior Naval Officer	Ensign	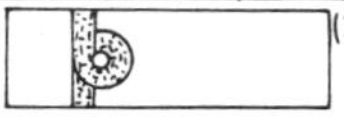 (2)
Chuan Uy	Student Officer	None (Cadet Naval Academy)	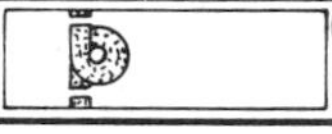 (2)
ENLISTED MEN			
Thuong Si Nhat(3)	Senior Grade Superior Petty Officer	Senior Chief Petty Officer	 (4)
Thuong Si	Superior Grade Petty Officer	Chief Petty Officer	
Trung Si Nhat	Senior Grade Petty Officer	Petty Officer First Class	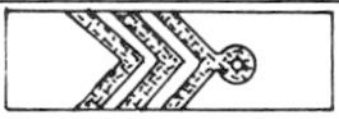
Trung Si	Intermediate Grade Petty Officer	Petty Officer Second Class	
Ha Si Nhat	Junior Grade Petty Officer	Petty Officer Third Class	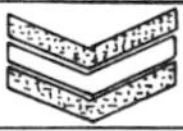 (5)
Ha Si	Low Junior Grade Petty Officer	Seaman	
Thuy Thu	Low Grade Seaman	Seaman Apprentice	

(1) Silver stars.
(2) Gold colored stripes.
(3) "Si," the Vietnamese term for "student," is also applied to NCO or petty officer.
(4) Center stripe: white.
(5) Center chevron: light blue.

Figure 15. Ranks and Insignia of the South Vietnamese Navy, 1966.

Vietnamese Title	Translation	United States Equivalent	Rank Insignia
OFFICERS			
Dai Tuong	Senior General	General	(1)
Trung Tuong	Intermediate General	Lieutenant General	(1)
Thieu Tuong	Junior General	Major General	(1)
Chuan Tuong	Sub General	Brigadier General	(1)
Dai Ta	Senior Grade Superior Officer	Colonel	(2)
Trung Ta	Intermediate Grade Superior Officer	Lieutenant Colonel	(2)
Thieu Ta	Junior Grade Superior Officer	Major	(2)
Dai Uy	Senior Grade Junior Officer	Captain	(3)
Trung Uy	Intermediate Grade Junior Officer	First Lieutenant	(3)
Thieu Uy	Junior Grade Junior Officer	Second Lieutenant	(3)
Chuan Uy	Student Officer	None (Cadet Air Force Academy)	(4)
Sinh Vien Si Quan	Student Officer Candidate	None (Officer Candidate)	(5)
ENLISTED MEN			
Thuong Si Nhat (6)	Senior Grade Superior NCO	Sergeant Major	(7)
Thuong Si (6)	Superior Grade NCO	First Sergeant	(8)
Trung Si Nhat (6)	Senior Grade NCO	Sergeant First Class	(9)
Trung Si (6)	Intermediate Grade NCO	Sergeant	(10)
Ha Si Nhat (6)	Junior Grade NCO	Corporal	(11)
Ha Si (6)	Low Grade NCO	Airman First Class	(12)
Binh Nhat	Private First Class	Airman	(13)
Binh Nhi	Private Second Class	Recruit	NONE
Trung Dinh	Able Bodied Man	None (Conscript)	NONE

(1) Silver stars.
(2) Silver plum blossoms.
(3) Gold plum blossoms.
(4) Gold disc with raised letter in gold.
(5) Gold disc with raised letter in red.
(6) "Si," the Vietnamese term for "student," is also applied to NCO's.

(7) Gold disc.
(8) Silver disc.
(9) Three silver chevrons.
(10) One silver chevron.
(11) One silver, two gold chevrons.
(12) Two gold chevrons.
(13) One gold chevron.

Figure 16. Ranks and Insignia of the South Vietnamese Air Force, 1966.

Pay

The base pay rates of the armed forces were established in 1957 and partially revised for the first time in 1964. In 1965 a 50 percent increase in enlisted pay went into effect. Base pay in all grades is supplemented by high cost-of-living family and food allowances, scaled according to grades and number of dependents. In addition, enlisted men, student officers and student officer candidates who possess special skills are granted a proficiency pay called supplemented technical allowance. There is a great variety of special allowances which are paid to military personnel who hold distinctive positions, are assigned technical duties or belong to a branch of service receiving particular emoluments. Among these special allowances are hazardous duty pay, special uniform grants and increased payments for duty involving extraordinary expenditures. Conscripts receive only nominal pay until they have completed 4 months of service, at which time their pay is raised to that of privates.

Rations

Enlisted men of the lower three grades are authorized a ration allowance consisting of a basic food allowance and an administrative food allowance. The basic food portion is intended to provide cash for the purchase of the fresh food component of the ration (meat, fowl, fish and vegetables). The administrative portion covering rice, salt, tea, sugar and shortening is issued in kind by the quartermaster and is worth about 4.50 piasters per man per day. The basic food allowance varies from 14 to 17 piasters per man per day, depending on the area of assignment.

Separate rations may be authorized when personnel are living with dependents or when the unit to which they are assigned does not operate mess facilities. In such cases the entire ration allowance is paid in cash. Servicemen wounded in line of duty and receiving treatment in a hospital or troop unit dispensary con ue to receive their ration allowance while being fed free of charge by the hospital mess.

Uniforms

The uniform worn by the armed forces are generally similar to those worn by the French in the tropics. United States Army influence, however, is quite strong and extends to a great number of articles of the uniform, including service caps, helmets, boots and fatigue clothing. Olive drab cotton garments are worn during most of the year, but woolen uniforms are supplied when needed. On special occasions officers and top-ranking noncommissioned officers wear dress uniforms—white for summer and light green gabardine for cooler weather.

Decorations

The Vietnamese tradition emphasized formal honors for achievement, and the attitude persists in the military service. Soldiers are proud of their medals and, when it is feasible, wear the full decoration rather than the ribbon bar on their duty uniforms. Decorations are customarily presented by the chief of state or the prime minister or their representatives at ceremonies which are held as soon as possible after the achievement for which they are awarded.

Five principal state decorations were authorized by statute in 1958: The National Order of Vietnam; the Medal of Military Merit; the Cross of Valor; the Wound Medal; and the Medal of Honor of Vietnamese Merit.

The National Order of Vietnam, the Republic's highest decoration, which resembles the French Legion of Honor, is composed of five classes—from highest to lowest: Grand Cross, Grand Officer, Commander, Officer and Knight. The medals of the two highest ranks are pinned on the left side of the chest below the breast pocket and are worn with a shoulder cord; the medal of the middle rank is suspended on a ribbon worn around the neck; the last two are suspended from ribbons pinned on the chest.

The Medal of Military Merit, comparable to the United States Silver Star, is awarded to student officers, noncommissioned officers and enlisted men for exceptional military valor. Under exceptional circumstances the medal may be awarded to service personnel of allied forces who have distinguished themselves in military action on Vietnamese territory.

The Cross of Valor resembles the French Croix de Guerre in appearance and is comparable to the United States Bronze Star. It is awarded in four grades, with bronze, silver and gold stars and with bronze palms.

The Wound Medal, comparable to the United States Purple Heart, is awarded to service personnel wounded in action against an enemy.

The Medal of Honor of Vietnamese Merit is awarded for outstanding service in either first or second class. First Class awards as a rule are made to officers and Second Class, to noncommissioned officers and enlisted men.

In addition to the state decorations various service awards are authorized. These include the Air Force Order, Air Force Honor and Air Merit medals, the Gallantry Medal, the Medal for Bravery and the Distinguished Flying Medal.

MILITARY JUSTICE

The basis of military justice in Vietnam is the Code of Military Justice, which was promulgated in 1951 and which, with relatively few amendments, remains in effect. The Code is based largely on French legal procedures and concepts and is administered centrally by the Minister of War and Reconstruction for all the armed forces. The Minister is assisted in discharging his responsibilities under the Code by a Military Justice Corps which is roughly equivalent to the United States Army Judge Advocate General's Corps. These men are generally law graduates, although some perform their duties while still serving the required probationary period before admission to the bar as qualified lawyers.

The South Vietnamese place considerable stress on pretrial investigation, which is performed by the Criminal Investigation Service of the Military Police. This function previously was performed by the National Gendarmerie, whose personnel were absorbed into the National Police and Military Police when it was abolished in January 1965.

The military court system provides for only two types of military courts: Regular Military Courts and Field Courts. These courts are generally similar to the American General Court-Martial in composition, jurisdiction and award of punishment. There are no South Vietnamese counterparts to the summary and special courts-martial of the United States Army. Regular Military Courts usually are convened at Hue for cases arising in I Corps, at Nha Trang for II Corps cases and at Saigon for those cases arising in the III and IV Corps areas and the Capital Military Region, except for those cases handled by the IV Corps Field Court at Can Tho.

A Regular Military Court is composed of a civilian president, four military members, a chief prosecutor and an examining magistrate, plus necessary administrative and clerical personnel. No defense counsel is provided the accused, although he may hire civilian counsel of his own choosing. If the accused cannot pay for counsel, a civilian lawyer is designated by the local bar association to defend him without pay.

The civilian president is usually a judge from the local court of appeals and is assigned to the military court for a period of 6 months. The four military members may be from any of the military services, are appointed from units within the area by the corps commander and are customarily senior in grade to the accused. Both the public prosecutor and the examining magistrate are generally officers appointed from the Military Justice Corps.

Cases referred to Regular Military Courts include offenses of moderate gravity (punishable by a fine and imprisonment not exceeding 5 years) as well as the most serious offenses (punishable by death or imprisonment for more than 5 years). An accused, if found guilty, may appeal to the Court of Cassation, the highest civilian court of appeals in the country. In cases where the death sentence has been imposed, the accused always has the right to petition for amnesty, even after this appeal has been rejected.

A Field Court has the same composition as a Regular Military Court, except that the president is a military officer instead of a civilian judge. Although the pretrial procedure is simplified and abbreviated much more than for cases appearing before a Regular Military Court, the same classification of offenses are assigned to it for trial. The characteristic features of cases assigned are that they must have arisen during an emergency and they must be of a *flagrante delicto* nature. The South Vietnamese, however, apply the *flagrante delicto* concept in a somewhat wider sense than is done under American law, in that greater latitude is permitted in the presumption that the accused was involved in a crime. While both military personnel and civilians can be brought before these courts, civilian cases usually are limited to the most serious crimes involving the security of the state. Sentences pronounced by Field Courts are final and not subject to appellate review as in the case of Regular Military Courts. As a matter of established procedure, however, death sentences are not carried out without the approval of the Chief of State.

Nonjudicial punishment is not recognized by the Code of Military Justice, but it has long been authorized by various directives and orders of the Minister of War and Reconstruction. In general, the permissible types and amount of punishment under this disciplinary action vary according to the grade of the offender and the rank of the person imposing the punishment. The usual type of punishment is restriction or confinement, the forfeiture of pay not being authorized by regulations. The lowest grade Vietnamese punishing authority is a corporal, who can impose a maximum of 2-days' restriction on any enlisted man under his command. The highest is the Minister of War and Reconstruction, who may order solitary confinement for up to 60 days. The Vietnamese soldier does not have the option of electing trial by court-martial in lieu of nonjudicial punishment.

BIBLIOGRAPHIES

Section I. Social

RECOMMENDED FURTHER READING

Among the sources consulted in the preparation of this section, the following are recommended as additional reading on the basis of quality and general availability.

Browne, Malcolm W. *The New Face of War.* Indianapolis: Bobbs-Merrill, 1965.

Buttinger, Joseph. *The Smaller Dragon: A Political History of Vietnam.* New York: Praeger, 1962.

Cadière, Leopold. *Croyances et pratiques religieuses des Vietnamiens*, I and II. Paris: Ecole Française d' Extrême-Orient, 1958.

————. "La Famille et la religion en pays annamite," *Bulletin de la Sociéte des Etudes Indochinoises*, XXXIII, 1958, 33–84.

Cady, John F. *The Roots of French Imperialism in Eastern Asia.* Ithaca: Cornell University Press, 1954.

————. *Southeast Asia: Its Historical Development.* New York: McGraw-Hill, 1965.

Canada. Department of Mines and Technical Surveys. Geographical Branch. *Indo-China: A Geographical Appreciation.* (Foreign Geography Information Series, No. 6.) Ottawa: 1953.

Carver, George A., Jr. "The Real Revolution in South Viet Nam," *Foreign Affairs*, XLIII, April 1965, 387–408.

Condominas, Georges. *Nous avons mangé la forêt de la Pierre-Genie Goo.* Paris: Mercure de France, 1957.

Dournes, Jacques (Dam Bo). "Les Populations montagnards du Sud-Indochine," *France-Asie* (Special Issue), V, 1949–50, 931–1204.

Fairbank, John K.; Reischauer, Edwin O.; and Craig, Albert M. *East Asia: The Modern Transformation.* Boston: Houghton Mifflin, 1965.

Fall, Bernard B. "Sociological and Psychological Aspects of Vietnam's Partition," *Journal of International Affairs*, XVII, No. 2, 1964, 173–187.

————. *The Two Viet-Nam's: A Political and Military Analysis.* (Rev. ed.) New York: Praeger, 1964.

Gourou, Pierre. *The Peasants of the Tonkin Delta*, I. (Human Relations Area Files "Behavior Science Translations.") New Haven: HRAF, 1955.

Great Britain. Admiralty. Naval Intelligence Division *Indo-China*. (Geographical Handbook Series.) London: 1943.

Halberstam, David. *The Making of a Quagmire*. New York: Random House, 1964.

Hall, D.G.E. *A History of South-East Asia*. New York: St. Martin's Press, 1955.

Hammer, Ellen J. *The Struggle for Indochina*. Stanford: Stanford University Press, 1954.

Hickey, Gerald C. *The Major Ethnic Groups of the South Vietnamese Highlands*. (Advanced Research Projects Agency, Memorandum RM-4-41-ARPA; ARPA Order No. 189-61.) Santa Monica: Rand Corporation, 1964.

————. "Making It On the Mekong," *Random News*, September 1964, 2-6.

————. "Problems of Social Change in Viet-Nam," *Bulletin de la Société des Etudes Indochinoises* (Nouvelle Série), XXXIII, No. 4, 1958, 1-12.

————. *Village in Vietnam*. New Haven: Yale University Press, 1964.

Huard, Pierre, and Durand, Maurice. *Connaisance du Viêt-Nam*. Hanoi: Ecole Française d'Extrême-Orient, 1954.

Joiner, Charles A. "South Vietnam's Buddhist Crisis: Organization for Charity, Dissidence and Unity," *Asian Survey*, IV, July 1964, 915-928.

Lancaster, Donald. *The Emancipation of French Indochina*. London: Oxford University Press, 1961.

LeBar, Frank M.; Hickey, Gerald C.; and Musgrave, John K. *Ethnic Groups of Mainland Southeast Asia*. New Haven: Human Relations Area Files Press, 1964.

Le Thanh Khoi. *Le Viet-Nam: histoire et civilisation*. Les Editions de Minuit. Paris: 1955:

Matsumoto Nobuhiro. *Indoshina no minzoku to bunka* (The People and Culture of Indochina). Tokyo: Iwanami Shoten, 1943.

Omori Minoru (ed.). *Doro to honoho no indoshina* (Mud and Flames in Indochina). Tokyo: Mainichi Shimbunsha, 1965. (Translated by U.S. Department of the Army, Washington: October 1965.)

Purcell, Victor. *The Chinese in Southeast Asia*. New York: Oxford University Press, 1951.

Republic of Vietnam. Ministry of National Economy. National Institute of Statistics. *Statistical Yearbook of Vietnam, 1964*. Saigon: June 1965.

Roberts, Adam. "Buddhism and Politics in South Vietnam," *World Today*, XXI, June 1965, 240–250.

———. "The Buddhists, the War, and the Vietcong," *World Today*, XXII, May 1966, 214–222.

Savani, A. M. *Visage et images du Sud Viet-Nam.* Saigon: Imprimerie Française d'Outre-Mer, 1958.

Schrock, Joann, *et al. Minority Groups in the Republic of Vietnam.* (Center for Research in Social Systems.) Washington: GPO, 1966.

Shaplen, Robert. *The Lost Revolution.* New York: Harper and Row, 1965.

Tac-Gia Chi. *Vietnam Vanhoa Su' cu'o'ng* (Vietnamese Culture: A General Outline). (Revised by Dao Duy Dinh). Vietnam: Bon Phuong (Four Corners of the Earth) Publishing Company, 1938.

Thompson, Virginia. *French Indo-China.* New York: Macmillan, 1942.

Tran-Van-Trai. "La Famille patriarcale annamite." (Thesè pour le Doctorat en Lettres Présentée à la Faculté des Lettres de l'Université de Paris). Paris: Lapagesse, 1942.

U.S. Army Special Warfare School. *Montagnard Tribal Groups of the Republic of Vietnam.* Fort Bragg: USASWS, March 1965.

Wood, Chalmers B. "An American View of the Vietnam Problem," *Journal of the Royal Central Asian Society*, LIII, February 1966, 6–16.

Yamamoto Tatsuro. *Annanshi kenkyu* (History of Annam), I. Tokyo: Yamakawa Shuppansha, 1950.

OTHER SOURCES USED

Benedict, Paul K. "Analysis of Annamese Kinship Terms," *Southwestern Journal of Anthropology*, III, 1947, 371–392.

———. "Languages and Literature of Indochina," *Far Eastern Quarterly*, VI, No. 4, 1947, 379–389.

Bezacier, L. "L'Art vietnamien." *Encyclopedie mensuelle d'outremer*, V, 1960–61.

Blake, Frank O. "Intercultural Communications Guide: Republic of Viet-Nam" Washington: The American University, Special Operations Research Office, 1966. (Unpublished manuscript not available for distribution.)

Bonn, Gisella. "The Grim Buddha," *Atlas*, October 1965, 207–210.

Briggs, Lawrence Palmer. *The Ancient Khmer Empire.* Philadelphia: American Philosophical Society, 1951.

Carthew, Anthony. "Vietnam is Like an Oriental Western," *New York Times Magazine*, January 23, 1966, 8–20.

Chau Kim Dinh. "An Introduction to Vietnamese Art," *Vietnam Today*, I, 1966, 67–69.

Chesneaux, Jean. *Contribution à l'histoire de la nation vietnamienne.* Paris: Editions Sociales, 1955.

Coedis, Georges. *Les Etats hindouisés d'Indochine et d'Indonésie.* Paris: E. de Boccard, 1948.

————. *Les Peuples de la peninsule indochinoise: histoire-civilisation.* Paris: Dunod, 1962.

————. *Pour mieux comprendre Angkor.* Paris: Adrien Maisonneuvre, 1947.

Cole, Allan B. (ed.). *Conflict in Indo-China and International Repercussions: A Documentary History, 1945–1955.* Ithaca: Cornell University Press, 1956.

"Comments on Recent GVN Legislation Concerning Montagnard Common Law Courts in the Central Vietnamese Highlands." (The Rand Corporation, Memorandum for Record OSD/ARPA R & D Field Unit.) San Francisco: June 8, 1965 (mimeo., not available for public distribution).

Condominas, Georges. "The Mnong Gar of Central Vietnam." Chapter 2 in George Peter Murdock (ed.), *Social Structure in Southeast Asia.* Chicago: Quadrangle Books, 1960.

————. "Racial Problems in Indochina: Aspects of a Minority Problem," *Far Eastern Economic Review,* XI, August 23, 1951, 238–240.

Condon, Catherine. *Foreign Fellowship Report: South Vietnam.* N.pl.: Smith, French and Kline, 1962.

Cressey, George B. *Asia's Land and Peoples.* New York: McGraw-Hill, 1951.

Cuisinier, Jeanne. *Les Muong: geographie humaine et sociologie.* Paris: Institut d'Ethnologie, 1948.

Devereaux, George. "Functioning Units in Ha (rh) Ndea (ng) Society," *Primitive Man,* X, No. 1, 1937, 3–7.

————. "The Potential Contributions of the Moi to the Cultural Landscape of Indochina," *Far Eastern Quarterly,* VI, No. 4, 1947, 390–395.

Doan Quan Tan. "The Evolution of the Civilization of Vietnam and the Problem Between Vietnam and France," *Asia,* I, March 1951, 47–61.

Donoghue, John D. *Cam An: A Fishing Village in Central Vietnam.* Washington: Michigan State University Vietnam Advisory Group. Agency for International Development, n.d.

————. *My Thuan: The Study of a Delta Village in South Vietnam.* Washington: Michigan State University Vietnam Advisory Group, Agency for International Development, 1961.

————. "The Rhade of South Viet Nam: A Preliminary Report," *Current Anthropology,* IV, October 1963, 382–384.

Dorsey, John T., Jr. "The Bureaucracy and Political Development in Viet Nam." Pages 318–359 in Joseph LaPalombara (ed.), *Bureaucracy and Political Development*. Princeton: Princeton University Press, 1963.

Dournes, Jacques (Dam Bo). *En suivant la piste des hommes sur les Hauts-Plateaux du Viet-Nam*. Paris: Rene Juillard, 1955.

Dowdy, Homer E. *The Bamboo Cross*. New York: Harper and Row, 1964.

Doxiadis Associates. *Saigon Metropolitan Area Urban Development Program and Plan*, I. N.pl.: January 26, 1965.

Dunn, William B. "American Policy and Vietnamese Nationalism: 1950–1954." Unpublished Doctoral dissertation, Faculty of the Division of the Social Sciences, University of Chicago, 1960 (Microfilm 7003E, Reel 6726).

"Education in Vietnam: Progress and Prospects," *Vietnam Review*, I, August 9, 1962, 8–13.

"L'Eglise au Sud-Vietnam," *Informations Catholiques Internationales* (Paris), No. 188, March 15, 1963.

Elegant, Robert S. *The Dragon's Seed: Peking and the Overseas Chinese*. New York: St. Martin's Press, 1960.

Ennis, Thomas E. *French Policy and Developments in Indochina*. Chicago: University of Chicago Press, 1936.

———. "Vietnam: Land Without Laughter," *Current History*, XLVI, February 1964, 101–106.

Fall, Bernard B. "Indochina Since Geneva," *Pacific Affairs*, XXVIII, March 1955, 3–25.

———. "The Political-Religious Sects of Viet-Nam," *Pacific Affairs*, XXVIII, September 1955, 235–253.

———. "South Viet-Nam's Internal Problems," *Pacific Affairs*, XXXI, September 1958, 241–260.

———. "Viet-Nam's Chinese Problem." *Far Eastern Survey*, XXVII, April 1958, 65–72.

Fifield, Russell H. *Southeast Asia in United States Policy*. New York: Praeger, 1963.

Fishel, Wesley R. "American Aid to Vietnam," *Current History*, XLIX, November 1965, 294–299.

Fishel, Wesley R. (ed.). *Problems of Freedom: South Vietnam Since Independence*. Glencoe: Free Press, 1961.

Fitzgerald, C. P. "Overseas Chinese in South East Asia," *Australian Journal of Politics and History*, VIII, No. 1, 1962, 66–77.

"Folklore indochinois: le marriage annamite," *France-Asie*, V, August 1946, 222–225.

Foy, Felician A. *1966 National Catholic Almanac*. Patterson: St. Anthony's Guild, 1966.

Funakoshi Yasuhisa. *Tonanazia bunkakenshi* (History of Southeast Asian Cultural Sphere). Tokyo: Sanseido, 1943.

Gobron, Gabriel. *History and Philosophy of Caodaism.* Saigon: Tu Hai Publishing House, 1950.

Guilleminet, Paul P. *Coutumier de la tribu Bahnar des Sedang et des Jarai (de la province de Kontum), XXXII.* Paris: Ecole Française d'Extrême-Orient, 1952.

————. "La Tribu Bahnar du Kontum," *Bulletin de l'Ecole Française d Extrême-Orient* (Paris), XLV, 1952, 393–561.

Hastings, Adrian (ed.). *The Church and the Nations.* New York: Sheed and Ward, 1959.

Hay, Stephen N., and Case, Margaret H. *Southeast Asian History: A Bibliographic Guide.* New York: Praeger, 1962.

Hendry, James B. *The Small World of Khanh Hau.* Chicago: Aldine Publishing House, 1964.

————. *The Work Force in Saigon.* Saigon: Michigan State University Vietnam Advisory Group, 1960.

Ho, Le van. *La Mère de famille annamite.* (L'Université de Paris, Institut de droit comparé: études de sociologie et d'ethnologie juridiques, XVI, published under the direction of René Maunier.) Paris: Les Editions Domat-Montchrestien, 1932.

Hoang Van Chi. *From Colonialism to Communism: A Case History of North Vietnam.* London: Pall Mall Pres, 1964.

Honey, P. J. "The Outlook in Indo-China." Pages 142–159 in Alastair Buchan (ed.), *China and the Peace of Asia.* New York: Praeger, 1965.

Hoskins, Marilyn W., and Shepherd, Eleanor M. "Life in a Vietnamese Urban Quarter." Carbondale: Southern Illinois University, Graduate School, Office of Research and Projects, 1965.

Hsu, Francis L. K. *Under the Ancestors' Shadow: Chinese Culture and Personality.* New York: Columbia University Press, 1948.

Ishizuka, Shunjiro. "Mud and Flame: Under Thick War Clouds in Indochina," *Mainichi Daily News,* January 4, 1965–February 1, 1965.

Janse, Olov R. T. "The People of French Indochina." (Smithsonian Institution War Background Studies, No. 19, Publication 3768.) Washington: June 12, 1944.

Japan. Ministry of Foreign Affairs. *Dai shichijūkyū gikai ni okeru gaikōkankei shitsugi ōtōyōshi, juichigatsu 1942* (The Summary of Question and Answer on Foreign Relations at the 79th Diet Session, November 1942). Tokyo: n.d.

————. *Futsuin ni kansuru nichifutsukan (fukōhyō o fukumu) jōyakushū, shigatsu 1943* (List of Treaties Between Japan and France [Including Those Unpublished] Pertaining to French Indochina, April 1943). Tokyo: n.d.

————. *Jōsei no henka ni ōzura futsuin shorimondai: Indoshina dokuritsu, gunbi, kōshu-wan setsushūmondai, kugatsu 1944-sangatsu*

1945 (The Problem of Actions to Be Taken Regarding French Indo-China in Order to Meet the Changed Situations: The Independence of French Indo-China, Military Expenses, and the Occupation of Kwangchow Bay, September 1944-March 1945). Tokyo: n.d.

————. *Nampō bunkaseisaku—daitōa sensō to bunkakōsaku* (Cultural Policy Toward Southeast Asia: Great East Asia War and Cultural Operations). Tokyo: n.d.

————. *Taifutsuin tai shisakuyōkō, ichigatsu 30, 1941* (Basic Policies Toward French Indochina and Thailand. January 30, 1941). Tokyo: n.d.

Joiner, Charles, *Public Administration in the Saigon Metropolitan Area.* Saigon: Michigan State University Vietnam Advisory Group, n.d.

Jones, P.H.M. "Factories for the Center," *Far Eastern Economic Review*, XLVIII, April 15, 1965, 130, 131.

Jumper, Roy. "Sects and Communism in South Vietnam," *Orbis*, III, April 1959, 85–96.

Kahin, George McTurnan (ed.). *Governments and Politics of Southeast Asia.* Ithaca: Cornell University Press, 1962.

Katayama Shinkicho. *Nampo Minzokuundoshi* (History of Nationalist Movement in South and Southeast Asia). Tokyo: Modan Nipponsha, 1942.

Kaufman, Howard K. "Cu-Lao: A Preliminary Socio-Economic Study of a Fishing Village and Its Cooperative." Saigon: Cooperative Research and Training Center, October 1963 (mimeo.).

Ky, Luong Nhi. "The Chinese in Vietnam: A Study of Vietnamese-Chinese Relations with Special Attention to the Period 1862–1961." Unpublished Doctoral dissertation, University of Michigan, 1962.

Lafont, Pierre Bernard. *Prières Jarai.* (Ecole Française d'Extrême-Orient: Collection de Textes et Documents sur l'Indochine, VIII.) Paris: Adrien Maisonneuve, 1963.

————. *To'lo'i djuat: coutumier de la tribu jarai.* (Publications de l'Ecole Française d'Extrême-Orient, LI.) Paris: Ecole Française d'Extrême-Orient, 1963.

Lam Le Trinh. "Village Councils: Yesterday and Today" (Pt. I), *Viet-My*, III, June 1958, 36–44.

Landon, Kenneth Perry. *Southeast Asia: Crossroads of Religion.* Chicago: University of Chicago Press, 1947.

Langrand, Gustave. *Vie sociale et religieuse en Annam: monographie d'un village de la côte Sud-Annam.* Lille: Editions Univers, 1945.

Levinson, John M. "Medicine in South Vietnam." *Journal of the American Medical Association*, CXCII, May 31, 1965, 156–158.

Levy, Roger; Lacam, Guy; and Roth, Andrew. *French Interest and Policies in the Far East.* New York: Institute of Pacific Relations, 1941.

Lindholm, Richard W. (ed.). *Viet-Nam: The First Five Years.* East Lansing: Michigan State University Press, 1959.

Lingat, Robert. *Les Régimes matrimoniaux du Sud-Est de l'Asie.* Essai de droit comparé Indochinoise.) Paris: Ecole Française d'Extrême-Orient, 1952.

Louka, Kathyrn T. *The Role of Population in the Development of Southeast Asia.* Washington: George Washington University, 1960.

Maillard, Jean. "Bilan de l'oeuvre medical et sanitaire de la France en Indochine," *Encyclopedie mensuelle d'outre-mer,* No. 67, March 1965, 126–129.

Maliks, Skaidrite, and Stowell, John H. *A Brief History of Ethnically Oriented Schools Within Vietnam's Educational System.* Washington: The American University Special Operations Research Office, Counterinsurgency Information Analysis Center, 1965.

Maurice, Albert, and Proux, Georges Marie. "L'Ame du Rix," *Bulletin de la Société des Etudes Indochinoises,* XXIX, 1954, 129–258.

Meillet, A., and Cohen, Marcel. *Les Langues du monde.* Paris: Société de Linguistique de Paris, Centre National de la Recherche Scientific, 1952.

Michigan State University Vietnam Advisory Group. Field Administration Division. "Preliminary Research Report on the PMS [Pays Montagnard du Sud]," by Gerald C. Hickey, assisted by Frederic Wickert. Saigon: June 1957 (mimeo.).

Ming, Ly-y. "The Chinese in Vietnam," *Viet-My,* III, Autumn 1960, 10–14.

Mitchison, Lois. *The Overseas Chinese: A Background Book.* Chester Springs: Dufour Editions, 1961.

Murray, Douglas P. "Chinese Education in South-East Asia," *China Quarterly,* XX, October–December 1964, 67–95.

Mus, Paul. *Le Viet Nam chez lui.* Paris: Centre d'Etudes de Politique Etrangère, 1946.

Nathan, Andrew. "'New Life' in Vietnam," *Far Eastern Economic Review,* XLIV, April 23, 1964, 200–203.

Nghiem-Lenh-Thiev. "The Role of Traditional Medicine in the Vietnamese Society." N.p.l.: n.d. (Unpublished manuscript not available for distribution.)

Nguyen Dac Khe. "The Independence of Viet-Nam and the French Union," *Asia,* III, September 1953, 216–230.

Nguyen Dinh Hoa. "Vietnamese Country Life," *Vietnam Today,* I, 1966, 11, 12.

Nguyen Huu Trong. *Les Origines du clergé vietnamien: le clergé national dans la fondation de l'eglise au Viet-Nam.* Saigon: Groupe Litteraire Tinh-Viet, Section Historique, 1959.

Nguyen Phuoc Thien. "The Theater of Vietnam," *Vietnam Today*, I, 1966, 71, 72.

Nguyen Thanh Giung. "Viet-Nam in Contact with French Culture," *Asia*, III, June 1953, 68–76.

Nguyen Van Thuan. *An Approach to Better Understanding of Vietnamese Society: A Primer for Americans.* Saigon: Michigan State University Vietnam Advisory Group, 1962.

Nguyen Xuan Ky. "Vietnamese Legends," *Vietnam Today*, I, 1966 59, 60.

Noss, John B. *Man's Religions.* New York: Macmillan, 1956.

Oka, Takashi. "Hill Tribes: Irritant to Saigon," *Christian Science Monitor*, December 24, 1965, 10.

————. "Hill Tribes Leader in South Vietnam," *Christian Science Monitor*, December 27, 1965, 2.

Pham Viet Tuyen, "Asian Cultural Relations and the Evolution of National Ideology," *Asian Culture*, I, Spring 1959, 27–54.

Pike, E. Royston. *Encyclopaedia of Religion and Religions.* New York: Meridian Library, 1958.

Poncins, Contran de Montaigne, Viconte de. *From a Chinese City.* New York: Doubleday, 1957.

Reischauer, Edwin O., and Fairbank, John K. *East Asia: The Great Tradition.* Boston: Houghton Mifflin, 1960.

Republic of Vietnam. Directorate General of Information. *Vietnam's Strategic Hamlets.* Saigon: 1963.

Republic of Vietnam. Directorate of Cultural Affairs. Department of National Education. *Democracy in Traditional Vietnamese Society*, by Nguyen Dang Thuc. (Vietnam Culture Series No. 4.) Saigon: 1961.

————. *Higher Education in the Republic of Vietnam*, by Nguyen Dinh Hoa. (Vietnam Culture Series No. 6) Saigon: n.d.

————. *Introduction to Vietnamese Culture*, by Nguyen Khac Kham. (Vietnam Culture Series No. 1.) Saigon: 1961.

Republic of Vietnam. Embassy in Washington. *Viet-Nam at the Crossroads of Asia.* Washington: n.d.

Republic of Vietnam. Laws, Statutes, etc.

"The Buddhist Question: The Position of the Government of the Republic of Vietnam," *Basic Documents*, I (May 6 to August 21, 1963) and II (August 22 to September 2, 1963). Saigon: Vietnam Press, n.d.

Cho do tai san trong gia dinh Viet Nam (Law Regulating Family Property), I and II. Saigon: 1960.

Sac-luat so 15/64 ban hanh ngay 23 thang 7 nam 1964, qui dinh gia thu, tu he va tai san cong dong (Decree Law No. 15/64 of July 23, 1964, Regulating Marriage, Descent and Community Property, published in the Official Gazette). Saigon: 1964.

Republic of Vietnam. Ministry of Education. *Education in Viet-nam, 1963–1964.* (Presented at the 27th International Conference on Public Instruction.) Geneva : 1964.

————. Department of Research and Planning. *Education in Viet-nam, 1965.* Saigon : 1965.

Republic of Vietnam. Ministry of National Economy. National Institute of Statistics. *Statistical Yearbook of Vietnam, 1962,* X. Saigon : 1964.

————. *Vital Statistics, 1963.* Saigon : 1963.

Republic of Vietnam. Secretariat d'Etat a l'Economie Nationale. *Enquete demographique a Saigon en 1962.* Saigon : Institut National de la Statistique, 1963.

————. *Recensement des etablissements au Viet Nam,* I and II. Saigon : Institut National de la Statistique, 1962 and 1963.

Riessen, René. *Jungle Mission.* New York : Crowell, 1958.

Sabatier, Leopold (ed.). *Recueil des coutumes Rhadées du Darlac.* Hanoi : Imprimerie d'Extrême Orient, 1940.

Saunders, Kenneth J. *Buddhism and Buddhists in Southern Asia.* New York : Macmillan, 1923.

Scigliano, Robert G. *South Vietnam: Nation Under Stress.* Boston : Houghton Mifflin, 1964.

Shaffer, H. L., Jr. "Literary Examinations in Old Viet Nam." *Viet-My,* VIII, March 1963, 38–45.

Shen-yu Dai. *Peking, Moscow, and the Communist Parties of Colonial Asia.* Cambridge : Center for International Studies, Massachusetts Institute of Technology, 1954.

Sien-chong, Niu. "The Overseas Chinese," *Military Review,* XLV, August 1965, 29–35.

Simoniya, N. A. *Overseas Chinese in Southeast Asia: A Russian Study.* N.pl. : n.d. (Translated by U.S. Joint Publications Re-search Service, JPRS : 3,443, New York : June 28, 1960.)

Sinanoglou, Paula A. "The History of Buddhism in Vietnam." New Haven : Yale University, n.d. (Unpublished manuscript not available for distribution.)

"Social Institutions in Ancient Vietnam," *Vietnam Fights and Builds,* No. 4, March 1965, 28, 29.

Spencer, R. F. "The Annamese Kinship System," *Southwestern Journal of Anthropology,* I, 1945, 371–392.

Stamp, L. Dudley. *Asia: A Regional and Economic Geography.* New York : Dutton, 1957.

Sugimoto Naojiro. *Tōnan aziashi kenkyū* (Studies in Southeast Asian History), I. Tokyo : Nippon Gakujutsu Shinkokai, 1956.

Sutter, John O. *Scientific Facilities and Information Services of the Republic of Vietnam.* (Pacific Scientific Information No. 3, pub-

lished for the National Science Foundation.)   Honolulu: Pacific
Scientific Information Center, 1961.

Thomas, David D. "Mon-Khmer Subgroupings in Vietnam."
Grand Forks: University of North Dakota, Summer Institute of
Linguistics, 1962 (mimeo.).

Thompson, Virginia. *Labor Problems in Southeast Asia.* New
Haven: Yale University Press, 1947.

Topping, Seymour. "Peking Pressing Overseas Chinese," *New
York Times*, July 10, 1965, 3.

Trager, Frank N. (ed.). *Marxism in Southeast Asia: A Study of
Four Countries.* Stanford University Press, 1959.

"Les Traits caracteristiques dans les moeurs et coutumes des tribus
montagnards au Sud au Vietnam." N.pl.: Management of Social
Welfare for the Montagnard Regions, n.d. (Translated by U.S.
Joint Publications Research Service, JPRS: 13,443, Washington:
April 13, 1962.

Tran Long. "How to be Liked in Vietnam," *Vietnam Today*, I, 1966,
9, 10.

Tran Quang Thuan. "Some Aspects of Vietnamese Society,"
Asian Culture, II, July–December 1960, 47–67.

Tran Van Tung. *Viet-Nam.* New York: Praeger, 1959.

Tue Giac. *Viet-nam phat-giao tranh-dau su* (History of Buddhist
Struggles in Viet Nam). Saigon: Hoa Nghiem Publishing House,
1964.

Tuyet Nguyet Markbreiter. "Vietnamese Dilemma," *Far Eastern
Economic Review*, XLVII, March 25, 1965, 552–555.

U.S. Agency for International Development. *A Nation's Progress:
The Story of U.S.-Vietnamese Cooperation in Economic Develop
ment.* Washington: AID, 1964.

U.S. Congress. 89th, 1st Session. Senate. Committee on Foreign
Relations. *Background Information Relating to Southeast Asia
and Vietnam.* (Rev. ed.) Washington: GPO, 1965.

U.S. Department of Defense. Military Assistance Institute. *Country Study: Republic of Vietnam.* Washington: American Institutes for Research, 1965.

U.S. Department of Health, Education and Welfare. Social Security
Administration. Division of Research and Statistics. *Social Security Programs Throughout the World, 1964.* Washington: GPO,
1964.

U.S. Department of Labor. Bureau of International Labor Affairs.
Directory of Labor Organizations: Asia and Australasia, II
Washington: GPO, 1963.

U.S. Department of Labor. Bureau of Labor Statistics. *Summary of
the Labor Situation in the Republic of Vietnam, 1957.* Washington:
GPO, 1957.

U.S. Department of State. Bureau of Public Affairs. Office of Media Services. *Fact Sheet: Vietnam.* (Far Eastern Series 116.) Washington: GPO, 1963.

U.S. United States Information Agency. Research and Reference Service. "The Vietnamese Peasant: His Value System." Washington: October 1965 (mimeo.).

U.S. United States Operations Mission to Vietnam. *The U.S. Assistance Program for Vietnam.* N.pl.: January 1965.

————. Agency for International Development. *USOM Vietnam: Operational Report, 1963–64.* Saigon: USOM, 1965.

U.S. United States Operations Mission to Vietnam. Division of Agriculture and Natural Resources. *Studies on Land Tenure in Viet Nam*, by J. P. Gittinger.. (Terminal Report.) Saigon: USOM, 1959.

U.S. United States Operations Mission to Vietnam. Economic and Financial Planning Division. *Annual Statistical Bulletin.* (No. 7.) Saigon: 1964.

U.S. United States Operations Mission to Vietnam. Education Division. *Student Record from Vietnam.* (Rev. ed.) Washington: Agency for International Development, 1964.

Vu Quoc Thuc. "The Influence of Western Civilization on Economic Behavior of the Vietnamese," *Asian Culture*, I, Winter 1958, 45, 46.

Vu Tam Ich. "A Historical Survey of Educational Developments in Vietnam," *Bulletin of the Bureau of School Service* (University of Kentucky), XXXII, December 1959, 1–135.

Vu Trong Tien. "The Origin of the Vietnamese Village Communities," *Viet-My*, II, March 1957, 49, 50.

Vuong Hong Sen. "Comments on Vietnamese History," *Viet-My*, I August 1956, 25–27.

Walter Reed Army Medical Center. Institute of Research. *The Republic of Vietnam.* (Health Data Publication No. 6.) Washington: 1963.

Ward, Barbara E. *Women in the New Asia.* Paris: United Nations Educational, Scientific and Cultural Organization, 1963.

Warner, Denis. *The Last Confucian: Vietnam, Southeast Asia and the West.* Baltimore: Penguin Books, 1964.

————. "Vietnam's Militant Buddhists," *Reporter*, XXXI, December 3, 1964, 29–31.

Woodruff, Lloyd W. *Local Administration in Vietnam: Its Future Development.* Saigon: Michigan State University Vietnam Advisory Group and National Institute of Administration, 1961.

World Confederation of Organizations of the Teaching Profession. *Impact on Education of Terrorist Activities in Viet Nam.* (Presented at the WCOTP Commission of Inquiry, May 18–26, 1962.) N.pl.: n.d.

The Worldmark Encyclopedia of the Nations: Asia and Australasia.
New York: Harper and Row, 1963.

(In addition to the above sources, various issues of the following periodicals, from January 1963 through May 1966, were used in the preparation of this section: *Asian Recorder, Deadline Data, Front Lines, Keesing's Contemporary Archives, The Guardian, Le Monde, New York Times, Saigon Daily News, Times, Wall Street Journal, Washington Post* and *Washington Star.*)

Section II. Political

RECOMMENDED FURTHER READING

Among the sources consulted in the preparation of this section, the following are recommended as additional reading on the basis of quality and general availability.

Ben, Philip. "Russia and Vietnam," *New Republic*, CLIII, July 10, 1965, 5.

Browne, Malcolm W. *The New Face of War*. Indianapolis: Bobbs-Merrill, 1965.

Carver, George A., Jr. "The Faceless Viet Cong," *Foreign Affairs*, XLIV, April 1966, 347–372.

————. "The Real Revolution in South Viet Nam," *Foreign Affairs*, XLIII, April 1965, 387–408.

Cattell, David T. "Soviet Foreign Policy: A Broad View," *Current History*, XLIX, October 1965, 208–213.

Chen, King. "North Vietnam in the Sino-Soviet Dispute, 1962–64," *Asian Survey*, IV, September 1964, 1023–1036.

Deutscher, Issac. "Russia vs. China: Clash over Vietnam," *Nation*, CCI, July 5, 1965, 3, 4.

Dorsey, John T., Jr. "The Bureaucracy and Political Development in Viet Nam." Pages 318–359 in Joseph LaPalombara (ed.), *Bureaucracy and Political Development*. Princeton: Princeton University Press, 1963.

Fall, Bernard B. "The Political-Religious Sects of Vietnam," *Pacific Affairs*, XXVIII, September 1955, 235–253.

————. *The Two Viet-Nam's: A Political and Military Analysis.* (Rev. ed.) New York: Praeger, 1964.

————. *Vietnam Witness: 1953–1966.* New York: Praeger, 1966.

Fifield, Russell H. *The Diplomacy of Southeast Asia: 1945–1958.* New York: Harper, 1958.

Fishel, Wesley R. "Vietnam: The Broadening War," *Asian Survey*, VI, January 1966, 49–58.

Fishel, Wesley R. (ed.). *Problems of Freedom: South Vietnam since Independence.* Glencoe: Free Press, 1961.

Halberstam, David, *The Making of a Quagmire*. New York: Random House, 1964.

Hammer, Ellen J. "South Vietnam: The Limits of Political Action," *Pacific Affairs*, XXXV, Spring 1962, 24–36.

Hammer, Ellen J. *The Struggle for Indochina.* Stanford: Stanford University Press, 1954.

Joiner, Charles A. "Administration and Political Warfare in the Highlands," *Vietnam Perspectives,* I, November 1965, 19–37.

————. "South Vietnam's Buddhist Crisis: Organization for Charity, Dissidence, and Unity," *Asian Survey,* IV, July 1965, 915–928.

Jumper, Roy, and Normand, Marjorie Weiner. "Vietnam." Pages 375–524 in George McTurnan Kahin (ed.), *Governments and Politics of Southeast Asia.* (2d ed.) Ithaca: Cornell University Press, 1964.

Lacouture, Jean. *Vietnam: Between Two Truces.* New York: Random House, 1966.

Lancaster, Donald. *The Emancipation of French Indochina.* London: Oxford University Press, 1961.

Lansdale, Edward G. "Viet Nam: Do We Understand Revolution?" *Foreign Affairs,* XLIII, October 1964, 75–86.

Larteguy, Jean. "Notre Indochine: dix ans apres," *Paris Match,* September 25, 1965, 52–57.

Lichtheim, George. "Vietnam and China," *Commentary,* XXXIX, May 1965, 58, 59.

Marr, David. "Political Attitudes and Activities of Young Urban Intellectuals in South Viet-Nam," *Asian Survey,* VI, May 1966, 249–263.

McLane, Charles B. "U.S.S.R. Policy in Asia," *Current History,* XLIX, October 1965, 214–220.

Morgenthau, Hans. "Dilemma—Russia, the U.S. and Vietnam." *New Republic,* CLII, May 1, 1965, 12, 13.

Morris, Roger. "Russia's Stake in Vietnam," *New Republic,* CLII, February 13, 1965, 13–15.

Roberts, Adam. "Buddhism and Politics in South Vietnam," *World Today,* XXI, June 1965, 240–250.

————. "The Buddhists, the War, and the Vietcong," *World Today,* XXII, May 1966, 214–222.

Scalapino, Robert A. "Moscow, Peking and the Communist Parties of Asia," *Foreign Affairs,* XLI, January 1963.

Scigliano, Robert G. "Political Parties in South Vietnam," *Pacific Affairs,* XXXIII, December 1960, 327–346.

————. *South Vietnam: Nation Under Stress.* Boston: Houghton Mifflin, 1964.

————. "Vietnam: Politics and Religion," *Asian Survey,* IV, January 1964, 666–673.

Shaplen, Robert. *The Lost Revolution.* New York: Harper and Row, 1965.

U.S. Department of State. *Aggression from the North: The Record of North Viet-Nam's Campaign to Conquer South Viet-Nam.* (Department of State Publication 7839.) Washington: GPO, 1965.

————. Bureau of Public Affairs. Office of Public Services. *A Threat to the Peace: North Viet-Nam's Effort to Conquer South Viet-Nam,* Pt. 1. (Department of State Publication 7308, Far Eastern Series 110.) Washington: GPO, 1961.

U.S. United States Information Agency. Research and Reference Service. "The Vietnamese Peasant: His Value System." Washington: October 1965 (mimeo.).

Warner, Denis. *The Last Confucian: Vietnam, Southeast Asia and the West.* Baltimore: Penguin Books, 1964.

OTHER SOURCES USED

Ben, Philip. "Opinion in Paris: China Won't Fight," *New Republic,* CLIII, September 25, 1965, 18.

Bouscaren, Anthony Trawick. *The Last of the Mandarins: Diem of Vietnam.* Pittsburgh: Duquesne University Press, 1965.

Bukkyo Dainenkan Kankokai (ed.). *Bukkyo Dainenkan 1961* (Buddhist Yearbook 1961). Tokyo: Bukkyo Dainenkan Kankokai, 1961.

Cady, John F. *Southeast Asia: Its Historical Development.* New York: McGraw-Hill, 1965.

Cole, Allan B. (ed.). *Conflict in Indo-China and International Repercussions: A Documentary History, 1945–1955.* Ithaca: Cornell University Press, 1956.

Corley, Francis J. "The President in the Constitution of the Republic of Viet-Nam," *Pacific Affairs,* XXXIV, Summer 1961, 165–174.

Dang Van Sung. "Dilemmas in Vietnam." Saigon: n.d. (mimeo.).

Devillers, Philippe. "The Struggle for the Unification of Vietnam," *China Quarterly,* IX, January-March 1962, 2–36.

Doan Quan Tan. "The Evolution of the Civilization of Vietnam and the Problem Between Vietnam and France," *Asia,* I, March 1951, 47–61.

Dorsey, John T., Jr. "South Viet-Nam in Perspective," *Far Eastern Survey,* XXVII, December 1958, 177–182.

Fairbank, John K. (ed.). *Chinese Thought and Institutions.* Chicago: University of Chicago Press, 1957.

Fall, Bernard B. "Blitz in Vietnam: A Report on the Impersonal War," *New Republic,* CLIII, October 9, 1965, 17–21.

————. *Street Without Joy: Indochina at War, 1946–1954.* Harrisburg: Stackpole, 1961.

————. "That Geneva Agreement: How the French Got Out of Vietnam," *New York Times Magazine,* May 2, 1965, 28, 29.

Fall, Bernard B. "What de Gaulle Actually Said About Vietnam," *Reporter*, XXXI, October 24, 1964, 39–41.

Finkle, Jason L., and Tran Van Dinh. *Provincial Government in Viet Nam: A Study of Vinh Long Province.* Saigon: Michigan State University Vietnam Advisory Group and National Institute of Administration, 1961.

Fishel, Wesley R. "Political Realities in Vietnam," *Asian Survey*, I, April 1961, 1–7.

Gettleman, Marvin E. *Vietnam.* New York: Fawcett Publications, 1965.

Gorrell, Frank. "Accomplishment of Mendes-France," *New Republic*, CXXXI, July 26, 1954, 6, 7.

Grant, J. A. C. "The Vietnam Constitution of 1956," *American Political Science Review*, LII, June 1958, 437–462.

Hall, D. G. E. "Vietnam's Political History: A Review Article," *Pacific Affairs*, XXXII, March 1959, 94–96.

Hammer, Ellen J. *The Struggle for Indochina Continues.* Stanford: Stanford University Press, 1955.

Hendry, James B. *The Study of a Vietnamese Rural Community: Administrative Activity*, I and II. (Michigan State University Vietnam Advisory Group.) Washington: U.S. Agency for International Development, 1960.

Hickey, Gerald C. *The Study of a Vietnamese Rural Community: Sociology.* Saigon: Michigan State University Vietnam Advisory Group, 1960.

————. *Village in Vietnam.* New Haven: Yale University Press, 1964.

Higgins, Marguerite. *Our Vietnam Nightmare.* New York: Harper and Row, 1965.

Hinton, Harold C. *China's Relations with Burma and Vietnam: A Brief Survey.* New York: Institute of Pacific Relations, 1958.

Japan. Ministry of Foreign Affairs. *Jōsei no henka ni ōzuru futsuin shorimondai: Indoshina dokuritsu, gunbi, kōshu-wan setsushumondai, kugatsu 1944 sangatsu 1945.* The Problem of Actions to be Taken Regarding French Indo-China in Order to Meet the Changed Situations: The Independence of French Indo-China, Military Expenses, and the Occupation of Kwangchow Bay, September 1944–March 1945). Tokyo: n.d.

Johnson, Lyndon B. *Patterns for Peace in Southeast Asia.* (Department of State Publication 7872, Far Eastern Series 132.) Washington: 1965.

————. Viet-Nam: *The Third Face of the War.* (Department of State Publication 7897, Far Eastern Series 134.) Washington: 1965.

_____. *We Will Stand in Viet-Nam.* (Department of State Publication 7937, Far Eastern Series 137.) Washington: 1965.

Joiner, Charles A. *Public Administration in the Saigon Metropolitan Area.* Saigon: Michigan State University Vietnam Advisory Group, n.d.

Jumper, Roy. "Mandarin Bureaucracy and Politics in South Vietnam," *Pacific Affairs,* XXX, March 1957, 47–58.

Klein, Wells C., and Weiner, Marjorie. "Vietnam." Pages 315–387 in George McTurnan Kahin (ed.), *Governments and Politics of Southeast Asia.* Ithaca: Cornell University Press, 1962.

Le Thanh Khoi. *Le Viet-Nam: histoire et civilisation.* Paris: Les Editions de Minuit, 1955.

Lindholm, Richard W. (ed.). *Viet-Nam: The First Five Years.* East Lansing: Michigan State University Press, 1959.

Martin, Paul. "If You Wonder How the U.S. Got into the War in Vietnam," *U.S. News & World Report.* LIX, September 13, 1965, 56–62.

Michigan State University Vietnam Advisory Group. Field Administration Division. "Preliminary Research Report on the PMS [Pays Montagnard du Sud], by Gerald C. Hickey, assisted by Frederic Wickert. Saigon: June 1957 (mimeo.).

"Minorities Under the Viet Minh," *Eastern World,* IX, November 1955, 17, 18.

Modelski, George. "The Viet Minh Complex." Pages 185–214 in Cyril E. Black and Thomas P. Thornton (eds.), *Communism and Revolution: The Strategic Uses of Political Violence.* Princeton: Princeton University Press, 1964.

Muramatsu Takeshi. "Minami betonamu no bukkyoto no yakuwariwa nanika? (What is the Buddhists' Role in South Vietnam?), *Chuokoron,* XXC, June 1965, 104–106.

Mus, Paul. "The Role of the Village in Vietnamese Politics," *Pacific Affairs,* XX, September 1949, 265–272.

Nakano Kyotoku. "Minami betonamu mondai o meguru shukyoshiteki haikei" (Religious Historical Background Involving the South Vietnamese Problem), *Shukyo Koron* (Review of Religion), XXXV, April 1965, 7–14.

Nguyen Ngoc Bich. "Vietnam: An Independent Viewpoint," *China Quarterly,* IX, January-March 1962, 105–111.

Nguyen Thanh Giung. "Viet-Nam in Contact with French Culture," *Asia,* III, June 1953, 68–76

Omori Minoru (ed.). *Doro to honoho no indoshina* (Mud and Flames in Indochina). Tokyo: Mainichi Shimbunsha, 1965. (Translated by U.S. Department of the Army, Washington: October 1965.)

Osborne, Milton E. *Strategic Hamlets in South Viet-Nam: A Survey and a Comparison.* (Department of Asian Studies, Southeast Asia

Program: Data Paper No. 55.)   Ithaca: Cornell University Press, 1965.

Pauker, Guy J.   "Southeast Asia as a Problem Area in the Next Decade," *World Politics*, XI, April 1959, 325–345.

Pham Viet Tuyen.   "Asian Cultural Relations and the Evolution of National Ideology," *Asian Culture*, I, Spring 1959, 27–54.

Pike, Douglas.   "How Strong is the NLF?"   *Reporter*, XXXIV, February 24, 1966, 20–24.

Platridge, Shane.   "Australia and the Defense of Southeast Asia," *Foreign Affairs*, XLIV, October 1965, 49–61.

The Psywar Society, VI, September 1965.

Raskin, Marcus G., and Fall, Bernard B. (eds.).   *The Viet-Nam Reader*.   New York: Random House, 1965.

Republic of Vietnam.   *The Bogus War of Liberation in South Vietnam*.   Saigon: June 1965.

————.   *Communist Aggression Against the Republic of Vietnam*.   Saigon: July 1964.

————.   Information Printing Office.   *Eight Years of the Ngo Dinh Diem Administration, 1954–1962*.   Saigon: 1962.

————.   *Seven Years of the Ngo Dinh Diem Administration, 1954–1961*.   Saigon: 1961.

Republic of Vietnam.   Laws, Statutes, etc.

"The Buddhist Question: The Position of the Government of the Republic of Vietnam," *Basic Documents*, I (May 6 to August 21, 1963) and II (August 22 to September 2, 1963).   Saigon: Vietnam Press, n.d.

Republic of Vietnam.   Ministry of Foreign Affairs.   *The So-Called War of Liberation in South Viet-Nam*.   Saigon: 1965.

————.   *The Viet-Nam-Cambodia Border Issue Before the U.N. Security Council*.   Saigon: 1964.

Republic of Vietnam.   National Institute of Administration.   Research and Documentation Division.   *Supplement to Government Organization Manual, 1957–1958*.   Saigon: 1960.

————.   *Viet Nam Government Organization Manual, 1957–1958*.   Saigon: 1958.

Rose, Dale L., and Vu Van Hoc.   *The Vietnamese Civil Service System*.   Saigon: Michigan State University Vietnam Advisory Group, 1961.

Saigon Daily News, June 20, 1965.

Shaplen, Robert.   "Letter from South Vietnam," *New Yorker*, XLII, March 12, 1966, 58–108.

"South Vietnam's Chinese Problem," *Far Eastern Economic Review*, XXXIII, July 20, 1961, 146–148.

Tanham, George K.   *War Without Guns: American Civilians in Rural Vietnam*.   New York: Praeger, 1966.

Tonan Azia Chosakai (Research Institute on South and Southeast Asia). *Tonan azia yoran* (South and Southeast Asia Factbook), *1962*. Tokyo: Tonan Azia Chosakai, 1962.

_____. *Tonan azia yoran* (South and Southeast Asia Factbook), *1964*. Tokyo: Tonan Azia Chosakai, 1964.

_____. *Tonan azia yoran* (South and Southeast Asia Factbook), *1965*. Tokyo: Tonan Azia Chosakai, 1965.

Trager, Frank N. (ed.). *Marxism in Southeast Asia: A study of Four Countries.* Stanford: Stanford University Press, 1959.

Tue Giac. *Viet-nam phat-giao tranh-dau su* (History of Buddhist Struggles in Viet Nam). Sagion: Hoa Nghiem Publishing House, 1964.

U.S. Agency for International Development. *A Vietnamese District Chief in Action,* by Luther A. Allen and Pham Ngoc An. Washington: AID, n.d.

U.S. Congress. 88th, 2d Session. Senate. *Report of the United Nations Fact-Finding Mission to South Vietnam.* Washington: GPO, 1964.

U.S. Congress. 89th, 1st Session. Senate. Committee on Foreign Relations. *Background Information Relating to Southeast Asia and Vietnam.* (Rev. ed.) Washington: GPO, 1965.

U.S. Department of Commerce. Office of Technical Services. Joint Publications Research Service. *Military Report of the National Front for the Liberation of South Vietnam,* by Tran Nam Trung. Washington: 1964.

_____. *Viet Cong and the National Liberation Front of South Vietnam: Communist Political-Military Organizations.* Washington: 1965.

U.S. Department of Defense. Military Assistance Institute. *Country Study: Republic of Vietnam.* Washington: American Institutes for Research, 1965.

U.S. Embassy in Saigon. Joint United States Public Affairs Office. *Vietnam in Profile.* Saigon: March 1966.

U.S. United States Operations Mission to Vietnam. Public Administration Division. *Public Administration Bulletin,* No. 15, August 31, 1964; No. 17, October 31, 1964; No. 18, November 30, 1964; No. 19, December 31, 1964; and No. 23, May 21, 1965.

_____. "Summary of Local Administration: Seminar." N.p.l.: n.d. Von der Mehden, Fred R. "Southeast Asia Relations with Africa," *Asian Survey,* V, July 1965, 341–349.

Warner, Denis. "Behind the Battlefront: A Search for Stability," *Reporter,* XXXIV, February 24, 1966, 25–29.

Wint, Guy. "China and Asia," *China Quarterly,* I, January-March 1960, 61–71.

Wolfe, Thomas W. "Military Policy: A Soviet Dilemma," *Current History*, XXXXIX, October 1965, 201-F.

Woodruff, Lloyd W. *Local Administration in Viet-Nam: Its Future Development*. Saigon: Michigan State University Vietnam Advisory Group and National Institute of Administration, 1961.

————. *Local Administration in Vietnam: Village Finance*. Washington: Michigan State University Vietnam Advisory Group and Agency for International Development, n.d.

Y Bham. *Declaration pour le Haut Comité du Front Unifié pour la Libération des Races Opprimées*. Champa: 1964.

————. *Proclamation*. Champa: 1964.

Zasloff, Joseph J., and Nguyen Khac Nhan. *A Study of Administration in Binh Minh District*. Saigon: Michigan State University Vietnam Advisory Group and National Institute of Administration, 1961.

(In addition to the above sources the following periodicals were used in the preparation of this section: *Saigon Daily News*, from June 1965 through May 1966; *New York Times*, from June 1962 through May 1966; *Washington Post*, from January 1965 through May 1966; *Christian Science Monitor*, from January 1965 through May 1966; *Keesing's Contemporary Archives*, from 1955 through May 1966; *Deadline Data on World Affairs*, from 1957 through 1965; *Economist*, from June 1965 through May 1966; *Far Eastern Economic Review*, from June 1965 through May 1966; *Facts-on-File*, from February 1, 1963, through August 1965; *Department of State Bulletins*, from January 1, 1963, through November 20, 1965; *Foreign Policy Briefs*, from January 1, 1963, through November 20, 1965; *Newsweek*, from January 1, 1963, through November 20, 1965; *Time* and *U.S. News & World Report*, from January 1, 1963, through November 20, 1965; *Wall Street Journal*, from June 1965 through May 1966; *Vietnam Illustration*, from January 1965 through April 1966; and *Viet-Nam* [a bimonthly news bulletin published by the Embassy of Vietnam in Washington], from June 1965 through May 1966.)

Section III. Economic

RECOMMENDED FURTHER READING

Among the sources consulted in the preparation of this section, the following are recommended as additional reading on the basis of quality and general availability.

Bennett, Alan. "Moving the Montagnards," *Far Eastern Economic Review*, XLIX, July 15, 1965, 127.

"Le Budget de 1964," *Kinh-te tap-san* (Bulletin economique), X, June 1964, 8–11.

Buu-Hoan. "Impact of Military Expenditures on the South Vietnamese Economy," *Far Eastern Economic Review*, XXV, December 25, 1958, 839–842.

———. "Vietnam: Economic Consequences of the Geneva Peace," *Far Eastern Economic Review*, XXV, December 11, 1958, 753–757.

———. "Vietnam: Structure of a Dependent Economy," *Far Eastern Economic Review*, XXV, December 18, 1958, 789–798.

———. "Vietnam's Economic Structure: The Impact of Aid," *Far Eastern Economic Review*, XXVI, May 14, 1959, 677–680.

Canada. Department of Mines and Technical Surveys. Geographical Branch. *Indo-China: A Geographical Appreciation.* (Foreign Geography Information Series, No. 6.) Ottawa: 1953.

Close, Alexandra. "Vietnam's Rice War," *Far Eastern Economic Review*, XLIX, September 2, 1965, 423–463.

Fall, Bernard B. "Vietnam: The New Korea," *Current History*, L, February 1966.

Gittinger, J.P. "Agrarian Reform in Free Viet Nam." (Saigon: United States Operations Mission to Vietnam, n.d. (mimeo.).

———. "Progress in South Vietnam's Agrarian Reform," *Far Eastern Survey*, XXIX, January 1960, 1–5; February 1960, 17–21.

Gourou, Pierre. *The Peasants of the Tonkin Delta*, I and II. (Human Relations Area Files "Behavior Science Translations.") New Haven: HRAF, 1955.

Great Britain. Admiralty. Naval Intelligence Division. *Indo-China.* (Geographical Handbook Series.) London: 1943.

Halberstam, David. *The Making of a Quagmire.* New York: Random House, 1964.

Hendry, James B. "Economic Development Under Conditions of Guerrilla Warfare: The Case of Viet Nam," *Asian Survey*, II, June 1962, 1–12.

Hendry, James B. "Land Tenure in South Viet Nam," *Economic and Cultural Change*, IX, No. 1, Pt. 1, October 1960, 27–44.

———. *The Small World of Khanh Hau*. Chicago: Aldine Publishing House, 1964.

———. *A Study of a Vietnamese Rural Community: Administrative Activity*. (Michigan State University Vietnam Advisory Group.) Washington: U.S. Agency for International Development, 1960.

———. *The Study of a Vietnamese Rural Community: Economic Activity*. Saigon: Michigan State University Vietnam Advisory Group, 1959.

Henry, Yves. *Economie agricole de l'Indochine*. Hanoi: Gouvernement Général de l'Indochine, Inspection Générale de l'Agriculture, de l'Elevage et des Forêts, 1932.

Hickey, Gerald C. "Montagnard Agriculture and Land Tenure." Saigon: The Rand Corporation OSD/ARPA R&D Field Unit, April 2, 1965 (mimeo.).

———. "Problems of Social Change in Vietnam," *Bulletin de la Société des Etudes Indochinoises* (Nouvelle Série), XXXIII, No. 4, 1958, 1–12.

———. *Village in Vietnam*. New Haven: Yale University Press, 1964.

Huard, Pierre, and Durand, Maurice. *Connaissance du Viet-Nam*. Hanoi: Ecole Française d'Extrême-Orient, 1954.

"Les Impots en vigueur au Viet-Nam," *Kinh-te tap-san* (Bulletin economique), XI, March 1965, 4–11; April 1965, 4–14.

Kaufman, Howard K. "Cu-Lao: A Preliminary Socio-Economic Study of a Fishing Village and Its Cooperative." Saigon: Cooperative Research and Training Center, October 1963 (mimeo.).

LeBar, Frank M.; Hickey, Gerald C.; and Musgrave, John K. *Ethnic Groups of Mainland Southeast Asia*. New Haven: Human Relations Area Files Press, 1964.

Le Thanh Khoi. *Le Viet-Nam: histoire et civilisation*. Paris: Les Editions de Minuit, 1955.

Lindholm, Richard W. (ed.). *Viet-Nam: The First Five Years*. East Lansing: Michigan State University Press, 1959.

Mende, Tibor. "The Two Viet-Nam's," *Listener*, LVII, May 2, 1957, 701, 702.

Musolf, Lloyd D. "Public Enterprise and Development Perspectives in South Vietnam," *Asian Survey*, III, August 1963, 357–371.

Nivolon, François. "Foreign Trade," *Far Eastern Economic Review*, XXXVI, May 31, 1962, 462, 463.

———. "Uncertain Supplies," *Far Eastern Economic Review*, XLIX, September 9, 1965, 504.

"Les Organismes de credit traditionnels et modernes au Viet-Nam."
Kinh-te tap-san (Bulletin economique), XI, May 1965, 14–22.

Ortiz, Elizabeth. "The Mekong Project of Vietnam," *Far Eastern Economic Review*, XXV, November 6, 1958, 596, 597.

Osborne, Milton E. *Strategic Hamlets in South Viet-Nam: A Survey and a Comparison.* (Department of Asian Studies, Southeast Asia Program: Data Paper No. 55.) Ithaca: Cornell University Press, 1965.

Pham Minh Duong. "Vietnamese Railways and Their Reconstruction," *Marchés tropicaux et méditerranéen* (Special Issue in English: *Vietnam 1958*), XIV, November 29, 1958, 25–31.

Pham-van-Hoang. "Le Budget de 1963," *Kinh-te sap-san* (Bulletin economique), IX, July 1963, 4–9.

"Le Regime des changes au Viet-Nam," *Kinh-te tap-san* (Bulletin economique), XI, May 1965, 4–13.

Savorin, André. "Mining Resources of Southern Vietnam," *Marchés tropicaux et méditerranéens* (Special Issue in English: *Vietnam 1958*), XIV, November 29, 1958, 16–20.

Scigliano, Robert G., and Snyder, Wayne W. "The Budget Process in South Vietnam," *Pacific Affairs*, XXXIII, March 1960, 48–60.

"South Vietnam," *Far Eastern Economic Review Yearbook, 1962* Hong Kong: Far Eastern Economic Review, 1962.

"South Vietnam," *Far Eastern Economic Review Yearbook, 1963.* Hong Kong: Far Eastern Economic Review, 1963.

"South Vietnam," *Far Eastern Economic Review Yearbook, 1964.* Hong Hong: Far Eastern Economic Review, 1964.

"South Vietnam," *Far Eastern Economic Review Yearbook, 1965.* Hong Kong: Far Eastern Economic Review, 1965.

"South Vietnam," *Far Eastern Economic Review Yearbook, 1966.* Hong Kong: Far Eastern Economic Review, 1966.

Tac-Gia Chi. *Vietnam Vanhoa Su' cu'o'ng* (Vietnamese Culture: A General Outline). (Revised by Dao Duy Dinh.) Vietnam: Bon Phuong (Four Corners of the Earth) Publishing Company, 1938.

Trinh Ngoc Sanh. "Highway Construction Projects of Vietnam," *Marchés tropicaux et méditerranéens* (Special Issue in English: *Vietnam 1958*), XIV, November 29, 1958, 32–36.

Trued, M.N. "South Viet-Nam's Industrial Development Center," *Pacific Affairs*, XXXIII, September 1960, 250–267.

U.S. Army Special Warfare School. *Montagnard Tribal Groups of the Republic of Vietnam.* Fort Bragg: USASWS, March 1965.

U.S. Department of Commerce. Bureau of Foreign Commerce. *Basic Data on the Economy of Viet-Nam.* (World Trade Information Service: "Economic Reports," Pt. 1, No. 59–52.) Washington: Bureau of Foreign Commerce, 1959.

U.S. Department of Defense. Military Assistance Institute. *Country Study: Republic of Vietnam*. Washington: American Institutes for Research, 1965.

U.S. Joint Publications Research Service (trans.). *Three-Year Industrial Plan is an Important Step in Industrial Socialization of North Vietnam*. (JPRS: 595–D.) Washington: JPRS, 1959.

U.S. United States Information Service. Field Service Center. "Land Tenure in South Vietnam." (Field Reporting Series.) Saigon: n.d. (mimeo.).

U.S. United States Operations Mission to Vietnam. Division of Agriculture and National Resources. *Studies on Land Tenure in Vietnam*, by J. P. Gittinger. (Terminal Report.) Saigon: USOM, 1959.

U.S. United States Operations Mission to Vietnam. Economic and Financial Planning Division. *Studies in Vietnamese Economy*, I. Saigon: 1964.

U.S. United States Operations Mission to Vietnam. Public Administration Division. *An Analysis of Property Tax Compliance in Vietnam: Number of Property Tax Assessments and Number of Property Tax Payments, 1960–1964*, by Ray E. Davis. Saigon: 1965.

————. *An Analysis of the Property Tax in Vietnam*. Saigon: 1965.

————. *End of Tour Report of Internal Taxation in Vietnam, April 1964*. Saigon: 1964.

"Le Viet-Nam et le credit international," *Kinh-te tap-san* (Bulletin economique), X, January–February 1964, 5–8.

(In addition to the above sources, the *Far Eastern Economic Review*, published weekly in Hong Kong, has been a basic source of information in the preparation of this section.)

OTHER SOURCES USED

Agricultural Credit and Cooperatives. (Proceedings of the Fifth Far East Agricultural Credit and Cooperative Workshop, May 10–22, 1965.) Seoul: 1965.

"Agricultural Credit in Viet-Nam," *International Financial News Survey*, XII, March 18, 1960, 289, 290.

"La Balance des paiements exterieurs du Viet-Nam en 1962," *Kinh-te tap-san* (Bulletin economique), IX, February 1963, 7–10.

"La Balance des paiements exterieurs du Viet-Nam en 1963," *Kinh-te tap-san* (Bulletin economique), X, March 1964, 4–7.

"Banking Operations in Viet-Nam," *International Financial News Survey*, XVI, December 4, 1964, 449, 450.

Barber, Charles H. "Business Boom in Saigon," *Far Eastern Economic Review*, LI, March 10, 1966, 443–447.

Barnum, Robert C. "Strategic Hamlet: The Rural Foundation," *Military Police Journal*, XIII, December 1963, 14–16.

Bowen, Thomas W. "The Misunderstood Man," *Army*, XV, August 1964, 41–44.

Brown, Thomas K. *A Model for the Economic Development of the Republic of Vietnam.* Provo: Brigham Young University, 1963.

"Budget of Viet-Nam," *International Financial News Survey*, XIII, June 23, 1961, 189, 190.

Bui Van Thinh. "Central Banking in Viet-Nam." Chapter 11 in S. Gethyn Davies (ed.), *Central Banking in South and East Asia.* Hong Kong: Hong Kong University Press, 1960.

"Busy Week for Ky—and Troops," *Newsweek*, LXVI, September 20, 1965, 44, 47.

Chinese FCA Technical Mission. "Report on Technical Service to Farmers' Cooperative Associations in Vietnam (March 1 to April 30, 1963)." Saigon: n.d. (mimeo.).

"Correlation entre la masse monetaire, les credits a l'economie et les avances a l'etat," *Kinh-te tap-san* (Bulletin economique), X, March 1964, 17–31.

"Danhim Power to Reach Capital in September," *Viet Nam*, No. 39, June 22, 1965, 16E.

Dorsey, John T., Jr. "South Viet-Nam in Perspective," *Far Eastern Survey*, XXVII, December 1958, 177–182.

"Economic Progress in Viet-Nam," *International Financial News Survey*, XIII, August 18, 1961, 254, 255.

"Evolution monetaire en 1962," *Kinh-te tap-san* (Bulletin economique), IX, February 1963, 11–14.

"Financial and Economic Reforms in Viet-Nam," *International Financial News Survey*, XIV, January 19, 1962, 19, 20.

Fishel, Wesley R. "American Aid to Vietnam," *Current History*, XLIX, November 1965, 294–299.

The Forests of Free Viet-Nam: A Preliminary Study for Organization, Protection, Policy and Production. With a foreword by Thomas W. McKinley, Forest Resources Advisor, United States Operations Mission to Vietnam. Saigon: USOM, March 1957.

"France in South Vietnam," *Asian Review*, LV, January 1959, 62–64.

Hendry, James B. "American Aid in Vietnam," *Pacific Affairs*, XXXIII, December 1960, 387–391.

Hickey, Gerald C. "Making It On the Mekong," *Random News*, September 1964, 2–6.

"Industrial and Financial Development Co. Set Up," *Vietnam Press*, Bulletin No. 218, December 17, 1961, 7.

"Industrial Development Center's Contributions to Local Industry." *News from Vietnam*, X, October 1961, 16, 17.

"Industrial Development in Viet-Nam," *International Financial News Survey*, XIII, October 20, 1961, 33.

481

"Industrial Investments Increase in Vietnam: Trade Sluggish," *Foreign Commerce Weekly*, LXVI, September 25, 1961, 15, 16.

"Insurgency Disturbs Viet-Nam Economy: U.S. Exports Increase," *Foreign Commerce Weekly*, LXVII, January 1, 1962, 24, 28.

International Monetary Fund. *Thirteenth Annual Report: Exchange Restrictions.* Washington: IMF, 1962.

————. *Sixteenth Annual Report: Exchange Restrictions, 1965.* Washington: IMF, 1965.

————. *Supplement 1965–1966 to International Financial Statistics.* Washington: 1965.

International Voluntary Services Vietnam. *Annual Report, June 1960–June 1961.* Saigon: IVS, 1961.

Jacoby, Erich H. *Agrarian Unrest in Southeast Asia.* Bombay: Asia Publishing House, 1961.

"Joint Communique by United States and South Viet Nam," *New York Times*, January 5, 1962.

Jones, Emily and Alan. "Taming the Mekong," *Far Eastern Economic Review*, XLIX, September 2, 1965, 418–420.

Jones, P.H.M. "In Short Supply," *Far Eastern Economic Review*, LI, March 18, 1966, 512, 529, 530.

————. "Rural Stagnation," *Far Eastern Economic Review*, XLIV, May 21, 1964, 370–373.

Labor Digest, No. 35, 1963.

Lacouture, Jean. "Neutralisme et communisme en Indochine," *Le Monde*, L, January 10, 1961, 3.

Ladejinsky, Wolf. "Agrarian Reform in Free Vietnam." Pages 144–173 in *Viet-Nam, 1960: Studies on National and International Affairs.* (Special issue of *Viet-Nam in World Affairs*.) Saigon: n.d.

Lafont, Pierre Bernard. "The 'Slash-and Burn' (Ray) Agriculture System of the Mountain Populations of Central Vietnam." Pages 56–59 in *Proceedings of the Ninth Pacific Science Congress of the Pacific Science Association, 1957.* Bangkok: 1959.

"The Lansdale File," *Economist*, CCXVII, October 2–8, 1965, 29.

Lindholm, Richard W. "Taxation in South Viet-Nam," *Public Finance*, XIV, No. 3–4, 1959, 236–247.

Lindley, Ernest K. "An Ally Worth Having," *Newsweek*, June 29, 1959.

"Le Marche noir des changes au Viet-Nam," *Kinh-te tap-san* (Bulletin economique), XI, June 1965, 8–12.

McAleavy, Henry. "Dien in China and Vietnam," *Journal of Asian Studies*, XVII, 1957–58.

Mecklin, John. *Mission in Torment.* Garden City: Doubleday, 1965.

"Mekong Committee Endorses Five Year Development Program," *Viet Nam*, No. 61, June 25, 1965, 18.

Michigan State University Vietnam Advisory Group. Field Administration Division. "Preliminary Research Report on the PMS [Pays Montagnard du Sud]," by Gerald C. Hickey, assisted by Frederic Wickert. Saigon: June 1957 (mimeo.).

"Mr. Diem's Town for Peasants," *Economist*, CXCVII, No. 6129, 1961, 575.

"NACO Announces New Loan Rates," *Vietnam Press*, Bulletin No. 223, January 21, 1962, 4, 5.

Nathan, Andrew. " 'New Life' in Vietnam," *Far Eastern Economic Review*, XLIV, April 23, 1964, 200–203.

"New Banknotes and Coins To Be Issued," *Vietnam Press*, Bulletin No. 223, January 21, 1962, 5.

"New Customs Tariff in Viet-Nam," *International Financial News Survey*, XIII, September 1, 1961, 271.

"New 500 and 20 Piastre Bank Notes," *Vietnam Press*, Bulletin No. 230, March 11, 1962, 9, 10.

Nguyen-bich-Hue. "Depots, credits et multiplicateur de credit au Viet-Nam," *Kinh-te tap-san* (Bulletin economique), X, April 1964, 4, 5.

———. "L'Evolution monetaire depuis 1955 and les perspectives d'avenir," *Kinh-te tap-san* (Bulletin economique), IX, November–December 1963, 9–14.

Nguyen-Ngoc-Ne. "The Historical Evolution of the Hamlet in Vietnam." (Lecture given at the Public Administration Seminar organized by USOM, September 24–25, 1964.) Saigon: n.d. (mimeo.).

Nguyen-thi-Nguyen. "Les Comptes nationaux du Viet-Nam en 1960–1962," *Kinh-te tap-san* (Bulletin economique), X, October 1964, 7–59.

Nivolon, François. "Curbing the Rackets," *Far Eastern Economic Review*, XLIX, September 9, 1965, 506.

———. "Massive Aid," *Far Eastern Economic Review*, XLIX, July 8, 1965, 96, 97.

———. "New Industrial Complex," *Far Eastern Economic Review*, XXXIII, September 21, 1961, 547.

———. "Steps in Prospect," *Far Eastern Economic Review*, L, December 9, 1965, 454, 455.

———. "Strong Measures," *Far Eastern Economic Review*, LI, March 18, 1966, 494–496.

———. "Taiwan-Vietnam Friendship," *Far Eastern Economic Review*, XLV, July 16, 1964, 119, 120.

———. "Trouble in Vietnam," *Far Eastern Economic Review*, XLIX, July 15, 1965, 151, 152.

———. "Two Mills for Vietnam," *Far Eastern Economic Review*, XXXIV, October 5, 1961, 74, 75.

"The Other Enemy," *Economist*, CCXVII, November 6, 1965, 603, 604.

"The 'Other War' in Vietnam: Fight Against Inflation," *U.S. News & World Report*, LIX, August 30, 1965, 32, 33.

Pham-van-Bao. "Quelques notes sur la nouvelle loi bancaire du Viet-Nam," *Kinh-te tap-san* (Bulletin economique), X, December 1964, 26–38.

Pham-van-Hoang. "L'Impot à la production," *Kinh-te tap-san* (Bulletin economique), IX, January 1963, 7–11.

Rawlings, E. H. "Decline of French Power in Vietnam," *Eastern World*, X, April 1956, 11, 12.

"The Relief of Duc Co," *Newsweek*, LXVI, August 23, 1965, 28–30.

Republic of Vietnam. Bo Cai-Tien Nong-Thon (Department of Rural Affairs). So Thong-Ke Va Kinh-Te Nong-Nghiep (Agricultural Economics and Statistics Service). *Nien-ciam thong-ke nong-nghiep, 1963* (Agricultural Statistics Yearbook, 1963). Saigon: n.d. (In both Vietnamese and English.)

Republic of Vietnam. Bo Canh-Nong (Department of Agriculture). So Thong-Ke Va Kinh-Te Nong-Nghiep (Agricultural Economics and Statistics Service). *Nien-ciam thong-ke nong-nghiep, 1964* (Agriculture Statistics Yearbook, 1964). Saigon: n.d. (In both Vietnamese and English.)

Republic of Vietnam. Bo Kinh-te Quoc-gia (Ministry of National Economy). Vien Quoc-gia Thong-ke (National Institute of Statistics). *Thong-ke nguyet-san* (Monthly Bulletin of Statistics), No. 8, August 1965. (Includes sections in Vietnamese, English and French.)

————. *Vietnam nien-giam thong-ke* (Statistical Yearbook of Viet-Nam, 1962), X. Saigon: 1964.

Republic of Vietnam. Commissariat Général à la Coopération et au Crédit Agricole. *Le Mouvement cooperatif au Vietnam.* Saigon: 1960.

Republic of Vietnam. Department of Land Registration and Agrarian Reform. *Agrarian Reform in Viet-Nam.* Saigon: 1958.

Republic of Vietnam. Directorate General of the Budget and Foreign Aid. *National Budget Fiscal Year 1958.* Saigon: 1958.

————. *National Budget: Fiscal Year 1959.* Saigon: 1959.

————. *National Budget: Fiscal Year 1960.* Saigon: 1960.

————. *National Budget: Fiscal Year 1961.* Saigon: 1961.

Republic of Vietnam. Ministry of Agriculture. *The National College of Agriculture, Biao.* Saigon: 1960.

Republic of Vietnam. Ministry of Labor. *Labour Code, 1965.* Saigon: n.d.

Republic of Vietnam. National Institute of Administration. Research and Documentation Division. *Viet Nam Government Organization Manual, 1957–1958.* Saigon: 1958.

Republic of Vietnam. Presidential Press Office. *President Ngo Dinh Diem and the Election of April 9, 1961.* Saigon: 1961.

Republic of Vietnam. The Secretariat of State for Information. *Cai San: The Dramatic Story of Resettlement and Land Reform in the "Rice Bowl" of the Republic of Viet-Nam.* Saigon: n.d.

Rose, Jerry A. "A Fight for Rice in Divided Vietnam," *Reporter*, V, October 12, 1961, 37, 38.

"Saigon Shipping Shake-Up," *U.S. News & World Report*, LIX, November 29, 1965, 110.

Sandrin, Christian. "Les Hameaux strategiques au Sud-Vietnam," *Revue de defense nationale*, VII, December 19; 1963, 1836, 1846.

Scigliano, Robert G., and Fox, Guy H. *Technical Assistance in Vietnam: The Michigan State University Experience.* New York: Praeger, 1965.

Shah, Sirdar Ikbal Ali. *Viet-Nam.* London: Octagon Press, 1960.

Shigeto Kawano. "Socio-Economic Significance of Land Reform in Southeast Asian Countries," *The Developing Economies*, Preliminary Issue No. 1, March-August 1962, 26–47.

"Situation des banques commerciales au 21 decembre 1964," *Kinh-te tap-san* (Bulletin economique), XI, June 1965, 5–7.

Smith, William A., Jr. "Strategic Hamlets in Vietnam," *Military Review*, XLIV, May 1964, 17–23.

Snyder, Wayne W. *Budgetary and Financial Administration in Vietnam.* Saigon: Michigan State University Vietnam Advisory Group, 1956.

"Tax Increases in Viet-Nam," *International Financial News Survey.* XIII, September 8, 1961, 278.

"Taxes sur l'importation frappant certains groupes de produits,' *Kinh-te tap-san* (Bulletin economique), X, March 1964, 36–47.

Taylor, Milton C. *The Patente (Business License Tax) in Vietnam.* Saigon: Michigan State University Vietnam Advisory Group, 1959.

——. "South Vietnam: Lavish Aid, Limited Progress," *Pacific Affairs*, XXXIV, Fall 1961, 242–256.

——. *The System of Excise Taxes in Vietnam.* Saigon: Michigan State University Vietnam Advisory Group, 1960.

——. *The System of Indirect Taxes in Viet-Nam.* Saigon: Michigan State University Vietnam Advisory Group, 1960.

——. *The Taxation of Income in Vietnam.* Saigon: Michigan State University Vietnam Advisory Group, 1959.

——. *The Taxation of Real Property in Viet-Nam.* Saigon: Michigan State University Vietnam Advisory Group, 1959.

——. *Taxes of Vietnam.* Saigon: Michigan State University Vietnam Advisory Group, 1960.

Ton That Thien. "Inflation Ahead?" *Far Eastern Economic Review*, L, October 21, 1965, 10, 11.

485

Ton That Thien. "Saigon's Worries," *Far Eastern Economic Review*, LI, February 17, 1966, 270, 271.

"Treasury Bill Issue in Viet-Nam," *International Financial News Survey*, XVII, January 29, 1965, 33.

United Nations. Economic Commission for Asia and the Far East. *Economic Survey of Asia and the Far East, 1957*. Bangkok: UN, 1958.

―――――. *Economic Survey of Asia and the Far East, 1958*. Bangkok: UN, 1959.

―――――. *Economic Survey of Asia and the Far East, 1959*. Bangkok: UN, 1960.

―――――. *Economic Survey of Asia and the Far East, 1960*. Bangkok: UN, 1961.

United Nations. Food and Agriculture Organization. *World Forest Inventory, 1958*. Rome: FAO, 1958.

United Nations. Technical Assistance Programme. *Toward the Economic Development of the Republic of Vietnam*. (ST/TAO/K/VIET–NAM/1 ILO/TAP/VIET–NAM/R.4 FAO/Report No. 539.) New York: TAP, 1959.

U.S. Agency for International Development. *Evaluation Survey of USOM Participant Training Program: Vietnam, 1954–1960*. Washington: 1964.

―――――. *A Nation's Progress: The Story of U.S.-Vietnamese Co-operation in Economic Development*. Washington: AID, 1964.

―――――. Advisory Committee on Voluntary Foreign Aid. *Voluntary Foreign Relief Programs: Activities of Registered American Voluntary Agencies*, January 1–December 21, 1961. Washington: AID, 1962.

U.S. Department of Commerce. Bureau of Foreign Commerce. *Licensing and Exchange Controls: Viet-Nam*. (World Trade Information Service: "Operations Reports," Pt. 2, No. 57–77.) Washington: Bureau of Foreign Commerce, 1957.

U.S. Department of Commerce. Bureau of International Commerce. *Basic Data on the Economy of Viet-Nam*. (Overseas Business Reports, OBR, 63–5.) Washington: 1963.

U.S. Department of Defense. Military Assistance Institute. *Republic of Vietnam*. (Station Report.) N.pl.: 1959.

U.S. Department of Labor. Bureau of International Labor Affairs. *Directory of Labor Organizations: Asia and Australasia*, II. Washington: GPO, 1963.

U.S. Department of Labor. Bureau of Labor Statistics. *Summary of the Labor Situation in the Republic of Vietnam, 1957*. Washington: GPO, 1957.

U.S. International Cooperation Administration. "Far East Conference of Food and Agriculture Officers." Hong Kong: April 6–11, 1959, 82, 83 (mimeo.).

————. Office of Statistics and Reports. *U.S. Foreign Assistance and Assistance from International Organizations*. Washington: ICA, 1961.

U.S. United States Operations Mission to Vietnam. "Agriculture Division Monthly Report for September 1961." (AGR–61–2652.) Saigon: USOM, October 16, 1961. (Photocopy of typed memorandum.)

————. *Annual Report for Fiscal Year 1959*. Saigon: USOM, 1959.

————. *Building Economic Strength: Annual Report for the 1958 Fiscal Year*. Saigon: USOM, 1958.

————. *USOM Vietnam: Operational Report, 1963–1964*. Saigon: USOM, 1965.

————. *Vietnam Meets Its Challenge: Annual Report for Fiscal Year 1961*. Saigon: USOM, 1961.

————. *Vietnam Moves Ahead: Annual Report for Fiscal Year 1960*. Saigon: USOM, 1960.

————. Economic and Financial Planning Division. *Annual Statistical Bulletin*. (No. 7.) Saigon: 1964.

————. *Annual Statistical Bulletin*. (No. 8.) Saigon: 1965.

————. *Monthly Statistical Bulletin* (Supplement No. 11 to *Annual Statistical Bulletin*, No. 7), March–April 1965.

————. *Monthly Statistical Bulletin* (Supplement No. 1 to *Annual Statistical Bulletin*, No. 8), May–July 1965.

U.S. United States Operations Mission to Vietnam. International Voluntary Services. "Forage Crops in Vietnam," by Harvey C. Neese. Saigon: 1960 (mimeo.).

U.S. United States Operations Mission to Vietnam. Program Office Research and Statistics Section. *Annual Statistical Bulletin*. (No. 4—Data through 1960.) Saigon: USOM, May 1961.

"Viet Industrialists Meet U.S. Investors," *Front Lines*, III, October 15, 1965, 8.

"Vietnam," *Far Eastern Economic Review*, XLVII, March 18, 1965, 503.

"Viet-Nam," *Foreign Commerce Weekly*, LXVI, September 18, 1961, 4.

"Viet-Nam," *International Financial Statistics*, XV, March 1962, April 1962 and July 1962, 280–283; XIX, January 1966, 308, 309.

Viet-Nam: A Breeding Country (Special Edition of *Review Horizons*) (Saigon), December 1958.

"Vietnam: A Market Study," *International Trade Review*, April 1958, 12, 60.

"Vietnam Institutes Fiscal Reforms by Revising Import Tariff, Taxes," *Foreign Commerce Weekly*, LXVII, January 22, 1962, 135.

"Vietnam Rural Electrification." (Prepared by the NRECA Rural Electrification Team for U.S. AID Mission/Saigon.) N.pl.: July 1, 1965 (mimeo.).

"The Vietnamese-American Textile Company," *News from Vietnam*, VII, June 1961, 17.

"Viet-Nam's Foreign Debt," *International Financial News Survey*, XVI, May 29, 1964, 176, 177.

"Viet-Nam's Supplementary Budget for 1961," *International Financial News Survey*, XIII, November 17, 1961, 362, 363.

White, Gilbert F. "The Mekong River Plan," *Scientific American*, CCVIII, April 1963, 49–59.

Wolfstone, Daniel. "The Measure of the Mekong," *Far Eastern Economic Review*, XXXII, April 20, 1961, 125–131.

Woodruff, Lloyd W. *Local Finance in South Viet Nam*. (Local Administration Series, Report No. 2.) Saigon: Michigan State University Vietnam Advisory Group and National Institute of Administration, 1961.

Wurfel, David. "Agrarian Reform in the Republic of Vietnam," *Far Eastern Survey*, XXVI, No. 6, 1957, 81–92.

Zasloff, Joseph J. "Rural Resettlement in South Viet Nam: The Agroville Program," *Pacific Affairs*, XXXV, Winter 1962–63, 327–340.

(In addition to the above sources, the following periodicals were used in the preparation of this section: *Washington Post*, from January 1, 1960, to July 15, 1966; *New York Times*, from January 1, 1960, to July 1966; *Christian Science Monitor*, from January 1, 1960, to July 15, 1966; *Keesing's Contemporary Archives*, from January 1, 1955, to July 15, 1966; *Deadline Data*, from January 1, 1957, to July 15, 1965; *Economist*, from January 1, 1960, to July 15, 1966; *Vietnam Press* (Viet-Nam Thong Tan Xa), from January 1964 to July 1966; *Saigon Daily News*, from January 1, 1965, to July 1966; *Labor Developments Abroad*, for January and February 1965; and *Quarterly* [formerly *Three-Monthly*] *Economic Review: Continental S.E. Asia* [published in London by The Economist Intelligence Unit, Ltd.], from December 1961 through December 1965.)

Section IV. National Security

RECOMMENDED FURTHER READING

Among the sources consulted in the preparation of this section, the following are recommended as additional reading on the basis of quality and general availability.

Browne, Malcolm W. *The New Face of War.* Indianapolis: Bobbs-Merrill, 1965.

Buttinger, Joseph. *The Smaller Dragon: A Political History of Vietnam.* New York: Praeger, 1962.

Corley, Francis J. "Freedom in Indo-China: A Review Article," *Pacific Affairs*, XXXIV, Winter 1961–62, 375–380.

————. "The President in the Constitution of the Republic of Viet-Nam," *Pacific Affairs*, XXXIV, Summer 1961, 165–174.

Fall, Bernard B. *The Two Viet-Nam's: A Political and Military Analysis.* (Rev. ed.) New York: Praeger, 1964.

Fishel, Wesley R. "The Eleventh Hour in Vietnam," *Asian Survey*, V, February 1965, 98–107.

Halberstam, David. *The Making of a Quagmire.* New York: Random House, 1964.

Jordan, Amos A. *Foreign Aid and the Defense of Southeast Asia.* New York: Praeger, 1962.

Kahin, George McTurnan (ed.). *Government and Politics of Southeast Asia.* Ithaca: Cornell University Press, 1962.

Lancaster, Donald. *The Emancipation of French Indochina.* London: Oxford University Press, 1961.

Mecklin, John. *Mission in Torment.* Garden City: Doubleday, 1965.

Newman, Bernard. *Background To Viet-Nam.* New York: The New American Library, 1965.

Republic of Vietnam. Information Printing Office. *Eight Years of the Ngo Dinh Diem Administration, 1954–1962.* Saigon: 1962.

————. *Seven Years of the Ngo Dinh Diem Administration, 1954–1961.* Saigon: 1961.

Republic of Vietnam. National Institute of Administration. Research and Documentation Division. *Supplement to Government Organization Manual, 1957–1958.* Saigon: 1960.

————. *Viet Nam Government Organization Manual, 1957–1958.* Saigon: 1958.

Scigliano, Robert G. "Vietnam: A Country at War," *Asian Survey*, III, January 1963, 48–54.

Scigliano, Robert G., and Fox, Guy H. *Technical Assistance in Vietnam: The Michigan State University Experience.* New York: Praeger, 1965.

Shaplen, Robert. *The Lost Revolution.* New York: Harper and Row, 1965.

Sloane, Charles F. "More About Vietnam," *Police Chief*, XXV, March 1958, 16–32.

―――――. "The Police in Vietnam," *Police Chief*, XXV, January 1958, 12–24.

―――――. "Vietnam Continues to Reorganize," *Police Chief*, XXV, February 1958, 22–32.

Trumbull, Robert. *The Scrutable East.* New York: David McKay, 1964.

U.S. Department of State. Bureau of Public Affairs. Office of Public Services. *A Threat to the Peace: North Viet-Nam's Effort to Conquer South Viet-Nam*, Pts. I and II. (Department of State Publication 7308, Far Eastern Series 110.) Washington: GPO, 1961.

U.S. United States Operations Mission to Vietnam. Public Safety Division. *National Police Plan for Vietnam*, by Frank E. Walton. Saigon: USOM, 1964.

―――――. *The Police and Resources Control in Counter-Insurgency*, by E. H. Adkins, Jr. Saigon: USOM, 1964.

Warner, Denis. *The Last Confucian: Vietnam, Southeast Asia and the West.* Baltimore: Penguin Books, 1964.

OTHER SOURCES USED

Republic of Vietnam. Embassy in Manila. *The Republic of Viet-Nam.* Manila: 1962.

Republic of Vietnam. Embassy in Washington. *Viet-Nam at the Crossroads of Asia.* Washington: n.d.

"Republic of Vietnam Armed Forces Medical Services." Saigon: n.pub., n.d. (typewritten copy).

Scigliano, Robert G. *South Vietnam: Nation Under Stress.* Boston: Houghton Mifflin, 1964.

Tonan azia yoran 1964 nehan (General Survey of Southeast Asia, 1964 Edition). Tokyo: Tonan Azia Chosaki (Southeast Asia Research Institute), 1964. (Translated by the U.S. Department of the Army from Japanese.)

Tonan azia yoran 1965 nenhan (General Survey of Southeast Asia, 1965 Edition). Tokyo: Tonan Azia Chosaki (Southeast Asia Research Institute), 1965. (Translated by the U.S. Department of the Army from Japanese.)

U.S. Department of Defense. Military Assistance Institute. *Country Study: Republic of Vietnam.* Washington: American Institutes for Research, 1965.

U.S. Military Assistance Command, Vietnam. Civil Affairs Division. *Information on Local Levels of Government of South Vietnam.* Saigon: n.pub., n.d.

U.S. United States Operations Mission to Vietnam. *End-of-Tour Reports.* Washington: May–August 1965.

————. *Monthly Report.* Washington: February 1965.

————. Economic and Financial Planning Division. *Annual Statistical Bulletin.* (No. 8.) Saigon: 1965.

U.S. United States Operations Mission to Vietnam. Public Administration Division. *Public Administration Bulletin,* No. 15, August 31, 1964; No. 18, November 30, 1964; No. 22, April 1, 1965; and No. 24, August 31, 1965.

U.S. United States Operations Mission to Vietnam. Public Safety Division. *Briefing Material.* Saigon: 1964.

Westerman, George F. "Military Justice in the Republic of Vietnam," *Military Law Review,* XXXI, January 1966, 137–158.

Woodruff, Lloyd W. *Local Administration in Viet Nam: Its Future Development.* Saigon: Michigan State University Vietnam Advisory Group and National Institute of Administration, 1961.

(In addition to the above sources, the following periodicals were used in the preparation of this section: *Washington Evening Star,* from December 1965 through February 1966; *Christian Science Monitor,* from January through March 1966; *Manchester Guardian,* from August 1965 through February 1966; *Saigon Daily News,* from June through December 1965, and *U.S. News and World Report,* from June 1965 through April 1966.

GLOSSARY

AID—Agency for International Development.

Annam—Name of former protectorate forming part of French Indochina; its area conformed roughly with that of the Central Lowlands and Central Highlands of Vietnam, between Cochin China and Tonkin.

ARVN—Army of the Republic of Vietnam.

bang—See *congregation*.

Binh Xuyen—A political and racketeering organization that flourished during the Bao Dai regime after World War II.

Buddhist Institute for Secular Affairs—See *Vien Hoa Dao*.

Buddhist Lay Institute—See *Vien Hoa Dao*.

Can Lao Nhan Vi Cach Mang Dang—The Revolutionary Personalist Labor Party, popularly known as the Can Lao. It was the progovernment party headed by Ngo Dinh Nhu, brother of the late President Ngo Dinh Diem.

Cao Dai—A religious group, commonly spoken of as a reformed Buddhist sect, but in fact it represents a synthesis of tenets drawn from several religious and philosophical traditions. Politically active, its center is in Tay Ninh, northwest of Saigon, but groups of varying sizes are found in all the other provinces of the Mekong Delta.

Cap St. Jacques—See *Vung Tau*.

CARE—Cooperative for American Remittances to Everywhere, Inc.

CGT—Confédération Générale du Travail (General Confederation of Labor). A Communist-led French labor organization.

Chieu Hoi—Lit., open arms. A government program designed to induce the Viet Cong to shift their allegiance to the government side. Administered by the Department of Information and Open Arms.

Cochin China—Former French colony which formed part of French Indochina; its area comprised roughly what is now the southern third of South Vietnam.

Colombo Plan—The Colombo Plan for Cooperative Economic Development in South and Southeast Asia was published by the Commonwealth Consultative Committee on South and Southeast Asia on November 29, 1950, and was to be effective from July 1, 1951, to June 30, 1957. The terminal date was extended to 1961 and later to 1966. The Plan is an international cooperative effort to assist countries of the area to raise their living standards. Member nations in 1966 were Afghanistan, Australia, Bhutan, Burma, Cambodia, Canada, Ceylon, India, Indonesia, Japan, Korea Laos, Malaysia, the Maldive Islands, Nepal, New Zealand, Pakistan, the Philippines, Thailand, the United Kingdom, the United States and South Vietnam. By mid-1966 no action regarding membership had been announced by the newly formed Republic of Singapore.

Con Son—An island in the South China Sea off the coast of South Vietnam; formerly called Poulo Condore. Well known as a penal island, the site of a maximum security prison and historically as a place for exiling political prisoners. Its status as a separate province changed in 1965 when its provincial government was replaced by an administrative delegation directly subordinate to the central government in Saigon.

congregation—The name commonly applied by the French to associations (in Vietnamese, *bang*) of Chinese in Vietnam. The associations are based on dialects spoken in the areas in China from which their members had emigrated, and they usually serve as focal points for the social, economic and political activities of the respective groups.

CSTV—Confédération des Syndicats des Travailleurs Viêtnamiens (Confederation of Unions of Workers of Vietnam). A South Vietnamese labor organization.

CVTC—Confédération Viêtnamienne du Travail Chrétien (Vietnamese Confederation of Christian Labor). The largest of the labor organizations in South Vietnam.

Dang Lao Dong Viet Nam—See *Lao Dong Party*.

Demarcation Line—The line dividing South and North Vietnam. It does not coincide exactly with the seventeenth parallel but approximates it closely enough so that the terms are used interchangeably in many contexts throughout this book.

dharma—Ideal truth, especially as taught by Buddha.

FAO—Food and Agriculture Organization. A Specialized Agency of the United Nations.

franc—Basic unit of French currency. Annual averages of the exchange rate for US$1: from September 1949 to August 1957, 350 francs; from August 1957 to December 1958, 420 francs; from December 1958 through December 1959, 493.7 francs; on January 1, 1960, the par value of the franc per US$1 was established at 4.937 new francs.

hectare—2.471 acres.

ho—Term used to refer to a named descent group—a group consisting of persons able to trace descent from a common ancestor. Can refer to either the group or the name.

Hoa Hao—A reformed Buddhist sect founded in 1939. Politically

494

active, it has gained importance as a religious and political force in the Mekong Delta region, especially in the northwestern provinces of Chau Doc and An Giang, where much of its membership is concentrated.

huong hoa—Land set aside; the income from it is dedicated to the support of the Cult of Ancestors.

IBRD—International Bank for Reconstruction and Development. A Specialized Agency of the United Nations.

ICAO—International Civil Aviation Organization. A Specialized Agency of the United Nations.

ICC—International Control Commission. A commission appointed under the provision of the Geneva Agreement of 1954 to check on the observance of its clauses by the contending sides.

IDA—International Development Association. A Specialized Agency of the United Nations.

ILO—International Labor Organization. A Specialized Agency of the United Nations.

IMF—International Monetary Fund. A Specialized Agency of the United Nations.

Institute for the Execution of Dharma—See *Vien Hoa Dao.*

ITU—International Telecommunications Union. A Specialized Agency of the United Nations.

Lao Dong Party—Dang Lao Dong Viet Nam (The Workers' Party of Vietnam). The Communist Party of North Vietnam.

MACV—Military Assistance Command for Vietnam.

Mat Tran Dan Toc Giai-phong Mien-Nam—See *National Front for the Liberation of South Vietnam.*

matrilocal—A term used to describe a society in which the husband and wife, at marriage, take up residence in the house or community of the bride's parents.

MEDCAP—Medical Civic Action Program.

Mekong River Project—A project for developing the irrigation, hydroelectric and navigational potentials of the Mekong River. Preliminary surveys were initiated in 1957 when Laos, Cambodia and South Vietnam joined Thailand and formed a four-nation Mekong Committee to direct planning for the project. Besides maintaining a year-round office in Bangkok staffed by United Nations technicians, the Committee has held several meetings a year in the capitals of the four countries, despite military operations or diplomatic difficulties. By mid-1965, 18 non-Communist nations as well as some United Nations agencies supplied funds or technical assistance to the Project.

MILPHAP—Military Public Health Assistance Project of the United States Army.

montagnard—Mountaineer. A French word frequently applied to the ethnically diverse peoples of the Central Highlands region.

mui—Vietnamese word for cape or point.

Nam-bo—A term initially used to denote the Cochin China area; now used by Vietnamese, North and South, to mean South Vietnam as a whole.

National Front for the Liberation of South Vietnam—Mat Tran Dan Toc Giai-phong Mien-Nam. Commonly known by the English contraction, National Front, or by the abbreviation NFLSV. A Communist political-front organization set up in December 1960 by North Vietnam and used by the Communists to give the appearance of popular non-Communist support to their insurgency activities in South Vietnam. Not given recognition or credence by the governments of South Vietnam or the United States.

NFLSV—See National Front for the Liberation of South Vietnam. Most often adopted by American journalists.

nuoc mam—A pungent fish sauce.

ong lang—Chinese traditional medicine.

Open Arms Program—See *Chieu Hoi*.

patrilocal—A term used to describe a society in which the husband and wife, at marriage, take up residence in the house or community of the bridegroom's parents.

piaster—The basic unit of currency in South Vietnam. Called the dong in Vietnamese, it is referred to as the piaster in all other languages. The official rate of exchange, established in May 1953, is 35 piasters to US$1. The exchange system was modified in January 1962 and a new rate established which, in effect, devalued the piaster. Technically the official rate stands, but a premium of 25 piasters to US$1 on purchases of foreign exchange and a tax of 25 piasters to US$1 on piaster sales introduced an effective rate of 60 piasters to US$1. This rate was made applicable to all trade transactions and to the ordinary transfers of funds. As before the 1962 modification, the controlled rate of 73.5 piasters to US$1 applies to certain specified transfers of funds.

Poulo Condore—See *Con Son*.

quoc ngu—A system of writing Vietnamese in Roman letters. Originally devised by a French missionary, it is now the common method of writing the language.

sangha—Any order or community of Buddhist monks. Sometimes used to refer to the total body of Buddhist monks everywhere.

SEATO—Southeast Asia Treaty Organization. Member nations (Australia, France, New Zealand, Pakistan, the Philippines, Thailand, the United Kingdom and the United States) are committed to resist aggression to the treaty area. Established in September 1954.

SOFIDIV—Société Financière pour le Développement de l'Industrie au Viet-Nam (Financial Company for the Development of Industry in Vietnam). An investment bank in South Vietnam. Created in November 1961.

song—Vietnamese word meaning stream or river.

Tonkin—Name of former French protectorate forming part of French Indochina; its area conformed roughly to the basin of the Red River System.

truong toc—The head of a lineage.

UNESCO—United Nations Educational, Scientific and Cultural Organization. A Specialized Agency of the United Nations.

UNICEF—United Nations Children's Fund. A Specialized Agency of the United Nations.

Unified Buddhist Church of Vietnam—Formed at Saigon in January 1964 by a group of Buddhist leaders, the most active of whom were Thich Tam Chau and Thich Tri Quang; it is the primary organization behind the Buddhist movement in South Vietnam.

UOV—Union Ouvrière du Viêtnam (Vietnam Labor Union). A South Vietnamese labor organization.

UPU—Universal Postal Union. A Specialized Agency of the United Nations.

USIA—United States Information Agency. Its representatives in embassies overseas form the USIS (United States Information Service).

USIS—United States Information Service. See *USIA*.

USOM—United States Operations Mission. Overseas mission of the Agency for International Development (AID).

Vien Hoa Dao—The Institute (or High Council) for the Execution of Dharma, an agency of the Unified Buddhist Church of Vietnam. Also known as the Buddhist Institute for Secular Affairs and as the Buddhist Lay Institute.

Viet Cong—Condensed from the term Viet Nam Cong San, meaning Vietnamese Communists (sometimes translated as Vietnamese Communism). It is the term generally applied to the supporters and participants in the Communist-controlled subversive insurgency in South Vietnam. Communists, including the insurgents themselves, avoid use of the term, preferring to operate under the guise of nationalists.

Viet Minh—See *Viet Nam Doc Lap Dong Minh*.

Vietnam Buddhist Force—The political arm of the Unified Buddhist Church of Vietnam.

Viet Nam Cong San—Vietnamese Communists; usually contracted to Viet Cong, *q.v.*

Viet Nam Doc Lap Dong Minh—The Vietnam Independence League, usually called the Viet Minh. A Communist-led organization, represented as a coalition of nationalist groups, which actively opposed the French and Japanese during World War II and spearheaded Vietnamese resistance to French rule in the early years of the Indochina War; in 1951 it incorporated its key elements into the newly formed Lao Dong Party.

Vietnam Nationalist Party—See *Viet Nam Quoc Dan Dang*.

Viet Nam Quoc Dan Dang—Vietnam Nationalist Party, formed in 1927. Commonly known by the abbreviation, VNQDD. It advocated a program for Vietnam similar to that of the Chinese Nationalist Party, the Kuomintang.

vinh—Vietnamese word for bay. See *vung*.

VNQDD—See *Viet Nam Quoc Dan Dang*.

vung—Vietnamese word for bay. See *vinh*.

Vung Tau—A town on the coast about 75 miles south of Saigon, formerly called Cap St. Jacques.

WHO—World Health Organization. A Specialized Agency of the United Nations.

WMO—World Meteorological Organization. A Specialized Agency of the United Nations.

Workers' Party of Vietnam—See *Lao Dong Party*.

INDEX

Bao Dai—Continued
    of state, 201; and civil service, 210;
    ex-emperor, 1; and Geneva Agree-
    ment, 257; and independence, 50–
    52, 54, 55, 57, 200; and labor Code,
    351; and *montagnards*; 76; nation-
    alist regime, 410–411; relations
    with United States, 261
Bien Hoa : 25, 73
Binh Dinh Province : 65, 80, 316
Binh Duong Province : 141
Binh Long Province : 82
Binh Nguyen Loc : 167
Binh Xuyen Province : 57, 411
birth rate : 60
black-marketing : 135, 425–426
Bo Ho Su : 9
Bong Mieu : 22
books : 281, 289
boundaries : 2, 9–10
Buddhists : 159, 179–184; and armed
    forces, 234; and education, 145, 153,
    155, 158; and government relations,
    6, 225, 227–229; and history, 38, 169,
    170, 172–176; and labor movement,
    348, 360; and Diem regime, 161, 219,
    225; as political force, 235–238, 253;
    in population, 5, 63, 70, 90, 171; and
    social values, 191, 195; and student
    groups, 242; and uprisings, 58, 194,
    217, 222–224, 227, 230, 234, 236
budgets : 392–395; 396–397 (table 9);
    deficit, 309; military, 430–431
Bui Hoanh : 253
Bui Quang Chieu : 46
Burma : 13

cabinet : 206–207, 224, 227, 228, 229
cai: 353
Cai San project : 64, 321, 327
Cam Ranh Bay : 25, 27
Cambodia : attitude toward, 278; de-
    scription, 2, 9, 13, 15, 24, 25, 69;
    and French rule, 1, 10, 96; and
    Geneva Conference, 56; history,
    30, 36, 38, 40, 41, 42; and "protocol"
    states, 262; relations with, 266–268,
    379
Can Lao (Revolutionary Personalist
    Labor Party) : 219
Can Tho : 25
Canada : International Control Com-
    mission : 258–259; relations with,
    266

Cao Dai faith : 57, 87, 169, 184–186, 189;
    and Catholics, 239; history, 175;
    landownership, 321; number in
    population, 5, 63; and political
    force, 240–242, 411
Cao Hoai Sang : 242
Cao Nguyen Dac Lac : 15–16
Caravelle Group : 220
Catholic : (*see also* refugees) : 187; and
    armed forces, 234; and education,
    158; and family life, 118–119, 189;
    and government relations, 172, 219,
    222, 225, 227–230, 232; and history,
    169–170, 174–176; as political force,
    217, 238–240, 254; in population, 5,
    39, 63, 70, 171; and student groups,
    242
censorship : newspapers, 225, 281–286;
    and campaign speeches, 255
census : 59
Central Executive Committee (The War
    Cabinet) : 199, 206–207
Central Highlands : and agriculture,
    308, 311, 314, 316, 320–322, 325–329;
    and Annam, 3; description, 15, 16,
    24, 27, 126, 128; geographic region,
    212; and labor force, 66; and nat-
    ural resources, 338, 387; and popu-
    lation, 4, 61, 84; and refugees, 64,
    187
Central Lowlands : and agriculture, 314,
    316, 320, 325; and Annam, 3; cli-
    mate, 17; description, 7, 130; and
    geographic region, 10, 16, 212; his-
    tory, 318; population, 61, 62, 63,
    69, 307; port facilities, 27; and
    refugees, 64, 65; and social rela-
    tions, 107, 112
Chaîne Annamitique : 2, 12, 17, 24, 314;
    geographic region, 10, 15–16; popu-
    lation, 61, 62, 73
Champa Kingdom : history, 30, 35–38,
    160; and *montagnards*, 12, 84
Chams : 77; as ethnic group, 69, 82, 90–
    91; history, 63, 75, 428, 429; and
    language, 70
China : history, 29–34, 37, 428; and
    North Vietnam, 51–54; relations
    with, 270–271; trade with, 378
Chinese (*see also* Cho Lon) : attitude
    toward, 277; and Communists, 49–
    50; and culture, 2, 3, 9, 159, 165;
    and education, 153; as ethnic group,
    4, 5, 12, 62, 69, 87–89; and family

Da Nang: and Buddhist disturbances, 217, 237; description, 22, 24, 25, 211; demonstrations, 225, 230; history, 40, 41; and population, 61, 65, 75; port, 26, 27, 374
Da Nhim River: 340, 386
Dai Co Viet: and Buddhism, 173
dams: 125, 340
Dao Phu Quoc: 10, 22, 25
Darlac Province: 62, 85; history, 75; and *montagnards*, 77, 245, 246; and population, 84
death rate: 60
Demarcation Line: 1, 2, 7, 56, 73, 201, 257, 259, 310, 411; and description, 9, 10, 16; and transportation system, 24
Democratic Republic of Viet Nam: 51–52, 53, 259
Department of Revolutionary Development: and rural reconstruction, 207, 312, 385, 431
Dhyana school: 173, 180
Diem: *See* Ngo Dinh Diem
Dien Bien Phu: 31, 55
diet: 102, 123, 124
Dinh dynasty: 35
Directory, The: *See* National Leadership Committee
disease: 122–124, 126–129; and *montagnards*, 81; in refugee camps, 136
divorce: 111, 142
doctors: 122, 132, 134
Dong Ha: 24, 308
Dong Minh Hoi: and National Assembly, 52
drainage systems: 226, 314, 319, 327; under French rule, 45; and Mekong River, 3, 13, 36
Duong Van Minh, Major General: 334; and censorship, 284, 285; coup d'etat, 58, 202–203, 224, 225, 227; and Revolutionary Military Committee, 202

Economic Commission for Asia and the Far East (ECAFE): 275
education: (*see also* elementary education, mandarinate, schools, secondary education): 143–158; adult education, 153–154; attendance, 144, 146, 147, 149; and elite, 100–101; and French rule, 97, 99, 100; and lower class, 102; and middle class, 101; in rural areas, 104; and scholarship funds, 386
elections: 228, 230; general, 56, 255; and law, 203, 205
electric power: 136, 281, 337, 340
elementary education: 143, 146, 147–149
elite: 70; and education, 95, 100–101, 152, 157; and French rule, 93–97; and landownership, 94–99; and religion, 171, 187
employers: 353, 354, 363
employment: 65–67
English language: 74, 100, 167; in education, 144, 152; as second language, 5, 92
ethnic groups: (*see also* Americans, Behnars, Chams, Chinese, French, Khmers, *montagnards*, Rhades, Vietnamese): Arabs, 63; Bih, 86; Eurasians, 69, 91; Europeans, 69; Hindus, 63; Hre, 245; Indians, 63, 278; Jarai, 62, 74, 76, 77, 84–85, 244, 245; Katu, 78–79, 373; Kil, 83; Koho, 82–83, 244; Ma (Cau Ma), 83; Malays, 63; Mnong, 62, 74, 77, 83–84, 87, 373; Nung, 87; Pakistanis, 63, 69, 70, 88, 91; Raglai, 77, 86; Rengao, 74; Sedang, 62, 74, 77, 79–80, 373; Sre, 83; Stieng, 74, 77, 82
Europe: 4, 266
expenditures, government: 309, 395, 396–397 (table 9)
Export-Import Bank: 385
exports: (*see also* rice, rubber): 310, 328, 330, 368–370, 377, 378–380, 381 (table 5), 382–383

farmers: 307, 310, 313
fertilizers: 20, 22, 135, 139, 311–313, 316, 328
films: 294, 296, 298
Financial Company for the Development of Industry in Vietnam (Sociètè Financière pour le Développement de l'Industrie au Viet Nam—SOFIDIU): 405
fishing: 16, 331, 332; and credit facilities, 312, 313; and diet, 102; and labor force, 65, 66; resources, 22
Five-Year Plan: 312, 339
floods: 66, 382; and Mekong River, 13, 324, 326

507

Revolutionary Military Council: 202, 224

Revolutionary Personalist Labor Party (Can Lao Nhan Vi Cach Mang Dang): *See* Can Lao

Rhades: 76, 77; as ethnic group, 62, 85–86; language, 74; social customs, 75, 120; trade, 373; uprising, 244; and Viet Cong, 245

rice: cultivation, 61, 66, 315 (fig. 11); in economy, 4, 12, 307; export crop, 26, 307, 309, 313, 369, 377, 378, 380, 382; marketing, 370–372; and Mekong Delta, 3, 326–327; and *montagnards*, 79, 83; production, 20, 307, 326–327; ricelands, 10, 13, 16, 22, 36, 311, 318; and trade, 89, 99, 369; and Viet Cong, 307–308

rivers: (*see also* Mekong River), 13, 14 (fig. 3), 15, 25–26

roads: 24, 308, 309, 368; and agriculture, 20; in Central Highlands, 79

rubber: and Agriculture Code, 351; and export crop, 307, 309, 328, 369, 377, 378, 380, 382–383; and labor force, 66; and land concessions, 318, 320, 326; and plantations, 16, 20, 45, 76, 277, 308, 326, 352, 357; and production, 329

Rural Reconstruction Budget: 394

rural reconstruction program: *See* Department of Revolutionary Development; Revolutionary Development Program

Rusk, Dean: 257, 260

Saigon: Buddhist disturbances, 217, 237; capital, 57, 308; Catholic demonstrations, 225; description, 2, 9, 17, 20, 26, 100, 106, 124–128, 132, 136, 167, 211, 410, 413, 416; education in, 149, 210; history, 41; industry, 66; labor force, 60, 65, 98; language, 70; population, 4, 61, 63, 70, 90; port, 26, 374; refugees, 64; transportaion, 24, 25; Viet Cong, 7

Saigon Post: and Dai Viet, 254

Saigon River: 125

sanitation facilities: 122, 124–126, 136

scholarship: 157, 160

schools: (*see also* education); and building program, 121, 143, 148, 149; dropouts, 143; enrollment, 143; private, 152–153; and terrorism, 221

script: (*see also chu nom, quoc ngu*): and *montagnards*, 80, 91

sculpture: 41, 159, 165–166

secondary education: 143, 144, 146, 149, 152, 158

skilled workers: 347, 350

smuggling: 425–426

Soc Trang: Chinese population, 62

Social Democratic Party (Dan Chu Xu Hoi Dang): 186, 254

Social and Political Research Service (So Nghien Cuu Xa Hoi Chinh Tri): 220

social security: 356

soils: 20; in Mekong Delta, 314, 316; in Central Lowlands, 316

Song Dong Nai River: 13, 83, 125

Song Hau Giang River: description, 13, 15, 20; and religion, 169; and resettlement project, 321

Song Sai Gon River: 13, 15, 26

South China Sea: 2, 13, 66, 469

South Korea: aid, 439

Southeast Asia: 9, 60, 121, 123, 273

Southeast Asia Treaty Organization (SEATO): and military aid, 6, 257–258; and "protocol states," 261–262; and foreign relations, 264, 265, 269, 273

Southern Montagnard Country (Pays Montagnard du Sud—PMS): 76

Soviet-bloc countries: 53

Soviet Union: 31, 50, 258–260; relations with, 265

Special Court: 409, 424

spirits and magic: 64, 70, 72, 75, 81, 84, 117, 133–134, 162, 170, 172, 174, 178, 180, 185

standard of living: 135, 385

Strategic Hamlet Program: 231–232

strikes: 225, 236, 348, 365–366

student groups: 223, 228, 236, 242–243

suffrage: 255

sugar: 329; in Central Lowlands, 16; crop, 314; and export, 328

superstitions: (*see* spirits and magic)

Tan Son Nhut Airport: 25, 26

Taoism: 170, 178; and Chinese, 5; and cultural influence, 159; history, 172; in population, 63, 70

tariffs: 377–378

taxes: 215, 309, 391–393, 398, 399 (table 10), 400

Tay Ninh Province: 63, 90, 185, 186

PUBLISHED AREA HANDBOOKS

550–65	Afghanistan	550–38	Liberia
550–44	Algeria	550–85	Libya
550–59	Angola	550–45	Malaysia and Singapore
550–73	Argentina	550–76	Mongolia
550–20	Brazil	550–49	Morocco
550–61	Burma	550–64	Mozambique
550–83	Burundi	550–88	Nicaragua
550–50	Cambodia	550–81	North Korea
550–26	Colombia	550–57	North Vietnam
550–60	Communist China	550–48	Pakistan
550–91	Congo (Brazzaville)	550–72	The Philippines
550–67	Congo (Kinshasa)	550–84	Rwanda
550–90	Costa Rica	550–51	Saudi Arabia
550–22	Cyprus	550–68	Senegal
550–54	Dominican Republic	550–86	Somalia
550–52	Ecuador	550–55	South Vietnam
550–29	Germany	550–27	Sudan
550–78	Guatemala	550–47	Syria
550–82	Guyana	550–62	Tanzania
550–21	India	550–53	Thailand
550–39	Indonesia	550–89	Tunisia
550–31	Iraq	550–80	Turkey
550–68	Iran	550–74	Uganda
550–25	Israel	550–43	United Arab Republic
550–30	Japan	550–71	Venezuela
550–34	Jordan	550–75	Zambia
550–56	Kenya	550–	Peripheral States of the
550–41	Republic of Korea		Arabian Peninsula
550–58	Laos		
550–24	Lebanon		

☆ U.S. GOVERNMENT PRINTING OFFICE: 1974 O—533-351